THE ROUTLEDGE HANDBOOK OF DIGITAL MEDIA AND GLOBALIZATION

In this comprehensive volume, leading scholars of media and communication examine the nexus of globalization, digital media, and popular culture in the early 21st century.

The book begins by interrogating globalization as a critical and intensely contested concept, and proceeds to explore how digital media have influenced a complex set of globalization processes in broad international and comparative contexts. Contributors address a number of key political, economic, cultural, and technological issues relative to globalization, such as free trade agreements, cultural imperialism, heterogeneity, the increasing dominance of American digital media in global cultural markets, the powers of the nation-state, and global corporate media ownership. By extension, readers are introduced to core theoretical concepts and practical ideas, which they can apply to a broad range of contemporary media policies, practices, movements, and technologies in different geographic regions of the world—North America, Europe, Africa, the Middle East, Latin America, and Asia.

Scholars of global media, international communication, media industries, globalization, and popular culture will find this to be a singular resource for understanding the interconnected relationship between digital media and globalization.

Dal Yong Jin is Distinguished SFU Professor at Simon Fraser University in Canada. After working as a journalist for many years, he completed his PhD in the Institute of Communications Research at the University of Illinois in 2005. Jin's major research and teaching interests are on digital platforms and digital games, globalization and media, transnational cultural studies, and the political economy of media and culture. He is the founding book series editor of *Routledge Research in Digital Media and Culture in Asia*.

THE ROUTLEDGE HANDBOOK OF DIGITAL MEDIA AND GLOBALIZATION

Edited by Dal Yong Jin

Routledge
Taylor & Francis Group

NEW YORK AND LONDON

First published 2021
by Routledge
605 Third Avenue, New York, NY 10158

and by Routledge
2 Park Square, Milton Park, Abingdon, Oxon OX14 4RN

Routledge is an imprint of the Taylor & Francis Group, an informa business

Library of Congress Cataloging-in-Publication Data
A catalog record for this title has been requested

ISBN: 978-0-367-41579-2 (hbk)
ISBN: 978-0-367-77074-7 (pbk)
ISBN: 978-0-367-81674-2 (ebk)

Typeset in Bembo
by Newgen Publishing UK

CONTENTS

Contents

ACKNOWLEDGMENTS

This book had its genesis in my conversation with Erica Wetter—the former editor of Routledge—at the International Association for Media and Communication Research (IAMCR) conference, which was held at the University of Oregon in June 2018. While checking other publication topics, she suggested I edit this particular volume. Later, Sheni Kruger and Emma Sherriff have helped me organize and finalize this book, and I, first, would like to thank their professionalism and patience. I also want to express my sincere gratitude to the contributors to this volume for their hard work and generosity. Also thanks to Taeyoung Kim, who is a PhD candidate at Simon Fraser University, for editorial assistance and to Michael Borowy for his fine proofreading and copyediting.

I also acknowledge that an early version of one chapter by Sophia McClennen in this book appeared in another publication.

CONTRIBUTORS

Ji-Hyun Ahn is Associate Professor of Communication in the School of Interdisciplinary Arts & Sciences at the University of Washington Tacoma USA. Her research interests include global media studies, critical mixed-race studies, national identity and racial politics in contemporary East Asian media and popular culture. She is the author of *Mixed-Race Politics and Neoliberal Multiculturalism in South Korean Media* (Palgrave Macmillan, 2018). She has published many articles on race, multiculturalism, and South Korean media in highly acclaimed journals in the field such as *Media, Culture & Society, International Communication Gazette, Cultural Studies*, and *Asian Journal of Communication*. Her recent project studies anti-Korean sentiment and the rise of (new) nationalism in East Asia.

Ahmed Al-Rawi is Assistant Professor of News, Social Media, and Public Communication at the School of Communication at Simon Fraser University, Canada. He is the Director of the Disinformation Project, which empirically examines fake news discourses in Canada on social media and news media. His research expertise is related to social media, global communication, news, and the Middle East. He has authored five books and over 80 peer-reviewed book chapters and articles published in a variety of journals like *Information, Communication & Society, Online Information Review, Social Science Computer Review, Telematics & Informatics*, and *Social Media+Society*.

Luiz Guilherme Duarte is a Brazilian journalist with a Bachelor's degree from the University of Sao Paulo. After completing a Master's degree in Telecommunications and a PhD focused on International Marketing Communications from Michigan State University, he pursued a career as a media researcher, having worked for companies like DIRECTV, WGBH, Sony Pictures, and TiVo. He has been awarded by the Advertising Research Foundation for his pioneer development of television ratings service in the US and Latin America. Dr. Duarte is currently the principal of the consulting group Cense and an adjunct faculty at the Nicholson School of Communication and Media in the University of Central Florida.

Evan Elkins is an assistant professor of film and media studies at Colorado State University who specializes in digital media industries and technologies, globalization, access, and cultural geography. He is the author of *Locked Out: Regional Restrictions in Digital Entertainment Culture* (NYU Press, 2019), and his work has appeared in the *International Journal of Cultural Studies, Media, Culture & Society, Television and New Media*, the *Fibreculture Journal*, the *Historical Journal of Film, Radio, and Television, Critical Studies in Media Communication*, and several edited collections. He is currently researching the historical relationship between the internet and the US American West.

Nissrine Fariss is a PhD candidate and teaching assistant at Paris 3 Sorbonne Nouvelle, in Paris, France. She is passionate about history, consumer behavior, and environmental studies. Since this year 2020/2021, she has also begun teaching a course entitled "Introduction to Media Studies." Her PhD dissertation topic, "the corporatization of environmentalism since the 1970s: the case of ExxonMobil," explores the conciliation between businesses' environmental discourse and their bottom line after the advent of corporate social responsibility, with ExxonMobil as a case study. Her contribution to *The Routledge Handbook of Digital Media and Globalization* looks at the ritualization of caffeine in the United States through a comparative study of Starbucks and Coca-Cola, from her Master's thesis (defended with highest honors). She pursues the career of a university professor.

David J. Gunkel is an award-winning educator, scholar, and author, specializing in the philosophy and ethics of emerging technology. He is the author of over 80 scholarly articles and book chapters and has published 12 internationally recognized books, including *Thinking Otherwise: Philosophy, Communication, Technology* (Purdue University Press, 2007), *The Machine Question: Critical Perspectives on AI, Robots, and Ethics* (MIT Press, 2012), *Of Remixology: Ethics and Aesthetics After Remix* (MIT Press, 2016), *Robot Rights* (MIT Press, 2018), and *An Introduction to Communication and Artificial Intelligence* (Polity, 2020). He currently holds the position of Distinguished Teaching Professor in the Department of Communication at Northern Illinois University (USA). More info at http://gunkelweb.com

Vanessa de Macedo Higgins Joyce is an associate professor in the School of Journalism and Mass Communication at Texas State University. Born in São Paulo, Brazil, she worked for two major public opinion research companies in that city. She received her doctorate degree from The University of Texas at Austin (December 2009) with a dissertation focusing on the consensus-building function of agenda setting, analyzing national and transnational news media in Europe. Her research lies in the intersection of transnational media, Latin America digital journalism, and consensus building. Her research has been published in top journals including *Journalism Practice, International Communication Gazette, Journalism Studies* and the Latin American journals *Cuadernos.info, Palabra Clave, Brazilian Journalism Review*, and others.

Koichi Iwabuchi is Professor of Media and Cultural Studies at the School of Sociology, Kwansei Gakuin University. His research interests are trans-Asian cultural flows, connections, and dialogue; diversity, multicultural questions, and cultural citizenship. His recent English publications include *Resilient Borders and Cultural Diversity: Internationalism, Brand Nationalism and Multiculturalism in Japan* (Lexington Books, 2015); "Migrancy and Diplomacy: Fostering Cross-Border Dialogue and Collaboration in the Age of Hyper-Mobility" (*The Brown Journal of World Affairs*, 25: 1, 2018); "Trans-Asia as method: a collaborative and dialogic project in a globalized world", in *Trans-Asia as Method: Theory and Practices* (Rowman & Littlefield International, 2019).

Dal Yong Jin is Distinguished SFU Professor at Simon Fraser University in Canada. After working as a journalist for many years, he completed his PhD in the Institute of Communications Research at the University of Illinois in 2005. Jin's major research and teaching interests are on digital platforms and digital games, globalization and media, transnational cultural studies, and the political economy of media and culture. He is the founding book series editor of *Routledge Research in Digital Media and Culture in Asia*.

Michael Keane is Professor of Chinese Media and Communications at Curtin University, Perth, Australia. He is Program Leader of the Digital Asia Research Node within the Centre for Culture and Technology. Professor Keane's key research interests are digital transformation in China; East Asian cultural and media policy; television in China, and creative industries and cultural export strategies in China and East Asia.

Roy Kheng is a PhD candidate with the Humanities, Arts and Social Sciences at the Singapore University of Technology and Design. A former journalist and editor, he has published across a wide swath of topics, from business intelligence, human resources, leadership, and computer gaming. His research interests are in video games, digital history, building a deep understanding of fake news to counter its ill effects and communications issues impacting youth.

Ju Oak Kim is an assistant professor of the Department of Psychology and Communication at Texas A&M International University. Her research interests include global media systems and industries, production studies, media representations of race, gender, ethnicity, and nationality, and East Asian media and culture. Her work has appeared in *Continuum: Journal of Media & Cultural Studies*, *International Journal of Communication, Culture, Theory and Critique*, *International Journal of Korean Studies*, *The Journal of Popular Culture*, and *Journal of Fandom Studies*. Kim is currently working on her book manuscript that examines the production culture of Korean television and pop industries in the context of the Korean Wave phenomenon.

Taeyoung Kim is a PhD candidate in the School of Communication at Simon Fraser University. He studies the nexus of nation-state systems and forces of neoliberal globalization in cultural and creative industries. His research has appeared in several journals including the *International Journal of Communication* and the *Journal of Arts Management, Law and Society*. His dissertation project focuses on the Korean state's continuing presence in the cultural industries and the process by which said industries become increasingly subject to globalization and neoliberalization.

Claire Shinhea Lee is an assistant professor in the Department of Social, Cultural, and Media Studies at the University of the Fraser Valley. Her research interests include digital migrant studies, qualitative audience studies, and feminist media studies. Her work appears in peer-reviewed journals including *Television & New Media*, *Social Media + Society*, *Media, Culture, & Society*, and *International Journal of Communication*.

Micky Lee is a professor of media studies at Suffolk University, Boston. She has published in the areas of feminist political economy, information, technologies, and finance. Her latest books are *Understanding the Business of Global Media in the Digital Age* (co-authored with Dal Yong Jin, Routledge, 2018), *Bubbles and Machines: Gender, Information, and Financial Crises* (University of Westminster Press, 2019), and *Alphabet: The Becoming of Google* (Routledge, 2019). Two forthcoming books are *Information* (Routledge) and *Media Technologies for Work and Play in East Asia: Critical Perspectives on Japan and the Two Koreas* (co-edited with Peichi Chung, Bristol University Press).

Sun Sun Lim is Professor of Communication and Technology and Head of Humanities, Arts and Social Sciences at the Singapore University of Technology and Design. She has extensively researched the social impact of technology, focusing on technology domestication, digital disruptions, and smart city technologies. She recently published *Transcendent Parenting—Raising Children in the Digital Age* (Oxford University Press, 2020) and co-edited *The Oxford Handbook of Mobile Communication and Society* (Oxford University Press, 2020). She serves on 11 journal editorial boards and three book series. She frequently offers her expert commentary in diverse outlets including *Nature*, *Scientific American*, and *South China Morning Post*.

Jue Lu, PhD (Shanghai University), is an assistant professor in the School of Communication and Arts at Shanghai University of Sport. She was a visiting scholar at the University of Kentucky. Her research interests focus on game studies and media history.

Robin Mansell is Professor in the Department of Media and Communications, London School of Economics and Political Science, board member and Secretary of The Research Conference on Communications, Information, and Internet Policy (TPRC), and past President of the International Association for Media and Communication Research (IAMCR). Her research focuses on technology innovation, digital platform governance, and its socio-political and economic consequences. She is author of *Imagining the Internet: Communication, Innovation and Governance* (Oxford University Press), and co-author of *Advanced Introduction to Platform Economics* (Edward Elgar Publishing, 2020).

Richard Maxwell is Professor of Media Studies at Queens College, City University of New York. His publications include *The Spectacle of Democracy, Culture Works: The Political Economy of Culture, Herbert Schiller, Global Hollywood* (co-author), *Greening the Media* (with Toby Miller), *The Routledge Companion to Labor and Media, Media and the Ecological Crisis* (co-editor), and *How Green is Your Smartphone?* (with Toby Miller).

Sophia A. McClennen is a professor of international affairs and comparative literature at the Pennsylvania State University and founding director of the Center for Global Studies. She studies human rights, media, satire, and politics, with two recent books on related topics, *Globalization and Latin American Cinema* and *The Routledge Companion to Literature and Human Rights,* co-edited with Alexandra Schultheis Moore. She also has a column with Salon.com where she regularly covers politics and culture.

Toby Miller is Stuart Hall Professor of Cultural Studies, Universidad Autónoma Metropolitana—Cuajimalpa and Sir Walter Murdoch Distinguished Collaborator, Murdoch University. He was a professor at the University of California Riverside for a decade and New York University for eleven years. The author and editor of over fifty books, his work has been translated into Spanish, Chinese, Portuguese, Japanese, Turkish, German, Italian, Farsi, French, Urdu, and Swedish. His most recent volumes are *Violence* (2021), *The Persistence of Violence: Colombian Popular Culture* (2020), *How Green is Your Smartphone?* (co-authored, 2020), *El trabajo cultural* (2018), *Greenwashing Culture* (2018), *Greenwashing Sport* (2018), *The Routledge Companion to Global Cultural Policy* (co-edited, 2018), *Global Media Studies* (co-authored, 2015), *The Routledge Companion to Global Popular Culture* (edited, 2015), *Greening the Media* (co-authored, 2012) and *Blow Up the Humanities* (2012). *A COVID Charter, a Better Future* is in press. Formerly the editor of the *Journal of Sport & Social Issues, Social Text, and Television & New Media*, he currently edits *Open Cultural Studies* and is co-editor of *Social Identities: Journal of Race, Nation and Culture*. Toby is Past President of the Cultural Studies Association (US).

Wonjung Min is an adjunct assistant professor of the History Department and Executive Committee Member of the Asian Studies Center at the Pontificia Universidad Católica de Chile. She holds a PhD in Latin American Literature. Her research focuses on the fandom of Asian pop culture in the Spanish-speaking world, identity formation of Latin American societies, and comparative culture between Asia and Latin America. She is the editor of the book *Estudios Coreanos para hispanohablantes: un acercamiento crítico, comparativo e interdisciplinario (Korean Studies for Spanish-speakers: A Critical, Comparative and Interdisciplinary Approach)* (Ediciones UC, 2015). She has published numerous articles and book chapters on the reception of Asian pop culture in Latin America. Between September 2020 and July 2021, she is a Kyujanggak Fellow at the International Center for Korean Studies of the Seoul National University.

Tanner Mirrlees is the president of the Canadian Communication Association (CCA) and director of Communication and Digital Media Studies in the Faculty of Social Sciences and Humanities,

Ontario Tech University. He is the author/co-editor of books such as *The Television Reader* (Oxford University Press), *Global Entertainment Media: Between Cultural Imperialism and Cultural Globalization* (Routledge), *Hearts and Mines: The US Empire's Culture Industry* (University of British Columbia Press), *Media Imperialism: Continuity and Change* (Rowman & Littlefield), and *EdTech Inc.* (Routledge).

David C. Oh is Associate Professor of Communication Arts at Ramapo College of New Jersey. He is the author of *Second-Generation Korean American Adolescent Identity and Media: Diasporic Identifications* and several articles on Asian/American representation vis-a-vis Whiteness, Asian American identity and media, intersectional representations of multiculturalism in South Korean popular media, and transnational audience reception of Korean media.

Melissa Santillana is a PhD candidate in the Department of Radio-Television-Film at the University of Texas at Austin. Her research focuses on international media flows, border studies, activist movements, feminist activism, digital media, and digital inequality.

Ralph Schroeder is Professor in Social Science of the Internet at the Oxford Internet Institute and director of its M.Sc. program. He has authored or co-authored more than 150 papers and his books include *Social Theory after the Internet: Media, Technology and Globalization* (UCL Press, 2018) *Knowledge Machines: Digital Transformations of the Sciences and Humanities* (MIT Press, 2015, co-authored with Eric T. Meyer), *An Age of Limits: Social Theory for the Twenty-First Century* (Palgrave Macmillan, 2013), *Being There Together: Social Interaction in Virtual Environments* (Oxford University Press, 2010), and *Rethinking Science, Technology and Social Change* (Stanford University Press, 2007). His current research interests include digital media and right-wing populism, and the social implications of big data.

Sergio Sparviero is an assistant professor of the Department of Communication Studies, University of Salzburg, Austria, since March 2011, and the coordinator of the EU-funded, Digital Communication Leadership (DC Lead) master's program since 2015. He holds a PhD in communication from Dublin City University (DCU, Ireland), where he was also employed as a postdoctoral researcher for three years. He has also degrees also from University College Dublin (UCD, Ireland) and the Université libre de Bruxelles (ULB, Belgium). He specializes in media economic theory, particularly in alternative economic theories, media management, and economic studies of different types of media industries, including audio-visual media services, music, and news. He edited the book *Media Convergence and Deconvergence* with Gabriele Balbi and Corinna Peil, published by Palgrave and the International Association for Media and Communication Research (IAMCR). More recently, he focused on studying the business model of non-profit and hybrid media and communications organizations.

Wendy Su is Associate Professor of the Department of Media and Cultural Studies at University of California Riverside. Her research falls along the intersections of global communication, Chinese media studies, and cultural studies. Specifically, she is interested in China's communication and cultural policy study, cultural industries research, transnational film studies, audience research, and Asian modernity. She is the author of *China's Encounter with Global Hollywood: Cultural Policy and the Film Industry, 1994–2013* (University Press of Kentucky, 2016), and co-editor of *Asia-Pacific Film Co-productions: Theory, Industry and Aesthetics* (Routledge, 2019). She has published in a number of high-ranking academic journals including *Pacific Affairs, International Journal of Cultural Policy, Critical Studies in Media Communication, Journal of International and Intercultural Communication, Global Media and Communication, Journal of International Communication*, and *Asian Journal of Communication*. She was a winner of the 2014 William L. Holland Prize for the best article granted by Pacific Affairs.

Joseph Straubhaar is the Amon G. Carter Sr., Centennial Professor of Communication in the Radio-Television-Film Dept. at the University of Texas at Austin. His current research concerns the globalization of television and new media, the BRICs, television in Brazil and Latin America, and the digital divide in Brazil and Texas. He is co-author of *Television in Latin America* (BFI, 2013), the author of *World Television: From Global to Local* (Sage Publications, 2007), and editor of *Inequity in the Technopolis: Race, Class, Gender and the Digital Divide in Austin* (University of Texas Press, 2011), and numerous journal articles on these topics.

Zixue Tai, PhD (Minnesota), is an associate professor in the School of Journalism and Media at the University of Kentucky, where he is sequence head of the Media Arts and Studies program. His research interests mostly pertain to the new media landscape in China. He is the author of *The Internet in China: Cyberspace and Civil Society* (Routledge, hardback in 2006; paperback released in 2013). Besides contributions to about two dozen edited volumes, his numerous publications can also be found in journals such as *International Communication Gazette, Journalism & Mass Communication Quarterly, New Media & Society, Journal of Communication, Sociology of Health & Illness*, and *Psychology & Marketing*.

Gordon Kuo Siong Tan is Faculty Early Career Award Fellow of Humanities, Arts and Social Sciences at the Singapore University of Technology and Design. A geographer by training, Gordon is interested in studying the impact of technological changes on urban financial centers, as well as how technology shapes the nature of financial work in terms of human capital (skills) requirements. He is also keen to explore the influence of financial technology (FinTech) on the increased financialization of society. With his interest in examining the spatialities of (mis)information production, dissemination, and consumption on the internet, he is co-author of a forthcoming book *Misinformation in the Digital Age* (Edward Elgar).

Mandy Tröger, born in East Berlin, is an assistant professor at the University of Munich (LMU). She received her PhD from the Institute of Communications Research of the University of Illinois at Urbana-Champaign (UIUC) in 2018. Her research focuses on post-socialist and German media history, political economy of media and communications, and Critical Theory.

Dwayne Winseck is Professor at the School of Journalism and Communication, with a cross-appointment to the Institute of Political Economy, Carleton University, Ottawa, Canada. His research interests include the political economy of media, internet and telecommunications, media history, and media theory. He is also the Director of the Canadian Media Concentration Research Project.

Huan Wu is a research associate working for the Digital Asia Research Node project in the Centre of Culture and Technology at Curtin University. She received her Doctoral Degree in Communication from The Chinese University of Hong Kong. She was an Associate Professor in the School of Media and Communication at Shanghai Jiao Tong University, China. Her research interests include the interaction between new media and disadvantaged groups, and the development of creative industries in Asia-Pacific area. She has been awarded the Endeavour Chueng Kong Scholarship and studied in The ARC Centre of Excellence for Creative Industries and Innovation (CCI).

1

INTRODUCTION

Dal Yong Jin

Globalization has become more complicated than ever as several actors, such as nation-states, international agencies, transnational corporations, and consumers, whether Western-based or non-Western based have become increasingly involved, in recent years. Globalization and media are especially well-connected because media, both traditional media like broadcasting and digital media, such as social media and smartphone technologies, have greatly facilitated the globalization process. While several significant dimensions, including economy, culture, migration, and consumption, have played pivotal roles in globalization, media, and in particular, digital technologies, are always facilitating and expediting the process. From the invention of the internet to the expansion of smartphones and to the dominant role of platform technologies, digital media in addition to traditional media are fundamental tools and means to actualize globalization, which is the integration and/or interdependence of the globe. In the early 21st century, there are some signals that globalization as an economic and geopolitical reality may be coming to an end, as can be seen in Brexit (Sharma, 2016); however, digital media have redirected the contour of current affairs in relation to globalization.

Using digital technology has indeed helped many corporations and individuals create global networks, new ways to work, and more data than ever. Digital technology also brings people together in newfangled ways, allows them to get insights that were never before possible, and enables massive disruption across the supply and demand chains of multiple industries (Forrester, 2020). During the COVID-19 era starting in late 2019, for example, several videoconferencing technologies, including Zoom, have fundamentally changed people's interactions from face-to-face to virtual gatherings, both nationally and globally, and therefore "there are signs that the relatively free movement of ideas"—called "Zoom globalization"—might persist in our contemporary society (Staley, 2020). Of course, this new trend provides broad benefits to many but at the cost of others who lose their jobs (Forrester, 2020).

As such, in the early 21st century, with the rapid growth of digital technologies and relevant socio-economic dimensions, including political, economic, and cultural elements, globalization has continued to become one of the most popular concepts in all academic fields. In other words, with the rapid growth of digital media, such as the internet, satellite, social media (e.g., Facebook and YouTube), search engines (e.g., Google), digital games, smartphones, and Netflix, the global economy and cultural markets have been more closely connected and interdependent than ever (Kerr and Flynn, 2003; Miller and Kraidy, 2016; Flew, 2018; Jin, 2019). Digital technologies have especially played a key role in the realm of popular culture as cultural producers and cultural distributors, although the boundary between production and distribution is getting blurry.

Due to the significance of digital media for both the national economy and global integration, several countries, both in the Global North like the US and the UK and the Global South, including Brazil, South Korea, and China, have developed their own digital technologies, and consequently tensions between the Global North and the Global South in the realm of digital media have continued or even intensified in recent years. On the one hand, digital media like the internet, iPhone, YouTube, and Facebook in the US have substantially increased their market shares to continue and extend their hegemonic dominance around the globe. On the other hand, several emerging markets in the Global South like India, China, and Korea have developed their local-based digital media to become major actors of the global society. The majority of countries around the globe, including these countries mentioned above, however, utilize American-based digital media to disseminate their popular culture to both regional and global markets, and therefore, they are still under American influences in most cases. As Goggin and McLelland (2017, 5) point out, "a further problem is that dominant notions of the Internet… are still modeled on a limited range of experiences, deployments, and conceptions of the Internet, largely based on the perspectives of Anglophone users, especially North Americans, who featured prominently among early pioneers (as well as some European nations)." Regardless of shifting power dynamics in politics and economy, globalization brings about continuing disparities between the Global North and the Global South.

How to comprehend globalization and media in the 21st century, therefore, relies on people's understanding of several major dimensions in conjunction with the natures of the flow of people, culture, and capital in the globalization process. Most of all, as digital media partakes in its increasing role in facilitating and expediting globalization, global networks provide unfathomable opportunities to many people. As availability spreads, people use digital media to their advantage to begin a social and global movement (Bieber, 2014). Therefore, it is crucial to comprehend the close relationships between globalization and media, in particular digital media.

This edited volume discusses global transformations in tandem with media, both traditional and new media with its emphasis on digital media, including social media, smartphone technologies, and digital platforms, in historical and contemporary terms. It begins the discussion by interrogating globalization as a critical and intensely contested concept, and then proceeds to explore how digital media have influenced "a complex set of globalization processes" in broad international and comparative contexts (Giddens, 1999). During the process, it addresses a number of key political, economic, cultural, and technological issues relative to globalization, such as the USMCA (United States-Mexico-Canada Agreement starting in 2018)—a new regional free trade agreement in North America—vs. Brexit (the British exit from the European Union starting in 2016), cultural imperialism (H. Schiller, 1976; also see Boyd-Barrett and Mirrlees, 2019) vs. heterogeneity, contra-flow of media products vs. increasing dominance of American digital media in the global cultural markets, the powers of the nation-state, and global corporate media ownership.

Purpose and Scope

The Routledge Handbook of Digital Media and Globalization contains nearly 30 chapters providing an empirically rich analysis of globalization processes, histories, texts, and state policies as they relate to the global media. Its goal is to introduce researchers and students to core theoretical concepts and practical ideas which they should apply to a broad range of contemporary media policies, practices, movements, and technologies in different geographic regions of the world—North America, Europe, Africa, the Middle East, Latin America, and Asia—with a view to determining how they shape and are shaped by globalization. It examines the nexus of globalization, media, and popular culture in the early 21st century. This book especially maps out the increasing role of digital media as they have shifted the contours of globalization in that they are not only distribution channels but also production tools, which greatly influence people's daily activities.

More specifically, this volume aims to provide an overview of globalization theories and stories as analytical frameworks for understanding globalization and media. It also examines our contemporary world surrounded by the use of digital media, while discussing the evolution of media technologies in conjunction with globalization. This means that this volume addresses the role of digital media in the globalization process so that readers are able to compare several different media technologies and cultures with each other. In addition, it addresses several examples from different regions and/or countries, both in the Global North and the Global South, to illustrate how globalized has influenced and has been influenced by historical, political, economic, and social factors. The power relations between global media and information technologies are ambiguous at local, regional, and international levels. Therefore, it illustrates these relations by giving regional examples from North America, Europe, Asia, Latin America, and Africa. Last, but not least, it is to help undergraduate and graduate students envision their careers in the communication industries in the globalized society. In other words, I expect that this book will help researchers, students, and policy makers who study of and work in the global media industries by discussing the relation between labor and the industries, and academic discourses and industrial discourses on the global media industries.

There have been several monographs and edited volumes on globalization and media; however, only a few books have touched on the shifting milieu occurring due to digital media. Several existing books (Hafez, 2013; Mirrlees, 2013; Birkinbine et al., 2016; Lechner and Boli, 2014; Lule, 2015; Miller and Kraidy, 2016; Flew, 2018; Jin, 2019) address terrain similar to what will be covered in this book. However, there are no direct competitor titles for this reference work. Although the books mentioned above are valuable sources, and many scholars and students have learned the concept and scope of globalization and media through these fine books, none of them analyzed the entire scope of digital media and globalization trends. Also, none of them seriously analyzed the significance of digital platforms and mobile communication, given that they are new technologies developed in the early 21st century. This may be a reflection of the short history of digital media technologies, like blockchain, digital platforms, and smartphones. Therefore, the current volume makes a significant contribution to the literature, primarily due to its comprehensive analysis of the emergence of the digital media. I also believe that the book puts new ideas on the agenda. The comprehensive and significant analyses of the dynamic changes and persistent features of digital media in the global context within the broader notion of global modernity will make this book an ideal selection for such disciplines.

Overall, this *Routledge Handbook of Digital Media and Globalization* will provide an authoritative overview of the maturing scholarly area of globalization and digital media. It will be international in its scope as it includes contributors, examples, or cases from North America, South America, Europe, the Middle East, Asia-Pacific, and Africa. It balances distinguished, established, and leading scholars with emerging, next-generation researchers and students.

Overview of the Volume

The organization of the book is as follows. To encourage the reading of the chapters alongside other cognate areas, I have organized the contents across six broad thematic points. Part I documents history and theory in the context of globalization, consisting of four chapters. To begin with, Chapter 2 written by Dwayne Winseck identifies the core elements of global communication in the late-19th and early-20th centuries and shows that they were more global and organized as a system than previously thought. These elements included investment and ownership, corporate identity, international and national laws, the careers of experts and engineers, views of modernization, and imperial strategy. The onslaught of World War I threw all of this into disarray, however. The chapter concludes by pointing to efforts after the war's end to reconstruct the earlier "belle époque of liberal internationalism" that had seized the minds of a small group of "communications experts" in the US State Department and a few other countries, including Britain, France, Italy, and Japan. As this chapter concludes, they were not enough to keep the mounting nationalism and the economic collapse of the late 1920s and 1930s at bay—all of which put the final nail in the coffin of "the empire of capitalist modernity" and led to incessant struggles for control over resources that bequeathed to us the calamity of another World War.

Chapter 3 by Joseph Straubhaar explores the evolution of the theory referred to as cultural proximity, which predicts that audiences will prefer national or, secondly, regional television. It also empirically examines it in terms of preferences for national and regional programming in Latin America during 2004–2014, based on a series of annual surveys conducted in eight Latin American countries. The first major prediction of cultural proximity—that audiences will tend to prefer local or national programming—is confirmed from the strong, fairly stable preference that the overall audience shows for national programming in the years studied. However, counter to the second major prediction of cultural proximity, that Latin American audiences would favor regional programming next, study found instead that US programming was their second choice. The chapter examines why that seems to be the case and why it has become stronger in the cable TV era.

Chapter 4 by Richard Maxwell and Toby Miller discusses environmental media materialism, which seeks to understand the history of communications technologies from cradle to grave, paying special attention to their environmental effects. The chapter asks questions about the labor process, extractive industries, and the manufacturing, distribution, use, and disposal of devices and texts. This is particularly important for understanding globalization. When it looks at the entire commodity chain, the life history, of our favorite genres or technologies, it uncovers uncomfortable material truths, with serious environmental implications.

In Chapter 5, Tanner Mirrlees examines how the US Department of Defense (DoD) assisted Marvel Studios' *Captain Marvel* (2019), a film whose production, storyline, and marketing exemplify a 21st century "DoD–Hollywood complex" militainment product. The chapter probes *Captain Marvel*'s production (as assisted by the DoD), content (the story, plot, characters, and themes), and marketing (publicity and cross-promotion), and shows how *Captain Marvel* helped the US Air Force to promote itself, and helped Hollywood turn a global profit. The chapter critiques the notion that *Captain Marvel* is a "progressive" and "feminist" film and considers its significance to US "cultural imperialism."

Part II mainly discusses capitalism, structure, and institutions, with three chapters. Chapter 6 by Sergio Sparviero defines ethical capitalism as a philosophy connecting a variety of institutions supporting a shared idea of good society. The good society is shaped by the values of sustainability: equality, harmony, and self-determination. Ethical capitalism institutions include abstract ideas of general economic systems, theories of organizational design, principles of management, but also "real-world" legal frameworks for enterprises that are "purpose-driven". This chapter explains how ethical capitalism is permeating local and global media and communications markets. It is embraced, but also shaped, by some of the most innovative and visionary organizations of the ICT revolution, including Wikimedia, Mozilla, and Creative Commons.

In Chapter 7, Micky Lee offers a feminist political economic understanding of the global digital divide by offering a critique from a Global South standpoint. It first summarizes how feminists theorize the divide: some believe digital technologies promote gender equality, whereas others believe they exacerbate gender inequality. It next examines how international organizations implemented programs that are embedded with a neoliberal agenda. Lastly, it shows how transnational companies such as Google appear to provide public services for the digitally disconnected, yet their motivations are driven by profits.

Chapter 8 by Ju Oak Kim aims to bring US–Korean collaborations to the fore of debates over media globalization, and the overarching structural dimensions of transnational media cultures and practices. In particular, this chapter analyzes the factors behind the latest phase of Korean media culture and practice, exploring the theoretical implications of the non-Western actor's media production and distribution in the globally networked society. It discusses the rise of Korean television formats in the US media industries and then proposes the third Korean Wave as a reflection of the structural transformations in global media production and distribution systems. This chapter highlights the salience and urgency of decolonizing scholarly discussions concerning the Korean Wave phenomenon in order to comprehend the centrality of Korean creators and practitioners in the global media market within the logic of the new global media economy.

Part III analyzes popular culture and globalization, with five chapters. Chapter 9 by Koichi Iwabuchi argues that the globalization of media and culture brings about complicated impacts. On the one hand, the flow and connection beyond national borders has promoted new kinds of cross-border exchange, alliance, and dialogue. On the other, however, what is even more conspicuous is the fortification of national cultural borders. This chapter examines how such introverted forces gain momentum in the 21st century context of market-driven globalism by examining the rise of cyber-driven neo-nationalism, nation branding, and commercial nationalism in Japan. It shows how the protection and promotion of national interest has become a governing code that works hand in hand with the intolerance of "anti-Japanese" and eventually overwhelms the transgressive and dialogic dynamism of globalization.

In Chapter 10, Nissrine Fariss explores Starbucks' dream of a global taste through the prism of American history and culture. It first expands on the changes in the American market that allowed Starbucks' proposition to gain traction, from bad supermarket coffee to the rise of "subculture brands", and the ensuing homogenizing tendency of the American food and beverage industry. It then analyzes the brand's synthetic authenticity in relation to what ex-CEO. Howard Schultz called "the people business." Last, it explores Starbucks' sustained associations with Ray Oldenburg's communal "Third Place" concept to ensure a uniform and reproducible experience capable of subsuming different cultures and communities on a global scale. Using Boorstin's terminology, this chapter essentially approaches Starbucks as an American "pseudo-event;" an illusory receptacle of subculture, authenticity, and community where patrons trade off ideals for ready-to-consume images.

Chapter 11 by Wendy Su draws on empirical focus group discussions and historical document analysis and inquires into how young Chinese audiences' reception of Japanese pop culture enhances their cultural imagination in a rapidly globalized world. The chapter argues that the reception process functions as an effective way of self-expression and escapism from the hardship of real life. Through engaging in Japanese media culture, Chinese fans not only actuate a deep reflection on their own society, but also form an imaginary cultural identity that negotiates through the political and social constraints of the Chinese society. Accordingly, the reception process is a site of contestation, negotiation, and even resistance, in which transnationalism triumphs and a cross-border Asian modernity is in the making.

In Chapter 12, Ji-Hyun Ahn discusses the power of inter-Asia media/cultural studies to explain the current wave of media globalization. It begins by introducing the concept of "Asia as method" that has been facilitating the development of an increasingly nuanced and rich understanding of the region. Next, the chapter contextualizes the development of inter-Asia media/cultural studies and discusses concepts developed by scholars in this field that have shed much-needed light on transnational media and cultural flow in East Asia. Lastly, Ahn draws attention to new challenges posed by the intersection of current geopolitical changes in East Asia with digitalization and the concomitant demand for new lines of inquiry by these scholars.

Meanwhile, Chapter 13 by David Oh examines transnational popular culture's counter-flows. In 2016, *Family Guy* aired "Candy, Quahog, Marshmallow," an episode that satirizes Korean popular media. Oh believes that the inclusion of the episode signals that counter-flows of global popular culture have become recognizable within the US cultural terrain. For him, its inclusion especially produces counter-hegemonic potential with recognizable, ethnically specific images of Korea and its popular culture, but its use of "pseudosatire" functions to largely discipline interest in Korean media and White fans by overdetermining both as a gendered feminine Other. Thus, counter-flows are disciplined within the US cultural terrain by drawing upon readily available racialized discourses, but, at the same time, it simultaneously provides materials for counter-hegemonic resistance.

Part IV discusses digital platforms and globalization. Chapter 14 by Robin Mansell examines whether Europe can achieve sufficient leverage to achieve protection for public values in the face of dominant digital platforms and its simultaneous support for digital economy strategies. European regulatory moves are intended to achieve the "right" balance between competing economic values and values such as privacy and freedom of expression. Based on a discussion of contemporary European Union initiatives to strengthen digital platform governance, the chapter assesses whether a "digital sovereignty" regulatory strategy is likely to protect or override a citizen's rights. It concludes that a radical approach will be needed if Europe is to ensure that platforms do not perpetuate exploitative business practices.

In Chapter 15, Evan Elkins analyzes Netflix's domestic politics and foreign policy. In its programming, branding strategies, and attempts to influence media policy around the world, Netflix promotes a broad vision of globalized cultural and economic liberalism geared toward humanist principles, cosmopolitan branding, international free trade, technological disruption, and economic deregulation. This chapter traces Netflix's politics across the company's recent partnerships with powerful Democratic Party figures, its attempts to gain DC influence, and its international diplomatic and cultural policy apparatus. It argues that Netflix's institutional politics encourage deregulatory platform-imperialist practices, while its cosmopolitan brand promotes the platform as a responsible, progressive global actor. The publicly visible elements of the latter both practice ease and mask the behind-the-scenes wheeling and dealing of the former.

Chapter 16 by Michael Keane and Huan Wu examines how Chinese online platforms have assumed a leading role in disseminating Chinese values and ideas. The chapter begins by providing some background to China's culture "going out" (also called "going global") program, which was instigated in 2002. Following this, the chapter considers some of the problems associated with evaluating soft power globally, noting how metrics are biased toward liberal democracies. With regard to media reception, the chapter examines the reliability of online recommendation sites and social media as a barometer of success. The final section illustrates how Chinese commercial entertainment industries are expanding beyond China and in doing so draws on data from a research project on online consumption of Chinese entertainment content in the Asia-Pacific region. The results show that the free platform YouTube, which is banned in China, is effectively benefiting China in its messaging to the world.

In Chapter 17, Dal Yong Jin employs a critical political economy approach and platform imperialism theory to analyze OTT services, in particular Netflix's global dominance, in order to determine the ways in which Netflix newly constructs platform imperialism as a new form of imperialism. It discusses the major characteristics of Netflix in the global cultural industries, which controls the vicious chain of the broadcasting and film industries. Second, it examines the ways in which Netflix influences the content production sector, as well as consumption in the Asian cultural and platform industries, as Asian countries have shifted their methods of production and exhibition by learning from Netflix. Finally, it examines how Netflix promotes imperialism which expands asymmetrical power relations between the US and other parts of the world. In other words, it articulates whether Netflix actualizes platform imperialism, referring to an asymmetrical relationship of interdependence between the West, primarily the US, and many developing countries, based on its crucial role in reshaping the global cultural industry.

Part V mainly focuses on digital media and social media in the globalization process. This part consists of five chapters. Chapter 18 by Ralph Schroeder explains that digital media have been seen as a force for democratization but they have recently come to be seen more as a source of disinformation and polarization. This chapter examines populism, particularly in China and India but also in Western democracies. There are similarities in populist uses of digital media, challenging traditional media and circumventing gatekeeping mechanisms, but also differences in how populists operate that depend on the particularities of media systems. Online media enable protest, but these counter-public spheres also promote anti-elite ultranationalist exclusionism. The chapter concludes by outlining approaches to counteracting populists and their supporters, offline and online.

In Chapter 19, Gordon Kuo Siong Tan, Sun Sun Lim, and Roy Kheng discuss fake news. The rising ubiquity of mobile-enabled devices has greatly accelerated the spread of online disinformation. Media production and dissemination capabilities are within easy reach of consumers, who may become key nodes in sharing fabricated information. Social media platforms' advertisement-driven revenue models have encouraged the proliferation of viral and inflammatory content, where journalistic best practices are de-emphasized. Furthermore, opaque algorithms favor fake stories that elicit greater emotional responses from users. Increased deregulation has given mobile media companies considerable freedom over content moderation policies. Finally, emerging mobile technologies have enabled more sophisticated and richer forms of fabricated content to be circulated among a global audience.

Chapter 20 by David Gunkel analyzes machine translation in the era of globalization, as one of the challenges of globalization is linguistic difference. As different human populations speak different languages and these differences can impede international communication and cooperation, machine translation (which initially developed as a result of a famous memorandum written by Warren Weaver after the conclusion of World War II) seeks to remediate this world-wide translation problem by way of computer technology, producing automatic translation between different human languages. This chapter investigates the concept, origin, and destination of machine translation. It considers the mythic origins of both linguistic difference and efforts to overcome the problem; the Weaver memo and the project of machine translation by computer; and the opportunities and challenges of translation and technology in the era of globalization.

In Chapter 21, Zixue Tai and Jue Lu offer a panoramic view of video games in China in the context of globalization. It starts with an examination of the development of the online game market, followed by an analysis of the rapid rise of esports, and then dissects the miscellaneous challenges and struggles in the tangled console game sector. The discussion is aligned with the contextual factors of state policymaking, market structure, and corporate strategies. The chapter places an emphasis on the multitude of glocalities (that is, how the global is refracted in the local waves) as manifested in these three areas over the past two decades.

Chapter 22 by Ahmed Al-Rawi discusses the Arab Spring on Twitter. This chapter empirically examines over 1.2 million tweets referencing the Arab Spring. Theoretically, the study is situated within the discussion of online trolling, and the preliminary findings show that there are two main active groups. The first shows support for the Arab Spring event as a catalyst for democratic change, often calling the protests "revolutions" leading to positive political progress. On the other hand, the second online community discusses the Arab Spring in the framework of foreign conspiracies, social chaos, and political regression, framing it as a pathway for political Islam to take over Arab countries. This community focuses its attacks on Qatar and its Doha-based Al Jazeera channel, accusing them of engineering popular protests in different countries with the help of the Muslim Brothers. The chapter contextualizes the findings to provide more insight into political developments in relation to the public discourses on the Arab Spring.

In Chapter 23, Wonjung Min examines transnational culture in Latin America in the digital age. Asians in Chile are often referred to as *chinos* (Chinese), and Chilean society tends to consider fans of Asian popular culture as outsiders—those who like *chinos* are akin to *chinos*. Fans recognize their *chino*-ism when they like Asian popular culture, and many Chilean Asian pop culture fans identify themselves as Westerners rather than Latin Americans. This chapter explores how fans of Asian popular culture in Latin America, and particularly Chile, form an imaginary society based on media depictions. Based on in-depth interviews conducted in Santiago from July to November 2019, this chapter maps out the ways in which fans of Asian popular culture in Chile share a fanciful bond created by an unfamiliar culture and develop imaginary cultural intimacy specific to digital media, primarily in the realm of social media.

Part VI as the final part of the volume collects chapters on migration and mobility in globalization. Chapter 24 by Joseph Straubhaar et al., discusses multilayered identities and coexistence of preferences for national and US television. This chapter is based on secondary analysis of data from TGI Latina, a biannual marketing and media consumption survey conducted in eight Latin American countries by the Miami-based marketing intelligence firm Kantar Media, with fieldwork by IBOPE (Instituto Brasileiro de Opinião Pública e Estatística, in Portuguese) and its other subsidiaries in Mexico and South America. This chapter also uses TGI Latina data to analyze major changes over time in respondents' self-reported interest in television programming from their own nation, the region, the US, and Europe.

In Chapter 25, Sophia A. McClennen discusses globalization and coproduction in Latin America. Latin American cinema has a long and complex history of cinematic coproduction. Generally, critical assessments of coproduction in the region have tended to assume that these arrangements mirror colonial hegemony, thereby replicating relations of power where Latin America is influenced and creatively controlled by Europe. Yet, this chapter shows that in the era of neoliberal globalization, coproductions are more financial than content-based. This chapter offers data and statistics on coproductions across a range of Latin American nations and shows that many of the assumptions that had grounded previous critiques of coproduction—namely that with financial investment comes ideological pressure—no longer hold true.

Chapter 26 by Claire Lee overviews the emerging field of digital migration studies and conceptualizes time, temporality, and temporariness within the migration and media field. Based on quasi-ethnographic research of 36 Korean visa-status migrants, the chapter investigates how media shape national and daily temporality in transnational lives, how a life course approach applies to different migration stages and media practices, and how temporary migrants experience "contingent" and "indentured" temporality during the "staggered" migration process. In doing this, the chapter argues that migration decision-making is a complex process which includes not only economic, political, demographic, and environmental features but also temporal factors. Moreover, transient migrants' daily lives are often disrupted and restructured by constant juggling of the biographic timescale across the dynamic institutional timescale.

Chapter 27 by Mandy Tröger provides a historical analysis of the early post-socialist transition of the press in Central and Eastern Europe (CEE) in 1989–1990. Based on extensive archival research, it focuses on the question of how Western (in particular West German) newspaper publishers built market structures to their favor. Starting with the press in the German Democratic Republic (GDR) and Hungary, West German newspaper publishers soon entered other CEE markets, establishing lasting economic dependencies. This chapter gives an overview of these developments. It helps us understand the conditions within which media systems develop in transitioning countries.

In Chapter 28, Taeyoung Kim examines the characteristics of SVOD (subscription video-on-demand) services by analyzing the catalogs of Netflix Canada. While the analysis focuses on the status of Canadian television programs on Netflix, it also explores the position of Canadian films in various international catalogs to cross-check the findings. Considering the roles and responses from local broadcasters and the Canadian government as major stakeholders in the nation's mediascape, the findings are expected to shed light on the interactive dynamics of television landscapes in Canada in the era of SVOD that would reshape the nature of a key pillar in the nation's cultural politics.

References

Bieber, J. (2014). Impact of the Globalization of Social Media. *Medium*. 30 April. https://medium.com/@jessbiebss/impact-of-the-globalization-of-social-media-7f8e956c10ae
Birkinbine, B., Gomez, R., and Wasko, J. (2016). *Global Media Giants*. Routledge.

Boyd-Barrett, O. and T. Mirrlees (eds) (2019). *Media Imperialism: Continuity and Change*. Lanham, MD: Rowman & Littlefield.

Flew, T. (2018). *Understanding Global Media*. New York, NY: Palgrave.

Forrester (2020). In A Time Of Crisis, Can Digital Technology Save Globalization? *Forbes*. 10 April. www.forbes.com/sites/forrester/2020/04/10/in-a-time-of-crisis-can-digital-technology-save-globalization/#6852c6463b72

Giddens, A. (1999). Comment: the 1999 Reith Lecture: New world without end. *The Observer*, 11 April. https://canvas.sfu.ca/courses/41615/files/folder/Week%202?preview=8617131

Goggin, G., and McLelland, M. (2017). Globalization: Global Coordinates of Internet Histories. In Goggin and McLelland (eds.). *The Routledge Companion to Global Internet Histories*, 1–19. London: Routledge.

Hafez, K. (2013). *The Myth of Media Globalization*. Cambridge, UK: Polity

Jin, D.Y. (2019). *Globalization and Media in the Digital Platform Era*. London: Routledge.

Kerr, A., and Flynn, R. (2003). Revisiting Globalisation Through the Movie and Digital Games Industries. *Convergence: The International Journal of Research into New Media Technologies* 9(1): 91–113.

Lechner, F., and Boli, J. (eds.) (2014). *The Globalization Reader*. Fifth Edition. Hoboken, NJ: Wiley.

Lule, J. (2015). *Globalization and Media: Global Village of Babel*. Third Edition. Lanham, MD: Rowman & Littlefield.

Miller, T., and Kraidy, M. (2016). *Global Media Studies*. Hoboken, NJ: Wiley.

Mirrlees, T. (2013). *Global entertainment media: Between cultural imperialism and cultural globalization*. London: Routledge.

Schiller, H. (1976). *Communication and Cultural Domination*. White Plains, NY: International Arts and Sciences Press.

Sharma, R. (2016). Globalisation as we know it is over—and Brexit is the biggest sign yet. *The Guardian*. July 28. www.theguardian.com/commentisfree/2016/jul/28/era-globalisation-brexit-eu-britain-economic-frustration

Staley, D. (2020). NEXT: Zoom Globalization. *Columbus Underground*. 14 September. www.columbusunderground.com/next-zoom-globalization-ds1w

PART I

History, Theory, and Globalization

2

THE STRUGGLE FOR CONTROL IN THE AGE OF IMPERIALISM VS THE BELLE ÉPOQUE OF LIBERAL INTERNATIONALISM AND THE MODERN WORLD ECONOMY IN COMMUNICATIONS HISTORY

Dwayne Winseck

Just over a decade ago, Robert Pike and I published *Communication and Empire* (2007), in which we showed that modern communications media had developed within the context of the "belle époque of liberal internationalism", circa 1860 to 1930, rather than as a reflex of national interests, as had long been asserted. Since this period was the closest prede-cessor to our own times, we believed that examining it offered insight into the 21st century version of globalization—and its precarity.

(O'Rourke & Williamson, 1999; Jones, 2005; Rosenberg, 2012: Topik & Wells, 2012)

This chapter picks up where we left off by reprising and synthesizing our work since the publica-tion of *Communication and Empire* in 2007, and that of others who have also added to the new lines of analysis that we tried to open up or, conversely, who have posed significant challenges to it. It identifies the core elements of global communication in the late 19th and early 20th centuries, and shows that they were more global and organized as a *system* than previously thought. These elements included, for example, investment and ownership, corporate identity, international and national laws, the careers of experts and engineers, views of modernization, and imperial strategy. The onslaught of World War I threw all of this into disarray, however. Finally, the chapter concludes by pointing to efforts after the war's end to reconstruct the earlier "belle époque of liberal internationalism" that had seized the minds of a small group of "communications experts" in the US State Department and a few other countries, including Britain, France, Italy, and Japan. While the much-heralded plan for a World Communications Conference where such issues were to be dealt with never came to fru-ition, some of the desired results were achieved in a piecemeal fashion: i.e., the breaking up of mon-opoly concessions throughout the Atlantic region, new investment in submarine cable and emerging wireless technologies and greater competition, regulators less beholden to industry and corporate interests, and improved services at more affordable prices than previously available. Nonetheless, as this chapter concludes, despite these successes, they were not enough to keep the mounting nationalism and the economic collapse of the late 1920s and 1930s at bay—all of which put the final nail in the coffin of "the empire of capitalist modernity" and led to incessant struggles for control over resources that bequeathed to us the calamity of another World War.

Reflections on "Methodological Nationalism" and the Turn to Global Histories

Pike and I began our research for *Communication and Empire* right before the turn of the 21st century, just as the processes of globalization were in full gallop—and a decade after the Cold War had ended. It was also a decade after Daniel Headrick's (1991) seminal book *The Invisible Weapon: Telecommunications and International Politics, 1851–1945* was published. According to Headrick and Pascal Griset (2001) in a later article, during the era of the new imperialism and rising nationalism, circa 1880–1910, the field of submarine telegraphy was one of "great power rivalries" (p. 543). Other proponents of this "imperial thesis" of great power rivalries included Paul Kennedy (1971), Peter Hugill (1999), Jill Hills (2002), Joseph Tulchin (1971), and Daqing Yang (2011). These scholars fostered an approach that had held sway from the 1920s (Shreiner, 1924), with recent contributions stressing the extent to which communications media served primarily as "weapons of politics" and "tools of empire" (Headrick, 1991, 1981).

This literature focused on how geopolitics, imperialism, and a struggle for control for resources between Britain, France, Germany, and, later, the US and Japan had defined the historical development of international communication. The story was ultimately one where the hegemony of *Pax Britannica* over international communications was consolidated in the late 19th century but subsequently lost to the US after World War II—albeit with crucial moves in this direction taking place by the 1910s. Such claims have influenced a generation of scholars ever since, all of whom stress the importance of both submarine telegraphs and news agencies like Reuters for "Britain's ascendency as a world power" (Müller-Pohl, 2013, p. 104).

However, new lines of thinking have also gained traction in the interim (Fari, 2015; Müller, 2016; Barton, 2014; Bonea, 2016; Mann, 2017; Müller & Tworek, 2015; Rosenberg, 2012; Topik & Wells, 2012). The critique of "methodological nationalism" that underpins the "struggle for control model" has also taken hold more broadly across academic disciplines amidst efforts to write history in a more global register (Beck, 2005; Conrad, 2015). There is also a strong move toward writing transnational histories of communications media, technology, politics, and culture as well (Badenoch & Fickers, 2010; Fickers, 2009). In sum, there is lively ferment in the field and it is a stimulating time to be doing communications history.

In *Communication and Empire*, Pike and I dubbed the conventional approach to writing communications history the "struggle for control" model of communication, and contrasted it to an analysis that showed the global communications system—consisting of underseas cables interlinked with national and urban telegraph networks, news agencies, and the commercial press—to be far more global, in terms of ownership, cartels, corporate identity, expertise, policy, and imperial strategy, than often assumed. Our work also drew from David Harvey's (2003) idea that "territorial imperialism" cannot be understood properly independently of "capitalist imperialism", a process whereby markets, technology, law, competition, cartels, and ideas about modernization all combine in an elusive gambit to create a universal space of economic development. Such a view also seemed to mesh well with contemporaries' accounts of the times (Feis, 1934; Reinsch, 1911; Conant, 1898; Hobson, 1902).

We began our research at the end of the 1990s with the expectation that we would fill in some missing gaps in the existing literature. However, as we neared the end of our research it became clear that we needed to shift gears rather abruptly.

Times had changed, and as products of the historical milieu in which we wrote, so too had the way we were thinking about things. By the late 1990s, two decades of regulatory liberalization had unleashed economic globalization and a technocratic view of the world, while the geopolitical context of the Cold War slipped further into the past. The "revolution" in communications—pervasive computing, the melding of telecommunications and computing, and the rise of the internet—was also in full swing. In other words, politics, economics, and communications were all intertwined in the current mode of globalization, so perhaps that was the case in the past too?

New archival material had also become available that had not been incorporated into the scholarly literature. In particular, two Record Groups at the US National Archives and Records Administration (NARA), RG43 and RG59, had been declassified and made available at this time (US National Archives and Record Administration). They offered fundamentally new insights into the US's conflicted stance on international communication policy and prospects for a Universal Electrical Communication Union after World War I and into the 1920s. In addition, after spending much time at the British National Archives at Kew Gardens, and those of Cable and Wireless,[1] we also realized that we had to look elsewhere.

Scholars had used the Cable and Wireless Archives a lot, and no wonder. The archivists there were generous, knowledgeable, and kind. Its original location in London was convenient and an attractive place to conduct research. The company's source material informed a generation of research on the firm's complex history and organizational structure, its approaches to new technologies such as wireless, and its connections to the British government and national security interests. The firm's official corporate history had also been widely used by many as a starting point for their own research (Barty-King, 1979; Headrick, 1991). Researchers' interest seemed to dwindle when the Cable and Wireless Archives were moved to the company's new headquarters in Porthcurno in the south of the UK, but staff continued to be amazingly helpful and any researcher worth their salt still went there to do research. We benefited greatly from all of this.

At the same time, however, it also struck us—again, rather late in the game—that there was another important resource that had not been used much until that point by researchers, including us: Guildhall Library. The Library specializes in business and corporate history, specifically materials from the London Stock Exchange (LSE) such as the prospectuses and annual reports of companies quoted on the LSE between 1824 and 1964 (Guildhall Library, n.d.). Since London was *the* center of world finance during this period, many submarine cable, telegraph, and wireless companies were listed there (Feis, 1934; Müller-Pohl, 2013; Müller-Pohl & Tworek, 2015). However, just because firms were listed on the LSE did not mean they were quintessentially British. Indeed, as we discovered, many of these companies featured a combination of investments from a variety of international sources, as we will see, and thus exemplified the multinational nature of business at the time. In short, discovering Guildhall Library was a boon. It took on a decisive importance in our work and has since become a valuable resource for subsequent researchers, who have used it extensively to write histories of Marconi and the communications industry more generally (Raboy, 2017; Elmer, 2016; Müller-Pohl, 2013).

A Short History of Global Communications and the Empire of Capital

Informed by these considerations, we eschewed the idea of the nation-state as the "natural" unit of analysis, while instead moving the role of investment, business interests, markets, and technology further up the ladder of intellectual priorities than had been the case in the conventional "struggle for control" model. Both moves were consistent with recent criticisms of "methodological nationalism" and theoretical trends in terms of writing history in a more global register. We did so, however, not because of fashionable scholarly trends but, as Giovanni Arrighi has observed (1994), because capital has been a globalizing force from its very inception, with developments in communication and transportation fundamentally bound up with such processes. As Karl Marx (1867/1972) famously observed,

> ... Capital by its nature drives beyond every spatial barrier. Thus the creation of the physical conditions of exchange—of the means of communication and transport—*the annihilation of space by time*—becomes an extraordinary necessity for it ... [T]he production of cheap means of communication and transport is a condition for production based on capital, and promoted by it for that reason (p. 459).

The key, however, is not to develop a one-dimensional focus on either the globalizing force of capital *or* the territorial geography of imperialism, but to grasp the interplay between *both*. One way to do so is to combine David Harvey's distinction between *territorial* and *capitalist* imperialism with a *structuralist view* of the global system (Long & Schmidt, 2005; Harvey, 2003; Lukes, 2005; Hills, 2002).[2] As David Long and Brian Schmidt (2005) write, for example, contemporaries often saw these two forces as two sides of the same coin, or the pivots upon which the woof and warp of the modern era turned (p. 2).

According to Harvey (2003), *territorial imperialism* is a "distinctly political project ... based in the command of territory and ... the strategies used by a state to assert its interests and achieve its goals in the world at large" (p. 26). While territorial imperialism *was* important, it mainly targeted "weak states" in Africa, the Caribbean, and Asia. Yet, to stop here is akin to "judging the size and character of icebergs solely from the parts above the water-line," as John Gallagher and Ronald Robinson (1953) put it in their seminal article, "The Imperialism of Free Trade" (p. 1). The spaces of capital and communication were *not* coterminous with the space of territorial-based empires, but part and parcel of a much larger framework of *capitalist imperialism*. Harvey (2003) defines *capitalist imperialism* as a system of power that aims to allow "economic power to flow across and through continuous space," where dominant models of development are emulated and consent preferred to coercion (p. 26). He also suggests that while power is usually the preserve of single states under territorial imperialism, capitalist imperialism relies upon "the *collective accumulation of power* as the ... basis of hegemony" (*emphasis added*, p. 37). Furthermore, Harvey does not view corporate interests as subordinate to state interests, nor does he see nation-states as mere handmaidens of capital. State and corporate interests and relationships are much more complex than that instrumentalist conception of power implies. So, too, is technology, hence our critique of it as "weapons of politics" and "tools of empire".

Harvey's views are of recent vintage but they overlap remarkably well with the theory of "capitalist investment imperialism" put forth by the first international economic advisor to the US government, Charles Conant (1898), and broader intellectual currents that linked the German Historical School to the newly emerging fields of economics, political science, and sociology in North America. Conant saw advances in communication and transportation as underpinning the creation of a world market and opening new outlets for a super-abundance of capital in Britain, Europe, and the US. He also warned, however, that while more universal communication synchronized world markets, it could also magnify the scale and expand the reach of *financial* crises. In addition, he argued that weak states were unstable and needed to be rationally managed, similar to how international financial commissions and public debt administrations had been imposed on the Balkans, Egypt, the Ottoman Empire, and Spain by British and European interests in the late 19th century—considerations which did not figure much, if at all, in the existing communications history literature (Feis, 1934). However, Conant also thought that sweeping reforms could be used to modernize the entire administrative and social systems of weaker states in order to bootstrap them into the modern world while countering their potential to generate instabilities that could threaten the world economy.

Like Harvey, Conant distinguished capitalist imperialism from territorial imperialism, but on the grounds that the former did not seek permanent control of foreign lands and people, just a transitional period of directed modernization during which weak countries would be remade in the image of capitalist modernity (Rosenberg, 2012; Sklar, 1988). Such views are also of a piece with the British theorist of imperialism, John Hobson (1902), as well as the German Historical School, which took the relationship between culture and economic development as its focus of analysis while seeing the world economy as emerging in an evolutionary process that involved ever larger political units (Young, 2009; Müller & Tworek, 2015; Reinsch, 1911).

For two or three decades before World War I, American scholars had traveled in flocks to Europe, many of whom studied with members of the German Historical School. They brought this experience back to the US, where some of them played formative roles in creating the new disciplines of sociology, political science, and economics. These ideas also filtered into the US by way of figures like the Secretary of State under President Ulysses Grant, Hamilton Fish. Fish was the architect of the country's first formal international communication policy statement in 1869 and a member of the International Institute of Law (US Secretary of State, Hamilton Fish, 1869–1906). The Institute, in turn, was a European-led effort to remodel international law in light of the realities of the modern capitalist world. When Fish announced the US's "free trade in cables" policy, the two doyens of the Institute, Louis Renaud of France and Dutch legal scholar Tobias Asser, lauded it as "très comprehensive." Given that Renaud and Asser had written some of the founding documents of the International Telegraph Union (ITU) and, as an aside, had each won the Nobel Peace Prize in 1907 and 1911, respectively, their views on the US policy carried some weight (Kokiennemi, 2004, pp. 1–5, 12–17, 274–278). This particular example also suggests that the US played a bigger role in international affairs and had a more international outlook than has been commonly assumed, and well before it emerged as an economic powerhouse during and after World War I.

Increased interdependence between large-scale technical systems, markets, and governments was also shaped by parallel developments in international law. The International Telegraph Union, most notably, led the way in this regard, bringing together two earlier predecessors into the unified ITU in 1865. By 1919, the number of multilateral unions had soared to 45 as *institution building* proceeded full-tilt to match the emerging new international order (Mattelart, 1994, p. 26; Reinsch, 1911, p. 4). Many observers argue that the ITU was purely a creature of the European governments that had created it (John, 2020). However, European-based companies had been active even in the organizations that preceded the ITU in the 1850s and, unsurprisingly, began participating in the then new organization's affairs by the early 1870s (Fari, 2015). The New York-based printer and backer of the Anglo American Telegraph Company Cyrus Field also appealed (without success) to the ITU to enshrine "cable neutrality" during its 1872 conference. In addition, despite not yet being a formal member, the US government participated in the ITU's affairs from the 1875 Moscow conference onwards, while the US-based Western Union and Commercial Company attended their first ITU conferences in 1882 and 1885, respectively. They continued to do so long before the US joined the International Radio-telegraph Union in 1906 and the reformed International Telecommunications Union in 1932 (ITU, 1868, p. 33, 1872–1908; Codding, 1952/1972, pp. 22–30).

Wiring the World: A Global History of Late 19th and Early 20th Century Communications

The initial ventures to build submarine cable telegraph links before 1866 from Britain across the Atlantic and to India and the Far East all failed. However, in the following decade the technology became reasonably well understood and financed, while the consolidation of domestic telegraph industries in Britain, Europe, and North America at this time also yielded large corporate entities with the means needed to "wire the world". The British government's nationalization of domestic telegraph systems in 1868 transferred £6 million (equivalent to ~$40m US dollars at the time) into the coffers of those who parlayed their early domestic experience into the conquest of global markets, notably John Pender and Julius Reuter. Reflecting these realities, by 1865, a system of telegraph lines and submarine cables linking Britain and Europe to India had been completed, followed by the crossing of the North Atlantic the next year.

Many new companies were launched at this time. Many of them failed but others became key players for decades to come, such as the Anglo American Telegraph Company (1866); the French Atlantic Telegraph Company (1869); the Great Northern Telegraph Company (1870); the Submarine Telegraph Trust Company (1871); the Eastern Telegraph Company (1872–1873); the Western & Brazilian Telegraph Company (1872); the Direct United States Cable Company (1873); and Globe Telegraph and Trust Company (1873). These companies alone represented over four-fifths of the capital of the industry in 1874—about £18.3 million ($100 million) (US, 1892, pp. 50–59). Private enterprise, moreover, ruled the industry. Even at the height of the new imperialism (1880–1910), state ownership accounted for less than 20 percent of cables in service (Britain, 1902, Appendix J; US, HR Committee of Interstate and Foreign Commerce, 1902).

Throughout the belle époque of liberal internationalism, London was the absolute center of investment in the submarine cable industry and remained so well into the 20th century. As Müller and Tworek state (2015), "by the late nineteenth century, telegraph companies had become major multi-national enterprises. They not only provided the infrastructure for faster stock-market interactions but were themselves traded on the stock exchange. Such firms formed a vital cornerstone in the rise of Western managerial capitalism" (p. 264).

The EATC was the biggest company of the era and it was clearly British in terms of the capital behind it, the composition of its board of directors, the technology it used, and its close ties to the British government, although even it had alliances with other firms and local directors at its affiliates around the world. Moreover, revealing just how complex these matters were, in 1911 the aptly named Anglo American Telegraph Company ceded *control* of its trans-Atlantic cables to the US-based Western Union, much to the consternation of some British cable experts. Nonetheless, Western Union proved to be a reliable ally in World War I as it handed over all trans-Atlantic messages to the British government for reasons of national security (Bright, 1911; Winseck & Pike, 2007, pp. 189–190).

Crucially, however, the fact that companies were registered on the London Stock Exchange *did not* mean that they were *British*. This was because London was not just the center of British capital investment but the hub of world finance. As Herbert Feis (1934) observed in his seminal book *Europe: the World's Bankers*: "London was the center of a financial empire, more international, more extensive in its variety, than even the political empire of which it was the capital" (p. 5; also see Müller-Pohl, 2013, p. 118). Economic historian Geoff Jones (2005) concurs: "London was exceptional in the degree of cosmopolitanism in the 19th century, although the lack of concern about the nationality of ownership *was general*—a stance that did not shift … before World War I" (p. 282). Simone Müller-Pohl's (2013) research over the past decade has led her to a similar conclusion (p. 118).

Many of the companies that were registered in the UK consisted of a mixture of British, European, and North American capital, and their boards of directors and management reflected this fact. From the beginning, the Anglo American Company, for instance, combined capital, directors, and concessions from Britain and the US. The Great Northern Telegraph Company and its affiliate, the Western and Brazilian Telegraph Company, was formed "in 1869 through an amalgamation of Danish, Norwegian, Russian, and English interests" (Müller-Pohl & Tworek, 2015, 266). The French Atlantic Cable Company in the 1870s also combined French and British capital as well as two boards of directors, one in London, the other in Paris. That practice set a precedent for the French Post and Telegraph Authority after 1902 when, after taking control of the South American Cable Company from its former British owners, it kept separate boards of directors in London and Paris until the outbreak of World War I. The Direct United States Cable Company is another example, with a shareholder list at its founding in 1873 that included major investors from the Siemens family, the Anglo-Austrian Bank, the Deutsche Bank, the Banque Centrale Anversoise, and stock brokers and merchants from Germany, Belgium, France, and the UK. The Commercial Cable Company was also backed by capital and directors from the US, Britain, and Canada, and opportunistically exploited the ambiguities around its national identity by claiming to be wholly British when it successfully sought subsidies for its two "British" affiliates—the Halifax Bermudas Telegraph Company (1890) and the Direct West India Cable Company (1898)—and as "American as apple pie" when standing before the US. Congress to argue why it should be chosen to lay the first US-owned cable across the Pacific (1904). It struck a similar stance on numerous other occasions thereafter (Müller & Tworek, 2015, 266; Müller-Pohl, 2013, p. 119; Winseck & Pike, 2007, p. 53).

Prior to the turn toward global history, however, these realities were obscured by the tendency to refer to the companies generically as British, American, German, French, Japanese, and so forth, as if their national identity dictated that they served as tools of the state. In fact, however, the multinational complexion of the business would have made realist assessments of the national basis of power difficult to achieve because nation-states and corporate actors often pursued their interests independently of one another—although this faded as World War I yoked the two closer together than ever before. Even scholars who have been reluctant to accept the full sweep of the global history thesis agree that the connections between national and corporate interests were much weaker than once thought and imperial administrators not as purposeful in pursuing their aim as previously assumed (Wenzlhuemer, 2013, p. 83).

Cartels: Private Structures of Cooperation and Avoiding Ruinous Competition

Cable and wireless firms also forged cartels with one another—or joint purse agreements, as they were called—on account of the high capital costs of submarine cable construction, the tendency for many nation-states to grant monopolistic concessions, and a desire to avoid "ruinous competition". Indeed, the combination of these factors led to all of the world's main communication markets becoming dominated by cartels in the last third of the 19th century, although in some instances such as the North Atlantic, there were two rival alliances, one led by the Anglo American Company and another led by the Commercial Company—*despite* the British and US governments' "free trade in cables" policies during this era. As a *rule*, however, the cartels were thoroughly multinational in nature and consisted of a mixture of British, US, Chinese, Danish, French, German, Japanese, Turkish, and Persian enterprises—depending on the market and/or region (Ahvenainen, 2004; Müller and Tworek, 2015, 273; US, 1921, pp. 89–92; Winseck & Pike, 2007, pp. 57–61, 168–174).

Cartels were also a defining feature *across* the global media. Building on earlier agreements going back to 1859, the "ring circle agreement" of 1870 expanded the terms of the global news cartel consisting of Reuters, Havas, and Wolff (revised to include Associated Press in 1893) (Rantanen, 2006, p. 21). Swiftly after World War I, the big four commercial wireless firms—Marconi, Compagnie Générale de Télégraphie sans Fil, RCA, and Telefunken—adopted the same methods, and with the surprising goal of quickly reintegrating Germany back into the international fold. The same was true of the new German Atlantic Telegraph Company, which was also brought into a joint-operating agreement with the Western Union and Commercial Company in 1927 (Winseck & Pike, 2007, pp. 288–290).

Building on Michael Hogan's (1977) work, we referred to these arrangements as "private structures of cooperation and control". They helped to manage not only "ruinous competition" but also the many tensions that periodically flared up between companies and between them and the governments whose territories they served. While Hogan sees these private structures of control as essential to trans-Atlantic commerce and diplomacy after 1918, they functioned globally rather than just in the trans-Atlantic economies and they emerged earlier, and with a greater range of national interests, than even he suggests. They also lasted well into the 20th century. The news cartel collapsed only in 1934 and the wireless cartel expired in the 1940s, while the cable cartels have been refashioned into the multinational consortia that own and operate the majority of the fiber optic cables that make up the internet infrastructure in our own time. In sum, these observations strongly suggest that it is the "*globalization* of control" rather than the "*struggle* for control" that defined the early global media.

Telegraphs and submarine cables integrated local markets into the global economic system, synchronized the financial markets of London, New York, Paris, Berlin, and Buenos Aires, and reshaped the geography and temporality of long-distance trade. As Christopher Hoag (2006) also observes based on his study of New York and London capital markets, "the telegraph shortened the information lag by about nine or ten days," and brought prices in both markets closer together as a result (p. 350). As the Secretary of Lloyds of London also observed, the "cables and telegraph increase the *information component of business transactions* and provide business with knowledge about markets before they enter them" (quoted in Britain, 1899, p. 156). Beyond financial markets, however, as submarine cable telegraphs reached new frontiers, the international news wire services—e.g., Reuters, Havas, Wolff, and, later, Associated Press—quickly established news bureaus in major world cities as soon as they were connected to the cable system. Thus, as the London-based Eastern and Associated Telegraph Companies extended their cables outwards from the British capital, Reuters news agency followed in near lock-step, setting up hubs for news gathering and dissemination in Bombay (1870), Hong Kong (1872), Shanghai (1873), and Buenos Aires (1874), for example.

While these developments clearly expanded the worldwide system of communications and information flows it is also true that, even more than being the "rich man's post," as domestic telegraphs were often called (John, 2010), international submarine telegraph cables were even more expensive and exclusive in terms of who could afford to use them. As a case in point, a mere 400 users accounted for the lion's share of the Central and South American Telegraph Company revenue, for example, with the vast majority of the messages sent over its cables going to just 90 recipients in 18 North American, British, and European cities. In short, far from creating a universal space of communication, these were networks of power that simultaneously included and excluded based on geography and wealth. Exclusivity, in turn, conferred enormous advantages on the precious few who could afford to use them.

Over time, however, some newspapers and news agencies became fierce critics of cable monopolies and cartels, especially as wireless communication (radio) took-off in the 1910s and 1920s. In fact, the US and British press and newswire services led the charge against monopoly concessions and cartels in the lead up to the World Communications Conference after World War I. For the most part, however, the press and news agencies were indifferent to whether press messages were carried over the wires or through the air, so long as service was affordable, reliable, and available wherever and whenever they needed it. Walter Lippmann (1920) underscored the point in *Liberty and the News* when he remarked that "the real censorship on the wires is the cost of transmission. This in itself is enough to limit any expansive competition or any significant independence" (p. 43).

Some Concluding Thoughts: The Triumph of the Struggle for Control Worldview and the End of the Belle Époque of Liberal Internationalism

There was much hope, and no shortage of energy, put into rebuilding the "belle epoque of liberal internationalism" at the end of World War I. Of particular note in this regard was an ambitious effort to reform the global media system that sought to eliminate monopolistic concessions and cartels, expand access of the press and news agencies to more affordable international communications by cable and wireless, and break down the status of the world's telegraph and wireless communications systems as "the rich man's post" into more accessible means of communication. On one level reformist efforts failed because the planned-for World Communications Conference where they were to be pursued in an integrated fashion was never held. On another level, however, some of these aims were achieved in bits and pieces over the next decade. Monopoly concessions in South American and the North Atlantic, for example, were broken up. A flood of new investment in new facilities did occur in the 1920s, just as the call by the "Great Powers" for a World Communications Conference had demanded. Greater competition between submarine cable telegraph companies and between them and the shortwave wireless services of Marconi, RCA, Telefunken, TSF, and others that emerged in the 1920s also took place, even though it would be some years yet before the cartels themselves were dismantled (as in the case of wireless and the news agencies) or remade into the multinational consortia that still own and operate so much of the global internet infrastructure today (Winseck, 2017). Improved services at more affordable rates resulted from the changes that did take place, even if that did not turn the cable and wireless services into means of *mass* communication. All of this, however, was not enough to reverse the tide against rising nationalism and authoritarianism at the end of the 1920s and throughout the 1930s—or the Great Depression—all of which combined put the final nail in the coffin of "the empire of capitalist modernity" and led to the horrors of World War II.

Notes

1 Cable and Wireless was the successor firm to the Eastern and Associated Telegraph Companies (EATC), a giant in the cable communications industry in the 19th and 20th centuries. It continued to be a key figure up until the 1990s before being cut down to a shadow of its former self and sold in 2016 to the US-based Liberty Global): Liberty Global, *Liberty Global Completes Acquisition of Cable & Wireless Communications Plc.*, May 16, 2016. www.libertyglobal.com/pdf/press-release/05-16-Closing-CWC-Acquisition-FINAL.pdf.

2 This view draws on Lukes' distinction between three views of power: (1) an *instrumentalist view* in which power is based on distinctive interests and the ability of one group or individual to realize their interests in the face of opposition from others; (2) an *agenda-setting view* in which power is a function of being able to shape the agenda around which debates, decisions, and conflict occur; and (3) a *systems view* in which power is a function of the ability of actors to forge relationships with others, exercise control over resources (material and symbolic), set the "rules of the game" and deform the acceptable range of action that is open to all actors as part of the *system* (Lukes, 2005). Jill Hills offers an excellent explanation of Lukes and the structuralist view, although her reliance on secondary sources and the struggle for control view seems to me to be at odds with her theoretical stance.

References

Ahvenainen, J. (2004). *The European Cable Companies in South America*. Helsinki: Finnish Academy of Science and Letters.

Arrighi, G. (1994). *The Long Twentieth Century: Money, Power and the Origins of our Time*. London: Verso.

Badenoch, A., & Fickers, A. (2010). *Materializing Europe: Transnational Infrastructures and the Project of Europe*. Basingstoke: Palgrave.

Barton, G. (2014). *Informal empire and the rise of one world culture*. New York: Oxford University.

Barty-King, H. (1979). *Girdle round the Earth*. London: Heinemann.

Beck, U. (2015), *Power in the Global Age*. London: Polity.

Bonea, A. (2016). *The news of empire: Telegraphy, journalism, and the politics of reporting in colonial India c. 1830–1900*. New Delhi: Oxford University.

Bright, C. (1911). *Imperial Telegraphic Communication*. London: P.S. King and Son.

Britain (1902). *Second Report of the Interdepartmental Committee on Cable Communications*, Cmd 1056, Appendix J. London: Her Majesty's Stationary Office.

Britain, Pacific Cable Committee (1899). *Report, Minutes and Proceedings, etc.*, London: Her Majesty's Stationary Office.

Codding, G. (1952/1972). *The International Telecommunication Union: An experiment in International cooperation*. New York: Arno Press.

Conant, C. (1898). The Economic Basis of Imperialism, *North American Review*, 326–46.

Conrad, S. (2016). *What is Global History?* Princeton, NJ: University of Princeton.

Elmer, G. (2016). A new medium goes public: The financialization of Marconi's Wireless Telegraph & Signal Company, *New Media & Society*, *19*(11), 1829–1847.

Fari, S. (2015). *The Formative Years of the Telegraph Union*. Newcastle: Cambridge Scholar.

Feis, H. (1934). *Europe: The World's Banker, 1870–1914*. New Haven: Yale University.

Fickers, A. (2009). Radio. In P.Y. Saunier & A. Iriye (eds). *Palgrave Dictionary of Transnational History*. New York: Springer.

Gallagher, J. & Robinson, R. (1953). The Imperialism of Free Trade, *The Economic History Review*, *6*(1) 1–27.

Guildhall Library (n.d.). *Business History*. London: Guildhall Library.

Harvey, D. (2003). *The New Imperialism*. New York: Oxford University.

Headrick, D. (1981). *Tools of Empire: Technology and European Imperialism in the 19th Century*. New York: Oxford University.

Headrick, D. (1991). *The Invisible Weapon: Telecommunications and International Politics, 1851–1945*. New York: Oxford University.

Headrick, D., & Griset, P. (2001), Submarine Telegraph Cables. *Business History Review*, *75*(autumn), 543–578.

Hills, J. (2002). *The Struggle for Control of Global Communications*. Chicago: University of Illinois.

Hoag, C. (2006). The Atlantic Telegraph Cable and Capital Market Information Flows. *The Journal of Economic History*, *66*(2), 342–353.

Hobson, J.A. (1902). *Imperialism: A Study*. New York: James Pott & Co.

Hogan, Michael (1977). *Informal Entente*. London: University of Missouri.

Hugill, P. (1999). Global Communications Since 1844: Geopolitics and Technology. Baltimore, MA: The Johns Hopkins University Press.

International Telecommunications Union (1868). *International Telegraph Conference (Vienna)*. Geneva, Switzerland: Author. Available at: http://handle.itu.int/11.1004/020.1000/4.2.51.fr.200.

International Telecommunications Union (1872–1908) *Conferences Collection*. Geneva, Switzerland: Author. Available at: www.itu.int/en/history/Pages/ConferencesCollection.aspx.

John, R. (2010). *Network Nation*. Cambridge, MA: Harvard University.

John, R. (2020). When Techno-Diplomacy Failed: Walter S. Rogers, the Universal Electrical Communications Union, and the Limitations of the International Telegraph Union as a Global Actor in the 1920s. In Balbi, G. & Fickers, A. (eds.). History of the International Telecommunications Union: Transnational techno-diplomacy in Modern Europe (pp. 55–76). Berlin: De Gruyter.

Jones, G. (2005). *Multinationals and Global Capitalism*. New York: Oxford University.

Kennedy, P. (1971). Imperial Cable Communications and Strategy, 1870–1914, *English Historical Review*, 728–748.

Lippmann, W. (1920). *Liberty and the News*. New Brunswick: Transaction.

Long, D., & Schmidt, B. (eds.) (2005). *Imperialism and Internationalism in the Discipline of International Relations*. Albany, New York: State University of New York.

Lukes, S. (2005). *Power: A Radical View*, 2nd ed. London: Palgrave Macmillan.

Mann, M. (2017). *Wiring the nation: Telecommunication, newspaper-reportage, and nation building in British India, 1850–1930*. New Delhi: Oxford University.

Marx, K. (1867/1972). *Capital: Volume One. A Critical Analysis of Capitalist Production*. Reprinted in Tucker, R., ed., *The Marx-Engels Reader*. London: W.W. Norton & Co.

Mattelart, A. (1994). *Mapping World Communication*. Minneapolis, MN: University of Minnesota.

Müller-Pohl, S. (2013). Working the Nation State: Submarine Cable Actors, Cable Transnationalism and the Governance of the Global Media System, 1858–1914. In I. Löhr & R. Wenzlhuemer (eds.), *The Nation State and Beyond: Governing Globalization Processes in the Nineteenth and Early Twentieth Centuries* (pp. 101–123). Berlin: Springer.

Müller-Pohl, S.M. (2016). *Wiring the world: The social and cultural creation of global telegraph networks*. New York: Columbia University.

Müller-Pohl, S., & Tworek, H.J. (2015). The telegraph and the bank: on the interdependence of global communications and capitalism, 1866–1914. *Journal of Global History*, 10(2), 259–283.

O'Rourke, Kevin & Williamson, J. (eds.)(1999). *Globalization and History*. Cambridge, MA: MIT, 1999.

Raboy, M. (2017). *Marconi: the Man Who Networked the World*. New York: Oxford.

Rantanen, T. (2006). Foreign Dependence and Domestic Monopoly: The European News Cartel and U.S. Associated Presses, 1861–1932, *Media History*, *12*(1), 19–35.

Reinsch, P. (1911). *Public International Unions*. Boston: Atheneum Press.

Rosenberg, E. (eds). (2012). *A World Connected*. Boston, MA: Harvard University.

Shreiner, G. (1924). *Cable and Wireless and their Role in the Foreign Relations of the United States*, Boston.

Sklar, M. (1988). *The corporate reconstruction of American capitalism, 1890-1916: The market, the law and politics*. New York: Cambridge University.

Topik S. & Wells, A. (2012). *Global Markets Transformed*. Boston, MA: Harvard University.

Tulchin, J. (1971). *The Aftermath of War*. New York: New York University.

US National Archives and Record Administration (n.d.) *Reports, Correspondence, and Other Documents* (Record Group 43 and Record Group 59, 574 D1 and D11). Washington: NARA.

US Secretary of State, Hamilton Fish to foreign governments (October and November, 1869). *Digest of International Law* (1906) Washington, DC: US Govt Printing Office.

US Hydrographic Office (1892). *Submarine Cables*. Washington: Government Printing Office.

US House of Representatives Committee of Interstate and Foreign Commerce (1902), *Pacific Cable*, Washington: US Government Printing Office.

US Congress (1921). *Cable Landing Licenses Hearings, 66th Congress, 3rd Session*. Washington, DC: US Government Printing Office.

Wenzlhuemer, R. (2013). *Connecting the nineteenth-century world: The telegraph and globalization*. New York: Cambridge University.

Winseck, D. (2017). The Geopolitical Economy of the Global Internet Infrastructure. *Journal of Information Policy*, 7(3), 228–267.

Winseck, D., & Pike, R. (2007). *Communication and Empire: Media, Markets and Globalization, 1860–1930*. Durham, NC: Duke University.

Yang, D. (2011). *Technology of Empire: Telecommunications and Japanese Expansion in Asia, 1883–1945*. Boston, MA: Harvard University.

Young, C. (2009), The emergence of sociology from political economy in the United States. Journal of the History of the Behavioral Sciences, 45(2), 91–116.

3

CULTURAL PROXIMITY

Joseph Straubhaar

Why Audiences Turned to National and Regional Broadcast Television

During the 1960s and 1970s, many studies reported a one-way flow of media, particularly television programs, films, and news, from the US and a few other European countries to the rest of the world. Herbert Schiller (Schiller, 1976), estimated that 65% of all world communications originated in the USA UNESCO study in 1973 found that over half of the world imported most of their TV shows, mostly entertainment from the US (Nordenstreng & Varis, 1974), while other studies indicated the dominance of four large news agencies (AP, UPI, Agence France Presse, and Reuters) in the production of news worldwide (Boyd-Barrett, 1977) and the strong dominance by Hollywood of world film distribution and exhibition (Guback, 1984).

However, this was not to be a permanent trend in many countries. As early as 1965, the brand-new TV Globo in Brazil nearly failed when it tried a program strategy heavy with US imports on the advice of its joint venture partner, Time-Life (Straubhaar, 1984). It only began to succeed over the next four years as it dumped that strategy and hired local producers to create national shows (Wallach, 2011).

Throughout the 1970s and 1980s, several of the larger and/or wealthier countries in Latin America, the Mid-East, and Asia began to produce far more of their own television programs (Lee, 1980; Sinclair, Jacka, & Cunningham, 1996; Straubhaar, 1984). Some, like Brazil, Hong Kong, and Mexico, were beginning to export them, both regionally and globally (Sinclair & Straubhaar, 2013). This surprised Hollywood, scholars, and industry analysts, since up until that time most people supposed that a combination of control over distribution, high production values, and cultural familiarity, dating from the huge outflow and consumption of Hollywood films since the 1920s, would also keep US television programs in prime time indefinitely (Guback, 1984; Toby Miller, 2001). One British critic expected "Wall to Wall *Dallas*," US television everywhere across the world (Collins, 1986). In reality, most Latin American countries rejected *Dallas* and preferred either national or regional telenovelas to US prime time melodramas (Antola & Rogers, 1984). By the beginning of the 1980s, a number of scholars began to observe that, at least in television, international production and flow was beginning to change (Lee, 1980; Straubhaar, 1984).

One theory to explain this was cultural proximity—the idea that audiences would prefer either their own local or national television, or if that was lacking in the genres audiences wanted, television from similar, nearby cultures (Straubhaar, 1991). However, this theory also seemed to have limits, even in the 1970s–1990s. Audience research noted that upper class or upper middle class audiences in Latin America were more likely to prefer television from dissimilar cultures than were middle class, lower middle class, or working class audiences (Straubhaar, 1991, 2007). A parallel theory from media economics, the cultural discount, made the logical opposite proposition that audiences would tend to discount and avoid programming that was too culturally unfamiliar or irrelevant (Hoskins & Mirus, 1988).

Dependency on US in Television

Deriving from Marx, for whom culture serves as the ideological support for dominance by capitalist ruling classes, cultural dependency theory looked primarily at the role of media as part of the economic relations of dependency. In this analysis, Third World countries depended on the industrialized world for capital, technology, and most manufactured goods, while exporting low-cost primary products or cheap manufactured goods, which added little benefit to the local economy (Baran & Sweezy, 1968). Speaking primarily of Latin America, Fox (1992) observed that, "Cultural dependency generally was taken to mean the domination of content, financing, and advertising of the domestic media by foreign, specifically US companies." Audience choices were not really considered, as a logic of economic domination was assumed to prevail. Fox noted that critiques of cultural dependency theories centered upon three areas: (1) the failure of state-directed policy aimed at countering dependency, (2) the allure of free trade, and (3) the apparent success of some large Third World broadcasters, such as Mexico's Televisa and Brazil's TV Globo in producing their own programs on a large scale (1992).

Waisbord offers a vision of the historical development of Latin America that builds subtly on ideas like dependency. He defines three eras of television in Latin America in which the relationship with the US is always a defining feature: early US support for and equipment sales to Latin American television businesses, a stage of direct investment that had largely failed by the 1970s with US firms withdrawing, and a stage in which US firms re-enter Latin America through cable and satellite television (Waisbord, 1998a).

Cultural Imperialism

Cultural imperialism tends to see culture as part of a holistic system, in which imported television programs and films, local adaptations of American entertainment media genres, local as well as imported advertising and commercial media models all combine to encourage increased consumption and acceptance of the framework of consumer capitalism among viewers (Oliveira, 1993; Schiller, 1991). Indeed, if we separate cultural imperialism into economic and cultural layers, despite its holistic claims, we find that the economic predictions of cultural imperialism have largely come true. From the revolutionary days of the late 1950s–1970s, when capitalism was actively contested across the region and defeated in Cuba, most Latin American countries have become capitalist consumer economies, facilitated as much by nationally produced television as by US imports (Oliveira, 1993; Schiller, 1991).

However, in the cultural sphere, imperialism tended to assume a dominance of imported television, which would lead to a homogenization of culture. Tunstall observed: "The cultural imperialism hypothesis claims that authentic, traditional, and local culture in many parts of the world is being battered out of existence by the indiscriminate dumping of large quantities of slick commercial and media products, mainly from the United States" (Tunstall, 1977). These programs were assumed to be attractive because of their higher production values, their quality of acting and writing, and the appeal of their portrayals of US life (Straubhaar, 1981).

National Production

One of the first major empirical arguments against dependency and cultural imperialism rested in the success of emerging Third World producers: TV Globo in Brazil (Straubhaar, 1984), Televisa in Mexico (Sinclair, 1992), TVB in Hong Kong (Ma, 2005), Egyptian national television (Abu-Lughod, 2005), and other stations and networks in pushing imported programs out of prime time, substituting imported programs in favor of local or national television production. Their growth and commercial success came from attracting large national audiences to their nationally produced programs, such as telenovelas, other dramas, music, comedy, and large variety shows (Tunstall, 2008), and successfully drawing the advertising required to support the cost of that programming (Mattos, 1984; Straubhaar, 1984). Further, these countries (Brazil, Mexico, Hong Kong, Egypt) and others, like India, pushed forward to export to other countries within their geo-cultural regions, such as Latin America, East and Southeast Asia, and the Arabic-speaking Middle East (Sinclair et al., 1996), or to cultural-linguistic markets, like the Lusophone linguistic space, where Brazil exported telenovelas to Portugal starting in 1976 and Lusophone Africa after that (Cunha, 2011). Thus, one strong empirical observation against the logic of dominated cultural flows was the emergence of culturally similar regional television markets (Sinclair et al., 1996; Wilkinson, 1995).

Cultural Proximity

The theory of cultural proximity (Straubhaar, 1991) tries to explain why television production is growing within Latin America and other regions of the world at both the national and regional levels. The argument, building on de Sola Pool (1977), is that all other things being equal, audiences will tend to prefer programming which is closest or most proximate to their own culture, starting with national programming, if it can be supported by the local economy. Localized or nationalized cultural capital, identity, and language tend to favor an audience desire for cultural proximity, which leads audiences to prefer local and national productions over those which are globalized and/or American. Cultural proximity is created by a feeling of cultural closeness or similarity, perceived in specific things like humor, gender images, dress, style, lifestyle, knowledge about other lifestyles, ethnic types, religion, and values that seem familiar or comfortable. It could also be seen as a desire to see national cultures reflected on television (Waisbord, 1998b).

A similar desire for the most relevant or similar programs also seemed to lead many national audiences to prefer cultural-linguistic regional programming in genres that small countries cannot afford to produce for themselves. For instance, audiences in smaller countries, such as the Dominican Republic, have shown a preference for national programming. However, when there is a lack of availability within certain genres, there is a tendency to look next to Latin American regional programing, which may be relatively more culturally proximate or similar than those in the US (Straubhaar 1991). This second level of cultural proximity has been embraced as a useful explanation for the rise of regional cultural markets, particularly in television (Iwabuchi, 2001), but has been cited for music as well (Colista & Leshner, 1998). This will be expanded upon below.

Anthropologist Conrad Kottak, a longtime observer of culture in Brazil, observed in 1990 that "common to all mass culture successes, no matter what the country, the first requirement is that they fit the existing culture. They must be *preadapted* to their culture by virtue of cultural appropriateness [emphasis in the original]. If a product is to be a mass culture success, it must be immediately acceptable, understandable, familiar, and conducive to mass participation" (p. 43). The Brazilian case shows how strong the preference is for national programming. The major channel, TV Globo, produces over 12 hours a day of programming for itself, including over 85% of its prime time programming (Sinclair & Straubhaar, 2013). This kind of production can only be achieved when the domestic market is large enough to support the products and when the cultural industries are sufficiently developed to manufacture them.

Hoskins and Mirus (1988) have also created a useful parallel concept for examining the attraction of national programming to national audiences: the cultural discount.

> A particular programme rooted in one culture, and thus attractive in that environment, will have a diminished appeal elsewhere as viewers find it difficult to identify with the style, values, beliefs, institutions and behavioural patterns of the material in questions. Included in the cultural discount are reductions in appreciation due to dubbing or subtitling… As a result of the diminished appeal, fewer viewers will watch a foreign programme than a domestic programme of the same type and quality, and hence the value to the broadcasters, equal to the advertising revenue induced if the broadcaster is financed from this source, will be less… the cultural discount explains why trade is predominantly in entertainment, primarily drama, programming
>
> *(Hoskins & Mirus, 1988, pp. 500–501)*

Primary, Local or National, Cultural Proximity

Cultural proximity has evolved since 1991 into what might be seen as national and regional versions of the theory. At the national level, it seems to have become commonplace that most (but not all) national publics prefer nationally based television programming. Research by Milly Buonanno in Western Europe since the 1990s has shown an evolving preference for national programming, when available (1999, 2002). Similar national preferences seem to have evolved in many parts of Asia. That might initially have been due to fairly strong protectionism (Chan, 1994), but as quotas and other protections were relaxed in the later 1990s and 2000s in many countries, national preferences seem to have persisted, notably in India, China (Sinclair & Harrison, 2004), Korea (Hyun, 2007), Japan (Ito, 1991), and others.

One could argue that the kind of national or local preference predicted by cultural proximity is latent but dynamic, depending on the evolving sense of collective identity in a given cultural space, and how cultural industries evolve in that space. Many countries were created artificially by colonial powers during the colonization process, such as the composition of Iraq from separate Kurdish, Sunni, and Shiite provinces (under the Turkish empire) after World War I (Lapidus, 2014). A survey of "Third World" broadcasting in 1976 showed that using radio and television to try to establish national identity in newly established nations that had not had identities focused on those territories was both a goal of almost all countries and a challenge for many (Katz & Wedell, 1976).

Artificially defined borders can, over time, come to house strongly felt national identities, as in Latin America. Anderson showed how states could often do much with their own tools (schools, holidays, museums, maps, anthems, military service) and could do even more in cooperation with cultural industries and artists to create imagined communities (1983). However, the imagined national communities of Latin America have been evolving since the 1820–1830s, whereas in many other states they date to changes after World War I or World War II, post-colonial struggles in the 1960s–1970s or even later. So, while Latin American countries have national cultures that prefer national broadcasts, many other states have not yet achieved that.

Secondary, Regional (Geo-Cultural), or Cultural-Linguistic Cultural Proximity

Cultural proximity is thus very dynamic, as it evolves with both national and transnational developments. It should not be seen as a static, inherent quality, as Iwabuchi (2001) has pointed out. The perceived cultural proximity of Japan to other Asian nations grew slowly after World War II, despite the resentment many other Asian peoples felt toward Japanese colonialism in the war, as it came to be seen instead as an attractive model of Asian modernity. To some degree, Japan has now been supplanted in that position by Korea (Hyun, 2007).

One of the ways in which potential cultural proximity, based in earlier historical interactions and shared cultural resources, can be developed in the television era is by the growth of a country as an early producer and exporter of television, as in the case of Brazil and Mexico (Sinclair, 1998). The regional aspect of cultural proximity has been a useful insight for scholars in Latin America, where regional television markets grew, starting with the exporting of scripts in the 1950s, and whole programs in the 1970s, including across language lines (Sinclair & Straubhaar, 2013). Brazilian telenovelas, for instance, were exported into Spanish-speaking Latin American countries starting in 1975. Strong intra-regional flows continue (Lopes, 2014), even as content from other regions, such as Korean wave dramas, has begun to show up in some markets. This goes to show that regional cultural proximity still works to some degree, but that genre proximity—like the appeal of melodrama—across cultures is part of a set of competing proximities (La Pastina & Straubhaar, 2005).

Although some authors see cultural proximity as a factor in intra-European television co-production and flows (Trepte, 2008), most European scholars, such as Buonanno (1999), Schlesinger (1993), and others have noted that there is little common cultural basis for TV flow or demand across language and cultural barriers within Europe, despite such ambitious projects to encourage these exchanges as Television Without Frontiers (Presburger & Tyler, 1989).

Ongoing Competition with Imported US Television Programs and Channels

Even though the growth of national television producers and regional producers/exporters may have actualized a sense of cultural proximity by appealing to aspects of identity and history, they have to contend with the continued export power of the US. The US had been exporting television world-wide since the early 1950s (Bielby & Harrington, 2008), building on films, many produced by the same companies, widely exported since the 1920s (Miller et al., 2005). Thus, there has been a long cultivation of a kind of cultural familiarity with the US, particularly in Western Europe and Latin America, which has led some to call the US "everyone's second culture" (Gitlin, 1998). Buonanno (1999) found that while European countries were producing and consuming more of their own national dramas and other programming, their second preferences were US programs and channels, not regional ones; cultural proximity only applied at the national level (Buonanno, 2004).

While US television programs had receded to the margins of television schedules for the largest television networks in Brazil and Mexico, for competing stations in those countries and for many smaller networks around Latin America US programs were always a widely and cheaply available resource to fall back on. A new stream of US programs and entire cable channels flowed into Latin America and the rest of the world in the late 1980s–early 1990s with the growth of pay TV (Duarte, 2001). While the uptake of cable or satellite pay TV was initially low in most of Latin America (Reis, 1999), it was higher in Argentina (Park, 2002) and Colombia (Forero et al., 2009) due to government limits on the development of commercial broadcast television networks. Pay TV and television over the internet began to grow, as we note below, as more Latin Americans moved into the lower middle and middle classes in the 2000s.

Cultural Capital and Cultural Proximity

This chapter will use cultural capital as a concept to sum up a series of identifiable sets of knowledge and disposition that people tend to use when deciding what they want to watch on television. Earlier work by Straubhaar (1991, 2003) tried to define and demonstrate a number of the cultural factors that also define audiences' cultural capital in terms of specific things like humor, gender images, dress, style, lifestyle, knowledge about other lifestyles, ethnic types, religion, and values. Those factors emerged from in-depth interviews from 1989 to the present. Cultural groups defined by their differences on these kinds of factors often overlap greatly with language groups, which has been emphasized by economists studying the definition of television and film markets (Wildman & Siwek, 1988).

According to Bourdieu (1986), cultural capital exists in the institutionalized state, objectified as educational and academic qualifications. As such, it can be acquired with educational gains but is, however, connected with other forms of capital. Cultural capital can be learned from parents, from peers, from work, but tends to be heavily linked to things learned in formal or informal education (Bourdieu, 1984). Cultural capital is established with an understanding and navigability of the dominant culture, norms, and, indeed, social language in a society (Sullivan, 2001). It can thus vary by social class (Sullivan, 2001).

Television can be understood as a cultural good, or the objectified state of cultural capital (Bourdieu, 1986). Certain types of televised content, and origin of television (national, regional, and international) will be more accessible culturally, linguistically, and economically to certain groups and not to others. International foreign television consumption would thus require a material appropriation (assuming economic capital) and symbolic appropriation (assuming cultural capital), which are two forms of cultural goods appropriation described by Bourdieu (1986). This chapter states that linguistic capital would also be necessary for seeking, understanding, and enjoying this particular form of cultural good.

Economic Capital

Economic capital then, is "money or assets that can be turned into money" (Benson, 2006, p. 189) necessary to access a particular cultural good, such as television and, specifically in the case of this study, foreign television. Bourdieu stated that economic capital is at the root of other types of capital (1986), such as cultural and linguistic capitals. They can, however, act independently. In Latin America, the past couple of decades have brought a substantial growth in the economy of many of its nations and, with that, a particular fluctuation of social class, marked mainly by increased purchasing power of the lower middle class.

After a decade with marginal middle class fluctuations in the 1990s, Latin America's middle class grew exponentially, from 100 million people in 2000 to around 150 million by 2010 (Ferreira, Messina, & Rigolini, 2012, xi). This growth has allowed a whole new segment of the Latin American population to have the economic capital necessary to subscribe to and access multichannel television, and with that more televised cultural goods, including international television. Although this new-found economic capital by a large group of individuals in Latin America does enable them to have considerable new purchasing power, they may not have as much cultural capital or social capital as previous middle classes (Bourdieu, 1986). And indeed, as Benson stated, "the social world is structured around the opposition between two forms of power: economic and cultural capital" (2006, p. 189).

Linguistic Capital

A third capital applicable in identifying an audience's preferences of television as a cultural good is linguistic. According to Morrison and Lui "Linguistic capital can be defined as fluency in, and comfort with, a high-status, worldwide language which is used by groups who possess economic, social, cultural, and political power and status in local and global society" (2000, p. 473). According to the authors, Linguistic capital has exchange value in markets (Morrison & Lui, 2000). The "disposition about language acquired in the course of learning to speak in particular context," or linguistic habitus (Chávez, 2014, p. 28), is a form of linguistic capital which can be used as an advantage in social and market contexts. Being part of a contextual speech community or knowing foreign languages well enough to understand the cultural norms transmitted through them gives individuals access and, in some cases, power and can serve as a commodity.

This chapter argues, however, based on an analysis of survey interviews in eight Latin American countries, that the proportion of people whose identity is deeply globalized is actually still quite small, and that the traditional layers of identity at the local, regional, and national levels are still the strongest for the large majority of people, with the cultural-linguistic region rapidly becoming very important for some cultures.

Capitals, Class, Viewing Options, and Viewing Choices

Cultural proximity is also limited by factors largely related to social class stratification. It also evolves with the changing nature of television, which has moved from dominance by a few broadcast channels to a much larger, more fragmented universe of competing pay TV and internet channels, as well (Lotz, 2014). One of the remarkable things about most Latin American countries was that pay TV or multichannel television penetration had been very low (Porto, 1998) by global standards for middle income countries until the mid-to-late 2000s, other than Argentina and Colombia, where multichannel penetration had been much higher, above half, much longer (Straubhaar et al., 2016). However, that seems to be changing, which is likely to have a complex interaction with cultural proximity, which had been notably high in Latin America, both for national and regional television productions (Sinclair & Straubhaar, 2013).

National audiences or other cultural groups originally united by language and/or culture in ways that gave rise to the theory of cultural proximity (Straubhaar, 1991) seem to be increasingly fragmented by economic, cultural, and linguistic capital in the senses defined by Pierre Bourdieu (1984, 1991). Economic capital (Bourdieu, 1984) has long given some people in the economic elite of many countries access to multiple television channels, particularly those delivered by satellite or cable, that the vast majority of the population could not afford (Porto, 1998), when they were originally diffusing rapidly in other countries. Changing income distribution in key Latin American countries seems to be expanding these possibilities well beyond the elite. In Brazil, for example, prior to the economic slowdown that began in 2014, estimates were that close to 40 million people had risen from the working class or working poor into the ranks of the lower middle class, where it was now feasible for them to have pay TV or broadband internet, to use internet-based television more easily. Similar economic expansion in China, other BRICS countries, and other middle income countries such as Turkey, South Africa, Nigeria, and others, seem to be producing similar changes in access to media, while some countries once considered developing, like South Korea and Singapore, now have among the highest multichannel, internet, and digital media penetrations in the world (ITU, 2019).

Increased economic capital gives audiences greater access to more kinds of television, which may challenge the kind of loyalty implied by cultural proximity by providing many more alternatives. Increased cultural capital gained from family background, education, travel, etc. may give audiences the cultural knowledge that might make previously unfamiliar, foreign television programs more interesting or relevant. Increased linguistic capital would work in a manner very similar to cultural capital, but based specifically on language learning leading to broader interest in other cultures' television.

Cultural proximity also evolves with the changing nature of television, which has moved from dominance by a few broadcast channels to a much larger, more fragmented universe of competing pay TV and internet channels (Lotz, 2014). In most countries, at least until the major economic growth of the lower middle classes in the 2000s, only elites or upper middle classes have had the education, employment experiences, travel opportunities, and family backgrounds that give them the cultural (Bourdieu, 1984) or linguistic (Bourdieu, 1991) capital required to seek, understand, and enjoy programs in other languages, from other countries (Straubhaar, 2007). One remarkable feature about most Latin American countries was that pay TV or multichannel television penetration remained very low (Porto, 1998) by global standards for middle income countries until the mid-to-late 2000s, with the exception of Argentina and Colombia, where multichannel penetration had been much higher for a long time (Straubhaar et al., 2016). People in the economic elite in many Latin American countries had long been able to access foreign programming through subscription services that were mostly unaffordable for the majority of the population (Porto, 1998).

This chapter posits that this wealth enables more parts of the audience to obtain more viewing choices and options increased (until recent recessions caused by Covid-19) across more parts of the population in Latin America, particularly in Brazil, Chile, and Mexico, and in similar countries in Asia, the Middle East, and Africa in most countries. This rapidly increasing economic capital is a major factor in the evolution of cultural proximity.

Conclusion

Cultural proximity at the national or local level seems well established in most countries. Research generally shows that most local or national audiences favor national programming, but not every country has the ability to produce in all genres or to produce enough for all dayparts. As Iwabuchi (2001) cautioned about the dynamic historical construction of cultural proximity, even a general favorable disposition toward national production will not necessarily save it from competition by attractive imported programs, channels, or streaming options, especially when these come in genres historically underrepresented in national production, such as dramatic or comedy series, action adventure series, police and detective series, or feature films.

Cultural proximity at the regional or cultural-linguistic level seems very strong in some regions. Television programs and satellite channels within certain regions, like Latin America (Straubhaar, 1991), East Asia (Iwabuchi, 2001), the Arabic-speaking Middle East (Amin, 1996), and South Asia (Burch, 2002), as well as trans-regional cultural-linguistic spaces like the Lusophone world (Davis, Straubhaar, & Ferrin Cunha, 2016), build on cultural proximity based in common languages, like Arabic or Spanish, as well as similar histories, colonial experiences, etc. However, in some regions, like Europe, there are so many language and cultural differences that intra-regional trade in television has been sparse, despite efforts by the European Union to build a common market in television (Philip, 1993).

References

Abu-Lughod, L. (2005). *Dramas of nationhood: the politics of television in Egypt.* Chicago: University of Chicago Press.

Amin, H. (1996). Egypt and the Arab world in the satellite age. In J. Sinclair, E. Jacka and S. Cunningham (eds), *New Patterns in Global Television: Peripheral Vision.* Oxford: *Oxford University Press,* 101–125.

Anderson, B. (1983). *Imagined Communities: Reflections on the origin and spread of nationalism.* New York: Verso.

Antola, A. & Rogers, E.M. (1984). Television Flows in Latin America. *Comm Res, 11*(2), 183–202.

Baran, P.A., & Sweezy, P. (1968). *Monopoly capital; an essay on the American economic and social order.* New York: Modern Reader Paperbacks.

Benson, R. (2006). News media as a "journalistic field": What Bourdieu adds to new institutionalism, and vice versa. Political Communication, 23(2), 187–202.

Bielby, D.D., & Harrington, C.L. (2008). *Global TV: Exporting television and culture in the world market:* New York: NYU Press.

Bourdieu, P. (1984). *Distinction: A social critique of the judgement of taste.* Cambridge, MA: Harvard University Press.

Bourdieu, P. (1986). The Forms of Capital. In J.G. Richardson (Ed.), *Handbook of Theory and Research for the Sociology of Education* (pp. 241–258). New York, Westport Connecticut, and London: Greenwood Press.

Boyd-Barrett, O. (1977). Media Imperialism: Towards an International Framework for the Analysis of Media Systems. In J.E.A. Curran (Ed.), *Mass Communication and Society.* London: Arnold.

Buonanno, M. (Ed.) (1999). *Imaginary dreamscapes: television fiction in Europe: Eurofiction first report 1997*. Luton, Bedfordshire: University of Luton Press.

Buonanno, M. (Ed.) (2002). *Convergences: Eurofiction fourth report*. Napoli: Liguri.

Buonanno, M. (2004). Alem da proximidade cultural: não contra a identidade mas a favor de alteridade (Beyond cultural proximity: not against identity but in favor of alterity). In M.I. Vassalo de Lopes (Ed.), *Telenovela—Internacionalização e interculturalidade* (pp. 331–360). São Paulo: Edições Loyola.

Burch, E. (2002). Media Literacy, Cultural Proximity and TV Aesthetics: Why Indian Soap Operas Work in Nepal and the Hindu Diaspora. *Media, Culture & Society, 24*, 571–579.

Chan, J.M. (1994). National Responses and Accessibility to STAR TV in Asia. *Journal of Communication, 44*(3), 70–88.

Colista, C., & Leshner, G. (1998). Traveling Music: Following the Path of Music Through the Global Market. *Critical Studies in Mass Communication, 15*, 181–194.

Collins, R. (1986). Wall-to-wall Dallas? The US-UK Trade in Television. *Screen* (May–August), 66–77.

Cunha, I.F. (2011). *Memórias de Telenovela: Programas e recepção*. Lisbon: Livros Horizonte.

Davis, S., Straubhaar, J., & Ferrin Cunha, I. (2016). The construction of a transnational Lusophone media space: A historiographic analysis. *Popular Communication: The International Journal of Media and Culture*. Vol. 14(4), p. 212–223

Duarte, L.G. (2001). *Due South: American Television Ventures Into Latin America*. (PhD). East Lansing, M.I.: Michigan State University.

Ferreira, F.H., Messina, J., Rigolini, J., López-Calva, L.F., Lugo, M.A., & Vakis, R. (2012). Economic mobility and the rise of the Latin American middle class. The World Bank.

Forero, G.A., Coba, L.G., Gutiérrez, A.F., Valderrama, J.V., Penagos, R.P., Avellaneda, L.C.B., & De Reyes, A.G. (2009). The media in Colombia. *The Handbook of Spanish Language Media*, 63.

Fox, E. (1992, August). Cultural dependency thrice revisited. Paper presented at *Conferência Anual da International Association for Mass Communication Research*, Guarujá. SP, Brasil.

Gitlin, T. (1998). Under the Signs of Mickey Mouse and Bruce Willis. *New Perspectives Quarterly, 15*, 4–7.

Guback, T. (1984). International Circulation of US. Theatrical Films and Television Programming. In G. Gerbner & M. Siefert (Eds.), *World Communications* (pp. 153–163). New York: Longman Incorporated.

Hoskins, C., & Mirus, R. (1988). Reasons for the US dominance of the International Trade in Television Programmes. In N.J. Smelser (Ed.), *Handbook of Sociology*: NewburyPark, CA: SAGE.

Hyun, K. (2007). *New Asian Cultural Proximity, Korean Modernity in Between, and Reception of Korean TV Drama in the East Asia*. Paper presented at the Intercultural/Developmental Communication division, International Communication Association, San Francisco, US.

Ito, Y. (1991). The Trade Winds Shift—Japan's Shift From an Information Importer to an Information Exporter. In *Communication Yearbook*, 14, pp. 430–465. Beverly Hills: Sage.

I.T.U. (2019). Measuring digital development: Facts and figures 2019. Geneva: I.T.U. Retrieved from www.itu.int/en/ITU-D/Statistics/Documents/facts/FactsFigures2019.pdf

Iwabuchi, K. (2001). Becoming "Culturally Proximate": The a/scent of Japanese Idol Dramas in Taiwan. In B. Moeran (Ed.), *Asian Media Productions*. Honolulu: University of Hawai'i Press.

Katz, E., & Wedell, G. (1976). *Broadcasting in the Third World*. Cambridge: Harvard University Press.

Kottak, C. (1990). *Television and family size in Brazil*. Media, Politics and Popular Culture.

La Pastina, A., & Straubhaar, J. (2005). Multiple Proximities between Television Genres and Audiences: The Schism between Telenovelas' Global Distribution and Local Consumption. *Gazette, 67*(3), 271–288.

Lapidus, I.M. (2014). *A history of Islamic societies*: Cambridge, UK: Cambridge University Press.

Lee, C. (1980). *Media Imperialism Reconsidered*. Beverly Hills, CA: Sage Publications.

Lopes, M.I.V.d. (2014). Mediation and reception. Some theoretical and methodological connections in Latin American communication studies. *Matrizes, 8* (1), 1–18.

Lotz, A.D. (2014). *The television will be revolutionized*. NYC: NYU Press.

Ma, E.K.-w. (2005). *Culture, politics and television in Hong Kong*. London: Routledge.

Mattos, S. (1984). Advertising and Government Influences on Brazilian Television. *Communication Research, 11*(2), 203–220.

Miller, T. (2001). *Global Hollywood*. London: British Film Institute.

Miller, T., Govil, N., McMurria, J., Maxwell, R., Wang, T., Shohat, E., & Corrigan, T. (2005). *Global Hollywood 2*. New York: Pearson Longman.

Morrison, K., & Lui, I. (2000). Ideology, linguistic capital and the medium of instruction in Hong Kong. Journal of multilingual and multicultural development, 21(6), 471–486.

Nordenstreng, K., & Varis, T. (1974). *Television Traffic—A One-Way Street*. Paris: UNESCO.

Oliveira, O.S.d. (1993). Brazilian Soaps Outshine Hollywood: Is Cultural Imperialism Fading Out? In K. Nordenstreng & H. Schiller (Eds.), *Beyond national sovereignty: international communication in the 1990s*. Norwood, NJ: Ablex Pub. Co.

Park, D.J. (2002). Media, democracy, and human rights in Argentina. *Journal of Communication Inquiry, 26*(3), 237–260.

Philip, S. (1993). Wishful thinking Cultural politics Media and collective identities in Europe. *Journal of Communication, 43*(2), 6–14.

de Sola Pool, I. (1977). The changing flow of television. Journal of Communication, 27(2), 139–149.

Porto, M.P. (1998). Telenovelas and politics in the 1994 Brazilian presidential election. Communication Review (The), 2(4), 433–459.

Presburger, P., & Tyler, M.R. (1989). Television Without Frontiers: Opportunity and Debate Created by the New European Community Directive. *Hastings Int'l & Comp. L. Rev., 13*, 495.

Reis, R. (1999). What Prevents Cable TV from Taking off in Brazil? *Journal of Broadcasting & Electronic Media, 43.*

Schiller, H.I. (1976). *Communication and Cultural Domination.* White Plains, NY: International Arts and Sciences Press.

Schiller, H.I. (1991). Not yet the Post-Imperialist Era. *Critical Studies in Mass Communication, 8*, 13–28.

Schlesinger, P. (1993). Wishful thinking: Cultural politics, media, and collective identities in Europe. Journal of Communication, 43(2), 6–17.

Sinclair, J. (1992). The Decentering of Globalization: Televisa-Ion and Globo-Ization. *Continental Shift: Globalisation and Culture*, 99–116.

Sinclair, J. (1998). Latin American television: A global view. Oxford: OUP.

Sinclair, J., & Harrison, M. (2004). Globalization, Nation, and Television in Asia: The Cases of India and China. *Television New Media, 5*(1), 41–54.

Sinclair, J., & Straubhaar, J. (2013). *Television Industries in Latin America.* London: BFI/Palgrave.

Sinclair, J.S., Jacka, E., & Cunningham, S. (1996). Peripheral Vision. In J. Sinclair, E. Jacka & S. Cunningham (Eds.), *New Patterns in Global Television* (pp. 1–15). New York: Oxford University Press.

Straubhaar, J.D. (1981). *The Transformation of Cultural Dependency: the Decline of American Influence on the Brazilian Television Industry.* (PhD). Fletcher School of Law and Diplomacy, Tufts University.

Straubhaar, J.D. (1984). The Decline of American Influence on Brazilian Television. *Communication Research, 11*(2), 221–240.

Straubhaar, J.D. (1991). Beyond Media Imperialism: Asymmetrical Interdependence and Cultural Proximity. *Critical Studies in Mass Communication,* (8), 39–59.

Straubhaar, J.D. (2003). Choosing national TV: Cultural capital, language, and cultural proximity in Brazil. *The impact of international television: A paradigm shift.* London: Routledge, 77–110.

Straubhaar, J.D. (2007). *World television: From global to local.* Newbury Park, CA: SAGE.

Straubhaar, J., Spence, J., Higgins, V.D.M., Sinta, V., Mora, A.A., García, V.M., & Duarte, L.G. (2016). The Evolution of Television: An Analysis of Ten Years of TGI Latin America (2004–2014). Austin, TX: Program in Latin American and Latino Media Studies, University of Texas.

Sullivan, A. (2001). Cultural capital and educational attainment. Sociology, 35(4), 893–912.

Trepte, S. (2008). Cultural proximity in TV entertainment: An eight-country study on the relationship of nationality and the evaluation of US prime-time fiction. *Communications, 33*(1), 1–25.

Tunstall, J. (1977). *The media are American.* New York, NY: Columbia University Press.

Tunstall, J. (2008). The media were American: US mass media in decline (p. xi). Oxford: Oxford University Press.

Waisbord, S. (1998a). Latin America. In A. Smith & R. Paterson, (Eds.), *Television: an international history.* NYC, USA: Oxford University Press.

Waisbord, S. (1998b). The Ties that Still Bind: Media and National Cultures in Latin America. *Canadian Journal of Communication, 23*, 381–401.

Wallach, J. (2011). *Meu capítulo na TV Globo.* Rio de Janeiro: Editora Topbooks.

Wildman, S., & Siwek, S. (1988). *International Trade in films and television programs.* Cambridge, MA: Ballinger.

Wilkinson, K. (1995). *Where culture, language and communication converge: The Latin-American cultural linguistic market.* (PhD disertation.). Austin, TX: University of Texas-Austin.

Zizola, F. (2014). Brazil's new middle class. Retrieved from http://noorimages.com/feature/brazils-new-middle-class/

4

ENVIRONMENTAL MATERIALISM AND MEDIA GLOBALIZATION

Richard Maxwell and Toby Miller

Globalization began as it would continue: with a dazzlingly catastrophic blend of conquest, destruction, and storytelling. Ripping yarns were told about environments, even as they were smashed to smithereens. Latin America's *conquistadores*, for example, relished heroic tales detailing their destruction of indigenous life at the same time as they developed a bizarre aesthetic appreciation of the natural world they had encountered and blitzed (Colmenares 1996; Acosta Peñaloza 2014).

A mixture of artistic production and rural transformation was crucial to that first wave of globalization, and ideologized in an interconnected way. Spain's *conquista de América*, Portugal's *missão civilizadora*, France's *mission civilisatrice*, and Britain's civilizing mission were overtly linked to ideas of *terra nullius* or *baldíos* (empty space). Such doctrines sought to justify appropriating land from native peoples by claiming that indigenous ideological and pragmatic lives harmonized with nature and hence were incapable of transforming, marking, and thereby truly owning it.[1] The capacity to communicate in sustainable written and pictorial form—to make permanent semiosis—was considered crucial to endow humans with territorial legitimacy. Relatedly, when colonial efforts directed at rural development failed, this was because "peoples of low social efficiency" predominated. They required either extermination or ideological transformation (AKA Christianity) (Kidd 2009: 311).

Semiosis within the Global South has also ventured deep into the environment, but in a more positive form. Consider Gabriel García Márquez's use of the Río Magdalena. Fifteen hundred kilometers long, the river passes through 11 of Colombia's 32 departments to its mouth in the Caribbean Sea, draining much of the Colombian Andes along the way. Because most Colombians have lived in the basin formed by the Magdalena, García Márquez could not think of a more fitting background to the magical lives of his characters than the natural scenery and human welfare it provided (Salazar *et al.* 2018). He based his description of the region's exuberant fauna and flora on participant observation, knowledge of untold numbers of adventurers, migrants, traders, and romantics, and an interpretation of 19th-century artworks that represented zones already subject to malevolent ecological transformation at the time he wrote (Williams 2013; Anda 2015).

The protagonists of *Love in the time of cholera* (1988) travel the River to heal the pain in their hearts. *El general en su laberinto* (*The general in his labyrinth*, 2015) explains the meaning of the Magdalena for the people living on its shores and the suffering they and other creatures experience as a consequence of its deterioration: "fish will have to learn to walk on land because the water will end." García Márquez describes how "alligators ate the last butterfly, and gone are the maternal manatees, parrots, monkeys, peoples" (1988: 55, 185).

But he insists the Magdalena can be reborn, through the power of love; for life is always stronger than death, as per his fantasy of returning to his youth living in a boat on the river, where he learnt more than in school. Like that memory, the Magdalena is capable of renewal—but only via lengthy reforestation after the disasters of private ownership and pollution. This will restore the river and make life palatable for those who rely on its long-contaminated water (García Márquez 1981).

The sense of an indomitable spirit incarnate in the Magdalena has influenced many other Latin American writers, as well as artists, filmmakers, and composers.[2] JAM Gómez counts 16 Colombian and four foreign feature films, three videos, 56 short movies, and four television series about the river (n.d.).[3] For example, the video artist Carolina Caycedo works with anti-extractive industry groups to record the destruction wrought by damming (Gómez-Barris 2017).

Environmental Materialism

It is clear from the above that globalization, the media, and the environment have been inexorably intertwined for many centuries. And just like past imperial desires for gold, silver, people, and provisions, contemporary globalization involves a restless search for things, leading to lamentations right across the Global South, from epidemiologists to environmentalists to activists.

These latter-day objects involve even more ecologically devastating plunder—and form part of our favorite media gadgets. In 1965, the industrial world used fewer than a dozen materials: "wood, brick, iron, copper, gold, silver, and a few plastics." Today, there is a comprehensive "materials basis to modern society": the computer chips that enabled us to type this chapter each contain more than 60 of them. Developments in the alloys that bind these materials together and form new ones have frequently led to greater efficiency, and sometimes even diminished greenhouse-gas emissions. But faith in endless growth fails to acknowledge that unearthing these things drains natural resources: we have a finite supply of the basic ingredients of modern material life (Graedel *et al.* 2015).

Meanwhile, the colonial lust for human conquest as part of the quest for materials continues today: over the past two decades, Filipin@ and Colombian environmental defenders have been assassinated by agents of legal and illegal miners at greater rates than the deaths of British and Australian subalterns serving in the Afghanistan and Iraq wars (Butt *et al.* 2019).

Environmental materialism is a response to this terrible past and our destructive present. It is both a political orientation and a method, extant if not exactly thriving since Marx and Engels' pioneering work about nature (Fisk 1980; Foster 1999; Miller 2019). Centrally opposed "to any political system that sees nature only through the lens of demands for unlimited economic growth," it analyzes environmental problems arising from "the organization of human society through the material conditions of capitalist (or state capitalist) economies" (Light 1998: 345, 348). Tying nature to capital and labor, it favors the regulation of business and work to comply with ecological principles (O'Connor 1998; Benton 1996).

Environmental materialism is a tendentious syntagm, for it brings together concepts from science and Marxism. That combination was far from unusual in the first 50 years of the 20th century. It fell victim both to Cold War ideology, which saw many scientists suffer Red-baiting, and state-socialist human-rights violations, which forced progressives to re-evaluate the Second World. Today it attracts opprobrium from essentialist ideologues who wish to associate environmental hazards with a putative human nature rather than actually existing social systems. Nevertheless, renewed interest in environmental materialism is emerging across the human sciences (Barber *et al.* 2018; Davis 2017; Bertrand 2019).

But the syntagm has *never* been important in disciplines that focus on the media. Their discussions of the environment usually concentrate on how well or ill the *bourgeois* media cover environmental science, while globalization is understood as a struggle between small and large nations and Hollywood versus everyone else. For its part, materialism generally refers to media ownership and control. So when we use the expression "environmental media materialism," we are close to new, perhaps perverse, coinage.

Although environmental materialism as applied to the media has been propounded in numerous venues,[4] it is yet to become a central concern of media, communication, or cultural studies. You will look in vain for mandatory classes on the environmental impact of the media, references to it in omnibus survey courses, or dedicated textbooks. There are some recent and notable book-length studies (Bozak 2011; Rust *et al.* 2016; Rauch 2018; Starosielski & Walker 2016; Gabrys 2013; Vaughan 2019; Kääpä 2018) and specialist journals (*Media+Environment*[5]; *Journal of Environmental Media*). But this is a marginal concern, if that, alongside the central priorities decreed by film theory, journalism history, audience research, regulation, and their kind.

Environmental media materialism is held back by the limited preparation of scholars in those fields: they need to read beyond their epistemological zones and the newspaper puff pieces, governmental niceties, cybertarian fantasies, and conventional industry research that characterize our media knowledge. Then they can learn about the science of climate change, lifecycle assessment, and the physics, chemistry, and epidemiology associated with the production, use, and disposal of media technologies—and must acknowledge their complicity in our urgent ecological crisis.

As things stand, we are likely to encounter two principal debates over globalization within orthodox communication, cultural, and media studies, depending on whether the disciplinary housing is in the humanities or social sciences: What do transnational media produce? And what impact do they have on people? If the approach is political-economic, the focus is likely to be on ownership and control: oligopolies, oligarchies, and the role of the state. These tendencies generate an understandable, legitimate, and predictable focus on the exchange of texts (particularly between wealthy and less-wealthy nations/Hollywood and the rest of the world) and the power of multinational corporations. *Contra* those critical tendencies, sunnier, more positive accounts highlight new entrants to the international exchange of culture and the prospects for technological disruption of traditional power bases.

All these approaches look at media technologies in terms of their textual relationship to realism or their use by governments, corporations, and customers. They rarely address the experience, politics, science, and theory of work or the environment. The political economy of the media, a field supposedly driven by economic inequality and Marxism, barely interrogates the labor process (Maxwell 2016). Instead, it remains within the safe house of a functionalist leftism, where state and capital are everything and class conflict is rarely seen or sensed.

Industriousness, exploitation, and precariousness are routinely present in cinema as themes, but rarely discussed in scholarly literature on the topic (Mazierska 2013: 2). Film studies, for example, looks with greater interest at cultural policies supporting national cinemas in the struggle against foreign domination than it does at working conditions within them or their carbon footprint.

So what is environmental media materialism, and what might it do for us? Consider what happened to your analog television set with the arrival of digital alternatives, or where your old smartphone goes to die once it has ceased to function or you've been seduced by marketing campaigns for the latest model. This electronic waste is quietly removed from Japan, the US, and Western Europe and dumped illegally in Asia, Latin America, and Africa. And it's significant that most research into this topic comes not only from outside the humanities and social sciences, but also from beyond the Global North. One must turn to environmental studies and occupational health research to find sizable and distinguished contributions to relevant knowledge, largely emanating from, and concerned with, West Africa, East and South Asia, and Latin America (da Silva *et al.* 2006; Ray *et al.* 2004; Mukherjee *et al.* 2003; Nnorom and Osibanjo 2009; Srigboh *et al.* 2016; Ni *et al.* 2014; Premalatha *et al.* 2014; Devi *et al.* 2014; Reis de Oliveira *et al.* 2012).

Taking its cue from such research, environmental media materialism seeks to understand the history of communications technologies from cradle to grave, with special attention to their environmental effects. It asks questions about the labor process, the extractive industries, and the manufacturing, distribution, use, and disposal of devices and texts. This is particularly important for understanding globalization. When we look at the entire commodity chain, the life history, of our favorite genres or technologies, we uncover uncomfortable material truths, with serious environmental implications. This chapter seeks to model such efforts, across two zones: mobile telephony and digital journalism.

Mobile Telephony

The cell phone's governing mythology of technological innovation and commercial design mixes the sublime—the awesome, the ineffable, the uncontrollable, the powerful—with the beautiful—the approachable, the attractive, the pliant, the soothing. In philosophical aesthetics, the sublime and the beautiful are generally regarded as opposites. They meet in the "technological sublime," a totemic, quasi-sacred quality that industrial societies cathectically ascribe to modern machinery, engineering, design, and marketing, as simultaneously powerful and pretty (Nye 1994; 2006).

Yet whether overtly or implicitly, each new media device is presented as a march toward increased realism, driven by audience desires and corporate plans. But many of these innovations emerge from governments funding scholarship to help them wage war (Virilio 1989). Like the internet, today's media technologies mostly derive from the militarized US state and associated Research 1 schools, inventing things and processes for use in global warfare then handing them over to an indolent corporate sector growing ever more corpulent and lazy courtesy of tax dollars subsidizing and displacing putatively capitalist research and development.

Consider click wheels, multi-touch screens, global positioning systems, lithium-ion batteries, signal compression, hypertext markup language, liquid-crystal displays, Siri, cellular technology, and microprocessors. Did they derive from customer desire, capitalist competition, *laissez-faire* talent, and a global division of labor?

No. They mostly originated in US universities, funded by the military as part of the Federal Government's global warlike designs: the iPhone was essentially brought to you by tenured faculty on grants from the Defense Advanced Research Projects Agency, the Department of Energy, the CIA, the National Science Foundation, the Navy, the Army Research Office, and the Department of Defense, *inter alia* (Mazzucato 2015). Nothing to do with spectators, entrepreneurs, or corporations; everything to do with military interests sponsoring scholars, then gifting the results to capital.

There is another, equally material, origin to the extraordinary global march of mobile telephony: 70 elements from the periodic table. For instance, copper, gold, platinum, silver, and tungsten are the main metals in basic microelectronic components, wires, and solder. Aluminum and cobalt are used in casings and batteries. Numerous rare-earth metals enhance smartphone functions through speakers, microphones, vibrations, and colors (Crowston 2018: 9; Jardim 2017: 4).

These metals are mined under extremely hazardous conditions by workers in Asia, Africa, and South America. Miners may experience radioactivity and respiratory diseases, often in places where industries are unregulated or laws barely enforced. Underground sites put them at risk from ore-dust inhalation, leading to bronchitis, silicosis, and cancer. Other hazards include fires and site collapses (Grossman 2016: 67–68). The tin, gold, tantalum, and tungsten that smartphones need are mostly found in the Democratic Republic of Congo. These conflict minerals have financed a civil war that has cost millions of lives—armed groups control mining through violence, sexual abuse, and rape, merrily profiting from a workforce comprising thousands of pre-teen children (Laudati & Mertens 2019). These militias sell the minerals to Chinese and Indian smelting companies (Maxwell & Miller 2020). The testimony of those suffering in this brutal industry is available from numerous documentaries and video journalism (*Conflicted* 2019; *Conflict minerals* 2012; *Special report* 2017; *Congo* 2011).

During the manufacturing process that follows, which is mostly undertaken in Asia, silicon wafers, semiconductors, batteries, and other smartphone components expose workers to toxic chemicals linked to brain cancer, leukemia, lymphoma, infertility, miscarriages, and birth defects (Grossman

2016: 70; Kim *et al*. 2014). Data from silicon carbide smelters indicate elevated risks of stomach and lung cancer by contrast with the wider population as a consequence of exposure to crystalline silica, dust fibers, and silicon carbide (Romundstad *et al*. 2001). Many diseases do not manifest themselves for years. Because the industry only reports work accidents, the available statistics underreport the health risks facing workers and their families. Employees receive little or no training in how to handle the deadly chemical elements to which they are exposed (Grossman 2016: 71–72).

Component manufacture and smartphone assembly generally take place in China (Jardim 2017: 5). Corporate control of the labor process in the factories-cum-dormitories exacts a terrible toll on emotional wellbeing; consider the mass suicides in 2010–2011 at the Chinese factory making iPhones. It is owned by Foxconn Technology Group, a transnational Taiwanese corporation that boasts half the global market in electronics manufacturing. After the first spate of suicides at its high-rise compounds in 2010, the company union remarked that "suicide is foolish, irresponsible and meaningless." Another six attempts followed, and there were over two dozen deaths that year. Foxconn's reaction? It increased automation and built new factories in low-wage interior regions of the country (Chan *et al*. 2016).

The firm's principal client, Apple, called for improved wages, safety measures, and counseling services at Foxconn and acknowledged poisonings and other code-of-conduct violations, including the employment of underage girls by some subcontractors. But Apple declined to meet, rehabilitate, or compensate the workers affected (Chan *et al*. 2016). That's media globalization working for you—and us. We are the consumers in whose name these atrocities occur day after day, from Congo to China.

Of course, ecological problems go beyond the occupational health and safety of mining and manufacture: one hour of video streaming to a mobile device via the cloud uses more electricity than two new refrigerators (Mills 2013), while the energy expended on mobile devices in standby mode in 2014 exceeded Canada's entire power use (International Energy Agency 2014). Expanded streaming is increasing demand for storage and high-speed processing in data centers, which raises the specter of the cloud's carbon footprint. Some, but by no means all, clouds operate sustainably. Nations with unsustainable electricity sources rely extensively on coal-fueled power. Barriers to a greener data future include the fossil-fuel lobby's plaything politicians and resistance from powerful industries for whom instantaneous data transmission is deemed critical. They include the news media (Shehabi *et al*. 2016; Lewis 2014; Zook & Grote 2017). We turn now to what happens when these global systems are used by media workers and audiences.

Digital Journalism

From the development of print to the era of mobile telephony, technologies used by writers and publishers have drawn upon, created, and emitted dangerous substances, generating cross-generational risks for ecosystems and employees. An environmental-materialist history of journalism is required that foregrounds those issues.

Such an account would begin with the systematic deforestation, conflict mining, perilous extraction, and unsustainable industrialization that characterize obtaining the raw materials of journalism over the last two centuries, from paper to computers. Print labor has long contended with poisonous solvents, inks, fumes, dust, and tainted wastewater. We have seen how today's wonderfully weightless world of new media is equally perilous.

Many of these risks are invisible to journalism, because they are separated from the labor process that disseminates stories from newsrooms and other reporting sites, or appear at different stages of the life cycle of the technologies used. Today's reporters often luxuriate in the rapid and profound research, communication, and publication guaranteed by new media technologies.

But the recent crisis in employment for journalists in the Global North has alerted them to problems with the digital world. The Associated Press maintains that robot journalism will create new jobs with greater diversity of everything from skills to cultural backgrounds. Many reactionary scholars have grown heady with this next cybertarian gift (Galily 2018). But a survey of BBC, CNN, and Thomson Reuters employees who use "robo-writing software" suggests they are doubtful about the new technology's ability to sense the qualitative import of stories, although they are certain of its appeal to their employers (Thurman *et al.* 2017).

Consider the current data fetish within sports coverage. The Associated Press uses Automated Insights 'Wordsmith' program to cover fixtures to which it does not send employees. Yahoo! Sports does so to generate millions of match reports aimed at Fantasy Football participants, inviting advertisers to feast on "over 100 years of incremental audience engagement."[6] Entities such as Canada's Postmedia Network of newspapers have institutionalized round-the-clock digital reportage, but only of the major leagues.[7] Postmedia relies on outsourced global labor, delivering unoriginal analysis and bloated bloviation (Daum & Scherer 2018).

While jobs may be lost or impoverished, there remains a huge environmental impact. Global television coverage of World Cup Finals is a major contributor to ecological irresponsibility. The UK's National Grid promotes its management of peak electricity usage based on audience activity during half time in big matches, when people head for the kitchen and bathroom and power use surges by 10%. When Brazil's games in the 2014 World Cup Finals were televised, UK surges totaled 4348 megawatts, the equivalent of over a million and a half kettles being turned on at the same time. The Carbon Trust has shown that people watching football via mobile telephony multiply their footprint tenfold in comparison with television or WiFi signals (Miller 2018).

Reporters are not very forthcoming or self-reflective about their ecological impact. The Society of Professional Journalists has made no discernible reference online to the carbon footprint of its members since 2007. The National Union of Journalists adopted a policy calling for greener workplaces that same year, but shows no taste for problematizing its complicity in the problem. The International Federation of Journalists is silent on the topic.[8]

The Guardian is one of the few media organizations to stimulate debate in this area, and has permitted public, scholarly scrutiny of its environmental impact (Dodd 2007; Wood *et al.* 2014). The paper has highlighted the issue of airplane travel by reporters, which is frequently undertaken by junketeering "travel writers" and adrenaline-fancying "war correspondents." To its credit, the B.B.C., a major contributor to energy misuse thanks to its thousands of employees and global over-reach, has convened researchers and organized studies of its own footprint in order to reform both policies and programs (West & Crowther, 2013).

Conclusion

The tales we have told above are vivid descriptions of a global media world that is responsible for enslavement and pollution—just like the *conquistadores* with whom we began. During that global European suzerainty, Kant wrote vivid descriptions of the natural world. He saw it as a terrifying place where "the shadows of the boundless void into the abyss before me." That horrifying specter raises an apocalyptic vision: a moment when we look out and realize there is nothing left, nothing else, nothing beyond (2011: 17).

It is past time for those of us enjoying action adventure, queer documentary, 24-hour news channels, or tricked-out smartphones to recognize that the abyss lies before us, partially disguised yet also revealed by a series of material contradictions: the Global South's proletariat and informal sector bring us media devices then relieve us of them, even as its scholars and activists seek to educate us about their environmental impact.

Environmental materialists run the risk of being called "vulgar" (Pluciennik 2001: 751). So be it. There are worse monikers in a time of such urgency; we could do with some crude Marxism resetting media, communications, and cultural studies in order to highlight the impact of technology on the environment.

Notes

1 www.migrationheritage.nsw.gov.au/exhibition/objectsthroughtime/bourketerra/.
2 Consider the variety of these exhibitions: www.arteinformado.com/agenda/f/el-rio-magdalena-109949; www.citytv.com.co/videos/340548/exposicion-en-museo-de-arte-del-quindio-rindo-homenaje-al-rio-magdalena; www.vkgaleria.com/es/exposicion/el-rio-magdalena.
3 A selection of films is excerpted in Calderón (2015).
4 Maxwell *et al.* (2015); Maxwell & Miller (2012, 2013, and 2020); Miller (2018); the monthly column "Greening the Media" in the magazine *Psychology Today* (www.psychologytoday.com/us/blog/greening-the-media).
5 https://mediaenviron.scholasticahq.com/#fn4.
6 https://automatedinsights.com/customer-stories/yahoo/.
7 www.postmedia.com/.
8 www.google.com/cse?cx=016561358561312553625:jrlnopll9n0&q=carbon%20footprint#gsc.tab=0&gsc.q=carbon%20footprint&gsc.page=1; https://www.nuj.org.uk/news/nuj-signs-environmental-pledge/; www.google.be/search?q=site%3Aifj.org+carbon%20footprint.

References

Acosta Peñaloza, C.E. (2014). "Remá, remá": Las literaturas del río Magdalena. *Credencial Historia* 292 www.banrepcultural.org/blaavirtual/revistas/credencial/abril-2014/rema-rema.
Anda, M.P. (2015). Homenaje: Del río Magdalena, al río de aguas diáfanas: Aracataca. *Revista Estudios* 30: 280–303.
Barber, D.A., Stickells, L., Ryan, D.J., Koehler, M., Leach, A., van der Plaat, D., Keys, C., Karim, F., & Taylor, W.M. (2018). Architecture, environment, history: Questions and consequences. *Architectural History Review* 22(2): 249–286.
Benton, T., (ed.). (1996). *The greening of Marxism*. New York: Guilford.
Bertrand, A. (2019). A rupture between human beings and earth: A philosophical critical approach to coviability. In O. Barrière, M. Behnassi, G. David, V. Douzal, M. Fargette, T. Libourel, M. Loireau, L. Pascal, C. Prost, V. Ravena-Cañete, F. Seyler, & S. Morand, (eds.) *Coviability of social and ecological systems: Reconnecting mankind to the biosphere in an era of global change. Vol. 1: The foundations of a new paradigm*. Cham: Springer. 269–284.
Bozak, N. (2011). *The cinematic footprint: Lights, camera, natural resources*. New Brunswick: Rutgers University Press.
Butt, N., Lambrick, F., Menton, M., & Renwick, A. (2019). The supply chain of violence. *Nature Sustainability* 2: 742–747.
Chan, J., Pun, N., & Selden, M. (2016). Chinese labor protest and trade unions. In R. Maxwell (ed.) *The Routledge companion to labor and media*. New York: Routledge. 290–302.
Colmenares, G. (1996). La formación de la economía colonial (1500–1740). In J.A. Campo (ed.) *Historia económica de Colombia*. Bogotá: Tercer Mundo Editores. 2–22.
Conflict minerals, rebels and child soldiers in Congo. (2012, May 22). *Vice* www.youtube.com/watch?v=kYqrflGpTRE.
Conflicted: The fight over Congo's minerals. (2019, March 3). *Al Jazeera* www.aljazeera.com/programmes/faultlines/2015/11/conflicted-fight-congo-minerals-151118084541495.html.
Congo: Blood, gold and mobile phones. (2011, September 6). *The Guardian* www.youtube.com/watch?v=gGuG0Ios8ZA
Crowston, B. (2018). Smartphones: Behind the screen. *Resonance* 8: 9–10.
da Silva, M.C., Fassa, A.G., & Kriebel, D. 2006. Minor psychiatric disorders among Brazilian ragpickers: A cross-sectional study. *Environmental Health* 5(17) www.ncbi.nlm.nih.gov/pmc/articles/PMC1482695/.
Daum, E. & Scherer, J. (2018). Changing work routines and labour practices of sports journalists in the digital era: A case study of postmedia. *Media, Culture & Society* 40(4): 551–566.
Davis, W. (2017). Visuality and vision: Questions for a post-culturalist art history. *Estetika: The Central European Journal of Aesthetics* 54(2): 238–257.
Devi, K.S., Swamy, A.V.V.S., & Krishna, R.K. (2014). Studies on the solid waste collection by rag pickers at Greater Hyderabad Municipal Corporation, India. *International Research Journal of Environment Sciences* 3(1): 13–22.
Dodd, C. (2007, April 9). Carbon copy. *The Guardian* www.theguardian.com/environment/2007/apr/09/travelsenvironmentalimpact.mondaymediasection.
Fisk, M. (1980). Materialism and dialectic. *Critique: Journal of Socialist Theory* 12(1): 97–116.
Foster, J.B. (1999). Marx's theory of metabolic rift: Classical foundations for environmental sociology. *American Journal of Sociology* 105(2): 366–405.
Gabrys, J. (2013). *Digital rubbish: A natural history of electronics*. Ann Arbor: University of Michigan Press.
Galily, Y. (2018). Artificial intelligence and sports journalism: Is it a sweeping change? *Technology in Society* 54: 47–51.

García Márquez, G. (1981, March 25). El río de la vida. *El País* https://elpais.com/diario/1981/03/25/opinion/354322807_850215.html.

García Márquez, G. (1988). *Love in the time of cholera.* Translated by E. Grossman. New York: Alfred A Knopf.

García Márquez, G. (2015). *El general en su laberinto.* Literatura Random House www.educando.edu.do/files/8914/0932/5229/Garcia_Marquez_Gabriel_-_El_general_en_su_laberinto.pdf.

Gómez-Barris, M. (2017). *The extractive zone: Social ecologies and decolonial perspectives.* Durham: Duke University Press.

Gómez, J.A.M. (n.d.) Presencia del río Magdalena en el audiovisual. *Patrimonio Fílmico* www.patrimoniofilmico.org.co/anterior/noticias/163.htm.

Graedel, T.E., Harper, E.M., Nassar, N.T., & Reck, B.K. (2015). On the materials basis of modern society. *Proceedings of the National Academy of Sciences of the United States of America* 112(20): 6295–6300.

Grossman, E. (2016). The body burden: Toxics, stresses and biophysical health. In R. Maxwell (ed.) *The Routledge companion to labor and media.* New York: Routledge. 65–77.

International Energy Agency. (2014). *More data, less energy: Making network standby more efficient in billions of connected devices* www.iea.org/publications/freepublications/publication/MoreData_LessEnergy.pdf.

Jardim, E. (2017). From smartphones to senseless: The global impact of 10 years of smartphones. Greenpeace www.greenpeace.org/usa/wp-content/uploads/2017/03/FINAL-10YearsSmartphones-Report-Design-230217-Digital.pdf.

Kääpä, P. (2018). *Environmental management of the media: Policy, industry, practice.* London: Routledge.

Kant, I. (2011). *Observations on the feeling of the beautiful and sublime and other writings.* P. Frierson & P. Guyer (eds.) Cambridge: Cambridge University Press.

Kidd, B. (2009). *Social evolution.* Cambridge: Cambridge University Press.

Kim, M.-H., Kim, H., & Paek, D. (2014). The health impacts of semiconductor production: An epidemiologic review. *International Journal of Occupational and Environmental Health* 20(2): 95–114.

Laudati, A. & Mertens, C. (2019). Resources and rape: Congo's (toxic) discursive complex. *African Studies Review* 62(4): 57–82.

Lewis, M. (2014). *Flash boys.* New York: W.W. Norton & Company.

Light, A. (1998). Reconsidering Bookchin and Marcuse as environmental materialists: Toward an evolving social ecology. In A. Light (ed.) *Social ecology after Bookchin.* New York: Guilford Press. 343–384.

Maxwell, R., (ed.). (2016). *The Routledge companion to labor and media.* New York: Routledge.

Maxwell, R. & Miller, T. (2012). *Greening the media.* New York: Oxford University Press.

Maxwell, R. & Miller, T. (2013). Cultural materialism, media and the environment. *Key Words: A Journal of Cultural Materialism* 11: 90–106.

Maxwell, R. & Miller, T. (2020). *How green is your smartphone?* London: Polity Press.

Maxwell, R., Raundalen, J., & Vestberg, N.L., (eds.). (2015). *Media and the ecological crisis.* New York: Routledge.

Mazierska, E. (2013). Introduction. In E. Mazierska (ed.) *Work in cinema: Labor and the human condition.* Houndmills: Palgrave Macmillan. 1–25.

Mazzucato, M. (2015). *The entrepreneurial state: Debunking public vs. private sector myths.* New York: Public Affairs.

Miller, T. (2018). *Greenwashing sport.* London: Routledge.

Miller, T. (2019). La crisis ambiental: El Marxismo contra el antropocentrismo filosófico. In P. Aroch Fugellie, E.G. Gallegos, M.M.S. Madureira & F. Victoriano (eds.) *Das Kapital. Marx, actualidad y crítica.* Mexico City: Siglo Veintinuo/Universidad Autónoma Metropolitana, Unidad Cuajimalpa. 200–214.

Mills, M.P. (2013). *The cloud begins with coal: Big data, big networks, big infrastructure, and big power.* National Mining Association and American Coalition for Clean Coal Electricity www.tech-pundit.com/wp-content/uploads/2013/07/Cloud_Begins_With_Coal.pdf?c761ac.

Mukherjee, S. with Central Department for Development Studies, Tribhuvan University. (2003). *Child ragpickers in Nepal: A report on the 2002–2003 baseline survey.* Bangkok: International Labour Organization.

Ni, W., Chen, Y., Huang, Y., Wang, X., Zhang, G., Luo, J., & Wu, K. (2014). Hair mercury concentrations and associated factors in an electronic waste recycling area, Guiyu, China. *Environmental Research* 128: 84–91.

Nnorom, I.C., & Osibanjo, O. (2009). Toxicity characterization of waste mobile phone plastics. *Journal of Hazardous Materials* 161(1): 183–188.

Nye, D.E. (1994). *American technological sublime.* Cambridge, Mass: MIT Press.

Nye, D.E. (2006). Technology and the production of difference. *American Quarterly* 58(3): 597–618.

O'Connor J. (1998). *Natural causes: Essays in ecological Marxism.* New York: Guilford.

Pluciennik, M. (2001). Archaeology, anthropology and subsistence. *Journal of the Royal Anthropological Institute* N.S.(7): 741–758.

Premalatha, M., Tabassum-Abbasi, Abbasi, T., & Abbasi, S.A. (2014). The generation, impact, and management of e-waste: State of the art. *Critical Reviews in Environmental Science and Technology* 44(14): 1577–1678.

Rauch, J. (2018). *Slow media: Why "slow" is satisfying, sustainable, and smart.* New York: Oxford University Press.

Ray, M.R., Mukherjee, G., Roychowdhury, S., & Lahiri, T. (2004). Respiratory and general health impairments of ragpickers in India: A study in Delhi. *International Archives of Occupational and Environmental Health* 77(8): 595–598.

Reis de Oliveira, C., Bernardes, A.M., & Gerbase, A.E. 2012. Collection and recycling of electronic scrap: A worldwide overview and comparison with the Brazilian situation. *Waste Management* 32(8): 1592–1610.

Romundstad, P., Andersen, A., & Haldorsen, T. (2001). Cancer incidence among workers in the Norwegian silicon carbide industry. *American Journal of Epidemiology* 153(10): 978–986.

Rust, S., Monani, S., & Cubitt, S., (eds.) (2016). *Ecomedia: Key issues.* Abingdon: Routledge.

Salazar, A., Sanchez, A., Villegas, J.C., Salazar, J.F., Carrascal, D.R., Sitch, S., Restrepo, J.D., Poveda, G., Feeley, K.J., Mercado, L.M., Arias, P.A., Sierra, C.A., del Rosario Uribe, M., Rendón, A.M., Pérez, J.C., Tortarolo, G.M., Mercado-Bettin, D., Posada, J.A., Zhuang, Q., & Dukes, J.S. (2018). The Ecology of Peace: Preparing Colombia for New Political and Planetary Climates. *Frontiers in Ecology and the Environment* 16(9): 525–531.

Shehabi, A., Smith, S.J., Horner, N., Azevedo, I., Brown, R., Koomey, J., Masanet, E., Sartor, D., Herrlin, M., & Lintner, W. (2016). *United States data center energy usage report,* Lawrence Berkeley National Laboratory, Berkeley, California. LBNL-1005775 http://eta-publications.lbl.gov/sites/default/files/lbnl-1005775_v2.pdf.

Special report: Inside the Congo cobalt mines that exploit children. (2017, February 27). *Sky News* www.youtube.com/watch?v=JcJ8me22NVs.

Srigboh, R.K., Basu, N., Stephens, J. Asampong, E. Perkins, M., Neitzel, R.L., & Fobil, J. 2016. Multiple elemental exposures amongst workers at the Agbogbloshie electronic waste (e-waste) site in Ghana. *Chemosphere* 164: 68–74.

Starosielski, N. & Walker, J., (eds.) (2016). *Sustainable media: Critical approaches to media and environment.* New York: Routledge.

Thurman, N., Dörr, K., & Kunert, J. (2017). When reporters get hands-on with robo-writing. *Digital Journalism* 5(10): 1240–1259.

Vaughan, H. (2019). *Hollywood's dirtiest secret: The hidden environmental costs of the movies.* New York: Columbia University Press.

Virilio, P. (1989). *War and cinema: The logistics of perception.* Translated by P. Cammiler. London: Verso.

West, J. & Crowther, B. (2013, April 19). Sustainability in broadcast and digital media. *BBC.co.uk* www.bbc.co.uk/rd/blog/2013/04/sustainability-in-broadcast-event-summary.

Williams, R. L. (2013). Rural and urban rivers: Displacements and replacements in the modern Latin American novel. *Hispanic Issues Online* 12: 195–211.

Wood, S., Shabajee, P., Schein, D., Hodgson, C., & Preist, C. (2014). Energy use and greenhouse gas emissions in digital news media: Ethical implications for journalists and media organisations. *Digital Journalism* 2(3): 284–295.

Zook, M. & Grote, M.H. (2017). The microgeographies of global finance: high-frequency trading and the construction of information inequality. *Environment and Planning A: Economy and Space* 49(1): 121–140.

5

"MARVELING" THE WORLD WITH HOLLYWOOD MILITAINMENT

The US Air Force and *Captain Marvel* Go Higher! Further! Faster!

Tanner Mirrlees

Introduction: Global Hollywood's Superheroes, Serving the US DoD?

For the past decade, Hollywood's North American and global box office has boomed thanks in part to the release of films derived from DC comic book heroes (e.g., Superman and Batman) and those by Marvel (e.g., Iron Man, Captain America, Black Panther, and The Avengers). While Hollywood's box office superpowers are widely recognized, perhaps less obvious is how the US. Department of Defense (DoD) has been assisting Hollywood's production of superhero films for more than a decade. The DoD supported DC. Entertainment's production of *Man of Steel* (2013), as well as Marvel Studio's *Iron Man* (2008), and *Iron Man 2* (2008), *Captain America: The First Avenger* (2011), and *The Avengers* (2012) (Secker 2019). Increasingly, Hollywood releases movies that depict superheroes joining forces with DoD personnel to defeat threats to US and global security. The most recent of these collaborations is *Captain Marvel* (McCrae 2019; Secker 2019).

This chapter focuses on how the DoD assisted Marvel Studios' *Captain Marvel* (2019), a film whose production, storyline, and marketing exemplify a 21st century "DoD–Hollywood complex" product. Part of a steady supply of globally popular militainment products, *Captain Marvel* serves both DoD publicity goals and Hollywood's bottom line. The chapter examines *Captain Marvel*'s production (as assisted by the DoD), content (the story, plot, characters, and themes), and marketing (publicity and cross-promotion), and shows how *Captain Marvel* helped the US Air Force communicate a positive image of itself to the world, and helped Hollywood turn a global profit.

The chapter's first section highlights Hollywood's worldwide dominance and *Captain Marvel*'s global box office success. The second section defines the "DoD–Hollywood complex" and explains how the Air Force Entertainment Liaison office assisted Marvel Studios' production of *Captain Marvel*. The third section probes how *Captain Marvel*'s content and marketing synergistically supported Air Force publicity and recruitment goals. The conclusion critiques *Captain Marvel*'s politics, especially the notion that this militainment is "progressive" and "feminist," and considers *Captain Marvel*'s significance with regard to US "cultural imperialism."

Global Hollywood Unmatched: An MCU for Men, until *Captain Marvel*

The US is the world's dominant economic, military, and media-technological power, and Hollywood has long been significant to US empire and cultural imperialism (Mirrlees 2016). Today, Hollywood's "big five" studios are subsidiaries of convergent global conglomerates: Walt Disney Studios and 20th Century Studios (Walt Disney Company); Warner Bros. (AT&T-WarnerMedia); Universal Pictures (Comcast-NBC Universal); and Paramount Pictures (Viacom CBS). These studios produce films across borders, capitalizing on the subsidies, cultural labor, distribution chains, exhibition networks, and consumers of many countries (Miller et al. 2005). Hollywood giants exert immense economic and cultural influence within non-US film industries and box offices, and without proportionate reciprocation of influence by them.

For example, Hollywood is behind all but one of the top 100 highest grossing worldwide films of all time, the top one being China Film Group's *Wolf Warrior 2* (Box Office Mojo 2020a). In 2019, Hollywood's total box office closed out at $42.5 billion, an all-time high: the North American box office returned $11.4 billion and the international box office took in $31.1 billion (Guerrasio 2020). In 2019, Hollywood made all ten of the highest grossing worldwide films, and the Walt Disney Company owned eight of those: *Avengers: Endgame* (#1), *The Lion King* (#2), *Frozen II* (#3), *Spider-Man: Far From Home* (#4), *Captain Marvel* (#5), *Toy Story 4* (#6), *Star Wars: The Rise of Skywalker* (#8), and *Aladdin* (#9) (Box Office Mojo 2020b). 2019's top grossing film—*Avengers: Endgame*—set over 30 box office records in China, while China's major blockbuster—*The Wandering Earth*—only placed #152 on 2019's list of highest grossing US box office films (Davis 2019). Evidently, Hollywood continues to be a global powerhouse.

Walt Disney Studio leads Hollywood, and its 2009 acquisition of Marvel Entertainment and the Marvel Cinematic Universe (MCU) for $4 billion added to its intellectual property-owning powers. With a combined worldwide gross of over $20 billion, the MCU is the most significant global entertainment franchise of all time (McSweeney 2018) and encompasses global mega-hits such as *Iron Man 1* (2008), *Captain America: Civil War* (2016), *Avengers: Infinity War* (2018), *Avengers: Endgame* (2019), and *Black Panther* (2018) (Wood 2019). That said, the MCU is very male-centric, as its films are frequently made by men, star male actors, and tell stories about men (Barrett 2018). Since 2008, the MCU has largely scripted women to play romantic interests of men (e.g., Pepper Potts in *Iron Man* and Dr. Jane Foster in *Thor*) or "sidekicks" to men (e.g., Valkyrie in *Thor: Ragnarok* and Natasha Romanova in *Captain America*). Nonetheless, on International Women's Day 2019, Marvel Studios released *Captain Marvel*, its first female superhero film.

Produced with a budget over $150 million, and garnering a box office return over $1.1 billion, *Captain Marvel* was the fifth highest grossing film of 2019, the ninth highest grossing superhero film ever, and the 26th highest grossing worldwide film of all time. News stories such as "*Captain Marvel* Ends Box Office Myths about Female Superheroes" (Rubin 2019) and "*Captain Marvel* Is The First Female Superhero Movie To Gross $1 Billion Worldwide" (Bowenbank 2019) celebrated *Captain Marvel*'s empowerment of women (especially the female actors looking for more gigs in Hollywood and the female viewers searching for new role models). However, this female-friendly superhero film was also made to serve the Air Force's publicity and recruitment goals and, as such, extolled a militarized version of "girl power."

The DoD–Hollywood Complex: Producing *Captain Marvel* as Militainment

The US DoD does not own Hollywood's major studios and distribution networks, nor does it force Hollywood to make commercially viable war propaganda films on its behalf. Nonetheless, the DoD and Hollywood studios have collaborated on military-themed entertainment products for over 100 years (Alford 2010; Mirrlees 2016; Alford and Secker 2017; Robb 2004; Stahl 2010).

The "DoD–Hollywood complex" is a useful concept for identifying the symbiotic relationships between the DoD and Hollywood that underlie the making of commercial "militainment" (Mirrlees 2016, 2017b). The DoD operates a Special Assistant for Entertainment Media (DoDSAEM) to assist Hollywood's production of militainment commodities and DoD. Instruction 5410.16 (US Department of Defense 1985/2015) is the DoD's "cultural policy" for guiding its support for military-themed TV shows, films, and digital games (Mirrlees 2017a).

The DoDSAEM frequently assists Hollywood studios by granting them access to installations (bases and barracks), personnel (officers and soldiers), software (knowledge about military protocol, chain of command, systems operation, troop lingo, and drill routines), and hardware (battleships, jet fighters, tanks, helicopters, and guns), so long as the studio's script meets DoD requirements (Alford and Secker, 2017; Mirrlees 2017a, 2017b; Robb 2004; Stahl 2010). Most often, Hollywood scripts that seem to positively promote the DoD to the public and serve the DoD's recruitment campaigns tend to get DoD assistance. Scripts that fail to meet these stipulations, do not. From 1911 to 2007, the DoD assisted Hollywood's production of 814 films (Alford and Secker, 2017, 2). Currently, each DoD branch (the Army, the Navy, and the Air Force) runs its own entertainment liaison office to support the production of the militainments they appear in. The Air Force's office supported the making of *Captain Marvel*, so a brief description of it is useful.

Located at 10880 Wilshire Boulevard Suite 1240, Los Angeles California, the Department of the Air Force Entertainment Liaison Office (DAFEL) is the "primary contact for scripted and unscripted entertainment production requests seeking support from the United States Air Force and/or the United States Space Force" (DAFEL 2020). The DAFEL and its project officers support "documentary, television, film, streaming media, video game and music video production at all phases from research through the final product" (DAFEL 2020). DAFEL (2020) may assist Hollywood by:

- acting "as a local, authoritative source of information about the US Air Force and US Space Force";
- "providing authentication, verification and limited research for producers, directors, writers, property masters, wardrobe supervisors, film editors";
- giving "advice to scriptwriters during initial writing phases," reviewing "rough drafts or treatments";
- making "suggestions prior to script finalization";
- arranging for "the use of Air Force and Space Force aircraft and equipment not commercially available";
- coordinating "requests for stock footage";
- organizing "with Air Force and Space Force installations or properties for location filming"; and,
- managing requests "for appearances of Air Force and Space Force personnel as extras or show participants."

Captain Marvel was made by Marvel Studios with DoD and DAFEL assistance. In the "Special Thanks" component of *Captain Marvel*'s credit roll, Marvel Studios thanks the DoD, Phil Strub of the Office of Secretary of Defense for Public Affairs, the Air Force's Secretary of the Air Force Public Affairs, Air Force Material Command, Air Combat Command, Air Education and Training Command, Air Force Bases, the Air Force Thunderbirds, numerous Air Force public affairs officers (e.g., Lt. Col. Nathan Broshear), and airmen (e.g., Brig. Gen. Jeanne M. Leavitt and Lt. Col. Kristin "Mother" Hubbard). The DoD assisted Marvel Studios' *Captain Marvel*, but how?

One way the DoD assisted *Captain Marvel* was by arranging for on-location shooting of scenes at Edwards Air Force Base, in a hanger and on a flight line. Also, actual US Airmen operated F-15C jets for Marvel Studios' camera (Losey 2019). Furthermore, the DoD helped Marvel Studios prepare star actors for their roles. General Jeanne M. Leavitt, head of the Air Force Recruiting Service, met with actor Brie Larson (who plays Carol Danvers–Captain Marvel) at Nellis Air Force base, and instructed Larson about how a fighter pilot salutes, interacts with her crew chief, puts on flight gear, carries a helmet bag, and climbs the ladder into the cockpit of a jetfighter (Losey 2019). Additionally, some actual US Air Force pilots—Matthew "Spider" Kimmel and Stephen "Cajun" Del Bagno—appear as themselves in *Captain Marvel*, on base, in bars, and in jets.

In sum, the DoD-Hollywood complex produced *Captain Marvel*, as the DoD clearly assisted Marvel Studios' production, and Marvel Studios solicited and welcomed DoD support. The following section probes how this militainment links with the DoD's publicity and recruitment goals.

Telling and Selling *Captain Marvel*'s American Exceptionalism: DoD PR and Recruitment, Mission Accomplished

At its core, *Captain Marvel* is a superhero origin story about a female US Air Force pilot named Carol Danvers (Brie Larson) who becomes Captain Marvel, the most powerful superhero in the galaxy. The story begins on planet Hala in 1995, and Danvers has been brainwashed to believe she is Vers, a Starforce soldier and member of the Kree, an alien race. The Kree worship a supreme artificial intelligence (S.A.I.), preside over a military Empire that extends across thousands of worlds, and seek the genocide of the Skrull, a refugee alien race that the Kree frame as a terrorist threat. Vers is sent on a mission by Kree Starforce Commander Yon-Rogg (Jude Law), but is captured by Skrull leader Talos (Ben Mendelsohn), who then extracts from her memories the location of a super energy source he is searching for to help the Skrull escape the Kree. Danvers escapes to earth, but Skirmishes between Danvers and the Skrull piques the interest of SHIELD agent Nick Fury (Samuel L. Jackson), whose job it is to "figure out" where the US's "future enemy is coming from." Fury and Danvers team up in search of the super energy source sought by the Skrull, and travel to a US Air Force base. There, they investigate project PEGASUS, which was headed by Dr. Wendy Lawson (Annette Benning), a rebel Kree named Mar-Vell, who had worked undercover as an Air Force scientist to protect technology to "end all wars." Danvers and Fury learn that Lawson had tried to convert the super energy source (derived from the Tesseract) into a light-speed time-travel engine for a US Air Force super jet. They also find an old photo of Danvers boarding an Air Force jet, and discover she is not really Vers, nor part of the Kree race, but instead a US citizen and female Air Force pilot who was presumed to have been killed in a 1989 jet crash. After more battles with the Skrull, Danvers and Fury escape the Air Force base to a farm in Louisiana, where they search for more information about Danvers' past.

There, Danvers reunites with her best friend Maria Rambeau (Lashana Rasheda Lynch) and her daughter Monica (Akira Akbar). Shocked that Danvers is alive and confused about why she does not remember her origins in the US Air Force, Maria and Monica try to help her remember by showing Danvers old Air Force pilot photos of herself and giving her an Air Force flying jacket and dog tags. As Danvers begins to remember who she is, Talos shows up to the farm, and pleads with Danvers to help his Skrull people find a new home planet where they can live in peace and freedom. Talos explains the Skrull are not "terrorists," but space refugees who have been hunted by the Kree's Star Command ever since they resisted the Kree's authoritarian rule over their planet. Talos explains that the Kree killed Lawson "because she realized she was on the wrong side of an unjust war" against the Skrull, and rebelled against the Kree in hopes of liberating the Skrull. To help Danvers remember who she is, Talos plays a black box recording of Danvers' jet crash. Listening to that, Danvers remembers flying in a Tesseract-powered jet fighter with Lawson, and then Yon-Rogg shooting her down, killing Lawson, and almost killing her. Danvers also remembers how she absorbed the energy from her special jet engine's explosion, and gained superpowers that Yong-Rogg and the Kree had tried to control for their own ends.

Soon after remembering who she really is (a US Air Force pilot!), Danvers chooses to use her superpowers to liberate the oppressed Skrull from the tyranny of the authoritarian Kree. Danvers and Rambeau take flight to Lawson's earth orbiting laboratory to meet the Skrull refugees and acquire the Tesseract. But the Kree show up. They take Danvers, Rambeau, and the Skrull captive, and threaten to kill the Skrull (including women and children). In a climatic final battle, Danvers liberates herself from the Kree's S.A.I. and Starforce Commander Yon-Rogg by ripping from her neck an implant that allowed the Kree's patriarchal techno-military dictatorship to subdue her emotions and control her superpowers. As Danvers is freeing herself from the Kree, she has flashbacks to her childhood and experience with Air Force basic training, and she remembers herself falling down and picking herself back up again. Freed from the oppressive Kree, and her sense of self restored and empowered, Danvers tells the Kree, the Skrull, and the galaxy who she really is ("My name is Carol!" and "Look what happens when I am finally set free!"). Superpowers unfettered, Carol explodes into Captain Marvel, swiftly obliterates a Kree warship and humiliates and defeats Yon-Rogg. In the film's denouement, Danvers flies off into the galaxy with the Skrull to help them find a new home planet, and SHIELD agent Fury begins piecing together a new US security project called the "Avengers" (named after Danvers' US Air Force call sign, "Avenger").

Captain Marvel's story does a lot of positive publicity work for the DoD and the Air Force. The film represents Captain Marvel, the galaxy's most powerful superhero, as one and the same with the Air Force (Loughrey 2019). The character of Carol Danvers was based upon General Jeannie Leavitt, the Air Force's first female fighter pilot and currently the commander of the Air Force Recruiting Service. Blurring history and fantasy, *Captain Marvel* conflates a fictional superhero with a real Air Force leader. "The core of her [Danvers–Captain Marvel] is the Air Force," said Larson (Whalen 2019). *Captain Marvel* fuses the values and characteristics of Danvers–Captain Marvel to the Air Force, and in Larson's words, makes Danvers "the spirit of the Air Force" (Whalen 2019). Importantly, Danvers' superhero origin story begins in the Air Force. After all, Danvers got her powers from a superpowered fighter jet spun out of a secretive Air Force technological research and development project headed by a female scientist. Nearing its climax, *Captain Marvel*'s blending of Captain Marvel with the Air Force is direct. Copying the colors of an old Air Force T-shirt worn by Monica (Maria's pilot-aspiring daughter), Danvers changes the color of her power suit from green to red, white, and blue—she is basically wrapped in the American flag.

In *Captain Marvel*, the US Air Force is the symbol and source of Captain Marvel, and both are exceptionally powerful. Moreover, the film conveys the US foreign policy doctrine of American exceptionalism: like Captain Marvel, the US is a good superpower with a unique role to play in the world, protecting and promoting the cause of oppressed yet freedom-loving people everywhere against evil threats. When Danvers realizes the Kree is an authoritarian Empire perpetrating genocide against the homeless Skrull, she takes up arms against the Kree on behalf of the Skrull. Danvers choses to use her superpowers for benign ends. Battling alongside Danvers are Fury, a former CIA agent, and Rambea, a Black American Air Force pilot. Read allegorically, these three American characters are the US security state and DoD Of course, *Captain Marvel*'s allegory of American exceptionalism is contradicted by the many historical examples of the US security state and military undermining the freedom of oppressed peoples. With regard to its own empire, the US is more akin to the Kree, but *Captain Marvel* represents the US as a freedom force, and even more dubiously, as a peace-loving anti-imperialist superpower.

From World War II to the present day, the US has been at war, and a military empire that is permanently at war requires a permanent recruitment campaign using all means available, and Hollywood's *Captain Marvel* is just one of these. Prior to the film's release, the Air Force had experienced a downturn in female recruits, perhaps due to the many reported sexual assault cases (e.g., male personnel harassing, assaulting, and raping female personnel) (Fuster 2019; Kirby 2019). In response, the Air Force Recruiting Service tried to rebrand the Air Force as a female-friendly institution unlike the macho male-centered one mythologized in the Reaganite film *Top Gun* (1986). In support of its rebranding and recruitment campaign, the Air Force assisted *Captain Marvel*. After watching the film, Air Force Chief of Staff General Dave Goldfein declared: "More than anything I hope that young women see themselves as future Air Force members" (cited in Insinna 2019). Air Force Recruitment Service head Leavitt said: "[Danvers] represents a role that so many young ladies could strive to do, in terms of becoming an officer, becoming an airman, [and] joining our Air Force" (cited in Losey 2019). For Larson, *Captain Marvel* combated the underrepresentation of female heroes in the M.C.U. and in the Air Force. "You can't be what you can't see," said Larson. "I really do hope that it inspires girls and women" (cited in Braslow 2019).

To "inspire" girls and women to become pilots, the Air Force made sure that *Captain Marvel*'s theatrical release was accompanied by a 30-second recruitment ad called "Origin Story" (Braslow 2019). Placed in 3,600 theaters across the US and spread across the internet and social media platforms such as Facebook, Twitter, and YouTube, "Origin Story" depicts F-15C jets zipping through the sky and firing off rockets, Air Force bases flooded with sunshine, and lots of actual female fighter pilots saluting. Overlaying these images is the voice of a female narrator: "Every superhero has an origin story. We all got our start somewhere. For us, it was the US Air Force." Nearing its conclusion, the ad asks its target female audience "What will your origin story be?", encourages these women to "Aim High," and wraps up with a display of the US Air Force logo and a URL for a digital recruitment platform (US Air Force 2020). Director of DAFEL Lt. Colonel Nathan Broshear (and *Captain Marvel*'s project officer) said "Origin Story" aims to "highlight Air Force female aviators" and "encourage young women to pursue careers in aviation" (cited in Braslow 2019). "Origin Story" is a not-so-subtle attempt to cross-promote Air Force recruitment through *Captain Marvel*. Given that Danvers' superhero origin story started in the Air Force, the ad seems to say to its subjects, "Aim high," your story can begin there too!

The girls and women who visited the "Origin Story" website encountered an even more elaborate pitch:

> Female pilots serving in the US Air Force reach new heights every day. They inspire everyone they meet and serve as reflections for young girls to set their sights higher than they think possible. Join them, wear the uniform, and know you'll be inspiring the next generation.
>
> *(US Air Force 2020)*

The "We're Ready for You" page of this site gave site visitors a panoply of interactive enlistment options. They were invited to set up a meeting with a local recruiter, chat live with a recruiter online, request more information, call a recruitment station, and even fill out and submit an application to join. The DoD also leveraged *Captain Marvel* with an online interactive quiz called "Higher! Further! Faster!—Test Your Superhero Knowledge." The caption for the quiz read: "How much do you know about the inspiration behind *Captain Marvel*? Test your Carol Danvers and Air Force knowledge."

The Air Force even inserted itself into *Captain Marvel*'s premiere screenings at Hollywood and Disneyland with Air Force Thunderbirds flyovers. "This flyover is a unique moment to honor the men and women serving in the Armed Forces who are represented in *Captain Marvel*," said Lt. Colonel John Caldwell, the Thunderbirds Commander. CBS's Super Bowl L.III broadcast also featured an Air Force flyover during the National Anthem performance and during commercial breaks from the game, and Marvel Studios aired the premier TV ad for *Captain Marvel* (Marvel Entertainment 2019a). In this ad, Danvers and her friend and fellow pilot Monica Rambeau walk toward their jets. Rambeau asks "How do we do it?" Danvers replies with a smirk: "Higher, further, faster baby." A rapid-fire montage of action sequences cut from the film follows while the slogan "Higher! Further! Faster!" repeats. To directly praise the Air Force's assistance to *Captain Marvel*, Marvel Studios also released an online video called "Monday Motivation: Taking Flight" (Marvel Entertainment 2019b). In it, the film's director-screenwriters Anna Boden and Ryan Fleck exclaim "the Air Force was welcoming and amazing" and Larson tells Leavitt she is "so cool" (Whalen 2019). Boden and Fleck participated in a screening of *Captain Marvel* and media roundtable centered on the film at the Pentagon, in Arlington, Virginia while actors promoted *Captain Marvel* on late-night TV, often accompanied by real Air Force pilots (Braslow 2019).

Apropos the logics of "synergistic media" (Hardy 2010) and the "Disney-model" of Hollywood entertainment (Wasko 2001), *Captain Marvel* cross-promoted myriad ancillary commodities through franchising, merchandising, and licensing deals with other corporate entities. Alaska Airlines placed a 63-panel decal of *Captain Marvel* across a Boeing 737–800 aircraft. Dole Food Company's "Powering the Hero Within" campaign inserted *Captain Marvel* imagery into millions of price tag stickers for its bananas. Retail merchandizers sold *Captain Marvel* action figures, LEGO sets, lunchboxes, pajamas, swimsuits, iPhone covers, birthday party supplies, and more. These *Captain Marvel* co-brandings and spin-off products increased returns to Hollywood and further cross-promoted the Air Force, tacitly interlinking with its publicity and recruitment goals.

In sum, *Captain Marvel* was instrumentalized by the DoD to promote itself and recruitment to women, and Marvel Studios helped the DoD to do this. But was this DoD–Hollywood symbiosis effective?

Conclusion: *Captain Marvel*, Militarized "Popular Feminism", and Cultural Imperialism

The DoD's use of *Captain Marvel* in support of its "Origin Story" campaign seems to have worked. Less than a year after the campaign, Military.com reported a "*Captain Marvel* effect" on Air Force recruitment (Pawlyk 2020). Lt. Colonel Jacob Chisolm, of the Air Force Recruitment Service, said the "Origin Story" was "the most popular piece of social media promotional content published by any service in 2019" as it had received "173,000 visits, 11 million views, and 200 million impressions" (cited in Pawlyk 2020). Media effects are difficult to gauge, so it would be a mistake to conclude that *Captain Marvel* is a "magic bullet" for DoD recruitment. Yet, the DoD would likely not assist this film unless it was itself convinced of its potential efficacy.

In any case, *Captain Marvel* is a militarized expression of "popular feminism." According to Banet-Weiser (2018), "popular feminism" is the incorporation and mainstreaming of gender equality projects across governments, corporations, media, and entertainment industries and non-profit organizations. These mostly extol "confidence building" exercises in support of a neoliberal meritocratic society wherein the institutions of the state and capital recognize, include, and give individual women the opportunity to show off their utility and prove their functionality to what-ever ends these institutions serve whilst maintaining the social power relations they perpetuate without genuine intersectional solidarity with other women. *Captain Marvel* may indeed help build the confidence of women dreaming of careers in Hollywood and piloting for the Air Force, two historically patriarchal institutions. But it has also made Hollywood's mostly male owners more confident that female superhero movies will serve their bottom line and assured the DoD's mostly male leadership that their assistance to Marvel Studios will help fill their ranks with more women.

Disconcertingly, the DoD recognizes and enlists women to fight its wars via policies, programs, and popular marketing that emphasize equal access to DoD jobs and career mobility (Spade and Lazar 2019), but wars often perpetuate patriarchy and sexual violence against women, in the military, in military families, and in the countries the US attacks. Far from being allies to feminism for the 99%, the DoD's female leaders now make big decisions about state violence in pursuit of a security agenda which often harms more than helps women (Spade and Lazar 2019). In this regard *Captain Marvel*'s militarized "popular feminism" is not so progressive. In fact, it has already been incorporated by the military-industrial complex. Four out of five of the DoD's largest defense contractors are now headed by women CEOs, and these capitalists annually take in millions when overseeing the production and sale of weapons for use by the DoD and militaries elsewhere (Spade and Lazar 2019).

A boon for Hollywood's global box office, *Captain Marvel* militarizes popular feminism and weds its female superhero to the military-industrial complex.

After all, the DoD assisted Marvel Studios' *Captain Marvel* to shape women's perceptions of and behavior toward the DoD, and to achieve a response that supported its publicity and recruitment goals. Together, the DoD and Marvel Studios' production, storytelling, and marketing of *Captain Marvel* may have indeed inspired many girls and women to venerate the DoD and consider a career in the Air Force. But based upon a comic book, *Captain Marvel* is no substitute for historical knowledge about the DoD, and it is useless as a primer on what real Air Force service (and sacrifice) for empire involves. While *Captain Marvel* lauds American exceptionalism and idealizes the DoD as an institution that includes, recognizes, and empowers women to become national and galactic superheroes, it elides the real geopolitical and economic interests that drive (and disproportionately benefit from) the US empire's ongoing and controversial global military and capitalist expansion. That occlusion or obscuration may be the real "*Captain Marvel* effect."

The DoD–Hollywood complex's power to marvel the women of the world with *Captain Marvel* may in some liberal quarters of international relations be lauded as a benefit to American "soft power," or, "the ability [of the US State] to get what it want[s] through attraction rather than coercion or payments" (Nye 2004). For critics of this euphemism, *Captain Marvel* can be conceptualized as a novel expression of the old state-corporate project of cultural imperialism, which is advanced by a symbiosis of the propaganda agencies of the US security state (which strive to win consent to ideas about America and US war policy around the world) and the trans-national corporations of the cultural industries (which seek to make money by producing and selling cultural goods to consumers in global markets). *Captain Marvel* is the concrete outcome of this cultural imperialist symbiosis, as it derives from and serves the institutions of the DoD and Hollywood.

Even though the DoD is currently at war, or, engaged in "anti-terrorist" activities in about 80 nation-states (Savell 2019), *Captain Marvel* deflects its viewers' attention away from these conflicts. It makes the DoD look good by showcasing a militarized feminist superhero saving planet earth and a refugee minority species from a macho alien Empire without identifying or vilifying the real countries and peoples the US security state is actually at war with, perhaps so as not to culturally offend or alienate any of the specific consumers in the nationally specific audio-visual markets that Hollywood now presides over. In this regard, *Captain Marvel* may attract some women to the DoD and Hollywood's MCU but at the cost of distracting from knowledge of and critical deliberation about where the US's real wars are being fought, why, for whom, and with what social consequence.

References

Alford, M. (2010). *Reel Power: Hollywood Cinema and American Supremacy.* London: Pluto Press.

Alford, M. and Secker, T. (2017). *National Security Cinema.* New York: Create Space Publishing.

Banet-Weiser, S. (2018). *Empowered: Popular Feminism and Popular Misogyny.* Durham and London: Duke University Press.

Barrett, G. (2018, July 6). Marvel feminism: real or comic fantasy? *BBC News.* www.bbc.com/news/newsbeat-44643477

Bowenbank, St. (2019, April 4). *Captain Marvel* is the first female superhero movie to gross $1 billion worldwide. *Elle.* www.elle.com/culture/celebrities/a27041715/captain-marvel-one-billion-box-office-record/

Box Office Mojo. (2020a, January 1). Top Lifetime Gross. Box Office Mojo. www.boxofficemojo.com/chart/top_lifetime_gross/?area=XWW

Box Office Mojo. (2020b, January 1). 2019 worldwide highest grossing films. Box Office Mojo. www.boxofficemojo.com/year/world/2019/

Braslow, S. (2019, March 8). *Captain Marvel*'s feminism is all tangled up with military boosterism. *Los Angeles Magazine.* www.lamag.com/culturefiles/captain-marvel-military/

DAFEL (Department of the Air Force Entertainment Liaison Office). 2019. US Department of Defense—Air Force. Retrieved from www.airforcehollywood.af.mil/

Davis, R. (2019, April 29). China Box Office: *Avengers Endgame* breaks a host of records. *Variety.* https://variety.com/2019/film/news/china-box-office-avengers-endgame-record-opening-1203199993/

Fuster, J. (2019, March 8). Air Force's use of *Captain Marvel* to recruit women ignores a grim record on sexual assault. *The Wrap.* www.thewrap.com/air-force-captain-marvel-recruit-women-sexual-assaults-martha-mcsally/

Guerrasio, J. (2020, January 11). 2019 broke the record for biggest global box office year of all time with $42.5 billion. *Business Insider.* www.businessinsider.com/2019-box-office-was-highest-global-ever-record-2020–1

Hardy, J. (2010). *Cross-media Promotion.* New York: Peter Lang.

Insinna, V. (2019, March 8). In *Captain Marvel,* Air Force leaders see tribute to the spirit of female airmen. *Air Force Times.* www.airforcetimes.com/news/your-air-force/2019/03/08/in-captain-marvel-air-force-leaders-see-tribute-to-the-spirit-of-female-airmen/

Kirby, J. (2019, May 3). Pentagon report shows sharp rise in military sexual assaults. *Vox.* www.vox.com/world/2019/5/3/18528148/pentagon-military-sexual-assault-report-shanahan

Losey, S. (2019, March 5). *Captain Marvel* pays tribute to Air Force history—and a fallen soldier. Air Force Times. www.airforcetimes.com/news/your-air-force/2019/03/05/captain-marvel-pays-tribute-to-air-force-history-and-a-fallen-thunderbird

Loughrey, C. (2019, March 8). *Captain Marvel* Exclusive: Brie Larson hopes new film will inspire women to become pilots. *Independent.* www.independent.co.uk/arts-entertainment/films/news/captain-marvel-brie-larson-interview-cast-women-pilots-air-force-a8810131.html

Marvel Entertainment. (2019a, February 3). Marvel Studios' *Captain Marvel*—"Big Game" TV Spot. YouTube. www.youtube.com/watch?v=NCoPycawxUk

Marvel Entertainment. (2019b, February 25). Marvel Studios' *Captain Marvel*—Monday Motivation. YouTube. www.youtube.com/watch?v=5b8rukjThTs

McRae, J. (2019, March 8). Higher, further, faster: *Captain Marvel* embodies the warrior ethos. *Air Force News.* www.af.mil/News/Article-Display/Article/1780631/higher-further-faster-captain-marvel-embodies-the-warrior-ethos/

McSweeney, T. (2018). *Avengers Assemble! Critical Perspectives on the Marvel Cinematic University.* New York: Wallflower Press.

Miller, T., Govil., N, McMurria, J., Maxwell, R., and Wang, T. (2005). *Global Hollywood 2.* London: Palgrave MacMillan.

Mirrlees, T. (2016). *Hearts and Mines: The US Empire's culture industry.* Vancouver: UBC Press.

Mirrlees, T. (2017a). The DoD's cultural policy: Militarizing the cultural industries. *Communication + 1,*1(3), 1–26.

Mirrlees, T. (2017b). Transforming *Transformers*: The DOD-Hollywood complex. *The American Journal of Economics and Sociology,* 76(2), 405–434.

Nye, J. (2004). *Soft Power: The Means to Success in World Politics.* New York: Public Affairs.

Pawlyk, O. (2020, January 5). Captain Marvel Effect? Air Force Academy Sees Most Female Applicants in 5 Years. Military.com. www.military.com/daily-news/2020/01/05/captain-marvel-effect-air-force-academy-sees-most-female-applicants-5-years.html

Robb, D. (2004). *Operation Hollywood.* New York: Prometheus Books.

Rubin, R. (2019, March 11). *Captain Marvel* Ends Box Office Myths about Female Superheroes. *Variety.* https://variety.com/2019/film/news/captain-marvel-box-office-opening-weekend-record-1203160002/

Savell, S. (2019). This map shows where in the world the is military is combatting terrorism. *Smithsonian Magazine.* www.smithsonianmag.com/history/map-shows-places-world-where-us-military-operates-180970997/

Secker, T. (2019, March 16). Captain Marvel: The Latest Propaganda Collaboration between the military and the MCU. *InsideOver.* www.insideover.com/politics/captain-marvel-the-latest-propaganda-collaboration-between-the-military-and-the-mcu.html

Spade, D. and Lazare, S. (2019, January 12). Women Now Run the Military-Industrial Complex. That's Nothing to Celebrate. *In These Times.* https://inthesetimes.com/article/21682/women-military-industrial-complex-gina-haspel-trump-feminism-lockheed-marti

Stahl, R. (2010). *Militainment, Inc.* New York: Routledge.

US Air Force (2020). Every hero has an origin story. www.airforce.com/OriginStory

Wasko, J. (2001). *Understanding Disney: The Manufacturing of Fantasy.* Malden, MA: Polity.

Whalen, A. (2019, February 28). Captain Marvel Latest Superhero Movie to Promote Air Force in Trend Stretching Back to Comics. *Newsweek.* www.newsweek.com/captain-marvel-superhero-movies-air-force-comic-book-military-promotion-1348486

Wood, J.M. (2019, March 18). 10 Highest-Grossing Movie Franchises of All Time. *Mental Floss.* www.mentalfloss.com/article/70920/10-highest-grossing-movie-franchises-all-time

PART II

Capitalism, Structure, and Institutions

6

THE CONTRIBUTION OF GLOBAL MEDIA TO ETHICAL CAPITALISM

Sergio Sparviero

Introduction

In October 2019, Twitter announced that it would ban political advertising from its services because "political message reach should be earned, not bought" (Conger, 2019, para. 3), and thereby diverged from the neutral platform ideal that social media companies traditionally advocate for themselves. In May 2020, Twitter also became the first social media platform to constrain President Trump's political messages by adding labels warning users when his tweets lacked information accuracy or glorified violence. A month later, Reddit banned the community "The_Donald" for consistently allowing members to target others with hate speech. This community had more than 790,000 members and was influential in nurturing President Trump's online base (Isaac, 2020). Critical of Twitter's decisions, Facebook's Chief Executive Officer (CEO) Mark Zuckerberg initially backed the company's primary commitment to free speech (Isaac & Kang, 2020). However, pushed by a protest from its own employees, but also by hundreds of companies adhering to the "Stop Hate for Profit" initiative by "pausing" their advertising spending on the platform, Facebook engaged in negotiations with the civil society organizations behind such initiatives. At the time of writing, these organizations are demanding that Facebook hires a top executive with a civil rights background, regularly submits to independent audits, and updates its community standards to avoid the diffusion of hate speech (Isaac & Hsu, 2020).

These examples show that powerful corporations in the field of communication have to come to terms with the opinions and values of a variety of stakeholders, including users, employees, business partners, and other people affected by their actions. In general, these types of dynamics are very much embedded in the role that business organizations play in society. Already in August 2019, nearly 200 corporate CEOs and members of the Business Roundtable, a powerful lobby, seemed to agree that the primary purpose of a corporation should no longer be to advance the interests of its shareholders. Instead, corporations should invest in their employees, protect the environment and deal fairly and ethically with suppliers (Gelles & Yaffe-Bellany, 2019).

Although the solutions are likely to underestimate the problems, there are concrete possibilities that social media organizations will henceforth consider more seriously the consequences that their own "rulebooks" have for the electoral process, democracy, and society at large. More generally and in line with the position of the Business Roundtable, corporations are likely to intensify their corporate social responsibility (CSR) strategy and take into account the increased attention paid by civil society organizations to their operations. Already in the 1950s, Bowen (1953) defined CSR as the obligation of a businessperson to pursue policies, make decisions, and follow lines of action that are desirable in relation to the objectives and values of (our) society (Raczkowski et al., 2016). Nowadays, CSR is publicly espoused by almost all the major corporations of the world (Banerjee, 2008), as they demonstrate interest in a wide set of social and ethical concerns that include the protection of the environment, fostering an improved society, supporting economic development, and sustaining good corporate relationships (Tsourvakas, 2016). CSR strategies produce efforts that go beyond compliance (Kolk, 2016)—including donations to, or cooperation with, civil society organizations—yet they are voluntary and evaluated internally. Companies embrace CSR principles because they are thought to be "good for business": they allow them to improve their reputation, enhance their learning capabilities (e.g., including exploring and finding new markets; Michelini & Fiorentino, 2012), and attract talented employees (Lüdeke-Freund et al., 2016).

For some observers, unethical business practices can alienate a company from the rest of society, resulting in reduced reputation, increased costs, and decreasing shareholder value through erosion of its (socially constructed) license to operate. According to this viewpoint, CSR practices are in between voluntary and mandatory (Steurer et al., 2005). However, corporations are obliged by law in the US to prioritize the interests of shareholders—hence, to focus on profits above all. Therefore, critical viewpoints suggest that stakeholders who do not adopt the corporate line are either co-opted or marginalized (Banerjee, 2008) and that CSR strategies lead to "glossy corporate social responsibility reports" trying to "greenwash" the "grim realities that lie behind them" (Banerjee, 2008, p. 64). Demonstrating this viewpoint is the publication of corporate citizenship and social performance reports by tobacco companies, weapons manufacturers, and other "bad" corporate citizens (Banerjee, 2008).

Therefore, the declaration recently delivered by Business Roundtable is not a binding contract for positive social impact. It is unlikely that this will be a turning point and a milestone in the history of the relationship between corporations and the rest of society. Nonetheless, it is of significance because it shows that there is a shared understanding of a good society's values—its fundamental goals—among corporations, officials, civil society, and citizens. Corporations agree with the rest of society which directions their social efforts should take. For example, the elimination of discrimination among ethnicities and genders, or balanced, comprehensive considerations of private interests and social concerns. However, corporations and other stakeholders tend to have different viewpoints regarding the steps that should be taken toward these agreed goals.

This chapter argues that the concept of sustainability provides a universal understanding of a good society's values. Sustainability also defines ethical capitalism, a "philosophy"—"a particular system of beliefs, values, and principles" (*Cambridge English Dictionary*, 2020)—connecting a variety of institutions supporting the same social goals. As the chapter shows, these institutions include abstract ideas of general economic systems, theories of organizational design, principles of management, and "real-world" legal frameworks for enterprises that are "purpose-driven". Many of these institutions affect media and communication organizations, and many of the latter are models of, and shape, ethical capitalism.

Sustainability, Sustainable Development, and the Foundations of the Good Society

Sustainability and sustainable development (SD) are concepts shaped throughout what was referred to as the "Rio process" (e.g., in Tulloch & Neilson, 2014), a collaboration between representatives of governments and intergovernmental organizations, civil society, and businesses under the coordination of the United Nations (UN). The first step of the Rio process was the World Commission of Environment and Development (WCED), which was tasked by the UN to come up with a "global agenda for change" (WCED, 1987, p. 5). The work of what became known as the Brundtland commission, from the name of its chairperson, was informed by the simulations included in the *Limits to growth* report (Meadows et al., 1972) prepared for the Club of Rome. Founded in 1968, this club was an informal, international association of scientists, educators, economists, humanists, industrialists, and national and international civil servants united by the conviction that the major problems facing mankind were interrelated and of such complexity that traditional institutions and policies were no longer able to manage them (Meadows et al., 1972). The report investigated five major trends of global concern: accelerating industrialization, rapid population growth, widespread malnutrition, depletion of non-renewable resources, and a deteriorating environment (Meadows et al., 1972).

There are three takeaways from the Brundtland commission's report *Our Common Future* (WCED, 1987), which are important for the present argument. First, solutions to sustainability problems had to be found in human needs and value orientations (van Egmond & de Vries, 2011). Second, the report became a "political answer to the Limits to Growth analysis" (van Egmond & de Vries, 2011, p. 853). In fact, the commission also concluded that the answer to present and future problems created by the—scientifically observed—imbalances between growth of natural resources and demographic and economic trends would require a redistribution of resources, and so a political answer. Third, beside the existence of many critical assessments and alternatives, the WCED is still credited with the most popular definition of SD (Steurer et al., 2005). This defines UN as a process of change "in which the exploitation of resources, the direction of investments, the orientation of technological development; and institutional change are all in harmony and enhance both current and future potential to meet human needs and aspirations" (WCED, 1987, p. 43).

Many events of the Rio process that followed the WCED contributed to the current understanding of sustainability and SD, but also attempted to operationalize them into practical goals. The UN Conference on Environment and Development, or "Earth Summit", (1992) in Rio de Janeiro produced the Rio Declaration, which covered a wide range of issues including poverty, demography, the economy, gender, youth, indigenous people, and peace, while remaining primarily focused on the natural environment (Fuchs, 2017). The UN Millennium Summit in 2000 produced the Millennium Declaration (UN General Assembly, 2006) and the eight Millennium Development Goals (Cavagnaro & Curiel, 2012). These were later replaced by 17 sustainable development goals (SDGs) described in the "2030 Agenda for Sustainable Development" (UN, 2015), resulting from the UN Conference on Sustainable Development, Rio+20, held in Rio de Janeiro in 2012.

Understanding the principles of the Rio process is crucial to grasp the concepts of sustainability and SD. This process is *pragmatic*, because it is goal-oriented: it starts from the message of the WCED that humanity is engaged in a structural, self-destructing spiral threatening its existence. It seeks to move forward from present conditions toward the universally accepted goal of survival. This process is also *inclusive* because the response to a global problem can only be universal. Therefore, it involves a variety of nationalities and interests. Finally, this process is *collaborative*, as it attempts to accommodate rather than prioritize different positions into a common agenda. This process's downsides are intrinsic to its characteristics and lengthy timespan: even key concepts are necessarily vague, and the interdependent goals represent trade-offs and conflicting interests and values (Mensah & Ricart Casadevall, 2019; van Egmond & de Vries, 2011).

Therefore, it is it not surprising that sustainability and SD led to the publication of more than 3,000 papers annually (Kajikawa et al., 2007) and that SD is also seen as a buzzword in development discourse, associated with different definitions, meanings, and interpretations (Mensah & Ricart Casadevall, 2019). Frequently, the terms sustainability and SD are used interchangeably in both academic and popular discourses (Banerjee, 2008). However, many scholars who separate these terms see sustainability as the goal and SD as the process (Mensah & Ricart Casadevall, 2019; Steurer et al., 2005). By adopting Rokeach (1968), sustainability can be understood as a cluster of *terminal values*, beliefs concerning desirable end-states. These are the individual and social values introduced by the WCED (1987) and shaped in the successive steps of the Rio process. They are primarily individual before being social (Cavagnaro & Curiel, 2012), but they are also universal because they are scientifically based responses to human needs, and necessary conditions for solving the ecological and social challenges affecting humanity.

In no hierarchical order, the first of these values is *equality*. Two main considerations justify this value. The first is intergenerational equality: for humanity to endure, current and future generations should be able to fulfill their needs. Second, intergenerational equality implies that the current generation does not overexploit natural resources, a condition that is incompatible with poverty. People from the current generation who lack resources cannot be persuaded to save resources for future generations. The second of these values is *harmony*: humanity's survival depends on a balance between the size of the population and the productive potential of the ecosystem. Harmony is the ideal, end-state of a balanced approach and a collaborative process. A response to the ecological and social crises affecting humanity can only be produced by a universal collaboration. The third of these values is *self-determination*. Self-determination is a human right and the end-state of empowerment, the capability of being in control of one's own environment. According to the WCED (1987), only people who are free can participate in the protection of the environment.

If sustainability is a cluster of terminal values preserving humanity from self-destruction, SD is a cluster of *instrumental values*. These are the contested intermediary objectives or processes, political and ideological, leading to the terminal goals. According to Tulloch and Neilson (2014) the Brundtland Report already puts economic growth, eradication of poverty, and ecological integrity on an equal footing. For Fuchs (2017), it was the World Summit on Sustainable Development (WSSD) in 2002 that shaped the current understanding of SD based on three equal dimensions: environmental, economic, and social. This development is important because critics see the elevation of the economic dimension of SD to the equivalent of the social and environmental ones as controversial. It is interpreted as an attempt to position free market capitalism as central to the protection of nature and the eradication of poverty (Tulloch & Neilson, 2014) or to foster the growth of private businesses' profits (Fuchs, 2017). Furthermore, Fuchs (2017) defines sustainability as ideological, because it is immensely positive and allows diverse groups with opposing interests to project their political goals into it. While certainly insightful, these criticisms stressed that the pragmatic, inclusive, and collaborative characteristics of SD allowed for the involvement of corporations and their business practices, and for parallel narratives privileging the economic dimension. However, they criticize S.D., not sustainability. They do not dispute the existence of universal values beyond the concept of S.D., and they focus on the instrumentalization of such values.

Ethical Capitalism: Re-thinking Economy and Business

The label "ethical capitalism" does not imply that capitalism is ethical and carries the values of a good society. The notion of ethical capitalism suggested here is broad and concerns a variety of institutions, or systems of embedded social rules (Hodgson, 2019): organizations, policies, and regulations, but also more academic and abstract concepts, like visions of economic systems and principles for the management of organizations. It is ethical, because these institutions incorporate the idea of sustainability as a universal standard for ethical principles. For example, sustainability is thought now to provide the normative foundations of CSR (Steurer et al., 2005), although CSR dates before the WCED and was once focused on societal issues, but not environmental concerns. Ethical capitalism also inherits the pragmatism of sustainability: even when abstract, these institutions aim at defining a practical way forward. Hence, the capitalism of "ethical capitalism" indicates the starting point, while equality, harmony, and self-determination—i.e., sustainability—represent features of a desirable end-state.

The *circular economy* (CE) is seen as a concept that operationalizes sustainable development for businesses: it describes an economic system that is based on "business models which replace the 'end-of-life' concept with reducing, alternatively reusing, recycling and recovering materials in production/

distribution and consumption processes" (Kirchherr et al., 2017, p. 224). In line with the C.E. is the policy-oriented concept of the *green economy* by the UN Environment Programme (UNEP, 2011), which describes an economic system that reduces environmental risks and ecological scarcities to improve human well-being and social equity. Alternative to CSR principles, but still conceptual and focused on the role of enterprises are the concepts of *business sustainability, stakeholder theory*, and *shared value*. Business sustainability refers in general to the integration of principles and values of sustainable development into a firm's strategy, operations, and business models. Key to this idea is the notion of "balance" referring to processes of economic, social, and environmental value creation (see Massa et al., 2017) and to the short, medium, and long terms (see Lüdeke-Freund et al., 2016). Freeman's (1984) stakeholder theory, considered one of the theoretical foundations of CSR (Raczkowski et al., 2016), stipulates that business executives who create value for customers, suppliers, employees, communities, and financiers (or shareholders) act in the best interest of the companies they manage. Along similar lines, Michael Porter and Mark Kramer (2006) argue that companies should concentrate on using their potential, resources, and capabilities to develop innovative solutions to environmental and social problems, and by doing so turn these issues into market opportunities. This is what they called the creation of shared value.

Since the 1990s, with the popularization of CSR strategies, the marketization of non-profit organizations, and the emergence of hybrid organizational forms (Sparviero, 2019), the distinction between for-profit and non-profit has been blurring. An exemplary illustration of this is the *social enterprise*, an organization that addresses social problems by means of markets (Mair, 2020). Social enterprises are entities active in markets for public purpose, which are social spaces covering private and public efforts to address social problems of public interest, like poverty, inequalities, or drug addiction. In the "real world", social enterprises exist in different legal forms (e.g., for-profit, non-profit, cooperatives), but also as combinations of legal forms. They merge a welfare logic and a commercial logic while pursuing both a double (social and economic) or triple bottom line (social, economic, and environmental). In management research, work focused on social enterprises is investigating how they achieve balance by managing the tensions created by the multiple approaches embraced (Mair, 2020).

Legal Forms for Media and Communication Organizations Embracing Ethical Capitalism

There is a variety of ethical capitalism organizations incorporated using different legal forms. On one end of the spectrum, there are weak proposals. These are for-profit companies including CSR principles in their business strategy. Although it is certainly true that, as critics put it (e.g., Banerjee, 2008), CSR is a public relation instrument instead of a genuine strategy for societal purpose for many large corporations, these represent only a small fraction of existing for-profits. For example, in 2015, large corporations produced about 60% of total receipts, but represented less than 5% of business in the US (calculated from IRS, 2020). Hence, CSR strategies can still improve the relationship with the community and the business perspectives of a large number of small and medium-sized companies.

On the opposite end of the spectrum, there are strong proposals: non-profit organizations financed by foundations, government grants, and individual supporters, dedicated to pursuing goals within the scope of sustainability without market involvement. In between these two types, there are organizations that adopt hybrid legal forms. In the US, there are (at least) three of them: the benefit corporation, the social purpose corporation, and the low-profit limited liability company (L3C). These forms allow an organization to prioritize social goals instead of profits (Murray, 2017), like non-profits do, and to redistribute economic value, like for-profits do.

A benefit corporation is a for-profit organization designed to follow the principles of CSR, business sustainability, and stakeholder theory. Its primary attributes are (Shackelford et al., 2019): (1)

its purpose must include either a general or a specific public benefit; (2) broader stakeholder interests as well as profit as part of directors' fiduciary duties; and (3) performance in the delivery of social benefits must be assessed annually by a third-party organization. The benefit corporation is a legal form established first in Maryland in April 2010. At the time of writing, legislation forming the status of benefit corporation has been passed in 36 states in the US (Benefit Corporation, 2020b), in Italy, and in Puerto Rico, and is also moving forward in Australia, Argentina, Chile, Colombia, and Canada (Benefit Corporation, 2020a). The social purpose corporation is similar to the benefit corporation, although it allows for the definition of a narrower social purpose. It is available only in California and in the state of Washington (Murray, 2017).

The benefit corporation represents the codification of B-Labs' B Corporation certification standards into articles of incorporation (Cooney, 2012). Unlike the benefit corporation legal status, the B Corporation certification is available to any organization around the world that obtains 80 points in the B Impact Assessment (B.I.A.). It is a public score based on the evaluation of the way in which a company's operations and business model impact workers, community, environment, and customers (Certified B Corporation, 2020a). Over 3,100 companies from 71 countries have obtained a B Corporation certification standard (Certified B Corporation, 2020b). Some are media or communications companies, including the news media *National Observer* in Canada and the *Guardian Media Group* in the UK, the crowdfunding platform *Kickstarter*, the networking website *Ello*, the lifestyle network *Evox*, many book publishers, and marketing and communication agencies.

In the US, an L3C company is a non-profit organization that is allowed to remunerate capital investments (i.e., to redistribute profits). Similar to non-profit organizations, an L3C must fulfill the following three criteria (Cooney, 2012; Schmidt, 2010): (1) it must significantly further the accomplishment of one or more charitable or educational purposes, which include social and environmental causes, but also art, religion, education, literary activities, scientific ventures, and the prevention of cruelty to animals; (2) the production of income or the appreciation of property is not a significant purpose of the company; and (3) it does not aim at accomplishing any political or legislative purpose—i.e., it is not a lobbying organization. Contrary to non-profit organizations, L3Cs can have a layered capital structure with different tiers of investors from low/non-remunerated donations or program-related investments (PRIs), to private investments remunerated at market rate (Florin & Schmidt, 2011; Schmidt, 2010). Clear advantages of this type of status are access to "cheaper capital" and the reduced risk enabled by the possibility of subsidizing the return paid to private investors from the donations paid by social investors (Florin & Schmidt, 2011).

There are similar legal forms around the world, which attempt to favor the establishment of social enterprises and organizations with a non-profit mission, competing in markets with for-profit counterparts and requiring capital from private investors. These include the community interest company (CIC) in the UK. In France, Portugal, Spain, and Greece, social enterprises tend to be particular forms of cooperatives (Defourny & Nyssens, 2012). Although the social enterprise model is an interesting one for media companies, and in particular, for struggling news organizations (Pickard, 2011) it has not yet been widely adopted.

Wikipedia and Other Non-Profit Media

There are many non-profit media and communications organizations around the world primarily focused on social goals, competing for users and resources with for-profit organizations. Notably, public service media (PSM) are non-profit organizations with social goals that in many countries compete with commercial broadcasters and online services. However, media and communications organizations that emerged from private entrepreneurship and the diffusion of digital media and communications are more interesting for understanding the relationship between information and communications technology (ICT) and ethical capitalism. Although these ethical capitalism organizations remain relatively small in terms of reach and resources compared with their competing for-profit counterparts, they are driven by a vision of how digital technologies can advance sustainability. In other words, they are high-impact forces of change in the domains and markets in which they operate.

The Mozilla foundation and Creative Commons are two good examples of ethical capitalism organizations that have a global reach and a high impact on media and communications environments. Mozilla is a non-profit foundation that in 2018 alone generated more than 400 million dollars and is one of the most famous advocates of the open-source software movement. Mozilla uses most of its resources, generated to a large extent from integrating access to search engines in its browser, for software development (Mozilla, 2018). Creative Commons is the organization that has made it easier for creators to share intellectual properties over the internet. Incorporated in the US, it leads the Creative Commons Global Network, a network of members clustered into 43 country chapters (CC Global Network, 2020), and in 2017 it generated a revenue of 1.6 million dollars (ProPublica, 2020).

Furthermore, many successful, ethical capitalism organizations that emerged in recent years are non-profit online news providers. The combination of digital news production and distribution coupled with the non-profit status allowing for reduced tax costs made the non-profit status particularly appealing for small news organizations. In the US, for example, many non-profit news organizations are local and hyperlocal. However, there are important success stories around the world of non-profit and hybrid news organizations that established themselves on a national level include *ProPublica* in the US, *The Hong Kong Free Press*, *Mediapart* in France, and *El Diario* in Spain (Sparviero, 2020).

Considering the involvement of volunteers around the world, the amount of resources generated, and the reach of its content, Wikipedia is certainly one of the most significant ongoing ethical capitalism projects. Wikipedia is an online encyclopedia of the non-profit Wikimedia foundation (Wikipedia, 2019). Based on quantifiable measures of success, it is commonly compared to media and digital platforms that are services or organizations of digital media and/or communications giants, like YouTube, MySpace, Facebook, and Twitter. In fact, in January 2020, the English version of Wikipedia had over 6 million articles and 38 million registered users (Wikimedia, 2020a). Furthermore, although English is certainly the most developed site on the platform, Wikipedia also exists in another 299 active languages (Wikimedia, 2020a). Thanks to its large volume of content and number of contributors, Wikipedia was ranked ninth by Alexa in the list of most-used global websites. It emerged as a more popular website than those of many powerful brands, including Yahoo.com (ranked 10th), Amazon.com (12th), Instagram.com (29th), and Twitter.com (37th) (Alexa, 2019).

The purpose of Wikipedia is to "to create a web-based, free content encyclopedia of all branches of knowledge, in an atmosphere of mutual respect and cooperation" (Wikipedia, 2020b, para. 2). This echoes the mission of the Wikimedia foundation, which is to "empower and engage people around the world to collect and develop educational content under a free license or in the public domain, and to disseminate it effectively and globally" (Wikimedia Foundation, 2018, para. 1). Therefore, many of sustainability's key values, such as self-determination (through knowledge and education) and harmony (through mutual respect and cooperation) are at the center of the project and the organization's mission. Furthermore, the efforts to include the largest possible variety of languages in the encyclopedia, the efforts spent in considering diversity within its workforce (Williams, 2019), and the publication of an environmental sustainability assessment by a third-party organization (Wikimedia Foundation Inc., 2019), clearly indicate that the organization considers equality, and sustainability values more generally.

Finally, the Wikimedia foundation and the activities that go into the creation of Wikipedia are interesting examples of ethical capitalism because, like its counterpart for-profit, ICT giants, it is a truly global organization. For example, Amazon has offices in more than 30 countries (Aboutamazon.com, 2018) and Facebook in 33 countries (Facebook Careers, 2020). Similar to Creative Commons, the Wikimedia foundation counts on chapters which are geographically spread out, and local hubs of activities led and managed by professionals (C. Garad, personal communication, 24 January 2020). Wikimedia's chapters are independent non-profit organizations with access to funding and other type of support (Wikimedia, 2019). Currently, there are 39 chapters in the network. Furthermore, in addition to the chapters, there are (currently) 124 user groups. These groups are local, but also thematic hubs of activities, which are related to the mission of Wikimedia foundation. Along with groups dedicated to art and feminism, math, academic publishing, or supporting the LGBT+ community, there are groups of contributors from Belarus, Greece, Ireland, and Iran, for example, which aim at becoming chapters (Wikimedia, 2020b).

Conclusion

Carlota Perez (2010) investigates the relationships between technological changes, business, economy, and society more generally, following the evolutionary economics tradition. She theorized that institutional innovations would slowly catch up with the more rapid technological innovations spurred by the ICT revolution, so that a sustainable and global knowledge-society can become possible. Institutional innovations are norms, rules, and policy objectives, but also ideas, models, and blueprints that are in line with a new "common sense" permeating the business world and society, "turning to 'normal' many processes, practices and expectations that would have been inconceivable only decades before" (Perez, 2015, p. 196). However, Perez did not consider that, while the ICT revolution unfolds, there are also many institutional innovations being designed and implemented, which adhere to a globally spreading common sense calling for less commercialism and more socially conscious and ethical behavior from corporations, smaller companies, and entrepreneurs. This chapter describes the most important of these institutional innovations, from abstract academic concepts to concrete legal frameworks governing different types of business entities. Together, these institutions were referred to here as ethical capitalism, because they share a normative and forward-looking vision of a sustainable society, characterized by the values of equality, harmony, and self-determination. Ethical capitalism also contributes to define the widespread, new common sense, although clearly, its role is relatively limited.

Moreover, media and communication industries and the ethical capitalism are two sites, partly overlapping, that benefit from cross-fertilization. Organizations such as Wikimedia, Mozilla, Creative Commons, and many non-profit news media are activist organizations that embed sustainability in their visions of using ICT for a better society. Simultaneously, they are key stakeholders of the ICT and ethical business revolutions. Whereas the visions that these organization advance, and the principles underpinning them (e.g., open source, public commons of knowledge and culture, public journalism) are very much debated among scholars of media and communications, their business models have so far attracted little attention. Yet, since these organizations that are models of a new common sense are permeating the economic and business domains, this chapter suggests that there is still a lot to learn from the ways in which they successfully combine sustainability principles with participation, collaboration, revenue models, and other features of their activities.

References

Aboutamazon.Com (2018, March 30). Our global offices. www.aboutamazon.com/working-at-amazon/our-global-offices

Alexa. (2019). The top 500 sites on the web. www.alexa.com/topsites

Banerjee, S.B. (2008). Corporate Social Responsibility: The Good, the Bad and the Ugly. *Critical Sociology, 34*(1), 51–79. https://doi.org/10.1177/0896920507084623

Benefit Corporation. (2020a). International Legislation. https://benefitcorp.net/international-legislation

Benefit Corporation. (2020b). State by State Status of Legislation. https://benefitcorp.net/policymakers/state-by-state-status

Bowen, H.R. (1953). *Social Responsibilities of the Businessman*. Harper and Brothers.

Cambridge English Dictionary (2020). Philosophy. https://dictionary.cambridge.org/dictionary/english/philosophy

Cavagnaro, E., & Curiel, G.H. (2012). *The Three Levels of Sustainability*. Sheffield, UK: Greenleaf Publishing Limited.

C.C. Global Network (2020). Chapters Archive. https://network.creativecommons.org/chapter/

Certified B Corporation (2020a). Certification. https://bcorporation.net/certification

Certified B Corporation (2020b). Directory. https://bcorporation.net/directory

Conger, K. (2019, October 30). Twitter Will Ban All Political Ads, CEO Jack Dorsey Says. *The New York Times*. www.nytimes.com/2019/10/30/technology/twitter-political-ads-ban.html

Cooney, K. (2012). Mission Control: Examining the Institutionalization of New Legal Forms of Social Enterprise in Different Strategic Action Fields. In B. Gidron & Y. Hasenfeld (Eds.), *Social enterprises: An organizational perspective* (pp. 198–221). London & New York: Palgrave Macmillan.

Defourny, J., & Nyssens, M. (2012). Conceptions of Social Enterprise in Europe: A Comparative Perspective with the United States. In B. Gidron & Y. Hasenfeld (Eds.), *Social enterprises: An organizational perspective* (pp. 71–90). London & New York: Palgrave Macmillan.

Facebook Careers. (2020). Facebook Careers. www.facebook.com/careers/v2/locations

Florin, J., & Schmidt, E. (2011). Creating Shared Value in the Hybrid Venture Arena: A Business Model Innovation Perspective. *Journal of Social Entrepreneurship*, 2(2), 165–197. https://doi.org/10.1080/19420676.2011.614631

Freeman, R.E. (1984). *Strategic Management: A Stakeholder Approach*. London, UK: Pitman Publishing

Fuchs, C. (2017). Critical Social Theory and Sustainable Development: The Role of Class, Capitalism and Domination in a Dialectical Analysis of Un/Sustainability. *Sustainable Development*, 25(5), 443–458. https://doi.org/10.1002/sd.1673

Garad, C. (2020, January 24). *A conversation about Wikipedia, the Wikimedia foundation and the Austrian Chapter* (S. Sparviero, Interviewer) [Teleconference].

Gelles, D., & Yaffe-Bellany, D. (2019, August 19). Shareholder Value Is No Longer Everything, Top CEOs Say. *The New York Times*. www.nytimes.com/2019/08/19/business/business-roundtable-ceos-corporations.html

Hodgson, G.M. (2019). Prospects for institutional research. *RAUSP Management Journal*, 54(1), 112–120. https://doi.org/10.1108/rausp-11-2018-0112

I.R.S., S. of I.D. (2020). *Table 1. Number of Returns, Total Receipts, Business Receipts, Net Income (less deficit), Net Income, and Deficit, by Form of Business, Tax Years 1980–2015*. Internal Revenue Service (I.R.S.). www.irs.gov/statistics/soi-tax-stats-integrated-business-data

Isaac, M. (2020, June 29). Reddit, Acting Against Hate Speech, Bans "The_Donald" Subreddit. *The New York Times*. www.nytimes.com/2020/06/29/technology/reddit-hate-speech.html

Isaac, M., & Hsu, T. (2020, July 7). Facebook Fails to Appease Organizers of Ad Boycott. *The New York Times*. www.nytimes.com/2020/07/07/technology/facebook-ad-boycott-civil-rights.html

Isaac, M., & Kang, C. (2020, May 29). While Twitter Confronts Trump, Zuckerberg Keeps Facebook Out of It. *The New York Times*. www.nytimes.com/2020/05/29/technology/twitter-facebook-zuckerberg-trump.html

Kajikawa, Y., Ohno, J., Takeda, Y., Matsushima, K., & Komiyama, H. (2007). Creating an academic landscape of sustainability science: An analysis of the citation network. *Sustainability Science*, 2(2), 221–231. https://doi.org/10.1007/s11625-007-0027-8

Kirchherr, J., Reike, D., & Hekkert, M. (2017). Conceptualizing the circular economy: An analysis of 114 definitions. *Resources, Conservation and Recycling*, 127, 221–232.

Kolk, A. (2016). The social responsibility of international business: From ethics and the environment to CSR and sustainable development. *Journal of World Business*, 51(1), 23–34. https://doi.org/10.1016/j.jwb.2015.08.010

Lüdeke-Freund, F., Massa, L., Bocken, N., Brent, A., & Musango, J. (2016). *Business models for shared value*. Network for Business Sustainability. www.nbs.net.

Mair, J. (2020). Social Entrepreneurship: Research as Disciplined Exploration. In W.W. Powell & P. Bromley (Eds.), *The Nonprofit Sector: A Research Handbook* (pp. 333–357). Stanford, US: Stanford University Press

Massa, L., Tucci, C.L., & Afuah, A. (2017). A Critical Assessment of Business Model Research. *Academy of Management Annals*, 11(1), 73–104. https://doi.org/10.5465/annals.2014.0072

Meadows, D.H., Meadows, D.L., Randers, J., & Behrens, W.W. (1972). *The limits to growth* (Vol. 102). New York, US: Universe Books.

Mensah, J., & Ricart Casadevall, S. (2019). Sustainable development: Meaning, history, principles, pillars, and implications for human action: Literature review. *Cogent Social Sciences*, 5(1). https://doi.org/10.1080/23311886.2019.1653531

Michelini, L., & Fiorentino, D. (2012). New business models for creating shared value. *Social Responsibility Journal*, 8(4), 561–577. https://doi.org/10.1108/17471111211272129

Mozilla. (2018). *The State of Mozilla: 2018 Annual Report*. www.mozilla.org/en-US/foundation/annualreport/2018/

Murray, J.H. (2017). Social Enterprise and Investment Professionals: Sacrificing Financial Interests. *Seattle University Law Review, 40*(2), 765–792.

Perez, C. (2010). The financial crisis and the future of innovation: A view of technical change with the aid of history. *The Other Canon Foundation and Tallinn University of Technology Working Papers in Technology Governance and Economic Dynamics,* 1–42.

Perez, C. (2015). 11. Capitalism, Technology and a Green Global Golden Age: The Role of History in Helping to Shape the Future. *The Political Quarterly, 86,* 191–217. https://doi.org/10.1111/1467-923X.12240

Pickard, V. (2011). Can government support the press? Historicizing and internationalizing a policy approach to the journalism crisis. *The Communication Review, 14*(2), 73–95. https://doi.org/10.1080/10714421.2011.573430

Porter, M.E., & Kramer, M.R. (2006). Strategy and society: The link between corporate social responsibility and competitive advantage. *Harvard Business Review, 84*(12), 78–92.

ProPublica, M.T., Wei, S., Schwencke, K., Roberts, B., & Glassford, A. (2020). *Creative Commons Corporation—Nonprofit Explorer.* ProPublica. https://projects.propublica.org/nonprofits/organizations/43585301

Raczkowski, K., Sułkowski, Ł., & Fijałkowska, J. (2016). Comparative Critical Review of Corporate Social Responsibility Business Management Models. *International Journal of Contemporary Management, 15*(2), 123–150. https://doi.org/10.4467/24498939IJCM.16.014.5554

Rokeach, M. (1968). *Beliefs, attitudes, and values: A theory of organization and change.* San Francisco, US: Jossey-Bass

Schmidt, E. (2010). Vermont's Social Hybrid Pioneers: Early observations and questions to ponder. *Vermont Law Review, 35,* 163.

Shackelford, S.J., Hiller, J.S., & Ma, X. (2019). Unpacking the Rise of Benefit Corporations: A Transatlantic Comparative Case Study. *Virginia Journal of International Law.* https://doi.org/10.2139/ssrn.3326852

Sparviero, S. (2019). The Case for a Socially Oriented Business Model Canvas: The Social Enterprise Model Canvas. *Journal of Social Entrepreneurship, 10*(2), 232–251. https://doi.org/10.1080/19420676.2018.1541011

Sparviero, S. (2020). Hybrids before Nonprofits: Key Challenges, Institutional Logics and Normative Rules of Behavior of News Media Dedicated to Social Welfare. *Journalism & Mass Communication Quarterly, OnlineFirst.* https://doi.org/10.1177/1077699020932564

Steurer, R., Langer, M.E., Konrad, A., & Martinuzzi, A. (2005). Corporations, Stakeholders and Sustainable Development I: A Theoretical Exploration of Business–Society Relations. *Journal of Business Ethics, 61*(3), 263–281. https://doi.org/10.1007/s10551-005-7054-0

Tsourvakas, G. (2016). Corporate Social Responsibility and Media Management: A Necessary Symbiosis. In *Managing Media Firms and Industries* (pp. 143–158). Springer, Cham. https://doi.org/10.1007/978-3-319-08515-9_8

Tulloch, L., & Neilson, D. (2014). The Neoliberalisation of Sustainability. *Citizenship, Social and Economics Education, 13*(1), 26–38. https://doi.org/10.2304/csee.2014.13.1.26

UN. (2015). *Transforming Our World: The 2030 Agenda for Sustainable Development.* United Nations. https://doi.org/10.1891/9780826190123.ap02

UNEP. (2011). *Towards a Green Economy: Pathways to Sustainable Development and Poverty Eradication.* United Nations Environment Programme (U.N.E.P.). www.unep.org/greeneconomy

UN. General Assembly. (2006, December 29). Millennium Summit Declaration. Wayback Machine—Internet Archive. https://web.archive.org/web/20061229095816/http://www.rcgg.ufrgs.br/msd_ing.htm

van Egmond, N.D., & de Vries, H.J.M. (2011). Sustainability: The search for the integral worldview. *Futures, 43*(8), 853–867. https://doi.org/10.1016/j.futures.2011.05.027

WCED. (1987). *Report of the World Commission on Environment and Development: Our Common Future.* World Commission of Environment and Development (WCED). www.un-documents.net/our-common-future.pdf

Wikimedia. (2019). Wikimedia chapters/Creation guide—Meta.Wikimedia.Org. https://meta.wikimedia.org/wiki/Wikimedia_chapters/Creation_guide

Wikimedia (2020a, March 1). List of Wikipedias—Meta. https://meta.wikimedia.org/wiki/List_of_Wikipedias

Wikimedia. (2020b). Wikimedia chapters. https://meta.wikimedia.org/wiki/Wikimedia_chapters

Wikimedia Foundation. (2018, May 31). Wikimedia Foundation Mission. https://wikimediafoundation.org/about/mission/

Wikimedia Foundation Inc. (2019). Sustainability Assessment and Carbon Footprint. Strategic Sustainability Consulting. https://commons.wikimedia.org/wiki/File:Wikimedia_Foundation_Sustainability_Assessment_and_Carbon_Footprint.pdf

Wikipedia. (2019, October 21). Wikipedia: About. https://en.wikipedia.org/w/index.php?title=Wikipedia:About&oldid=922393621x

Wikipedia. (2020a, February 10). Statistics. https://en.wikipedia.org/wiki/Special:Statistics

Wikipedia. (2020b). Wikipedia: Contributing to Wikipedia. https://en.wikipedia.org/w/index.php?title=Wikipedia:Contributing_to_Wikipedia&oldid=933640971

Williams, A. (2019, October 1). Wikimedia Foundation diversity and inclusion information about our workers—2019 by the numbers. *Wikimedia Foundation*. https://wikimediafoundation.org/news/2019/10/01/wikimedia-foundation-diversity-and-inclusion-information-about-our-workers-2019-by-the-numbers/

7

FEMINIST SCHOLARSHIP ON THE GLOBAL DIGITAL DIVIDE

A Critique of International Organizations and Information Companies

Micky Lee

Introduction

Digital divide is commonly defined as the discrepancy of internet access across different populations at the local, regional, national, and global levels.[1] At all levels, the poorest populations in rural areas tend to have less internet coverage than those living in affluent, populated areas. At the local level in California, African Americans and Latinx who are low-income, less educated, or live in rural areas tend not to have broadband subscriptions at home (Goss, Lee, & Gao, 2019). At the national level, the poorest US households are less likely to have a smartphone, desktop computer, or broadband services (Anderson & Kumar, 2019). At the regional level, less affluent countries in a single region have lower telecommunications penetration rates than their wealthier neighbors. For example, more than half of individuals in South Africa used the internet in 2017, but less than ten percent did so in Congo.[2] At the global level, Europe has the most individuals using the internet while Africa has the least.[3]

I assert in this chapter that the digital divide should not be narrowly defined as internet access and digital device ownership. Digital divide should also include discrepancy in skills such as reading and writing competencies in one or more languages as well computer and information literacies (Ford, 2000). I also assert in this chapter that digital divide refers to unequal opportunities in the production and ownership of information. Some related questions are: who produces content by using consumer-grade software? Who creates or modifies a programming language? Who contributes to the internet architecture? Who owns intellectual property of digital content and code? If these questions are taken into account, then it is clear that the huge gulf between the "information-haves" and the "information-have-nots" cannot be merely explained by individuals' financial, cultural, or intellectual abilities to go online and acquire technological products. The gulf can only be explained by *structural political economic arrangements that systematically exclude certain populations from accessing, understanding, creating, or owning digital media, technologies, and knowledge.* In other words, the disparities in internet access are not about individuals' inabilities to pay for them, but about public and private institutions actively excluding populations who are deemed to have little political, economic, and cultural power. Such disparities are also not about individuals' intellectual failure to grapple technical knowledge, but about institutions singling out some knowledge as being more useful than others (Lee, 2006). Similarly, intellectual property is not about protecting individuals' rights to their own creations, but about protecting the concentrated power of private corporations (Lessig, 2005).

If the discussion of digital divide is shifted from individuals' lack to institutional exclusion, then we need an analytical approach that could connect the phenomenon of digital divide to broader political, economic, and cultural injustices such as global wealth disparities, power imbalance, and the erosion of public life. The analytical approach that I explore in this chapter is called a feminist political economy. A feminist political economic approach recognizes that gender differentiates the production, distribution, and consumption of wealth and resources. At the same time, gender is used to justify why such imbalances in wealth and resources should be legitimized (Lee, 2006). For example, some societies will only send boys, not girls, to schools because parents believe girls should help out at home and learn to be good wives. In another example, women still earn less than men doing the same jobs because women are not seen as the main breadwinners (Hegewisch & Tesfaselassie, 2019). Gender is not only about women, but all historically constituted social relations, including those between races, ethnicities, social classes, geographical locations, religions, and physical and mental abilities. These historically constituted social relations tend to promote social hierarchy rather than equality. Even though the focus of this chapter is the social relation between women and men, by no means does it assume other social relations are less important in the analytical framework of a feminist political economy.

In the following, I will first examine what feminists say about the digital divide. Then I will suggest why a feminist political economic approach will shed light on the digital divide at the global level. Next, I will explore how three international organizations—UNESCO (the United Nations Educational, Scientific and Cultural Organization), ITU (the International Telecommunications Union), and the World Bank—define, explain, and tackle digital divide. Lastly, I will examine how Alphabet (the parent company of Google) appears to play the role of international organizations by promising universal internet access to the world's population.

What Would Different Feminist Approaches Say about the Digital Divide?

A feminist political economic approach is but one of many feminist approaches that explain why the divide exists and how technologies may be used to narrow this divide. In addition to a feminist political economy, I will also summarize three other schools of thought: liberal feminism, post-feminism, and technofeminism. When compared with the three other approaches, a feminist political economic approach pays more attention to: first, how goods and resources are produced, distributed, and consumed at the global level; second, how macrostructures such as the economy and politics reinforce an unequal distribution of goods and resources; and third, how gender ideology is used to legitimize this inequality (Lee, 2006).

Liberal Feminism

Liberal feminists would explain the digital divide between the genders with inequalities in education, employment, and income between the two genders.[4] Similar to bridging all divides, liberal feminists advocate that laws and regulations be implemented to ensure girl children and women have the same opportunities to learn and use digital technologies (Madgavkar, Ellingrud, & Krishnan, 2018; Robertson & Ayazi, 2019). They also believe that when women have access to digital technologies, they will produce content to better represent themselves and to participate more in public life. However, liberal feminists are wary that digital technologies make online sexual harassment and pornography pervasive, thus further reinforcing gender inequality (Broadband Commission for Digital Development, 2015). In short, liberal feminists believe that digital technologies, when used appropriately, are tools that help women close the education and income gaps. When they are used inappropriately, these tools perpetuate gender inequality.

Because liberal feminists mostly focus on how women use technologies, they do not always take into account how digital technologies may transform gender relations, such as challenging power relations between the two genders. They also do not always pay attention to *who* benefits from the production and consumption of digital technologies and content. In other words, as long as girl children and women have equal access to technologies and content as their male counterparts, it does not matter whether commercial or public/non-profit entities provide these technologies and content.

Post-Feminism

Post-feminists believe that gender equality has already been achieved so they would disagree with liberal feminists that digital divide exists. They believe that young girls and women have the power, agency, and creativity to use digital technologies for self-expression and representation (see discussion of a post-feminist view of digital media in Benn, 2013; Harvey & Fisher, 2015). Therefore, even if they use technologies differently from their male counterparts, they are as technologically apt; even if women use technologies in an apparently self-exploitative ways (such as taking "sexy" pictures of themselves and posting them online), they are exercising their agency and being playful. Unlike liberal feminists, post-feminists believe that gender relations are not fixed but can be transformed by digital technologies which challenge how gender is understood, experienced, and performed. However, like liberal feminists, post-feminists pay little attention to *who* benefits from the production and consumption of technologies and content.

Technofeminism

A technofeminist perspective critiques how digital technologies are designed and how these designs are supposed to solve women's problems. Technofeminists such as Wajcman (1991) pointed out that technologies are predominately designed by men for men. When men design technologies for women, they often misconstrue the problems that women face; therefore, technologies do not solve women's problems, but instead create new realities that differentiate male users from female users (Webster, 1995). Unlike liberal feminists and post-feminists, technofeminists point out *who* designs technologies but do not usually explicate *who* economically benefits from these technologies. There remains a question whether women inventors and programmers will create more women-friendly technologies *if* the organizations for which women work have the prime motive of profit-making.

Although liberal feminists, post-feminists, and technofeminists have offered ways to theorize women and technologies, a feminist political economist would critique them to be Global North-centric. Traditionally, Global North refers to wealthy, democratic countries in the Northern hemisphere as well as Japan, Australia, and New Zealand. Global South refers to countries in Central and South America, Eastern Europe, the Middle East, and most of Asia (Royal Geographical Society, n/a). However, the line between Global North and Global South became blurry when some countries in the Global South became wealthy (such as South Korea and Qatar) and when wealth disparities became more pronounced between rural and urban areas in a country, between residents living in gated communities and slums in a city. The Global North concept is more useful if it does not merely refer to specific regions and countries, but populations with sufficient income and resources to access food, shelter, schooling, healthcare, and other daily necessities regardless of geographical location. When the Global North is redefined as a population's access to resources, then there is a Global North in the poorest countries in the world, and a Global South in the wealthiest countries in the world. With this definition, I assess liberal feminists, post-feminists, and technofeminists to be Global North-centric because they assume societies have sufficient resources to allocate for women and girls to produce, distribute, and consume technologies and content; all women and girls need are laws and regulations, training and education, will and creativity to bridge the digital divide between them and the male counterparts.

A Global North-centric view of digital divide needs to be critiqued from a Global South position that is compatible with a feminist political economic perspective because digital divide is not seen as an isolated inequality from other inequalities (such as income, education, workplace) or merely an inequality between men and women. A feminist political economic perspective argues that gender relations reflect and constitute unequal power relationships between the Global North and Global South. This perspective also acknowledges that gender relations are deliberately kept unequal because those who have the most resources have the power to make decisions for those who have the least resources.

At the global level, men of the dominant racial and ethnic groups from the upper-middle-class have the most power to make decisions about technological development. These decisions are implemented as international treaties, national policies, macroeconomic policies, and company policies. These decisions not only affect populations in their own countries, but also those in other countries. For example, the North American Free Trade Agreement signed by the US, Canada, and Mexico in 1992 has had devastating effects on women factory workers in Mexico. On the premise of facilitating free trade in the region, US-based companies moved audiovisual hardware manufacturing south of the border to take advantage of cheaper labor costs. In the name of economic development, the government encouraged women to leave their farms and homes to work at factories where sexual harassment and hazardous environments are common (Quintero-Ramírez, 2002). Similar situations are found in Chinese factories that manufacture Apple Computers (Qiu, 2009). Migrant workers moved from rural areas to economic zones where they work long hours making goods that they can barely afford.

A feminist political economic perspective not only occupies a Global South position, but also connects the political economic conditions between the Global South and Global North. For example, the harsh realities that Global South factory workers face should be understood in the context of economic recession experienced by the Global North since the 1970s. Economic recession led to wage stagnation in lower-class and middle-class families. To make ends meet, women often have to work part-time or full-time to bring in extra income. Women working outside the home may reflect women's empowerment and gender equality but they face systematic discrimination in the workplace: they tend to earn less than men doing the same job (Hegewisch & Tesfaselassie, 2019), work in less-well-paid industries such as education and human services (Stone & Southerlan, 2019; Wong, 2019), work in part-time and temporary positions (Sands, 2014), and have a harder time getting promoted to managers (Fuhrmans, 2019).

Ironically, the rise of two-income households also brought consumerism in the Global North. Supply-side economic theories believe that consumption will lead the Global North to dig out from recession (Yamamura, 2018). An image-saturated media environment also persuades two-income families that they deserve an upper-middle-class lifestyle (Schor, 1993). Advertisers and marketers promote the idea that multiple television sets and the latest technological devices are no longer luxury items, but necessities in the average household. The alluring images in the marketing and advertising of technologies obscure the harsh, mundane, and hazardous work environment experienced by Global South women. Some of the alluring images, ironically, ask women in the Global North to see technologies as empowerment tools. For example, some smartphone advertisements show a carefree woman roaming a new city with the aid of a smartphone, her freedom contrasting with the constrictive work conditions of factory workers.

To sum up, a feminist political economic perspective that takes a Global South position examines the unequal production and consumption of goods at the global level. It also asks what kind of gender ideology is used to legitimize this inequality. Feminist political economists believe that digital divide between the Global North and Global South *is* deliberately maintained so that those who have the power to control the resources can continue doing so. In this sense, unlike liberal feminists, post-feminists, and technofeminists, technologies are not seen as neutral political economic tools that, when designed and used appropriately, will advance gender equality.

In the following section, I will use a feminist political economic perspective to critique international policies that aim to bridge the digital gap between men and women, developed economies and developing ones. I argue that these policies implemented by international organizations rarely address the question of power. Instead, they point their finger at the "have-nots" by first defining for them the problem (i.e., digital divide), then blaming them for not solving this problem on their own. In addition, these policies often have a neoliberal agenda that aims to transform the "disadvantaged" populations into workers and consumers so that they can produce more surplus value for the national economy. To give an example, homemakers—very often women—are said to be potential wage earners who can contribute to the household and national income. When women have their own income, they are asked to see themselves as empowered consumers. From a feminist political economic perspective, women making their own money does not automatically liberate them; it in fact burdens them with work both inside and outside home, making them less available for the extended family and community even though they are still expected to play the primary caretaker role. The extra money that women bring in is advertised to be best spent on consumer goods such as smartphones so that they can better connect with their family and friends. By asking the "disadvantaged" populations to see themselves as individual workers and consumers, this neoliberal agenda weakens structures—such as family, community, and the public—that provide common goods and social network during economic downturns.

Bridging or Widening the Gap? International Efforts to Solve the Digital Divide

In this section I focus on three international organizations that assist national governments to bridge the digital divide between women and men, Global South and Global North. They are UNESCO, the ITU, and the World Bank. Even though they have different expertise, all believe that international development is essential to combat global issues from religious violence, income disparity, to climate change. Despite their noble goals, I will conclude this section by arguing that their digital gap-bridging projects are embedded with a neoliberal agenda. Hence, they will widen the gap rather than narrowing it.

UNESCO

UNESCO was established at the end of WWII It believes that economic and political negotiation is insufficient to solve world problems. Instead, international dialogue through education, cultural, and scientific collaboration is essential to maintain world peace. The organization acknowledges that poor nations are left out of information and communication technologies; at the same time, it believes that the disadvantaged populations must have information literacy and internet access for education, civic participation, and scientific exchange (UNESCO, 2002).

UNESCO's strategy to combat digital divide has failed to point out a few things. First, it did not mention who creates the digital divide. To UNESCO, digital divide is like a "thing" that exists on its own; it was not seen as a result of human actions. For example, it stated that "the so-called 'digital divide' [...] threatens to deny [the promise of cultural dialogue and mutual understanding] from entire regions" (UNESCO, 2002, para. 2).

Second, it did not point out who the disadvantaged populations are; it only pointed out that digital divide is a gap between "rich and poor nations" (ibid.). It is relatively mute about whether gender, race/ethnicity, and social class differentiate information access. Moreover, UNESCO sees Global North and Global South as groups of countries; it does not acknowledge that there is a Global North in the Global South, and a Global South in the Global North. Ignoring this obscures the unequal power relations between the "haves" and the "have-nots" in every country. When all populations in the most developed countries are believed to be the "haves" rather than "have-nots", it is difficult to establish global coalition between the "have-nots" in different countries.

Third, it sees nation-states as the primary actors to bridge the gap and fails to suggest what transnational corporations might gain in bridging this gap. UNESCO is aware that information is not a commercial good—"education as well as cultural goods and services cannot be treated as mere commodities" (UNESCO, 2002, para. 6)—but it does not point out that the technologies through which information is provided are very often commodities produced for profits.

The UNESCO website illustrates the unequal power structure between powerful corporations and this relatively poorly funded international organization. First, it is with some irony that the website uses the Google search engine, a "free" service provided by a company that is known for information commodification (Fuchs, 2011; Lee, 2011). However, UNESCO probably does not have an alternative but to incorporate the Google search engine or its competitors' ones because it does not have the resources to develop one. Second, interested readers who want to read more about UNESCOs project on Western China are led to a "page not found" destination. These two instances show that although Google has enough money and resources to provide fast and accurate information, it does not have enough human resource to locate broken links.

ITU

The ITU was founded in the late 19th century to regulate international radio spectrum. Since then it has been advising nation-states about providing information and communication technologies (ICTs) to underserved communities worldwide. International development is a major area of the ITU's work, and bridging the digital divide is one major responsibility.

The ITU Secretary-General wrote in a digital divide progress report that ICTs have been driving global development, transforming both society and the economy (Zhao, 2015). He believed that the digital divide is narrowing for most of the world's populations because of technological progress, infrastructure deployment, and lower costs. Similar to UNESCO, the ITU sees the digital divide as one between the developed world and the developing world rather than the Global North and the Global South as differentiated by gender, race/ethnicity, social class, and geographical location. In the developing world, the ITU specifically named women and young girls, school children, and people with disabilities as the populations whose information access relies on sound public policies.

The ITU's digital divide progress report stated that the digital divide between women and men has been closing. It believes that a narrower gap is desirable because an uptick of women and girl users correlates to an increase of the global GDP. Accordingly, the organization has an initiative called ITU's International Girls in ICT. Day to promote girls' online participation. On this day, member-states are encouraged to organize events to encourage girls to consider studies and careers related to ICTs. I argue that the ITU. believes an ICT career benefits women because not only does it lift them up from poverty, but it also makes women's mid-level careers fulfilling and paves the way for top leadership. At another level, technologically apt women and girls are good for business: the ITU wrote, "ICT companies are looking to attract and promote women because achieving greater workforce diversity is good for business".[5]

Similar to UNESCO, the ITU did not name the actors who create and maintain the digital gap. Likewise, it sees digital divide as a gulf between nation-states even though it acknowledges that in developing countries, women and girls, school children, and people with disabilities tend to lag behind in the use of information and communication technologies. Unlike UNESCO, which sees information access as a key to world peace, the ITU believes that left-behind populations should be online for economic reasons. For example, its progress report page has a link to an Intel report *Women and the web* in which underserved women and girls are considered "consumers of Internet products and services" (Intel, 2012, p. 27) as well as potential workers who can "produce gains for their families, communities, and nations" (p. 28). The ITU is blatant in stating that women are potential economic beings; I.C.T.s can transform women and young girls from social beings with no market value to high-value consumers and workers. Their economic contribution is not only for individual gains, but also for the national and global economies.

The World Bank

The World Bank was founded in 1944 to re-build western European countries after WWII. It has since metamorphosed into a development bank for the developing world. The two missions of the Bank are to end extreme poverty and to promote shared wealth by bolstering the income of the bottom 40% population in every country. Two of its areas of expertise are: (1) providing low-interest loans, zero- to low-interest credit, and grants to developing countries; (2) assisting developing countries with policy advice, research and analysis, and technical assistance.[6]

The World Bank recognizes that digital technology benefits an economy, governments, and the general population. But it also acknowledges that there are technological disparities between countries largely due to cost. Without internet access, the World Bank believes that individuals who are already poor and vulnerable will miss out on information access, opportunities to work and learn online, and healthcare support. The Bank believes that countries ought to provide universal broadband access and skills training to their citizens to become "digital rich".[7] The Bank funded projects that are directly related to a digital economy, such as financing infrastructure, financial services, innovation and entrepreneurship, digital platforms, and online skills for employment.[8]

Similar to UNESCO and the ITU, the World Bank sees digital divide as that between countries, in particular between the developed and the developing worlds. It also does not discuss how gender, race, and geographical locations constitute one's economic status. The projects that the Bank had funded did not mention women as exclusive or preferred recipients, nor did they have a gender dimension in their projects. Therefore it is unknown if women and girls benefit as much as their male counterparts.

On the World Bank's page about gender, it recognizes that the wealth gap between males and females is closing, but women and girls tend to fare worse because of gender discriminatory policies, customs, and norms. The Bank believes that these practices impede women as agents of economic growth.[9] Despite this belief, the Bank's projects to reduce gender inequality focus on girls' education, women's leadership, women's shelters, and insurance more than economic development. While these projects undoubtedly promote women's rights, they do not directly address how women can be agents in a digital economy.

In conclusion, even though UNESCO, the ITU, and the World Bank have different beliefs about how world peace can be maintained and promoted, they share some similar ideas of the digital divide. First, these three international organizations view digital divide as existing chiefly between countries in the developed and developing countries. Second, none of them named *who* is responsible for creating and maintaining the divide. To them, the divide appears to be an autonomous "thing" that exists in a political economic vacuum. It is more like a natural disaster that needs to be managed and overcome, not a consequence of unbalanced power relationship between the "haves" and the "have-nots", transnational corporations, and impoverished governments. Third, apart from UNESCO, whose stance on gender and digital divide cannot be deduced due to the lack of information, both the ITU and the World Bank have a neoliberal agenda in closing the digital divide. In other words, they see some populations not as citizens or members of the public, but potential workers and consumers who help the global economy grow. In the case of the ITU, it encourages girl students to learn "masculine" subjects (such as mathematics and computer sciences) so that they can get jobs with higher pay. Girls are seen as raw resources that need to be refined for value extraction not only for themselves, but also for their family and the country. The World Bank's digital development projects aim to bolster national economies through investments in infrastructure and digital platforms. Other projects aim to invest in human capital, training "underutilized" humans to become workers for the digital economy. Because these projects are gender-blind it is hard to assess if they further widen gender inequality of digital development, especially because a gender-blind approach would channel limited resources to men rather than women. Furthermore, the Bank's projects on women tend to confine them to the private domains (such as early childhood education and the household) rather than the public domains (such as the workplace and politics), thus excluding them from the Bank's digital development projects that facilitate economic development through state agencies and private enterprises.

Where International Efforts Fail, Google Can Fill in

In the previous section, I argued that the digital gap-bridging projects of the ITU and the World Bank are embedded with a neoliberal agenda because they advocate the "disadvantaged" populations to see themselves as individual workers and consumers through international development projects. A neoliberal agenda weakens community fiber and public services that provide common goods to these populations. In a broader context, how these two organizations can effect global change is probably incomparable to transnational private corporations such as Alphabet (the parent company of Google). Even though Alphabet is a corporation, it often uses language to present itself as a benevolent organization that provides "free" services for global internet users. In the rest of the chapter, I assert that a transnational corporation cannot bridge the digital gap because its main purpose is to expand the market by connecting "untapped" populations to the internet so that more people can conduct their searches on Google.

The revenue of Alphabet in the third quarter in 2019 was US$40.49 billion (Li, 2019). In contrast, the operating budget of the ITU was only US$178 million in 2016 (ITU, 2018). In addition, the name "Google" also has more cultural influence on the world's populations since it is the dominant search engine in most countries (Lee, 2019). With such economic power and cultural influence, Alphabet has a better chance to implement large-scale infrastructure projects that have profound impact on digital divide.

For example, Alphabet has an innovation lab called X that carries out "moon shot projects" that "build and launch technologies that aim to improve the lives of millions, even billions, of people"[10]. One of the lab projects is to use stratospheric balloons to deliver the internet to half of the world populations that are not yet online. Google deems internet access to be important because "[r]ight now, billions of people across the globe still do not have Internet access. They are completely left out of a digital revolution that could improve their finances, education, and health".[11] The language that Alphabet uses is closer to that of international organizations such as the ITU and the World Bank than corporations; it is as if they are now in the business of international development.

An instance where the stratospheric balloons filled in a void is communication during natural disaster, an area that is traditionally seen as a role played by the government. When Puerto Rico was devastated by a hurricane in 2017, Alphabet worked with AT&T and T-Mobile to bring internet connection to Puerto Ricans for rescue efforts (Mattise, 2018). While these corporations may appear to pay back to communities, they also send a message that private entities are more efficient at solving problems that are pushed to the side by governments. Private corporations stepping in where the government has failed further reinforces the neoliberal agenda that they can replace the government by providing privatized public utilities. From a Global South perspective, Alphabet's stratospheric balloons project already shows that not-yet-connected populations are likely to be recruited online by corporations before governments or international organizations can provide internet access as a public service. These populations may hardly have a chance to experience online citizenry because they arrive in cyberspace as digital consumers. From a feminist political economic perspective, a neoliberal agenda of digital divide embraced by private corporations and international organizations will not achieve gender equality or women's empowerment, and it will instead marginalize the Global South.

Conclusion

This chapter advocates for a broader definition of global digital divide by: first, acknowledging that there is a Global North in the Global South, and a Global South in the Global North; second, broadening up the definition of digital divide by including disparities in the creation and development of programming languages and internet infrastructure. From a Global South position, digital divide is not only a result of power inequalities shaped by gender, race/ethnicity, and geographical location, but is also *deliberately* maintained so that the "have-nots" can be uplifted to become the "haves". The process of uplifting requires the "disadvantaged" populations—in particular women—to enter into an "earn and spend" cycle; they are supposed to work outside home to generate income which will be spent on sensible necessities, such as fast internet connections and smartphones.

An examination of three international organizations (UNESCO, the ITU, and the World Bank) shows that they strictly see the digital divide as one between the developed and developing worlds; they do not problematize how gender, race/ethnicity, and geographical locations shape the digital divide in one single country. These organizations have few projects that have a gender dimension to bridge the digital divide. For the few projects that involve girls and women, these populations are seen as "untapped" resources that can be developed for the job market. Making women into better workers reinforces a neoliberal agenda because citizens are supposed to be self-sufficient and less reliant on public goods and community resources.

However, the political economic power and cultural influence of international organizations are dwarfed by those of transnational corporations such as Alphabet, Google's parent company. Transnational corporations adopt the language of international organizations to play a role in international development. Alphabet, a company whose profits depend on a continuous increase in internet users, has come to see itself as a benevolent organization that uses technology to bring the internet to the yet "untapped" populations. While it is yet to be seen whether a transnational corporation can close the digital divide in terms of internet access, an examination of job stratification and sexual harassment in the company has revealed that women and non-whites are less likely to be promoted as leaders (Lee, 2019). In other words, a digital divide is perpetuated by Alphabet that systematically excludes some populations to own and control technologies even though it believes it is closing the digital gap.

Notes

1 Digital divide. Glossary of statistical terms. O.C.E.D. Retrieved from: https://stats.oecd.org/glossary/detail. asp?ID=4719
2 Percentage of individuals using the internet (Excel). International Telecommunication Union. Statistics. www. itu.int/en/ITU-D/Statistics/Pages/stat/default.aspx
3 Download time series of I.C.T. data for the world, by geographic regions and by level of development, for the following indicators. International Telecommunication Union. Statistics. www.itu.int/en/ITU-D/Statistics/Pages/stat/default.aspx
4 Studies guided by liberal feminist thought are predominately conducted by think tanks, policy-making bodies, and advocacy groups rather than feminist scholars in the academia.
5 Why girls in ICT day? International Girls in ICT Day. Retrieved from https://www.itu.int/en/ITU-D/Digital-Inclusion/Women-and-Girls/Girls-in-ICT-Portal/Pages/Why-a-Girls-in-ICT-Day.aspx

6 What we do. The World Bank. Retrieved from: https://www.worldbank.org/en/about/what-we-do

7 Context. Digital development. The World Bank. Retrieved from: https://www.worldbank.org/en/topic/digitaldevelopment/overview#1

8 Strategy. Digital development. The World Bank. Retrieved from: https://www.worldbank.org/en/topic/digitaldevelopment/overview#2

9 Context. Digital development. The World Bank. Retrieved from: https://www.worldbank.org/en/topic/digitaldevelopment/overview#1

10 The moonshot factory. X. Retrieved from https://x.company/

11 Loon. X. Retrieved from https://x.company/projects/loon/ This project was discontinued as of early 2021.

References

Anderson, M., & Kumar, M. (2019, May 7). Digital divide persists even as lower-income Americans make gains in tech adoption. Pew Research Center. Retrieved from: www.pewresearch.org/fact-tank/2019/05/07/digital-divide-persists-even-as-lower-income-americans-make-gains-in-tech-adoption/

Benn, M. (2013). After post-feminism: Pursuing material equality in a digital age. *Juncture, 20*(3), 223–227.

Broadband Commission for Digital Development. (2015). *Cyber violence against women and girls: A world-wide wake-up call.* Geneva and Paris: ITU and UNESCO.

Ford, B.J. (2000). Libraries, literacy, outreach and the digital divide. *American Library Association.* Retrieved from: www.ala.org/aboutala/offices/olos/olosprograms/jeanecoleman/00ford

Fuchs, C. (2011). A contribution to the critique of the political economy of Google. *Fast Capitalism, 8*(1). Retrieved from: www.fastcapitalism.com/.

Fuhrmans, V. (2019, October 15). Where women fall behind at work: The first step into management. *Wall Street Journal.* Retrieved from: www.wsj.com/articles/where-women-fall-behind-at-work-the-first-step-into-management-11571112361

Goss, J., Lee, C., & Gao, N. (2019, March). California's digital divide. *Public Policy Institute of California.* Retrieved from: www.ppic.org/publication/californias-digital-divide/

Harvey, A., & Fisher, S. (2015) "Everyone can make games!": The post-feminist context of women in digital game production. *Feminist Media Studies, 15*(4), 576–592.

Hegewisch, A., & Tesfaselassie, A. (2019, September 11). The gender wage gap: 2018; earnings differences by gender, race and ethnicity. *Institute for Women's Policy Research.* Retrieved from: https://iwpr.org/publications/annual-gender-wage-gap-2018/

"How is ITU funded?" (2018, October 25). *ITU News.* Retrieved from https://news.itu.int/how-is-itu-funded/

Lee, M. (2006). What's missing in feminist research in new information and communication technologies? *Feminist Media Studies, 6*(2), 191–210.

Lee, M. (2011). Google ads and the Blindspot Debate. *Media, Culture, and Society, 33*(3), 433–448.

Lee, M. (2019). *Alphabet: The becoming of Google.* New York: Routledge.

Lessig, L. (2005). *Free culture: The nature and future of creativity.* New York: Penguin.

Li, A. (2019, October 28). Alphabet reports Q3 2019 revenue of $40.49 billion. *9T5 Google.* Retrieved from https://9to5google.com/2019/10/28/alphabet-q3-2019-earnings/

Madgavkar, A., Ellingrud, K., & Krishnan, M. (2018, July 30). How can digital technology speed up gender equality? *McKinsey Global Institute.* Retrieved from: www.mckinsey.com/mgi/overview/in-the-news/how-can-digital-technology-speed-up-gender-equality

Mattise, N. (2017, February 18). Project Loon team gave Puerto Rico connectivity—and assembled a helicopter. *Ars Technica.* Retrieved from: https://arstechnica.com/science/2018/02/project-loon-engineer-sees-a-tool-for-future-disaster-response-in-puerto-rico/

Qiu, J.L. (2009). *Working-Class network society: Communication technology and the information have-less in urban China.* Cambridge, MA: The MIT Press.

Quintero-Ramírez, C. (2002). The North American Free Trade Agreement and women. *International Feminist Journal of Politics, 4*(2), 240–259.

Robertson, D., & Ayazi, M. (2019, July 15). How women are using technology to advance gender equality and peace. *United States Institute of Peace.* Retrieved from: www.usip.org/publications/2019/07/how-women-are-using-technology-advance-gender-equality-and-peace

Royal Geographical Society. *A 60 second guide to the Global North/South divide.* Retrieved from: www.rgs.org/schools/teaching-resources/a-60-second-guide-to-global-north-south-divide/

Sands, D. (2014, August 20). Women working in low paid, insecure or temporary roles on the rise. *The Guardian.* Retrieved from: www.theguardian.com

Schor, J. (1993). *The overworked American: The unexpected decline of leisure.* New York: Basic Books.

Stone, T., & Southerlan, E. (2019, April 1). Women make up 65 percent of health care workers—but only 13 percent of CEOs. Why? *Brink: The edge of risk*. Retrieved from: www.brinknews.com/women-make-up-65-percent-of-healthcare-workers-but-only-13-percent-of-ceos-why/

UNESCO. (2002). UNESCO outlines strategy to combat digital divide (Press release No. 2002–62). Paris: UNESCO.

Wajcman, J. (1991). *Feminism confronts technology*. State College, P.A.: Penn State University Press.

Webster, J. (1995). What do we know about gender and information technology at work? A discussion of selected feminist research. *The European Journal of Women's Studies, 2*(3), 315–334.

Women and the Web. (2012). *Intel*. Retrieved from: www.intel.com/content/dam/www/public/us/en/documents/pdf/women-and-the-web.pdf

Wong, A. (2019, February 20). The US teaching population is getting bigger, and more female. *The Atlantic*. Retrieved from www.theatlantic.com

Yamamura, K. (2018). *Too much stuff: Capitalism in crisis*. Bristol, UK: Bristol University Press.

Zhao, H. (2015, August 26). Digital divide progress report: 15 year review. *ITU News*. Retrieved from: https://news.itu.int/digital-divide-progress-report-15-year-review/

8

THE KOREAN WAVE AND THE NEW GLOBAL MEDIA ECONOMY

Ju Oak Kim

In the late 2010s, noticeable changes were identified in the US media industries in alignment with the ongoing expansion of Korean popular culture and practice. Transnational media conglomerates (power holders in the global media market) established collaborative partnerships with Korean media industries (the world's seventh-largest content creator), by making various deals with Korean networks to purchase Korean television formats and by producing original Korean series with local production companies and creators (Yonhap, 2017).

The US commercial television networks have taken the initiative in establishing this new media landscape: NBC aired two seasons of the TV series *Better Late than Never* (2016–2018), based on the Korean variety show format, *Grandpas over Flowers* (tvN, 2013–2018). ABC's medical drama series, *The Good Doctor* (2017–), which was initially created by Korea's leading network, KBS, in 2013, has achieved high viewership, resulting in the renewal of its fourth season in 2020. Fox chose the third season of *The Masked Singer* (2019–)—the latest Korean unscripted format that has penetrated the US television industry—for a post-Super Bowl slot and had 23.7 million total viewers following the Super Bowl LIV (Maglio & Maas, 2020).

Netflix—the global on-demand entertainment service—has invigorated US–Korean media connections with investment in distribution agreements with Korea's major networks and in local-bound film and original series productions. In 2019, Netflix agreed to engage in a multi-year content distribution deal with the Korean media entertainment conglomerates CJE&M and JTBC to stream their prime-time dramas and reality shows. Also, Netflix has made efforts to create original films and series with local creators. This new production ecosystem emerged with the release of Bong Joon-ho's film *Okja* in 2017. Since then, Netflix has invested heavily in producing and distributing original Korean series, including *Kingdom* (2019–2020) and *Extracurricular* (2020).

The recent expansion of US entertainment giants into Korean television content is, by and large, driven by Korea's content creators and celebrities, who have played central roles in empowering Korean products and services in the global media market.[1] For example, at the turn of the 2020s, the K-pop boy group BTS and Bong Joon-ho have shown the impact of the Korean Wave phenomenon—the transnational spread of Korean popular culture—in the US media sphere. The BTS sensation has resulted in four million preorders worldwide for BTS' album, *Map of the Soul: 7*, which is a rare achievement "for any musician, even the most successful in the industry" (McIntyre, 2020, para. 3). Also, the Oscar-winning movie *Parasite* grossed $376,264 in the US box office during its opening weekend, and its per-venue average of $125,421 is the best ever for an international film (Ramos, 2019).[2]

Notably, both BTS and Bong have deconstructed long-standing ideological barriers of language and culture between the West and the non-West, demonstrating the power of universally appealing messages along with Asian creativity and sensibility (Kim J., 2021). BTS exemplifies how Korean celebrities have established a sense of belonging with global audiences in an age of social media, while Bong has proven that the local creator's personal experience and autonomy are critical in the production of global culture.[3] These two Korean cultural acts have not only enhanced the visibility of Korean popular culture, but have also reshaped the relationship between the US and Korean media industries.

When the Korean Wave swept over Asian societies in the mid-1990s, few scholars expected this cultural fad to penetrate the US media industries. Such a skeptical perspective maintained that the Korean Wave was a temporary, intraregional phenomenon that would eventually follow the trajectory of Japanization and the Hong Kong Wave in the 1980s and 1990s (Kim J., 2016b). However, in recent years some global media scholars have discussed the phenomenon as an anchoring point in deconstructing the long-standing binary approach of global (West) vs. local (non-West) to media businesses and in empowering local practitioners and creators in the production of global media cultures and flows (Lee & Nornes, 2015; Jin, 2016; Jin & Kim, 2018).

In this chapter, I chronicle the ongoing expansion of the Korean Wave, focusing on the recent visibility of unscripted and scripted Korean television formats and the increasing presence of Korean filmmakers, actors, and pop celebrities in the US media industry. US–Korean media connections have become an unexplored subject of study in media industry scholarship. A lack of research on the changing dynamics between the US and Korean media industries is not only a result of Hollywood's dominance in the global media market, but also of Anglo-driven media industry scholarship. Haven's (2006) critique regarding the failure of academics to grasp the global distribution and marketing of media products and services has not been sufficiently acknowledged; meanwhile, formerly marginalized and currently rising national actors from countries such as Korea, Turkey, India, Brazil, and China have led to reshaping global media interactions (Thussu, 2007). This study responds to the inquiry, suggesting a new approach to the periodization of the Korean Wave phenomenon.

Media Globalization: An Angle of Political Economy

US-based media conglomerates have dominated the global media industries since the 1980s; additionally, neoliberal capitalism has been employed in the operations of the global media system, transforming the structures and patterns of media production, distribution, and consumption (Herman & McChesney, 1997). Global media scholars have critically pointed out the centralization of US media conglomerates in shaping one-way cultural flows from Western countries to the rest of the world (Fejes, 1981; Schiller, 1975; Tomlinson, 1991; Tunstall, 1977; Wallerstein 1974). This cultural imperialism thesis has considered the transnational interaction between cultures as the spread of Western values and ideas, which is intensely promoted by political and economic systems (Tomlinson, 1991). Havens (2006) sustained this perspective by pointing out multinational gigantic media conglomerates' tactics in invading the not-yet-touched local markets, which reaffirms the substantial presence of European–US television programming in regional markets.

Some media scholars have challenged the domination of the cultural imperialism thesis in the discussion of global culture, pointing out the local impetus of cultural production and distribution. Tunstall (2008) admitted the discontinuity of US dominance in the global media landscape, indicating the rise of Chinese and Indian media markets. His main argument maintains that, although the visible presence of US media content is ongoing in various areas of the world, such as Canada, Mexico, and Europe, many local audiences, in particular, Asian societies, have revealed their preference for the consumption of media content created with familiar sociocultural backgrounds. Key thinkers in this academic strand have emphasized the impetus of locality in the production and consumption of media products and services. For instance, Straubhaar (1991) called attention to the sociocultural intimacy and geographical gravity in transnational media interactions. Thussu (2007) devoted attention to the global media system in invigorating industrial connections between spatially and culturally separated authors and distributors in the media businesses. In his view, this new media ecology has allowed non-Western production companies to facilitate transnational productions within the logic of the global media economy and to make local television programming more appealing to multiple markets.

The Korean Wave: From the Regional to the Global

Korean popular products—TV drama, reality shows, film, pop music, and online gaming—are penetrating various societies of the world, employing new media platforms and aspirational fan communities. The Korean Wave is a salient example showing how a historically and culturally marginalized nation has created global consumption of its popular products through the deployment of cultural hybridity in production and digital networks in distribution. Previous research has emphasized political economy, social media, and participatory culture in the scholarship of this cultural phenomenon and has brought East Asian connections to the fore of debates regarding media globalization (Huat & Iwabuchi, 2008).

Korean media scholars have thoroughly discussed the development of the Korean Wave during the past two decades; this phenomenon has expanded from a regional to a global scale in a geographic context and has experienced changes in the key genres for cultural exportation. For instance, television dramas and films initiated the popularity of Korean popular culture in the late 1990s (Shim, 2008). At that time, the Korean media industry made efforts to develop interregional partnerships with neighboring countries, including China, Japan, and Taiwan. Such East Asian media connections intensified the Korean media industry's exportation-driven development. However, digital games and K-pop have become the central engine for expanding the Korean Wave phenomenon to multiple societies outside of the region in the 2000s (Jin, 2016; Lee & Nornes, 2015; Yoon & Jin, 2017;). Since then, scholars have pointed out the Korean Wave as a global phenomenon in the context of digital media and fan participatory culture. This phase references the influence of Western cultures and values in the Korean Wave, claiming K-pop as a hybrid form of Western and traditional elements (Kim J., 2016a; Ryoo, 2009; Shim, 2006). In their view, the mixture of Western and non-Western elements was critical in the globalization of K-pop culture and practice.

In the late 2010s, certain global media scholars shifted the discussion of the Korean Wave, examining the power dynamics between Western and non-Western cultures. Jin (2016) argued that Korea had become the first non-Western actor to export its cultural content to both Western and non-Western countries to a considerable degree. According to him, while a few countries have previously penetrated the global market with single or limited cultural forms, such as Mexico and Brazil's telenovelas and Japan's animations and console games, the global visibility of Korea's multiple cultural forms is an unprecedented phenomenon (Jin, 2016). Kim (2016b) suggested that Korean Wave scholarship should go beyond the binary approach of global (West) vs. local (non-West) in the discussion of Korean cultural production and distribution. In this view, it is problematic to sustain the terminological amalgamation of the global and the West because this ideological framework discourages media scholars from situating non-Western players at the center of media globalization (see Kim J., 2021).

Television Revolution: From Format Adaptation to Original Series

In the late 2010s, Korean and US media industries developed partnerships in the television format trade, in which US major networks and streaming services either purchased Korean television formats or coproduced original Korean series. The US adaptation of Korean television formats and the US–Korean coproduction of original television series unveiled fundamental changes in the relationship between the two media industries. Over the decades, the US media industry has maintained one-sided media flows with Korean partners, similar to other non-Western nations.[4] Although long-standing asymmetrical media flows are still ongoing between them, the past years have observed the visibility of Korean television content on American television.

Major networks such as ABC, NBC, and Fox have contributed to the arrival of the Korean Wave in the US media landscape by purchasing Korean unscripted and scripted television formats. In February 2016, ABC announced a ten-episode straight-to-series plan for an American remake of the Korean television drama series *Somewhere Between*, based on the Korean drama *God's Gift: 14 Days* (Rodriguez, 2017). Later that year, another news report came out, indicating that CBS had bought the scripted Korean format *My Lawyer, Mr. Jo,* in order to develop the legal drama *Exhibit A.* (Andreeva, 2016). The more surprising news was ABC's adaptation of the Korean medical series *The Good Doctor*. In the promotional video, David Shore and Daniel Dae Kim noted that ABC decided to produce the US version of the KBS drama series due to the unique characters and stories (ABC, 2017). They identified Korean television programs as an artifact containing different sentiments and creativity from US television series (A.B.C., 2017). These US remakes of the Korean television formats, including *The Good Doctor* and *The Masked Singer*, have successfully attracted attention from the domestic US audience during the late 2010s.

Netflix has accelerated changes in the landscape of the US media industry by making direct investments in Korean production companies. The production of original Korean series has been promoted based on mutual benefits between the multinational video-on-demand streaming service and Korean media creators. The recent Netflix original series *Kingdom* is a clear example that reveals the newly shaped partnership between the US online-based streaming service and Korean production companies and practitioners. This zombie-thriller was devloped by Eun-Hee Kim, who is one of the most influential writers in the Korean television industry. It has been said that, due to the unpopularity of the zombie action-thriller genre in the Korean media market, the country's major networks hesitated to accept her proposal (Song, 2019). However, Netflix made a different decision, with the view that the new content would attract global audiences who are interested in that television genre (Kim H.-j., 2019). Likewise, Netflix offered Korean production companies and media creators the opportunity to create globally appealing and big-budget productions (Kim S., 2020). Although the arrival of the global entertainment giant has, to some degree, threatened the Korean television production ecosystem, Netflix's original Korean series has emerged as a new engine for the Korean Wave, based on mutual benefits between the multinational streaming service and Korean media creators (Kim S., 2020).

The growth of Korean media consumers has helped the US media industries to recognize the market power of Korean media content. On the one hand, large international audiences are seeking something different from their own cultures and practices (Park & Lee, 2019). Video-on-demand streaming services have offered them the material condition for enjoying a variety of media content produced outside of the homeland. Rob Roy, Vice President of Content at Netflix, values these subscribers who have transcended language barriers and geographic borders to consume media content in the era of post-network television (White, 2019). On the other hand, the US Asian population has grown remarkably in the past two decades, reaching 28% of all immigrants in 2018 (López, Ruiz & Patten, 2017; Budiman, 2020). This population growth may have invigorated the consumption of Korean television dramas in the US, launching online streaming services such as *DramaFever* and *Viki* in the end of the 2000s, both of which focused on East Asian popular content. Korean broadcasters—KBS, MBC, and SBS—have also identified the potential of the US media market and have joined the competition by providing a streaming service called KOCOW (Spangler, 2018). In a similar vein, US-based video streaming services, including Netflix, Hulu, and Amazon Prime, have recognized audience segmentation and have developed a line-up of Korean dramas and films.

Against this backdrop, I propose that the Korean Wave opened up its third phase in the late 2010s; Korean popular content, including television formats, original series, films, and K-pop, has penetrated the mainstream US media industries. During its second phase, Korean media products went beyond the Asian region with the support of online media platforms. While media scholars considered the Korean Wave as a global phenomenon during its second phase, the Korean Wave was still one of the subcultures that specific fans of various societies consumed. However, the new phase of the cultural phenomenon has been promoted by industrial practices through which US major networks and streaming services have become proactive in securing the transnational flow of Korean media content.

The Third Korean Wave? From BTS to Bong Joon-ho

It is important to mention that US media industries have promoted this cultural turn by actively celebrating the economic power of Korean cultural acts. BTS and Bong Joon-ho are representatives showing that the Korean Wave has advanced to challenge Western hegemony in the global culture sphere. *Parasite* took in more than $501,000 at movie theaters on the day after the Oscars ceremony, placing it sixth in the list of foreign-language film sales in the US market (Pulver, 2020). BTS became the first music artist group since the Beatles to top the Billboard 200 album chart three times within a year.[5] This penetration of US mainstream entertainment markets shows that Korean cultural products are is no longer restricted to the subcultural terrain.

More to the point, these Korean cultural acts have subjectivized themselves while working in the US media industries. For instance, when asked about the absence of Korean film nominations at the Academy in October 2019, Bong jokingly described the Oscars as a "very local" event (Jung, 2019). Similarly, after appearing on Lil Nas X's performance at the Grammys, BTS members revealed their willingness to showcase their performance on the Grammy's stage in the near future (BTS, 2020). Bong and BTS have not succumbed to the ideologies of Western values and cultures. Instead, they showed their confidence to the outcome of local production. These cultural subjects confirm that Korean media industries have become a salient space for alternative creativity and sensibility in the global media market, echoing the claim that a global culture is "the outcome of 'dialectic' between self-development and socioeconomic structures" (Tomlinson, 1991, p. 141).

I argue that some, Korean creators and practitioners have inspired their counterparts in the West by offering Asian sensibility and creativity (see Kim J., 2021). After collaborating with Netflix for his film *Okja,* Bong produced the Korean film *Parasite* reflecting on his personal experiences (Lee, 2019). Unlike other K-pop stars, BoA, Seven, and Rain, who attempted to penetrate the US pop industry in the late 2000s, BTS focused on producing Korean albums without moving to the US (Kim J., 2021). They showed that the power of messages takes precedence with respect to the power of communication tools in deconstructing the ideological hierarchies of global media culture (Kim J., 2021). In this new phase of the Korean Wave, locally encoded creativity and sensibility can be effective in attracting larger audiences in the US media markets; moreover, they have inspired audiences to embrace non-English media products (Kim J., 2021).

The unprecedented achievement of *Parasite* not only conveys the direction that the Academy has taken to diversify competition submissions, but also unveils the fundamental transformations through which the media industries have passed in the era of digitalization and convergence. During a media conference after the Oscars ceremony, Bong revisited his acceptance speech about "the 1-inch-tall barrier of subtitles" at the Golden Globes (MBC NEWS, 2020). In so doing, he wanted to modify his claim that media audiences have already enjoyed varied international media content beyond barriers. As indicated in his remarks, structural and technical innovations have fundamentally reshaped the landscape of media flows and interactions. The construction of diverse and inclusive sensibilities is also identified in the popularization of BTS in the world—the group has become one of the most influential music groups in the era of social media (Kim J., 2021).

Notably, government-led institutes and Korean media enterprises have mutually engaged in the third phase of the Korean Wave, in which they have held meetings and conventions to boost the exportation of Korean cultural products to the US media industries. For instance, the US branch house of the Korean Creative Content Agency (KOCCA) has held annual screening events in order to provide meeting spaces between US syndicators and buyers, and Korean television networks and agents (Kim & Kim, 2016). Gonsik Yu, former CEO of KBS America, who had made a deal with A.B.C. to remake the drama series *The Good Doctor*, mentioned that these meeting sites were helpful in working with American networks and production companies (Keum, 2018; Yu, 2017).[6] Similarly, BTS is a beneficiary of the annual music festival KCON CJE&M has organized this music convention to offer American fans an affordable opportunity to consume K-pop live performances. By performing in this music event from 2014 to 2017, BTS developed its fandom in the Americas (KCON USA, n.d.).

Discussion

Due to differences in philosophical and cultural roots, US television has not been proactive in purchasing Korean media content in the past. However, established media industries have revisited the potential of non-Western content creators in the global media system. The rise of the Korean–US format trade reflects not only the intensification of media globalization, but also the complicated relationship between domestic and international media industries. Considering that the inequality of the West–East television trading system has continued over the decades, the US adaptation of scripted and unscripted Korean formats reveals the changing views of US broadcasters toward Korean media culture and practice.

The increasing flows of East Asian people and cultures have constructed minority communities in the US, who have become essential in spreading local cultures to the mainstream society. Digital technologies allow them to maintain their cultural identities through the consistent consumption of media content created by their homeland cultures (Lee, 2018); these digital technologies also allow media industries to find other consumer segments that are interested in consuming foreign cultures. In this sense, the growth of Korean media fandom has led to the popularization of Korean media content in numerous parts of the Western world.

This changed audience segmentation has influenced the production process; thus, US media producers have attempted to bring Korean television formats to the US mainstream media. Korean government-affiliated institutes, media enterprises, media practitioners, and artists have developed collaborative relationships to expand this phenomenon, and US–Korean media connections are part of their actions. In this sense, media industry scholars should adopt dewesternized and delocalized approaches in discussing the visibility of Korean television formats and media creators in the US By doing so, media industry scholarship can contextualize the Korean case in the process of media globalization and can explain how and why Asian values, norms, and creativity have become more visible in US society.

Notes

1 Bong's return to the Cannes International Film Festival with Neflix has produced controversies over the streaming service's commitment to theatrical releases in France (Wilkinson, 2018).

2 Bong's film *Parasite* made history at the Oscars by becoming the first non-English film to win the category of Best Picture.

3 He directed two films with American production companies, *Snowpiercer* (Bong, 2019) and *Okja* (Bong, 2017). He often expressed his experiences with the Hollywood production system. After returning to the Korean film industry, he made the film *Parasite* encoding his personal experiences and beliefs in the story (Lee, 2019).

4 According to Kim's report (2017), "USM&E exports to South Korea increased from $393.11 million in 2014 to $465.67 million in 2016" (para. 3).

5 Liu (2020) of *The Washington Post* declared that the Korean boy group, BTS had established its own empire for merchandising and endorsement, to the extent that no other group has achieved in the Western pop music industries.

6 According to Yu (2017), one of the most challenging situations involved persuading KBS to accept a shopping agreement. Korean television networks have preferred to receive a minimum guarantee when selling their television formats to foreign networks or production companies. Cultural differences between the US and Korean television industries have resulted in delays with respect to reaching mutual agreements in the process (Yu, 2017).

References

A.B.C. (2017, August 28). *Now in production: The Good Doctor.* Retrieved from YouTube.com: www.youtube.com/watch?v=qLTj9JR0PWI&t=22s

A.B.C. (2020, February 9). *Bong Joon Ho accepts the Oscar for directing.* Retrieved from YouTube.com: www.youtube.com/watch?v=ftz-BPqCiZU

Andreeva, N. (2016, October 11). *CBS developing drama about Korean-American lawyer from Alexi Hawley, Daniel Dae Kim & Ben Silverman.* Retrieved from https://deadline.com/2016/10/exibit-a-cbs-drama-korean-american-lawye-alexi-hawley-daniel-dae-kim-ben-silverman-1201834425/

Bong, J. (Director). (2013). *Snowpiercer* [Film]. The Weinstein Company.

Bong, J. (Director). (2017). *Okja.* [Film]. Netflix.

Bong, J. (Director). (2019). *Parasite* [Film]. Barunson E&A.

BTS (2020). *Map of the soul: 7* [Album]. BigHit Entertainment.

BTS (2020, January 26). *We're back from the 2020 Grammys~!* Retrieved from VLIVE: www.vlive.tv/video/172521?channelCode=FE619

Budiman, A. (2020, August 20). *Key findings about U.S. immigrants.* Retrieved from Pew Research Center: www.pewresearch.org/fact-tank/2020/08/20/key-findings-about-u-s-immigrants/

Chalaby, J.K. (2016). *The format age: Television's entertainment revolution.* Cambridge: Polity.

Fejes, F. (1981). Media imperialism: An assessment. *Media, Culture & Society, 3*(3), 281–289.

Han, J. (Executive Producer). (2014). *God's gift: 14 days* [TV series]. Content K: SBS.

Havens, T. (2006). *Global television marketplace.* London: Palgrave Macmillan.

Herman, E.S., & McChesney, R.W. (1997). *The global media: The new missionaries of corporate capitalism.* London: Continuum Books.

Huat, C. B., & Iwabuchi, K. (Eds.). (2008). *East Asian pop culture: Analysing the Korean Wave.* Hong Kong: Hong Kong University Press.

Jin, D.Y. (2016). *New Korean Wave: Transnational cultural power in the age of social media.* Urbana: University of Illinois Press.

Jin, D.Y., & Kim, J. O. (2018). The U.S. adaptation of Korea's unscripted format in the new Korean Wave Era: A case study of Grandpas Over Flowers. *International Journal of Korean Studies, 22*(2), 75–96.

Jung, A.E. (2019, October 7). Bong Joon-ho's dystopia is already here. The Korean director's ruthless, bleak new film Parasite is the most fun you'll have in theaters this fall. *Vulture.* Retrieved from www.vulture.com/2019/10/bong-joon-ho-parasite.html

Jung, H. (Executive Producer). (2016). *My lawyer, Mr. Jo* [TV series]. SM Culture & Contents; KBS2.

KCONUSA (n.d.). BTSXKCON-from 2014 to 2017. *KCONUSA.* Retrieved from https://www.kconusa.com/bts-kcon-usa-debut/

Keum, J.-k. (2018, October 25). *How did the Korean drama, Good Doctor penetrate the U.S. media market?* Retrieved from Media Today: www.mediatoday.co.kr/news/articleView.html?mod=news&act=articleView&idxno=145139

Kim, H.-j. (2019, November 25). Netflix to further join hands with S. Korean, Asian content providers: CEO. *Yonhap News Agency.* Retrieved from https://en.yna.co.kr/view/AEN20191125005400320

Kim, J.O. (2016a). Establishing an imagined SM Town: How Korea's leading music company has produced a global cultural phenomenon. *The Journal of Popular Culture, 49*(5), pp. 1042–1058.

Kim, J.O. (2016b). *The Korean Wave as a localizing process: Nation as a global actor in cultural production.* Philadelphia: Temple University.

Kim, J.O. (2021). BTS as method: A counter-hegemonic culture in the network society. *Media, Culture & Society.* January 2021. doi:10.1177/0163443720986029

Kim, J.O., & Kim, I. (2016). An art of remaking television drama. In Seok-Keyong Hong (ed.), *All about Korean television dramas* (pp. 171–199). Seoul: Culture Look.

Kim, S. (2020, October 30). Is Netflix a double-edged sword? *Pressian.* Retrieved from www.pressian.com/pages/articles/2020102911543023740?utm_source=naver&utm_medium=search - 0DKU

Kim,Y.-R. (2017,August 10). *The First U.S. remake of a Korean drama debuts this summer.* Retrieved from www.huffpost. com/entry/the-first-us-remake-of-a-korean-drama-debuts-this-summer_b_598c6ea6e4b030f0e267ca54

Lee, C.S. (2018). Making home through cord-cutting: The case of Korean transient migrants' postcable culture in the United States. *Television & New Media*, 21(3), 278–296.

Lee, Y.-L. (2019, May 30). "Parasite" director talks Palme d'Or win: Bong Joon-ho says film was inspired by his time tutoring a rich student. Korea JoongAng Daily. Retrieved from https://koreajoongangdaily.joins. com/2019/05/30/movies/Parasite-director-talks-Palme-dOr-win-Bong-Joonho-says-film-was-inspired-by-his-time-tutoring-a-rich-student/3063736.html? detailWord=

Lee, M. (Executive Producer). (2013–2018). Grandpas over flowers [TV series]. tvN.

Lee, S. (Executive Producer). (2019–2020). *Kingdom* [TV series]. AStory; Netflix.

Lee, S., & Nornes, A.M. (Eds.). (2015). *Hallyu 2.0: The Korean Wave in the age of social media*. Ann Arbor: University of Michigan Press.

Liu, M. (2020, January 30). The branding genius of K-pop band BTS. *The Washington Post*. Retrieved from www. washingtonpost.com/business/2020/01/30/bts-kpop-bighitentertainment/

López, G., Ruiz, N.G., & Patten, E. (2017, September 8). Key facts about Asian Americans, a diverse and growing population. *Pew Research Center*. Retrieved from www.pewresearch.org/fact-tank/2017/09/08/ key-facts-about-asian-americans/

Maglio,T., & Maas,J. (2020, February 3). *'The Masked Singer' season 3 premiere lands 23.7 million viewers after Super Bowl LIV*. Retrieved from www.thewrap.com/the-masked-singer-season-3-premiere-ratings-lil-wayne-robot-super-bowl-liv/

M.B.C. NEWS. (2020, February 10). *Bong Joon-ho onsite interview: "Parasite" winners including the best picture, a new history for the first foreign language film*. Retrieved from YouTube.com: www.youtube.com/watch?v= uzdtT3IWlSQ

McIntyre, H. (2020, January 7). BTS announces new album 'Map Of The Soul: 7'. *Forbes.com*. Retrieved from www.forbes.com/sites/hughmcintyre/2020/01/07/bts-announces-new-album-map-of-the-soul-7/ #1e131d482a9d

Park, J., & Lee, A.-g. (Eds.). (2019). *The rise of K-drama: Essays on Korean television and its global consumption*. Jefferson, NC: McFarland & Company.

Pestis, G. (Executive Producer). (2019–). *The masked singer* [TV series]. Endemol Shine North: FOX.

Pulver, A. (2020, February 12). *Parasite's box office figures surge after Oscar triumph*. Retrieved from www.theguardian. com/film/2020/feb/12/parasite-box-office-figures-surge-after-oscar-triumph

Ramos, D.-R. (2019, October 13). "Parasite's peachy debut breaks records, "Pain and Glory" has noteworthy expansion-Specialty Box Office. *Deadline*. Retrieved from https://deadline.com/2019/10/parasite-neon-premiere-pain-and-glory-judy-specialty-box-office-1202758973/

Rodriguez, C. (2017, August 12). The US starting to adapt Korean dramas into their own. *The Christian Post.*. Retrieved from www.christianpost.com/trends/the-us-starting-to-adapt-korean-dramas-into-their-own. html

Ryoo, W. (2009). Globalization, or the logic of cultural hybridization: the case of the Korean wave. *Asian Journal of Communication, 19*(2), pp. 137–151.

Schiller, H. (1975). Communication and cultural domination. *International Journal of Politics, 5*(4), 1–127.

Shim, D. (2006). Hybridity and the rise of Korean popular culture in Asia. *Media, Culture & Society, 28*(1), pp. 25–44.

Shim, D. (2008).The growth of Korean cultural industries and the Korean Wave. In *East Asian pop culture: Analysing the Korean Wave* (pp. 15–32). Hong Kong: Hong Kong University Press.

Shore, D. (Executive Producer). (2017–). *The good doctor* [TV series]. Shore Z Productions; ABC.

Song, S.-j. (2019, March 8). *Writer of Kingdom, Eun-hee Kim*. Retrieved from Korean Film Council: www.kobiz. or.kr/new/kor/03_worldfilm/news/news.jsp?mode=VIEW&seq=2830

Spangler, T. (2018, October 18). With Drama Fever's demise, other services step up to cater to K-drama fans. *Variety.com*. Retrieved from variety.com/2018/digital/news/dramafever-demise-other-korean-drama-streaming-services-1202984586/

Straubhaar, J. D. (1991). Beyond media imperialism: Assymetrical interdependence and cultural proximity. *Critical Studies in Mass Communication, 8*, 39–59.

Thussu, D.K. (Ed.). (2007). *Media on the move: Global flow and contra-flow*. London: Routledge.

Tomlinson, J. (1991). *Cultural imperialism*. Baltimore: Johns Hopkins University Press.

Tunstall, J. (1977). *The media are American*. New York: Columbia University Press.

Tunstall, J. (2008). *The media were American: U.S. mass media in decline*. New York: Oxford University Press.

Wallerstein, I.M. (1974). *The modern world-system*. New York: Academic Press.

White, P. (2019, September 5). Netflix orders slew of Korean originals including supernatural action drama 'The School Nurse Files' & 'Kingdom' S2. *Deadline*. Retrieved from https://deadline.com/2019/09/ netflix-orders-slew-of-korean-originals-kingdom-s2-1202711328/

Wilkinson, A. (2018, April 13). Netflix vs. Cannes: why they're fighting, what it means for cinema, and who really loses. *Vox.com*. Retrieved from www.vox.com/culture/2018/4/13/17229476/netflix-versus-cannes-ted-sarandos-thierry-fremaux-okja-meyerowitz-orson-welles-streaming-theater

Winkler, H. (Executive Producer). (2016–2018). *Better Late Than Never* [TV series]. Storyline Entertainment: NBC.

Yonhap. (2017, February 5). *S. Korea stands as world's 7th biggest media content creator.* Retrieved from Yonhap News: http://english.yonhapnews.co.kr/news/2017/02/05/0200000000AEN20170205001600315.html

Yoon, S. (Executive Producer). (2020). *Extracurricular* [TV series]. Sudio 329; Netflix.

Yoon, T.-j., & Jin, D.Y. (2017). Introduction: In retrospect of the Korean Wave. In T.-j. Yoon, & D.Y. Jin (Eds.), *The Korean Wave: Evolution, fandom, and transnationality.* Lanham: Lexington Books.

Yu, G. (2017). A full story of KBS' drama Good Doctor from pitching to broadcasting. *Broadcasting Trend & Insight, 11*(2), 7–16.

PART III

Popular Culture and Globalization

9

IN THE NAME OF NATIONAL INTEREST

Globalization and Media Culture in 21st Century Japan

Koichi Iwabuchi

Introduction

Globalization has engendered the interplay of centrifugal and centripetal forces to promote various modes of cross-border connection, translation, exchange, and dialogue, at the same time newly highlighting the relevance of national borders. How the development of globalization has an impact on the reproduction of the exclusive idea of the nation, one of the most powerful cultural forms in the modern world, is a key issue for media and cultural studies. Globalization processes have significantly activated cross-border flows and interpenetration of capital, people, and media communication all around the world, which amplify various kinds of connection, exchange, shared-ness, and rivalry. Development of digital communication technologies and social media and their affect-driven capacity further generates the tendency. Globalization apparently disregards national borders and dilutes exclusively constructed national identities by generating hybridized identification, transnational dialogue, cosmopolitan consciousness, and mediated collectivities beyond and across the nation (Hall, 1996; Pieterse, 2003; Beck 2006; Iwabuchi, 2002, 2014).

However, these developments do not necessarily bring about the weakening of national imaginations and frameworks. We have seen the resilience of national identity, the strengthening of national frameworks, and the resurgence of nationalism in many parts of the world. In the age of globalization, the nation is still firmly instituted and conceived, socially and personally as a most significant unit of identification and belonging, as "a pervasive way of imagining the world—a sort of grammar and syntax that allow people to speak about and act in the world" (Antonsich & Skey, 2017, 6). While advancing the construction of mediated connectivity and collectivity beyond and within the nation, the internet also amplifies the occasions of media contacts that encourage people to talk about the nation via diverse platforms in a standard national language (Mehelj, 2011). Its border-transgressing ability also enables migrants and diaspora overseas to contact and identify with the nation, while governments are keen to regulate the internet and social media for their own nationalistic purposes (Eriksen, 2007; Morozov, 2011).

These developments are reminiscent of the reproduction of "imagined communities", but the rise of digital communication and intensifying cross-border connections have seriously brought in question key features of an imagined community paradigm—the centrality of mass media representation and the narrative of a nation to be shared, with a stress on historical continuity and the presumed coherence and comradeship, and collective practices of consuming and conversing over mediated representations that produce a national public. One approach to make sense of the nation operating as a pervasive syntax in a globally (over)connected world is to reconsider the international nature of imagined communities, which institutes "a globally intelligible grammar of nationhood (Mehelj, 2011, 28)". The interplay of national and international has long been a significant part of the discursive and imaginative construction and reproduction of the nation. It discursively constructs the nation through a clearly demarcated boundary of "us" and "them" and facilitates the reproduction of the nation as a most significant local unit of the composition of the world (Robertson, 1995; Iwabuchi, 2015a). As the flows of money, people, and media communication have become rather rogue and interpenetrating, the demarcation of the internal and the external has become complicated and the autonomy of the nation-state has been subordinated to cross-border mobility and connectivity that globalized market forces intensify. This creates a situation in which, as Subramanian (2017) points out, "a nation's identity, for the first time, had to pull the rest of the world in" and an impulse "to regain or construct a more distinctive version of a country's self" has been newly intensified. It takes two associated forms—a commercialized shape, driven by marketing dynamism of selling and branding the nation to the world and the populace, and a reactive shape of exclusionary nationalism, jingoism, and populism, joined with growing antipathy against migration, multiculturalism, and globalism.

Despite significant differences—the latter is hot, divisive, protective, and social media-driven with anti-mass media posture, while the former is banal, encompassing, promotional, and involving various cultural industries including traditional mass media—the two forms are "mirror images of a sort," reflecting on growing national identity apprehension in a globalized world (Subramanian, 2017).

This chapter considers how the two associated forms of commercialized brand nationalism and hate-driven jingoism take shape in tandem with the work of digital communications and traditional mass media in the Japanese context. The progression of media globalization, it will be suggested, spawns renationalization whose driving impetus is the protection and promotion of national dignity and national interest rather than underlining the comradeship of the nationhood or national identity crisis.

Branding the Nation: Commercial Nationalism

Intensifying international cultural encounters and communication has been strengthening the discursive and performative framework of the nation in market terms. Especially since the early 1990s, after the end of the Cold War, the market-oriented process of cultural glocalization has been further pushing forward this momentum. The number of occasions of international media spectacle and cultural exhibition and festival has substantially increased, such as sports events, film festivals, TV/music awards, food expos, pageants, and tourism, as well as the proliferation of satellite and cable broadcasting and audio-visual internet sites (Roche, 2000; Edensor, 2002). The key players of this process include international organizations such as the International Olympic Committee (IOC) and UNESCO and, more significantly, media and cultural industries which transnationally and locally work with/for them (Ichijo, 2017).

Accordingly reciprocated international gazes have come to play a key role in re-highlighting the nation as the most meaningful cultural entity of collective identification. A plethora of international events and spectacles facilitate mundane occasions when people are reminded of the nationhood with which they identity. The amplification of actual or virtual participation in the number of international occasions prompts people to implicitly comprehend cross-cultural encounters as those among mutually exclusive national cultures with the delimited boundaries. This push has been joined and reinforced by increasing interest in enhancing the nation's brand image and states have become rather keen to take an initiative by joining forces with media culture industries. With the global spread of the market-driven economy and accompanied international competition, the management of the nation's image in the world has been developing to "a strategically planned, holistic and coherent activity" (Szondi, 2008, 4) by incorporating marketing techniques since the late 1990s.

The international improvement of a nation's brand images via the circulation of media culture in a digitalized multiplatform environment has been widely regarded as a serious business for states to enhance national interests, politically to enhance national brand images, and economically for developing service sectors in which creative/content industries play a significant role. Many states in East Asia too began assertively pursuing the idea of exploiting the economic and political utility of media culture to win the international competition, by interchangeably using terms such as soft power, nation branding, creative industries, and cultural diplomacy.

In Japan, it was under the Koizumi government (2001–2006) that policy concern with the uses of media culture to enhance national interests was firmly instituted for the first time. Koizumi was the first prime minister to refer to the advancement of cultural policy that aimed to promote media culture export and nation branding, stating in an address to the Diet that the government would strengthen the international projection of Japan's attractive brand images by advancing the content industries such as film, animation, and fashion (Koizumi, 2005). In the course of this development, the expression "Cool Japan" thus gained currency as an umbrella policy term to incorporate diverse areas of interest of various ministries and government departments.[1] The Cool Japan policy was developed as a sort of nation branding strategy, with a substantial budget to promote Japanese culture overseas and enhance the image of Japan (Iwabuchi, 2015b). Meanwhile, there is still no single ministry that plans and implements a coherent cultural diplomacy policy.

The Ministry of Foreign Affairs (MOFA) has been actively incorporating the idea of promoting Japanese media culture overseas into its public diplomacy program and officially adopted a policy of pop-culture diplomacy in 2006, which aims to further the understanding and trust of Japan by using pop-culture as a key tool (MOFA, n.d.). The Ministry of Economy, Trade, and Industry (METI) has been taking the initiative in implementing the Cool Japan policy as it established the Cool Japan promotion office in June 2010. In 2013, the Cabinet Secretariat also set up "the Council for the Promotion of Cool Japan" and 50 billion yen was allocated in the national budget for infrastructure promoting Japanese content overseas to spread the charm of Japanese culture internationally (which also includes food, fashion, tourism, and traditional crafts).

Nation branding is not an easy business. It is hard to prove how it is successful and it often takes incoherent and contradictory policy actions among various actors such as the states, public relations advisory organizations, and media and cultural industries (Aronczyk, 2013). Nevertheless, nation branding does matter not just due to substantial fiscal funding. The international projection of attractive images of the nation is conceived as the key aim of nation branding, but nation branding is actually not just externally oriented but also internally projected toward the national citizen (Kaneva, 2011; Aronczyk, 2013). Nation branding domestically generates the mobilization of citizens into "nationalistic consumers" using multiple digital platforms (Volcic & Andrejevic, 2016), as they are encouraged to join in (including participating in international events as a member of the nation) as "representatives, stakeholders and customers of the brand" (Varga, 2014, 836). "The mundane practices of nation branding do serve to perpetuate the nation form…Because they perpetuate a conversation about what the nation is *for* in a global context" (Aronczyk, 2013, 176)" And the development and implementation of nation branding policy broadly propagates an idea among the populace that the promotion of national branding is a serious business for the international enhancement of national prestige and interests. This tendency is also discerned in Japan. Despite huge investment, the Cool Japan policy's efficacy has been deeply questioned and the Cool Japan policy has attracted much criticism for not enhancing the creativity of cultural industries by improving working conditions (Iwabuchi, 2017).

However, the significance of using culture to enhance national prestige and interests has come to be widely accepted. According to Tokyo Polytechnic University's 2014 survey, 60% of respondents know about the Cool Japan policy, doubled that in a 2010 survey, and animation and manga as well as washoku (Japanese food) are ranked above traditional cultures as Japanese culture to be introduced internationally. Furthermore, more than 90% of respondents approved of the promotion of the Cool Japan policy and 65% believed that Cool Japan-related industries will be key industries for the Japanese economy (Tokyo Polytechnic University, 2014).

Nation branding elucidates the significance of the nation as a form to be filled with distinctive cultural assets of the nation to win an international competition of enhancing national prestige and interest. As Jensen puts it, "Branding not only explains nations to the world but also reinterprets national identity in market terms and provides new narratives for domestic consumption" (2008, 122). The representation of the nation in market terms tends to be highly image-driven, superficial, and ahistorical, lacking substantial depth and coherence of national narratives. Nevertheless, an exclusive conception of the nation as a cultural entity is reproduced and "core" national culture is re-demarcated, without giving due attention or even suppressing socio-cultural diversity as constitutive of the nation (Kaneva, 2011; Aronczyk, 2013). In Japan, this tendency can be seen in a striking gap between the rapid development of the Cool Japan policy and the un-engagement with immigration and multicultural diversity (Iwabuchi, 2015a). One policy maker of the "Japan Brand project" states that it is required to reassess "Japan's distinctive cultural DNA to strategically apply it to the creation and marketing of Japanese products and services" (Ito, 2002).

As the Japan country report of the EU's recent *Preparatory Action Culture in the EU's external relations* states, the Cool Japan policy aims to "enhance awareness of the 'uniqueness' of Japan" by taking "an approach which is based on Japan's portrayal of itself as ethnically and linguistically homogeneous and culturally unique" (Fisher, 2014, 3–4). The substantial development of the Cool Japan policy in the past decade focuses upon the projection of a selected national image by exporting appealing cultural products for the sake of the national interest and does not engage with or even suppresses crucial questions of who is the actual beneficiary, how cross-border dialogue can be further advanced, and how growing cultural diversity within Japan is fostered. The public good, increasingly, is being made to serve business, and this in the name of putative national interests.

Furthermore, nation branding works in tandem with the straightforward mobilization of nation-alistic sentiments, in which traditional mass media play a significant role. Volcic and Andrejevic (2016, 4) conceptualize "commercial nationalism" as the reproduction of nationalism in market terms through a paired advancement of "the ways in which states come increasingly to rely on commer-cial techniques for self-promotion, diplomacy, and internal national mobilization on the one hand and, on the other, the ways in which new, emerging, and legacy forms of commercial media rely on the mobilization of nationalism for the purpose of selling, ratings, and profit." As Turner (2016, 24) points out, the development of commercial nationalism enables mass media to "be uncompli-catedly dedicated to prosecuting its own commercial interests without being bothered about such old-fashioned regulatory issues as 'the public good' as long as the content is in line with the enhance-ment of nation branding".

International sports events such as the FIFA World Cup and Olympics are great occasions for the dual purposes of selling nations to the world and to the populace, and Japanese TV industries enthusiastically broadcast events to stir up nationalistic feeling. Currently, the forthcoming Tokyo Olympics, which have been postponed to July 2021 due to the COVID-19 pandemic, are considered a great occasion to enhance national dignity and interest. The comment of a chief editor of NHK, a semi-public national broadcaster in Japan, in a morning news program clearly showed that the merit of hosting the Olympics is significant in terms of the enhancement of national dignity, and strengthening Japan's international standing and economic benefits.[2] For mass media to survive the digital era, "generating, or embedding already existing, performances of nationalism within its enter-tainment formats" (Turner, 2016, 25) is an effective strategy. This takes the shape of the rise of "*Nihon Sugoi*" (Japan is great) TV programs and publications that claim the distinctiveness and excellence of Japanese culture and show how it is praised through the eyes of foreigners (*Tokyo Newspaper*, 2016, December 23; Hayakawa, 2017). An emphasis on the global popularity of Japanese cool culture indicates the influence of the Cool Japan policy. Actually, such media discourses surged around 2012–2014, a period that corresponds with the further activation of the Cool Japan policy.

It should also be noted that it was in the same period that the antipathy against China and South Korea became more noticeable, and that Japanese TV programs and books praising Japanese culture and tradition flourished (Hayakawa, 2017). Many programs and publications represent the excellence of Japan and Japanese culture in comparison to its Chinese and South Korean counterparts. In this regard, the "Japan is Great" genre overlaps what is called "hate-books" *(heitobon)* against Korea, resident Koreans, and China. As will be discussed shortly, with the rise of cyber-right movements and anti-sentiments against China and South Korea, Japanese publishing industries have actively marketed nationalistic sentiments. Various kinds of anti-China and anti-Korea books and journal articles have been put in the front corner of major bookshops and publishers heavily advertise the books in trains, train stations, and newspapers. More than 200 hate-books against Korea, resident Koreans, and China had been published since 2013–2014. Criticism led to a relative decline in the most aggressive hate-books, but the "Japan is Great" genre takes over its key tone from them. Some editors of hate-books self-critically confessed that they published the books only for the purpose of hitting the niche market in which people's sense of depression can be shaken off (Kimura and Kise, 2015). Jingoistic contents and titles tend to attract more attention and thus more advertisement on the internet and this is even more the case with mass media (Kyodo Tsushin, 2018).[3] Mass media's commercial nationalism is closely linked not just to the Cool Japan policy but also to the marketing of hate-driven jingoism to capitalize on a niche royal market of nationalism, to which we will now turn our attention.

For the Sake of the Nation: Spawning Cyber-Driven Jingoism

In Euro-American contexts, the intensified human mobility and socio-economic predicaments induced by the globalized market economy have evoked a sense of insecurity and even antipathy to cultural diversity within. Migration and multiculturalism policy have been under strong attack, especially since 9.11 2001—a terrorist attack against the US—because they are considered divisive to national unity and harmful to national security. Governments accordingly have reinforced national border control and stressed national integration. More recently, we are observing the rise of anti-globalism isolationist nationalism and populist movements to protect economic interests, prevent "unwanted" migrants from crossing national borders, and regain national autonomy to recover national dignity and protect national interest, as exemplified by the UK's exit of the EU and the US's "we first" policy. Rhetoric of national populism that underlines the regaining of national autonomy to counter globalized market forces and excessive migration captures people's socio-economic uneasiness, sense of neglect, and frustration against transnational-minded elites (Eatwell & Goodwin, 2018). And digital communications and social media play an active role in facilitating national populism. Affect-driven story telling mobilizes people into a collectivity and a public (Papacharissi, 2014). Whether and how the formation of "affective public" leads to the reconstruction of the nation is an intriguing question to be further examined, but what has become noticeable is digitalization amplifying, if not causing, reactive nationalism and jingoism and generating the expression of hate and jingoism, with intensifying antipathy to immigration and globalism, rather than promoting a sense of unity and solidarity of the nation. Political figures and parties subtly capitalize on these trends through populist speeches and performance to pursue more affective and sensory impacts to win the consent of the populace, as clearly shown by Euro-American cases (Moffitt, 2017). Billig (1995, 38) argues that banal nationalism "operate[s] mindlessly, rather than mindfully" but these are instances of how people's unreflexive and mindless reproduction of and identification with imagined communities in everyday life are breached politically, so "the nation is made explicit and its foundations are fortified" (Fox, 2017, 38). This breach has become the rule rather than the exception in many parts of the world.

Though populist politics and anti-migration movements are not yet the central feature in Japan, as immigration policy has not yet been developed, the rise of nationalism, jingoism, and the recent spawning of hate speech movements in Japan has shown similar features of national populism: antipathy against (leftist) intellectuals and mass media, anti-foreign movements, and a sense of socioeconomic deprivation. Historical revisionism in the 1990s that condemned the "self-torturing" historical view of Japan's colonialism in East Asia, which leftist intellectuals and mass media were supposed to develop, was very influential in the rise of this movement in Japan. The launch of an internet forum *Ni-Channerru* (2 Channel) in 1999 gave further momentum to trigger the upsurge of what is called *netto uyoku* (cyber right-wingers).

The rise of cyber nationalism in Japan shows how digitalized communication affectively encourages people to change from passive consumers to active subjects. Access to the internet urged them to open up their eyes to the hidden "historical truth" about Japan's colonial history and the idea that Japan did not do anything wrong to colonies and "comfort women" were a fabrication. Cyber right-wingers self-claim their mission as alternative media activists to debunk the falsehood of "self-torment" historical perception that mass media and leftist intellectuals have fabricated (Tsuji, 2008; Ito, 2015; Sakamoto, 2011). Cyber right-wingers stubbornly cling to and actively dispatch "affective facts and truths (Massumi, 2010)", which they have found on the internet, and aggressively and anonymously engage with the conduct of internet trolling, which amplifies the culture of dislike or hate as it attacks those who express views or ideas that they do not agree with and tolerate (Stein, 2016). The number of cyber right-wingers is small. Several surveys show that they make up about 1–1.7% of the population.[4] However, their energetic internet activities make their comments very visible as they make up 20% of all comments on political and social issues (Kimura, 2017). The number of those who have some sympathy with their claims also seems to be gradually expanding and the key issue shifts from historical revisionism to jingoism and hate speech. Tsuji points out that another 5.3% are sympathetic to cyber right-wingers' comments (2018). Recent research found that another 3%, whom Nagayoshi calls "online jingoists," also actively made jingoistic comments despite not having particular political stances (Nagayoshi, 2018).

Nagayoshi (2018)'s study also shows that 21.5% of all respondents show jingoistic tendencies, especially against China, Korea, and resident Koreans. The activities of cyber right-wingers and hate speech movements have been driven by the aversion to China and Korea, which are perceived to recurrently and deceitfully demand Japan to make sincere apology and compensation for colonial rule. Growing international political tensions and economic rivalry with China and South Korea further energized cyber right-wingers to claim the regaining of national dignity. The post-Cold War era has generated the globalized expansion of the market-driven economy, including in many parts of Asia, but Japan's experience has been marked by the struggle with economic slump after the collapse of the so-called bubble economy. In addition, the Japanese economy is confronting serious domestic problems in the aging and shrinking population and substantial reduction of workforces in the decades to come. This has accompanied various kinds of socio-economic anxiety, contradiction, and discordance—such as a widening gap between the haves and the have-nots, and the increasing sense of insecurity regarding full-time employment and the gloomy prospects of the maintenance of the social welfare system and a public pension plan.

In the 21st century, the growing economic and cultural power of China and South Korea have raised nationalistic sentiments in an aggressive manner. While Japan had long enjoyed the special status of a highly industrialized non-Western country until the early 1990s, the substantial expansion of global capitalism in the post-Cold War context has accompanied the ascent of Asian economies, most exemplified by China. Japanese media culture has become favorably received internationally, but even more notable is the rise of its South Korean counterparts. Japan's antagonistic relationship with them has been further exacerbated by anti-Japanese sentiments over unresolved historical issues and territorial disputes over the Diaoyu/Senkaku Islands with China and Dokdo/Takeshima with South Korea. Public opinion surveys conducted by the government every year clearly showed a sharp decline in the sense of intimacy that people in Japan felt toward China and South Korea in this period.[5] The surge not only coincided with the above-mentioned rise of hate-books against China and South Korea, but also generated hate speech movements targeting resident Koreans.[6] Cyber right-wingers' activities turned to street jingoistic hate speech demonstrations against resident Koreans in Japan around 2009.[7] Resident Koreans are attacked because they are considered anti-Japan people who align with and support Korea. Moreover, resident Koreans are condemned for unfairly enjoying the special privileges of receiving social welfare. Such special privileges for resident Koreans do not exist and the claim was based on a series of false information circulating on the internet (Oizumi et al., 2015). Yet the affective fact has eventually become a key motivation of the hate speech movement against resident Koreans.[8]

Jingoists (*haigai shugisha*, who include both cyber right-wingers and hate speech activists) in Japan seek to reclaim national dignity and protect national interests, but show no concern with national integration and comradeship. Unlike historical revisionist movements in the 1990s, the current jingoistic movements do not care for any historically embedded national narrative, either. As Yamazaki (2015) argues, nationalism is ambiguous as it is at the same time inclusive and exclusive as well as universalistic and particularistic, but the hate movements too radically stress exclusiveness at the cost of national integration and coherence. The sole purpose of jingoism seems to be the discovery and attack of enemies who supposedly damaged and condemned Japan, even if they might claim they are doing the right thing for the sake of the nation. Bringing "traitors to Japan" (*han-nichi*), such as resident Koreans, mass media, leftist intellectuals, China, and Korea, which allegedly damage Japan's national dignity and interests, to a kangaroo court appears the key purpose. A significant feature underlying the impetus of jingoists other than antipathy against China and Korea is a sense of fury against the socially vulnerable who receive or claim social welfare payments (Kimura, 2017; Tsuji, 2018). This is exemplified by the attack on resident Koreans for receiving special privileges while blaspheming Japan, but a hunt for traitors eventually expands its target to various socially vulnerable people such as LGBTQI+, disabled people, Ainu, Okinawa, and welfare recipients (Yasuda, 2012, 2015). It can be argued that the sense of neglect and victimhood due to socio-economic marginalization is an important factor in the spawning of cyber jingoism and hate speech in Japan. Those who participate in the hate speech movement in Japan were supposed to be socio-economically underprivileged persons—mostly men with low incomes, no full-time job, and no partners—but many studies show that there are also many women of various age groups who join the demonstrations and middle class, full-time workers and even well-to-do elite people are participating in and supporting the activities, as well (Tsuji, 2013; Higuchi, 2014; Kitahara & Paku, 2014; Tsuji, 2013, 2018). This is reminiscent of the globally witnessed trend of modern symbolic racism by the violent effects of globalized capitalism, which makes many people in a majority position in terms of ethnicity, gender, and sexuality feel so distressed and neglected that they claim that ethnic minority people are not much discriminated against but demand too much and "we first" need to be protected and attended to by the government (Sears & Henry, 2002). In the case of Japan, the key tone is the condemnation of the socially vulnerable for requesting social welfare rather than people in a majority position demanding the government's care for themselves. What is unpardonable for the participants in and supporters of cyber jingoism and hate speech is that the socially vulnerable are playing the victim and unreasonably and unjustly demanding social protection and benefit. This demand is considered sly as many people are forced to endure harsh realities without receiving such benefits. A sense of frustration and suffocation with life has been diffusing under intensifying market-driven globalization, which coincides with the relative decline of Japan, especially after the 3.11 earthquake, and the sense of powerlessness is released in the shape of intolerance of the socially vulnerable. And digital media are used to amplify the negative energy to attack them under the name of national dignity and national interest.

Beyond Narrowly Focused National Interests

In a globalized world, the nationhood has been actively evoked and reproduced in many parts of the world to commercially deal with and jingoistically counter rogue flows of people, capita, and media culture for the sake of enhancing national dignity and protecting national interest. Digital communications and social media are utilized to boost jingoistic expressions and traditional mass media are apt to survive the competitive digitalized market by selling nationalism. However, we need to remember that digital media also advance progressive actions and connections beyond the dominance of traditional mass media, such as highlighting hitherto marginalized voices and concerns and fostering international exchange and cosmopolitan consciousness. Such potential does not negate the promotion of the national interest but expands the scope of the national interest in a more open, dialogic, and inclusive way that goes beyond the pursuit of narrowly focused economic and political objectives.

To further actualize the progressive potential of media communication, it is crucial to promote dialogue with and listening to others of different values and thoughts and foster collective imagination to make the nation more inclusive and egalitarian against the odds of market-driven globalism. Calhoun (2007)'s point is relevant, here that the nation functions as the most important unit of collective organization and plays an indispensable role in facilitating democracy and social solidarity through which the populace deals with globalization challenges. The current situation shows that the democratic potentials of national improvement are overpowered by a divisive and market-driven impetus that promotes exclusionary and closed-minded ways of re-highlighting the nationhood. Such development urges us to give renewed attention to whether and how the nation-state can be reconstituted as an open society so as to counter jingoistic populism that capitalizes on anti-globalism sentiments, progressively engage with "the crisis of the neoliberal hegemonic formation" (Mouffe, 2018), and serve the public interest beyond narrowly focused national interests and foster the sense of living together in diversity (Iwabuchi, 2015a; Judis, 2018). And conceiving how to use media communication to pursue the democratic potentials of the national society is rather a crucial issue in a globally connected world.

Note: Earlier versions of some parts of this chapter were included in "Globalization, Digitalization, and Renationalization: Some Reflections from Japanese Cases", *Situations: Cultural Studies in the Asian Context*, 12 (1), 2019, pp. 1–22.

Notes

1 A TV program titled *Cool Japan* (N.H.K. B.S.2) also started in 2006.
2 NHK's *Good Morning Japan*, August 21, 2018. TV coverage of international sport events in Japan features theme songs to inspire a sense of national identification and pride among audiences, which are originally created by popular singers. Shiina Ringo's *Nippon* (for the Rio De Janeiro Olympics 2014) and Radwimps' *Hinomaru* (for the 2018 FIFA World Cup) are two recent instances of how theme songs use contentiously nationalistic words and expressions, which reminisce about war-time frenzied chauvinism, though these singers seem to be motivated by their frank desire to express a sense of pride as a member of the nation (Masuda, 2018).
3 Recently, TV stations have produced many programs in entertainment formats dealing with the Immigration Bureau of Japan's cracking down on illegal long-stayers. Working closely with the Bureau, the programs sensationally depict foreigners as if all of them are criminals without explaining wider backgrounds and contexts.
4 Tsuji (2008) defines *netto uyoku* as those with the following traits: 1) anti-South Korea and anti-China, 2) support for politicians who honor the Yasukuni Shrine, revision of Article 9 of the Japanese Constitution, and patriotism education in Japanese schools, and 3) actively participating in online discussions about political and social issues.
5 The percentage of respondents who feel a sense of intimacy toward South Korea declined from 62% to 39% between 2011 and 2012. And that to China sharply declined in 2004 and 2010 due to anti-Japan movements and the heat-up of the dispute over the territorial ownership of Senkaku Island. According to the latest survey

conducted in January 2016, only 14% of respondents feel a sense of intimacy toward China and 33% to South Korea (www2.ttcn.ne.jp/honkawa/7900.html).

6 According to a governmental survey, there had been 1,152 hate speech demonstrations between April 2012 and September 2015 (The Mainichi, 2016).

7 It should be noted that the first large hate speech demonstration was organized to attack the family of illegal over-stayers in 2009.

8 Japanese mass media such as major newspapers and TV stations tended to ignore rising hate speech against resident Koreans mainly because they considered it ephemeral and their coverage would result in acknowledging their significance and gratifying them, and even be used for their own publicity and ostentation. Yet this eventually showed how mass media did not consider racist hate speech as a highly grave social issue and thus implicitly endorsed the movement (Sato, 2014).

References

Antonsich, M. & Skey, M. (2017). Introduction: The persistence of banal nationalism. In M. Antonsich & M. Skey (eds.) *Everyday Nationhood: Theorising Culture, Identity and Belonging after Banal Nationalism* (pp. 1–13). London: Palgrave Macmillan.

Aronczyk, M. (2013). *Branding the Nation: The Global Business of National Identity* Oxford: Oxford University Press.

Beck, U. (2006). *Cosmopolitan Vision* (translated by C. Cronin). Cambridge: Polity.

Eatwell, R. & Goodwin, M. (2018). *National Populism: The Revolt against Liberal Democracy.* London: Penguin Press.

Billig, M. (1995). *Banal Nationalism.* London: Sage.

Calhoun, C. (2007). *Nations Matter: Citizenship, Solidarity, and the Cosmopolitan Dream.* Oxford: Routledge.

Edensor, T. (2002). *National identity, popular culture and everyday life.* London & Oxford: Bloomsbury Publishing.

Eriksen, T.H. (2007). Nationalism and the Internet. *Nations and Nationalism,* 13(1), 1–17.

Fisher, R. (2014). *Japan Country Report: Preparatory Action "Culture in EU External Relations".* Brussels: European Commission.

Fox, J.E. (2017). The edges of the nation: A research agenda for uncovering the taken-for-granted foundations of everyday nationhood. *Nation and Nationalism,* 23(1), 26–47.

Hall, S. (1996). The question of cultural identity. In S. Hall, D. Held, D. Hubert & K. Thompson (eds.) *Modernity: An Introduction to Modern Societies* (pp. 595–634). London: Blackwell.

Hayakawa, T. (2017). National narrative of "Japan is Great" ("Nihon sugoi" to iu kokumin no monogatari). In K. Nakano & H. Tsukada (eds.) *Thorough examination of Japan's turning rightist (Tettei kenshou Nihon no ukeika)* (pp. 236–255). Tokyo: Chikuma Shobo.

Higuchi, N. (2014). *Japanese Style of Jingoism: Zaitokukai, Foreigners' Voting Right, East Asian Geopolitics (Nihongata Haigaishugi: Zaitokukai, Gaikokujin Sanseiken, Higashi Asia Chiseigaku).* Nagoya: Nagoya Daigaku Shupankyoku.

Ichijo, A. (2017). Banal nationalism and UNESCO's intangible cultural heritage list: Cases of *Washoku* and the gastronomic meal of the French. In M. Antonsich & M. Skey (eds.) *Everyday Nationhood: Theorising Culture, Identity and Belonging after Banal Nationalism* (pp. 259–284). London: Palgrave Macmillan.

Ito, H. (2002). Retrieved from http://blogs.yahoo.co.jp/hiromi_ito2002jp/57705983.html (accessed February 10, 2019).

Ito, M. (2015). What is cyber right-winger?" (Nettouyoku towa nanika). In N. Yamazaki (eds.) *Strange Nationalism: Against Jingoism (Kimyou na nashonarizumu: Haigaishugi ni koushite)* (pp. 25–68). Tokyo: Iwanami Shoten.

Iwabuchi, K. (2002). *Recentering Globalization: Popular Culture and Japanese Transnationalism.* Durham, NC: Duke University Press.

Iwabuchi, K. (2014). De-Westernization, inter-Asian referencing beyond. *European Journal of Cultural Studies,* 17(1), 44–57.

Iwabuchi, K. (2015a). *Resilient Borders and Cultural Diversity: Internationalism, Brand Nationalism and Multiculturalism in Japan.* Lanham, M.L.: Lexington Books.

Iwabuchi, K. (2015b). Pop-culture diplomacy in Japan: Soft power, nation branding and the question of "international cultural exchange". *International Journal of Cultural Policy,* 21 (4), 419–432.

Iwabuchi, K. (2017). Creative industries and Cool Japan. In A. Fung (eds.) *Global Game Industries and Cultural Policy* (pp. 33–52). Cham: Palgrave Macmillan.

Jensen, S.C. (2008). Designer nations: Neo-liberal nation branding—Brand Estonia. *Social Identities,* 14(1), 121–142.

Judis, J. (2018). *The Nationalist Revival' Trade, Immigration, and The Revolt against Globalization.* New York, NY: Columbia Global Reportism.

Kaneva, N. (2011). Nation branding: Toward an agenda for critical research. *International Journal of Communication,* 5, 117–141.

Kimura, T. (2017). Reason why conservative voices prevails in internet public opinions" (Netto yoron de hoshu ni tatakareru riyu). *Chuo Koron* 132(1), 134–141.

Kimura, Y and Kise, T. (2015, July 28). 売れるという理由だけで醜悪なヘイト本が生まれた構造。ヘイトスピーチは表現ではない! Retrieved from http://wpb.shueisha.co.jp/2015/07/28/51312/ (accessed February 10, 2019).

Kitahara, M. & Paku, S. (2014). *Patriotic Housewives (Okusama Wa Aikoku)*. Tokyo: Kawadeshoboushinsha.

Koizumi, J. (2005, January 20). Policy Address at the National Diet.

Kyodo Tsushin heito mondai shuzaihan (2018, November 7). 悪質な中傷、ネットで減らない理由： 弱者たたく〝差別ビジネス〟も　検証・ヘイトスピーチ対策法（１）. Retrieved from https://this.kiji.is/432453601786446945 (accessed February 9, 2019)

Massumi, B. (2010). The future birth of the affective fact: The political ontology of threat. In G. Seigworth & M. Gregg (eds.) *The Affect Theory Reader* (pp. 52–70). Durham, NC: Duke University Press.

Masuda, S. (2018, July 8). Looking back on patriotic songs for the last 30 years (Aikoku Songu 30nenshi wo furikaeru). *Gendai Bijinesu*. Retrieved from https://gendai.ismedia.jp/articles/56365?page=3 (accessed February 10, 2019)

Mehelj, S. (2011). *Media Nations: Communicating Belonging and Exclusion in the Modern World*. Basingstoke & New York: Palgrave Macmillan.

Ministry of Foreign Affairs (n.d.). www.mofa.go.jp/policy/culture/exchange/pop/ (accessed February 10, 2019).

Moffitt, B. (2017). *The Global Rise of Populism: Performance, Political Style, and Representation*. Stanford, CA: Stanford University Press.

Morozov, E. (2011). *The Net Delusion: The Dark Side of Internet Freedom*. New York, NY: Public Affairs.

Mouffe, C. (2018). *For a Left Populism*. London: Verso.

Oizumi, M., Kimura, M., Kato, N. & Kajita Y. (2015). *Good-bye Hate-Books! Debunking the Boom of Hate-Korea and Anti-China Publications (Saraba heitobon! Kenkan hanchu bon bumu no uragawa)*. Tokyo: Korokara.

Nagayoshi, K. (2018, October 7). ネトウヨ像覆す８万人調査　浮かぶオンライン排外主義者. Asahi Shinbun. Retrieved from www.asahi.com/articles/ASLB37DGLLB3UCVL01V.html (accessed 10 February 2019)

Papacharissi, Z. (2014). *Affective Publics*. New York, NY: Oxford University Press.

Pieterse, J.N. (2003). *Globalization and Culture: Global Mélange*. London: Rowman & Littlefield.

Robertson, R. (1995). Glocalisation: Time-space and homogeneity-heterogeneity. In M. Featherstone (eds.) *Global Modernities* (pp. 25–44). London: Sage.

Roche, M. (2000). *Mega-events and modernity: Olympics and expos in the growth of global culture*. London: Routledge.

Sakamoto, R. (2011). Koreans, go home! Internet nationalism in contemporary Japan as a digitally mediated subculture. The Asia-Pacific Journal, 10(2). Retrieved from http://apjjf.org/2011/9/10/Rumi-SAKAMOTO/3497/article.html.

Sato, K. (2014) Investigating the actual situation of racial discrimination to overcoming it (Sabetsu no jittai wo ukabiagarase sabetsu wo norikoeteiku). *Journalism*, 282, 74–75.

Sears, D. & Henry, P.J. (2002). *Race and Politics: The Theory of Symbolic Racism*. Los Angeles, CA: University of California Press.

Stein, J. (2016, August 29). Tyranny of the mob. *Time*, 26–32.

Subramanian, S. (2017, November 7). "How to sell a country; the booming business of nation branding". *The Guardian*, Retrieved from www.theguardian.com/news/2017/nov/07/nation-branding-industry-how-to-sell-a-country (accessed February 10, 2019)

Szondi, G. (2008). Public diplomacy and nation branding: Conceptual similarities and differences. *Discussion Papers in Diplomacy*. Hague: Clingendael Netherlands Institute of International Relations.

The Mainichi (2016, March 31). Hundreds of hate speech rallies held across Japan annually: Justice Ministry report. The Mainichi. Retrieved from https://mainichi.jp/english/articles/20160331/p2a/00m/0na/003000c (accessed 10 February 2019)

Tokyo Polytechnic University (2014, February 12). クールジャパンに関する調査(2014). Retrieved from www.t-kougei.ac.jp/static/file/cool-japan.pdf (accessed February 10, 2019)

Tsuji, D. (2008, September 10) A report and summary on an empirical study on the right wing tendencies in the Internet" (Intanetto ni okeru "ukeika" gennshoni kannsuru jisshokenkyuchousakekka gaiyo houkokusho). Retrieved from www.d-tsuji.com/paper/r04/report04.pdf (accessed February 10, 2019)

Tsuji, D. (2018, November 4). "Actual situation of cyber-right wingers" (Netto uyoku: Imeiji to kotonaru jittai). *Asahi Shinbun*.

Turner, G. (2016). Setting the scene for commercial nationalism: The nation, the market and the media. In Z. Volcic & M. Andrejevic (eds.) *Commercial Nationalism: Selling the Nation and Nationalizing the Sell* (pp. 14–26) London: Palgrave Macmillan.

Varga, S. (2014). The politics of nation branding: Collective identity and public sphere in the neoliberal state. *Philosophy and Social Criticism*, 39(8), 825–845.

Volcic, Z., & Andrejevic, M. (2016). Introduction. In Z. Volcic & M. Andrejevic (eds.) *Commercial Nationalism: Selling the Nation and Nationalizing the Sell* (pp. 1–13) London: Palgrave Macmillan.

Yamazaki, N. (2015). "Kinyou na nashonarizumu?" (Strange nationalism?). In N. Yamazaki (eds.) *Kimyou na nashonarizumu: Haigaishugi ni koushite (Strange nationalism: Against jingoism)* (pp. 1–28). Tokyo: Iwanami Shoten.

Yasuda, K. (2012). *Internet and Patriotism: Exploring the Dark Side of Zaitokukai (Netto to Aikoku: Zaitokukai no Yami wo Oikakete)*. Tokyo: Kodansha.

Yasuda, K. (2015). Endless Expansion of Enemy Hunt (Dokomademo hirogaru tekinintei). *AERA* 28 (34), 34–35.

10

STARBUCKS' DREAM OF A GLOBAL TASTE

Nissrine Fariss

The rapid rise of Starbucks and its unprecedented command of the global coffee "experience" stirred an enduring fascination amongst commentators eager to decipher its recipe for success. For the past 40 years, business insiders have pored over the company's corporate culture and unadvertised visibility, while social critics saw it as a purveyor of consumerist values to impressionable demographics. But how does a siren hailing from countercultural waters, celebrating its 25th Anniversary in 1996 with "in-store posters, tie-dyed T-shirts, and buttons with slogans such as 'make latte, not war,'" (McDowell, 1996) substantiate its unchallenged coffee conquest today?

This chapter explores Starbucks' dream of a global taste through the prism of American history and culture. It first expands on the changes in the American market that allowed Starbucks' proposition to gain traction, from bad supermarket coffee to the rise of "subculture brands," and the ensuing homogenizing tendency of the American food and beverage industry. It then analyzes the brand's synthetic authenticity in relation to what ex-CEO Howard Schultz called "the people business." Last, it explores Starbucks' sustained associations with Ray Oldenburg's communal "Third Place" concept to ensure a uniform and reproducible experience capable of subsuming different cultures and communities on a global scale. Using Boorstin's terminology, this chapter essentially approaches Starbucks as an American "pseudo-event;" an illusory receptacle of subculture, authenticity, and community where patrons tradeoff ideals for ready-to-consume images.

From Caffeinating Counterculture to Changing Q.S.R.

When interviewed at Draper University in 2017, Jerry Baldwin, one of Starbucks' three original founders, professed his early distaste for corporations: "the only thing I could say with any certainty," he declared, "was I didn't really want to work for a big company." Conversely, he expressed the passion he shared with his co-founders, Gordon Bowker and Zev Siegl, for "unfunded great ideas," "organic" entrepreneurship, and the unincorporated philosophy of "doing other things." (Draper TV, 2017) This moderately insurgent mindset, groomed by a post-hippie desire to counterbalance uniformity with authenticity, typified the existing need for a cultural revision of consumer products after the bromidic mass production of the 1950s in the US.

The political tumult of the following decade had stretched the declinist specter into a national crisis of confidence, fomented by leader assassinations, the ongoing Vietnam debacle, and the Santa Barbara oil spill in 1969, an environmental disaster that prompted the first Earth Day a year later. This conjunction of circumstances reverberated as antinomian detachment among Americans. The threat of impending doom, be it nuclear or ecological, prepped consumers into an irreverent retreat to psychic self-improvement, from practicing spiritualisms to overcoming "the fear of pleasure;" (Lash, 1979) in the reigning uncertainty, Americans began to disengage from establishing themselves in a sense of longevity—sturdy, stable, predictable lives—and turned to products for self-expression instead—hippies being the visible archetype.

Formalizing the association of what people consumed to what they believed, the modern environmental movement entered the 1970s with its discourse of responsibility oscillating between "supply-side," with Barry Commoner's call to reform production in *The Closing Circle* (1971), and "demand-side," with Stewart Brand and his Whole Earth Catalog's "shopping for change" countercurrent. (Wight, 2017) On the one hand, the role of businesses no longer boiled down to creating jobs; they were now expected to produce differently. On the other hand, the role of consumers was no longer confined to boosting the economy; they were now expected to consume differently. At the intersection of both, the commodity became imbued with more than its pragmatic value; the act of consumption gained an ideological dimension. This paved the way for the institutionalization of "countercultural capitalism," (Simon, 2009) wherein a form of dissent could be integrated in the capitalist system it opposed through commodification, a concept the political analyst, historian, and journalist Thomas Frank broached extensively in his works.

Against this background, what Warren Belasco described as an "appetite for change" culminated in a health foods movement that transmuted political agency into acts of "countercuisine" since the 1960s—defined as alternative food beliefs, practices, and institutions. (Belasco, 1993) Belasco traced the co-optation of hippie food, an edible scion of the pursuit of unprocessed, decentralized authenticity, into a lucrative business model for more distinguished, non-subversive palates.

Since the 1953 "Fourth of July Frost" in Brazil reduced the coffee harvest and drove up the prices, (Patnaik, 2009) the big American coffee brands that vied for housewife allegiance on the supermarket turf had begun mixing Robusta beans into their scarce Arabica, which had done an enduring disservice to the taste of American coffee. (Clark, 2007) Starbucks, which emerged in 1971 as an "unfunded great idea" but brimmed well over its "organic" beginnings under Howard Schultz, instantiates Belasco's countercuisine-gone-mainstream premise beautifully. Its countercultural appeal was clear: if what you ate could become an outlet for self-expression, why couldn't Americans, who ran on coffee as their work hours stretched longer than their forebears', enjoy a palatable cup of joe that reflected their individuality? The Man's putridly processed coffee needed its untelevised revolution—and it first found one in Starbucks' predecessor: Alfred Peet. Peet's, first opening for business in 1966, Berkeley, California, associated Dutch roasting savvy to experiential marketing. The aroma filtering from his shops was a dematerialized advertisement, while demonstrations on coffee roasting science and occasional taste tests further fed the gourmet concept. Alfred Peet didn't offer seating or a menu; he was an independent retailer who roasted his beans longer, his discerning ear growing so well-versed in their secret language as to pick up on how they "wanted" to be roasted. (Clark, 2007) Hippies and Beatniks found a kindred spirit in Peet, who, in removing what few stools his shop had in a dissuasive effort to keep them out, couldn't stop his "Peetniks" from taking the floor. "The funny thing was," he recalled, "they understood what I was doing. It was big business they were fighting, and they appreciated that I had a good product at modest prices. So spiritually, I was one of them." (Clark, 2007) Spiritual seemed like a good qualifier for Peet's. When Howard Schultz, a salesman on the lookout for the American Dream, first set foot at the Pike Place Market Starbucks location, it impressed him as a "temple for the worship of coffee." (Schultz and Yang, 1997) That wasn't a coincidence: Starbucks was, back then, the unambiguous heir of the Peet's coffee legacy; the original founders had honed their roasting skills under Alfred Peet's aegis during an informal internship. Wanting to join the good business of offering decent coffee in a country where demand was high and supply close to nonexistent, Schultz negotiated a hired position with the owners for close to a year, becoming Starbucks' director of retail operations and marketing in 1982. After Baldwin decided to buy Peet's chain, his ideological underpinning businesswise, he found himself financially unable to hold on to both chains and decided to sell Starbucks. That is when Schultz stepped in to seize the chance of a lifetime.

In 1987, Howard Schultz completed his acquisition of the six-store coffee chain, after an in-person interjection from the father of Microsoft's founder, Bill Gates Sr., to stop an unnamed Seattle investor from beating Schultz to the deal. After this highly opportune footnote in Starbucks' history, Schultz rewired it for growth. He began by promising his investors 125 new stores in five years—instead, he opened 150, and Starbucks was ready to issue its IPO (initial public offering) in 1992. (Schultz and Yang, 1997)

Schultz never jibed with the original founders' mildly anti-corporate politics, (Simon, 2019) but he recognized the auriferous potential of specialty coffee in the US. During a Starbucks business trip to Italy in 1983, he understood that learning bean language at Peet's and revolutionizing the taste of coffee at Starbucks was incomplete without an image, a "romance," and he modeled his around the Milanese espresso bar culture. His transatlantic simulation of the bona fide Italian coffee scene, he knew, would be a place where coffee, no longer the main attraction, became in the service of something bigger: "We are not in the coffee business serving people," he averred, "we are in the people business serving coffee." (Schultz and Yang, 1997)

As vaguely cryptic as "the people business" was, it constituted a break from Peet's coffee-centered vision. It put an end to the time when the siren, before becoming a globalist leviathan, claimed sailors of the countercultural persuasion and donned peace signs on its stores. (Frank, 1997) As the sacredness of subversive caffeine was dissipating along "back-to-nature yippies" to accommodate "well-trimmed yuppies," (Belasco, 1993) Starbucks became an emblem of post-need capitalism—(Simon, 2009) an order of businesses that inaugurated group identities "where before there had been nothing but inchoate feelings of common responses to pollsters' questions." (Frank, 1997) In this repertoire, Pepsi had claimed authorship over an entire generation of baby boomers, inviting them to fold their desire for liberation and youth ideals into a matrix of "hip" consumption. (Frank, 1997) Likewise, in deciding to divest coffee of its original priority and invest in consumer behavior, Starbucks—dealing in the "people business"—brought hip to a commodity formerly abused by mainstream brands from Folgers to Maxwell House. Nike, for Schultz, was the only company that "did something comparable." The cheap low-quality sneakers market, he explained, was revolutionized by Nike's "world-class running shoes" and the atmosphere of "top-flight athletic performance and witty irreverence" woven around them. (Schultz and Yang, 1997) In other words, both brands made sure the atmosphere was interwoven with the product. Naomi Klein, whose book *No Logo* (2000) marked the second millennium with a sober indictment of "New Age" brands, called it the "branding renaissance;" wherein "the ostensible product was mere filler for the real production: the brand." (Klein, 2000) Under Schultz, Starbucks transmuted the concept of good coffee into what Boston Consulting Group (BCG) called the "New Luxury"; a category of brands that produce "artisanal quality at middle-market quantity;" (Silverstein et al, 2005) or, in Naomi Klein's diction, "Extra-premium 'attitude brands' that provide essentials of lifestyle and monopolize ever-expanding stretches of cultural space." (Klein, 2000)

The New Luxury existed to align high markup with mass production. To fit the bill, the product needed to be augmented on three levels: technical differentiation to suggest quality, functional improvement to make a difference in the customer's life, and emotional leveraging to incite a desire of association with the brand—what BCG called the "ladder of benefits." Delivering on all three points explains why brands like Starbucks "catch fire." (Silverstein et al, 2005) Unlike supermarket coffee, which laced Arabica with Robusta, the more bitter bean variety, and light-roasted the beans so as not to lose in product weight, Starbucks paid more for premium Arabica coffee beans and roasted them dark the way Alfred Peet did. It provided patrons with good coffee and an atmosphere of bookish distinction and jazz music, all in a physical "third place" between work and home, which made a difference in the patrons' day. It sourced its coffee "ethically," extended health coverage to part-time workers, and the ability to afford their order and display it to fellow metropolitans gratified customers with a sense of sophistication. This model was then built into a reproducible, exportable culture, one that Schultz ran with across the planet to meet the needs of a globally "life-stylized" clientele.

In *Nobrow* (2000), John Seabrook illustrates that the marketplace's apparent renouncement of highbrow distinctions is due to their reformulation, not disappearance. High culture, essentialized and monolithic, was replaced by subculture, multiplied and postmodern. Pepsi created its own subculture of "those who think young" and referred to it as "The Pepsi Generation." So did Nike, allying athleticism to the "witty irreverence" of urban culture. As Starbucks placed itself directly into this pigeonhole, selling caffeinated vouchers to its way of life, Scott Bedbury, who helped launch the Just Do It campaign as Nike's worldwide advertising director, joined as Starbucks' chief marketing officer in 1995 and was later quoted affirming Starbucks' intention to "align ourselves with one of the greatest movements toward finding a connection to your soul." (Klein, 2000) A year later, Pepsi embarked on a 50/50 joint venture to bottle and distribute Starbucks' caffeinated cold drinks—Frappuccinos—in supermarkets in the US and Canada, then across the world. (Schultz and Yang, 1997)

But how did Starbucks do it? Schultz didn't franchise, yet the chain's store count was proliferating. It was a mystery in plain daylight. Eric Flamholtz, an ex-Starbucks CFO (Chief Financial Officer), remarked that what the company was doing had been, all along, invisible to its competitors: "It's like the stealth bomber—if you can't see it, how can you copy it?" (Clark, 2007)

But this festive mystification is misleading. Beside the "Stealth Starbucks" experiments taking place beginning 2009—non-logoed indie coffee shops that were Starbucks-implanted to conduct market research after the "luxflation" incurred from growing too fast and the 2008 crisis curtailing its American store count by 600—Starbucks' growth strategy was never invisible; it was transcendental—it transcended and sidestepped coffee people to synergize with retail operations people, hiring executives from Wendy's, Pathmark, or Taco Bell. (Simon, 2009) In fact, visibility was always a crucial aspect of Starbucks' expansion, even if it meant developing a growth-by-cluster system—multiple Starbucks stores opening in close vicinity to each other to "cannibalize" competition. This visible ubiquity has led the chain to develop a nondescript, factual feel, ingrained in the urban backdrop of 78 countries and driven by what Schultz considers his "obligation to add value to humanity." (Bloomberg QuickTake Originals, 2017) But what is this "obligation" adding up to in reality?

Naomi Klein called companies like Nike or Starbucks "meaning brokers;" but what does their existence mean? Starbucks is a specialty coffee chain. McDonalds, the spiritual opposite, is a fast-food chain. While these are discrete categories, Starbucks is now, 50 years after its inception, the second most valuable "fast-food brand" after the Golden Arches. (Lock, 2019) In China, Starbucks' biggest growing market, commentators labor under the impression that Starbucks' main competition is the cheap, local-based Luckin Coffee—which would be axiomatic if Starbucks were in "the coffee business." Yet, in 2018, when Starbucks devised its growth in the Chinese market to the rhythm of a new store every 15 hours until 2022, it effectively entered a competition against KFC for the title of China's fastest-growing foreign fast-food chain—(Bloomberg News, 2018) three years after China's KFC had launched its own coffee menu to compete with Starbucks in China. (Bloomberg News, 2015) So is American QSR (Quick Service Restaurant) competition still containable by categorical compartmentalization?

The year 2018 graced Starbucks with an important distinction: the title of the fifth most admired company worldwide—first in the food and beverage industry (Starbucks Newsroom, 2018). The same year, as if to translate this admiration into skating where the Starbucks puck is going, McDonalds partnered with Coke to bottle its McCafé coffee beverages. Nestle swapped $7.15 billion for the rights for Starbucks' packaged roasts; now the supermarket coffee Starbucks was created to replace. Coke embarked on these neo Coffee Wars by purchasing Costa Coffee, the second biggest coffee chain after Starbucks, for £3.9 billion. Dunkin' announced a $100 million renovation blueprint that involved broadening its coffee menu à la Starbucks. This concatenation of business moves indicates that the food and beverage industry is blurring lines in a nebulous inception of fast-food imperialism, with Starbucks in the branding forefront. Even Peet's Coffee, a chain of 200 stores today, finds its coffee menu severely reformed to meet today's trends. In the QSR realm, Starbucks' first-mover advantage in transforming consumer aspirations into a coffee-flavored drink menu explains why it has become its spiritual leader. Is it the lack of competition—or the virtual inefficacy of anti-trust when it comes to ousting fledgling competition—that is reducing the scope for excellence and driving global food and beverage homogenization? Or is Starbucks and its subculture brand ilk simply an answer to the new "harried leisure class," (Linder, 1970) brought up in the wake of a "graphic revolution" (Boorstin, 1962) that liquefied commodity value into prints, pixels, and imagination work?

Synthetic Authenticity and the People Business

"Authenticity," Shultz declared in his autobiography, "is what we stand for." (Schultz and Yang, 1997) But in its intangible splendor, authenticity can hardly be pointed at inside a Starbucks. Is it the "dark-roasted flavor profile" that "differentiated" the coffee and "made it authentic?" (Schultz and Yang, 1997) Is it the exposed beams and pipes, the music, the distinct smell inside a shop, the chatty baristas, or the pictures of coffee farmers that remind the customer they are helping them by consuming from Starbucks? (Simon, 2009) Or is an image more than the sum of its parts? Daniel J. Boorstin wrote extensively about the place of "the image" within the American experience. The ideal, he explained, needed to be strived toward, while the image—its synthetic replacement—could be fitted into. (Boorstin, 1962) Is Starbucks just an image, a "pseudo-event," an artificial happening of synthetic authenticity, hip, and planet consciousness that consumers can fit into at their convenience? How does being in the "people business" make this achievable?

The appreciation for authentic foods fostered by the 1960s health movement vested sustenance with a new dimension in the US. It became, in defining itself as the counternarrative of drab supermarket consumables, an "edible identity." (Brulotte and Di Giovine, 2014) In *A New Branding World* (2003), Scott Bedbury wrote that "we all want to belong to something larger than ourselves (…) it means that the mere possession of a product can make customers feel as if they are somehow deeply connected to everyone else who owns that product, almost as if they were together in a family." This branded revision of the purpose of life in a postindustrial, postmodern, postwar society is the backbone of what BCG called "the personal brand;" a concept companies like Starbucks exist to valorize, helping consumers "trade up" from the "unassuming and unsophisticated person of modest means and limited influence into a sophisticated and discerning customer with high aspirations and substantial buying power and clout." (Silverstein et al, 2005) The passage from "person" to "customer" is read here as an all-empowering process; a middle-market revolution. In a materialist order that advertises self-selling as the key to success, the "personal brand" blurs the line between what you buy and who you are; as a consumer, buying authentic means being authentic, hence Starbucks's role takes on full significance, feeding the personal brands of all those who populate Bedbury's "new branding world."

Starbucks marketed its authenticity by replicating the Italian coffee experience into atmospheric stores with "a strategic association with books, blues and jazz." (Klein, 2000) Wanting to set Starbucks apart from cracker-and-cereal companies after deciding that his main capital would be the people, Schultz extended health benefits to part-timers, made diversity a permanent fixture in the company mission statement, and began dabbling in philanthropy with the Starbucks Foundation, created in 1997 to promote literacy in the US and Canada.

However, just like Nike—Schultz's favorite status symbol—learned to sell sneakers to people who didn't play basketball, post-I.P.O. Starbucks began to expand its appeal to people who didn't drink coffee. Howard Behar, founding president of Starbucks International in 1995 and author of a book on Starbucks called *It's Not about the Coffee* (2007), sensed that a move toward different milk options and syrupy drinks would be more on a par with American taste, (Clark, 1997) which, at its "tastiest"—other American food chains have shown—enjoys exportable potential. Since their inception, the Caffè Latte in 1985 and the Frappuccino a decade later have been implacable bestsellers. People who hadn't developed a taste for bitter espressos, namely younger demographics, could still partake in the conspicuous "cool" of buying a Starbucks drink: "these beverages enabled us to introduce great coffee to people who normally didn't even drink coffee." (Schultz and Yang, 1997) Swerving further off Starbucks' pre-Schultz minimalism, drink options were expanded until the company could claim to provide "more than 170,000 ways to customize beverages at Starbucks stores." (Starbucks, 2019) In 2010, free AT&T-powered Wi-Fi was introduced in its American and Canadian stores, tuning in with the concept of the cybercafé, and the words "Starbucks" and "coffee" were taken off the brand logo a year later, as though cancelling the association. In 2013, patrons began having their name marked on their individuality-empowering cup—an innovation replicated by Coke a year later for its Share a Coke campaign. Throughout this timeline, Starbucks' authentic veneer was cracking as the siren, year after year, "somatized" its anxiety for growth with symptoms of "McDonaldization," from the replacement of barista demonstrations of coffee knowhow with automated machines to maximizing its drive-through orders. (Ritzer, 2011) Authenticity, it seemed, wasn't very scalable against the imperatives of relentless growth. 2,498-stores-large and counting, this idea dawned on Starbucks when some of its Seattle locations were vandalized by anti-WTO (World Trade Organization) protestors in 1999. At that time, NGOs (non-governmental organizations) were rising to fill the trust void, champion the vox populi, and hold the excesses of capitalism in check. After its diatribe against Nike's sweatshop labor conditions, Global Exchange, an NGO created in 1988, San Francisco, California, wanted Starbucks to go Fair Trade or suffer the ultimate backlash of buying power: a national boycott. (Argenti, 2004) Starbucks, seeing that its physical growth had outpaced its cultural capital, the novelty of its coffee proposition being somewhat exhausted, needed now, like all the big brands, to realign its image with what trended as "authentic" in the tertiary sector. The same year of the protests, it went about it like a brand extension, partnering with Conservation International, a non-profit that helped other big brands make "greener" choices, to devise its very own "ethical sourcing" program. This created "Starbucks Farmer Support Centers" in nine coffee-sourcing spots around the world. Named "Coffee and Farmer Equity" (CAFE) Practices, these tailor-made guidelines involved, like the Fair Trade certification, eschewing large middlemen and privileging smaller farmer co-ops. In 2017, Starbucks celebrated having 99% of its coffee "ethically sourced," so to investigate this self-awarded distinction, Arte produced a film called *Starbucks Unfiltered* (Herman & Bovon, 2018) where it acted as Starbucks' default compliance verification engineer in one of the sourcing spots; Chiapas, Mexico. The filmmakers realized that Starbucks, after showing real engagement in the beginning and rewarding the most compliant farmers, eventually cut back on its promises and turned to AMSA, a middleman roasting factory in the region. This decision, though non-compliant with its own program, stemmed from its need for mass-produced coffee beans to fuel its dream of 37,000 global locations by 2021. (Starbucks, 2016)

Like Gresham's law maintained that bad money drives out the good, Boorstin maintained that the image drives out the ideal. So authenticity, as an ideal, was dispensed with, but as an image, no failures were deplored, since Starbucks' graphic references to ethical sourcing existed, like all the constituents of its meticulously designed branding, to feed people's "personal brands;" which people depend on, in turn, to "fit in". As Starbucks expanded, shedding the "niche" aspect but gaining access to the international mass market without compromising its markups, it consistently awarded its patrons a form of cultural belonging. A culture is shaped around a place—be it physical or digital—a language, sartorial markings, and participants come together in a stage of togetherness. Starbucks ticks all four. A Third Place between work and home, "Euro-latte lingo" that is only privy to the regulars, (Klein, 2000) logoed cups that serve to complete a look, employees—"partners"—and the patrons they serve. Schultz, making it clear from the offset that he was in the people business, not the coffee business, stated that "people connect with Starbucks because they relate to what we stand for." (Schultz and Yang, 1997) Showcasing this cultural belonging, people learned to clutch their logoed cups like walking billboards down the street, whether they were 1980s yuppies displaying an air of sophistication, or millennials posing with a Starbucks drink with their name on it on social media.

In an age where, as Landor famously stated, "products are made in the factory, but brands are created in the mind," investing in people's psyche—making them want to associate with Starbucks for its psychographic attributes, i.e., its culture—ends up disqualifying the coffee. "To be honest," Bedbury said, "you could train a monkey to pull a double shot. It's not that hard. The coffee wasn't the hard part." (Clark, 2007)

To demonstrate Bedbury's point, one can measure the "graphic" capacity of the contract between the consumer and the subculture brand by studying consumer behavior, namely as it shows people gauging the same harm differently based on what logo stamps it. For instance, while Coke and McDonalds are blamed for promoting global obesity, Starbucks' signature caramel hot chocolate, sized Venti (20 oz), with oat milk and whipped cream, packs 23 teaspoons of sugar, 758 calories, and rouses little public offense for it. (Action on Sugar, 2019) For reference, there are 550 calories in a Big Mac. Instead of inspiring the kind of outrage reserved for fat, the saccharine, caloric intake is received by many as a self-gift; (Simon, 2009) the steep price "luxurizing" the same thing that Coke and the Golden Arches are constantly blamed for. This difference in liability stems from the tacit, graphic "deal" between the brand and the customer. Because what Starbucks is retailing is in fact a visible culture, it can only incur customer displeasure by visibly striking a cultural false note. Conversely, Coca-Cola, like McDonalds, is not a subculture brand but the surviving vestige of brand universalism (Tedlow, 1996). In the US, it is the anointed companion of American soldiers in WWII by command of Eisenhower, with remnants of its cure-all past driving its mystique. (Pendergrast, 1993) Once Coke and Starbucks have placed themselves on this graphic spectrum, consumer response meets them halfway. As a patriotic heirloom, Coca-Cola enjoys a fair laissez-passer with community rites which Starbucks does not. Coke, for instance, gets to celebrate Christmas and recommend Muslims break their fast with a fizz in Ramadan, but if Starbucks were to begin dealing in religious allusions in the US, it would most likely be flagged for cultural appropriation, tokenization, or anything in the free range of political incorrectness, in the light of the 2015 Christmas cup outrage which involved a handgun-equipped internet evangelist attacking Starbucks for taking "Christ and Christmas" off of their plain red cups—though their holiday cups had hitherto used secular iconographies. Starbucks, it was being reminded, does not have access to that aspect of American communities. Three years later, the Philadelphia scandal involving the arrest of two African Americans who were looking to use the restroom without placing orders reminded it that it was supposed to be inclusive, not racist. Similarly, Pepsi, placing itself as a youth generator by the can and a champion of diversity, was accused of "trivializing" Black Lives Matter in its 2017 advertisement where a Pepsi can was portrayed as the solution to end police brutality against African Americans. Pepsi's actual soda being sweeter than Coke is hardly making headlines. So does it really matter if Starbucks' hot chocolate is an oversweet, caloric scandal? Not in the people business.

Curating Community and Conquering Global Taste

While Starbucks mined its cultural capital as an American status symbol well into the new millennium, its clients, "spirits in the material world" of the bustling city, Schultz knew, depended on physical convenience; on a place to catch their breath between work and home. Starbucks was the first QSR to claim to engineer this society-healing "Third Place" by design. Coined by Oldenburg, the concept designates "informal public gathering places" that allow people to convene with strangers and boost their civic engagement in an atmosphere of locality. (Oldenburg, 1991) "Almost everywhere we open a store," Schultz enthused, "we add value to the community. Our stores become an instant gathering spot, a Third Place that draws people together. That's what community should be about." (Schultz and Yang, 1997) Schultz, frequently associating Starbucks with Oldenburg's "Third Place," insisted on de facto trade-marking it as a Starbucks Corporation creative concept. Though Oldenburg himself considered Starbucks stores a mere "imitation" of the more idiosyncratic, unpredictable open spaces he had in mind, (Simon, 2009) Schultz was determined to lend credence to his corporate Third Place as the new norm for urban hangouts. "Without such places," Schultz wrote, quoting Oldenburg, "the urban area fails to nourish the kinds of relationships and the diversity of human contact that are the essence of the city. Deprived of these settings, people remain lonely within their crowds." (Schulz and Yang, 1997) Taking it upon himself to fill the public place void in the metropolis, Schultz preached that "in an increasingly fractured society, our stores offer a quiet moment to gather your thoughts and center yourself. Starbucks people smile at you, serve you quickly, don't harass you. A visit to Starbucks can be a small escape during a day when so many other things are beating you down. We've become a breath of fresh air." People, he rephrased, "are looking for a Third Place, an inviting, stimulating, sometimes even soulful respite from the pressures of work and home." (Shultz and Yang, 1997) Starbucks stores were like little alcoves in the urban time continuum where the customer could "decelerate"; like a place of cult. In response, the curiosity of some cult leaders was piqued. In 2007, Evangelism Professor Leonard Sweet published *The Gospel according to Starbucks* where he enjoined churches to engage people the Starbucks way based on his "EPIC" model: Experience, Participation, Images that Throb with Meaning, and Connection. In 2014, Reverend Bill McBride, having led congregations for 35 years, decided to self-publish his own slim book entitled *The Church according to Starbucks* where he invited churches to start making use of Starbucks' "radical hospitality." When 300 young Catholic delegates met at the Vatican in 2018, they read a 12-page letter asking the church, oftentimes "associated with excessive moralism," to be "more welcoming" and "find creative new ways to encounter people where they naturally socialize: bars, coffee shops, parks(...)." These different invitations to "Cappuccino Catholicism" (Pullella, 2018) paint Starbucks as a virtuous community curator. But Starbucks stores are not predestined; they are justified by a powerful real estate strategy in which long-term leases and competition-ousting Starbucks clusters are replacing real community cafés that would have otherwise opened for business. The admiration accreting around Starbucks as it mass-produces an imitation of communal space precludes the fact that its business model does not thrive on people commandeering the seats for dragging reunions, but on fast foot traffic. Temple University Professor and Historian Bryant Simon visited hundreds of Starbucks locations before writing that, generally, the layout of the coffee chain "quietly discouraged conversation, setting tables apart, turning up the music, and making itself into a laptop alley." (Simon, 2009) Throughout the years, Starbucks remodeled its interior with uncomfortable furniture, increased drive-thrus, ramped up mobile app order and payment options, and partnered with Uber Eats; all tactical moves that favor speed. (Walton, 2012; Grill-Goodman, 2018) As Schultz warns that Americans are in danger of losing social interaction, Starbucks' real estate monopoly precipitates this social void, to then position itself as the solution by default—like a self-fulfilling prophecy.

But the ubiquity of its stores—and the gentrifying effect they were having on American neighborhoods—(Rascoff and Humphries, 2015) inevitably created cappuccino heretics. To keep Starbucks' expansion from being perceived negatively, the design department decided to enhance the in-store theatricality by espousing "local relevance" instead of cloning the same template in the US and worldwide. As though to uphold Ritzer's theory on Starbucks being a McDonalds-type organism retrofitted with an innovation in the realm of theatrics, (Ritzer, 2011) under Bill Sleethe, Starbucks' V.P. for store design & concepts, Starbucks scattered 18 design centers around the globe and began selectively rearranging its "core kit" with local input in touristy locations like the Chapultepec Starbucks in Mexico City, the Hamilton House Starbucks in New Delhi, the Utrechtsestraat Starbucks in Amsterdam, or the Ninenzaka Starbucks in Kyoto. (Re:co symposium, 2014) These locations became statement stores proving that Starbucks' Third Place was visually accommodating of different cultures, even if the coffee menu was predictably the same. On this same route of architectural performance, Starbucks entered the Italian market in 2018 with a Starbucks Reserve Roastery in Milan's historic Palazzo Delle Poste building. The 25,000-square foot interior, complete with opulent marble bar tops and handcrafted mosaic floors, recreated an industrial coffee roastery atmosphere in a jointventure with Percassi, an Italian licensing partner that worked with status brands like Gucci, or, indeed, Nike. Signing the completion of Schultz's Milan-born dream of a global taste, "every coffee we have served has led us here" was prophetically inscribed on the wall. The coffee menu, deliberately Frappuccino-free, was complemented with Princi's food menu, a high-end Italian bakery now present on global Starbucks roastery locations. This projection of an entirely different coffee narrative proved that Starbucks' global conquest is a contextualizable, shape-shifting force.

With the siren reaching the shores of Italy, Europe was conquered at last, but Starbucks' biggest market outside of North America was more to the East.

As a tea-drinking nation, China was not an easy conquest for the coffee peddler. The first triumph of caffeine in its territory after the normalization of US-China relations took place when Coca-Cola became the first American company to re-enter Beijing in 1979. Coke expands through franchise; local bottlers meant local product, and its Western provenance, as it had with Nike, sat well will the blooming trend of status consumption. (Zakkour and Chan, 2014) In a similar capacity, Starbucks' success strategy involved both localization and American glamour. In either Confucian China or Shinto Japan, Starbucks became the revival of the tea-house culture with a "modern, upscale sensibility," (Zakkour, 2017) filling the cultural gaps created, in part, by the same globalizing wave that carried the siren in. By enfolding its predictable experience with local adjustments in its two largest Asian markets, where K.F.C.'s immense success had already shown an enthusiasm for Western QSR, Starbucks demonstrated its capacity to adapt its Third Place vision to cultures where coffee drinking was not the national sport, luring international sailors with the song of sugar, status, and self-gifting. Its dream of a global taste finds itself somewhat stumped, however, in places like Seoul, South Korea, where effervescent conceptual cafés are interspersed along the urban scheme; unique happenings of café culture (not coffee culture; coffee in itself never survived the people business). They become prioritized for get-togethers—though Schultz's Starbucks menu undeniably redefined the South Korean café game—while Starbucks, generally deprived of the cultural advantage until it stirs in, say, a merchandise fad thanks to local partnerships with South Korean pop icons, faces the threat of being reduced to its individualist, cybercafé practicality; becoming the haunt of students and laptop-equipped workers. (Pearce, 2018) Surprisingly, Starbucks isn't losing revenue over this cultural demotion. Over the past decade, its Korean profit margins have been on a steady rise; perhaps because, behind the picture-perfect glitz South Korea advertises, its ultracompetitive society has plenty of individualist students and laptop-equipped workers to offer, making their existence and Starbucks' growth ironically linked. Since Seoul has the most Starbucks per city in the world, and the image of community Starbucks projects is actively driving out its ideal, this reality could very well be a work in progress in every other city hosting the ever-expanding siren.

In this optic, Starbucks "borrowed" the Third Place concept and reformulated community gathering around its stores, crafting the idea of an experience behind it, and disseminating it across the world to feed the lonely crowds that urban life shed in its trail as they, in turn, fed its growth. In an accelerating world where "change changed," (Postman and Weingartner, 1969) Starbucks exists within the "global imaginary" (Steger, 2008) as a pseudo-event; an image that can be stretched over the planet like a neo-universalist, global answer to everything, everywhere, except the coffee.

References

Action on Sugar. (2019, December 3). Festive Hot Drinks Loaded with Sugar & Calories Reveals Lack of Progress in Achieving Sugar Reduction Targets. Action on Sugar. www.actiononsugar.org/news-centre/press-releases/2019/festive-hot-drinks-loaded-with-sugar—calories-reveals-lack-of-progress-inachieving-sugar-reduction-targets-.html

Argenti, P.A. (2004). *Collaborating with Activists: How Starbucks Works with NGOs. California Management Review,* 47(1), 91–116. https://doi.org/10.2307/41166288Bedbury, S. (2003). *A New Brand World: Eight Principles for Achieving Brand Leadership in the Twenty-first Century.* New York, NY: Penguin Books.

Behar, H. (2007). *It's not About the Coffee: Leadership Principles from a Life at Starbucks*. New York, NY: Portfolio.

Belasco, W. (1993). *Appetite for Change: How Counterculture Took on the Food Industry*. Ithaca, NY: Cornell University Press.

Bloomberg News. (2015, March 04). *KFC aims to out-coffee Starbucks in China with lower-cost "premium" brew.* Financial Post. https://financialpost.com/news/retail-marketing/kfc-aims-to-out-coffee-starbucks-in-china-with-lower-cost-premium-brew

Bloomberg News. (2018, May 16). *Flush With Nestle Cash, Starbucks Unveils Bold China Plan*. Bloomberg. www.bloomberg.com/news/articles/2018-05-16/flush-with-nestle-cash-starbucks-wants-to-triple-china-revenue

Bloomberg QuickTake Originals. (2017, February 27). *CEO Says Starbucks Obligated to Add Value to Humanity* [Video]. YouTube. www.youtube.com/watch?v=IU0OYBSKdR0

Boorstin, D. (1962). *The Image: A Guide to Pseudo-Events in America*. New York, NY: Harper & Row.

Brulotte, R., & Di Giovine, M. (2014). *Edible Identities: Food as Cultural Heritage*. New York, NY: Routledge.

Clark, T. (2007). *Starbucked: a Double Tall Tale of Caffeine, Commerce, and Culture*. New York, NY: Little, Brown.

Commoner, B. (1971). *The Closing Circle*. New York, NY: Random House.

Draper TV. (2017, December 5). *Starters, Carriers, and Finishers | Jerry Baldwin* [Video]. YouTube. www.youtube.com/watch?v=XErPL8KHTp4

Frank, T. (1997). *The Conquest of Cool*. Berkley, CA: UC Press.

Grill-Goodman, J. (2018, May 5). *Starbucks Ramps Up Personalization, Drive-Thru and Delivery for 2019*. RIS. https://risnews.com/starbucks-ramps-personalization-drive-thru-and-delivery-2019

Hermann, L., & Bovon, G. (Directors). (2018). *Starbucks Unfiltered* [Film]. Arte France, Premières Lignes Télévision.

Klein, N. (2000). *No Logo: Brands, Globalization, Resistance*. Toronto: Knopf.

Lash, C. (1979). *The Culture of Narcissism: American Life in an Age of Diminishing Expectations*. New York, NY: Warner Books.

Linder, S.B. (1970). *The Harried Leisure Class*. New York, NY: Columbia University Press.

Lock, S. (2019, August 16). *Brand Value of the 10 Most Valuable Fast Food Brands Worldwide in 2019*. Statista. www.statista.com/statistics/273057/value-of-the-most-valuable-fast-food-brands-worldwide/

McBride, B. (2014). *The Church According To Starbucks: Radical Hospitality For Growing A Healthy Church*. Scotts Valley, CA: CreateSpace.

McDowell, B. (1996, December 9). *Starbucks is Ground Zero in Today's Coffee Culture Brand Goes Beyond Cup by Embodying Attitude*. AdAge. https://adage.com/article/news/starbucks-ground-today-s-coffee-culture-brand-cup-embodying-attitude/75420

Oldenburg, R. (1991). *The Great Good Place: Cafés, Coffee Shops, Bookstores, Bars, Hair Salons, and Other Hangouts at the Heart of a Community*. New York, NY: Marlowe.

Patnaik, D. (2009). *Wired to Care: How Companies Prosper When They Create Widespread Empathy*. London: Financial Times.

Pearce, T. (2018, September 17). *How the Coffee Shop Became King in South Korea*. World Coffee Portal. www.worldcoffeeportal.com/Latest/InsightAnalysis/2018/The-culture-behind-South-Korea-s-coffee-shop-boom

Pendergrast, M. (1993). *For God, Country and Coca-Cola: The Unauthorized History of the Great American Soft Drink and the Company That Makes It*. New York, NY: Scribner.

Postman, N., & Weingartner, C. (1969). *Teaching as a Subversive Activity*. New York, NY: Dell Pub. Co.

Pullella, P. (2018, March 14). The Catholic Church—coming to a Starbucks near you? Reuters. https://reut.rs/2Quf5K4

Rascoff, S., & Humphries, S. (2015). *Zillow Talk: The New Rules of Real Estate*. New York, NY: Grand Central Publishing.

Re:co Symposium. (2014, June 10). *Bill Sleeth: Locally Relevant Design* [Video]. YouTube. www.youtube.com/watch?v=56qT707SN4Q

Ritzer, G. (2011). *The McDonaldization of society* (6th edition). Los Angeles, CA: Pine Forge.

Schultz, H, & Yang, D.J. (1997). *Pour Your Heart Into It: How Starbucks Build a Company One Cup at a Time*. New York, NY: Hyperion.

Seabrook, J. (2000). *NoBrow: The Culture of Marketing the Marketing of Culture*. New York, NY: Knopf.

Silverstein, M.J., Fiske, N., & Butman, J. (2005). *Trading up: Why consumers want new luxury goods—and how companies create them*. New York: Portfolio.

Simon, B. (2009). *Everything but the Coffee: Learning about America from Starbucks*. Berkley, CA: UC Press.

Starbucks. (2016, December 7). *Starbucks Presents its Five-Year Plan for Strong Global Growth*. Starbucks. https://stories.starbucks.com/stories/2016/investor-day-2016-press-release/

Starbucks. (2019, April 8). *Top six ways to customize your favorite Starbucks drink*. Starbucks. https://stories.starbucks.com/press/2019/customizing-beverages-at-starbucks-stores/

Starbucks Newsroom. (2018, January 19). *Starbucks Named Fifth Most Admired Company Worldwide*. Starbucks. https://stories.starbucks.com/stories/2018/starbucks-fortune-most-admired-company-in-the-world/

Steger, M.B. (2008). *The Rise of the Global Imaginary: Political Ideologies from the French Revolution to the Global War on Terror*. New York, NY: Oxford University Press.

Sweet, L. (2007). *The Gospel According to Starbucks*. Colorado Springs, CO: WaterBrook Press.

Tedlow, R.S. (1996). *New and Improved: The Story of Mass Marketing in America*. Brighton, MA: Harvard Business School Press.

Walton, A.G. (2012, May 29). *Starbucks' Power Over Us Is Bigger Than Coffee: It's Personal*. Forbes. www.forbes.com/sites/alicegwalton/2012/05/29/starbucks-hold-on-us-is-bigger-than-coffee-its-psychology/#4c050f024aed

Wight, P. (2017). The Countercultural Roots of Green Consumerism. *Shopping for Change: Consumer Activism and the Possibilities of Purchasing Power*. Ithaca, NY: ILR Press.

Zakkour, M., & Chan, S. (2014). *China's Super Consumers: What 1 Billion Customers Want and How to Sell it to Them*. Hoboken, NJ: Wiley.

Zakkour, M. (2017, August 24). *Why Starbucks Succeeded In China: A Lesson For All Retailers*. Forbes. www.forbes.com/sites/michaelzakkour/2017/08/24/why-starbucks-succeeded-in-china-a-lesson-for-all-retailers/#d8442fe79232

11

"THERAPEUTIC AND INSPIRING"—JAPANESE POP CULTURE IN PRC AND THE ISSUE OF ASIAN MODERNITY

Wendy Su

Introduction

The immense popularity of Japanese pop culture products, including comics, anime, TV dramas, movies, cartoons, computer games, and pop music, in the world and especially in Asia is a remarkable phenomenon of transnational cultural flows. Although it has a different ideological and political system, Mainland China or the People's Republic of China (PRC) is no exception to this pop culture flow trend. The past two decades have witnessed numerous studies on the impact of Japanese pop culture on the societies of Hong Kong, Taiwan, Singapore, Thailand, South Korea, and other diaspora communities and regions, as well as the booming Asian cultural industries and transnational and inter-Asian cultural exchanges (Iwabuchi, 2002, 2004, 2010; Huat, 2004; Huat & Iwabuchi, 2008; Berry, Liscutin, & Mackintosh, 2009; Fung, 2007; Keane, Fung, & Moran, 2007; Lee, 2011; Taylor-Jones, 2012; Otmazgin & Ben-Ari, 2013; Jin & Otmazgin, 2014; DeBoer, 2014; Saluveer, 2014). Past research has also brought up the issue of "the shifting nature of transnational cultural power" (Iwabuchi, 2004, p. 6) and Japan's "soft power" (Otmazgin, 2012), as well as the natures of Asian modernity, "Asianness," and Asian values. However, research remains absent on the reception of Japanese pop culture by audiences in its biggest rival of the region—the People's Republic of China, and the possible role of the PRC and its audience in the formation of a pan-Asian cultural identity.

This chapter aims to fill this research gap in transnational audience reception studies, and to use the reception as a site of inquiry about the issue of Asian modernity. I first expound the theoretical exploration conducted by previous researchers on the nature of Asian values and Asian modernity, followed by a brief overview of the PRC's engagement with Japanese pop culture. I then discuss Chinese college students' reception of Japanese films and TV dramas, and the implications on the issue of Asian modernity.

The research method is a mixed historical document analysis plus ethnographic focus group discussion. Six focus groups were organized based on six universities in northern and southern China from February to December of 2019. In each university, one focus group composed of six to eight students was organized and discussions were launched and recorded. The transcripts were then decoded, and the themes and patterns were identified.

The chapter intends to inquire about how the reception of Japanese pop culture facilitates the transformation of social norms and values of the young generation of China, and enhances their cultural imagination in a rapidly globalized world. The chapter argues that the reception process functions as an effective way of self-expression and escapism from the hardship of real life. Through deeply engaging in Japanese media culture, Chinese fans not only actuate a deep reflection on their own society, but also form a new or imaginary cultural identity that negotiates through the political and social constraints of the Chinese society. Accordingly, the reception process is a site of contestation, negotiation, and even resistance, in which transnationalism triumphs and a cross-border Asian modernity is in the making.

Transnational Flow of Japanese Pop Culture and the Issue of Asian Modernity

In one of the pioneering articles on East Asian culture, Chua Beng Huat argued that the production, distribution, and consumption of popular cultural products that cross national and cultural boundaries have made it possible to imagine "a potential 'East Asian identity'" (Huat, 2004, p. 200) based on Confucianism and a "cultural China" (Tu, 1991). Within the common cultural sphere of Confucianism, and bounded by cultural proximity and the so-called Asian values of loyalty and duty to family and friends, a common East Asian cultural identity is imaginable. These Asian values are further elaborated by East Asian state leaders as the "embrace of peace and harmony," "Neo-Confucian tradition," and an "Asian pragmatism" that combines individualism and social well-being (cited from Berry et al., 2009, p. 5). This "post-industrial globalized consumerism" and "individual freedom" are seen as "contemporary, open, transnational, and … 'cool.'" "At the beginning of the 2000s, then, culture and the creative industries, it seems, have the capacity to effect historical reconciliation and shrink spatio-temporal distance to create a cosmopole of consumers who identify themselves as Asian" (Berry et al., 2009, p. 5).

Asian identity and Asian values are also related to the Japanese colonial and imperial legacy, which is intertwined with East Asia's desire for both technomodernity (DeBoer, 2014) and capitalist modernity. One vision of a pan-Asian identity and its cinematic representation was pioneered by the Japanese empire's concept of a "Greater East Asian Film Sphere," in accordance with its concept of the "Greater East Asian Co-prosperity Sphere" back in the 1930s (Taylor-Jones, 2012, pp. 127–128). The Japanese military empire and its brutal repression of other Asian nations aimed to create a pan-Asian sphere led by Japan to counter Western imperialism and domination. Since a number of East Asian regions were once conquered or fully colonized by the Japanese military empire— including Manchuria, Inner Mongolia, Taiwan, Korea, Hong Kong, Singapore, and the Philippines— the Japanese legacy lives on in many aspects of these societies (Chen, 2010). These places therefore share or mirror many elements of Japanese technomodernity and capitalist modernity. Furthermore, as Koichi Iwabuchi has pointed out, as these countries and regions skillfully mastered globalized styles and cultural expressions during the postwar and globalization eras, they established extensive transnational cultural connections and came to share "'our' East Asian (post)modernity" (2010, p. 151).

Japanese Pop Culture in the PRC

Japanese pop culture and technology have had an indisputable impact on China's cultural industries and audiences ever since the end of World War II and the founding of the People's Republic of China. The Chang Chun Film Studio (originally the Northeastern Studio), one of the PRC's oldest and most prestigious, evolved from the Japanese Manchukuo Film Association and was taken over by the Chinese Communist Party after the defeat of Japan. In the 1950s, almost every one of new China's red classics was produced by Chang Chun, with the assistance of a number of Japanese professionals from Manchukuo. These classics included *Minzhu Dongbei* (Democratic Northeast), *Bai Mao Nv* (The White-Haired Girl), *Gangtie Zhanshi* (Iron Soldiers), and *Zhao Yi-man,* depicting the famous anti-Japanese heroine (Wang, 2012). In 1979, seven years after the two countries normalized their diplomatic relationship, the Japanese Movie Week was launched as part of a cultural exchange program. Japanese movies *Kimi yo Fundo no Kawa o Watare* (Manhunt and Dangerous Chase), *Sandakan No.*

8, and *Fox Story* were introduced in China and caused quite a stir. After nearly 30 years of isolation from the international community, these Japanese movies widened the horizons of young Chinese audiences and connected them to the outside world. Japanese star Ken Takakura—with his tough, cool-guy image and dark glasses—immediately became a model of masculinity and individual freedom who was emulated and admired by young Chinese men. Well-known Chinese film director Zhang Yimou, who grew up during this era, became a huge fan of Ken Takakura and eventually developed a friendship with the Japanese actor. He invited Takakura to star in his 2011 film *Riding Alone for One Thousand Miles,* fulfilling his longtime dream of working with this Japanese icon (Wang, 2012).

The 1980s witnessed the import and wide spread in China of such Japanese TV dramas as *Akai Giwaku, Oshin,* and *Moero Atakku,* familiarizing the Chinese audience with Japanese iconic stars like Ken Takakura, Momoe Yamaguchi, Tomokazu Miura, Komaki Kurihara, and Ryoko Nakano. The earliest Chinese fan community of Japanese TV dramas was established during this period. The 1990s became the "Golden Age" for the distribution and circulation of Japanese TV dramas in China, romance dramas such as *Tokyo Love Story, Asunaro White Paper, Long Vacation,* and *Meguriai* attracted large number of young Chinese fans, and Japanese stars like Takuya Kimura, Takako Matsu, Yutaka Takenouchi, Takako Tokiwa. and Hideaki Takizawa became new icons of Chinese fans. Many young Chinese became Japanophiles (Wang, 2012).

Japanese movies and animated films (anime and manga) are equally popular in China, especially among younger loyal fans. After a relatively quiet time in the early 2000s because of Hollywood imports and the deteriorating relationships between Japan and China, Japanese pop culture rebounded in China by the mid-2000s. The anime *Stand by Me Doraemon* made 530 million yuan in China in 2015, becoming the highest grossing film ever at that time. In 2016, 11 Japanese imports poured into China, exceeding the total of the previous five years. Among them, *Your Name* led at the box office with 576 million yuan in receipts. Three others—*One Piece Film: Gold, Boruto-Naruto the Movie,* and *Doraemon: Nobita and the Birth of Japan*—exceeded 100 million yuan at the box office in China. The trend of growing Japanese imports continued in 2017. By September, *The 100th Love with You, Midnight Dinner 2, Gintama, A Silent Voice,* and *Sword Art Online the Movie: Ordinal Scale* had all been released in China (Wenchuangzixun, 2017). In total, Japanese films released in China took in more than $50 million in 2017. *Your Name* finished its run in China in January with nearly $85 million—a record for a Japanese title in China (Blair, 2017). In 2018 and 2019, 15 and 24 Japanese animations and films were released in China respectively, marking the new high in Japanese import record. Hayao Miyazaki's animated feature *Spirited Away* championed the import box office of 2019 with 488 million yuan (Wang, 2020).

The wide spread of Japanese pop culture in China and Asia brings up the research theme of transnational audience and fandom studies in the past decade with two new dimensions: the transnational and the digital. Many transnational audience studies have centered around particular audience groups in diasporas or geographically proximate regions focusing on the issue of social identities, assimilation, and alienation (Athique, 2016). This chapter acknowledges the significant contribution of the past decade's transnational audience studies on the issue of subjectivity and identity, but takes the research forward to explore the issue of "global imagination" (Appadurai 1996; Taylor 2002) and modernity for which transnational audiences make sense of the world they are living through.

Chinese College Students' Reception of Japanese Pop Culture

Chinese college students' appreciation of Japanese pop culture is mainly based on its unique "Asianness" or "Asian Flavor," which differentiates it from Hollywood or Western-style pop culture. In focus group discussions, the following components embedded in Japanese movies and TV dramas are identified: very refined and exquisite production; touching storylines and picturesque scenes that create a tranquil, warm, and delicate ambience easily for the audience to immerse itself in; the positive message and the spirit of working and struggling hard that inspire the audience to overcome their own difficulties and troubles; and a profound probing of human nature and the intricacy and complexity of human relationships that evokes the audience's self-reflection.

The exquisite and delicate style of Japanese movies and TV dramas leaves a lasting imprint on Chinese audiences' minds and hearts, and creates a very graceful, warm, and calm ambience that audiences willfully identify with and pleasantly integrate into so as to revitalize and refresh themselves to continue their battle in daily life. The Chinese audience has termed this kind of cultural product as "the healing (therapeutic) series," meaning they can have great emotional and mental catharsis in this type of movie or TV series, refreshing themselves and regaining the strength to move on with their journey. Japanese movie series *Little Forest, Midnight Dinner, Our Little Sister, Bunny Drop, 10 Promises to My Dog,* and *Sayonara bokutachi no youchien* are among these healing series.

One college student expressed her love for the Japanese healing series in the focus group discussion. She said the Japanese healing series, like *Little Forest,* are "especially warm and refreshing." "Such series always discover the kindness and humanity in ordinary people and daily life, making us feel good about life. The plots of such series are usually very simple, but with very deep implications and philosophy of life" (student participant Valerie). Another student commented that she often wanted to escape from the hustle-bustle of the noisy campus and demanding workload of her college life to "fully immerse into the world of *Little Forest,* so peaceful, tranquil, and close to the nature without much competition and pressures" (student participant Shiyou). Other students mentioned that simple but beautiful stories like *Midnight Dinner* describe the kindness and mutual understanding of common people, touching and full of positive energy, which makes audiences feel good about life and regain confidence in human society and interpersonal relationships, thus releasing and "curing" their anxiety, and revitalizing them.

The "therapeutic" series usually feature the unique Japanese way of life, the food, the ways of meditation, picturesque natural landscapes, neat and scenic urban and rural residential places, and kind and caring interpersonal or human–animal relationships. Embodied in these series are grace, gentleness, sophistication, and tranquility—a distinct Oriental wisdom and flavor.

Close to the "therapeutic" function is the "inspirational" function of Japanese movies and TV dramas. They often send the positive message of "'to strive and to struggle hard,' or 'ganbaru' in Japanese" (Leung, 2004, p. 90). This positive message has inspired audiences in a variety of regions and countries, and the mainland Chinese audience is no exception to the appreciation of this message. From the earliest dramas of the 1980s like *Akai Giwaku, Oshin,* and *Moero Atakku,* to the 21st century campus or youth dramas like *Gokusen, Jūhan Shuttai!,* and *Dragon Sakura,* Japanese pop cultural products have delivered strong spiritual inspiration themes and have greatly encouraged and uplifted Chinese college students. One focus group member said:

> I feel American super hero series are too distant from us. With a surreal power, these super heroes are born to save the earth and are not living in the same world with us. But Japanese series are much closer to our daily life. Their stories are very inspiring and touch our hearts.
>
> *(Student participant Valerie)*

Other students agreed and said that they all enjoyed watching Japanese inspirational dramas. When they felt lost and disoriented in their life journey, they especially wished to acquire strength through others' stories that can give them hope and spiritual uplifting. It is therefore unhelpful to watch Marvel series because superheroes are not very relatable to their daily life. Another student commented:

> Japanese dramas, like Korean dramas, have different styles. Some are dark and depressive (*Sang*); some are extremely romantic and inspiring. I do not like to watch dark dramas which make me very down and depressive. I am going to graduate and will make a living in

the society very soon. But look at our society, the housing prices are so high and job pay is not able to afford a house. When I turn 30 or 40 years old, I am still not able to buy a house and take good care of my parents. To watch dark dramas can only make me increasingly depressed. Therefore, I like to watch positive, inspiring dramas that can offer more hope and positive energy to me, or can offer day dreams that let me escape from the reality. Chinese mainstream movies, like *Operation Red Sea*, propagate a strong country, which is good, but is not relatable and cannot improve my personal life and help ease my personal anxiety. Japanese dramas are much more relatable at individual level and provide positive energy we so desperately need.

(Student participant Tiantian)

Japanese inspirational dramas portray ordinary people's daily struggles, and foreground their never-give-up spirit. Unlike Hollywood movies and Marvel superhero series that often highlight a mythic surreal power that saves human beings from disasters, Japanese dramas are earthier and more realistic, which can translate into Chinese audiences' real circumstances and thus inspire them to strive hard in their own journeys.

The third appreciation point of Japanese dramas is their deep probe of human nature and profound reflection on the intricacy and complexity of human relationships. Compared with Chinese movies and dramas that mainly construct morally superb or ideologically strong and politically correct heroes without any shortcomings, Japanese dramas foreground the complexity of human nature and often depict human beings with an all-around angle encompassing both evil and good natures. This complexity makes the audience think deeply and feel it's hard to make simple, black and white judgments. Several students cited the movie *Shoplifting Family* and TV dramas *Unnatural*, commenting that it is difficult to judge people by adopting conventional moral criteria, and specific circumstances must be taken into consideration. They also cited similar Korean movie *The Taxi Driver* to speak the hidden shining nature of ordinary people, which are more realistic and convincing. One student said:

Japanese dramas are both very enjoyable and educational. Unlike Chinese dramas that often construct black and white simplistic figures, Japanese dramas make you think about the complexity of human nature and the difficulty of judging people. One should stand at a higher level to reconsider which is good and which is bad and how to judge, by which standard. Human nature is both good and bad. Under certain circumstances, one's behavior is understandable. We cannot judge people just by one thing and need to redefine what is good and what is bad in specific contexts. This is the biggest impact that Japanese movies and dramas have on me.

(Student participant Valerie)

Taking about Japanese culture and compared with China's homegrown movies and TV programs, focus group discussions were often into the pungent criticism of the latter. Group members all agreed that Japanese and Korea dramas usually focus on the life of common people, or so-called "nobodies," but especially highlight the virtue and hidden good human nature of these ordinary people, such as kindness, self-sacrifice, and courage. That taxi driver in the Korea movie *The Taxi Driver* was frequently mentioned by group members in comparison with Chinese film and TV figures. This taxi driver has his own family burden and originally appears selfish and self-serving, but is gradually transformed after witnessing Korean students' protests and the government's bloody repression. He eventually goes beyond the confines of his personal interest and is elevated to a moral high level, demonstrating incredible courage and a noble nature. Focus group members believed such drama is more realistic and convincing, and especially touching. They said Japanese and Korea dramas have exceptionally profound inquiry into human nature, which is unmatchable by Chinese movies and dramas. One member said:

Chinese dramas always attempt to build correct and elevated heroes without any flaws, or extremely evil people without any merit, which make Chinese dramas appear especially unreal. But Japanese and Korean dramas always concentrate on common people with human weaknesses and flaws. They are one of us, but are turned into noble people under special circumstances. This makes me think that I can be one of them someday. China does not have "the healing series," always attempts to uplift you with hollow and artificial narratives. Japanese and Korean dramas, on the other hand, feature very deep exploration of human nature.

(Student participant Jiaqi)

Another member commented:

Japanese cultural products are deeply rooted in Japanese society and very localized with a distinguishable Japanese flavor. They deeply explore interpersonal relationships and often put forward powerful questions about human beings and human society with philosophical depth. They are very thought-provoking.

(Student participant Zang)

Focus group members also mentioned that Japanese drama series usually have 10 or 12 episodes of 45–50 minutes each, easy to follow and fit into their busy schedules; whereas Chinese TV dramas usually have 50–60 episodes, dragging on too long and full of redundant and pretentious plots that appear both boring and distracting.

If these focus group members are so fond of Japanese pop cultural products and are so critical of homegrown dramas, how would they regard China-made anti-Japanese invasion TV dramas? And what are their true feelings about Japan? Focus group members launched interesting and in-depth discussions.

Attitude toward China's Patriotic Education and Anti-Japanese TV Shows

Unlike middle school students, who often express animosity toward Japan while separating their passion for Japanese popular culture (Naftali, 2018), Chinese college students demonstrate more rational reflection on the "patriotic education" that they have received ever since their primary school age. One focus group member said:

We grow up by receiving a kind of education that is termed as "the Hatred for Japan Education." But I feel the historical past should not be brought into our daily interpersonal interactions. We should not elevate interpersonal interactions to the level of country to country and government to government. Of course, we should have our stances in terms of national sovereignty and our value system.

(Student participant Tingting)

Another member said:

Relatively fewer college students hate Japan. We have objective attitude toward Japan. But older generations may have long memories and strong emotions—they after all personally experienced the War.

(Student participant Guangyin)

Almost all focus group members admitted that they have far more good feelings and impressions of Japan than bad feelings, saying that younger generations like them are very open and like Japanese culture very much. They identified with them and believed what Japanese dramas depict is universal and transcends national boundaries. At the same time, they all expressed their disdain for those home-grown anti-Japanese television dramas, and felt those dramas are too phony and shoddy and are not worth their time watching. They see them as poor-quality dramas that indulge in cheap gimmicks.

In contrast, they admitted, some of their fellow schoolmates dislike Japanese culture very much, and display strong hostility toward Japan. College students' attitude toward Japan and Japanese culture varies to a great extent based on education, family backgrounds, and even geographical regions. For example, their fellow schoolmates from Shandong Province and Northeast China show strong resistance to Japanese and Taiwanese culture, but those schoolmates attending international schools from childhood and those who are eager to study abroad display indifference to the notion of nation and the state. Some of the latter claim that they are "world citizens" and even argue that "the country is but a spatial dimension." With increasingly frequent cultural exchanges worldwide and a more Westernized lifestyle trendy among part of Chinese youth, and still strong nationalistic mood prevailing among another part, there have been more difficulties in launching meaningful dialogues even between college students themselves.

Some group members held that both attitudes—indifference and nationalistic mood—have a lot to do with the "primitive and unsophisticated patriotic education" that they received from childhood. Such patriotic education does not distinguish between the concepts of the nation, the political entity like the government and the party, and the country and the land. Any criticism against a particular political entity is considered "non-patriotic," and the patriotic education is equivalent to love for the government and the party without much identification with the land, the people, and the civilization. Such primitive education has led to a polarized mentality among college students.

The above discussions are based on the relatively small sample size and focus group members who are well-educated, more Westernized, and cosmopolitan college students and Japanese pop culture lovers. There might be a vast number of "angry youth" who have strong nationalistic feelings and dislike, even completely reject, Japanese culture. A large-scale survey and a bigger sample size are needed to have a complete picture of mainland Chinese youth.

Conclusion: Imagined Asian Modernity

In his introduction to *Feeling Asian Modernities—Transnational Consumption of Japanese TV Dramas*, Koichi Iwabuchi asked key questions about the consumption of Japanese pop culture by Asian people:

> What is the nature of Japanese cultural power and influence in the region and how is it historically overdetermined? How is it similar to and different from "Americanization" and other Asiana cultural sub-centers? What kinds of images and sense of intimacy and distance are perceived through the reception of Japanese youth dramas? Do Japanese youth dramas cultivate some kind of transnational imagination and self-reflexive view toward one's own culture and society?
>
> *(Iwabuchi, 2004, p. 3).*

Iwabuchi argued that the transnational reach of Japanese TV dramas in Asia is unprecedented and significant in the sense that Asians "have learned to cope with the meanings of their own modern experiences through the urban lives depicted in Japanese TV dramas" (Iwabuchi, 2004, p. 2). Chinese college students' appreciation of Japanese pop culture resonates with Iwabuchi's argument and offers empirical clues to the issues of Japanese cultural power and Asian modernity.

For well-educated young Chinese audiences, Japanese pop culture is a comfort zone for them to escape the constraint and stress of their daily life; a haven to immerse into to get revitalized; a source of inspiration to acquire strength and courage to continue their struggle against the harsh reality of the Chinese society; and a mirror for their reflection on human nature, their own culture, and society.

American pop culture and Hollywood movies are not sufficient for them and sometimes unable to provide the same functions, power, and the amount of comfort and enjoyment as Japanese pop culture does. The unique glamour of Japanese culture suggests that Asian flavor, Asian values, and Asianness play an undeniable role in Asian audiences' appreciation of Japanese pop culture.

The PRC originally operated in a different realm, with its socialist and communist legacy, and once had attempted and is now still experimenting with another brand of modernity with Chinese characteristics. But it has been increasingly integrated into the global capitalist system economically, if not so much culturally, not to mention politically. However, transnational cultural flows and consumption transcend ideological and political boundaries, and have increasingly brought the world and people together. Pop culture may open up larger spaces for critical dialogues and mutual understanding. Young Chinese audiences make good use of Japanese pop culture to make sense of their own life and society, rethinking the issue of cultural modernity and the path that their country should go through. They bring their own experiences and reflection into the consumption and appreciation process, creating a space for effective self-expression, catharsis, and escapism from the hardship of their real life. Through engaging in Japanese pop culture, Chinese audiences form new or imaginary cultural identity that negotiate through the political and social constraints of the Chinese society. Accordingly, transnational audience reception functions as a site of contestation, negotiation, and even resistance, in which transnationalism triumphs and a cross-border Asian modernity is in the making.

References

Appadurai, Arjun. (1996). *Modernity at Large*. Minneapolis and London: University of Minnesota Press.

Athique, Adrian. (2016). *Transnational Audiences: Media Reception on a Global Scale*. UK & Malden, USA: Polity Press, Cambridge.

Berry, Chris, Liscutin, Nicola, & Mackintosh, Jonathan D. (2009). *Cultural Studies and Cultural Industries in Northeast Asia—What a Difference a Region Makes*. Hong Kong University Press.

Blair, Gavin J. (2017, October 24). Tokyo Film Festival Thrives Amid Diplomatic Thaw With China. *The Hollywood Reporter*. Retrieved from www.hollywoodreporter.com/news/tokyo-film-festival-thrives-diplomatic-thaw-china-1049202 on 10/25/17).

Chen, Kuan-Hsing. (2010). *Asia as Method; Toward Deimperialization*. Durham: Duke University Press.

DeBoer, Stephanie. (2014). *Coproducing Asia: Locating Japanese-Chinese Regional Film and Media*. Minneapolis: University of Minnesota Press, 2014.

Fung, Anthony (2007). Intra-Asian Cultural Flow: Cultural Homologies in Hong Kong and Japanese Television Soap Operas. *Journal of Broadcasting & Electronic Media, 51*:2, 265–286.

Huat, Chua Beng (2004) Conceptualizing an East Asian Popular Culture, *InterAsia Cultural Studies*, 5:2, 200–221, DOI: 10.1080/1464937042000236711.

Huat, Chua Beng, & Iwabuchi, Koichi. (2008). *East Asian Pop Culture: Analyzing the Korean Wave*. Hong Kong, PRC: Hong Kong University Press.

Iordanova, Dina, Martin-Jones, David, & Vidal, Belén. (2010). Introduction: A Peripheral View of World Cinema. In Martin-Jones Iordanova and Belén Vidal (Eds.), *Cinema at the Periphery* (pp. 1–19). Detroit: Wayne State University Press.

Iwabuchi, Koichi. (2002). *Recentering Globalization: Popular Culture and Japanese Transnationalism*. Durham and London: Duke University Press.

_____(2004) (ed.). *Feeling Asian Modernities: Transnational Consumption of Japanese TV Dramas*. Hong Kong University Press.

_____(2010). Globalization, East Asian Media Cultures and their Publics, *Asian Journal of Communication*, 20:2, 197–212, DOI: 10.1080/01292981003693385.

Jin, Dal Yong, & Lee, Dong-Hoo. (2007). The Birth of East Asia—Cultural Regionalization through Co-Production Strategies, in Hybrid Media, Ambivalent Feelings Media Co-Productions and Cultural Negotiations, Special edition of *Spectator* 27:2 (Fall 2007): 31–45.

Jin, Dal Yong, & Otmazgin, Nissim. (2014). East Asian Cultural Industries: Policies, Strategies and Trajectories. *Pacific Affairs*. Vol. 87: No. 1, pp. 43–51.

Keane, Michael, Fung, Anthony, & Moran, Albert. (2007). *New Television, Globalizations, and the East Asian Cultural Imagination*. Hong Kong, PRC: Hong Kong University Press.

Lee, Vivian P.Y. (ed.) (2011). *East Asian Cinemas—Regional Flows and Global Transformations.* Palgrave Macmillan.

Leung, Lisa Yuk-ming (2004). Ganburu and Its Transcultural Audience: Imaginary and Reality of Japanese TV Dramas in Hong Kong, in Koichi Iwabuchi (ed.), *Feeling Asian Modernities: Transnational Consumption of Japanese TV Dramas.* Hong Kong University Press.

Naftali, Orna. (2018). "These War Dramas are like Cartoons": Education, Media Consumption, and Chinese Youth Attitudes Towards Japan, *Journal of Contemporary China,* 27:113, 703–718, DOI: 10.1080/10670564.2018.1458058

Otmazgin, Nissim. (2012). Japan Imagined: Popular Culture, Soft Power, and Japan's Changing Image in Northeast and Southeast Asia, *Contemporary Japan* 24 (2012), 1–19.

Otmazgin, Nissim and Ben-Ari, Eyal. (2013). Popular Culture Co-Productions and Collaborations in East and Southeast Asia. Singapore: National University of Singapore.

Saluveer, Sten-Kristian. (2014). *East Asia in Production: Media space, Film Markets & Co-Productions in Japan, Hong Kong, and South Korea,* Master's Thesis, University of Tokyo.

Taylor, Charles. (2002). Modern Social Imaginaries, *Public Culture* 14 (1): 91–124.

Taylor-Jones, Kate E. (2012). The Intra-East Cinema: the Reframing of an "East Asian Film Sphere," in *De-Westernizing Film Studies,* (eds.) Saer Maty Ba & Will Higbee, London and New York: Routledge.

Tu, Weiming. (1991). "Cultural China: the periphery as the center," The Living Tree: *The Changing Meaning of Being Chinese Today,* Daedalus; Spring 1991; 120, 2; pp.1–32. Retrieved from https://faculty.washington.edu/stevehar/culture-periphery.pdf

Wang, Xiaosa. (2020). Qiaoranzhizhong, riben xiaoaole pipianshichang (An overview of Japanese film market and China's import of Japanese movies), *Mtime,* February 6. Retrieved from http://news.mtime.com/2020/02/06/1601043-all.html On 2/28/2020.

Wenchuangzixun. (2017, September 15). Ribendianying zaizhongguo jiaohao you Jiaozuo, hanguodianying weihe jiu meiname shoudaijian (Japanese movies are both popular and critically acclaimed in China compared with Korea movies). Retrieved from www.tmtpost.com/2801207.html on 9/15/17.

Zhongyi, Wang. (2012). Riben dianying zai zhongguo de chuanbo ji zhongri dianying de hudong (The diffusion of Japanese movies in China). *Renmi Zhongguo.* Retrieved from www.scj.go.jp/en/sca/activities/conferences/conf_8_projects/pdf/p1.pdf on 8/7/17.

12

INTER-ASIA MEDIA/CULTURAL STUDIES IN THE ERA OF HATE

Ji-Hyun Ahn

Introduction

Media globalization facilitated by the development of communication technology has significantly de-Westernized knowledge production and the consumption of media content. As numerous scholars of global media studies have pointed out, the "West and the rest" or "core and the periphery" model is no longer adequate to explain the complex map of media flow in the current transnational and global environment owing to the rise of "contra-flow" and "multiple-flow" challenges to Western-centric media/cultural studies that are creating hybrid spaces in which the local meets the global (Iwabuchi, 2002; McMillin, 2007; Murphy & Kraidy, 2003; Parks & Kumar, 2003; Thussu, 2007). Asian countries vary greatly in terms of their cultures and social systems, and this variation has given rise to a fascinating landscape of transnational connectivity with regard to media and cultural production. As Asian media and cultural studies scholars have reported, the rise and fall of succeeding cultural "waves"—of Hong Kong action films in the 1980s, Japanese animation/drama in the 1990s, and the Korean Wave of the 2000s—have contributed to the development of an "East Asian sensibility," the key feature of which has been the active engagement of primarily young audiences or consumers with media and popular cultural content produced by East Asians and/or in the region (Berry, Liscutin, & Mackintosh, 2009; Chua & Iwabuchi, 2008; Erni & Chua, 2005; Keane, Fung, & Moran, 2007).

Here, I approach Asian media as a lens through which to view critical issues relating to globalization. In so doing, I emphasize the importance of an inter-Asian approach to media and cultural flow in and beyond East Asia that takes into account the growing geopolitical tension in the region. I begin with a discussion of the concept of "Asia as method" that was proposed and has been developed by some of the region's thinkers as a means to deconstruct the geographical notion of (East) Asia and to recreate it as a discursive space in which notions of Asian-ness, modernity, and (post-)coloniality are contested. This concept, I suggest, offers a useful theoretical framework for contemporary inter-Asia media/cultural studies. Next, I contextualize the emergence of inter-Asia media/cultural studies as an intellectual network and movement and briefly survey studies that have utilized such inter-Asian frameworks to examine the transnational circulation and consumption of media and popular culture in contemporary East Asia. Lastly, I draw attention to the impact of current geopolitical tensions on East Asian media and in particular the rise of nationalistic antagonism across the region. I consider in some detail the intersection of digitalization and media globalization with recent shifts in geopolitics in East Asia focusing on the importance of inter-Asian frameworks for the study of hate culture in the context of digital media.

Asia as Method: Rethinking Asia

"Asia" is obviously more than a geographical concept; as Chen and Chua (2000) explained the vast scope of the term,

> In different historical moments, 'Asia' has served different purposes, sometimes contradictory ones: as an abstract entity countering the 'west'/Europe; as a concrete geographical zone; as a physical space and an imaginary sign; as a mindset or a mood; as a unified civilization and non-unified sub-regions; as a location to be conquered; and as a method of constructing cultural identity.
>
> *(K.-H. Chen & Chua, 2000, p. 10)*

In terms of knowledge production, "Asia" is a discursive practice of producing particular types of knowledge about the region (Said, 1979). It is undeniable that the concept (or that of "the Orient") has long been considered conceptually as a counterpart of "the West," as if lacking autonomy and subjectivity. In an attempt to deconstruct Western colonial power, critique existing Western-centric approaches to Asia, and de-Westernize knowledge production generally, many thinkers in Asia have developed their own analytical concepts and frameworks to theorize (postcolonial) Asian modernity (Bhabha, 1990; Chakrabarty, 2000; Spivak, 2008). The concept of "Asia as method," first introduced by the Japanese scholar Yoshimi Takeuchi[1] in a 1960 lecture, is an early product of this attempt (2005).

Takeuchi, from his perspective as a Japanese scholar of Chinese literature, sought to rethink Japanese modernization; his consideration of China formed part of a larger project of developing a sort of pan-Asianism in the postwar world. His insight was to look beyond Asia as a specific geographical construct and to view it instead as a "method" for contemplating what modernity offered Asia and Asians by triangulating China, Japan, and the West (2005). While Takeuchi never fully explained what he meant by "Asia as method," his arguments were sufficiently suggestive to inspire many other scholars. Yuzo Mizoguchi, for example, another Japanese scholar of Chinese studies, adapted Takeuchi's perspective in his revealingly titled book *China as Method* (1989/2016), in which he theorized Chinese modernity in relation to European and Japanese notions of modernity and criticized approaches to these issues based on the linear, progress-oriented historical view that has informed traditional Japanese sinology. Mizoguchi's theorization of China as method represents an ambitious attempt to rewrite world history from a strictly Chinese perspective rather than through the lens of Western history.

Kuan-Hsing Chen, a Taiwanese scholar whose works have primarily concerned postcolonialism and Asian cultural studies, has also reworked and extended this approach to imagining a (new) postcolonial Asia. Making clear his debt to Takeuchi in his book *Asia as Method*, Chen (2010) proposed thinking of Asia as a polemical space through multiple historical junctures, such as periods of Western imperialism and Japanese colonialism. As he put it,

> Asia as method recognizes the need to keep a critical distance from uninterrogated notions of Asia, just as one has to maintain a critical distance from uninterrogated notions of the nation-state. It sees Asia as a product of history, and realizes that Asia has been an active participant in historical processes.
>
> *(Chen, 2010, p. 215)*

Asia as method, Chen further argued, could serve as an intellectual movement and practice and thus facilitate the crucial tasks of de-colonization, de-imperialization, and de-Cold War that

Asian nations need to perform. Because these three tasks are intertwined, indeed inseparable, they must be completed simultaneously so that each supports the others. More specifically, Chen (2010) insisted "using the idea of Asia as an imaginary anchoring point, societies in Asia can become each other's points of reference, so that the understanding of the self may be transformed, and subjectivity rebuilt" (p. 212). Approached this way, Asia as method should be perceived not only as a tool and a concept for use in criticism of Western constructions of Asia but also as an imaginative space in which various historical ruptures simultaneously overlap and compete and thereby offer meaningful reference points for each other. The arguments of Takeuchi, Mizoguchi, and Chen, therefore, suggest that "Asia" is better viewed as a concept than as a substance, the meaning and (conceptual) boundary of which are ceaselessly remade and reworked in the development of postcolonial, de-Cold War Asian nations.

The Significance of Inter-Asia Media/Cultural Studies

Chua (2004) argued that, because popular cultural products such as TV dramas and music have been finding audiences across national borders in East Asia since the 1980s, "East Asian popular culture" could be considered a meaningful subject for analysis. Indeed, with transnational media corporations and new media technologies now enabling the simultaneous circulation of media and popular cultural content throughout the region, East Asian popular culture has flourished and created an (imaginative) transnational cultural community, especially among the most recent generation of Asians.

Especially noteworthy in this respect is the emergence of a network of inter-Asia media/cultural studies scholars in East Asia since the late 1990s who have sought alternatives to the hegemony and normative status of the West. The launch of the peer-reviewed journal *Inter-Asia Cultural Studies* in 2000 exemplified this endeavor. In articulating its goals and scope, Chen and Chua (2007a), the key editors of the journal, wrote,

> One of the tasks of the journal is to build a platform for an "Inter-Asia" intellectual community by creating links between and across local circles. Therefore, the journal performs a double function: (1) linking together communities in Asia; and (2) linking Asia to the global community. (p. 2)

As part of this initiative, the Inter-Asia Cultural Studies Society was established in 2004 and in 2005 began organizing a biennial conference that has provided various venues and outlets for scholars to present their research and exchange ideas.

Thanks to these efforts, inter-Asia media/cultural studies thrived and grew throughout the 2000s in step with the increasing transnational circulation and consumption of media and popular culture, which was in turn fueled by new media technologies and the growth of creative industries in East Asia. Adapting the transnational approach to Asian media in various ways, scholars have tackled such important and pressing issues as (mass-)mediated identity, co-production, historical memory, Asian modernity, and geopolitics (Berry et al., 2009; K.-H. Chen & Chua, 2007b; Chua & Iwabuchi, 2008; Erni & Chua, 2005). These studies intentionally moved beyond the boundaries of individual nation-states and directed attention to the intersection of the transnational production and consumption of media and popular culture with local, regional, and global contexts of postcolonial Asia.

Scholars of inter-Asia media/cultural studies have naturally been eager to develop frameworks that can help them to sharpen their analysis of transnational and inter-Asian subjects. Building further on the Asia-as-method approach, some have proposed similar approaches and concepts, such as Chua's (2010) "East Asian pop culture studies," Cho's (2011) "East Asian sensibilities," Iwabuchi's (2013) "inter-Asian referencing," and Kloet, Chow, and Chong's (2019) "trans-Asia as method." These scholars have advanced cross-border dialogue and underscored the need for and utility of inter-Asian approaches. Thus, for instance, Cho and Zhu (2017) examined the adaptation of Korean TV formats in China through their reframing as cultural assemblages. Likewise, Jung and Hirata (2012) studied conflicting agendas among K-pop fans in Japan, K-pop management companies (and their marketing strategies), and Japanese mainstream media outlets (which have reinforced a male gaze on K-pop fandom) in the context of the influx of K-pop girl groups into Japan. Similar studies have offered trans-local readings of Japanese dramas across Asia (Iwabuchi, 2004), shed light on online Chinese fans of Japanese dramas (Hu, 2005), explored the consumption of Korean dramas by men in Hong Kong (Lin & Tong, 2007), and considered the daily cultural practices of Indonesian fans of Korean dramas and popular culture (Jeong, Lee, & Lee, 2017). This body of literature attests to the productivity of an approach founded on inter-Asian comparison and collaboration in a de-nationalized manner.

While Japanese popular culture provided the primary cultural texts for young (regional) audiences in the 1990s, in the present century, Korean popular culture has become increasingly popular and influential, producing content that has inspired the formation of transnational interpretive communities across and even beyond Asia. The Korean Wave has accordingly emerged as an important research field for media and cultural studies scholars in terms of providing perspectives on transnational media flow, media/cultural imperialism, transnationalism, and hybridity in culture and identity. Thus many studies of the Korean Wave have highlighted its transformation of the relationship between the local and the global and its creation of hybrid space for the media as an industry, for media content, and for audiences (Chua & Iwabuchi, 2008; Jin, 2016; Jung, 2011; Kim, 2013; Lee & Nornes, 2015).[2] More importantly, the popular cultural content produced by Korean media outlets has offered and generated meaningful reference points for "understanding modern trajectories of Asian countries in a new critical light" (Iwabuchi, 2013, p. 44) by showing national and regional specific images and markers of Asian modernity that are "neither identifiable nor incommensurate with Euro-American modernity" (Cho, 2011, p. 395). In sum, inter-Asia media/cultural studies has provided frameworks useful for examining the transnational flow of media and popular culture into and out of Asia and has nurtured cross-border dialogues, thereby yielding much grounded knowledge relating to cultural politics in Asia in the era of globalization.

Hate, Geopolitics, and Inter-Asia Media/Cultural Studies

The cross-border dialogue forged by inter-Asia media/cultural studies does not, however, necessarily yield a utopian vision of harmonious Asia. As Iwabuchi (2013) astutely pointed out, "East Asian media culture connection has brought about not just cross-boundary dialogues but also cross-boundary disparity, division, antagonism and marginalization in various overlapping ways" (p. 49). In recent years, the situation has become increasingly complicated as the development of digital media has enabled the rapid and easy circulation of information, some of it in the form of rumor and "fake news." In the meantime, power imbalances and the uneven flow of media/cultural content among Asian nations remain salient issues, and unshared-ness—particularly with respect to historical memories and territorial disputes—retains the capacity to generate (political) conflict at any time. As globalization proceeds and communication technology becomes increasingly sophisticated, the challenges that scholars face and the inquiries in which they engage evolve. I return to these considerations later in this chapter in a discussion of shifts in social conditions to which, I suggest, scholars of inter-Asia media/cultural studies must give serious consideration and of the key research questions and agendas in the current era of hate politics.

The Changing Political Landscape Worldwide and in East Asia

The rise of populism and isolationist nationalism across the globe, from Europe to North and South America to Asia, certainly casts globalization today in a different light than was the case earlier, when the belief was common that the result of globalization would be a brighter future with societies becoming increasingly open. The current moment is dominated by anti-globalist, anti-immigrant, and protectionist movements that are gaining power and popularity in many countries around the world, as reflected in, for example, responses to the Syrian refugee crisis in Europe, the Trump administration's plan to build a wall across the US-Mexico border, and the recent departure of Britain from the European Union known as "Brexit." These developments indicate that national borders, recently thought to be weakening, are in fact becoming increasingly rigid and salient. The resurgence of nationalism (or re-nationalization), then, demands close scrutiny of the manner in which globalization simultaneously propels and hinders mediated collectivities in spaces beyond nation-centered imaginations and frameworks.

Along with the rise of right-wing populism around the globe, the ever-evolving situation in East Asia—in particular, China's rise and its expanding cultural and political impact on the region and beyond—deserves further attention in this regard. Especially relevant to the present discussion, Ching (2015) argued regarding the emergence of neo-regionalism in East Asia, "two regional developments under global capitalism—the rise of China and the Korean Wave—have radically transformed the Japan-centric model of an imagined regional integration" (p. 39). In other words, the global success and popularity of Korean popular culture together with the rise of China in the world economy and international relations/politics have significantly de-Westernized the regional and global orders, and one result of this shift has been a decrease in—though to be sure not the withering away of—Japan's influence over regional politics. More broadly, this geopolitical shift has certainly caused or renewed tensions, conflicts, and antagonisms within the region.

The tense relationships among China, South Korea (hereafter simply "Korea"), and Japan over issues ranging from the presentation of history in school textbooks to territorial disputes (i.e., between Korea and Japan over the Dokdo/Takeshima Islands and between China and Japan over the Diaoyu/Senkaku Islands) well demonstrate the ongoing political and historical struggles in the region. The resolution of these conflicts is difficult to imagine, especially in the circumstances just described, with (physical) national borders being increasingly contested. In the case of China, in addition to the country's conflicts with neighboring countries, its relations with ethnic Chinese populations in Taiwan (the Republic of China) and Hong Kong have also been tense and have been generating geopolitical friction. Thus, for instance, the Sunflower Movement[3] in Taiwan (2014) along with the Umbrella Movement[4] (2014) and more recent extradition protests (2019) in Hong Kong clearly manifest anxiety (and fear) regarding Chinese opposition to the efforts of citizens of Taiwan and Hong Kong to control their own affairs, which inevitably undermines regional stability. As such, China's desire to be the next leading global powerhouse has resulted in various levels of antagonism toward China across the region.

It is, then, the task of inter-Asia media/cultural studies to examine how the evolving regional and international situations impact and are affected by the cultural consumption patterns of regional audiences. The popular cultural arena abounds with examples of the complex interplay between politics and culture in the context of China's rise and Korea's exertion of soft power through the Korean Wave. Noteworthy in this regard is the Chinese government's (temporary) ban on Korean media and popular culture and Chinese citizens' boycotting of the Korea-based conglomerate Lotte following Korea's announcement in 2016 of plans to deploy the controversial Terminal High Altitude Area Defense (THAAD) system; the ban demonstrated the potential for political tension at the state level to affect transnational media and cultural flow between the two countries (see L. Chen, 2017; Park, Lee, & Seo, 2019). In their study of state intervention in the consumption of Korean dramas in China, Park et al. (2019) argued that the regulations imposed on Korean TV programs following the THAAD dispute should be understood in the larger context of the Chinese government's control over the Internet and the inflow of foreign media content and of capitalist culture generally.

In a similar vein, K-pop is hybrid and transnational in every respect—including the capital that finances it, the composers of the songs, the origins of the members of the various groups, and the fashions and styles that it promotes. While its transnational nature facilitates its global spread, this aspect of K-pop can also be a source of controversy, so that K-pop stars' bodies at times serve as symbolic sites of cultural contestation where regional nationalisms flare and antagonistic geopolitics play out (Fedorenko, 2017). I and a colleague (see Ahn & Lin, 2019), for instance, have explored the specific case known as the "Tzuyu incident," in which a Taiwanese member of a K-pop girl group known as TWICE waved a Taiwanese flag during appearances on a Korean TV show, leading to a range of responses among the various audiences—Korean, Chinese, and Taiwanese—of K-pop. This incident, we argued, is another example of the complexity of the relationships among Korea, China, and Taiwan at the intersection of commercialism and nationalism. Again, the tension between politics and culture in the region requires keen attention in the form of analysis from a trans-Asian perspective in order to transcend perspectives dominated by simple deterministic conceptions, economic or political, of cultural flow.

Digitalization, Hate Culture, and Media Globalization

Digitalization and the ensuing rise of online hate culture have further complicated the geopolitical situation in East Asia. It is indisputable that the development of communication technologies and the availability of digital media platforms have promoted the exchange of ideas and interactions among cultures and have facilitated the organization of various types of social activism, thereby effecting meaningful social change. At the same time, however, online spaces have also mediated and fostered hate culture and cybercrimes and the spread of misinformation, including rumors and "fake news," and propelled the (systematic) organization and development of hate groups that target individuals on the basis of gender, sexuality, race/ethnicity, and/or nationality. It is not surprising, given the transnational flow of cultural content discussed above, that similar types of online forums have emerged across East Asia for individuals, especially young, digital media-savvy users, to express extreme hatred, anger, and discontent largely unfiltered. Thus *Ilbe* in Korea, *Nichanneru (2-channel)* in Japan, *Tianya* in China, and *PTT* in Taiwan are representative of websites that have served as arenas for hate speech.

Under conditions including the neoliberal transformation of East Asia, the rise of China as a world power, and the growing influence of Korean popular culture in the region, then, nationalistic antagonism has been especially apparent in the online spaces inhabited by young people in China, Japan, and Korea (see Takahara, 2006/2007). A telling example is *Zaitokukai*, a citizen's group that formed to oppose the ostensible granting of special rights to ethnic Koreans residing in Japan and has in fact become the most popular and the largest anti-Korean organization in the country. The group grew rapidly online, attracting members through the effective use and mobilization of digital media content (Hall, 2018; Yamaguchi, 2013). Other studies have similarly revealed ways in which online spaces and digital platforms serve to nurture cyber nationalism and channel nationalistic antagonism. Thus Liu (2006) examined Chinese netizens' active engagement in an anti-Japan movement in 2005 in response to what they perceived as Japan's irresponsible attitude regarding colonial rule, and Qiu (2015) investigated image-driven cyber nationalism among mainland Chinese students in Hong Kong, while I (Ahn, 2019) in an earlier study explored the collective expression and circulation of anti-Korean sentiment by Taiwanese netizens that resulted in the creation of an (online) affective community. These studies corroborate the conclusion that the de- and re-territorialization of nationalism have been taking place at the juncture of the burgeoning development of new media technology on the one hand and increasing geopolitical tensions on the other.

As another contribution to inter-Asia media/cultural studies, I have also been researching the rise of anti-Korean sentiment across East Asia. More specifically, I take a transnational approach to anti-Korean racism by studying the creation and circulation of anti-Korean sentiment in online and offline spaces and the politicization of this sentiment in ways that channel racial antagonism in distinct ways in China, Japan, and Taiwan. In particular, I have examined the framing of anti-Korean racism by mainstream media and popular online forums and the channeling of nationalistic aspirations to form a particular type of ethnic nationalism. Based on my fieldwork in Taipei and Tokyo, I have concluded that anti-Korean sentiment in East Asia should be understood within the broader context of the shifting media landscape, which is characterized by interdependence among China, Japan, and Taiwan, as well as the evolving geopolitical situation. Thus, for instance, I have found that the increase in anti-Korean racist comments in online spaces in both Taiwan and Japan is partly, if not primarily, due to the fact that Korean national daily newspapers have started to provide both Chinese- and Japanese-language services online. This seemingly paradoxical finding points to the multi-layered nature of the problem. In some cases, the translations were inaccurate; in others, anti-Korean groups in Japan and Taiwan purposely quoted out of context the original articles in order to slander Korea and Koreans; these malicious users' postings then circulated widely in online spaces with little in the way of filtering or fact-checking. What I want to emphasize here is that, in the absence of a trans-national perspective on the interdependent and changing media environment across these nations, it is difficult to capture the dynamics of the formulation of anti-Korean sentiment across "old" and "new" media platforms.

Conclusion

The year 2020 will doubtlessly be remembered for the outbreak of the worldwide COVID-19 crisis. As the pandemic has spread across the globe and profoundly affected the daily lives of individuals in so many countries on multiple levels, one of its impacts has been to inflame racism against Asians in general and Chinese in particular, both online and offline, as potential disease carriers. Thus social networking sites and web forums have been embroiled in controversies over such racist postings and comments against Asians (again, often ethnic Chinese), not only in the Asian countries most affected by the pandemic but wherever the disease has been reported (Cummins, 2020). Such incidents challenge and indeed dismantle the notion of Asia as a specific region or territory in the sense that they call for a rethinking of precisely who is Asian and of the status of Asia as an imaginative space in an age characterized by hate politics propagated through digital media. Also in this context, the notion of Asia as method and the practice of inter-Asia media/cultural studies as a discipline have become even more critical for engaging with current anti-Asian discourses around the globe, providing as they do fresh insights into digitally mediated hate culture that transcend the limits of methodological nationalism through analysis of trans-national media and cultural flow within and beyond Asia.

In this era of hate politics, extreme populism, and nationalistic antagonism, I consider it all the more important to carve out space in which to practice and imagine collaborative networks, shared conversational spaces, and communities that can assist in combating the various forms of hate. Just as the work of inter-Asia media/cultural studies scholars has highlighted the need for trans-national perspectives on media and cultural flow and suggested the possibility of promoting mutual understanding throughout the region, the same sort of effort should be made to study and engage with the antipathy that is increasingly characterizing cross-border interactions. While nationalistic antagonisms have occurred simultaneously across East Asia, their specific development and content have varied depending on the local context, so it is crucial to study the distinct modes of mutual antagonism among East Asian countries from an inter-Asia media/cultural studies perspective. Such a perspective offers meaningful anchoring points for considering each nation separately and in relation to others and thus provides a basis for complex and rich accounts of the intricate relations among geopolitics, history, and culture in the region.

Notes

1 All Asian names in this chapter follow the American style, with the personal name preceding (rather than following) the surname.
2 It is, of course, beyond the scope of this chapter to provide a comprehensive overview of the scholarship on the Korean Wave; my point here is rather that the Korean Wave has been a crucial area of research in global media studies (See Chua & Iwabuchi, 2008; Kim, 2013; Lee & Nornes, 2015; Yoon & Jin, 2017).
3 The Sunflower Movement is a social movement led by university students that has protested the rush by the ruling Kuomintang party to sign the Cross-Strait Service Trade Agreement with People's Republic of China on the grounds that the agreement threatens Taiwan's economy and political autonomy.
4 The Umbrella Movement is the name given to the series of sit-in protests that took place in 2014 against the central government's decision to select the candidates for the 2017 Hong Kong elections.

References

Ahn, J.-H. (2019). Anti-Korean sentiment and online affective community in Taiwan. *Asian Journal of Communication, 29*(6), 445–463.

Ahn, J.-H., & Lin, T.-w. (2019). The politics of apology: The 'Tzuyu Scandal' and transnational dynamics of K-pop. *International Communication Gazette, 81*(2), 158–175.

Berry, C., Liscutin, N., & Mackintosh, J.D. (Eds.). (2009). *Cultural Studies and Cultural Industries in Northeast Asia: What a Difference a Region Makes.* Hong Kong: Hong Kong University Press.

Bhabha, H. (1990). DissemiNation: Time, Narrative, and the Margins of the Modern Nation. In H. Bhabha (Ed.), *Nation and Narration* (pp. 291–322). London; New York: Routledge.

Chakrabarty, D. (2000). *Provincializing Europe: postcolonial thought and historical difference.* Princeton, NJ: Princeton University Press.

Chen, K.-H. (2010). *Asia as Method: Toward Deimperialization.* Durham: Duke University Press.

Chen, K.-H., & Chua, B.H. (2000). An Introduction. *Inter-Asia Cultural Studies, 1*(1), 9–12.

Chen, K.-H., & Chua, B.H. (2007a). Introduction: The *Inter-Asia Cultural Studies*: Movements project. In K.-H. Chen & B.H. Chua (Eds.), *The Inter-Asia cultural studies reader* (pp. 1–6). New York: Routledge.

Chen, K.-H., & Chua, B.H. (Eds.). (2007b). *The Inter-Asia cultural studies reader.* New York: Routledge.

Chen, L. (2017). The emergence of the anti-*Hallyu* movement in China. *Media, Culture & Society, 39*(3), 374–390.

Ching, L.T.S. (2015). Neo-regionalism and neoliberal Asia. In L. Hjorth & O. Khoo (Eds.), *Routledge Handbook of New Media in Asia (pp. 39–52).* Milton: Routledge.

Cho, Y. (2011). Desperately Seeking East Asia amidst the Popularity of South Korean Pop Culture in Asia. *Cultural Studies, 25*(3), 383–404.

Cho, Y., & Zhu, H. (2017). Interpreting the Television Format Phenomenon Between South Korea and China Through Inter-Asian Frameworks. *International Journal of Communication, 11,* 2332–2349.

Chua, B.H. (2004). Conceptualizing an East Asian Popular Culture. *Inter-Asia Cultural Studies, 5*(2), 200–221.

Chua, B.H. (2010). Engendering an East Asia pop culture research community. *Inter-Asia Cultural Studies, 11*(2), 202–206.

Chua, B.H., & Iwabuchi, K. (Eds.). (2008). *East Asian Pop Culture: Analyzing the Korean Wave.* Hong Kong: Hong Kong University Press.

Cummins, E. (2020, February 4). The new coronavirus is not an excuse to be racist, *The Verge.* Retrieved from www.theverge.com/2020/2/4/21121358/coronavirus-racism-social-media-east-asian-chinese-xenophobia

Erni, J.N., & Chua, S.K. (Eds.). (2005). *Asian Media Studies: Politics of Subjectivities*: Blackwell Publishing.

Fedorenko, O. (2017). Korean-Wave celebrities between global capital and regional nationalisms. *Inter-Asia Cultural Studies, 18*(4), 498–517.

Hall, J.J. (2018). Japan's Right-wing YouTubers: Finding a Niche in an Environment of Increased Censorship. *Asia Review, 8*(1), 315–347.

Hu, K. (2005). The power of circulation: digital technologies and the online Chinese fans of Japanese TV drama. *Inter-Asia Cultural Studies, 6*(2), 171–186.

Iwabuchi, K. (2002). *Recentering Globalization: Popular Culture and Japanese Transnationalism.* Durham, NC: Duke University Press.

Iwabuchi, K. (Ed.). (2004). *Feeling Asian Modernities: Transnational Consumption of Japanese TV Dramas.* Hong Kong: Hong Kong University Press.

Iwabuchi, K. (2013). Korean Wave and inter-Asian referencing. In Y. Kim (Ed.), *The Korean Wave: Korean Media Go Global* (pp. 43–57). New York: Routledge.

Jeong, J.-S., Lee, S.-H., & Lee, S.-G. (2017). When Indonesians Routinely Consume Korean Pop Culture: Revisiting Jakartan Fans of the Korean Drama *Dae Jang Geum. International Journal of Communication, 11,* 2288–2307.

Jin, D.Y. (2016). *New Korean wave: transnational cultural power in the age of social media.* Chicago: University of Illinois Press.

Jung, S. (2011). *Korean Masculinities and Transcultural Consumption: Yonsama, Rain, Oldboy, K-Pop Idols.* Hong Kong: Hong Kong University Press.

Jung, S., & Hirata, Y. (2012). Conflicting Desires: K-pop Idol Girl Group Flows in Japan in the Era of Web 2.0. *Electronic Journal of Contemporary Japanese Studies, 12*(2).

Keane, M., Fung, A., & Moran, A. (2007). *New television, globalisation, and the East Asian cultural imagination.* Hong Kong: Hong Kong University Press.

Kim, Y. (Ed.). (2013). *The Korean Wave: Korean Media Go Global.* New York: Routledge.

Kloet, J.D., Chow, Y.F., & Chong, G.P.L. (Eds.). (2019). *Trans-Asia as Method: Theory and Practices*: Rowman & Littlefield.

Lee, S., & Nornes, M. (Eds.). (2015). *Hallyu 2.0: the Korean wave in the age of social media.* Ann Arbor: University of Michigan Press.

Lin, A.M.Y., & Tong, A. (2007). Crossing Boundaries: Male Consumption of Korean TV Dramas and Negotiation of Gender Relations in Modern Day Hong Kong. *Journal of Gender Studies, 16*(3), 217–232.

Liu, S.-D. (2006). China's popular nationalism on the internet: Report on the 2005 anti-Japan network struggles. *Inter-Asia Cultural Studies, 7*(1), 144–155.

McMillin, D.C. (2007). *International media studies.* Malden, MA: Blackwell Pub.

Mizoguchi, Y. (2016). *Bang-beob-eu-lo-seo-ui Jung-gug* [China as Method]. (G. Seo & J. Choi, Trans.). Seoul: Sanjini. (Original work published 1989)

Murphy, P.D., & Kraidy, M.M. (Eds.). (2003). *Global Media Studies: Ethnographic Perspectives* New York: Routledge.

Park, J.H., Lee, Y.S., & Seo, H. (2019). The rise and fall of Korean drama export to China: The history of state regulation of Korean dramas in China. *International Communication Gazette, 81*(2), 139–157.

Parks, L., & Kumar, S. (Eds.). (2003). *Planet TV: A Global Television Reader.* New York: New York University.

Qiu, J. (2015). Image-Driven Nationalism, Generation Post-80s, and Mainland Students in Hong Kong. *Positions: East Asia Cultures Critique, 23*(1), 145–165.

Said, E. (1979). *Orientalism.* New York: Vintage Books.

Spivak, G.C. (2008). *Other Asias.* Malden, MA: Blackwell.

Takahara, M. (2007). *Hanjungil Inteonet Sedaega Seoro Miwohaneun Jinjja Iyu* [The real reason why Internet generations in Korea, China and Japan hate each other]. (H. Jung, Trans.). Seoul: Samin. (Original work published 2006)

Takeuchi, Y. (2005). Asia as method (R. Calichman, Trans.). In R. Calichman (Ed.), *What Is Modernity? Writings of Takeuchi Yoshimi* (pp. 149–166). New York: Columbia University Press.

Thussu, D.K. (Ed.). (2007). *Media on the move: global flow and contra-flow.* London, New York: Routledge.

Yamaguchi, T. (2013). Xenophobia in action: Ultranationalism, hate speech, and the internet in Japan. *Radical History Review,* (117), 98–118.

Yoon, T.-J., & Jin, D.Y. (Eds.). (2017). *The Korean Wave: evolution, fandom, and transnationality.* Lanham, Maryland: Lexington Books.

13

DISCIPLINING TRANSNATIONAL POPULAR CULTURE'S COUNTER-FLOWS ON *FAMILY GUY*

David C. Oh

In 2016, *Family Guy*[1] aired an episode titled "Candy, Quahog, Marshmallow." Despite the episode's arguable lack of enduring cultural value, it is an important text because it is the first major popular cultural text in the US to address head-on the presence of Korean popular culture within its borders. Previously, K-pop performances were seen intermittently on variety shows or as a fleeting moment in a television show. What is unique about this case is that *Family Guy* dedicates the entire episode to its protagonists' interactions with K-pop and Korean television (K-drama). Unlike the *Simpsons* episode in which the family travels to Japan or even a later *Family Guy* episode in which two characters travel to India, the jokes in "Candy, Quahog, Marshmallow" are primarily about Korea's media culture. This is captured in the episode's title, which mocks K-pop as nonsensical, superficial, and saccharine. As such, the episode can be read as an early response by the US cultural industries to the counter-flows of a non-Western country's media culture. I read the episode as reactive, ideological disciplining that is intended to position its viewers against Korean media culture and its transnational US fans. It portends future responses, at least in the near term, to a rising Asia that is poised to at least provide an alternative to the near-ubiquitous domination of US media culture for more than a half century.

In the episode, Peter Griffin, the show's anchoring character and patriarch, visits Korea with his friends Glenn Quagmire, Cleveland Brown, and Joe Swanson. The friends are there to find the last episode of *Winter Summer*, a Korean "drama" in which Quagmire (he is referred to by his last name) starred. When Quagmire runs into his former co-star, Sujin, he decides to stay with her, but his friends try to convince Quagmire to return home by performing a parody of "Bubble Pop," a song by a K-pop singer, Hyuna. Though they are unsuccessful, Quagmire chases after his friends when he learns that he will have to share his bedroom with more than 20 of Sujin's relatives. Optimistically, the episode can be read as US recognition of the multipolar nature of global media. I posit, however, that the episode works to assert US and White hegemonic dominance through the use of mockery that is masked by what Colpean and Tully (2019) refer to as "pseudosatire."

The episodes are instructive about US media's response to the media cultures of Asian others. In an analysis of the parodic web series *Dramaworld* (2016), the only US text of which I am aware that represents the encounter with Asian media cultures, Oh and Nishime (2019) argue that because the text expresses fan admiration for Korean television, it creates hybrid possibilities, albeit one that still favors the White American perspective of its writer-director and its White female lead. With global media, it is helpful to keep in mind Kraidy's (2005) argument that while global media produce hybridity, it is still structured by the dominance of the West. Today, there are an increasing number of media centers that act as regional and increasingly international hubs (Iwabuchi, 2007). Yet, global flows do not radiate evenly from these different, global media centers.

As counter-flows grow in number and strength, it is important to study the counter-hegemonic impacts in the West (Thussu, 2007a). Thussu (2007b) notes, "There is relatively little work being done on how the 'subaltern flows' create new transnational configurations and how they connect with gradually localizing global 'dominant flows'" (p. 20). What the limited research on counter-flows shows is a hegemonic policing of Western media superiority. In studies of news, the object of most, if not all, work on counter-flows, non-Western news agencies are treated as deviant, untrustworthy sources of information (Samuel-Azran, 2009). Xie and Boyd-Barrett (2015) point out that CCTV, RT, and Al Jazeera English were given only marginal distribution and that they had to gain mainstream credibility by hiring US-trained staff and by producing US-based news. As such, their ability to be disruptive counter-flows is highly curtailed.

To study counter-flows, Korea is an especially interesting case. The Korean media industries have become an important hub in the international circuit of media (Jin & Yoon, 2017; Joo, 2011). In just a few decades, it has already decentered US global culture and has arguably displaced Japan and Hong Kong as the leading media centers in the East Asian region (Schulze, 2013; Siriyuvasak & Shin, 2007; Wilson, 2007). This was particularly visible with *Parasite*'s multiple awards at the 2020 Academy Awards. As such, Korean media have become a powerful source of soft power (Yoon, 2016) that has upturned antagonistic views of Korean with more favorable ones (A.E. Kim, Mayasari, & Oh, 2013). It is such a noteworthy counter-flow that Ono and Kwon (2013) argue it has begun to "re-world" the global cultural order. As media cultures like Korea's develop and find distribution on the borderless streams of the internet, it is increasingly important to study their counter-flows (Jin & Yoon, 2017; Oh & Nishime, 2019).

What the *Family Guy* episode highlights is the ways Western media texts deal with emerging media centers and the ways it acts in its self-interest to discipline interest away from these centers by marginalizing its fans. Korea is not only global media competition but also a racially different threat that is managed through mocking representations. However, to disparage Korean texts straightforwardly would invite criticisms of the show as xenophobic or racist. Sienkiewicz and Marx (2009) note that "...*Family Guy* has been given a free pass by dint of its network, aesthetic style, and timing in television history" (p. 107). The show uses its mash-up like visual aesthetic to insert stereotypical jokes about marginalized others in order to privilege its primary audience of young, White men (Sienkiewicz & Marx, 2014). Indeed, it frequently trades in derogatory racist, sexist, and homophobic speech (Ricke, 2012), particularly by characters who are themselves White, middle-class, heterosexual, and male.

Because the show is understood as satire, *Family Guy*'s mocking playfulness of people of color and women can be dismissed as a critique of the stereotype rather than the target of the joke. Simply being satirical, however, does not make the humor anti-racist when using racist tropes; rather, it depends on how the jokes are positioned (Lacroix, 2011). With satire, racial humor can be problematic because the target of the satire often does not deconstruct the stereotype but furthers it (Sienkiewicz & Marx, 2009). "The joke can demand a suspension of empathy, with the target being an object of ridicule not sympathy" (Billig, 2001, p. 268). This can be problematic because it breaks taboos against overt racism that convert overt expressions of racism into pleasure for White audiences (Sienkiewicz & Marx, 2009).

The dismissal of the overtly problematic representations is likely rooted in what is called ironic racism or hipster racism. Viewers think because they recognize the representations as racist, then it is appropriate to laugh at the jokes because they understand their superficial reflexivity as an indication of their own lack of racism (Dubrofsky, 2013). However, instead of countering the intention of the joke, self-reflexivity obfuscates it (Dubrofsky & Wood, 2014). Though previous scholars have argued that *Family Guy* mocks people of color rather than deconstruct stereotypes, irony provides discursive space because of the ambiguity around its explicit versus its intended meaning (Colpean & Tully, 2019; Goltz, 2015). Thus, in counter-flows, transnational Asian threats to US media hegemony are disciplined through the use of mocking ethnic humor, which escapes criticism because of its literary use of irony. *Family Guy's* encounter with the Asian Other has ambivalence as it visually represents Korea in recognizable portrayals that show the appeal of the media culture of the Asian Other, in its mockery of US American fans and celebrities, and in its postracist guise of "equal opportunity" mockery of both the US American characters and South Korean media culture.

Recognizable Culture and Its Ambivalences

US media frequently racializes Asian cultures by mixing different cultural signifiers into a monolithic, undifferentiated mass (Hamamoto, 1994; Shim, 1998). Although Korea is no exception as it is Orientalized in this way (J. Kim, 2015; J.S. Lee, 2007), it is striking that *Family Guy* largely avoids this monolithizing tendency by representing Korea with recognizable, differentiated images of ethnic specificity. The Korean characters and Quagmire speak Korean, and words are written in legible hangeul script. Though the use of language is stilted, excruciatingly slow, and not native in pronunciation, it is at least recognizable as Korean being voiced by Korean American actors, Margaret Cho, Sung Kang, and C.S. Lee as well as Chinese American actor Robert Wu. In addition to language specificity, an establishing montage features recognizable attractions and landmarks such as a statue of King Sejong, the Olympic Stadium, the Han River, Gyongbokgung Palace, and Seoul Tower while a soundtrack plays of the song "Oh, Victory Korea," a rock anthem popularized during Korea's improbable path to the 2002 World Cup Semi-Finals. Its mundane background images of alleys lined with retail businesses, the airport, and a bar also evoke recognizable Korea-specific spaces.

The show's ambivalent relationship with Korean media culture also features a clip of an actual music video from the now-disbanded group Sistar and their hit "Touch My Body." A later parody music video also references Hyuna's "Bubble Pop." For fans of "K.-pop," these clips can legitimate Western fan interests, which are frequently maligned in their countries of reception (Otmazgin & Lyan, 2013; Lee et al., 2020). For Western fans of Korean dramas, the parody of *Winter Sonata* titled *Winter Summer* clearly references the film's title and generic melodramatic elements. These representations demonstrate that the producers of *Family Guy* have Korea-specific knowledge—i.e., "done their homework." Thus, one of the consequences of the US's interaction with the counter-flows of Asian popular culture may be a more nuanced understanding of Asian countries' specificities. This challenges prior racializing tendencies, but the ethnically specific images also provide postracist cover for mocking images of the Korean Other.

Postracist Strategies

Postracism[2] is the belief that structural racism no longer oppresses people of color (Bonilla-Silva, 2010; Cramer, 2016). By postracist logics, if racism no longer matters, then explicit, race-conscious casting and race-sensitive portrayals are no longer necessary, thus creating the space not only to continue racism but to roll back progressive gains that have been hard earned (Ono, 2010). "Enjoyment of the postracial is pegged to anxieties of a post-white society and the re-exertion of white (masculine) sovereignty as a mode of racial reclamation" (Watts, 2017, p. 325). One way in which postracism works itself into representation is by demonstrating that racism no longer structures interpersonal friendships while centering the White lead (Griffin, 2015; Oh & Banjo, 2012; Thornton, 2011). In addition, racial triumphs of anti-racist films suggest that racism is confined to the historical past (Schultz, 2014) or through heroic White people confronting racist White villains (Bineham, 2015; Griffin, 2015). White savior films like *Dangerous Minds* (1995) argue that the lack of educational success for students of color is not structural racism—i.e., the underfunding of urban schools—but, rather, the cultural deficiencies of communities of color, which are only overcome by the courage and dedication of individual White heroes (Giroux, 1997).

More relevant for this analysis are the ways that comedy is used for postracist purposes. Perez (2013) observed that comedians are taught to use self-deprecating humor in order to safely make racially inflammatory jokes. The appearance of humorous, self-reflexive satire, which Colpean and Tully (2019) refer to as "pseudosatire," functions to disguise problematic racist representations by reinforcing rather than critiquing power. In their conceptualization, they argue that actual satire, perhaps borrowing from Bakhtinian notions of carnival, subverts dominant power; thus, texts that use the aesthetics of satire such as "ironic racism" but that reinforce domination in substance, are pseudosatire (Colpean & Tully, 2019). Though Oh and Banjo (2012) did not use the term pseudosatire, they similarly argue that the short-lived NBC show *Outsourced* uses a superficial appearance of balanced humor that provides cover for its racism and advancement of White supremacy (Oh & Banjo, 2012).

One way that *Family Guy* mocks White America is through its representations of US celebrities and kitschy patriotism. Using *Family Guy*'s pastiche-like style (Sienkiewicz & Marx, 2014), the show inserts two fake commercials, one that features Ashton Kutcher as a pitchman for Dr. Lee's Pet Engine Cooking Bags. The commercial features an overtly racist claim of barbarism when Kutcher tells viewers they can eat dogs and that the bags are not meant for babies while winking and saying, "But, they can be used for babies." Though the commercial's mockery of Koreans as dog (and even baby) eaters is its primary function, it also ridicules celebrities who go to Asia (this is most likely a reference to Japanese commercials' occasional use of Hollywood celebrities) to act as spokespeople for a quick payday. In another satirical commercial, a Korean tech entrepreneur orders an imprisoned Hilary Duff to dance while wearing only a bikini and high heels. This is an even clearer case of the show's mockery of B.-list celebrities, who are reduced to objectifying themselves.

In the episode's most famous scene, a parody music video based on Hyuna's "Bubble Pop," Peter, Cleveland, and Joe insult Korea as strange, while also presenting unflattering, kitschy images of the US in their unsuccessful attempt to lure Quagmire from his renewed domestic bliss in Seoul. During the song, the men have multiple set and costume changes, including Cleveland wearing a white, sequined jump suit with coiffed black hair, and standing in front of a Las Vegas marquee sign, a clear allusion to Elvis Presley; Peter as Colonel Sanders holding a bucket of chicken decorated with the stars and stripes of the US flag; Cleveland as the Statue of Liberty; and a dancing eagle in the Oval Office that wears only underwear decorated as the US flag while doing hip thrusts. The jokes can be read as the US being an undesirable place of lowbrow tastes, thus providing enough self-deprecating humor to be able to present mocking, Orientalist jokes and images about Korea. The show's mockery of the US is specific and limited to unexceptional celebrities and kitschy patriotism that functions to present a superficial, meritocratic guise of equal derision that allows the audience to believe that the show offends both Korea and the US equally. As such, the jokes activate postracism, which provides cover to discipline US fans of Asian media cultures.

Peter, Cleveland, and Joe act as embodiments of obsessive, emotional fans. When the men learn that Quagmire was in a Korean drama, they watch the old episodes of the series on videocassette. While watching the show, Cleveland says, "…if Heesun and Bong-Hwa don't get together, I'm going to kill myself." This can be simultaneously read as the emotional appeal of Korean television but also as ridicule for Western fans' emotional investments. After watching the penultimate episode, the men are hysterical when they learn that the last episode is missing. Unable to find the episode, the men immediately buy airline tickets to find the last episode in Korea. In Seoul, Sujin, the actress who plays Heesun in the drama, finds Quahog, and Joe cries, repeating "She's so beautiful," while his voice cracks. When the men finally watch the last episode, they cry and interact with the drama, asking why American Johnny had to leave his life in Korea.

In each of these scenes, the overdetermined point is that US fans of Korean dramas have abnormal emotional investments in dramas. This representation invites polysemic interpretations—that the dramas are emotionally powerful, that the dramas are melodramatic and feminized, and that US fans become bizarre through their interests. Thus, this works as acknowledgment of the text's dramatic qualities, as postracist cover, and as a way to discipline fans of Korean media culture. In addition to being mocked for simply having fan interests, a common experience for fandoms (Fiske, 1992; Jenkins, 1992), non-Asian fans of Korean popular culture commonly note that they are insulted for having interests in what is perceived as a racially inferior Asian Other (Oh, 2017; Otmazgin & Lyan, 2013). The show functions to legitimize the gendered marginalization of Korean media fans.

Strange, Feminized Other

With the protections of postracism and under the guise of pseudosatire, *Family Guy* mocks Korean popular culture and Korea as a feminized and bizarre Other, using hegemonic strategies of trivialization and marginalization (Artz & Murphy, 2000). The construction of Korea as a feminized Other draws on the hyperfeminization of Asia in the Western imagination (Espiritu, 2004; Oh, 2012), and this overdetermination of Korea as feminized trivializes Korean culture. In a patriarchal system that devalues feminine tastes as lacking artistic merit, the association of Korea with the feminine is the problematic, taken-for-granted reason for its ridicule. The jokes, then, function to reinforce Whiteness and patriarchy simultaneously. They imply that masculinity is preferred in media texts and that Korea is bereft of it.

There are multiple gags that feminize Korea, such as a hotel named the "Grand Imperial Kitty Kat," Peter's plastic surgery that gives him over-sized, sparkly eyes, and his joke that he wants to giggle behind his hand. Though these are interesting on their own, for this analysis, the focus is on the feminization of Korean media culture, specifically. This is manifest in the representation of the drama *Winter Summer* and K.-pop. In addition to the earlier description of the men's emotional, obsessive fan behavior, which points to the gendered nature of the texts, the clips of the show itself feature exaggerated melodramatic elements, which are gendered in the West (Burwell, 2015).

The first clip features American Johnny and Heesun at their wedding. As Heesun walks down the aisle at an outdoor wedding ceremony, a bus driver loses control and crashes into the gathering, hitting Heesun. The clip cuts to an extreme close-up of a candle flame that is extinguished by the wind, an overwrought use of symbolic meaning. The scene returns to Heesun rolling limply in slow motion because of the force of the bus's impact with Johnny yelling in anguish. The episode ends with credits rolling and a melancholic ballad playing. In the other clip, American Johnny boards a plane on a tarmac, sharing his final farewell with Heesun. After the plane takes off, Heesun is framed in a close-up with tears rolling down her cheeks while the ballad plays again. The episode, then, cuts to the men, crying and Peter questioning American Johnny's choice to leave Heesun.

In addition to its exaggerations of gendered melodramas, *Family Guy* also feminizes men in Korean media. In the first instance, Quagmire explains that he was cast in the role after seeing an ad for auditions, looking for a leading man who was taller than 5 feet 4 inches. Though the joke is explicitly about height, in the context of US media's tendency to feminize Asian men, the joke also functions by portraying White men as more masculine, working through height's signification of masculinity. Later, while watching the episode of *Winter Summer*, Peter remarks that a man is handsome, and Quagmire responds that the person is a woman. Like much humor, there are polysemic possibilities with this joke. It can be read as a joke that references stereotypes of Asian inscrutability and confusion, and it can be interpreted as gender-breaking ambiguity; however, its most likely interpretation, particularly given the direction of the humor throughout the episode, is that Korean men are insufficiently masculine such that they cannot be distinguished from women. As Whiteness works in opposition, the representation of Asian male femininity functions to masculinize White men in implicit contrast

(Nakayama, 1994). As such, these jokes point to White American anxieties about the threats of an Asian Other's media in challenging White male desirability through mediated counter-flows.

When it comes to K.-pop, however, there is some ambivalence represented in the gendering of the videos. The episode features two songs—one is a short clip of Sistar's "Touch My Body" from the actual music video, and the other is the parody of Hyuna's "Bubble Pop." Despite "boy bands" being more internationally and domestically popular, the episode only features women, which further feminizes and sexualizes K.-pop. Its sexualization is represented as desirable for the male gaze as Peter says, "What is this, and how can I make the rest of my life about it?" Though the "Candy, Quahog, Marshmallow" parody video is not particularly feminized through its visual representations, it is feminized through the song's aural aesthetics and intertextual reference to "Bubble Pop." The original song is well known for its sexualized imagery, particularly with Hyuna's hip gyrations during the "Bubble Pop" lyrics while wearing short shorts and miniskirts, flipping her hair, and showing images of red lips. Aurally, the musical phrase, "uh, uh, uh, uh, uh, uh, ew" in which the last syllable slides from a high to a lower pitch, also sexualizes the video and is incorporated into the parody. Thus, its references to K-pop overdetermine it as sexualized femininity, constructing women in K-pop as desirable objects while also creating distance from K-pop as identifiable subjects.

It is important to note that the episode also constructs Korea as bizarre, disgusting, and barbaric. This is, of a course, a common representation of the Oriental Other (Said, 1978). Asian culture and people are frequently constructed as dirty and diseased, threatening to spread their moral and physical filth into White society (R.G. Lee, 1999; Ono & Pham, 2009). This happens throughout the episode, including the Ashton Kutcher commercial about eating pet dogs and babies, disgusting food, and retching at the smell of kimchi. Asianness is marked as an abject Other through discourses of indigestion as a metaphor for rejecting racial difference (Han, 2007). Korea is also constructed as nonsensical and strangely collectivistic, with everyone getting the same "psychopath haircut," and as bizarre as roughly two dozen extended family members sleep in the same room. Thus, this first response to Korean media culture's inroads into the US is to not only feminize Korean media culture in order to masculinize (White) US American media culture and to assert the existing White media/racial order but also to demonize Korean culture itself as revolting.

Conclusion

When there are attempts to "re-world" popular culture with Korean media culture, the US-mediated response is one of ambivalence that manifests awareness of the challenge and a sense of begrudging respect, seen in the recognizable images and language that give ethnic specificity to Korea and its popular culture. It is also a respect that recognizes opportunities and threats to White heterosexual masculinity. The feminizing of Asia has long acted to masculinize the West (Espiritu, 2004), to present Asian women as objects for White men's possession, and to act as a colonial metaphor that justified possessing Asian lands (Marchetti, 1993). As such, the overdetermination of Korea as hyperfeminine flatters and presents desirable objects for White heterosexual masculinity. At the same time, it disciplines the threat by overdetermining the feminine and, thereby, associating feminine media as appealing to unsophisticated tastes. Thus, enjoyment of Korean media becomes marginalized because of its gendering. As US media industries encounter the multidirectional flows of contemporary global media culture, it should be expected that their responses will draw upon salient racialized discourses in order to contain the counter-hegemonic threat and to maintain the global hegemony of US media and White heterosexual masculinity. Yet, the containment cannot fully foreclose counter-hegemonic possibilities. Ideological seepages threaten to leak out and break its containment, which might lead to a more multipolar mediated global media.

Notes

1 *Family Guy* is a popular US cartoon aimed at a predominantly adolescent male audience. It is often lumped together with cartoons such as *The Simpsons* and *South Park*, and reruns play on the Cartoon Network's line-up of adult-oriented cartoon humor called "Adult Swim." The show's entertainment is primarily based in its juvenile forms of satirical humor, which frequently use straightforward stereotypes (Sienkiewicz & Marx, 2014). The show's popularity has been enduring, staying on air since 1999 and leading to two spin-offs by the show's creator, Seth MacFarlane. These include *American Dad* and *The Cleveland Show.*

2 Some scholars may be more familiar with the term postracial. I use postracism, instead, to emphasize that the belief is not about the end of race but about the end of racism. Other than the emphasis in the concept's name, there is no difference in how postracialism and postracism are theorized.

References

Artz, L., & Murphy, B.O. (2000). *Cultural hegemony in the United States.* Thousand Oaks, CA: Sage.

Billig, M. (2001). Humour and hatred: The racist jokes of the Ku Klux Klan. *Discourse & Society, 12*(3), 267–289. doi:10.1177/0957926501012003001

Bineham, J.L. (2015). How *The Blind Side* Blinds us: Postracism and the American Dream. *Southern Communication Journal, 80*(3), 230–245. doi:10.1080/1041794X.2015.1030084

Bonilla-Silva, E. (2010). Color-blind racism. In P.S. Rothenberg & S. Munshi (Eds.), *Race, class, and gender in the United States* (pp. 113–119). New York, NY: Worth Publishers.

Burwell, C. (2015). You know you love me: *Gossip Girl* fanvids and the amplification of emotion. *Feminist Media Studies, 15*(2), 306–323. doi:10.1080/14680777.2014.919335

Colpean, M., & Tully, M. (2019). Not just a joke: Tina Fey, Amy Schumer, and the weak reflexivity of white feminist comedy. *Women's Studies in Communication, 42*(2), 161–180. doi:10.1080/07491409.2019.1610924

Cramer, L.M. (2016). The whitening of *Grey's Anatomy. Communication Studies, 67*(4), 474–487. doi:10.1080/10510974.2016.1205640

Dubrofsky, R.E. (2013). Jewishness, Whiteness, and Blackness on *Glee*: Singing to the tune of postracism. *Communication, Culture, & Critique, 6*(1), 82–102. doi:10.1111/cccr.12002

Dubrofsky, R.E., & Wood, M.M. (2014). Posting racism and sexism: Authenticity, agency and self-reflexivity in social media. *Communication and Critical/Cultural Studies, 11*(3), 282–287. doi:10.1080/1479120.2014.926247

Espiritu, Y.L. (2004). Ideological racism and cultural resistance: Constructing our own images. In M.L. Andersen & P. Hill Collins (Eds.), *Race, class, and gender: An anthology* (5th ed., pp. 175–184). Belmont, CA: Wadsworth.

Fiske, J. (1992). The cultural economy of fandom. In L.A. Lewis (Ed.), *The adoring audience: Fan culture and popular media* (pp. 30–49). New York: Routledge.

Giroux, H.A. (1997). Race, pedagogy, and whiteness in *Dangerous Minds. Cineaste, 22*(4), 46–49.

Goltz, D.B. (2015). Ironic performativity: Amy Schumer's big (white) balls. *Text and Performance Quarterly, 35*(4), 266–285. doi:10.1080/10462937.2015.1070194

Griffin, R.A. (2015). Problematic representations of strategic whiteness and "post-racial" pedagogy: A critical intercultural reading of *The Help. Journal of International and Intercultural Communication, 8*(2), 147–166. doi:10.1080/17513057.2015.1025330

Hamamoto, D.Y. (1994). *Monitored peril: Asian Americans and the politics of representation.* Minneapolis, MN: University of Minnesota Press.

Han, A. (2007). "Can I tell you what we have to put up with?": Stinky fish and offensive durian. *Continuum: Journal of Media & Cultural Studies, 21*(3), 361–377. doi:10.1080/10304310701460714

Iwabuchi, K. (2007). Contra-flows or the cultural logic of uneven globalization?: Japanese media in the global agora. In D.K. Thussu (Ed.), *Media on the move: Global flow and contra-flow* (pp. 67–83). New York, NY: Routledge.

Jenkins, H. (1992). *Textual poachers: Television fans & participatory culture.* New York, NY: Routledge.

Jin, D.Y., & Yoon, T.-J. (2017). The Korean Wave: Retrospect and prospect. *International Journal of Communication, 11,* 2241–2249. Retrieved from http://ijoc.org/index.php/ijoc

Joo, J. (2011). Transnationalization of Korean popular culture and the rise of "pop nationalism" in Korea. *The Journal of Popular Culture, 44*(3), 489–504.

Kim, A.E., Mayasari, F., & Oh, I. (2013). When tourist audiences encounter each other: Diverging learning behaviors of K-pop fans from Japan and Indonesia. *Korea Journal 53*(4), 59–82.

Kim, J. (2015). From Cold Wars to the War on Terror: North Korea, racial morphing, and gendered parodies in *Die Another Day* and *Team America: World Police. The Journal of Popular Culture, 48*(1), 124–138. doi:10.1111/jpcu.12238

Kraidy, M. (2005). *Hybridity, or the cultural logic of globalization*. Philadelphia, PA: Temple University.

Lacroix, C.C. (2011). High stakes stereotypes: The emergence of the "Casino Indian" trope in television depictions of contemporary Native Americans. *Howard Journal of Communications, 22*, 1–23. doi:10.1080/10646175.2011.546738

Lee, J.S. (2007). North Korea, South Korea, and *007 Die Another Day*. *Critical Discourse Studies, 4*(2), 207–235. doi:10.1080/17405900701464865

Lee, R.G. (1999). *Orientals: Asian Americans in popular culture*. Philadelphia, PA: Temple University Press.

Lee, J.J., Lee, R.K.Y., & Park, J.H. (2020). Unpacking K-pop in America: The subversive potential of male K-pop idols' soft masculinity. *International Journal of Communication*, 14, 5900–5919.

Marchetti, G. (1993). *Romance and the "yellow peril": Race, sex, and discursive strategies in Hollywood fiction*. Los Angeles, CA: University of California Press.

Nakayama, T.K. (1994). Show/down time: "Race," gender, and sexuality, and popular culture. *Critical Studies in Mass Communication, 11*, 162–179. doi:10.1080/15295039409366893

Oh, D.C. (2012). Black-Yellow fences: Multicultural boundaries and Whiteness in the *Rush Hour* franchise. *Critical Studies in Media Communication, 29*(5), 349–366. doi:10.1080/15295036.2012.697634

Oh, D.C. (2017). K-pop fans react: Hybridity and the White celebrity-fan on YouTube. *International Journal of Communication, 11*, 2270–2287. Retrieved from http://ijoc.org/index.php/ijoc

Oh, D.C., & Banjo, O.O. (2012). Outsourcing postracialism: Voicing neoliberal multiculturalism in *Outsourced*. *Communication Theory, 22*(4), 449–470. doi:10.1111/j.1468-2885.2012.01414.x

Oh, D.C., & Nishime, L. (2019). Imag(in)ing the post-national television fan: Counter-flows and hybrid ambivalence in Dramaworld. *International Communication Gazette, 81*(2), 121–138.

Ono, K.A. (2010). Postracism: A theory of the "post"-as political strategy. *Journal of Communication Inquiry, 34*(3), 227–233.

Ono, K.A., & Kwon, J. (2013). Re-worlding culture?: YouTube as a K-pop interlocutor. In Y. Kim (Ed.), *The Korean wave: Korean media go global* (pp. 199–214). New York, NY: Routledge.

Ono, K.A., & Pham, V.N. (2009). *Asian Americans and the media*. Malden, MA: Polity.

Otmazgin, N., & Lyan, I. (2013). Hallyu across the desert: K-pop fandom in Israel and Palestine. *Cross-Currents: East Asian history and Culture Review, 9*, 68–89.

Perez, R. (2013). Learning to make racism funny in the 'color-blind' era: Stand-up comedy students, performance strategies, and the (re)production of racist jokes in public. *Discourse & Society, 24*(4), 478–503. doi:10.1177/0957926513482066

Ricke, L.D. (2012). Funny or harmful?: Derogatory speech on Fox's *Family Guy*. *Communication Studies, 63*(2), 119–135. doi:10.1080/10510974.2011.638412

Said, E.W. (1978). *Orientalism*. New York, NY: Vintage Books.

Samuel-Azran, T. (2009). Counterflows and counterpublics. *The Journal of International Communication, 15*(1), 56–73. doi:10.1080/13216597.2009.9674744

Schultz, J. (2014). *Glory Road* (2006) and the White savior historical sport film. *Journal of Popular Film & Television, 42*(4), 205–213. doi:10.1080/01956051.2014.913001

Schulze, M. (2013). Korea vs. K-dramaland: The culturalization of K-dramas by international fans. *Acta Koreana, 16*(2), 367–397. doi:10.18399/acta.2013.16.2.004

Shim, D. (1998). From yellow peril through model minority to renewed yellow peril. *Journal of Communication Inquiry, 22*(4), 385–409. doi:10.1177/0196859998022004004

Sienkiewicz, M., & Marx, N. (2009). Beyond a cutout world: Ethnic humor and discursive integration in *South Park*. *Journal of Film and Video, 61*(2), 5–18. Retrieved from www.press.uillinois.edu/journals/jfv.html

Sienkiewicz, M., & Marx, N. (2014). Click culture: The perils and possibilities of *Family Guy* and convergence-era television. *Communication and Critical/Cultural Studies, 11*(2), 103–119. doi:10.1080/14791420.2013.873943

Siriyuvasak, U., & Shin, H. (2007). Asianizing K-pop: Production, consumption and identification patterns among Thai youth. *Inter-Asia Cultural Studies, 8*(1), 109–136. doi:10.1080/14649370601119113

Thornton, D.J. (2011). Psych's comedic tale of Black-White friendship and the lighthearted affect of "post-race" America. *Critical Studies in Media Communication, 28*(5), 424–449. doi:10.1080/15295036.2010.518621

Thussu, D.K. (2007a). Introduction. In D.K. Thussu (Ed.), *Media on the move: Global flow and contra-flow* (pp. 1–8). New York, NY: Routledge.

Thussu, D.K. (2007b). Mapping global media flow and contra-flow. In D.K. Thussu (Ed.), *Media on the move: Global flow and contra-flow* (pp. 11–32). New York, NY: Routledge.

Watts, E.K. (2017). Postracial fantasies, blackness, and zombies. *Communication and Critical/Cultural Studies, 14*(4), 317–333. doi:10.1080/14791420.2017.1338742

Wilson, R. (2007). Killer capitalism on the Pacific Rim. *Theorizing major and minor modes of the Korean global boundary 2, 34*(1), 115–133. doi:10.1215/01903659-2006-029

Xie, S., & Boyd-Barrett, O. (2015). External-national TV news networks' way to America: Is the United States losing the global "information war?" *International Journal of Communication, 9*, 66–83. Retrieved from http://ijoc.org/index.php/ijoc

Yoon, S. (2016). East to East: Cultural politics and fandom of Korean popular culture in Eastern Europe. *International Journal of Media and Cultural Politics, 12*(2), 213–227. doi:10.1386/macp.12.2.213_1

PART IV

Digital Platforms and Globalization

14

EUROPEAN RESPONSES TO (US) DIGITAL PLATFORM DOMINANCE

Robin Mansell

Introduction

Europe positions itself as a leader in curtailing harms associated with the dominant digital platforms, yet the European Union's (EU) digital strategy aims to benefit from digital services economically. When European Commission (EC) President Ursula von der Leyen started her term in 2020, "a Europe fit for the digital age—empowering people with a new generation of technology" was one of six policy priorities (EC, 2019a). The aim is to ensure that Europe has a choice to "pursue the digital transformation in its own way" (EC, 2020b, 2). In this chapter, I consider tensions in European moves to govern digital platforms—among them, Google, Amazon, and Facebook, using a selection of "the layers of governance relationships structuring interactions between key parties" (Gorwa, 2019, p. 2). My aim is to reflect on whether it is realistic to expect the EU to succeed in governing platforms in a way that is consistent with upholding public values such as privacy and freedom of expression. The question is: can public values "be forced upon the [commercial datafication] ecosystem's architecture" (Van Dijck *et al.*, 2018, p. 138) when this ecosystem is dominated by United States (US)-based platforms (de Streel *et al.*, 2019), even in the presence of some 7,000 online platforms in the EU (Fabo *et al.*, 2017)?

The first main section contextualizes the EU's approach, highlighting tensions in its economic and public values priorities. A discussion of contemporary initiatives in Europe to strengthen its governance of the digital economy follows, highlighting the positions of state and business stakeholders and the risk that a "rush to regulate" will override citizens' rights. In the conclusion, I reflect on whether there are grounds for optimism that a distinctive European response to the dominant commercial datafication business model employed by the digital platforms will successfully avert the platforms' rights threatening practices.

Contextualizing EU Platform Governance

A harmonized approach to the governance of platforms is favored on the global level (United Nations, 2019) and the EU's approach can be characterized as diverging both from neoliberal approaches in the US and China's approach to market capitalism. The European approach typically is depicted as having achieved success in moderating market outcomes to better align with public values including fairness, inclusivity, and rights to privacy and freedom of expression, but there is growing concern about harms in relation to digital platforms.

European policy on the digital economy can be traced to the EC's *White Paper on European Growth, Competitiveness and Employment* (EC, 1993). This noted that the EU's economy was challenged by a "new industrial revolution" in which the US had already taken the lead. The need to mitigate adverse consequences was recognized in view of the potential for "an increase in the isolation of individuals, intrusions into private life, and moral and ethical problems" (EC, 1993, p. 93). Protecting citizens and removing obstacles to the development of the EU's commercial market were to be achieved by opening up the market to competition, promoting universal service, setting common standards, protecting data and privacy and addressing the security of information and communication systems (EC, 1994). A series of e-Europe strategies followed (EC, 2015). Today's Digital Single Market Strategy aims to enable access to digital goods and services and ensure a harmonized regulatory environment that protects citizens and drives investment in digital technologies (EC, 2019c). A recurrent refrain has been that while "Europe has the capabilities to lead in the global digital economy … we are currently not making the most of them" (EC, 2015, p. 3); and the market power of "some online platforms" typically is noted (EC, 2015, p. 9).

Whether the digital platforms should be required to exercise "greater responsibility and due diligence"—a "duty of care"—are the subjects of ongoing policy debate (EC, 2015, p. 12). At the same time, the EU's competitiveness is said to depend on investments in "big data", cloud services and the Internet of Things. Enabling the "free flow of data" (other than personal data) has been central to Europe's digital strategy, which is expected to achieve the "right balance between legitimate business interests and the fundamental rights ensuring the protection of personal data and privacy" (EC, 2016a, p. 5). Despite the emphasis on achieving a balance, the policy discourse strongly emphasizes innovation, efficiency gains, competitiveness and consumer choice (EC, 2016c). Concern about the dominance of a small number of largely US-owned digital platforms has been met with measures to remove barriers to the growth of the Digital Single Market so as to develop a leadership position in artificial intelligence applications and in the capacity to monetize data.

Since 2018, European moves to legislate—as in jurisdictions in other Western regions—have had an added sense of urgency, often linked to the widely reported Cambridge Analytica scandal when Facebook platform users' data was given to third parties. This scandal and other concerns about the dominant digital platforms have led the EU increasingly to favor "digital sovereignty"; the idea that European users, as citizens or consumers—as well as companies—must have control over their data. In addition, populist moves in Europe and election interference have triggered a perception of "a problem" around digital platforms with strong momentum toward new forms of platform regulation (Trust Truth and Technology Commission, 2018). Whether described as a problem of misinformation, harms to children, or algorithm bias, an "information crisis" has been associated with hyperglobalization, distrust of elite authority, and growing economic and social inequality. In this context, the digital platforms are seen as escaping public accountability and threatening older business models, especially those of news producers, and as contributing to a loss of faith in democracy. Policy and regulatory responses aimed at protecting freedom of expression and individual privacy in Europe are influenced by the ways in which tensions between economic value generation and public values and rights are managed through Europe's governance institutions.

Citizen Rights—Freedom of Expression

Freedom of expression is protected by Article 10 of the European Convention on Human Rights, the European Charter of Fundamental Rights and by the constitutions of the EU member states. Concerns about the spread of mis- or disinformation and its impacts on the polarization of public opinion have increased, despite evidence in Europe that the spread of such information is more limited than is typically assumed in the press (Newman *et al.*, 2019). In response, the EC has defined disinformation as "verifiably false or misleading information created, presented and disseminated for economic gain or to intentionally deceive the public" (EC, 2018e; 2019h: n.p.) and put an action plan in place. The plan addresses online content and behavior that are legal under EU law, but potentially harmful (EC, 2018a). Any moves to intervene in the market must be informed by a fundamental rights framework with restrictions on speech rights prescribed in law and only in pursuit of a legitimate aim which is "proportional and necessary in a democratic society" (HLG, 2018; Nielsen *et al.*, 2019, p. 10), and a code of practice on disinformation with reporting requirements for the platforms has been introduced (EC, 2018d).

Audiovisual media legislation also has been updated to address the hosting of illegal or harmful content, bringing video-sharing platforms within the regulatory framework (EC, 2018c, 2018d). Other measures with a bearing on freedom of expression include those to promote "the availability and accessibility of the broadest possible diversity of media content as well as the representation of the whole diversity of society in the media" (CoE, 2018, p. II.3). It has been observed, however, that these initiatives may encourage new platform practices of censorship or create incentives to host propaganda (Helberger *et al.*, 2019).

Citizen Rights—Privacy Protection

Measures for data and privacy protection include the General Data Protection Regulation (GDPR) (EC, 2016b) and updated legislation regarding the processing of personal data (EC, 2016d). Despite the global attention received by the GDPR as businesses sought to comply with its provisions when it came into force in 2018, it applies only to certain kinds of sensitive personal data (EC, 2016b). Nevertheless, this legislation does aim to give consumers greater control over personal data by requiring explicit consent for use of their data. An Open Data Directive addresses the "free flow" of non-personal data, encouraging platform self-regulatory codes of practice, and there are some data-sharing restrictions designed to respond to artificial intelligence and machine-learning applications as they come on the market (de Streel *et al.*, 2019; EC, 2019f). Consumer rights legislation has been updated to emphasize data minimization, purpose limitation, and protections for special categories of sensitive data (EC, 2019b), there is a new Electronic Communications Code of Practice (EC, 2019e) and, on the security front, the European Union Agency for Cybersecurity operates with a Competency Centre.

Notwithstanding these measures and their implementation at the member state level, evidence is accumulating that methods of obtaining platform user consent are insufficient. Privacy notices still lack clarity and the scale of data-sharing has been found (in the UK) to be "disproportionate, intrusive and unfair" and, in the case of non-special category data, "unlawful" (ICO, 2019). As the UK Information Commissioner's Office (ICO) put it, "individuals have no guarantees about the security of their personal data within the [platform] ecosystem" (ICO, 2019, p. 23). The advertising industry claims, in contrast, that European legislation designed to protect individual privacy is overly protective (Marotta *et al.*, 2019) and, so far, these platform governance initiatives do not appear to be suppressing the drive toward the growth of the platforms' commercial datafication ambitions.

Competition Policy—Toward a Level Playing Field

Competition policy plays an important role in the European digital platform governance mix. The Treaty on the Functioning of the European Union prohibits the abuse of a dominant position that may affect trade and prevent or restrict competition in the Single Market (EC, 2012). There is considerable equivocation about whether competition policy interventions are needed to address platform dominance. While it may be acknowledged that multisided platforms make it more likely that a platform owner will price at a level "higher than is socially desirable" (Evans and Schmalensee, 2014, pp. 11–12) and that there may be "room for intervention" (UK, 2015, p. 408), the focus has been mainly on examining potential harms to a representative consumer—there is no citizen and there are no politics in the predominant discourse.

There have been signs, nevertheless, that competition authorities in Europe are starting to take non-price barriers to competition into account, especially when they involve privacy and data collection issues (CMA, 2019; Crémer *et al.*, 2019; Digital Competition Expert Panel, 2019; Just, 2018). Policy measures are under consideration to remove barriers to competition to achieve better data access for companies that use it as a resource to generate revenues and profits as well as to ensure that data can be ported from one platform to another so that consumers can switch to a different platform (Crémer *et al.*, 2019).

The EC has moved to strengthen competition policy enforcement and to introduce provisions for interim measures such as fines while lengthy proceedings are ongoing (EC, 2019d). It has used its power to fine Google €2.4 billion for abusing its dominant position, a measure that is being contested by Google at this writing. In 2019, an antitrust proceeding was opened against Amazon Marketplace and its potentially anticompetitive use of commercially sensitive data (EC, 2019g). Consideration is also being given to whether digital platforms suspected of anticompetitive behavior should be required to demonstrate gains for their users if they expect to avoid punitive measures and concern is growing about the dominant platform role as "*de facto* regulator" (Espinoza and Fleming, 2019). However, evidence of the decline of local and national traditional newspapers in Europe in the face of the dominant content aggregation platforms (Nielsen *et al.*, 2019, p. 1) has yet to result in market intervention measures to secure a level competitive playing field or provide subsidies sufficient to sustain the industry.

Toward Improved Platform Governance

The EC's new Digital (or data) Economy legislative program is intended to be "fit for the digital age." It is acknowledged that "it may be too late to replicate hyperscalers, but it is not too late to achieve technological sovereignty in some critical technology areas" (von der Leyen, 2019: n.p.). This means "balancing" investment in data flows and artificial intelligence applications including the Internet of Things and robotics with European privacy, security, safety, and ethical standards as well as sustainability goals. A consultation on new legislation, from February 2020, aimed to ensure that the EU's digital strategy benefits all citizens and enables businesses to grow, innovate, and compete on fair terms and to develop an open, democratic, and sustainable society (EC, 2020a, 2020b, 2020c). A new Data Act to support a "data agile" economy is planned alongside an updated artificial intelligence strategy and regulatory framework (EC, 2018b). The ambition is to ensure that Europe can "act and decide independently and reduce over-reliance on digital solutions created elsewhere" (EC, 2020b, p. 4). The EC is confident that since "many countries around the world have aligned their own legislation with the EU's strong data protection regime" (EC, 2020b, p. 6), it is well positioned to promote its model of a "safe and open global Internet" (EC, 2020b, p. 6).

The EC also introduced proposals for a new Digital Services Act and a Digital Markets Act at the end of 2020, and there are plans for a European Democracy Action Plan to address election integrity (EC, 2020d, 2020e; Kayali *et al.*, 2020). The new legislation may maintain a conditional liability exemption for the platforms, but it also may introduce some modifications to recognize the platforms' "editorial functions" and market dominance. Provisions for governing algorithms used in automated filtering are likely to be introduced so that obligations to remove illegal content become binding, albeit with safeguards. The aspiration is to introduce a "simple" set of rules for removing harmful content that is not illegal.

Within the existing accountability regime, Germany introduced the NetzD.G. (network enforcement law) in 2018 with a complaint management infrastructure. Reports indicate that more than

70 percent of complaints did not result in removal of content, but there are concerns about content overblocking (Heldt, 2019; Tworek and Leerssen, 2019). A new digital antitrust law is planned, which is expected to emphasize access rights to "data relevant for competition" (EAE, 2019; Schoening and Ritz, 2019). The German government favors the idea of "digital sovereignty" and is promoting a federated European cloud platform to compete with Alphabet/Google Cloud, A.W.S., and Microsoft's Azure services (B.M.Wi., 2019) and to secure European data from reach of US law enforcement under the US *Cloud Act* (US, 2018). In France, a new law aims to protect cultural sovereignty, copyright, and minors (France, 2019; Mission Facebook, 2019).

From January 2021, the UK will no longer be bound by EU legislation as its post-Brexit future unfolds. The government's *Online Harms White Paper* (UK, 2019b) which emerged following intensive debate (UK, 2019a, 2019c), contained a long list of harmful (not illegal) content, often blurring the boundary between illegal and harmful content. At this writing, there is no clarity about how over- or under-regulation will be avoided or how independent of the platforms the government's approach to governance will be when it does not need to align with EU policy. The expectation is that legislation will seek to clarify platform responsibilities to keep users safe online, with new codes of practice for online content management and expectations for balancing freedom of expression and safety, especially for children, with the platforms' economic interests. The media and telecommunications regulator, Ofcom, seems likely to be granted responsibility for any new forms of platform regulation (Hern and Waterson, 2020).

Overall, the predominant approach to European platform policy and regulation is to seek a balance between economic interests and public values using a combination of measures (Afilipoalie *et al.*, 2019), with the German approach gaining in prominence as Germany took up the EU presidency in mid-2020 (Tambini and Moore, 2019). Some of its policy initiatives are clearly echoed in the "European Strategy for Data" which was announced in February 2020 (EC, 2020a).

The industry response to EU-wide and member state governance approaches is suggested by the High Level Industrial Roundtable's vision of Industry 2030. This offers a model that aims to anticipate and develop skills, foster social fairness and well-being, and promote competitive and agile business. Claiming that "Europe risks falling behind in this transformation" (ERTI, 2019: 7), privacy and ethical issues are treated as a trade-off with corporate access to data. Some platforms, such as Amazon, argue that new platform regulations are "unnecessary, inappropriate and unworkable impediments to innovation" (UK, 2015, p. 54). Google supports the aims of Europe's digital economy strategy but argues "there is no evidence that specific online services have excessive market power" and that it cannot be open about the technical details of its algorithms for fear of security breaches (UK, 2015, p. 518). Facebook has called for regulation, but on its own terms and relying on its own "independent" Oversight Board (Collins, 2020).

Some academic analysts are cautious about "duty of care" approaches to platform governance arguing, for example, that problems associated with platform power have yet to be thoroughly investigated. Thus, the UK should stop moving along the road of a duty of care regime, as this will lead Britain to become what might be called a "Digital Nanny State", undermining privacy and freedom of expression (Dutton, 2020: n.p.). Instances of harmful (not illegal) online content should be treated as specific problems with multiple potential solutions and it is argued that this is not feasible when the government aims for regulatory simplicity and gives broad discretion to the platforms and to the state with the risk of chilling freedom of expression (Tambini, 2019; UK, 2015, p. 314).

Conclusion—Reflections on European Dependency and Grounds for Optimism

In the 1990s, there were warnings about the harms linked to private sector digital gatekeeping in relation to the development of web-based portal services (Mansell, 1999) and, as McGuigan (2018, p. 6) points out, "the melding of behavioral science and data analytics … is not a sudden and exogenous disruption." The commercial logic of today's digital platforms amplifies long-standing concerns about digitally mediated means of linking suppliers with consumers or citizens using their data (Couldry and Mejias, 2019; Mansell and Steinmueller, 2020; Zuboff, 2019). Criticism of the dominant platforms is increasingly visible in European policy discourses. For example, "clearer rules on the transparency, behaviour and accountability of those who act as gatekeepers to information and data flows are needed, as is effective enforcement of existing rules" (EC, 2020b, p. 5). In the domain of competition policy, "based on the single market logic, additional rules may be needed to ensure contestability, fairness and innovation and the possibility of market entry, as well as public interests that go beyond competition or economic considerations" (EC, 2020b, p. 4). But, can Europe achieve sufficient leverage to achieve protections for public values in the face of its simultaneous support for commercial datafication strategies?

The policy discourse does acknowledge that digital platforms do not operate in a bubble of supply and individualized demand and that public values are not simply the aggregation of individual preferences. At the same time, however, European legislative moves frame harms associated with the platforms in relation to consumers who typically are assumed to be sovereign and free to choose what they do online. Economic and public value considerations in relation to platform governance are treated as distinct, rather than as inextricably intertwined, issues.

There is a distinctive approach to governing the "European internet" and its digital platform ecology and there are world-leading European moves to enhance individuals' privacy protection. However, as geopolitical relationships change, these measures are unlikely to be sustainable unless the European approach is replicated, or at least respected, by the EU's trading partners. In addition, many of the remedies under the "duty of care" regime rely on digital literacy training and on burdening individuals with the problems created by digital platforms; they require people (including children) to empower themselves by enhancing their general and data science literacies (EC, 2020a). The EU's recognition of platform-related harms risks becoming a justification for state control that infringes on people's rights and freedoms (Kaye, 2019; Rozgonyi, 2018). It is fostering a "spiral of privatized regulation" with a mix of self-regulation with some state oversight (Helberger *et al.*, 2018; Wagner, 2018, p. 223). EU policy does not seek to suppress the advertising-supported drive toward commercial datafication as the dominant platform business model. What can be priced, quantified, and calculated in the marketplace is privileged, although there are exceptions. For example, a Dutch court has ruled that the use of artificial intelligence and automatic surveillance systems to detect welfare fraud violates human rights and has banned the practice (Henley and Booth, 2020).

A more radical approach will be needed if Europe is to safeguard its public values in the face of US—(and Chinese-)—owned platform competition. In encouraging EU-wide platform champions as envisaged in the proposals for legislative measures from 2020 onwards—e.g., the federated cloud proposal—the policy framework promotes business models similar to those employed by the now dominant platforms, even if they do comply with data and privacy protection legislation and put ethical codes in place. Many features of the EU's governance arrangements are complicit in perpetuating exploitative business practices. A more proactive approach to tackling the risks and harms associated with the dominant platforms in a way that respects public values is unlikely unless it emerges from a denaturalization of the norms that legitimize commercial datafication practices (Cammaerts and Mansell, 2020). Achieving this will require a consideration of the limits of commercial data markets and, in turn, the political will to privilege public values above, not just alongside, the EU's economic goals. This seems unlikely despite a policy discourse that positions Europe as a global role model for the digital economy (EC, 2020b).

There may be scope for optimism, however. If European governance processes are opened to contestation over what European citizens value in their digital platform-mediated lives, the outcomes of consultation may generate opportunities to legitimize a shift toward the supply of platform services using models that do not rely on evermore intensive use of commercial datafication. Platform services have become infrastructural components in the lives of European citizens. This means that responses to their operations are needed before, not after, harms—around which there is an independent consensus—have occurred. A failure in Europe—as elsewhere—to devise alternatives to the commercial datafication model will mean that private (and state), not citizen, interests in the development of the EU's digital economy will be normalized as the priority. This will happen notwithstanding a policy discourse that calls for a balancing of these interests. If this process of normalization of commercial datafication strategies is not disrupted, the result will be inconsistent with the values of fairness, solidarity, accountability, and democracy that have long distinguished European governance arrangements as compared to the US and other regions.

References

Afilipoalie, A., Donders, K., and Ballon, P. (2019) What are the pro-and anti-competitive claims driving the European Commission's platform policies? A case study based analysis of the European Commission's take on platform cases. Paper prepared for TPRC47, Washington, DC, 20–21 Sept.

B.M.Wi. (2019) Project GAIA-X: A federated data infrastructure as the cradle of a vibrant European ecosystem, Federal Ministry of Economic Affairs and Energy, Berlin, Oct.

Cammaerts, B. and Mansell, R. (2020) Digital platform policy and regulation: Toward a radical democratic turn. *International Journal of Communication, 14*: 1–19.

CMA. (2019) Online platforms and digital advertising: Market study interim report. Competition and Markets Authority, London.

CoE. (2018) Recommendation on media pluralism and transparency of media ownership, Council of Europe Recommendation CM/Rec (2018)1, Strassbourg, 7 Mar.

Collins, D. (2020) WIRED opinion: Facebook must not be allowed to dictate how it gets regulated. *WIRED*, 20 Feb.

Couldry, N. and Mejias, U.A. (2019) The Costs of Connection: How Data is Colonizing Human Life and Appropriating it for Capitalism. Standford, CA: Stanford University Press.

Crémer, J., de Montjoye, Y.-A., and Schweitzer, H. (2019) Competition policy for the digital era: Final report. Directorate-General for Competition, Brussels.

de Streel, A., Kramer, J., Bourreau, M., Broughton Micova, S., Donders, K., Feasey, R., and Lemstra, W. (2019) Ambitions for Europe 2024: CERRE White Paper. Centre on Regulation in Europe, Brussels.

Digital Competition Expert Panel. (2019) Unlocking digital competition, Report of the digital competition expert panel, London. March.

Dutton, W.H. (2020) Jettison the digital nanny state: Digitally augment users. *Billdutton.me blog*, 7 Jan.

EAE. (2019) GWB-digitization law. Federal Ministry for Economic Affairs and Energy, Draft Bill, Berlin, 7 Oct.

EC. (1993) Growth, competitiveness, employment: The challenges and ways forward into the 21st century (White Paper). European Commission, COM(93) 700 final, Brussels, 5 Dec.

EC. (1994) Europe and the global information society: Recommendations to the European Council (Bangemann Report). European Commission, Brussels, 16 Mar.

EC. (2012) Consolidated version of the treaty on the functioning of the European Union (TFEU). European Commission, C326/47, Brussels.

EC. (2015) A digital single market strategy for Europe. European Commission, COM(2015) 192 final, Brussels, 6 May.

EC. (2016a) Digitising European industry: Reaping the full benefits of a digital single market. European Commission COM(2016) 180 final, Brussels, 19 Apr.

EC. (2016b) General data protection regulation. European Commission, 2016/679, Brussels, 4 Apr.

EC. (2016c) Online platforms and the digital single market opportunities and challenges for Europe. European Commission, COM(2016) 288 final, Brussels, 26 May.

EC. (2016d) Protection of natural persons with regard to processing of personal data. European Commission, 2016/680, Brussels, 4 Apr.

EC. (2018a) Action plan against disinformation. European Commission, JOIN(2018) 36 final, Brussels, 5 Dec.

EC. (2018b) Artificial intelligence in Europe. European Commission, COM(2018) 237 final, Brussels, 25 Apr.

EC. (2018c) Audiovisual media services directive. European Commission, Amending 2010/13/EU, OJ/L 303/69, Brussels, 28 Nov.

EC. (2018d) Code of practice on disinformation. European Commission, Digital Single Market, Brussels, 26 Sept.

EC. (2018e) Tackling online disinformation: A European approach. European Commission, COM(2018) 236 final, Brussels, 28 Apr.

EC. (2019a) 6 Commission priorities for 2019–24. European Commission, Brussels, 16 Jul.

EC. (2019b) Better enforcement and modernisation of union consumer protection rules. European Commission Directive 2019/2161, Brussels, 18 Dec.

EC. (2019c) Copyright and related rights in the digital single market. European Commission, 2019/790, Brussels, 17 Apr.

EC. (2019d) Directive to empower the competition authorities of the member states to be more effective enforcers and to ensure the proper functioning of the internal market. European Commission Directive 2019/1, Brussels, 14 Jan.

EC. (2019e) European electronic communication code directive. European Commission 2018/1972, Brussels, 17 Dec.

EC. (2019f) Open data and the re-use of public sector information directive. European Commission 2019/1024, Brussels, 26 Jun.

EC. (2019g) Opening of proceedings. European Commission, Competition Directorate, Brussels, 17 Jul.

EC. (2019h) Tackling online disinformation. European Commission, Brussels.

EC. (2020a) A European strategy for data. European Commission, COM(2020) 66 final, Brussels, 19 Feb.

EC. (2020b) Shaping Europe's digital future. European Commission, Brussels, 19 Feb.

EC. (2020c) White paper—on artificial intelligence—a European approach to excellence and trust. European Commission, COM(2020) 65 final, Brussels, 19 Feb.

EC. (2020d) Proposal for a regulation on a single market for digital services (Digital Services Act). European Commission, COM(2020) 825 final, 15 Dec. https://eur-lex.europa.eu/legal-content/EN/TXT/PDF/?uri =CELEX:52020PC0825&from=en

EC. (2020e) Proposal for a regulation on contestable and fair markets in the digital sector (Digital Markets Act). European Commission, COM2020) 842 final, 15 Dec. https://eur-lex.europa.eu/legal-content/EN/TXT/ PDF/?uri=CELEX:52020PC0825&from=en

ERTI. (2019) Turning global challenges into opportunities—a chance for Europe to lead. European Round Table for Industry, Brussels, 19 Feb.

Espinoza, J. and Fleming, S. (2019) Margrethe Vestager eyes toughening "burden of proof" for big tech, *The Financial Times,* 30 Oct.

Evans, D.S., and Schmalensee, R. (2014) The antitrust analysis of multi-sided platform businesses. In R.D. Blair and D.D. Sokol (Eds). *The Oxford handbook of international antitrust economics, vol I,* (pp. 404–450). Oxford: Oxford University Press.

Fabo, B., Beblavý, M., Kilhoffer, Z., and Lenaerts, K. (2017) An overview of European platforms: Scope and business models. JRC Science for Policy Report, Luxembourg.

France. (2019) Projet de loi relatif à la communication audiovisuelle et à la soveraineté culturelle à l'ère numérique. French Ministry of Culture, No. 2488, Paris.

Gorwa, R. (2019) What is platform governance? *Information, Communication & Society*, Published online 11 Feb: 1–10.

Helberger, N., Leerssen, P., and Van Drunen, M. (2019) Germany proposes Europe's first diversity rules for social media platforms. Media@lse blog, London School of Economics and Political Science, London, 29 Apr.

Helberger, N., Pierson, J., and Poell, T. (2018) Governing online platforms: From contested to cooperative responsibility. *The Information Society, 34*(1): 1–14.

Heldt, A. (2019) Reading between the lines and the numbers: An analysis of the first NetzDG reports. *Internet Policy Review, 8*(2): n.p.

Henley, J. and Booth, R. (2020) Welfare surveillance system violates human rights, Dutch court rules, *The Guardian,* 5 Feb.

Hern, A. and Waterson, J. (2020) Ofcom to be put in charge of regulating the internet in UK, *The Guardian,* 12 Feb.

HG. (2018) A multi-dimensional approach to disinformation: Report of the independent high level group on fake news and online disinformation. European Commission, Brussels, 12 Mar.

IO. (2019) Update report into AdTech and real time bidding. Information Commissioner's Office. London, 20 Jun.

Just, N. (2018) Governing online platforms: Competition policy in times of platformization. *Telecommunications Policy, 42*(5): 386–394.

Kayali, L., Heikkila, M., and Delcker, J. (2020) Europe's digital vision, explained', *POLITICO, 20* Feb.

Kaye, D. (2019) Speech police: The global struggle to govern the internet. Columbia Global Reports. New York.

Mansell, R. (1999) New media competition and access: The scarcity-abundance dialectic. *New Media & Society, 1*(2): 155–182.

Mansell, R. and Steinmueller, W.E. (2020) *Advanced introduction to platform economics.* Cheltenham: Edward Elgar Publishing.

Marotta, V., Abhishek, V., and Acquisti, A. (2019) Online tracking and publishers' revenues: An empirical analysis. Workshop on the Economics of Information Security, WEIS'19, Boston, May.

McGuigan, L. (2018) Selling the American people: Data, technology, and the calculated transformation of advertising. Publicly Accessible Penn Dissertations, 3159, University of Pennsylvania.

Mission Facebook. (2019) Creating a French framework to make social media platforms more accountable: Acting in France with a European vision: Interim report regulation of social networks—Facebook experiment. Submitted to the French Secretary of State for Digital Affairs, Paris, May.

Newman, N., with Fletcher, R., Kalogeropoulos, A., and Kleis Nielsen, R. (2019) Reuters institute digital news report 2019. Reuters Institute for the Study of Journalism, Oxford.

Nielsen, R.K., Gorwa, R., and de Cock Buning, M. (2019) What can be done? Digital media policy options for strengthening European democracy. Reuters Institute for the Study of Journalism, Oxford.

Rozgonyi, K. (2018). A new model for media regulation. *Intermedia, 46,* 18–23.

Schoening, F. and Ritz, C. (2019) Germany's proposed digital antitrust law: An ambitious project to regulate digital markets, *Hogan Lovels Focus on Regulation,* 31 Oct.

Tambini, D. (2019) Reducing online harms through a differentiated duty of care: A response to the online harms white paper. The Foundation for Law, Justice and Society, with Centre for Socio-Legal Studies and Wolfson College, University of Oxford, Oxford.

Tambini, D. and Moore, M. (2019) Dealing with digital dominance. Media@lse blogs, London School of Economics and Political Science, London, 5 Dec.

Trust Truth and Technology Commission. (2018) Tackling the information crisis: A policy framework for media system resilience. Report of the LSE Commission, London, Nov.

Tworek, H. and Leerssen, P. (2019) *An analysis of Germany's NetzDG law.* Transatlantic Working Group, UBC and University of Amsterdam, Apr.

UK. (2015) Online platforms and the digital single market: Oral and written evidence. House of Lords Select Committee on the European Union Internal Market Sub-Committee, London.

UK. (2019a) Disinformation and "fake news": Final report, eighth report of session 2017–19. House of Commons, Digital, Culture, Media and Sport Committee, London, 18 Feb.

UK. (2019b) Online harms white paper. Secretary of State for Digital, Culture, Media & Sport and the Secretary of State for the Home Department, London, 8 Apr.

UK. (2019c) Regulating in a digital world. House of Lords Select Committee on Communications, 2nd Report of Session 2017–19. London, 9 Mar.

United Nations. (2019) The age of digital interdependence. Report of the UN Secretary-General's High-level Panel on Digital Cooperation, New York, Jun.

US. (2018) *Cloud Act S.2383.* 115th Congress, 2nd Session, Washington, DC, 6 Feb.

Van Dijck, J., Poell, T., and De Waal, M. (2018) *The platform society: Public values in a connective world.* Oxford: Oxford University Press.

von der Leyen, U. (2019) *A Union that strives for more: My agenda for Europe.* Candidate statement for President of the European Commission, Brussels, 9 Oct.

Wagner, B. (2018) Free expression? Dominant information intermediaries as arbiters of internet speech. In M. Moore and D. Tambini (Eds). *Digital dominance: The power of Google, Amazon, Facebook and Apple,* (pp. 219–292). Oxford: Oxford University Press.

Zuboff, S. (2019) *The age of surveillance capitalism: The fight for a human future at the new frontier of power.* New York: Public Affairs.

15

STREAMING DIPLOMACY

Netflix's Domestic Politics and Foreign Policy

Evan Elkins

Netflix is a political organization. This is not to say that the platform's slate of content has a uniform or cohesive politics in the way that, say, Fox News does. Rather, the company engages directly in domestic and global struggles over ideological and technological power. In its programming, branding strategies, and attempts to influence global media content, trade, and infrastructure policies, the entertainment platform promotes a broad vision of globalized cultural and economic liberalism geared toward humanist principles, cosmopolitan branding, international free trade, technological disruption, and economic deregulation. The company maintains robust promotional and lobbying arms that promote a broadly progressive politics at home and abroad, while also using these principles to embolden the company's recent goal of moving into almost every national market around the world. That is to say, the company's alignment with liberal politics, both in the abstract and through its specific institutional relationships with the United States' Democratic Party, serves both public-relations and institutional/regulatory purposes. The company's espoused social and economic liberalisms signal its ostensible social values to the public and help build political influence at home and abroad.

Netflix attempts to promote its progressive brand while strengthening its foreign policy apparatus in order to gain footholds in global markets. To do so, the company has been working with international governments on issues like content and tax policies, peering with global ISPs to boost streaming quality, and engaging in other forms of behind-the-scenes diplomacy with state and private entities around the world. This chapter will explore the relationship between Netflix's cultural-liberal and economic-liberal politics in the context of the platform's globalization throughout the 2010s. More specifically, I will show how the platform embodies a blend of mainstream, 21st century, centrist-liberal domestic and foreign politics that help it achieve its corporate goals in the US and abroad.

Two of Netflix's connections to the Obama Administration underline the company's political ambitions. In March 2018, it appointed former US National Security Advisor and Ambassador to the United Nations Susan Rice to its Board of Directors, highlighting in a press release her ability to "[tackle] difficult, complex global issues" (though she has since left the Board in order to join Joe Biden's presidential administration as head of the Domestic Policy Council). A couple of months later, the company announced that Barack and Michelle Obama would sign a multi-year agreement to produce humanistic programs and documentaries for the platform through their Higher Ground production company. I argue that Netflix's relationships with powerful political actors and global encouragement of deregulation encourage platform-imperialist practices, while its cosmopolitan brand promotes the platform as a responsible, progressive global actor. The publicly visible elements of the latter practice at once ease and mask the behind-the-scenes wheeling and dealing of the former.

Netflix's Liberalisms

By claiming that Netflix is an organization built around a globalization-oriented liberalism, I use two different, but related, understandings of the term. One is an understanding of liberalism as a capitalist economic ideology based in free markets and a lack of regulatory oversight. I use this term broadly in ways that can incorporate variants and evolutions like neoliberalism, though I do not intend to understate the differences between these economic ideologies. Rather, Netflix embodies a reigning, late-20th and 21st century economic orthodoxy that involves the privatization of the digital commons, deregulation of technology and entertainment institutions, and cross-border free trade. The second is a more US-based, domestic understanding of the term as aligned with the center-progressive platform of the Democratic political party. Though it has shifted in important ways over the past 100 years, this liberal platform broadly promotes a combination of state- and market-based solutions to social problems, generally advocating for progressive civil-rights positions while not abandoning economic liberalism and capitalism.

In the United States, entertainment sectors have long been associated with this second form of liberalism through their political, financial, and promotional ties to the Democratic Party (Muscio, 1997). While conservative and right-wing figures certainly exist in Hollywood, movie stars, musicians, and Hollywood's trade unions have a history of advancing positions associated with liberal Democrats within the realms of civil rights and environmentalism—both superficially through promotional rhetoric and awards speeches, and more materially through political donations and partisan philanthropy. While stars and performers are the most visible line between liberal politics and the film and television industries, powerful figures like Jeffrey Katzenberg, Harvey and Bob Weinstein, and Steven Spielberg have long been cozy with Democrats. Furthermore, the Motion Picture Association of America (MPAA), Hollywood's major trade group and lobbying arm, was for much of the second half of the 20th century run by Jack Valenti, a former aide of president Lyndon Johnson. After Valenti stepped down in 2014, he was replaced by a successive series of former Democratic politicians: Secretary of Agriculture Dan Glickman in 2004, Connecticut Senator Chris Dodd in 2011, and Assistant Secretary of State for Economic and Business Affairs Charles Rivkin in 2017. As Netflix becomes an increasingly powerful player in Hollywood (it joined the MPAA in 2019), the same year the association dropped the "America" and rebranded as the MPA, it likewise becomes tied more closely to this political mechanism.

Netflix's espoused cultural liberalism does not simply come from its association with Hollywood's broadly Democratic institutional identity. The company's programming and branding practices reflect a generally progressive approach to cultural politics. Many of Netflix's highest-profile and most heavily promoted programs advocate feminism, anti-racism, and other forms of inclusivity. These include programs by alumna of *The Daily Show* such as *Patriot Act with Hasan Minhaj* and *The Break with Michelle Wolf*. The latter was particularly politically potent, due to it premiering not a month after its host performed a routine highly critical of the Trump Administration at the 2018 White House Correspondents' Dinner. The service has also released high-profile programming that highlights Democratic politicians and ideals. Many of these showcase famous and establishment Democrats, such as the series premiere of David Letterman's interview program *My Next Guest Needs No Introduction*, which featured a heavily promoted, hour-long chat with former President Obama. Others portray up-and-coming party figures. *Knock Down the House* (Lears, 2019) follows four Democrat women politicians across the US attempting to challenge incumbents, with its most notable example being New York Congresswoman Alexandria Ocasio-Cortez. So, while the documentary in some ways offers a critique of the Democratic Party establishment, it nevertheless highlights a vanguard in the party and places the platform—for a moment, anyway—at the center of zeitgeisty discussions about congressional politics and Ocasio-Cortez's political celebrity.

Netflix's patina of progressivism exists beyond its investment in US-based Democratic politics. More broadly, the company stresses cultural diversity and cosmopolitanism as central components of its brand image. For instance, it has recently promoted the power of its algorithmic recommendation systems to reveal previously unearthed affinities between people across cultural difference—an idea appealing to those with a progressive, liberal mindset. Specifically, over the past few years the company has made much of its suggesting that people from all walks of life might enjoy the same movie or program as part of a "taste cluster" or "taste community" (Adalian, 2018). Netflix brass routinely promote the taste cluster as non-stereotypical, because it does not lump people into taste groups based solely on their demographic identity (Roettgers, 2017). As I have argued elsewhere, the concept of the taste cluster presents the platform's algorithmic recommendations software and data-processing regime as a cosmopolitan force—something that is not purely cold and mathematical, but that also helps forge and reveal the commonalities that link people across demographic differences and geographic distances (Elkins, 2019). In other words, Netflix asks us to view its computational power, combined with the diverse slate of its programming, as a mechanism that promotes and celebrates cultural difference.

As this suggests, Netflix's politics stretch beyond its slate of films and programs. While the company's increasingly powerful place in Hollywood is consistent with the US cultural industries' ties to Democrats, the company's centrist-capitalist liberalism reflects the general political tenor of its original, primary institutional home: the Silicon Valley-based tech industry. These politics embody a neoliberal framework of individualist enterprise, privatization of internet infrastructure, globalized outsourcing of labor, and deregulation (Levina and Hasinoff, 2017; Marwick, 2013 pp. 5–6). Silicon Valley's politics are complicated and less overtly tied to the Democratic Party than Hollywood, often reflecting a more outwardly libertarian perspective. At the same time, it has long advanced a version of mainstream, capitalist liberalism with a humanist bent. To this end, the platform's politics are also characterized in part by Barbrook and Cameron's (1996) "Californian Ideology." This refers to the dominant political dogma of Silicon Valley that blends the social liberalism of the hippies with the economic liberalism traditionally associated with the right but, at least since the Clinton Administration's zeal for deregulation, increasingly a component of the Democrats' stated economic goals. This libertarian streak means that while the tech industry has long aligned with the Democrats, it also at times allied with powerful Republican and right-wing figures pushing deregulatory policies and supply-side economics, such as Newt Gingrich and George Gilder in the 1990s and Peter Thiel and Larry Ellison later on (Turner, 2006). Even if the tech industry's politics are a bit murkier than Hollywood's, with several powerful figures leaning libertarian and right, it is nevertheless packed with powerful figures who regularly promote and donate to Democratic politicians and liberal causes, like LinkedIn founder Reid Hoffman and Facebook co-founder Dustin Moskovitz (Schleifer, 2020).

As a tech and entertainment hybrid, Netflix is an avatar for this blend of liberal-but-not-radical cultural politics and deregulatory (neo)liberal economic policies. Its political activities are apparent not only in its institutional, branding, and programming practices, but also in its increasing attempts to influence political figures directly. In 2012, it formed FLIXPAC, a political action committee that would allow the company to contribute directly to politicians and political campaigns. It is difficult to find much information about the specific activities and issues that the service attempts to influence through this committee, and regulators have raised concerns about the increasing power and influence of the company (Novak, 2016, p. 35). However, news and trade sources have suggested that the committee helps the company promote policies consistent with its tech-entertainment corporate context—namely, a "pro-intellectual property, anti-video piracy agenda" (Levinthal, 2012). Other reports indicate that the company and its committee are largely invested in influences debates about technology policy (Romm, 2014).

Through its lobbying mechanism, the company has pushed for technology policies associated with the Obama Administration and liberal politics more broadly. Net neutrality is one example of this. The

2010s saw a series of battles in the United States over the issue, with the Federal Communications Commission in 2015 instilling net neutrality rules by reclassifying the internet as a common carrier (though these rules were overturned by the Trump Administration's F.C.C. two years later). Netflix had an institutional stake in this fight, since overturning net neutrality could not only result in customers having to pay more to service providers in order to access Netflix via high-speed internet "fast lanes," it could also force Netflix to pay I.S.P.s for interconnection deals. Throughout the decade, Netflix allied with other companies like Facebook and Google via the trade group the Internet Association in order to push for and protect common carrier classification. The push for net neutrality represented a visible alignment with regulatory policies that outwardly supported a program proposed by Democratic politicians—and one that favored government regulation over deregulation. Subsequently, in an indication of the platform's complicated relationship to both the traditional Democratic Party platform and its straddling of the tech and entertainment sectors, it was less vocal in its opposition to the later overturning of the rule (Pinsker, 2017). This shift occurred as the company established itself as more of a Hollywood company than a tech one—abandoning the Internet Association and joining the MPA in 2019 (Martineau, 2019).

I do not intend to suggest that these political stances and alignments point out something deeper about the political "soul" of the company. In some respects, much of the above represents a set of common political and philanthropic practices in the 21st century corporate culture-industry: lobbying, progressive P.R., and cosmopolitan brand identity. Furthermore, issues of media and technological (de) regulation are in many ways bipartisan—with Democrats also favoring deregulatory policies and a few Republicans promoting net neutrality. At the same time, Netflix has been more explicit than other major streaming entertainment platforms in aligning itself with ideologies and powerful figures within liberal politics. While the platform's corporate owners often deny that the service has an overt, stated politics, Netflix nevertheless appears to be self-presenting as a responsibly liberal and cosmopolitan actor in a world that is veering toward right-wing nationalism. This is true not only textually, via the kinds of programming the service chooses to highlight, but also paratextually and institutionally, through corporate P.R. and lobbying and philanthropic practices. It is also apparent in the more direct links that the service has to powerful political figures—including former President Obama himself.

Netflix, Democrats, and the Obama Administration

Netflix is not simply "liberal" in a vague, aesthetic sense; it has financial, institutional, and personal ties to mainstream US liberal politics via the Democratic Party. Netflix Chief Content Officer Ted Sarandos' wife, Nicole Avant, served as the US Ambassador to the Bahamas under President Obama. More famously, however, the company announced in 2018 that it had signed a lucrative deal with Barack and Michelle Obama to distribute programming from Higher Ground. While Higher Ground has only released a few productions as of this writing, its documentary *American Factory* (Bognar, Reichert, 2019) won the Directing Award at the 2019 Sundance Film Festival as well as the 2020 Academy Award for Best Documentary Feature. The film tells the story of Chinese company Fuyao Glass reopening a closed General Motors plant in Ohio. Though not extensively a film about US *politicians*, nor carrying a straightforwardly didactic or partisan political message, it nevertheless carries a political valence in its illustration of the consequences of the financial crisis caused largely by deregulatory excess in corporate banking (and by institutions and executives that, ironically enough, the Obama Administration ultimately neglected to hold accountable) as well as the effects of corporate globalization and the erosion of labor power. In a broad sense, Fuyao's own globalized business practices and self-presentation mirror those of Netflix. Early in the film, an executive tells a group of assembled job applicants about Fuyao's global operations, suggesting that the company is "melding two cultures together" in order to create a "truly…global organization." Like Netflix itself, the glass company presents its globalized business ambitions through the aesthetics of intercultural collaboration while masking the less savory dimensions of its global expansion.

Indeed, if much of Netflix's above-discussed political identity seems geared primarily toward United States political culture, one notable Netflix hire points to the platform's globally political ambitions. In 2018, the company announced that President Obama's former National Security Advisor and Ambassador to the United Nations Susan Rice would be joining their Board of Directors. That Rice is not only a career diplomat, but somebody well versed in international conflict suggests that the service understands the difficulties that come with major firms attempting to globalize their operations—and in Netflix's case, with a geographic reach comparable to major tech and entertainment corporations like Alphabet and Disney. Hastings suggested as much in the press release announcing the appointment: "For decades, she has tackled difficult, complex global issues with intelligence, integrity and insight and we look forward to benefiting from her experience and wisdom" (Spangler, 2018a). It also points to the longstanding importance of media content, industries, and infrastructure to geopolitics in the realms of international trade, national development, soft power, cultural policy around content quotas, and concerns of cultural imperialism.

Even if Rice's appointment and the Obama partnership was part of a more global strategy, domestic and far-right outlets like Fox News and Breitbart have routinely critiqued Netflix for its ostensibly liberal programming as well as the platform's partnerships with notably liberal and Democrat figures, treating the service as a proxy figure in a longstanding culture war against a perceived left-wing media and entertainment sector. Examples abound of right-leaning publications accusing the service of cozying up to Democrats and proffering liberal programming. In response to *American Factory*, Fox News published an aggregation of other op-eds suggesting that the documentary was "slammed" as a bit of left-wing propaganda and "an attack on … president [Trump]" (Flood, 2019). Somewhat more subtly, Breitbart News tends to aggregate stories that highlight Netflix failures, such as dwindling subscriber numbers and growing debt—often accompanied by the same Getty Images photograph of Reed Hastings shrugging his shoulders. Even these stories regularly mention the Obamas' production deal and the platform's alienation of conservatives (Ng, 2019a, 2019b). Such stories tend to rather flimsily blame phenomena like lost subscribers and increasing debt on the supposed liberalism of the platform, when they can be more readily attributed to the rise of competing platforms as well as the speculation- and dept-based Silicon Valley funding model. At the same time, there is at least some empirical evidence to suggest that conservative ire at the service was not simply an invention of right-wing media. Polling from research firm YouGov suggested that the platform's approval rating among Republicans dropped while it simultaneously rose among Democrats in 2018—during the period immediately following Rice's appointment, the Obamas' production deal, and the premier of *The Break with Michelle Wolf* (Spangler, 2018b). While these few data points should not indicate a comprehensively empirical understanding of the brand's perception among a wide swath of the population, they nevertheless point to the fact that Netflix is, in the United States at least, increasingly perceived as having a relationship with liberal political institutions.

For its part, Netflix has attempted to thread the needle of maintaining its close relationship to Democrat stalwarts while claiming outwardly that the service has no explicit, stated politics. Sarandos said in part as a response to the conservative backlash that the platform would not be "the Obama Network" and that "there's no political slant to the programming" even as he acknowledged "a left lean to the creative community" (Barr 2018). The point, however, is not to pin down Netflix as "liberal" or "left-wing" in the binaristic way that US politics tends to be framed. Rather, it is to show how the platform's politics are part of its larger aim of self-promoting as a corporate avatar of humanist globalism. For many reasons, it would be wrong to claim that *American Factory*'s political significance comes only from its association with the Obamas. That would be an overly simplistic way of understanding the importance of the platform's politics—one that ignores the service's complex political economy and more globally oriented ambitions. Indeed, the documentary's critique of neoliberal global capitalism is somewhat ironic, given that neoliberal global capitalism is the milieu in which Netflix aims to thrive. But this is part of what makes the platform's partnership with the

Obamas a keystone in the platform's approach to cultural policy. On one hand, it can enjoy the liberal brand that the Obamas and Higher Ground bring to the platform. On the other, it can use the partnership to solidify its brand image as a purveyor of progressive content to the world. That the economic policies of the Obama Administration were more neoliberal, centrist, and ambivalent about organized labor than those implicitly articulated by *American Factory* is beside the point. The platform has built a brand strategy pushing itself as a benevolent, diplomatic force attempting to edify and enlighten global audiences with the help of a president who presented himself as trying to do the same. The diplomatic dimensions of this project are not simply metaphorical; they point to the platform's intensifying global policy apparatus.

Netflix's Foreign Policy

Calling Netflix a left-liberal service due to its alignments with the Obama Administration should not suggest that the platform is a direct extension of the Democratic establishment. Rather, the service's hiring of Rice and the centralizing of Obama within the brand ensure that Netflix has a relationship with powerful figures who can increase the platform's stature and influence throughout the world. The production deal with the Obamas not only provided the platform with progressively oriented content, it enabled Netflix to promote that content through a politician who, at the end of his presidency, enjoyed a high level of international popularity (Wike, Stokes, Poushter, and Fetterolf, 2017). If Rice is less of a household name and her specific role on Netflix's board was less publicly known, she nevertheless helped direct the company's international strategy as it navigated an increasingly complex set of national and regional regulations.

These regulations involve content, economics, and technology, all of which Netflix has attempted to influence and shape in various international markets. Recently, as the platform has entered into almost every global market, it has shifted its lobbying resources away from DC and into areas like attempting to shape Latin American tax policies and content quotas in Europe (Keegan, 2019). The content regulation issue has been a particularly difficult one for the platform, with the service both responding to and attempting to influence complex content regulations that vary significantly from country to country and can be shaped by both national and regional governance bodies. For instance, the European Union recently imposed local content quotas for its member states which platforms like Netflix must abide by, and the service has lobbied the EU—both behind the scenes and publicly in the press—to try to ease or clarify these rules in ways that would benefit the platform (Alexander, 2018). Furthermore, when the service first announced that it would be introduced in Kenya, the country's Film Classification Board threatened to ban the platform due to inappropriate content (Warner, 2016). Occasionally, local content regulations can lead to some challenging PR for the company, as in a highly publicized incident when the service pulled an episode of *Patriot Act with Hasan Minhaj* in Saudi Arabia after the program criticized the country's Crown Prince Mohammed bin Salman for his alleged role in the murder of journalist Jamal Khashoggi (Griffiths and McKirdy, 2019). Though not a particularly proud moment for Netflix, it points to why the company requires a diplomatic apparatus to navigate political minefields now that it has a global presence.

The platform also aims to influence policy around the world regarding issues of technology and infrastructure (Lobato, 2019, p. 85). It does so in part by developing relationships with ISPs, promoting high-speed broadband in regions where internet penetration is low, and even developing its own infrastructures (Barrett, 2016). The privatization of infrastructure, particularly in developing countries and the Global South, has become a significant development project for tech and media sectors, and Netflix's promotion of global high-speed internet should be considered in this light (Chakravartty and Sarikakis, 2006, p. 133). After all, the service relies on two primary mechanisms of corporate infrastructure: Amazon Web Services and the company's own Open Connect system, which is a series of servers containing cached Netflix content that the service supplies to ISPs in order to ease streaming traffic (Lobato, 2019, pp. 94–100). As I have argued elsewhere, the company uses this fight for faster broadband not simply out of the goodness of its philanthropic and charitable heart, but largely as a way to gain ownership over technological and economic development practices (Elkins, 2018). Netflix's global ambitions are thus part of a broader phenomenon that Jin (2015, p. 12) refers to as "platform imperialism," or "an asymmetrical relationship of interdependence in platform technologies and political culture between the West, primarily the US, and many developing countries, including…both nation-states and transnational corporations." In its political and diplomatic operations, Netflix has developed a means by which it can assert power in, accumulate capital from, and influence the cultural policies of nations around the world.

The international sphere is thus where the platform's liberal-progressive cultural politics act as a lubricant for its liberal *economic* perspective. Outwardly, Netflix promotes itself as cosmopolitan. This is consistent with the platform's stated desire to become a truly universal "global television network," to use an oft-repeated phrase of CEO Reed Hastings. But when companies call themselves "global," this blends several understandings and implications of the term together. "Global" can indicate a particular approach to culture—one that is cosmopolitan, inclusive, and that lacks a taste for the geographic and cultural borders that separate people and places—as well as an approach to economics—one based in a neocolonial entrée into other markets in order to expand economies of scale and engage competition in a variety of countries around the world. Media and trade outlets tend to discuss the platform's global ambitions in more aggressive terms, often suggesting that Netflix wants to "conquer" or "rule the world" (Barrett, 2016; Owen, 2018; Roettgers, 2017). Though often benign or tongue-in-cheek in their intention, such phrases nevertheless speak to the relationship between the platform's business practices and a perceived global political power.

Netflix wants its globalism to embody both humanist cosmopolitanism and free-market economic might, using the former in order to put a positive image on the latter. Its global image is part of what Havens (2018, p. 28) calls the service's "translational" brand, or its ability to promote its programs, and by proxy the platform itself, to a wide variety of different kinds of global audiences. Although Netflix is not the only streaming entertainment platform with global ambitions, it has been the most successful in terms of introducing a version of the platform to the most countries around the world, centering a globally cosmopolitan perspective as part of its brand, and building a legitimate policy and diplomacy apparatus to help smooth out the expansion. As the service increases its infrastructural, institutional, and onscreen presence around the world, its parlay of national political clout into global influence will do much to shape the scale of its international power.

References

Adalian, J. (2018, June 10). Inside the binge factory. *Vulture*. Retrieved from www.vulture.com/2018/06/how-netflix-swallowed-tv-industry.html

Alexander, J. (2018, October 16). Netflix criticizes EU over "content quota. *The Verge*. Retrieved from www.theverge.com/2018/10/16/17986086/netflix-third-earnings-report-european-union-content-quote-international

Barbrook R. and Cameron A. (1996) The Californian ideology. *Science as Culture, 6*: 44–72.

Barr, J. (2018, May 29). Netflix's Ted Sarandos on Obama deal: "it's not the Obama Network." *Hollywood Reporter*. Retrieved from www.hollywoodreporter.com/news/netflixs-ted-sarandos-obama-deal-not-going-be-obama-network-1115402

Barrett, B. (2016, March 27). Netflix's grand, daring, maybe crazy plan to conquer the world. *Wired*. Retrieved from www.wired.com/2016/03/netflixs-grand-maybe-crazy-plan-conquer-world/

Chakravartty, P., and Sarikakis, K. (2006). Media policy and globalization. Edinburgh: Edinburgh University Press.

Elkins, E. (2018). Powered by Netflix: speed-test services and video-on-demand's global development projects. *Media, Culture & Society, 40*, 838–855. Doi: 10.1177/0163443443473178187755446649

Elkins, E. (2019). Algorithmic cosmopolitanism: on the global claims of digital entertainment platforms. *Critical Studies in Media Communication, 36*, 376–389. Doi: 10.1080/15295036.2019.1630743

Flood, B. (2019, August 20). Obamas' debut Netflix documentary slammed as 'lefty propaganda,' an attack on Trump. *Fox News*. Retrieved from www.foxnews.com/entertainment/obamas-netflix-documentary-american-factory

Griffiths, J., and McKirdy, E. (2019, January 2). Netflix pulls "Patriot Act" episode in Saudi Arabia after it criticized official account of Khashoggi killing. *CNN*. Retrieved from www.cnn.com/2019/01/01/middleeast/netflix-patriot-act-hasan-minhaj-jamal-khashoggi-intl/index.html

Havens, T. (2018). Netflix: Streaming channel brands as global meaning systems. In D. Johnson (Ed.), *From networks to Netflix: A guide to changing channels* (pp. 321–332). New York, NY: Routledge.

Jin, D.Y. (2015). *Digital platforms, imperialism and political culture.* New York: Routledge

Keegan, R. (2019, August 8). The Netflix lobbying machine: inside the effort to sway policy worldwide. *Hollywood Reporter.* Retrieved from www.hollywoodreporter.com/news/netflix-lobbying-machine-inside-effort-sway-policy-worldwide-1229622

Levina, M., and Hasinoff, A.A. (2017) The silicon valley ethos: tech industry products, discourses, and practices. *Television and New Media, 18,* 489–495. Doi: 10.1177/1527476416680454

Levinthal, D. (2012, April 7). Netflix forms PAC. *Politico.* Retrieved from www.politico.com/story/2012/04/netflix-forms-pac-074929

Lobato, R. (2019). *Netflix nations: the geography of digital distribution.* New York: New York University Press.

Martineau, P. (2019, January 23). Netflix now aligns itself with Hollywood, not Silicon Valley. *Wired.* Retrieved from www.wired.com/story/netflix-aligns-itself-with-hollywood-not-silicon-valley/

Marwick, A.E. (2013). *Status update: celebrity, publicity, and branding in the social media age.* New Haven, Yale University Press.

Muscio, G. (1997). *Hollywood's new deal.* Philadelphia: Temple University Press.

Ng, D. (2019a, October 17). Netflix misses subscriber mark for second straight quarter. *Breitbart.* Retrieved from www.breitbart.com/tech/2019/10/17/netflix-misses-subscriber-mark-for-second-straight-quarter/

Ng, D. (2019b, October 21). Netflix takes on $2 billion in debt as Disney, Apple launch competition. *Breitbart.* Retrieved from www.breitbart.com/tech/2019/10/21/netflix-takes-on-2-billion-in-debt-as-disney-apple-launch-competition/

Novak, A.N. (2016). Framing the future of media regulation through Netflix. In K. McDonald and D. Smith-Rowsey (Eds.), *The Netflix effect: Technology and entertainment in the 21st century* (pp. 33–48). New York: Bloomsbury.

Owen, R. (2018, November 21). Tuned in: Netflix wants to rule the world. *Pittsburgh Post-Gazette.* Retrieved from www.post-gazette.com/ae/tv-radio/2018/11/21/Tuned-In-Netflix-program-expansion-streaming-service/stories/201811190141

Pinsker, J. (2017, December 20) Where were Netflix and Google in the net-neutrality fight? *The Atlantic.* Retrieved from www.theatlantic.com/business/archive/2017/12/netflix-google-net-neutrality/548768/

Roettgers, J. (2017, March 18). How Netflix wants to rule the world: A behind-the-scenes look at a global TV network. *Variety.* Retrieved from https://variety.com/2017/digital/news/netflix-lab-day-behind-the-scenes-1202011105/

Romm, T. (2014, May 3). Netflix takes leading role in D.C. *Politico.* Retrieved from www.politico.com/story/2014/05/netflix-dc-106297

Schleifer, T. (2020, February 3). Tech billionaires are funding the Democratic Party whether Democrats like it or not. *Vox.* Retrieved from www.vox.com/recode/2020/2/3/21121243/silicon-valley-billionaires-reid-hoffman-dustin-moskovitz

Spangler, T. 2018a, March 28). Netflix names former Obama adviser and U.N. Ambassador Susan Rice to board. *Variety.* Retrieved from https://variety.com/2018/digital/news/netflix-ambassador-susan-rice-board-1202738289/

Spangler, T. (2018b, June 2). Netflix turning too blue? Republicans' perception of the brand Has dropped, data shows. *Variety.* Retrieved from https://variety.com/2018/digital/news/netflix-political-republican-approval-perception-decline-data-1202828735/

Turner, F. (2006). *From counterculture to cyberculture: Stewart Brand, the Whole Earth Network, and the rise of digital utopianism.* Chicago: University of Chicago Press.

Warner, G. (2016, January 21). Is Netflix chill? Kenyan authorities threaten to ban the streaming site. NPR. Retrieved from www.npr.org/sections/goatsandsoda/2016/01/21/463807063/is-netflix-chill-kenyan-authorities-threaten-to-ban-the-streaming-site

Wike, R., Stokes, B., Poushter, J., and Fetterolf, J. (2017) U.S. image suffers as publics around world question Trump's leadership. *Pew Research Center.* Retrieved from www.pewresearch.org/global/2017/06/26/u-s-image-suffers-as-publics-around-world-question-trumps-leadership/

16

ONLINE PLATFORMS, CULTURAL POWER, AND CHINA'S PAN-ASIAN STRATEGY

Michael Keane and Huan Wu

Introduction

The People's Republic of China (PRC) is the second largest economy globally by GDP (gross domestic product). Yet China still claims "developing nation" status under World Trade Organization (WTO) guidelines, which it joined in 2001. But if China is still developing, is it a world power? Many would concur with this perspective. A Charter Member of the United Nations Security Council, the founding member of the Shanghai Cooperation Organization, a member of ASEAN Plus Three, and the instigator of the Belt and Road Initiative (BRI), China's influence is challenging the liberal world order. In particular, Chinese participation in regional forums has reshaped regional relations by causing the eviction of the Republic of China, known to most people as Taiwan. But how does the nation-state's economic and political influence impact on China's soft power outside the PRC (Nye, 1990)?

The key question of this chapter is whether China's digital connectivity is leading to enhanced cultural standing, particularly the kind that registers as admiration. China's economic prowess is not a precondition for the exercise of soft power globally, nor are infrastructures of media diplomacy reliable evidence of success. China Central Television (hereafter CCTV) broadcasts in multiple languages in multiple overseas locations, and global circulation data of state-owned print media appears to show China's media "going global" (Thussu, de Burgh, & Shi, 2017). But is China's culture admired internationally and has China's state-supported culture "going out" project been successful?

The chapter begins by providing some background to the culture "going out" program, which was instigated in 2003, shortly after China joined the WTO While there are numerous channels of outward bound cultural activity including government-supported initiatives (e.g., Confucius Institutes and diplomatic delegations), commercial enterprises (e.g., publishing), artistic activities (state-funded performing troupes as well as international festivals and exhibitions), overseas students and academic exchanges, the chapter focuses on media output, noting how the supporting role of the state has to a large extent been counterproductive in changing negative images of China outside the PRC.

Using international reputational metrics, many scholars have turned to the ranking index known as "soft power," which purports to evaluate a nation's "attractiveness." Soft power was devised by Joseph Nye, who at the time of its conceptualization in 1990, was the Director of the Center for International Affairs at Harvard University. Of course, the soft power dice is loaded against the PRC, which is not entirely surprising when one considers its western origins. In 2019, the Portland Soft

Power 30, the most widely cited index, listed China at 27th, well behind Japan (8), South Korea (19) and Singapore (21). The second section of the chapter provides a brief discussion of the ways that soft power is adjudicated, as well as flaws endemic to the system. It then examines how the "going out" of media influence is conventionally measured, and the inherent flaws in data.

The final section illustrates how Chinese commercial entertainment industries are expanding beyond China. The success of Alibaba, Tencent, Baidu, and ByteDance within China is to a large extent based on the phenomenal growth of the internet. Reconnecting with overseas Chinese heritage communities has allowed these companies to assume the privileged role of ambassadors of Chinese culture. In this section we draw on data from a research project on online consumption of Chinese entertainment content in the Asia-Pacific (South Korea, Taiwan, Hong Kong, Singapore, and Australia).[1] The data attempts to shows how Chinese content is making inroads in the region and how people are using a variety of digital platforms to access content. The most successful platform for dissemination of Chinese content, including government messages, is YouTube, which is somewhat ironic as this western platform is banned within China. Overall, we find that attitudes toward China's cultural influence remain divided in the region. Chinese culture is going out and it is landing in overseas Chinese communities but it is not reaching out to "foreign" audiences in any meaningful way.

Going Out

The idea that Chinese culture should "go global" assumed critical importance in the early 2000s. International media content was readily accessible online, initially as free downloads on BitTorrent sites (Zhao and Keane, 2013) and as pirated DVDs and VCDs (Wang, 2003). In the previous two decades, Chinese audio-visual media, with the exception of dynastic costume television dramas such as *The Three Kingdoms* (1994), *The Water Margin* (1998), *The Dream of the Red Chamber* (1986), and *Journey to the West* (1988) (Zhu, 2008) had made few inroads into global or even regional markets. Fifth-generation filmmakers, including Zhang Yimou, Chen Kaige, and Tian Zhuangzhuang, had achieved a degree of respect and recognition but it wasn't until the success of *Crouching Tiger, Hidden Dragon* in 2000, that Chinese cinema achieved a measure of popular success, and this film was in fact directed by Li Ang (Ang Lee), a Taiwanese director who had graduated in film production from New York University.

While much of the sloganeering from Beijing has been about the need to achieve global success, "going regional" has become a pressing concern. From the mid-1990s, the trendiness of media products of Japan and South Korea, in addition to the already popular audio-visual content of Hong Kong S.A.R. and Taiwan, had generated widespread appreciation for these nations' (and regions') culture. These positive evaluations of China's smaller neighbors reflected poorly on audio-visual content produced in the PRC, which was invariably propaganda-heavy and formulaic. South Korea's success in winning a best picture Oscar in 2020 for *The Parasite* illustrates the inherent "softness" of China's soft power, namely the failure on the part of its film makers to directly criticize the hard power of the state, except through historical allusion.

The attractiveness of East Asian content—in particular TV drama, manga, anime, and games, combined with the greater sophistication of East Asian, producers, and artists, produced a flow-on effect, often characterized as a wave. In addition, the influence of East Asian audio-visual within the region led to numerous invitations to filmmakers, movie stars, singers, musicians, and technicians to work on coproduction projects with the PRC and to feature in PRC film and television shows (Keane, Yecies, & Flew, 2018; Jin & Su, 2019). The "wave" nature of East Asian popular culture (see Chua, 2012) had the effect of breaking down the dams, dykes, and (fire)walls erected to privilege national culture in China.

Acutely aware of these regional waves and the global reputation of Hollywood content, the Chinese government, and provincial and city governments, provided incentives to mainland media producers, including free rent for studio space, tax holidays, and access to cheap labor (Keane, 2015), while endeavoring to restrict the kinds of foreign content that could be accessed within China. Regulation also had a positive effect. As Wendy Su notes, the controlled introduction of international blockbusters after 1994 served as a means to build domestic audiences and encourage investment and new technologies in film production. Profits were siphoned into politically correct "main melody" films, which were heavy on propaganda, and which the state believed might counter foreign influence (2016, p. 20).

In contrast to the smaller regional territories that were generating trendy content, China possessed a trump card, a massive national audience. Added to the 1.3 billion people living in the PRC was a diaspora made up of overseas students and persons with Chinese heritage, numbering 50 million, who by the early 2000s were able to access content online. The potential of digital technology to connect China with its diaspora validates Michael Curtin's argument made as early as 2007: 'Although dispersed across vast stretches of Asia and around the world, this audience is now connected for the very first time via the intricate matrix of digital and satellite media' (2007, p. 2). Moreover, the acquisition by the Chinese private company Wanda of the international theater chains AMC and Hoyts, in 2014 and 2015 respectively, further raised opportunities for Chinese content to "go out," and for diasporic audiences to see made-in-China films screened at multiplex cinemas.

In addition to acquiring the infrastructure of overseas cinema chains, China's culture going out strategy has been enhanced by investment in Hollywood film studios. In 2016 the Wanda Group acquired Legendary Pictures but by late 2017 had relinquished its investment (Curtin, 2018). The overseas production of reality TV shows and films, meanwhile, had led to a visible Chinese presence outside the PRC, occasionally making the entertainment news overseas. Co-productions with foreign partners including the US (Kokas, 2019; Jin & Su, 2019; Keane, Yecies & Flew, 2018) were adding to the quota of talent coming into the PRC The key point here is skills transfer, notably creatives from South Korea and Hong Kong moving to China.

Moreover, as Keane (2016) has noted elsewhere, thanks to the internationalization of its online platforms, China was now able to reconnect with overseas Chinese, who may have adopted more "western" viewing habits. Overseas audiences could once again evaluate made-in-PRC content, especially newer offerings of commercial film and reality TV, which compared to those of the 1980s and 1990s were more professional. The same kind of creative know-how transfers that occurred in the film industry occurred with TV formats (Keane, 2015; Zeng & Sparks 2017; Nauta, 2018: Cho & Zhu, 2017). Overseas shoots of TV reality shows like *Where Are We Going, Dad?* (*baba qu na'er?*), *Running Man China* (*benpao ba xiongdi*)[2], and *If You Are the One* (*feicheng wurao*) helped to justify the claim that China's media was going out. Somewhat ironically, the above TV reality shows were copies of foreign programs, the first two being Korean. In fact, a large part of the mini-renaissance of made-in PRC content was due to the influence of the region. The development of China's pan-Asian strategy has therefore largely been a consequence of East Asian media success in China.

Upping the Ante: Soft Power and Metrics

Devised in the US in 1990 (Nye, 1990), "soft power" made its way into discussions of China's media and culture in the early 2000s, largely as a result of the inter-regional success of East Asian pop culture. The uptake of this western term was not immediate. China already had developed its own matrix called "comprehensive national power" (*zonghe guoli*), and cultural power was one part of this equation (see Zhang, 2010). The Chinese variant came to be referred to as "cultural soft power" (*wenhua ruanshili*), which as the name suggest prioritizes cultural influence. Cultural soft power departs somewhat from the work of Joseph Nye, whose much-cited definition states that it (soft power) relies on "the ability to shape the preferences of others" rather than influence (Nye, 2004, p. 5; for East Asia, see Rawnsley, 2012).

Nye's soft power model is in fact a resource-based approach (Pan et al., 2019). Nye says that a nation's soft power, i.e., its attractiveness to others, "rests on" three resources: its culture (in places where it is attractive to others), its political values (when it lives up to them at home and abroad), and its foreign policies (when they are seem as legitimate and having moral authority) (2004, p. 11). Nye has had very little to say directly about representational media, echoing Marshall McLuhan's focus on the medium rather than the message. Significantly, it is the representational aspects of Chinese media that have cruelled success in many parts of the world.

Before looking more closely at media reception, it is worth briefly considering the way that soft power is ranked, as this term is now widely contested. Soft power is a 20th-century invention, as are the many lists that purport to rank nations and regions. As Portugal (2019) notes, listings, indexes, measurements, and rankings are associated with the evolution of the economic press, the consolidation of mercantilism, and the development of financial capitalism in Europe from the 16th to the 18th century. A good score on an index can elevate a nation, or a region's reputation and standing, depending on the perceived veracity of the ranking system. Rankings are probably the most pertinent to cities, which are subject to competition for talent and investment. In the case of nations, longitudinal data has attempted to standardize a set of variables for measuring an observable phenomenon, and noting changes. The most pertinent index is the Portland Soft Power 30 Index.

A joint initiative between the strategic communications consultancy Portland and the University of Southern California's Center on Public Diplomacy, the Portland Soft Power 30 is widely cited in China. The survey purports to capture data from 60 nations; a range of data is collected from international polling and secondary sources, including respondents' "impressions" of the appeal of nations in categories including cuisine, tech products, friendliness, culture, luxury goods, foreign policy, and livability. With regard to culture, Portland has developed a "culture sub-index" that purports to measure both the quality and international reach and appeal of a country's cultural production. However, it is not media industry reception that counts, as one might expect, but the annual number of international tourists, the global success of a country's music industry, and a nation's international sporting prowess; hence New Zealand "punches above its weight" thanks to the All Blacks. Indicators are far too often arbitrary. As Zhang and Wu (2019) discuss, the 2017 addition of "the number of 'Michelin Restaurants'" to the index heavily biased the results toward European nations and particularly France. The *Michelin Guide* did not even make its way into China until 2016.

The notion of privileging the number of identifiable and measurable data points over actual reception is similar in some respects to the Chinese strategy of building radio and television infrastructure throughout the nation from the 1970s. It was assumed that important messages were getting through because of the sheer scale of repetition and the number of transmitters. In fact, there was no evidence to suggest otherwise. Likewise, many academic analyses of China's media and culture going out have taken this quantitative solution, while sidestepping the more significant qualitative question of how they are received. In a study of China's media going out by Hugo de Burgh, the author says that a Chinese historical drama serial, the 2015 *Nirvana in Fire* had over 13 billion views globally (de Burgh, 2017, p. 11). Of course, the fact that the serial had multiple episodes, combined with e-word of mouth, may have been the reason behind accumulated viewings. Elsewhere, reports claimed 3.3 billion views on iQIYI, China's version of Netflix by the end of the serial.[3] Another dynastic serial released in 2018, *Yanxi Palace*, is reported to have received 15 billion streams on iQIYI alone, an interesting release of industry data when one considers that the western streaming platform Netflix does not release such figures.[4] Unsurprisingly, Chinese media sources are quick to report on such online reports. Success, presumably much of it, is coming from the Asia-Pacific, and this suggests that Chinese culture is reaching out, even if it's not critically acclaimed by Hollywood reviewers.

Of course, reception is problematic when using the number of hits online as an indicator of success, or even adjudging the reach of China Global Television Network (CGTN) to be evidence of soft power. Chinese TV channels do reach overseas Chinese audiences but the fact is that the presence of China Central Television (CCTV) channels in international hotels and resorts frequented by Chinese tourists is more symbolic than real. Yet the "net effect" is something to take seriously. Some scholars have pointed out that engagement with content via online media can augment the power of the messaging if users interact by sharing and commenting favorably on social media platforms (see Gilardi et al., 2018; Moe, Poell & van Dijck, 2018). It is a strategy of marketers to get exposure through social media platforms in the first instance.

Part of the problem with recognition of Chinese content outside the PRC is reviews. Whereas a film, TV series, or online video may "go viral" among online communities, racking up millions of hits and shares in a few days, this does not always translate into commercial success. A case in point was the Chinese film *The Great Wall* (2016–2017), a coproduction with Hollywood and China. Universal Pictures reportedly spent US$80 million on promotion (McClintock and Galloway, 2017). The film's reception nosedived when reviews surfaced, receiving ratings of 6/10 on IMDB, 35 percent on the Rotten Tomatoes site, and 5.4/10 on Douban, the Chinese online rating site.[5] Such sites are also not reliable evaluators of critical acclaim as they can be overwhelmed by patriotic posters. In fact, the recommendation economy is a flawed metric as posts are mostly registered either by those who are fans, or those who feel disappointed by the product (Muller, 2018). Moreover, when it comes to actually paying for professional content, many consumers are inclined toward critical industry reviews. Fan reviews, such as those found on sites like IMDB or Douban, and personal recommendations from friends do help in generating interest, of course.

A report on Chinese film consumption in the US and Canada by a team at the Beijing Normal University has provided some useful insights, albeit not without methodological misgivings (Huang, Sun, Wang & Yang, 2019). Using a professional survey company to ensure the survey was as demographically broad as possible, the survey managed to collect 1,208 and 312 responses in the US and Canada respectively. The nominated ethnic groups were "white", Asian, African-American, and "other ethnic group." In fact, 68.4 percent of the respondents self-identified as "white." The survey found that overall 79.1 percent of people had watched one or more Chinese movies in the past three years, with 43.3 percent reporting they had watched five or more. The report concluded that movies were a better way to transmit understanding of China's national image than mainstream media or even the internet. Aside from the problematic methodology of ascribing race to viewing habits, the report made no distinction regarding "made-in-PRC" movies and those made in adjacent territories, or even co-productions; that is, it assumed that the respondents can identify a Chinese movie because it features Chinese actors and producers, including those from Hong Kong and Taiwan.

Online Platforms and the Reception of China's Message in the Asia-Pacific

The above-mentioned survey also did not seek to ascertain how people watch movies—for instance, in cinemas or at home, e.g., DVDs, streaming platforms, or video-on-demand. As with international media industries, China's audio-visual sector has been disrupted by the advent of online platforms. The key platforms with stakes in the audio-visual content sectors are Baidu, Alibaba, and Tencent, although the global phenomenon of the user-generated content video site TikTok is worth considering. Tencent Video provides audiences with exclusive copyright content from industry-leading companies like HBO and Time Warner. Baidu's iQIYI is well known for its Professionally Generated Content (PGC) and high premium self-made content, and has entered into collaborations with Netflix. Alibaba, which owns the platform Youku, also has its film production assets, known as Alibaba pictures.

In order to ascertain whether digital platforms are more effective in carrying China's message than traditional media, in 2018 and 2019 we conducted a series of online questionnaire surveys. The analysis was part of a three-year research project called "Digital China; from Cultural Presence to Innovation Nation" funded by the Australian Research Council. Surveys were authorized by Curtin University's Human Ethics Research Committee to assure confidentiality and anonymity prior to distribution. Most of the respondents were contacted by advertisements posted on Facebook and WeChat, as well as through local community organizations. In the survey introduction page, we specifically directed attention to "made-in-China" audio-visual content; we were aware that some respondents might conflate Hong Kong and Taiwanese Chinese-language content, or even Jacky Chan's Hollywood movies with PRC Chinese audio-visual content.

Our interest was platforms that distributed narrative forms of content. All of the surveys sought to discover the motivations for seeking out and viewing made-in-China entertainment products. We hypothesized that persons would seek out Chinese content, and even pay for access, if they had some personal connection—i.e., friends, family members who were Chinese, or if they had visited China or had studied Chinese. The survey was opt-in (i.e., persons chose to participate). Overall, the results confirmed that Chinese audio-visual content is engaging for persons who have an existing interest. From the results of the three surveys, it was difficult to show that Chinese audio-visual content was winning new audiences, as for instance, the recent case of South Korea's success in the Oscars.

The first survey, which was made available in Chinese, Malay, Indonesian, and Japanese, was conducted in April 2018 using Qualtrics software. In this survey the focus was on respondents' understanding of soft power and their perception of China's actual soft power. We asked people to nominate what they thought was the "most familiar indicator of soft power" (a single choice). Among 258 valid responses, 63.95 percent selected "a nation's cultural and creative output," followed by "a nation's political standing and leadership in the global community" (21.32 percent). The two other choices were "a nation's reputation as technologically innovative" and "a nation's foreign aid." The results appeared to confirm the significance of cultural and creative products, at least in the minds of our respondents. Of course, the title of the survey may have predisposed some people to answer this way.

The following question asked respondents to rank these four soft power attributes with respect to China; here cultural and creative output (33.96 percent) ranked second behind political standing (39.25 percent). Significantly, 27.55 percent of respondents listed "China's cultural and creative output" last, suggesting a wide discrepancy of opinion. The survey then asked respondents to rank eight countries' soft power. Among 262 respondents, the US was ranked first by most people (80.15 percent) while the PRC was ranked first by 6.97 percent. In this survey 39 percent of respondents self-identified as Chinese citizens.[6] Because many respondents avoided questions about soft power, and the fact that there appeared to be some uncertainty as to its meaning, we developed a second survey, in which we changed the wording "soft power" to "influence." We also sought to ascertain where people were living, not just their passport nationality.

In September 2018, we launched the second iteration. We were surprised to receive 1,063 valid answers within a month. Due to one of the platform distribution methods used (WeChat), a large number of respondents came from the PRC, which indicated an interest in sharing the survey within the WeChat community. Among the respondents, 47.98 percent expressed Chinese nationality. While this was a large demographic, 24.7 percent of these respondents were living overseas, which was of interest to us, as we were seeking to ascertain perceptions of China's media content when living overseas. 17.59 percent of respondents were South Korean, and all except 11 were living in South Koreas. Table 16.1 shows the country (or region) distribution of respondents.

This survey revealed that YouTube is the major platform for people living in Australia, Hong Kong, Indonesia, Malaysia, Singapore, Taiwan, and South Korea to access Chinese audio-visual content (see Table 16.2). However, Chinese online video platforms iQIYI and Tencent Video are familiar among Hong Kong and Taiwan audiences. Another Chinese video sharing website, Bilibili, is well known to audiences in Singapore and Malaysia.

Cognizant of the fact that most respondents in survey two identified as coming from the PRC, we initiated a third survey in August 2019 and promoted it among people living outside China. By this time, TikTok had appeared on the radar of possibilities. TikTok is the international version of the Chinese domestic video sharing platform Douyin; 28.6 percent of respondents from Singapore

Table 16.1 Where Were You Born (Country/Region)?

	Percentage	*Count*
Mainland China	47.98	510
South Korea	17.59	187
Singapore	5.83	62
Australia	5.36	57
Malaysia	5.27	56
H.K. S.A.R.	4.80	51
Taiwan	3.76	40
Indonesia	1.88	20
United States	0.85	9
Macau S.A.R.	0.19	2
Japan	0.09	1
Other (please specify)	6.40	68
Total	**100**	**1,063**

Table 16.2 Platforms for Accessing Chinese Content (Selected Cells, Results in Percentages)

	Australia	*H.K. S.A.R.*	*Indonesia*	*Japan*	*PRC*	*Malaysia*	*Singapore*	*South Korea*	*Taiwan*
Bilibili	1.6	32.8	0.0	0.0	42.2	17.4	13.2	0.96	2.4
Foxtel	3.3	0.0	0.0	0.0	0.57	0.0	0.0	0.0	0.0
Netflix	18.0	20.7	15.4	0.0	2.3	7.2	35.3	8.7	7.1
Tencent Video (v.qq)	0.0	12.1	0.0	0.0	49.3	8.7	11.8	2.4	14.3
Viki	1.6	0.0	3.8	0.0	0.43	1.4	8.8	0.0	0.0
Vue	0.0	1.7	0.0	0.0	0.57	2.9	4.4	0.48	0.0
YouTube	41.0	60.3	50.0	0.0	21.4	60.9	72.1	22.6	61.9
Youku	6.6	29.3	3.8	20.0	45.8	14.5	20.6	6.7	19.0
iQIYI	4.9	27.6	3.8	0.0	58.2	26.1	22.1	4.3	38.1

selected TikTok as a platform used to access entertainment content produced in mainland China; the percentage in Malaysia was 21.6 percent. It is important to bear in mind that our questions referred specifically to "made-in-China" video content and these results therefore do not reflect the actual percentage of TikTok users in the countries. Respondents from South Korea selected Netflix as their choice for viewing Chinese entertainment products. The Chinese video platform iQIYI performed well, with 47.2 percent of respondents from Malaysia and 40.5 percent of respondents from Taiwan nominating it as the "Chinese" platform of choice. 51.4 percent of Hong Kong respondents chose Bilibili. However, the survey confirmed our earlier finding that the free "western" platform YouTube is used the most in Australia, Hong Kong, Malaysia, Singapore, and Taiwan to access Chinese entertainment content.

Concluding Remarks: Not There Yet

Over and above box office data and online hits and shares, evaluations of success are ultimately contingent on who is doing the viewing. Global audience success, not regional audiences, translates into the kind of admiration equivalent to soft power. Winning an Oscar for "best film" or "best screenplay" surely helps the cause and Chinese producers will be feeling the pressure to perform with

South Korea's recent ground-breaking success. But if overseas Chinese communities are the target audience, then Chinese films and TV are surely doing well—regionally, that is. Chinese films, such as the patriotic *Wolf Warrior 2*, have scored spectacularly well. The numbers appear to tell a story of success. Likewise, *Monster Hunt*, the most popular movie in China in 2015, grossed $381 million in theater sales but when it opened in the US it earned a mere $21,000 in its debut weekend and closed after a week. The TV serial *Empresses in the Palace* was a huge hit in mainland China and Southeast Asia but achieved very moderate success when released on the Netflix platform. With both the above examples, the Chinese versions had probably exhausted the potential audience before global release.

Global results don't exactly make great reading. Efforts to "go out" on the cultural front have not been assisted by perceptions of the PRC as an authoritarian state, a mass purveyor of cheap goods, and a land of copyright infringers. On one level, government cultural export initiatives have assisted Chinese culture and media products to go into world markets. Chinese media has extensive foreign outposts and Chinese-language content is readily available on Chinese and Asian video platforms. But media content is predominantly landing in places where Chinese people live. In other words, quantity and consumption by the Chinese diaspora does not equate to cultural influence. It is evident that while China's traditional cultural resources are obviously deep, the world is not responding as Beijing would wish. The bad news is that film, television, music, and publication, the content industries, account for only small a quota of China's exports, which was about 2 percent in 2015 (Li, 2016). Overall, we can conclude that China's media is going out in large numbers, but these numbers are not adding substantially to China's soft power. The future might yet bring glory, a golden Oscar perhaps. As Sun Yat-sen once famously said, "The work of the revolution is not yet done."

Notes

1 The project did not investigate Japan due to the composition of the research team.
2 "Running man" is also translated as *Keep Running*.
3 https://en.wikipedia.org/wiki/Nirvana_in_Fire
4 www.bbc.com/news/world-asia-china-46630781
5 www.nytimes.com/2016/12/22/movies/the-great-wall-what-critics-and-filmgoers-are-saying-in-china.html
6 102 respondents reported that they were born in the PRC but had lived overseas more than three months. The longest time overseas was 33 years.

References

Cho, Y., & Zhu, H. (2017). Interpreting the television format phenomenon between South Korea and China through Inter-Asian frameworks. *International Journal of Communication* 11, 2332–2349.

Chua, B.H. (2012). *Structure, Audience and Soft Power in East Asian Pop Culture*. Hong Kong: Hong Kong University Press.

Curtin, M. (2007). *Playing to the World's Biggest Audience: The Globalization of Chinese Film and TV.* Berkeley: University of California Press.

Curtin, M. (2018) The new geography of the global blockbuster: Wanda scales up. In M. Keane, B. Yecies & T. Flew (Eds.). *Willing Collaborators: Foreign Partners in Chinese Media*. London and New York: Rowman & Littlefield International, pp. 31–46.

De Burgh, H. (2017). *China's Media in the Emerging World Order*. Buckingham: University of Buckingham Press.

Gilardi, F., Lam, C., Tan, K.C., White, A., Cheng, S., & Zhao, Y. (2018). International TV series distribution on Chinese digital platforms: Marketing strategies and audience engagement. *Global Media & China*, 3(3), 213–230.

Huang, H., Sun, Z., Wang, C., & Yang, Z. (2019). Zhongguo dianying yu guojia yingxiang chuanbo [Chinese film and the communication of national image], *Xiandai chuanbo* [Modern Communication], 1, 22–28.

Jin, D.Y. (2016). *New Korean Wave: Transnational Cultural Power in the Age of Social Media*. Urbana, University of Illinois Press.

Jin, D.Y., & Su, W. (Eds.). (2019). *Asia-Pacific Film Co-productions: Theory, Industry and Aesthetics*. London: Routledge.

Keane, M. (2015). *The Chinese Television Industry*. London: BFI Palgrave.

Keane, M. (2016), Disconnecting, connecting, reconnecting: How Chinese television got out of the box. *International Journal of Communication, 10*, 5426–5443.

Keane, M., Yecies, B., & Flew, T. (2018). *Willing Collaborators: Foreign Partners in China's Media.* London: Rowman & Littlefield International.

Kokas, A. (2017). *Hollywood Made in China.* Berkeley: University of California Press.

Li, H.L. (2016). Chinese culture "going out": An overview of government policies and an analysis of challenges and opportunities for international collaboration. In M. Keane (Ed.) *The Handbook of Cultural and Creative Industries in China.* Cheltenham: Edward Elgar Publishing, 129–143.

McClintock, P. & Galloway, S. (2017). Matt Damon's "The Great Wall" to lose $75 million: U.S.-China productions in doubt. *The Hollywood Reporter.* Retrieved from www.hollywoodreporter.com/news/what-great-walls-box-office-flop-will-cost-studios-981602

Moe, H., Poell, T., & van Dijck, J. (2018). Rearticulating audience engagement: Social media and television. *Television & New Media, 17*, 99–107.

Muller, J. (2018). *The Tyranny of Metrics.* Princeton: Princeton University Press.

Nauta, A. (2018) Localizing Korean television shows in China: the practice of production and censorship. In M. Keane, B. Yecies & T. Flew (Eds.). *Willing Collaborators: Foreign Partners in Chinese Media.* London and New York: Rowman & Littlefield International, 171–186.

Nye, J.S. (1990). Soft Power. *Foreign Policy* No.80, Twentieth Anniversary (Autumn, 1990), 153–171.

Nye, J.S. (2004). *Soft Power: The Means to Success in World Politics.* New York: Public Affairs.

Pan, C.X., Isakhan, B., & Nwokora, Z. (2019). Othering as soft-power discursive practice: China Daily's construction of Trump's America in the 2016 presidential election *Politics,* 1(16). Retrieved from https://doi.org/10.1177/0263395719843219

Portugal, A.C. (2019). The role of city rankings in local public policy design: Urban competitiveness and economic press. *Global Media & China, 4*(2), 162–178.

Rawnsley, G.D. (2012). Approaches to soft power and public diplomacy in China and Taiwan. *Journal of International Communication, 2*(18), 121–135.

Su, W. (2016). *China's Encounter with Global Hollywood. Cultural Policy and the Film Industry 1994–2013.* Lexington: University of Kentucky Press.

Thussu, D., de Burgh, H., & Shi, A.B. (2017). *China's Media Go Global.* London: Routledge.

Wang, S. (2003) *Framing Piracy: Globalization and Film Distribution in Greater China.* Lanham: Rowman & Littlefield.

Zeng, W., & Sparks, C. (2017). Localization as negotiation: Producing a Korean format in contemporary China, *International Journal of Digital Television, 1*(8), 81–98.

Zhang, C., & Wu, R. Q. (2019). Battlefield of global ranking: How do power rivalries shape soft power index building?' *Global Media & China, 4*(2), 179–202.

Zhang, W.H. (2010). China's cultural future: from soft power to comprehensive national power. *International Journal of Cultural Policy, 16*(4), 383–402.

Zhao, E.J. & Keane, M. (2013). Between formal and informal: the shakeout in China's online video industry. *Media Culture and Society, 35*(6), 724–741.

Zhu, Y. (2008). *Television in Post-Reform China.* London: Routledge.

17

NETFLIX'S CORPORATE SPHERE IN ASIA IN THE DIGITAL PLATFORM ERA

Dal Yong Jin

Introduction

In the early 21st century, several over-the-top (OTT) service platforms, including Netflix, Disney+, and Amazon Prime have become cornucopias. As the number of global users of platforms like these has rapidly increased over the past 10 years, OTTs, together with some of the largest commercial digital platforms like Facebook and Google, have influenced people's daily activities and cultural lives. Among these, Netflix has become one of the most significant OTT platforms in terms of monetization based on its soaring number of global customers. The subscription members in the US have been staggering in very recent years; however, international membership figures in Europe, Latin America, and Asia are rapidly increasing. While several OTT platforms still focus on the American market, Netflix has shown tremendous growth in global audio-visual markets.

As the most successful OTT service, Netflix has greatly influenced global entertainment systems. From content distribution to exhibition and to production, Netflix has substantially shifted the ecology of global entertainment industries. As people consume cultural content on digital platforms, Netflix has especially increased revenues through a monthly fee-based business model, unlike other digital platforms like Google and Facebook, which rely mainly on advertising. This status quo is crucial for the capitalization of Netflix, and as such, Netflix as a digital platform has fundamentally transformed cultural industries.

By employing a critical political economy approach and platform imperialism theory, this chapter analyzes OTT services, in particular Netflix's global dominance, in order to determine the ways in which Netflix newly constructs platform imperialism as a new form of imperialism. It discusses the major characteristics of Netflix in the global cultural industries, which controls the vicious chain of the broadcasting and film industries. Second, it examines the ways in which Netflix influences the content production sector, as well as consumption in Asian cultural and platform industries, as Asian countries have shifted their methods of production and exhibition by learning from Netflix. Finally, it examines how Netflix promotes imperialism which expands asymmetrical power relations between the US and other parts of the world. In other words, it articulates whether Netflix actualizes platform imperialism, referring to an asymmetrical relationship of interdependence between the West, primarily the US, and many developing countries, based on its crucial role in reshaping the global cultural industry (Jin, 2015). I expect that discussions in this chapter will shed light on the current debates on the increasing role of Netflix as a digital platform in the globalization context.

Netflix's Global Penetration in the OTT Markets

The history of Netflix started only 24 years ago when it was founded in the US in 1997 as a video rental service company, which offered offline movie rentals. Its streaming service began in 2007. Ever since it started its streaming service, Netflix has been the forerunner in the streaming television system and "its streaming service has become internationalized" (Ju, 2019, 33). Netflix introduced streaming, which allowed members to instantly watch television shows and movies on their personal computers and later on smartphones. Regardless of such a short history, Netflix has become the most successful OTT service. Netflix has especially utilized artificial intelligence (AI) supported by algorithms to develop the best recommendation system, which drives the company's global dominance.

Due to its diversification of business strategies, Netflix's global impact is not limited to the distribution sector, but the production sector and the OTT service industry. Netflix's business strategies have shifted to grab the customer's attention, from "its original business model as exhibitor of film content" to "the business of being producer of serialized drama" (Jenner, 2016, 261). Netflix has also "rewritten the rules of TV and movie deal-making, talent paydays, TV scheduling, film release windows, and marketing campaigns. It's an extraordinary level of influence exerted on a mature industry dominated by long-established stalwarts" (Littleton, 2018).

More importantly, Netflix has penetrated other countries since its successful launch in Canada in 2007. Netflix has continued to diversify its global markets. In 2011, Netflix launched throughout Latin America and the Caribbean. In 2012, Netflix became available in Europe, including the UK, Ireland, and in the Nordic countries. Netflix finally moved into the Asian market, including Japan and Korea, in the mid-2010s to become the biggest OTT platform around the globe (Netflix Media Center, 2020). Netflix entered Japan in 2015 and then entered several other Asian countries, including Korea in 2016, gaining a tangible presence in most Asian countries, with the exceptions of China and North Korea, although they planned to work in China (Team, 2015). According to Netflix (2020a), its subscribers with a streaming-only plan could watch TV shows and movies instantly in over 190 countries in December 2019. The content that is available to stream may vary by location, though.

Netflix kept getting bigger, but it was not growing quite as fast as it had been in the US, partially because of other competitors including Disney+. For Netflix, going global is its biggest asset, and how to increase international subscribers, in particular in Asia, in the midst of fierce challenges from late comers, is its concern. What is interesting is that Netflix shares have soared by more than 65% in the first half of 2020 during the COVID-19 era. The COVID-19 outbreak has led more people to subscribe to streaming services, including Netflix, and spend less on traditional cable TV and movies in theaters, which means that Netflix has been one of the major beneficiaries of the pandemic (La Monica, 2020).

With its soaring global penetration, Netflix has rapidly increased its revenues, from $11.7 billion in 2017 to $15.4 billion in 2018, and to $20.1 billion in 2019 as the number of subscribers has increased from 110 million in 2017 to 167.9 million in 2019. The number of international subscribers surpassed US subscribers in 2017, and it consisted of 63.5% in December 2019 (Netflix, 2017, 2020a). Asia Pacific was the smallest region, in both revenues and paid members; however, the growth rate was much higher than the US market. By comparison, the revenues in Asia in 2019 increased by 55.4% from 2018, while the revenues in North America increased 21%. The number of paid customers in Asia increased as much as 53% during the same period, while it was only 1.5% in North America (Netflix, 2020a).

As the *New York Times* (Lee, 2019) reports, Netflix is in fact an international business platform whose growth (and value) come from Brazil, Mexico, India, and elsewhere. The report continues to claim that "the Asia-Pacific region, which includes South Korea, Japan, and India, is the fastest-growing segment, with 14 million subscribers, more than triple what it had at the end of March 2017, the earliest period for which the numbers were made available." That region accounts for 9% of its total subscribers, after Netflix gave up on China. Due to its potential with a huge population and emerging economy, Asia has been the most significant target for Netflix, and perhaps later other global OTT service platforms, including Disney+.

Netflix Effects in Local OTT Content

Netflix's global influence can be easily identified in the OTT service industry and entertainment industry. Netflix has directly invested in local cultural production in several countries, while limiting its acquisition of other cultural companies, which makes it a unique media giant. While other mega-media giants have increased their global market shares and dominance through corporate integration, Netflix has not emphasized the significance of mergers and acquisitions (M&As). Of course, this does not mean that Netflix is totally uninterested in corporate convergence. Especially in recent years, its business model has slightly changed to focus on the potential of corporate convergence. Netflix made only one big deal when it acquired Millarworld, a comic-book publisher, in 2017. Netflix acquired Millarworld, founded by comic-book legend Mark Millar, the creative force behind a number of stories that were turned into films, including *Kick-Ass, Kingsman: The Secret Service, Logan,* and *Captain America: Civil War.* "Netflix said the deal, its first-ever acquisition, is a natural progression as the company looks to work more closely with filmmakers and creators" (Williams, 2017).

Regarding Netflix's relatively quiet M&A track record, two different plans have been stated by the company itself. On the one hand, Netflix's CEO Reed Hastings said in April 2019, the company "hasn't made many acquisitions to date, and doesn't plan to go on a shopping spree now. The company still has plenty of room to grow by just focusing on developing new shows and movies and improving its service" (Wolverton, 2019). On the other hand, as the acquisition of Millarworld shows, Netflix is open to making the right deal. Netflix chief content officer Ted Sarandos signaled his interest: "In terms of using M&A to acquire intellectual property, it could be a very useful tool" (Wallenstein, 2018). This is an especially significant statement because of upcoming competition from other OTT service platforms, in particular Disney+, which has an ample amount of cultural content. In order to compete against Disney+, Netflix must secure high-quality cultural content, and this can be achieved through two major tools: one is the acquisition of existing cultural industry firms, and the other is its investment in cultural production, both internally and externally.

In these circumstances, what is significant is that Netflix has worked with local entertainment companies, in particular in Asia, in order to secure quality content. Again, Netflix has its service in 190 countries, and it is not possible to attract all viewers with only American cultural content. Netflix has hugely invested in emerging cultural powers like India, Mexico, Japan, and Korea as they continue to develop their own unique cultural products, like Bollywood movies in India, Telenovelas in Mexico, and the Korean Wave in Korea, as well as several movies and animations in Japan.

To begin with, as Netflix inroaded Japan first in Asia, Netflix greatly increased its investment in Japanese cultural production. As ContentAsia (2019) points out, Netflix's 2019 originals slate out of Japan included the eight-part *The Naked Director* (premiered August 2019, directed by Masaharu Take), about pornography pioneer Toru Muranishi; *The Forest of Love* (premiered October 2019, produced by Hiroshi Muto), about the merciless Jo Murata; and *Followers* (2020, directed by Mika Ninagawa), about a group of Tokyo-ites crossing paths through social media. Netflix is also backing a Japanese original, *Alice in Borderland* (2020), based on Haro Aso's sci-fi manga about a life-or-death game directed by Shinsuke Sato (*Kingdom*). Netflix's 2019 commissions also included kids' animated comedy *Dino Girl Gauko* from Japanese creator/showrunner Akira Shigino, produced by Hitoshi Mogi (*Crayon Shin-chan, Line Town*). In addition, Netflix has inked partnerships with three local companies—Anima, Sublimation, and David Production—for titles such as *Altered Carbon: Resleeved* from Anima and *Dragon's Dogma* from Sublimation (Netflix, 2020b).

In Korea, Netflix has invested in several examples of cultural content, including *Okja,* a fusion of benign monster film, action comedy, and coming-of-age fable. Netflix funded $50 million for *Okja,* directed by Bong Joon-ho (2017). Netflix wanted to stand out as it had been struggling to gain

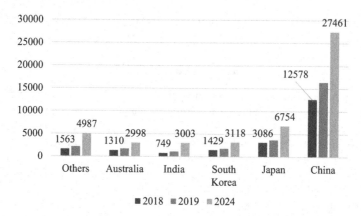

Figure 17.1 OTT TV and Video Revenues by Country in Asia-Pacific Region ($ million)
Source: Broadband TV News (2019).

ground in the Korean market during the early stages, which means that it hoped to increase Korean audiences (Kim, H.K, 2017). The investment seems like a lot, and therefore, industry analysts consider "Netflix's move as part of its rollout in Asia" (Pulver, 2015). In 2019, Netflix released its first original Korean drama series, *Kingdom,* which was set in the middle of the Joseon Dynasty (from 1392 to 1897). It took nearly eight years to produce the series, with its production cost reaching 2 billion Korean won, comparable to US$1.7 million per episode (Park, 2019). The second season of *Kingdom,* the zombie drama set in medieval Korea, started filming in February 2019.

In 2019, Netflix also announced that it planned to spend $420 million on Indian content for 2019 and 2020 to produce more local content in India. Netflix certainly understood the global acceptance of Bollywood movies, and the company indicated that some of the Indian content on the platform could find wider acceptance beyond India (Altstedter et al., 2019). Netflix cited Indian animated children's show *Mighty Little Bheem,* which was viewed by 27 million households outside of India. Since its launch in India in 2016, Netflix has been building up its local penetration in India, starting with its first Indian original *Sacred Games* (Bhushan, 2019).

Netflix's Asian penetration will continue as Asia is the largest future market based on its huge population and emerging economy. According to Broadband TV News (2019), Asia Pacific OTT TV episode and movie revenues will reach $48 billion in 2024, up from the $21 billion recorded in 2018. China and Japan will account for 71% of the region's total revenues by 2024. China will command a 57% share by 2024 from the 22 countries covered in the report (Broadband TV News, 2019) (Figure 17.1).

As this data clearly indicates, the growth rate of Asian OTT markets is very attractive, and Netflix and other global OTT platforms will be targeting Asian audiences in the 2020s. In particular, it is clear that global OTT platforms will continue to open the Chinese market, which is the largest in Asia. As of now, Netflix's attempt to penetrate China is not successful, but the streaming company cannot avoid this profitable market.

Netflix's Impacts on Global OTT Platforms

Over the past two decades, the Netflix effect across the entertainment sector has taken root in meaningful ways. Attempting to catch up with Netflix, many media firms, from the largest US media conglomerates to small and mid-sized local OTT platforms in non-Western countries, including Korea, are bent on reinventing part of their operations as a direct-to-consumer business model (Littleton, 2018). The direct-to-consumer (DTC) streaming video business model developed and advanced by Netflix is the reason why other media companies like Disney acquired 21st Century Fox with such fervor in 2018, which created one of the biggest shifts in the entertainment industry in decades (Littleton, 2018). In this regard, AT&T chairman-CEO Randall Stephenson stated in 2018:

> The modern media company must develop extensive direct-to-consumer relationships… We think pure wholesale business models for media companies will be really tough to sustain over time. Traditional media conglomerates indeed feel the urgency to act now out of fear that Amazon, Facebook, Apple and Google are also busy crafting global content platforms that will dwarf their operations. It's no surprise that Disney—the world's biggest media company—is leading the race among Hollywood's old guard to catch up with Netflix, et al. Disney chairman-CEO Bob Iger calls the planned launch of a suite of DTC services the biggest priority of the company during calendar [year] 2019.
>
> *(Littleton, 2018)*

In the Global South, Netflix's impact has been even bigger than expected. With no single acquisition by Netflix, local OTT service firms attempted to develop "Netflix-style algorithmic programming built into their software architecture" (Arya, 2020). However, due to their small sizes and limited funds, they could not compete against Netflix, which demanded they become local mega giants through corporate integration.

As ContentAsia (2019) discussed, Asia had at least 134 home-grown dedicated domestic streaming services in the first half of 2019, led by Taiwan, with 18 platforms (excluding regional/global streamers, although they are increasingly adding Chinese content) and Japan, which has 15 platforms (excluding Amazon Prime Video, which is focused almost entirely on Japan and India, and Netflix). Including regional/global players, we counted 24 platforms in Taiwan and 20 in Japan. Japan has three platforms on the list of the 15 biggest streaming earners in Asia Pacific identified by Media Partners Asia (MPA) in 2019. The three Japanese platforms are Hulu Japan, dTV, and Niconico. Hulu Japan places 9th, followed by dTV in 10th spot and Niconico at 12th. Combined, the 15 take 70% of total online video revenues in the region. The M.P.A. says Japan is the largest online video country by revenue (excluding China). In total, Asia Pacific advertising and subscription revenue this year (excluding China) is forecast to be US$11 billion. By 2024, this is expected to more than double to US$23 billion.

Global, regional, and local streaming services are all backing original production in Asia, some more than others but together driving up output, content spend, and opportunity.

Global streaming wars are already well under way in Japan—an Amazon stronghold—with Netflix upping its executive firepower on the ground and pushing forward with its anime and other originals. Apple TV+ included Japan in its 1 November roll out, but has not disclosed any content localization. Disney+ started its service in Japan in June 2020 (ContentAsia, 2019; Frater, 2020).

In Korea, a few OTT service corporations, including Oksusu (owned by S.K. Broadband), POOQ (owned by three network channels, KBS, MBC, and SBS), and Tving (owned by CJE&M), had been major actors until recent years. Due to Netflix's soaring market share, these local OTT firms decided to merge POOQ and Oksusu, which established the new service platform Wavve (Kim, S.Y., 2019). With the aim of taking on streaming giant Netflix, the broadcasters and the mobile carrier launched a unified platform that combines the media companies' POOQ streaming service with the latter's Oksusu service in September 2019. The joint venture Content Wavve said it will invest 300 billion won ($250 million) by 2023 to secure more than five million paid subscribers and annual sales of 500 billion won. Wavve planned to create its own Netflix-like original content, which means that the new streaming service platform has been highly influenced by the global OTT platform since its launch (Baek, 2019).

The recent mergers of local OTTs have brought new concerns as this consequently results in a lack of diverse voices, which hurts cultural democracy. The local OTT market certainly turns into an oligopoly market, which hurts diversity. As a handful of mega OTTs, both nationally and globally, focus on a few commercial genres in both production and distribution, locally produced genres focusing on culture, history, and general people's struggles will not be emphasized. Netflix's recent rush in Asian countries is not always positive, because it implies the possibility of the subordination of the local cultural industries to Netflix. Netflix's penetration in the Asian OTT markets will continue as new digital platforms like Disney+ focus on the American market, and Netflix needs to expand in the global market, and Asia is at the front line.

Platform Imperialism in OTT Platforms

Netflix's global dominance based on its massive amount of users has, again, continued since its international penetration started in Canada. Although there are several US-based digital platforms, such as Google, Facebook, and Instagram, people around the globe have never seen this kind of monopolistic dominance of a US-based platform, which has created an unimaginable capitalist system in terms of capital gains from user data. Several OTT platforms like Amazon Prime and Disney+ have competed against Netflix; however, their global presence, compared to Netflix's, is still marginal. While Netflix offers users a way to enjoy cultural content, it obscures economic relations that reflect larger patterns of capitalist development in the digital era based on the socio-cultural and economic relations present on it (Jin, 2013).

Most of all, it is crucial to understand Netflix as a digital platform in actualizing global dominance. There are several previous works that defined digital platforms as merely infrastructure. For example, as Ballon and van Heesvelde (2011, 703) point out, a platform is "a hardware configuration, an operating system, a software framework or any other common entity on which a number of associated components or services run." However, as I discussed elsewhere (2013; 2015), digital platforms have commercial values, because they not only provide opportunities for users to communicate with one another but also afford platform designers and owners the opportunity to sell their platforms as commodities. Digital platforms could not be fairly understood without contemplating three major areas: technological sphere, corporate sphere, and political sphere. What they commonly emphasize is that we need to understand Netflix through not only its technological aspects, but also its commercial and cultural aspects. As van Dijck (2012, 162) argues, digital platforms can also be analyzed from the corporate sphere because "their operation is substantially defined by market forces and the process of commodity exchange." Several critical scholars also argue that digital platforms need to be understood from a critical perspective related to a platform's value embedded in design. Indeed, some theoreticians (Feenberg, 1991; Salter, 2005; Lekka-Kowalik, 2010; Flanagin et al., 2012) point out that technology is not value neutral, as technology possesses a certain bias that embeds the values and communication preferences of designers and developers. In other words, Netflix offers several characteristics similar to digital platforms.

Netflix as a digital platform heavily relies on the increasing number of users and data gathered from those users. Netflix has become one of the most recent digital technologies that increasingly influences people's cultural activities. As van Dijck et al (2018, 9) point out "a platform is fueled by data, automated and organized through algorithms and interfaces, formalized through ownership relations driven by business models, and governed through user agreements." Netflix is the largest OTT service utilizing big data and algorithms to make commercial profit, and it is not only working as an intermediary, but is also playing a role as a mediator to control the vicious chain of cultural spheres (Jin, 2021).

More importantly, it is critical to understand them as mediators, not intermediaries. As van Dijck (2013) argues, platforms play a significant role in influencing people's daily lives as mediators, as they process big data through algorithms and massively commodify user data and user behavior (Fuchs,

2011). Digital platforms should be considered as mediators instead of intermediaries, mainly because digital platforms function as matchmakers, which is one of the most significant capitalist systems (Jin, 2017).

Of course, it is controversial to categorize Netflix as a digital platform like Facebook or Google, mainly because of their different dimensions. As Lobato (2019) especially claims:

> Netflix is not a platform in the same way as social media services like Facebook or Twitter are. Netflix is not open, social, or collaborative. One cannot upload content to Netflix or design software applications to run within it. In this sense, it is fundamentally different from video sites containing both user-uploaded and professionally managed content (YouTube, Youku, etc.)… Netflix is closed, library-like, professional; a portal rather than a platform; a walled garden rather than an open marketplace (31–32).

However, it is critical to understand several of its unique characteristics, such as it being data-driven, commercially oriented, and mediated, which imply that Netflix can be identified as a digital platform (Jin, 2021). Although people or companies could not run their software programs on Netflix, this OTT service platform plays a major role in developing new forms of business models and cultural activities. Elkins (2019) especially identifies Netflix as one of the most significant "digital entertainment platforms." Netflix has continued to transform its own major characteristics, and it is certain that we can analyze Netflix as one of the most significant digital platforms. This critical analysis of digital platforms helps determine challenges and opportunities in understanding digital platforms as a new driver of imperialism in the relationship between countries, in particular the very few Western countries as digital platform creators and owners and the vast majority of non-Western countries as digital platform users (Jin, 2015).

Platform imperialism is an asymmetrical relationship of interdependence between a handful of Western countries, in particular the US, and many non-Western countries, characterized by unequal technological exchanges and capital flows, which implies a technological and cultural domination of US-based digital platforms that have fundamentally influenced the majority of people and countries around the globe (Jin, 2015, 12). Netflix promotes "algorithmic culture as a pathway to global connection, thereby justifying it as essential to their global ambitions. At a key moment in the platforms' play for global dominance," this sells Netflix's globalization "as benevolently multicultural rather than cold, techno-corporate, and threatening to global cultural diversity" (Elkins, 2019, 385).

Although several countries like Japan, Korea, and China as some of the most advanced economic and technological powerhouses in Asia have developed digital platforms, including OTT platforms, it is clear that American-based OTT platforms, including Netflix, dominate the global OTT markets. A few US-owned platforms, from social media platforms to OTT service platforms, have fervently expanded their global dominance, resulting in the increasing asymmetrical gap in terms of technological growth and financial gains between the US and remaining countries. Power is not equally dispersed, and only a few countries, in particular the US, have expanded their global reach and capital accumulation in the OTT sector. The dominance of Netflix has intensified the asymmetrical power relations between the US and Asia and other regions.

Conclusion

This chapter has discussed the increasing role of Netflix as a digital platform in the global OTT markets. The influence of Netflix in the Asian market has been increasing. Netflix as a global OTT platform has built its own brand in Asia over the past several years, and its impact will continue to grow in the near future due to its unique business models in utilizing an ample amount of capital and manpower. Alongside several emerging OTTs, Netflix has greatly influenced the Asian market, which is potentially the largest entertainment market in the world.

In the early 21st century, the US has expanded its global dominance in the OTT markets with Netflix, which means that Netflix's global dominance has not been contested. Due to emerging markets, including China and Korea, several media scholars and popular media argue that the US is losing its dominant power in the global cultural markets. Instead, however, the US has intensified its monopolistic hegemony in the realm of OTT platforms. The emergence of non-US-based platforms in China and Korea has suggested new potential challengers to American hegemony may be forming. These countries have developed their own OTT services, and presumably competed with the US, and they are supposed to build a new global order with their advanced digital platforms. However, these countries have not, and likely cannot, construct a balanced global order, because Netflix is an indicator of the dominance of the US Netflix has penetrated the global OTT markets and expanded its global dominance in the early 21st century. Therefore, it is not contentious to claim that American imperialism has been continuing with OTT platforms, and in general digital platforms. As Mirrlees (2015, 11) also points out, "in the early 21st century, the US is still an Empire and the world system's dominant capitalist, military and communications power center."

Overall, Netflix has become one of the largest and most important OTTs for the Asian cultural industries. It has greatly influenced the entire chain of audio-visual industries in Asia, as elsewhere. Only six years after its launch in Asia, Netflix has already become a formidable force as a global OTT platform to transform Asian cultural and platform sectors. It has controlled the vicious circle of the cultural industries to actualize its status as a global empire, which reshapes local platform and cultural industries, triggering the tremendous shift of cultural consumption.

References

Altstedter, A., Saxena, R., and Nagarajan, S. (2019). Netflix Is Spending $420 Million on Indian Content, CEO Says. *Bloomberg*. December 6. www.bloomberg.com/news/articles/2019-12-06/netflix-is-spending-420-million-on-indian-content-ceo-says

Arya, K. (2020). Can AI improve the workflow in media & entertainment production and content distribution? LinkedIn. January 28. www.linkedin.com/pulse/can-ai-improve-workflow-entertainment-production-kiran-arya

Baek, B.Y. (2019). Wavve receives lukewarm responses. The Korea Times. September 25. www.koreatimes.co.kr/www/tech/2019/09/133_276169.html

Ballon, P., and van Heesvelde, E. (2011). ICT Platforms and Regulatory Concerns in Europe. *Telecommunications Policy* 35(8): 702–714.

Bhushan, N. (2019). Netflix to Invest $400M in Indian Content Over Two Years, CEO Reed Hastings Says. The Hollywood Reporter. June 12. www.hollywoodreporter.com/news/netflix-invest-400m-indian-content-says-ceo-reed-hastings-1260159

Broadband TV News (2019). Asia Pacific OTT to generate $48 billion. March 18. www.broadbandtvnews.com/2019/03/18/asia-pacific-ott-to-generate-48-billion/

ContentAsia (2019). STREAMING: OTT platforms in Japan & Taiwan. October 3. www.contentasia.tv/features/streaming-ott-platforms-japan-taiwan

Elkins, E. (2019). Algorithmic cosmopolitanism: on the global claims of digital entertainment platforms. *Critical Studies in Media Communication* 36 (4): 376–389.

Flanagin, A., Flanagin, C. and Flanagin, J. (2012). Technical Code and the Social Construction of the Internet. *New Media and Society* 12(2): 179–196.

Feenberg, A. (1991). *The Critical Theory of Technology*. London: Oxford University Press.

Frater, P. (2020). Disney Plus to Launch in Japan in June. Variety. 27 May. https://variety.com/2020/streaming/asia/disney-plus-japan-launch-june-1234618352/

Fuchs, C. (2011). *Foundations of Critical Media and Information Studies*. London: Routledge.

Fuchs, C. (2012). Critique of the Political Economy of Web 2.0 Surveillance. In C. Fuchs, K. Boersma, A. Albrechtslund, and M. Sandoval (eds.). *Internet and Surveillance: the challenges of Web 2.0 and Social Media*, 31–70. London: Routledge.

Gillespie, T. (2010). The Politics of Platforms. *New Media and Society* 12(3): 347–364.

Herrman, J. (2017). Platform Companies are Becoming More Powerful-but What Exactly Do They Want? *The New York Times*. March 21. www.nytimes.com/2017/03/21/magazine/platform-companies-are-becoming-more-powerful-but-what-exactly-do-they-want.html

Jenner, M. (2016). Is this TVIV? On Netflix, TVIII and binge-watching. *New Media & Society* 18(2) 257–273.

Jin, D.Y. (2013). The Construction of Platform Imperialism in the Globalization Era. *Triple C: Communication, Capitalism & Critique. Open Access Journal For a Global Sustainable Information Society* 11(1): 145–172.

Jin, D.Y. (2015). *Digital Platforms, Imperialism and Political Culture.* London: Routledge.

Jin, D.Y. (2017). Rise of Platform Imperialism in the Networked Korean Society: a critical analysis of corporate sphere. *Asiascape: Digital Asia* 4: 209–232.

Jin, D.Y. (2021). *Artificial Intelligence in Cultural Production: Critical Perspectives on Digital Platforms.* London: Routledge.

Jin, D.Y., and Feenberg, A. (2015). Commodity and Community in Social Networking: Marx and the Monetization of User-Generated Content. *The Information Society* 31(1): 52–60.

Ju, H.J. (2019). Korean TV drama viewership on Netflix: Transcultural affection, romance, and identities. *Journal of International and Intercultural Communication* 13(1): 32–48.

Kim, H.K. (2017). Why Did Netflix Make Okja. *Sisa Journal.* June 29. www.sisajournal.com/news/articleView.html?idxno=170155

Kim, S.Y. (2019). Wavve, Oksusu +Pooq New Local OTT Started Today. *Star Today.* September 18. www.mk.co.kr/star/hot-issues/view/2019/09/742015/

La Monica, P. (2020). Take that, Disney! Goldman Sachs is super bullish on Netflix. *CNN.* 10 July. www.cnn.com/2020/07/10/investing/netflix-stock-goldman-sachs/index.html

Lee, E. (2019). Netflix Looks Abroad as Growth Slows in the U.S. New York Times. December 16. www.nytimes.com/2019/12/16/business/media/netflix-us-subs-slowing-down-international-subs-growing.html

Lekka-Kowalik, A. (2010). Why Science cannot be Value-Free. *Science and Engineering Ethics* 16(1):33–41.

Littleton, C. (2018). How Hollywood Is Racing to Catch Up With Netflix. Variety. August 22. https://variety.com/2018/digital/features/media-streaming-services-netflix-disney-comcast-att-1202910463/

Lobato, R. (2019). *Netflix Nations: the geography of digital distribution.* New York: New York University Press.

Mirrlees, T. (2015). U.S. Empire and Communications, Today: Revisiting Herbert I. Schiller. *Political Economy of Communication* 3(2): 3–27.

Netflix (2017). 2016 Financial Statements. www.netflixinvestor.com/financials/financial-statements/default.aspx

Netflix (2020a). *Financial Statements.* Netflix.

Netflix (2020b). Netflix Bolsters Anime Programming Through New Partnerships with Four Leading Production Houses in Japan and Korea. October 23. https://about.netflix.com/en/news/production-line-partnerships-2020

Netflix Media Center (2020). Netflix Timeline. https://media.netflix.com/en/about-netflix

Park, W.I. (2019). Per Episode 2 billion Won? Netflix Investigates the Production Cost of a Korean Drama *Kingdom. Chosun Ilbo.* April 19. https://biz.chosun.com/site/data/html_dir/2019/04/18/2019041802659.html

Pulver, A. (2015). Netflix invests $50m in Snowpiercer director Bong Joon-ho's new film. *The Guardian.* November 11. www.theguardian.com/film/2015/nov/11/netflix-invests-50m-snowpiercer-director-bong-joon-ho-jake-gyllenhaal-tilda-swinton

Salter, L. (2005). Colonization Tendencies in the Development of the World Wide Web. *New Media and Society* 7(3): 291–309.

Team, T. (2015). A Look At Netflix's New Asian Target Markets (Part I)—South Korea. *Forbes.* September 16. www.forbes.com/sites/greatspeculations/2015/09/16/a-look-at-netflixs-new-asian-target-markets-part-i-south-korea/#1a9864a97c91

Van Dijck, J. (2012). Facebook as a Tool for Producing Sociality and Connectivity. *Television and New Media* 13(2): 160–176.

Van Dijck, J. (2013). *The Culture of Connectivity: A Critical History of Social Media.* New York: Oxford University Press.

Van Dijck, J., Poell, T., and de Wall, M. (2018). *The platform society: public values in a connective world.* New York: Oxford University Press.

Wallenstein, A. (2018). Netflix Says It's Open to Acquisitions, Stays Mum on Rumored Targets. Variety. April 16. https://variety.com/2018/digital/news/netflix-says-its-open-to-acquisitions-stays-mum-on-rumored-targets-1202754958/

Williams, T. (2017). Netflix just made its first acquisition ever—and it's a comic book enterprise. *MarketWatch.* August 9. www.marketwatch.com/story/netflix-just-made-its-first-acquisition-ever-and-its-the-dude-behind-kick-ass-2017-08-07

Wolverton, T. (2019). Reed Hastings says Netflix has "no big appetite, no big need" for mergers. *Business Insider.* April 17. www.businessinsider.sg/netflix-ceo-reed-hastings-mergers-2019-4/

PART V

Digital Media, Social Media, and Globalization

18

DIGITAL MEDIA AND THE GLOBALIZING SPREAD OF POPULISM

Ralph Schroeder

Introduction

Digital media, once seen as a worldwide force for democratization, have recently come to be regarded as promoting populism instead. What role do digital media play in the rise and entrenchment of populist politics? This chapter will examine populism in a range of countries, arguing that there are similarities in how digital media are used, hence there are global trends. It will also show that different media systems shape the distinctive openings and consolidations of populist online politics. The chapter will begin with two countries that are often seen as alternative models in the Global South: India and China. It will focus on online ultranationalism in both countries, and argue that WhatsApp and WeChat, but earlier also Twitter and bulletin board systems (BBS), have been fora for the dissemination of populist agendas and mobilizations. The chapter will then go on to make comparisons with other instances of the spread of populism, including in the US and Europe. It will highlight that there are similarities across these cases whereby digital media are used to challenge traditional media, as evidenced for example by the uses of Twitter by Modi and Trump. But apart from leaders, populist parties and movements also use online strategies to engage supporters, "from below," including by means of "alternative" newspapers and in small online groups. These online counter- public spheres can set the agenda, but in ways that depend on the particularities of the media systems. In the conclusion, I suggest that populism cannot be counteracted by means of online politics or media alone. Instead, the underlying strength of populist politics must also be addressed.

This chapter will proceed as follows: first, it will lay out how a rethinking of media is required in the light of how digital media have transformed political communication. Next, it will illustrate these changes for China and India, focusing in particular on how populists are circumventing traditional media. To do this, we will need in each case to look at the media system, then how digital media have transformed it, and then how populists use digital media to their advantage. At this point the chapter will turn to some brief comparisons with Western democracies, again focusing on populists in particular, before concluding with some suggestions for how to address some of the dysfunctions that have arisen with the uses of digital media in politics. It can be mentioned at the outset that "digital media" (or online media) will be used throughout to refer to social media—including the use of search engines for information and online-only alternative channels—in contrast to traditional media. Obviously this distinction is becoming harder to maintain, but it will be used here, first, to indicate that traditional news media are governed by journalistic professional standards and a role of reflecting societal concerns and furthermore that they are regulated regarding political communication (such as for electoral advertising). These rules and norms ensure the impartiality, objectivity, diversity, and inclusiveness of traditional media—roles and norms which do not apply to most online or digital media; although, as we shall see, they are becoming increasingly regulated.

Rethinking Media Systems Theory

Media systems theory (Hallin and Mancini, 2004) still provides an important point of departure when thinking about media in different parts of the world. The media systems framework highlights differences in how media operate in various regions of the world; for example, as between the "democratic corporatist model" found in Northern European countries with strong public sector broadcasting as against the Anglo- countries like the US with a "liberal model" where the private sector dominates. The theory points to the fact that media are primarily focused on national news and that the regulation of political communication is mainly nationally bounded. China's media system falls outside of the Hallin and Mancini schema, which was limited to Western democracies. China's media operate in a country with an authoritarian regime, and so they have limited autonomy even if they are increasingly commercialized (Stockmann 2013). India's media, on the other hand, operate in an imperfect democracy (Varshney, 2014), and although there are media that criticize the government, the media are also tied to political and economic elites who bend them to their will (Reddy, 2019). The media in Western democracies are autonomous from states and markets, and so strive, in their political function, to mediate between elites and civil society. With this autonomy, and however imperfectly, they uphold the news norms of objectivity, impartiality, and diversity or inclusiveness of social interests. The news media hold a mirror up to society, represent different groups, and perform a watchdog function.

During the post-war period, the media systems in China, India, and Northern Europe were dominated by public service broadcasters and newspapers. In recent decades, however, they have become increasingly commercialized. In the US, public broadcast has played a minor role, but the regulation of political communication, especially in relation to elections, has been extensive. Yet since the turn of the millennium, American-based digital media companies have come to dominate worldwide. They have largely outflanked national governments in terms of the regulation of political communication, though this is beginning to change. Ultimately digital media will eclipse traditional media. Media systems theory therefore needs to be expanded, not only beyond the original Hallin and Mancini schema to other parts of the world (see Hallin and Mancini, 2012), and not just to include commercialization, but also to include digital media, which add a layer of online political communication that includes targeting and tailoring messages to audiences, sharing messages, and providing non-gatekept channels.

Digital media have changed the political communications environment. The public arena (the term is preferred here to "public sphere" to include conflict, which "sphere" typically does not, Schroeder, 2018, p. 9) used to consist of traditional news with established journalistic norms plus mass media markets, but it has now been complemented by a digital public arena. Traditional media now have competition—for revenue and attention—from online media that can tailor and target their audiences. Apart from the decline of traditional media vis-à-vis digital media (Newman et al., 2019), digital media are driven by audience metrics which may skew them away from their traditional function—as we shall see. But a second change is that news media, even if they continue to be dominant, are no longer the exclusive gatekeepers of the public arena: people share news and alternatives to news, politically active partisans post and disseminate messages, and political leaders and journalists and influencers push their messages via social media that translate into traditional media and into the news agenda (Schroeder, 2018, esp. Chapter 3).

An alternative way to characterize this shift is to point to disinformation, polarization, filter bubbles, and the like. But this is misleading: in relation to disinformation, which we can take here as an umbrella term to include misinformation, propaganda, media manipulation, and the like, the question of the illegal or improper use of media during elections (as with foreign interference) or defamation falls under the rubric of regulation or self-regulation of digital media. In relation to whether digital media have led to polarization or filter bubbles and the like, the evidence is at best elusive, as with claims about the role of disinformation (for example, Schroeder, 2019). The reason why these debates and claims have arisen is because digital media have added a layer, outside of traditional media, to the public arena. This layer does not conform to the standards of news journalism in traditional media, including objectivity, impartiality, and inclusiveness or diversity. Nor does it conform to official communication by parties and leaders and social movement organizations or how they are covered in traditional media. Instead, online politics is often partisan and confrontational. However, the content—apart from the aforementioned efforts externally to influence domestic politics, harm online, or defame—is not illegal, and could be regarded as the legitimate expression of inputs of public opinion into the political process. Traditional media and journalism have never had a monopoly on legitimate political inputs—since the public arena also included pamphlets, rallies, mass mailings, calls to voters, and the like—but they used to be dominant and gatekept. They still are, but this dominance has been challenged.

The recent successes of populists can be partly attributed to digital media, which are often used to challenge traditional media or circumvent them. Populists can be defined as anti-elite, favoring the people conceived in exclusivist terms against "others", and seeking more representation by "the people" (Mudde and Kaltwasser, 2017). Populists disproportionally take to digital media since they regard traditional media as elite and not representing their views. It is important not to exaggerate the populist challenge: not all countries have significant populist politics; for example, Ireland, Japan, and Singapore. And digital media have been used by challengers who are not populists, such as the Obama campaign (Kreiss, 2016), the Arab Spring protesters (Howard, 2010) and the Pirate Party (Jungherr, Stier, and Schroeder 2019). But wherever populists have recently gained strength, they have used digital media, though in quite different ways. Populists' uses of media have been well-documented in Western democracies but less so outside the West (but see Moffitt, 2017). Thus we can turn to two important non-Western cases, India and China, before making comparisons.

Twitter, WhatsApp, and Modi

Narendra Modi was not the first politician to use new media in Indian politics. Mayawati's successful election campaign in Uttar Pradesh used feature phones to mobilize voters and turn out voters (Doron and Jeffrey, 2013, pp. 148–54). Doron and Jeffrey have argued that this made a critical difference to the insurgent campaign of this Dalit (formerly known as untouchable) politician, who overcame the opposition of traditional elite media and of upper caste political dominance. In 2014, Modi similarly had to overcome opposition from within his own party elite to become the candidate for prime minister of the B.J.P. (the Bharatiya Janata Party or Indian Peoples' Party). But he used Twitter, and also vernacular language media (Neyazi 2018), effectively to promote his agenda outside of established media and elite channels, and succeeded both within his own party and then against the Congress Party. He did so not using Twitter alone, since digital media at the time were used only by a small fraction of the population. But the Rashtriya Swayamsevak Sangh (RSS), the extreme Hindu nationalist volunteer organization supporting the BJP, was galvanized on Twitter. Further, traditional media could not but broadcast Modi's tweets, as Chakraborty et al. (2018) have shown. Moreover, Pal, Chandra and Vydiswaran (2016) have documented how his ultranationalist message was toned down once he was candidate for prime minister and had to win votes, and even more so (at least officially) when he became prime minister and had to represent the whole nation. But by that stage he could leave the more extreme Hindu nationalist message to his proxies, and especially his second-in-command in the party (now home affairs minister) Amit Shah and other more out-spoken leading political figures like Yogi Adityanath (now chief minister of Uttar Pradesh), as well as the RSS and his vocal social media supporters.

In India, the role that digital media play in politics is still limited: The Lokniti report (2019) found that only a third of voters used social media in relation to the 2019 national election. But this underestimates the role of digital media for at least two reasons: the first is that digital media have been used to great effect to spread an extreme Hindu nationalist message that would be unsuitable in traditional media. There are exceptions to civility in traditional media, especially Republic TV, which is uncannily similar to Fox News in the US: they both have the largest national TV news audience share and often depart from impartiality in their support for their countries' leaders. The extreme online messages, however, often set the political tone and so the news agenda: the clearest example during the 2019 election was how flames were fanned in the wake of the terrorist attack in Kashmir and the Indian airstrike response: online nationalism reached a fever pitch during these events and helped Modi's victory. The second underestimation of digital media is that they were used during the election to mobilize supporters and spread messages and influence public opinion, including on WhatsApp (Aneez et al., 2019); illustrated by the continual smears against Congress leaders and other opposition politicians and the spread of anti-Muslim hate.

Thus while comparatively few may have used social media, they have been used to promote politics that are more extreme than the official pronouncements of the parties and leaders which, in turn, shaped the overall media agenda. The fact that the BJP was far more active and successful in this endeavor, partly because it had a far better-funded and more well-organized digital media campaign than its main rival, the Congress Party (Sardesai, 2020, pp. 226–267, 232–233), should not detract from the fact that this kind of mobilization could equally have been undertaken by other political forces, including challengers on the left.

In India, as mentioned, the press has never been entirely autonomous: it has been influenced by large businesses and by corrupt politicians, some of whom have bought their own media channels. India's public service media, especially NDTV, which dominated into the 1980s and 1990s, has since declined into insignificance. But this is not simply "neo-liberalism"; a similar commercialization of media has taken place in a range of countries from social-democratic Sweden to the party-state's marketization of the economy of China. Further, commercialization has gone hand in hand with a proliferation of online channels, some of which represent the interests of India's progressive civil society (Aneez et al., 2019). But Modi and the BJP have used digital media more successfully, both early on to take over the party and push it further toward ultranationalism, and in the 2019 election to consolidate its power. Even now, when he is solidly in power, Modi and the BJP use digital media, now primarily WhatsApp and digital media campaigns by supporters, to push a more extreme Hindu nationalist agenda than is possible in traditional media, which continue to provide a meek opposition.

China's Subterranean Online Sphere

Populism in China seems a contradiction in terms because opposition to elite rule is not tolerated. Nevertheless, the government in China, too, must be at least partly responsive to its citizens, and populists aim to pressure the regime's elites to put certain "people" first. In China, digital media are more important for responsiveness to citizens than traditional media because traditional media are more easily controlled by the state. Digital media, in contrast, constitute a relatively open public arena (for example, Rauchfleisch and Schäfer, 2015), within limits set by the party-state, but which the state can also monitor for discontent. This online realm can be called "subterranean", a realm where political expression is either unofficially tolerated (as long as it stays within limits or serves the regime) or under the radar of official public opinion formation. "Subterranean" online political discourse is thus an open "counter-public" (Schroeder 2018, p. 9, drawing on Nancy Fraser's concept) in democracies but it remains below the ground in China. And in India's partial democracy, as we have seen, it is open but faces large obstacles because of media ownership and the lack of autonomy of the media from government influence.

In China, online expression that goes against the official policies promoted by the party-state is sometimes tolerated, as long as (again) it remains within bounds. Wright (2018) has argued that nationalist protest has been the most successful among the various types of popular protest against the regime, which for her include environmental, property-related, labor, ethnic, and rural protests. These other protests have had at best partial or limited success. But Wright says that unlike these other protests, nationalist protest is mainly online and it is not driven by material interests but rather expressive ones. It is also more episodic rather than continuous; in other words, it is related to specific events such as the Beijing Olympics, the dispute over Japanese versus Chinese islands, flare-ups around Tibetan independence, and the like. But the main reason why nationalist protest is tolerated, according to Wright, is that it suits the regime—unless it goes too far, in a direction that goes counter to the regime's policies, and in that case it is quashed.

Intellectuals are a particular target for attack for Chinese populists, especially the "White Left". Zhang (2019) has discussed the "White Left", which populists see as consisting of Western-influenced "liberals" (in the American sense) who espouse progressive causes. Their netizen critics regard them as foolish, much in the way that populists in other countries criticize multicultural cosmopolitan elites. In criticizing the "White Left" elite, populist critics (ironically, themselves mostly elites) claim support from the public or from "the people". But there is a difference in China: in the West, populists criticize intellectuals for their views about domestic politics, while Chinese populists mainly criticize multicultural cosmopolitans because their attitudes are too foreign and Western. Another difference is that Chinese populists see a strong authoritarian state as a remedy against these "enemies of the people". Han has observed, in relation to public intellectuals (gongzhi, which can be a derogatory term): "Considering that the authoritarian regime has been struggling to dismiss the impact of public intellectuals with little success...popular denigration of the group has helped the state to achieve its goal. In particular, by embracing popular cyber culture and expressional elements, these netizens may have defended the regime more effectively than the state has' (2018: 1980). Again, we see that online expression can help the state, but again, this online contestation is subterranean.

Official media are thus more immune to populist beliefs than non-official ones, but that may not apply to commercial media. Wright (2018) notes, for example, that the *People's Daily*, the official propaganda organ, is more positive toward foreign powers than commercial media, which sometimes promote virulent nationalism to please their audiences. But there is another difference from Western democracies: unlike these democracies, China has had comparatively little immigration, which has often been the spark for populist protest since they are seen as "enemies." Yet relative to the small proportion of black immigrants, Chinese racism toward this group has been disproportionately strong, especially online (Cheng, 2011). Racist antagonism, apart from being directed against the black minority, is also directed against the state and against intellectuals whom racists regard as being too accommodating toward this group.

China's populism is both easy to control, because it is mainly online, and at the same hard to control since the online realm is the arena of strongest political contention. Chinese populists remain fragmented: there are several groups that can be identified as potential populists but they do not have a coherent constituency within the party and nor is there any coherence or coordination among social movements or non-governmental organizations that support them. The report by Shi-Kupfer et al. (2017) identifies several quite different groups: Mao Lovers and Equality Advocates, who are potentially "left-wing" populists, and Flagwavers, Traditionalists, Party Warriors, and China Advocates, potentially "right-wing" populists. Yet fragmentation applies to Chinese oppositional groups generally, not just to populists. And another weakness of potential populist mobilization and of digital politics in China generally is that the party has more powerful means to measure and target—and thus to manage—the strength of online sentiments than other countries do. This is a strength of the party-state, but it also comes with a danger: namely, that this source is an unreliable evidence base because it is "skewed" toward the population that is most vocal online.

Any conclusions about the role that populists will play in China are premature. Populists are among the most prominent and successful forces of popular political protest or mobilization in China, especially online. They need to be reckoned with, but have been largely overlooked to date because they are unlike two groups which are prominent in the study of Chinese politics, and with which they should not be confused: they are unlike the pro-democracy and pro-Western anti-party-state dissidents that are anti-elite, but they are also unlike the pro-party-state and anti-Western or anti-foreigner rabid nationalists that support the party-state's elite. Chinese populist enthusiasm goes against the regimes' Westernizing policies, including its moderate (as opposed to nationalist) economic policies and its pragmatic foreign policies. Yet it is also difficult to curb. Unlike other forms of popular protest, the regime cannot dismiss populists as a foreign-influenced meddling force. Populists seek more recognition for "the people", and so they are continuous with the "grassroots" tradition in Chinese politics. In this respect they are similar to other populists in the West (and beyond) that seek more "democracy from below." Populists are thus a force that the regime cannot easily suppress since it goes with the grain of Chinese political history. They are also not easily controlled since their main agitation is taking place online. It remains to be seen if they will follow a global pattern with Chinese characteristics.

China, India, and Western Democracies

It is not surprising that two geopolitically and economically rising powers like India and China should see increasing ultranationalism (Zhao, 2004) from above and from below—"ultra-" to indicate that, unlike traditional nationalist forces, this populist type of nationalism is directed against enemies from within (elites) and from without (rival powers). It is also not surprising that this ultranationalism should be especially vocal online, since official government policy is typically "diplomatic" and citizens' public everyday concerns are not particularly aggressive toward "others." Moreover, traditional media must be impartial and balanced toward all political actors. Online, however, and outside of established channels, such aggressive politics can be expressed. And apart from internal enemies, India's foreign arch rival is Pakistan whereas China's arch rivals (apart from Taiwan) are Japan and the US. In Western democracies, populism is less outward-facing, and mainly concentrates on alleged threats to culture and to economic well-being from within, again, mainly via online media.

Apart from attacking "others," populists attack traditional media. One reason why this attack is particularly pronounced outside of Western democracies is that media are often seen as supporting a dominant elite or a cosmopolitan consensus that does not reflect alternative views or political models from the Global South. Thus certain elites in India, China, and the Global South are regarded as sharing the views of Western elites, making them a target of online populist anti-elitism since the media agenda is dominated by elite viewpoints in leading national traditional media. A related point is that traditional media are not as autonomous in less-than-democratic societies as they are in democracies. Instead, they are controlled by a mixture of political-cum-business elites in India and by the party-state elite in China. In these (again) less-than-democratic societies, digital media provide a comparatively less controlled alternative to traditional media. Added to which, digital media also offer an alternative to Western-centric consumer or entertainment culture, more so than traditional media. And again, even if these alternatives in their current political form are often mobilized on behalf of an exclusivist—and in this sense an anti-progressive—agenda, they are also democratizing in providing more voices "from below" and providing more diverse political and cultural inputs.

Populists have used digital media to gain power. Once in power, populists in government have also found new ways to use digital media: President Trump's tweets were regularly broadcast via traditional media. This is a novel form of the mediatization (Hjarvard, 2008) of politics: previously, American presidents held press conferences, whereas Trump used Twitter to attack the media and his opponents as well as to announce his policies and plans. This new form of communication has not just come from his side; traditional media have accommodated the change: they regularly featured his tweets, and this mode of political communication now also occasionally extends to other leaders. Whether it will last beyond Trump's presidency is unknown. Trump was opposed by much of the public and of the media, but he used Twitter to amplify his criticism of this opposition, and the media obliged him (after all, Trumps tweets were newsworthy and also could not be ignored for the sake of keeping audiences). Note the contrast with Modi: Modi needed alternative channels to get into power, but he is now firmly ensconced and the media provide only weak opposition. Populists in power also need to be inclusive, at least "officially," and they are also now part of the elite even if they continue to be anti-establishment. But digital media are still used by Modi's allies and his supporters to promote a stronger Hindu nationalist message than Modi's own.

Trump and Modi are not alone. The anti-immigrant Alternative for Germany party (AfD) has a YouTube "news" channel (AfDTV), which was created because the party thinks that its agenda is ignored in traditional media. In Sweden, the anti-immigrant Sweden Democrat party relies not only on Facebook groups, like AfD supporters do, but it also has the support of several "alternative news" websites. These websites are not directly affiliated with the party, but they support its agenda and prominently feature anti-immigrant and anti-establishment stories. They can also be called "hyperpartisan" websites because they do not follow the journalistic standards of objectivity, impartiality, and inclusiveness. Such websites exist in several European countries. In China, populists are mainly in opposition and they have few allies among the ruling elite. But their subterranean use of digital media can also be used to attack traditional media and to provide alternatives to dominant views in the media. Digital media thus provide alternatives for populist leaders and parties and also for their civil society supporters in all cases, but how they do so differs as between the contexts of the media systems in China, India, and Western democracies. The differences are shown in table 1 below (Table 18-1 here):

Table 18.1 Media Systems and Populist Uses of Digital Media

	China	*India*	*Western Democracies*
Media System	Authoritarian control of state media and (partly audience-driven) commercial media	Mostly commercial, heavily shaped by politically corrupt influences	Hallin and Mancini's three Western types (liberal, democratic-corporatist, polarized pluralist)
Populist Politicians and Organizations	Elite ultranationalist activists	Modi and BJP politicians	Trump, far right and far left (Bernie Sanders)
Civil Society Supporters	Ultranationalist political activists and netizens—highly fragmented and "subterranean"	RSS, party workers, voter mobilization	Voters, activists, populist leader supporters
Populist Use of Digital Media	Grassroots use of Weibo, WeChat, bulletin boards	Modi's and his surrogates' tweets translated into other media, social media (WhatsApp), smartphone messages for party workers and supporters	Trump's tweets translated into traditional media (US), 'alternative news' websites and social media (esp. Facebook)

It can be noted how this chapter departs from other approaches to populism and digital media: much of the recent discussion about populist politics has revolved around filter bubbles, disinformation (or misinformation or propaganda), polarization, and the like. But the digital media uses by populists discussed here do not fall under those headers: populists have used digital media to push their agenda in legitimate—though often unconventional—ways. It is true that certain aspects of digital media require regulation, such as illegal foreign interference, bots, or targeting citizens in non-transparent ways. However, these techniques are not unique to populists. What should therefore be done, if the aim is to counteract populists, is to either seek to reassert the role of traditional media as autonomous and trustworthy—or to convince publics of political alternatives, online and offline. Combating online disinformation or curbing social media companies will do little to counter populists; this will require alternatives to populist politics too (Schroeder, 2020).

Counteracting the changed media conditions requires strengthening the objectivity, impartiality, and inclusiveness or diversity of news media, and avoiding inequality of access for political inputs; in other words, the legitimacy of traditional modes of conveying news and political communication. Even if political communication is now in online formats, the traditional role of media must be restored and adapted to the online realm. In India and China, the autonomy of the news and of freedom of expression of civil society must be strengthened against the state, and in Western democracies also against excessive market competition which has led to a pandering to audiences. Anti-elitism has been strengthened, but so too have the voices of a vocal part of the population. But these populist forces must also be countered on their own terrain of bypassing traditional gatekeepers. In other words, political alternatives to populism must also partake of digital opportunities. Online communication without gatekeepers will continue to have advantages, for good or ill. That applies not just to leaders and parties but also to social movements and to the public generally.

Although populists are currently in the ascendant and their online politics are particularly vocal, they are not the only ones who can benefit from circumventing traditional media gatekeepers. Circumventing gatekeepers can mobilize digital media on behalf of creating positive shared understandings which reestablish a fair public arena—not a public sphere in Habermas' sense of "rational agreement" but an arena where a certain common ground is shared that allows for reasonable conflict and disagreement. Civility online, whereby citizens and their leaders use the public arena for constructive engagement, may currently seem on the decline, but there is no reason why it cannot be strengthened. This is also where academic research and cosmopolitan elites can make common cause, in an objective understanding of the media which does not exaggerate their effects but points to weaknesses of populist strategies and opportunities for political alternatives. Zhang and Neyazi (2020) in their useful overview of approaches of communication theories from China and India, have rightly argued that research about the Global South should no longer only take the West as a reference point. Yet they go too far in therefore rejecting theories that try to generalize across cases: indeed, in view of the similarities and differences in how populists have gained advantages across "East" and "West", there is much to be learned from how they enable populists—but also how to counter them.

References

Aneez, Z., Neyazi, T.A., Kalogeropoulos, A., & Nielsen, R.K. (2019). *Reuters Institute India digital news report*. Reuters Institute for the Study of Journalism/India Digital News Report. Retrieved from https://reutersinstitute.politics.ox.ac.uk/sites/default/files/2019-03/India_DNR_FINAL.pdf

Chakraborty, S., Pal, J., Chandra, P. and Romero, D.M., (2018). Political Tweets and Mainstream News Impact in India: A Mixed Methods Investigation into Political Outreach. In *Proceedings of the 1st ACM SIGCAS Conference on Computing and Sustainable Societies*. ACM, June.

Cheng, Yinghong. (2011). From campus racism to cyber racism: Discourse of race and Chinese nationalism. *The China Quarterly* 207: 561–579.

Doron, A. & Jeffrey, R. (2013). *The Great Indian Phone Book: How the Mass Mobile Changes Business, Politics and Daily Life*. Harvard: Harvard University Press.

Hallin, D., & Mancini, P. (2004). *Comparing Media Systems: Three Models of Media and Politics.* Cambridge: Cambridge University Press.

Hallin, D., & Mancini, P. (eds). (2012). *Comparing Media Systems Beyond the Western World.* Cambridge: Cambridge University Press.

Han, Rongbin. (2018). Withering gongzhi: Cyber criticism of Chinese public intellectuals. *International Journal of Communication* 12: 1966–1987.

Hjarvard, S. (2008). The Mediatization of Society: A theory of the media as agents of social and cultural change. *Nordicom Review* 29(2): 105–134.

Howard, P. (2010). *The Digital Origins of Dictatorship and Democracy: Information Technology and Political Islam.* Oxford: Oxford University Press.

Jungherr, A., Stier, S., and Schroeder, R. (2019). Digital Media and the Surge of Political Challengers: Explaining the Political Success of Outsiders in the US, Germany and China', *Social Media + Society,* DOI:10.1177/2056305119875439.

Kreiss, D. (2016). *Prototype Politics: Technology- Intensive Campaigning and the Data of Democracy.* Oxford: Oxford University Press.

Lokniti—Centre for the Study of Developing Societies (CSDS). (2019). Social Media & Political Behaviour. www.csds.in/uploads/custom_files/Report-SMPB.pdf

Moffitt, B. (2017). *The Global Rise of Populism: Performance, Political Style, and Representation.* Stanford: Stanford University Press.

Mudde, C., and Kaltwasser, C.R. (2017). *Populism: A Very Short Introduction.* Oxford: Oxford University Press.

Newman, N et al. (2019). *Reuters Institute Digital News Report 2019.* Oxford: Reuters Institute for the Study of Journalism, University of Oxford, https://reutersinstitute.politics.ox.ac.uk/sites/default/files/2019-06/DNR_2019_FINAL_0.pdf

Neyazi, T.A. (2018). *Political Communication and Mobilisation: The Hindi Media in India.* Cambridge: Cambridge University Press.

Pal, J., Chandra, P., & Vydiswaran, V. (2016). Twitter and the Rebranding of Narendra Modi. *Economic & Political Weekly* 51(8): 52– 60.

Rauchfleisch, A., & Schäfer, M.S. (2015). Multiple public spheres of Weibo: A typology of forms and potentials of online public spheres in China. *Information, Communication & Society,* 18, 139–155.

Reddy, C.R. (2019). Media in Contemporary India: Journalism transformed into a commodity. In C. Jaffrelot, A. Kohli and K. Murali (eds), *Business and Politics in India.* New York: Oxford University Press, 183–207.

Sardesai, R. (2020). *2019: How Modi Won India.* Noida: Harper Collins.

Shi-Kupfer, K., Ohlberg, M., Lang, S., and Lang, B. (2017). Ideas and Ideologies Competing for China's Political Future. *Merics Paper on China 5.*

Schroeder, R. (2018). *Social Theory After the Internet: Media, Technology and Globalization.* London: UCL Press, www.ucl.ac.uk/ucl-press/browse-books/social-theory-after-the-internet

Schroeder, R. (2019) Digital Media and the Entrenchment of Right-wing Populist Agendas, *Social Media + Society.* 5 (4).

Schroeder, R. (2020): Political power and the globalizing spread of populist politics, *Journal of Political Power,* DOI: 10.1080/2158379X.2020.1720101

Stockmann, D. (2013). *Media Commercialization and Authoritarian Rule in China.* Cambridge: Cambridge University Press.

Varshney, A. (2014). *Battles Half Won: India's Improbable Democracy.* New Delhi: Penguin.

Wright, T. (2018). *Popular Protest in China.* Cambridge: Polity Press.

Zhang, C. (2019). Right-wing populism with Chinese characteristics? Identity, otherness and global imaginaries in debating world politics online. *European Journal of International Relations.* 23(1): 49–73.

Zhang, W. and Neyazi, T. (2020). Communication and technology theories from the South: the cases of China and India. *Annals of the International Communication Association.* 44(1): 34–49.

Zhao, S. (2004). *A Nation-State by Construction: Dynamics of Modern Chinese Nationalism.* Stanford: Stanford University Press.

19

LETHAL, VIRAL, GLOBAL

The Role of Mobile Media and the Growing International Scourge of Fake News

Gordon Kuo Siong Tan, Sun Sun Lim, and Roy Kheng

Introduction

The rising ubiquity of mobile phones and other mobile-enabled devices, even among bottom-of-pyramid users, has greatly accelerated the spread of online disinformation. Whereas news was previously shared via a one-to-many broadcast model in which incumbent news providers played a gatekeeping role and tried to adhere to journalistic standards, media production and dissemination capabilities are now within easy reach of everyday consumers. We have thus transitioned to an era of many-to-many communication, in which news is no longer the preserve of established media companies but can be produced and widely shared by media consumers themselves. This democratization of media production and dissemination has also contributed to the surge in online disinformation because consumers may become key nodes in sharing fabricated information that is calculated to be eye-catching, sensationalist, or titillating. This chapter will analyze the spread of fake news and the role that mobile media has played in exacerbating this pernicious trend in a globalized media landscape.

We examine the architecture of social media platforms built upon user engagement and sharing of content where advertisement-driven revenue models have encouraged the proliferation of viral and inflammatory content, with journalistic best practices like fact-checking and source verification being de-emphasized. We also explain the role of human factors and cognitive biases in spreading fake news, even as content production is within easier reach of everyday media consumers. Finally, we explore the role of emerging technologies such as social media bots and "deep fake" videos that facilitate the spread of fake news at much faster speeds to an ever-growing global audience.

Surveillance Capitalism and the Rise of Social Media

Contemporary capitalism has spawned a new breed of high-technology companies with entirely different business models. Technology titans like Facebook, Google, and Twitter serve users globally by offering complimentary services that are supported by advertising, through which they capture user data that can be monetized in multiple ways. Zuboff (2019) calls this "surveillance capitalism," where technology is used to surveil users and to commodify them as profit-making objects by monitoring and influencing their online behavior.

Social media firms in particular generate lucrative advertising revenue by "monetizing" attention through motivating users to stay longer and interact more intensively with their platforms. Social media platforms increase user engagement by using proprietary algorithms to personalize news (and advertising) content. These algorithms sort and organize content based on relevancy rather than chronological order and employ complex statistical models to track and aggregate voluminous amounts of user data to infer and predict user preferences and behavior. Information is then algorithmically curated to deliver customized content that captures user attention. The emergence of the always-on, always-connected multi-function smartphone gave social media a real shot in the arm (Westlund, 2014). With people increasingly tethered to their smartphones, their usage of social media increased both in quantity and in form, further invigorated by the rise of location-based services (Katz & Lai, 2014) that enable an even more precise delivery of personalized content.

One frequently cited example is Facebook's news feed function. It is powered by sophisticated algorithms in which "nearly every interaction with content on Facebook informs the algorithm to accommodate accordingly" (Wiggins, 2017: 19). Algorithms actively predict the information that users want to see by harvesting and analyzing data from their digital trail: users' profiles, the profiles of their friends, browsing and search histories, their locations, and virtually every trackable online activity within legally permissible limits. Trending stories are tailored to each user's preferences as determined by the algorithms. Content is refreshed and displayed in real time according to popularity, as measured by user engagement metrics such as "likes," "clicks," and "shares."

It is in precisely such a user-driven and commercially oriented architecture that falsehoods have thrived. Notably, Vosoughi, Roy, and Aral (2018) show that false stories are more captivating and spread faster than real news. Individuals react more to content that elicits stronger emotional responses like shock, amazement, fear, and disgust. Therefore, fake news is intentionally crafted to trigger emotional responses by being sensational, to ensure that it is liberally shared and widely circulated. Social media algorithms that heavily prioritize user engagement thus actively promote inflammatory content to users and those in their network. The act of sharing by users gives further traction to fake news because it confers implicit endorsement that makes the message appear compelling and plausible. As more people turn to social media as their main source of news (Shearer, 2018), these platforms have become the prime conduits for ill-intentioned actors seeking to disseminate falsehoods.

Human Agents and Cognitive Bias

Clearly, the digital infrastructures that enable the spread of fake news require the support of human agents to consume, comment, and share before traction mounts and virality is attained. Indeed, the human factor is crucial when examining the role of algorithms in perpetuating and diffusing fake news. Cognitive bias can influence our online behavior, which in turn modifies how these algorithms function (Borges & Gambarato, 2019). The effect of discourse in polarizing behavior is well studied in communication research. The theory of selective exposure (Stroud, 2017) describes how we are motivated to seek out information that parallels our beliefs and values. Such behavior is rooted in confirmation bias, where we are more persuaded by messages that are consistent with our existing opinions, and discount or ignore discordant information. Although the internet can facilitate both the search for like-minded individuals and exposure to diverse viewpoints, the inherent design of social media (and its business model) has gravitated toward the former. After all, our social media networks consist of friends, family, and co-workers who share similar interests and beliefs (Gaines & Mondak, 2009). Social media algorithms organize and filter information to customize the content delivery experience. This involves simultaneously selecting and prioritizing content that fits the user's cognitive preferences and screening out dissonant information by downgrading their prominence in the newsfeed. When a user clicks on a fake news link, the algorithm will respond accordingly to offer similar content that may be biased or fake under a continuous feedback loop. Social media essentially uses software code to supercharge selective exposure on a global scale (Waldrop, 2017).

The individualization of social media content has led to "filter bubbles" (Pariser, 2011) whereby users are exposed to homogeneous content that mirrors and reinforces their existing beliefs. "Filter bubbles" are akin to digital "echo chambers" (Zimmer, Scheibe, Stock, & Stock, 2019). Users become more entrenched in their current beliefs, which are further reinforced by continuous exposure to concordant content under a contagion effect that allows misinformation to quickly diffuse (Törnberg, 2018). Del Vicario et al. (2016) find evidence of segregated and polarized clusters of users within which biased stories circulate rapidly. Human "trolls" also play a contributing factor in sowing online discord and disrupting the norms of internet discourse. Trolls deliberately make controversial and inflammatory speech online to provoke emotional responses from unsuspecting readers that end up in bitter arguments and create divisiveness among users. Indeed, internet platforms have become the primary conduits where these cognitive biases are exploited by malicious agents for monetary, political, and other nefarious purposes.

Democratization of Content Production

The internet—and mobile media—have significantly lowered entry barriers for content production. All it takes is a mobile-enabled device and an internet connection to send a tweet and post on TikTok, or to create a phony news website that mimics the professional appearance of established news sources like the *New York Times*. In a discernible shift toward "produsing", users are no longer just passive consumers of content but have been co-opted as producers (creating and disseminating content) and evaluators (reviewing and sharing the content of others). The disintermediation of news production aided by the internet and ubiquity of social media has connected content producers to consumers directly, bypassing long-standing institutional gatekeepers like newspapers that counter misinformation (Lazer et al., 2018).

While the production and consumption of information have been democratized, this egalitarian approach has resulted in an explosion of digital content that is continuously produced by a global pool of users. When virtually anyone can become a content producer, it is difficult to assess the accuracy and credibility of information. At the same time, this new system of decentralized information production has meant that editorialization norms, news gathering ethics, and other journalistic standards are largely absent, especially in the rush to create more eye-catching content to attract higher readership and boost advertising revenues.

News making has thus become more amateur in its globalized transformation, turning into a lucrative business enterprise that is often geographically and politically detached from the subject being covered. Writers may be roped in from different parts of the world to churn out misleading articles that are targeted at overseas audiences. For instance, the small city of Veles in Macedonia has become infamous for its fledgling industry of fake news production, where residents make a living by writing articles and hosting websites that are either wholly fabricated or based on distortions of actual events (Oxenham, 2019). Sensational headlines function as advertising "clickbait," tricking users into following links to articles that present a warped worldview and reinforce existing prejudices. Those articles were meant to fuel disharmony among readers in the US and capitalize on the country's growing political divisiveness, especially leading up to the 2016 US Presidential election. With news production and consumption plugging into an internationalized juggernaut that defies and subverts geographical boundaries, fake news is indeed an intriguing by-product of media globalization.

Emerging Technological Twists: Bots and "Deep Fakes"

Just as the media landscape evolves ceaselessly, new technological innovations emerge constantly. Social media bots in particular compound the fake news scourge, playing a central role in the diffusion of misinformation (Shao et al., 2018a, 2018b). Social bots are fake accounts that impersonate real human users. Sporting human avatars on their account profiles, they can interact with other bots and human users autonomously. Bots expand their networks by connecting with influential, legitimate users with a large follower base to amplify their reach, so that they can target misinformation at those who are most susceptible to believing false narratives. They can create new posts, share content, follow, or reply to other users, all with the aim of influencing or manipulating public opinion. Bots are essentially algorithms that automate online tasks, generating content repetitively at much faster speeds than typical human users, making them highly efficient tools for spreading misinformation. It is estimated that between 9 and 15% of active Twitter accounts were run by bots in 2017 (Varol, Ferrara, Menczer, & Flammini, 2017), demonstrating their embeddedness in social media.

Despite their prominence, a Pew Research Center survey shows that most people are not confident of identifying social bots (Stocking & Sumida, 2018). By simulating human interaction, bots exploit our curiosity about popular trending topics, and our proclivity to be more trusting toward information from our social contacts (Turcotte, York, Irving, Scholl, & Pingree, 2015). Therefore, as Shao et al. (2018b) posit, bots and human users work in conjunction to spread false content, where the resharing of low-credibility information from bots is mostly performed by users who are unwittingly drawn into becoming active agents of fake news dissemination.

Besides bots, advancements in artificial intelligence have made it possible for newer and more sophisticated modalities of fake news dissemination to emerge. Of particular concern is "deep fake" technology. A portmanteau of "deep learning" and "fake," this technology makes use of artificial intelligence and machine-learning algorithms trained to insert faces and voices into video and audio recordings of actual people. Richer media content that appears more convincing and credible is easily produced, with hyper-realistic, digitized impersonations making it appear as if a person said or did something.

The sophistication of "deep fake" technology belies its easy accessibility; such technology has already begun to diffuse through society via tools that are freely available online. A free desktop application called FakeApp allows amateur users to create "deep fake" videos that are highly realistic without requiring much technical knowledge or skill. The sheer computing power in mobile devices allows the speedy production of realistic face-swapping videos with minimal input required. A Chinese app, Zao, requires just one photograph to superimpose a person's face onto TV and movie scenes. The uncanny realism of the output has made the app go viral, becoming the most downloaded app on the Chinese iOS app store (Porter, 2019).

Such easy access to sophisticated "deep fake" technology has led to homemade production of increasingly convincing audio and video impersonations that are becoming more difficult to detect and debunk. While such algorithmically driven "deep fake" videos may be entertaining, they can also be deployed for nefarious purposes. In 2018, a viral video showed former US President Obama cursing and calling President Trump names. It later emerged that the video was derived from digitally manipulated public footage of Obama and deliberately made to warn against the dangers of easily produced "deep fake" videos in exacerbating fake news and worsening political divisions.

Fundamentally, users favor novel and emotionally stirring content and thus circulate falsehoods more widely than real news (Vosoughi et al., 2018). This gives digitally fabricated videos the perfect opportunity to infiltrate the news ecosystem to sow confusion and destabilize society by deepening social divisions, undermining institutions of authority, and interfering with elections (Chesney & Citron, 2018). "Deep fake" videos inject richer performative elements to make false stories seem more credible. The interplay between our cognitive biases and revolutionary technological developments within a social media-focused news environment forebodes emerging threats in the burgeoning fake news problem.

Growing Reach and Heightening Hostility

In 2016, a man drove from his home in North Carolina to the Comet Ping Pong pizza joint in Washington DC Heavily armed, he was there on a rescue mission. The man had read conspiracy theories online that suggested kidnapped children from an underground pedophile ring were being hidden by Hillary Clinton in tunnels below the pizzeria. Interestingly, those conspiracy theories were widely retweeted by bots originating from Cyprus, the Czech Republic, and Vietnam (Fisher, Cox, & Hermann, 2016). Fortunately, no one was hurt in this "Pizzagate" incident and the man eventually surrendered to the police. However, other incidents have ended in grisly violence and bloodshed. Both the gunmen involved in the El Paso, Texas and Christchurch, New Zealand mass shootings had published manifestos that were inspired by the Great Replacement, a conspiracy theory originating in France. The Great Replacement warns of white genocide because of displacement by immigrants, particularly Muslims, fomenting racism and anti-immigrant attitudes that culminated in the two tragedies. These incidents show how false stories can originate in one place and lead to negative consequences in another in our interconnected world. Indeed, the unprecedented and unfettered circulation of misinformation in cyberspace has allowed the undesirable outcomes of fake news to unfold on national, regional, and global scales.

Social messaging apps have also been used to propagate falsehoods. In India, for example, there was a spike in the number of deaths resulting from lynchings arising from the viral spread of unfounded rumors about child kidnappings that circulated like wildfire on WhatsApp. The rumors stoked considerable public fear and anxiety that was further fueled by the local media's irresponsible sharing of these uncorroborated claims. Innocent victims have lost their lives in the waves of senseless mob violence that have seen random passers-by and individuals from marginalized groups such as the mentally challenged and the differently abled being disproportionately targeted by community vigilantes.

Beyond these fake news-related crises that unfold organically are those that result from deliberate orchestration, namely hostile information campaigns. While state-sponsored or state-enacted fake news campaigns go as far back as Rameses the Great, circa 13th century BCE (Dorman & Faulkner, 2019), today the internet and social media have become modern catalysts to transmute fake news from what might be nuggets of humor with a limited reach, to a virulent plague able to threaten immense swathes of modern economic, social, and political life (Tandoc, Lim, & Ling, 2018). In a global context where we are experiencing the rapid democratization of news, media consumption fragmentation, and a decline in trust of media and state institutions, fake news disseminated via social media is a clear and present danger magnified by the echo chambers that social media enables (Colleoni, Rozza, & Arvidsson, 2014; Jebril, Stetka, & Loveless, 2013). It does not help that political partisanship and social schisms are increasingly the norm across the developed world. This dividedness is very often fueled by consuming news from one-sided and biased media outlets that do more to harden perspectives than to facilitate healthy, civil discourse.

A good example would be US President Donald J. Trump, who skillfully exploits partisan media consumption with many of his pronouncements and tweets. President Trump's statements on Twitter often stray from the norms of previous presidential tweets. Trump was impeached by Congress in December 2019, and his party members have repeated Russian disinformation in a partisan effort to defend Trump. This has the chilling effect of giving state-sponsored disinformation airtime and efficacy when it is politically expedient (in defense of Trump) and when this happens, it fulfills the objectives the disinformation campaign was designed for (Zengerle & Freifeld, 2019). Finally, the COVID-19 pandemic of 2020 has uncovered Trump's use of disinformation for political gain by ignoring evidence-based best medical practice to mitigate the spread of the virus and even touting unproven remedies. This egregious tactic exacerbated the US's disastrous response to the disease, further politicizing a medical issue and dividing the nation on simple and efficacious strategies like mask wearing (Breuninger, 2020; Evelyn, 2020).

Accelerating this discord and making antagonistic publics even more hostile to each other, nations have weaponized fake news to fight low-cost, effective information wars by waging hostile information campaigns. Hostile information campaigns are the bane of free and fair elections. They attack the roots of many of our hallowed democratic values and systems, specifically measured discourse, and reasoned, respectful debate that fake news has transformed into opinion-based diatribes and passion-based polemical monologues. Russia is often named as a key sponsor of such campaigns to poison elections, sow uncertainty, and in some cases, induce government paralysis through fractured legislative houses like the US Congress. Numerous intelligence reports have presented credible evidence that Russia coordinated elaborate disinformation campaigns across multiple social media platforms to interfere in the political affairs of other countries, such as influencing important political events like the Brexit referendum and 2016 US Presidential election (McKew, 2018; Mueller, B., 2019; Mueller, R., 2019). There is also evidence that Russia is supporting the far-right political parties that have sprung up across Europe and the surge of nationalism globally in the last few years (Becker, 2019).

Oxford Internet Institute researchers have revealed that other countries besides Russia have also used disinformation to interfere in foreign affairs (Bradshaw & Howard, 2019). The researchers highlighted that about 70 countries have mounted disinformation campaigns to quell political dissent and advance domestic agendas, using an array of communication strategies such as creating false information, manipulating the media, and conducting state-sponsored trolling. This suggests a prevalence in the weaponization of disinformation, where fake news is deployed as a valuable political tool to further agendas both domestically and abroad. Ultimately, the palpable effects may be local, but the roots of interference are global.

Fighting Fake News

To tackle this growing scourge, governments worldwide have thus taken a variety of responses to fake news. These span the spectrum of draconian legislation and even jail terms, which opponents have accused of being used to target dissent; to a light-touch neoliberalist response that hardly seems to make a dent. The Poynter Institute has an interactive tracking tool that keeps abreast of developments all over the world in terms of how different countries' governments have dealt with and are dealing with fake news (Funke & Flamini, 2019). We will review the experiences of the US and Singapore to contrast two radically different responses to tackling fake news.

Facebook founder Mark Zuckerberg's refusal to police political advertisements in the run-up to the US 2020 Presidential elections on the widely used platform is a clear signal that the neoliberalist philosophy of letting businesses police themselves is not an effective strategy. Ideally, the state should hold enterprise accountable, especially when it concerns democracy itself (Milman, 2019). However, proposed legislation to combat fake news has reached a stalemate because of a divided Congress. For instance, federal law S.1989—Honest Ads Act, a proposed law that would require social media firms like Google and Facebook to maintain copies of political advertisements and allow public access to important disclosure information like the ad sponsors' identities, has been stalled in the US Senate since 2017 (US Congress, 2018). Other legislation relating directly to election security has also been stalled by US Senate majority leader Mitch McConnell (West & Gambhir, 2019). It would seem that partisanship and clinging on to power are more important than honoring and respecting the idea of the co-equal branches of government enshrined in the US Constitution.

With its multi-ethnic and multi-religious makeup, Singapore regards itself as being especially susceptible to disinformation and misinformation campaigns. The tiny nation's much-celebrated religious and racial tolerance is also its Achilles heel; an adversary can potentially use social media to sow discord and spark discontent among the different ethnic groups. Singapore has approached the tackling of fake news from many directions. This multi-pronged approach is to ensure that all the bases are covered, with the principal legislative response being the controversial Protection from Online Falsehoods and Manipulation Act (POFMA), involving fines as high as S$1 million (US$0.74 million). While critics have characterized POFMA as a heavy-handed law that threatens free speech and privacy, supporters have argued that it provides the establishment of essential fact-checking and news-correction mechanisms (Daskal, 2019; Kamil, 2019).

Singapore's community-based response focuses on raising awareness of fake news among religious and community groups. One aspect involves training that helps people to understand what fake news is and its impact on national security and society (Lee, 2019). The salience of defending the country against the insidious effects of online falsehoods has been underscored by the addition of a "Digital Defence" component to Singapore's Total Defence strategy. A national effort to protect and defend citizens and the country against various threats, Total Defence also encompasses the five original areas of military, civil, economic, social, and psychological defense (Singapore Ministry of Defence, 2019). Finally, a media literacy campaign was rolled out to teach youth to spot false news stories (Choo, 2019).

Besides individual state efforts, other actors such as scholars and intergovernmental organizations play important roles in combating fake news, such as developing sustainable and effective measures to inoculate publics against future misinformation campaigns. Amazeen and Bucy's (2019) study on facilitating resistance to fake news via inoculation with procedural news knowledge showed that there are viable tools to deal with fake news. Another effective yet simple strategy may be to directly inform people of the fact that scientific consensus supports a particular view. Communicating experts' consensus is protective against fake news and this work on mitigating misinformation with regards to climate change offers us a viable model to deal with organized disinformation campaigns (van der Linden, Leiserowitz, Rosenthal, & Maibach, 2017). Roozenbeek and van der Linden's (2019) study showed that playing an educational game, which simulated the creation of a fake news article, had protective and inoculative aspects against fake news among high school students. Cook, Lewandowsky, and Ecker's (2017) work determined inoculation messages that were effective against the negative aspects of misinformation. The United Nations, through its United Nations Educational, Scientific, and Cultural Organization (UNESCO) division has also rolled out an online publication, *Journalism, 'Fake News' and Disinformation: A Handbook for Journalism Education and Training*, whose core strategy is aimed at building resilience to fake news via media and information literacy training targeting journalists and those who train journalists (Ireton & Posetti, 2018).

Conclusion

Clearly, social media has heralded rich and complex permutations in one-to-one, one-to-many, many-to-one, and many-to-many communications in our interconnected world. Invigorated by the rising ubiquity and growing functionality of mobile media, social media has been a key conduit in the spread of fake news. The adverse effects of fake news are therefore more wide-ranging and globalized than before and developing remedies to this wicked problem is more challenging than ever. It is still early days in the struggle against this highly contagious information disease, but stamping it out requires the coordinated efforts of academics, politicians, media professionals, ordinary citizens, and of course, big technology companies. To this end, we must accelerate efforts on three critical fronts.

The first is to empower media consumers with media literacy competencies that can inure them to the adverse effects of fake news. This will involve public education efforts that sensitize consumers to the motivations, business models, and typical strategies of fake news purveyors, and to make them conscious of inherent cognitive biases that heighten their susceptibility to fake news.

The second front is to fortify research on diverse aspects of fake news, including the political economy surrounding its production and dissemination, the design and deployment of digital infrastructures that support its spread, and its effects on consumers and communities at large. Such research is vital for refining our societal response in the realms of education, regulation, and innovation to combat the wide-ranging effects of fake news.

The third front relates to a more strategic collaboration with big technology companies that create and sustain the digital arteries that oxygenate the flow of fake news. Whereas companies such as Facebook, Twitter, and Weibo have made piecemeal efforts at moderating the spread of fake news, these measures have been feeble at best. Greater state intervention must be undertaken to take these companies to task and secure more systematic and comprehensive compliance with regulations designed to construct a healthier and more robust digital information infrastructure. Ideally, with these big technology companies investing more heavily in digital solutions, fake news and its spread should be contained at source. Anti-trust regulations must also be initiated and enforced to prevent power concentration and the domination of the information landscape by a digital oligopoly. Political will is essential for tackling fake news on these three fronts, failing which we will continue on our current trajectory, which would make fake news even more lethal, viral, and global than it already is.

References

Amazeen, M.A., & Bucy, E.P. (2019). Conferring resistance to digital disinformation: The inoculating influence of procedural news knowledge. *Journal of Broadcasting & Electronic Media, 63*(3), 415–432. https://doi.org/10.1080/08838151.2019.1653101

Becker, J. (2019, August 10). The global machine behind the rise of far-right nationalism. *The New York Times*. Retrieved from www.nytimes.com/2019/08/10/world/europe/sweden-immigration-nationalism.html

Borges, P.M., & Gambarato, R.R. (2019). The role of beliefs and behavior on Facebook: A semiotic approach to algorithms, fake news, and transmedia journalism. *International Journal of Communication (19328036), 13*, 603–618.

Bradshaw, S., & Howard, P.N. (2019). *The global disinformation disorder: 2019 global inventory of organised social media manipulation* (Working Paper 2019.2; pp. 1–26). Retrieved from https://comprop.oii.ox.ac.uk/wp-content/uploads/sites/93/2019/09/CyberTroop-Report19.pdf

Breuninger, K. (2020, July 20). Trump says face masks are "patriotic" after months of largely resisting wearing one. *CNBC*. Retrieved from: www.cnbc.com/2020/07/20/trump-says-coronavirus-masks-are-patriotic-after-months-of-largely-resisting-wearing-one.html

Chesney, R., & Citron, D.K. (2018). *Deep fakes: A looming challenge for privacy, democracy, and national security*. Retrieved from https://papers.ssrn.com/abstract=3213954

Choo, C. (2019, March 11). Two new media literacy resources to teach youth how to spot fake news. *TODAY*. Retrieved from www.todayonline.com/singapore/two-new-media-literacy-resources-teach-youth-how-spot-fake-news

Colleoni, E., Rozza, A., & Arvidsson, A. (2014). Echo chamber or public sphere? Predicting political orientation and measuring political homophily in Twitter using big data. *Journal of Communication, 64*(2), 317–332.

Cook, J., Lewandowsky, S., & Ecker, UKH (2017). Neutralizing misinformation through inoculation: Exposing misleading argumentation techniques reduces their influence. *PLoS One, 12*(5), e0175799.

Daskal, J. (2019, May 30). This "fake news" law threatens free speech. But it doesn't stop there. *The New York Times*. Retrieved from www.nytimes.com/2019/05/30/opinion/hate-speech-law-singapore.html

Del Vicario, M., Bessi, A., Zollo, F., Petroni, F., Scala, A., Caldarelli, G., Stanley, H.E., & Quattrociocchi, W. (2016). The spreading of misinformation online. *Proceedings of the National Academy of Sciences, 113*(3), 554–559.

Dorman, P.F., & Faulkner, R.O. (2019). Ramses II: King of Egypt. In *Encyclopedia Britannica*. Retrieved from www.britannica.com/biography/Ramses-II-king-of-Egypt

Evelyn, K. (2020, April 22). Trump stops hyping hydroxychloroquine after study shows no benefit. *The Guardian*. Retrieved from www.theguardian.com/us-news/2020/apr/22/trump-hydroxychloroquine-study-coronavirus

Fisher, M., Cox, J.W., & Hermann, P. (2016, December 6). Pizzagate: From rumor, to hashtag, to gunfire in D.C. *The Washington Post*. Retrieved from www.washingtonpost.com/local/pizzagate-from-rumor-to-hashtag-to-gunfire-in-dc/2016/12/06/4c7def50-bbd4-11e6-94ac-3d324840106c_story.html

Funke, D., & Flamini, D. (2019, August 13). A guide to anti-misinformation actions around the world. Retrieved from www.poynter.org/ifcn/anti-misinformation-actions/

Gaines, B.J., & Mondak, J.J. (2009). Typing together? Clustering of ideological types in online social networks. *Journal of Information Technology & Politics, 6*(3–4), 216–231.

Ireton, C., & Posetti, J. (2018). *Journalism, "Fake news" and Disinformation: A Handbook for Journalism Education and Training*. Retrieved from https://en.unesco.org/fightfakenews

Jebril, N., Stetka, V., & Loveless, M. (2013). Media and democratisation: What is known about the role of mass media in transitions to democracy. Retrieved from https://reutersinstitute.politics.ox.ac.uk/sites/default/files/2017-11/Media%20and%20Democratisation.pdf

Kamil, A. (2019, April 2). All you need to know about Singapore's proposed fake news law. Retrieved from www.todayonline.com/singapore/all-you-need-know-about-singapores-proposed-fake-news-law

Katz, J.E., & Lai, C.H. (2014). Mobile locative media: The nexus of mobile phones and social media. In G. Goggin & L. Hjorth (Eds.) *The Routledge Companion to Mobile Media* (pp. 77–86). Routledge.

Lazer, D.M.J., Baum, M.A., Benkler, Y., Berinsky, A.J., Greenhill, K.M., Menczer, F., … Zittrain, J.L. (2018). The science of fake news. *Science, 359*(6380), 1094–1096.

Lee, V. (2019, January 13). 2 initiatives launched to help fight fake news, terrorism. *The Straits Times*. Retrieved from www.straitstimes.com/singapore/2-initiatives-launched-to-help-fight-fake-news-terrorism

McKew, M. (2018, February 16). Did Russia affect the 2016 election? It's now undeniable. *Wired*. Retrieved from www.wired.com/story/did-russia-affect-the-2016-election-its-now-undeniable/

Milman, O. (2019, December 2). Defiant Mark Zuckerberg defends Facebook policy to allow false ads. *The Guardian*. Retrieved from www.theguardian.com/technology/2019/dec/02/mark-zuckerberg-facebook-policy-fake-ads

Mueller, B. (2019, December 13). What is Brexit? A simple guide to why it matters and what happens next. *The New York Times*. Retrieved from www.nytimes.com/interactive/2019/world/europe/what-is-brexit.html

Mueller, III, R.S. (2019). Report on the Investigation into Russian Interference in the 2016 Presidential Election. Retrieved from www.justice.gov/storage/report.pdf

Oxenham, S. (2019, May 29). I was a Macedonian fake news writer. *BBC News*. Retrieved from www.bbc.com/future/article/20190528-i-was-a-macedonian-fake-news-writer

Pariser, E. (2011). *The Filter Bubble: What the Internet is Hiding from you*. London, UK: Penguin Press.

Porter, J. (2019, September 2). Another convincing deepfake app goes viral prompting immediate privacy backlash. *The Verge*. Retrieved from www.theverge.com/2019/9/2/20844338/zao-deepfake-app-movie-tv-show-face-replace-privacy-policy-concerns

Roozenbeek, J., & van der Linden, S. (2019). The fake news game: Actively inoculating against the risk of misinformation. *Journal of Risk Research, 22*(5), 570–580.

Shao, C., Ciampaglia, G.L., Varol, O., Yang, K.-C., Flammini, A., & Menczer, F. (2018a). The spread of low-credibility content by social bots. *Nature Communications, 9*(1), 1–9.

Shao, C., Hui, P.-M., Wang, L., Jiang, X., Flammini, A., Menczer, F., & Ciampaglia, G.L. (2018b). Anatomy of an online misinformation network. *PLoS One, 13*(4), e0196087.

Shearer, E. (2018, December 10). Social media outpaces print newspapers in the U.S. as a news source. Retrieved from www.pewresearch.org/fact-tank/2018/12/10/social-media-outpaces-print-newspapers-in-the-u-s-as-a-news-source/

Singapore Ministry of Defence. (2019, February 15). Fact sheet: Digital defence. Retrieved from www.mindef.gov.sg/web/portal/mindef/news-and-events/latest-releases/article-detail/2019/February/15feb19_fs

Stocking, G., & Sumida, N. (2018). Social media bots draw public's attention and concern. *Pew Research Center, Washington, DC*.

Stroud, N.J. (2017). Selective exposure theories. In K. Kenski & K.H. Jamieson (Eds.), *The Oxford handbook of political communication* (Vol. 1, pp. 531–548).

Tandoc, Jr, EC, Lim, Z.W., & Ling, R. (2018). Defining "fake news." *Digital Journalism, 6*(2), 137–153.

Törnberg, P. (2018). Echo chambers and viral misinformation: Modeling fake news as complex contagion. *PLoS One, 13*(9).

Turcotte, J., York, C., Irving, J., Scholl, R.M., & Pingree, R.J. (2015). News recommendations from social media opinion leaders: Effects on media trust and information seeking. *Journal of Computer-Mediated Communication, 20*(5), 520–535. https://doi.org/10.1111/jcc4.12127

US Congress. (2018). S.1989—115th Congress (2017–2018): Honest Ads Act (2017/2018). Retrieved from www.congress.gov/bill/115th-congress/senate-bill/1989

van der Linden, S., Leiserowitz, A., Rosenthal, S., & Maibach, E. (2017). Inoculating the public against misinformation about climate change. *Global Challenges, 1*(2), 1600008.

Varol, O., Ferrara, E., Menczer, F., & Flammini, A. (2017). Early detection of promoted campaigns on social media. *EPJ Data Science, 6*(1), 1–19.

Vosoughi, S., Roy, D., & Aral, S. (2018). The spread of true and false news online. *Science, 359*(6380), 1146–1151.

Waldrop, M.M. (2017). News feature: The genuine problem of fake news. *Proceedings of the National Academy of Sciences, 114*(48), 12631–12634.

West, D.M., & Gambhir, R.K. (2019, August 2). Why won't the Senate protect American elections? Retrieved from www.brookings.edu/blog/fixgov/2019/08/02/why-wont-the-senate-protect-american-elections/

Westlund, O. (2014). The production and consumption of news in an age of mobile media. In G. Goggin & L. Hjorth (Eds.) *The Routledge companion to mobile media*, (pp. 135–145). Routledge.

Wiggins, B.E. (2017). Navigating an immersive narratology: Factors to explain the reception of fake news. *International Journal of E-Politics, 8*(3), 16–29.

Zengerle, P., & Freifeld, K. (2019, November 22). Trump Russia adviser scolds Republicans for repeating Kremlin lies. *The Sydney Morning Herald*. Retrieved from www.smh.com.au/world/north-america/trump-russia-adviser-scolds-republicans-for-repeating-kremlin-lies-20191122-p53cz6.html

Zimmer, F., Scheibe, K., Stock, M., & Stock, W. (2019). Fake news in social media: Bad algorithms or biased users? *Journal of Information Science Theory and Practice*, 7(2), 40–53.

Zuboff, S. (2019). *The age of surveillance capitalism: The fight for a human future at the new frontier of power*. New York, NY: PublicAffairs.

20

MACHINE TRANSLATION

Mediating Linguistic Difference in the Era of Globalization

David J. Gunkel

Ten rozdział dotyczy tłumaczenia maszynowego. Unless you can read and understand Polish, the sentence that begins this chapter is probably confusing and virtually unintelligible. And this points to something important in the context of globalization. Human communication is dependent on language and natural human languages are different, diverse, and seemingly incompatible. It is currently estimated that there are somewhere in the range of 6,900–7,100 different languages in use world-wide. We typically contend with this linguistic diversity in one of two ways. We can seek to become proficient in more than one language, which is one of the reasons why the university curriculum in the United States and elsewhere typically has a foreign language requirement. Or we can translate, literally "carry over," the meaning that is expressed in one language to that of another. This can be accomplished either by applying the efforts of a human translator—an individual who has adequate knowledge of at least two different languages and considerable experience mediating between languages—or a computational mechanism. This chapter deals with machine translation (which is a translation into English of the Polish sentence provided above), which employs computational solutions to mediate linguistic difference.

Mythic Origins

Translation is needed in order to contend with and even overcome the fact that human beings speak a wide range of different languages. This is especially important as the world's people become more involved with each other through international trade and exchange, travel and migration, and daily involvements and interactions with each other on a global scale by way of telecommunications technology. But how and why is this a "problem" in the first place? How did we get here?

In the Judeo/Christian tradition, the fact that different human communities speak different languages is something that is explained by way of a myth or legend incorporated in the first book of the Holy Scriptures (in Jewish traditions this is called the *Torah*; for Christians, it appears in the Old Testament of *The Bible*). The story is usually titled "The Tower of Babel," and it can be found in the book of *Genesis* 11:1–9. "The Tower of Babel" story begins at a mythical point in time, when it is assumed that all of humanity lived in a single place on the planet and spoke one common language. This single language was a powerful tool of communication, because (according to the story) it facilitated cooperation between different individuals, so much so that the entire human population of planet earth could agree to work together and construct a city and a massive tower that reached all the way into the heavens.

Upon seeing this impressive undertaking, God begins to get nervous. He worries that humanity might get too powerful and do all kinds of other impressive things, and that nothing would be impossible for them achieve. In an effort to curb their ambitions, God puts an end to the building project by deliberately confusing the language: "The Lord said, 'If as one people speaking the same language they have begun to do this, then nothing they plan to do will be impossible for them. Come, let us go down and confuse their language so they will not understand each other.'" This linguistic confusion makes it virtually impossible for the human population to talk with one another and to complete work on the tower. As a result, they abandon the edifice, scatter over the face of the earth, and end up speaking different languages. This is why the place where this occurred was called *Babel*, because it was here that God confused the original human language, creating the babble of different languages that we currently live with.

The Task of Translation

The Babel narrative, it should be remembered, is just that. It is a story. It is not a statement of anthropological fact. In fact, the origins (in the plural) of human language and their remarkable diversity are studied and debated by linguists, anthropologists, neurobiologists, evolutionary biologists, behavioral scientists, etc. But the mythic narrative is informative, because it provides a way to characterize the rationale, task, and objective of translation. Because of linguistic difference—the catastrophic damage that was supposedly inflicted at the Tower of Babel—humans speak different languages. This difference often impedes communication and makes it difficult for a person who speaks one particular language to be understood by someone who speaks another. Translation is the process of remediating this difference by rendering into one language the meaning that is expressed by the words of another.

The work of translation typically requires a human intermediary or "translator," some individual who is knowledgeable in at least two different languages and can therefore represent in the target language what had been said or written in the source language. But this is more difficult than it initially sounds, even for individuals who would call themselves bilingual. In English, for example, one can say something like "Makes no difference to me" in response to questions concerning a choice between two alternatives. If we wanted to convey this in Polish, the English sentence could be translated as "Nie ma dla mnie znaczenia." Although this is an accurate word-for-word rendering of the initial English statement, it is unlikely that a native Polish speaker would ever say such a thing or understand what it is meant to convey. Instead, they might say, "Wszystko jedno," which literally means "Everything [is] one." In other words, the task of translation is not simply rendering the words of one language into the exact words of the other language. It involves more. It requires knowing the meaning and context of words in the source language in order to reproduce that same meaning (or at least a close approximation thereof) in the words of the target language.

If the Old Testament of the Christian *Bible* narrates the origin and *raison d'être* of translation between languages, the New Testament provides a clue concerning the ambitions and objectives of automatic, universal translation. This occurs during an event called "Pentacost," which is described in the second chapter of the *Acts of the Apostles*. After the crucifixion and death of their teacher, Jesus Christ, the Apostles hole up in a room in order to avoid suffering a similar fate. This changes when they receive the Holy Spirit, which is represented, both within the story and in subsequent religious iconography, in the form of tongues of fire that descend from heaven. After receiving the gift of the spirit, the Apostles leave their stronghold and began proselytizing in the streets. As they speak in their native language, everyone hears their words in his/her own language: "And the people were amazed and marveled saying: 'Are not all these men who are speaking Galileans? How is it that each of us hears them in our own language to which we were born?'" (Acts 2:7–8). The story of Pentacost, therefore, narrates the alleviation of Babelian confusion through automatic, real-time translation. In this way, Pentecost promises to reestablish universal understanding between humans despite the problem of linguistic difference that had been imposed at Babel. In other words, Pentecost repairs and remediates the babble of Babel.

Science Fiction

The promise of automatic, real-time translation is not just a part of our religious traditions. We also see versions of it in the techno-myths of science fiction. Consider, for example, a device called (not surprisingly) the "Babel fish." According to *The Hitchhiker's Guide to the Galaxy*—a title that names both a novel by Douglas Adams and an encyclopedic reference book cited within that novel: "The Babel fish is small, yellow, leech-like and probably the oddest thing in the universe. It feeds on brain wave energy, absorbing all unconscious frequencies and then excreting telepathically a matrix formed from the conscious frequencies and nerve signals picked up from the speech centers of the brain, the practical upshot of which is that if you stick one in your ear, you can instantly understand anything said to you in any form of language" (Adams 1979, 59–60). The Babel fish, therefore, reproduces the miracle of Pentecost for its host by providing automatic and real-time translations from and into any and all languages.

A similar device, called the Universal Translator, is part of the standard equipment of Star Fleet in the science-fiction television and film franchise *Star Trek*. According to the *Star Trek Encyclopedia*, the Universal Translator is a "device used to provide real-time two-way translation of spoken languages" (Okuda et al., 1994, p. 361). In the original series, which made its debut on US network television in the mid-1960s, the Universal Translator was a hand-held device about the size of a flashlight (a graphic representation can be found in Franz Joseph's *Star Fleet Technical Manual*, 1975, T0:03:02:04), and the device makes its initial and only appearance as a prop in the episode *Metamorphosis* (1967). In the sequel, *Star Trek: The Next Generation* (as well as its numerous spin-offs, *Deep Space Nine, Voyager, Enterprise, Discovery,* etc.), the Universal Translator is incorporated as an application residing in the ship's main computer. According to the *Star Trek Next Generation Technical Manual*, "the Universal Translator is an extremely sophisticated computer program that is designed to first analyze the patterns of an unknown form of communication, then to derive a translation matrix to permit real-time verbal or data exchanges" (Sternbach and Okuda, 1991, p. 101).

Though the Babel Fish and Universal Translator are the product of science fiction, these imaginative technologies supply researchers and developers with accessible examples that can and have been used to explain the efforts and objectives of machine translation for a non-technical audience. "The basic idea of machine translation" (M.T.), as Vanessa Enríquez Raído and Frank Austermühl describe (2003, p. 246), "is that of Star Trek's universal translator or a mechanized version of Douglas Adam's Babel Fish—a black box that converts the source language input into a (perfect) target language output without any human interaction."

The Weaver Memo

The idea of applying electronic computers to the task of translation was something initially formulated and presented in a memorandum written by Warren Weaver in 1949. For this reason, Weaver is often credited as "the father of machine translation." During World War II, Weaver was head of the Applied Mathematics Panel at the US Office of Scientific Research and Development. In this capacity, he had the opportunity to experience the application of electronic calculating machines—what we now call "computers"—to the task of *cryptography*, the coding and decoding of secret messages. One of the technologies that gave the Nazis a considerable advantage in the conduct of wartime operations was the Enigma machine—a sophisticated cryptography instrument, looking something like a rather large typewriter, that rendered messages issued by the German high command virtually unreadable when intercepted during transmission. The allies applied an impressive effort to decoding the Enigma code. This had been the wartime occupation of Alan Turing at Bletchley Park in the United Kingdom (dramatically represented in the 2015 film *The Imitation Game*), and the work of the Applied Mathematics Panel that Weaver oversaw in the US.

In 1949, Weaver, who had by that time returned to his pre-World War II position at the Rockefeller Foundation, wrote a brief memorandum in which he proposed that translation between languages might be a special instance of cryptography and therefore solvable using the same tools that had been developed during the war. In fact, Weaver's "Translation," as the memorandum has been called, introduced a number of important concepts that taken together frame the opportunity and challenge of machine translation.

1. *Linguistic Difference is a Problem.* Right at the beginning of the memorandum, Weaver operationalized an idea that proceeds directly from the "Tower of Babel" story, even if he does not mention it by name. He begins the memo by recognizing the "fact" that linguistic difference is a significant problem, impeding human communication and international cooperation: "There is no need to do more than mention the obvious fact that a multiplicity of language impedes cultural interchange between the peoples of the earth, and is a serious deterrent to international understanding" (Weaver, 1949, p. 1). So right at the beginning, in the first line of the memorandum, Weaver affirms and mobilizes the basic "problem space" that is described in the "Tower of Babel" story—confusion between different human languages is a barrier to intercultural exchange and a serious impediment to international understanding and cooperation.

2. *Technological Fix.* Weaver assumes that there must be a technological solution to this problem. In Weaver's case, that solution comes in the form of the new electronic technology of the digital computer: "The present memorandum, assuming the validity and importance of this fact, contains some comments and suggestions bearing on the possibility of contributing at least something to the solution of the world-wide translation problem through the use of electronic computers of great capacity, flexibility, and speed" (Weaver, 1949, p. 1). There are two things to note here. First, Weaver hedges against his proposal failing by recognizing that one first has to agree to the validity of the assumption that linguistic difference is, in fact, a problem to be solved. Although this might appear to be a mere rhetorical gesture, we will eventually see how this was a prescient insight and comment. Second, Weaver is entirely realistic about the importance of his work. He does not claim to solve everything once and for all; he simply offers the memorandum as a modest contribution in the direction of an eventual solution. He is, in other words, content to get things started by planting the seeds or the initial ideas of/for machine translation.

3. *Translation = Cryptography.* Based on his wartime experience, Weaver had surmised that linguistic difference and the task of translation could be addressed in terms roughly equivalent to that of cryptography. As he recounts in the memorandum, this idea was first developed and presented to Norbert Wiener in a letter from 4 March 1947: "One naturally wonders if the problem of translation could conceivably be treated as a problem in cryptography. When I look at an article in Russian, I say 'This is really written in English, but it has been coded in some strange symbols. I will now proceed to decode'" (quoted in Poibeau, 2017, p. 53). Whether Weaver's hypothesis (i.e., translation is a variant of cryptanalysis) is factually accurate or not is something that is still open to debate. What is not in question, however, is the idea of applying the experiences and tools of cryptography to process natural language. Consequently this sentence, and the memorandum in total, initiated what would become MT and, more generally, natural language processing (NLP).

4. *Universal language.* The memo was intended to be a short "think piece" and not a technical paper. So there is very little in Weaver's text that would be considered an actual methodology or approach. Despite this, Weaver does engage in some theorizing about basic procedures and his theory mobilizes both Babelian imagery and the dream of a "universal language" or *Characteristica Universalis* which had been developed by 17th century European philosophers and mathematicians.

> Think, by analogy, of individuals living in a series of tall closed towers, all erected over a common foundation. When they try to communicate with one another, they shout back and forth, each from his own closed tower. It is difficult to make the sound penetrate even the nearest towers, and communication proceeds very poorly indeed. But, when an individual goes down his tower, he finds himself in a great open basement, common to all the towers. Here he establishes easy and useful communication with the persons who have also descended from their towers. Thus may it be true that the way to translate…is not to attempt the direct route, shouting from tower to tower. Perhaps the way is to descend, from each language, down to the common base of human communication—the real but as yet undiscovered universal language…"
>
> *(Weaver, 1949, p. 11)*

Weaver's reformulation of the "Tower of Babel" story concerns not a single tower and the origin of linguistic diversity but a series of different towers and the problem of translation. He tells of a multiplicity of individual towers that indicate the isolation and incompatibility of each language. Translation therefore typically proceeds by trying to make one language understandable in terms of another—a difficult process that can be illustrated, as Weaver explains, by shouting from the top of one tower to another.

This problem can, Weaver continues, be circumvented by descending the individual towers to the common foundation or basement that underlies linguistic differences. The idea is simple. Instead of trying to translate from language to language—shouting from the top of one tower to another tower—one might make better progress in translation by way of "descending" to a more fundamental and universal representation that underlies particular linguistic differences. "Thus may it be true," Weaver (1949, p. 11) explains, "that the way to translate from Chinese to Arabic, or from Russian to Portuguese, is not to attempt the direct route, shouting from tower to tower. Perhaps the way is to descend, from each language, down to the common base of human communication—the real but as yet undiscovered universal language—and then re-emerge by whatever particular route is convenient."

The influence of Weaver's memorandum cannot be underestimated. The prospect of overcoming and putting an end to the problem of linguistic difference—or, fixing the babble of Babel—by way of applying computer technology to the problem of translation definitely had traction. As a result, Weaver's memo along with his access to lucrative funding sources in the US Federal government, launched a concerted effort in machine translation that has, since that time, gone through a number of different technical phases or iterations. The effort begins with simple rule-based systems, extending from direct translation methods suitable for dealing with pairs of languages to the use of interlinguas for expanded capabilities across multiple languages (Poibeau, 2017); progresses through example-based (Makato, 1984) and statistical MT (Brown et al., 1990 and 1993), which provide for better phrase- and sentence-level transfers by using existing parallel corpora or bilingual texts that are aligned sentence by sentence and available in digital form on the internet (Gunkel, 2020); and currently employs sequence-to-sequence recurrent neural networks (RNN) trained on large sets of linguistic data (Cho et al., 2014). Although MT technology has, at times, developed in fits and starts, current systems, like Google Translate, are able to provide users with reasonable translations into and out of over 100 different human languages.

Linguistic Difference in the Era of Globalization

Given recent technological progress with digital computers, one might ask whether we have finally achieved the means to repair and overcome, once and for all, the damage that had been narrated by the "Tower of Babel" story? Does MT represent a technologically enabled version of the miracle of Pentecost, in which no matter who is speaking and in what language, we can all understand what is being said in the language to which we were born? Was Warren Weaver's prediction from 1949 correct and accurate? Have we, in fact, devised a workable solution to the world-wide translation problem through the use of electronic computers of great capacity, flexibility, and speed? Or to formulate it in way that matters for university instructors and students, does MT make the foreign language requirement obsolete? Interestingly the answer to all these questions must be both "yes" and "no." It all depends on how we understand language, linguistic difference, and global interaction.

If language is understood as little more than a means of interpersonal communication, and if linguistic difference—or if you like, the diversity of languages that was the unfortunate legacy of the Tower of Babel—is understood as an obstacle to human communication and cooperation, then MT seem to promise a solution that is on a par with or at least very close to achieving what was experienced at Pentecost and has been imagined in science fiction with *Star Trek*'s Universal Translator or the Babel Fish from the *Hitchhiker's Guide*. One can, right now, travel the world and, by way of a smart phone app, simply point the phone's camera at some text—e.g., a sign or restaurant menu—and have Google Translate immediately render the unfamiliar words and phrases in one's native language. And by employing some augmented reality (AR) visualization techniques, the scene that is displayed on the phone's screen can look exactly like the world outside with one exception: the text is rendered in another language selected and understood by the user.

Likewise, by using Microsoft's Skype Translator, one can seamlessly interact with another individual, who speaks an entirely different language, in real time over the internet. In other words, a person in Australia who only speaks English can have an intelligible conversation with someone in Germany who only speaks Deutsch. The application renders spoken English into understandable German and vice versa, thus mediating the linguistic difference between the two participants. The application "can currently translate conversations in ten languages, including English, Spanish, French, German, Chinese (Mandarin), Italian, Portuguese (Brazilian), Arabic, and Russian" (Microsoft, 2020). And its capabilities are planned to be expanded in order to encompass a wider variety of languages in the not-too-distant future. Consequently, and looked at from this vantage point, it appears that these MT applications and tools do in fact remediate the babble of Babel and call for an end to or at least a significant re-evaluation of the need to learn other languages.

But not so fast. There may be more to it. Language is not just a tool of communication, it is also the expression and carrier of culture. In other words, languages are not just different ways of encoding thought, as Weaver had assumed in his "Translation" memo. They are also the means of thought such that different languages make available different ways of thinking about and engaging with the world. This alternative viewpoint is something that is rooted in the Sapir–Whorf hypothesis (named for two linguists who independently developed slightly different versions of it, Edward Sapir and Benjamin Lee Whorf)—the idea that language determines (or at least strongly influences) thought and that linguistic elements can limit and shape cognitive categories. A similar idea was put forward in the work of Ludwig Wittgenstein (1981, pp. 5.6) who famously argued that "*the limits of my language* mean the limits of my world." The proverbial illustration of this insight (something initially reported by the anthropologist Franz Boas and repeated with considerable regularity in both the academic and popular literature) is that the Inuit language of the Arctic contains many different names for what we, in English, call "snow," each one identifying a different aspect of the phenomenon not necessarily accessible to or able to be captured by the others.

Considered from this perspective, the linguistic diversity that had (supposedly) been instituted at Babel might not be a catastrophic loss of communicative ability; it could be an advantage and gain. Here is how George Steiner (1975, p. 233) explains it in his book-length examination of translation titled *After Babel*:

> The ripened humanity of language, its indispensable conservative and creative force live in the extraordinary diversity of actual tongues, in the bewildering profusion and eccentricity (though there is no center) of their modes. The psychic need for particularity, for "in-clusion" and invention is so intense that it has, during the whole of man's [sic] history until very lately, outweighed the spectacular, obvious material advantages of mutual comprehension and linguistic unity. In that sense, the Babel myth is once again a case of symbolic inversion: [hu]mankind was not destroyed but on the contrary kept vital and creative by being scattered among tongues.

Steiner's reading suggests an inversion of the traditional interpretation of the Babelian narrative. He argues that the so-called "catastrophe" of Babel, namely the confusion instituted by the multiplicity of languages that had divided humanity, does not constitute a kind of damage to be repaired but is instead a substantial advantage. At Babel, humankind was not destroyed by confusion but was "kept vital and creative" through linguistic diversification. Like bio-diversity, Steiner argues, linguistic diversity is a feature and not a bug. It has ensured human ingenuity and survival.

If we look at language from this perspective, the learning of more than one language and the task of translating between different languages is not just about efficient and effective communication. It involves learning about, experiencing, and living-in a particular way of seeing, conceptualizing, and engaging the world. What is interesting and important about MT, therefore, is that it can alleviate language learning of the assumption and burden of mere communication, opening up opportunities to see other ways to think about and work with languages. So instead of repairing linguistic difference and putting an end to the need to be proficient in more than one language, it is more likely that MT will have the effect of recontextualizing and reformulating—a process Jay David Bolter and Richard Grusin (1999) called "remediation"—the *raison d'être* for learning languages in the first place.

Consequently, automatic translation by way of digital computer is not the end of the task of translation; instead MT fundamentally resituates and reformulates how we think about translation and the diversity of languages in the era of globalization. As Jacques Derrida wrote in "Des Tours de Babel" (1985), an essay about translation that was written for translation: "The 'tower of Babel' does not figure merely the irreducible multiplicity of tongues; it exhibits an incompletion, the impossibility of finishing, of totalizing, of saturating of completing something on the order of edification, architectural construction, system and architectonics" (Derrida, 1985, p. 165). According to this re-interpretation, linguistic variation is not a mere empirical problem to be overcome by the application of technological mediation. It is a fundamental difference that renders the task of translation an interminable undertaking that is both necessary and impossible to finish.

References

Adams, D. (1979). *The Hitchhiker's Guide to the Galaxy*. New York: Pocket Books.

Bolter, J.D. and R. Grusin (1999). *Remediation: Understanding New Media*. Cambridge, MA: MIT Press.

Brown, P.F., Cocke, J., Della Pietra, S.A., Della Pietra, V.J., Jelinek, F., Lafferty, J.D., Mercer, R.L., and Roossin, P.S. (1990). A Statistical Approach to Machine Translation. *Computational Linguistics* 16(2): 79–85. www.aclweb.org/anthology/J90-2002

Brown, P.F., Della Pietra, S.A., Della Pietra, V.J., and Mercer, R.L. (1993). The Mathematics of Statistical Machine Translation: Parameter Estimation. *Computational Linguistics* 19(2): 263–311. www.aclweb.org/anthology/J93-2003

Cho, K.H., Merriënboer, B.v., Gulcehre, C., Bougares, F., Schwenk, H., Bahdanau, D., and Bengio, Y. (2014). Learning Phrase Representations using RNN Encoder-Decoder for Statistical Machine Translation. *Proceedings of the 2014 Conference on Empirical Methods in Natural Language Processing* (EMNLP), October 25–29: 1724–1734,

Derrida, J. (1985). *Des Tours de Babel*. In *Difference in Translation*, edited and translated by J.F. Graham. Ithaca: Cornell University Press.

Eco, U. (1995). *The Search for the Perfect Language*, translated by J. Fentress. Cambridge: Blackwell.

Gunkel, D.J. (2020). *An Introduction to Communication and Artificial Intelligence*. Cambridge: Polity.

Joseph, F. (1975). *Star Fleet Technical Manual*, New York: Ballantine.

Makato, N. (1984). A Framework of a Mechanical Translation Between Japanese and English by Analogy Principle. In *Artificial and Human Intelligence*, ed. A. Elithorn and R. Banerji, 173–180. Amsterdam: Elsevier Science Publishers. www.mt-archive.info/Nagao-1984.pdf

Microsoft (2020). Skype Translator. www.skype.com/en/features/skype-translator/

Okuda, M., Okuda, D, and Mirek, D. (1994). *The Star Trek Encyclopedia*. New York: Pocket Books.

Poibeau, T. (2017). *Machine Translation*. Cambridge, MA: MIT Press.

Raído, V.E. and Austermühl, F. (2003). Translation and Localization Tools: Current Developments. In *Speaking in Tongues: Language Across Contexts and Users*, ed. Luis Pérez González, 225–250. València: Universitat de València Press.

Steiner, G. (1975). *After Babel*. New York: Oxford University Press.

Sternbach, R. and Okuda, M. (1991). *Star Trek Next Generation Technical Manual*. New York: Pocket Books.

Weaver, W. (1949). Translation. The Rockefeller Foundation. www.mt-archive.info/Weaver-1949.pdf

Wiener, N. (1996). *Cybernetics: Or Control and Communication in the Animal and the Machine*. Cambridge, MA: MIT Press.

Wittgenstein, L. (1981). Tractatus Logico-Philosophicus. Translated by C. K. Ogden. New York: Routledge.

21

PLAYING WITH CHINESE CHARACTERISTICS

The Landscape of Video Games in China

Zixue Tai and Jue Lu

Introduction

Against the backdrop of the economic rise of China as a world powerhouse, the growth of the video game sector from virtual non-existence to a prominent global leader in the past two decades is nothing short of spectacular. Three important, albeit not exactly parallel, trajectories have defined the development of China's video game industry: steady explosion of the online gaming sector at the turn of the 21st century, followed by the fast-paced maturation of the mobile market, coupled by the recent expansion of the esports sector.

This chapter offers a panoramic view of video games in China in the prevalent perspective of globalization. It starts with an examination of the path of development of the online game market, followed by an analysis of the rapid rise of esports, and then dissects the miscellaneous challenges and struggles in the tangled console game sector. Discussion is aligned with the contextual factors of state policymaking, market structure, and corporate strategies. We place emphasis on the multitude of glocalities (that is, how the global is refracted in the local waves) as manifested in these three areas over the past two decades.

Transformation of Online Gaming in China: From Follower to Leader

China boasts the largest video game market in the world today, with a projected market size of US$27.8 billion in 2020, trailed by the US ($19.5 billion), and Japan ($12.2 billion) (Statistica, 2020). This is no small feat considering the humble start of the game industry in China. Electronic games were introduced to Chinese players in the 1980s, through smugglers on the Southern coast and pirated copycats of Japanese consoles by unauthorized vendors across the country. With the diffusion of the World Wide Web in the 1990s, multi-user dungeons (MUDs) were available online in China, similar in format to those played in the West but with content adaptions to the local appetite. MUD games from Taiwan, thanks to their cultural affinity, quickly became popular in the late 1990s. Korean online games broke into the Chinese market in the early 2000s and rapidly made their presence felt among Chinese fans (Chew, 2019). From the 1980s to the late 1990s, official media portrayed game arcades as "dens of evil" and equated online gaming to electronic opium that lured youth away from their legitimate daily responsibilities to degenerate doings and moral toxins (e.g., Zhang, 2013). Chinese web cafes, or Wangba, which were the primary venue for youngsters to congregate in playing games, became frequent targets of public denunciation and government scrutiny during this period.

The rapid surge of the internet economy in China in the early 2000s reshaped the official discourse, and the government changed its approach to online games. The prominent rise of South Korea as a global empire of online gaming (Jin, 2010) served as an inspiration, and created a sense of urgency for the Chinese leadership. This led to a series of legislative, executive, and policy acts in the early 2000s through both the State Council and the various ministries in charge of culture, information technology, and publishing in coordinating national planning and spearheading initiatives to foster a unique brand of gaming industry in the country (Tai, 2010). Online gaming was designated a pillar of China's internet economy, which facilitated the mobilization of national and local resources in supporting the expansion of online games from corporate initiatives to player activities.

In examining China's ascent as a global economic powerhouse in the reform era, Zheng and Pan (2012) note three phases of evolution between economic nationalism and policy changes: "Inviting In" (Phase I: 1978–1991) features the introduction of foreign capitalism into the Chinese market; "Gearing with the World" (Phase II, 1992–2001) characterizes pragmatic efforts to be geared to international practices and the global market; "Going Out" (Phase III, since China's entry into the WTO in December 2001) manifests in fierce exploration of overseas markets and vigorous integration with the global economy. The development of online games in China bears some similarity to this overall trajectory, but with important twists and a significant temporal lag in implementation. The era we describe above, from the 1980s to the early 2000s, can be characterized as the Phase I of online gaming development, although one noticeable deviation of video games from other economic activities is that their entry into the Chinese market is more of a bottom-up effort by fans to embrace them rather than a deliberate effort by the state to invite them in. The measures enforced by state regulators and policymakers were invariably reactive in nature in addressing issues as they emerged.

China's online game industry entered Phase II in the 2002–2003 period, as revealed by a number of indicators. Firstly, this was a time when online gaming embarked on a path of rapid growth (Chew, 2019), quickly leading China into the biggest online game market. This is actualized by three parallel developments in the ensuing decade: an extended stretch of explosion in online gaming as manifested in both fan size and revenue generation; a dramatic change in the industry structure from the domination of overseas game content in the previous phase to the saturation of homegrown games; and the maturity of domestic creative talent in the game industry. Secondly, having molded its own brand of neo-techno nationalism intermingling state commitments, public-private partnerships, and global-local collaboration (Jiang & Fung, 2019), China effectively worked out a unique business model and propagated home-bred titles by tapping into its creative talent and appropriating its rich cultural heritage. Although overseas games still had a visible presence in the market, localization by Chinese developers countered with competitive games to win over players. Thirdly, the market size and the exploding internet sector in China turned out to be an unrivaled blessing to the rising online gaming industry. The sheer population of netizens in China after a decade of internet expansion created a sturdy bedrock perfectly fitting for the online gaming environment once viable game titles became available. It is no surprise that the Big Three portals in China—Sohu, Netease, and Sina—all established their online gaming branches and have remained in the top ten of China's gaming businesses. In a similar vein, rapid growth in mobile services provided the ideal soil for China to quickly evolve into the leading mobile game market in the world during this period (Tai & Hu, 2017).

Shanda, one of the top game conglomerates in China, exemplifies the path of success for online gaming business at the time. Founded in Shanghai in 1999, the company first set its foot into the Chinese market by purchasing the localization rights of *Legend of Mir II* from South Korea. It went on in building partnerships with a national network of web cafes, followed by its in-house title *The World of Legend* (2003) and other productions. Shanda pioneered the freemium model (free play, with in-game purchase) in 2005, which soon became the online game standard in the whole country. Its mobile enterprise started with a partnership with Motorola, and its subsequent expansion included acquisitions, business alliances, and marketing agreements with both Chinese and overseas game entities. The Chinese regulatory regime dictates that foreign games can only enter the Chinese online market through a local game publisher, thus necessitating local partnerships for any overseas asset to gain entry into China. Boosted by the huge Chinese internet market, all major gaming companies in China have pursued multiple collaborative schemes with foreign partners, a trend that started during this phase and continues to this date.

Tencent's majority purchase of Riot Games in the US (best known for its *League of Legends*) in 2011 (which changed to full acquisition in 2015) can be marked as the start of Phase III ("Going Out"), in which branching off into overseas markets became a major hallmark. This is a remarkable switch from the "defensive" from outside approach in Phase I to the "offensive" strategy of reaching out to the overseas market. Thanks to over a decade of consolidation and transformation in the Chinese market, the game business has been aggregated to a small number of global conglomerates. By 2020, eight major companies collectively own over 80% of the gaming revenue, with the remaining 20% split among about 200 smaller enterprises (Gamma Data, 2020). Another trend that continued in the 2010s is the domination of domestic game titles, which shifted to an impressive 84% (cf. 57.3% in 2013) of the Chinese gaming market in 2019 (ibid).

The "Going Out" initiative by Chinese gaming companies has been accomplished with a concerted, well-orchestrated strategy of "securing advantages in Southeast Asia, gaining competitiveness in the US and EU" (Gong, 2018). Due to their regional proximity and cultural affinity, countries in Southeast Asia have been the targets of game exports by Chinese conglomerates since around 2006, through various partnerships and subsidiaries in these localities. Similar strategies have paid off in recent years in the Western market. In 2019, Chinese game products generated a net revenue of US$11.6 billion (cf. $570 million in 2012), an increase of 21% over the previous year (GPC & IDC, 2019). In terms of country distribution (the top four), sales in the US account for 30.9%, Japan for 22.4%, South Korea for 14.3%, and Germany for 7% of the total overseas revenue (ibid). Another area that has experienced explosive growth during this phase is esports, which we look at next.

Esports: From Naught to Global Prominence

Besides mobile gaming, esports has been the fastest-growing area in Chinese video games for the past decade. It is noteworthy that "China has not only taken on South Korea as the mecca of esports but also taken over North America and Europe as the world's largest esports market" (Yu, 2018, p. 89). The rise of China's esports spectacles plays nicely with its overall strategy in the global expansion of the digital economy in the country, accomplished through the seamless integration of "boundaryless infrastructural power and platform capitalism" (Zhao & Lin, 2020, p. 13) in spearheading creative game assets into a sustainable path of development.

Competitive gameplay started in the late 1990s, at the venue where most youngsters were introduced to the world of online games—web cafes that were on popular street corners throughout major Chinese cities. Because the most dominant activities in web cafes were for teenagers to play networked games, it was only natural that players would engage in competitive gameplay there. The professionalization of esports as a mainstream cultural and commercial undertaking in South Korea at the turn of the 21st century (Jin, 2010) served as an eye-opener for Chinese gamers, and inspired them to a brand-new mode of gameplay. The World Cyber Games (WCG), which originated in South Korea in 2000 and quickly evolved into one of the largest global events (known as the Esports Olympics), caught the attention of Chinese fans. In the initial years, however, participation was limited: unorganized for lack of sponsorship or affiliation, and amateurish, relying on dispersed hardcore enthusiasts. This would be dramatically changed by one landmark event, single-handedly accomplished by Li Xiaofeng, (better known among fans by his game ID "sky") who won the championship for two consecutive years (2005 and 2006) for playing *Warcraft III*.

In its latest report on China's esports industry from the late 1990s to the present, iResearch (2020) summarizes its development into four distinct phases. The nascent (or exploratory) era (Phase I) lasts from 1998 to 2008, and witnesses the formalization of esports as a legitimate profession alongside the emergence of the esports industry in the country. One pivotal achievement during this period was the installation of a regulatory framework in facilitating the professionalization of esports in China. This was first signified by the recognition of esports as a formal competitive genre in November 2003 by the General Administration of Sport of China (GACC), which is the state agency for regulating all sport-related activities and events. This was an important step in elevating esports to a reputable occupation, and in erasing and defacing the stigmatized image of playing games as a worthless and time-wasting pastime. In September 2006, the GACC issued its administrative provisions stipulating pathways for organizing esports competitions, paving the way for holding esports tournaments in China. Esports were included in the 2nd Asian Indoor Games held in the Chinese territory of Macau in October 2007, making history for being the first international games event that made room for esports. This was followed by the induction of the Esports National Team in 2009 to participate in the 3rd Asian Indoor Games in Vietnam. Moreover, the GACC established its Esports Bureau in 2009, which is authorized to specialize in overseeing electronic events and competitions. Notably, esports competitions by Chinese players at this time were dominated by participation in overseas tournaments. One notable breakthrough during this period was the formation of the first esports club, WNV, in July 2003, with the specific aim of competing in regional and global esports events through corporate sponsorship (Baidu Wiki, n. d.). This set the model for many other clubs to follow in the coming years.

Phase II (2009–2013) is the takeoff period, marking the maturity of esports in China as a formal competitive event through regular tourneys and organized series. An important development during this phase was the debut and fast consolidation of China as the venue for an expanding list of regional and global esport events, as opposed to previously, when Chinese gamers had had to seek out venues in other countries. A simultaneous development was the rapid emergence of an expanding list of home-grown game titles on the esports battleground, side by side with the broadening scope of participation of Chinese players in overseas competitions. Involvement in well-established and popular global tournaments such as *StarCraft II*, *League of Legends*, and *Dota2* in the early years served as an effective eye-opener and inspirer, especially for Chinese game producers and publishers at a time when esport was a novel enterprise in China. This naturally led to the exploration of similar events by Chinese game entities. It was within this context that Tencent Games started the TGA (Tencent Games Arena) series in 2010, which has since taken center stage as one of the most prominent esports championship series in the world. This also accentuated Tencent's supremacy as a pivotal player in China's esports arena. In particular, Tencent's *Honor of Kings* championship became one of the most coveted accolades for gamers. In response to the blossoming of mobile games, the Global Mobile Game Confederation (GMGC) was founded in September 2012 as "an international platform for [mobile] companies to form long lasting partnerships and access new markets" (Global Mobile Game Confederation, n. d.). The GMGC has since sponsored mobile game tournaments in a number of Southeast Asian countries beyond China. Triggered by the proliferation of esports clubs across the nation, the Association of China E-sports (ACE) was formed in 2011 to coordinate rule-making, player transfer, game scheduling, and other activities among member e-clubs. ACE has played an important role in smoothing the organizational structure of esports clubs as well as promoting the professionalization of e-athletes in the country, a momentous step in fostering batches of top-notch professional players, some of whom have gone on to stellar careers in competing at the international stage.

The next phase (2014–2017) is marked by rapid consolidation of the trends set in the previous period, and witnesses growing spearheads of emergent territories as the Chinese esports industry engages further with global alliances. In parallel with the staggering mass saturation of mobile games in China (Tai & Hu, 2017), one of the most landmark breakthroughs during this time was the shifting status of mobile games from ancillary to domination. This is illustrated well by the overall trend in the latest trajectories of game revenues, as summarized in the most recent gaming industry half-year report by the Gaming Publications Committee (GPC) and International Data Corporation (IDC) (2020): of the three major game genres, mobile game revenues stand out for maintaining a steady upward growth pattern in the first six months for each year from 2014 (RMB ¥12.5 billion) to 2020 (RMB ¥104.7 billion), while revenue derived from web-based games sustained the most dramatic downturn during this period (from RMB ¥9.2 billion in 2014 to RMB ¥4.0 billion in 2020). Distributed engine-based games, on the other hand, mostly plateaued, with slight year-to-year fluctuations from 2014's RMB ¥25.6 billion to 2020's RMB ¥28.2 billion (generated in the first six months). Clearly, mobile games lead the way into the future, and have featured prominently in esports events in recent years.

In company of the vibrant esports industry there emerges an ancillary economy in the service of an assortment of niche needs orbiting around esports activities. Live streaming of game-related content and esports events is right at the forefront in this category. Game streaming in China started with YY (yy.com), which kicked off its live audio streaming service among Chinese gamers shortly after Justin Kan released Justin.tv in 2007. YY debuted its video streaming service in 2012, with a focus on gaming-related content. A competing streaming service, Kuaishou (kuaishou.com) went live online in late 2012. YY evolved into Huya TV (Huya.com) in November 2014 with enhanced and expanded services in diverse areas of video gaming. The rising success of YY and Kuaishou trigged more competing services in the next few years, most notably Douyu TV (douyu.com) and Zhanqi TV (zhanqi.tv) in 2014. Penguin Gaming (egame.qq.com) was founded on July 26, 2016 under the auspices of Tencent. A chaotic spurt of streaming platforms between 2013 and 2016 resulted in over 100 venues in China representing diverse corporate and audience interests. Competition got so fierce that streaming was often hosted by sparsely clad girls, with nudity and sexually suggestive content becoming mainstream. Public outrage led to the intervention of the Ministry of Culture, the official state arm in regulating online content, in 2016 to set new rules of the game. Breakneck consolidation of the market from 2014 to 2017 has resulted in the concentration of the streaming business to four prominent platforms: Huya, Douyu, Bilibili, and Kuaishou make up 90% of the streaming business in China in 2019 (Forward Industry Research, 2019).

This phase also marks the maturation of esports events on two fronts: game developers and publishers continuously play pivotal roles in the esports ecology, while third-party partners have mapped out their own business model in building their branded esports events. This is a big contrast to the early two phases—foreign esports events served as the gateway for Chinese players in Phase I, whereas first-party game stakeholders (meaning game developers and publishers like Tencent and Perfect World) were the main sponsors of esports during Phase II. The elevated role of third-party entities in Phase III (i.e., businesses or entities that do not directly own game publishing or developing assets) magnifies the scope of participation through including more game titles, and more importantly, injects much-needed capital in boosting esports' reach to diverse constituents. Two prime examples in the latter are NEST and WESG, both of which have now become elite esports events. NEST, which stands for National Electronic Sports Tournament, was started in 2013 by the GACC in collaboration with a Shanghai-based company, and turned into a major tournament in the coming years. One of NEST's eye-catching brands is the *CS:GO* series. The WESG, or World Electronic Sports Games, was inaugurated in December 2016 by AliSports (the sports subsidiary of the Alibaba Group), with a prize pool totaling over US$5.5 million in its first edition. As a general trend, the expansion of participants in hosting and organizing e-tournaments has resulted in a dramatic increase in the amounts of cash awards tallied on these events, which in turn spices up the attraction of talent.

Phase III, from 2018 to the present, is the explosion stage. Esports are set in full throttle thanks to the developments in the prior years, partly propelled by state policymaking and government support. In January 2019, the China Employment Training Technical Instruction Center (CETTIC), the state agency for certifying professions and employment, included two esports-related jobs in its 15 new professional lines: esports technicians, and esports athletes. In April 2019, China's National Bureau of Statistics added esports as a formal competitive sport category, similar to what is called the "Three Balls" in China—professional basketball, volleyball, and soccer. These official measures are important in mobilizing social, educational, local, and other resources in training, educating, and hiring esports-related personnel. Maneuvers by the central government have been followed closely by local governments in recent years in laying out and supporting esports initiatives of their own, as esports are eyed as a vital area in revitalizing the local economy.

In January 2019, Tencent and Riot Games jointly founded TJ Sports, a corporate endeavor specializing in spearheading regional and global tournaments under the *League of Legends* brand. This is the first esports endeavor of its kind in the world, and is poised to lead in its innovative approaches in exploiting commercial and esports opportunities. It also signifies efforts to promote esports in the same way as has been done for conventional sports, and how it fares in the years to come will most likely shape the contours of the esports landscape.

The multifaceted efforts to incubate esports have paid off lately, as attested by two fronts. Firstly, Chinese players have had a dominant presence and proud achievement in esports in Asia and on global stages, with stellar records of sweeping major esports championships in recent years. Secondly, in the first six months of 2020, when the whole country was caught in an unprecedented lockdown due to the Covid-19 pandemic, even though most other economic activities were reduced to historical lows, the esports sector turned into a money grabber by experiencing a drastic 55% revenue outburst over the same period last year, generating RMB ¥72.9 billion (GPC & IDC, 2020).

Console Games: From Predicament to Flashes of Hope

Compared with the steady rise of online games, console games have followed a rather tortuous path in gaining acceptance in the Chinese market. Their future, at the same time, is very much uncertain. According to the China gaming industry report jointly released by the GPC and IDC (2019), although console games experienced annual growth of 8.9% in 2019, their market value of RMB ¥5.36 billion (approximately USD $0.78 billion) only accounts for 2.3% of the overall Chinese gaming market. The import of the status quo is twofold: compared with other major global game markets, Chinese players' penchant for mobile and online games is well-entrenched and will not be easy to budge; on the other hand, the console game sector is at a rather nascent stage, and has great potential to grow in the coming decades.

Console games made their debut in the Chinese market in the 1980s through unauthorized imports and pirated products, mostly of consoles and cartridges originated in Japan (Liao, 2016). Bands of dealers smuggled the goods into China's southeast coastal lines from neighboring Hong Kong and Taiwan, which were then sold in the black market to consumers. The most dominant console in the 1980s was the Nintendo Family Computer (FC), nicknamed the "Red-White Machine" in China and sold significantly below its market price in Japan. Game titles, once released in Japan, were pirated almost overnight and would become available to Chinese players in no time.

The staggering interest in its consoles in mainland China led to Nintendo's decision in 1994 to contract its overseas wholesale right to Mani Limited as its strategy to break into the Chinese market. Mani, a Hong Kong-based marketing company, was already a highly prospering partner with Nintendo in hardware and software sales in Hong Kong and Taiwan. Its success elsewhere, however, did not transfer into the mainland market. In retrospect, two factors led to the FC marketing fiasco in China. Firstly, there was no effort to adapt the products for Chinese consumers—the console machines sold in China were manufactured in Hong Kong, for players there, with instructions and manuals written in English. Secondly, Chinese players already had easy access to pirated counterparts and cheap counterfeits, and it was hard to sway them over to the authorized but higher-priced items (GameTHK, 2017).

Another insurmountable challenge for Nintendo at the time was the widespread presence of cheap knockoff imitators. One of the household name was Subor Famiclone (FC). Founded in 1987 in China's southern province of Guangdong (Canton), Subor thrived in its business model as a blatant copycat of the Nintendo Family Computer when the legal framework for intellectual property protection was not in place in China. Popularly known as the "Jackie Chan Computer" (because he was hired as the spokesperson in Sudor's household television and print commercials), the FC was formally branded as a "Learning Machine" to target the vast population of school-age youth. Marketed at a much lower price than its Nintendo counterpart, the Sudor console had basic word processing and programming functionalities as well as being compatible with Nintendo's game cartridges.

Console games hit an impasse in China with an executive order regulating video game venues and practices announced by seven ministry-level government agencies, led by the Ministry of Culture, and promulgated on June 15, 2000 (PRC Central Government, 2000). Clause VI of the decree explicitly bans the manufacturing or distribution of electronic equipment or accessories in the service of video games, which was justified by the overall goal of rectifying a multitude of consequences of video gameplay including the "harm of adolescent health" and "disruption of social order." This is no surprise considering the widespread "moral panic" practice in Chinese society to equate video games to a special type of "spiritual opium" or "electronic drug" (Golub & Lingley, 2008).

This ban would remain in place for the ensuing 13-plus years until the government gave permission to the Shanghai Free Trade Zone to produce and market game consoles to the Chinese market on April 21, 2014. Since then, the Big Three of game consoles (Microsoft, Sony, and Nintendo) have established their presence in the Chinese market, and the player base has experienced steady growth. Nonetheless, console gameplay still constitutes an inconspicuous presence on the overall Chinese game market, accounting for only about 0.3 percent of market share as of 2019 (GPC & IDC, 2019), and monumental hurdles still exist side by side with looming opportunities in the coming years. At this stage, three pivotal factors have shaped (or hindered) the development of console games in China. Firstly, the official blockade of console games in China during the critical era when console technology experienced phenomenal growth in the outside world has drastically distanced Chinese players from this game genre, both in terms of its mechanics and content. Meanwhile, the steady rise of online games first and the domination of mobile games later among Chinese players in the 21st century have influenced their taste and play style so much that it is going to take something monumental beyond marketing for them to make the switch to console games. Secondly, the prevalent model of free play in China—players have free access to the games while making in-game purchases through virtual transactions—has become entrenched in China's game culture. In contrast, the console game model, which necessitates the purchase of the game console ranging from RMB¥2899 (PS4) to RMB¥4299 (Xbox One), plus the cost of the game title (typically at a few hundred *yuan*), is totally alienating for Chinese players. Thirdly, the current copyright management practice of region locking not only presents a nuisance for players but also limits their choice to the small pool of game titles that have received official authorization in the Chinese market. At the same time, the rather strenuous criteria for approval by state regulators create an extra burden on game producers/distributors to localize and adapt, a potentially costly procedure disincentivized by the small percentage of players interested in console games. Moreover, popular genres in console games such as first-person shooters, racing, and sports that dominate in other parts of the world do not align squarely with the preferred tastes or play styles of most Chinese players. As a result, for those players who are attracted to console games, there is a very limited pool of titles to choose from.

There are, however, flashes of promise for console games in China. Nintendo leads in its presence among the Big Three. Although its Switch debuted in China in 2019, about three years later than in most other regions, sales reached 3 million as of early 2020, making up about 6% of its global market share (Guancha Zhe, 2020). Part of its success may be attributable to Nintendo's strategy of partnering with Tencent, the tech giant leading China's online market. Another agent of change in facilitating future console game uptakes is the steadily increasing base of core console gamers, a trend in recent years showing patterns of expanding.

Concluding Remarks

The evolution of video games in China from a foreign invasion in the 1980s to the current status of a prominent global leader in the 21st century is in alignment with the overall rise of China as a technological and economic powerhouse. The despised image of video games as unproductive, low-taste playthings in the popular discourse in the 1980s and 1990s gave way to the state-orchestrated eulogy of the economic and cultural potential residing in online games in the 2000s, through a coordinated set of administrative measures and policy incentives in the new millennium. China's embrace of online gaming, however, is predicated on officially set regulatory and ideological boundaries. Games are classified as cultural products, and are subject to vigorous scrutinization by state censors. Entry into the Chinese market is also dictated by stringent stipulations ranging from story lines and graphic content to venue of publishing and distribution. These terms have facilitated the formation of business alliances between Chinese game enterprises and their foreign counterparts. This overall national strategy is most likely to continue in the years ahead.

Powered by their success in the Chinese market in the first decade of the 21st century, Chinese gaming conglomerates have embarked on an aggressive pathway of establishing and consolidating their presence in overseas markets. The further integration of Chinese gaming into the global market points to a direction that will be more vigorously pursued in the future. The unique edge that China has garnered through esports in recent years will work as a distinct advantage in promoting its business interest worldwide. One area in which China deviates from most other countries, nonetheless, is the console game sector. The stagnancy of console games in China during the pivotal years when this genre took off in other parts of the world serves as a formidable roadblock for consoles to gain critical mass in the country. How the future will pan out for console games is all but assured.

It is useful to cast the development of video games in China through the lens of glocality, which argues that local cultural entity is "influenced by global trends and global consciousness" (Meyrowitz, 2005, p. 23). Glocalization, as Roudometof (2016) contends, is an outcome of the refraction of the global formation through intense interaction with the local market. With regard to China's video game industry, as delineated in this chapter, the acculturation of game content is driven by the government mandate to regulate what goes into the game space, while market entry of overseas game titles is dictated by terms and conditions through government decrees. State policymaking, on the other hand, has been shaped to a great extent by developments in global markets. Corporate strategies and goal setting, meanwhile, prioritize the needs of "going out" into overseas markets. The tortuous trajectory of console games in China illustrates eloquently how the regulatory state can sink or boost a sector, irrespective of global trends. The current and new formations in these dynamics are bound to mold the future contours of the Chinese empire of video games.

References

Baidu Wiki (n. d.). wNv. Available: https://baike.baidu.com/item/wNv

Chew, M.M. (2019). A critical cultural history of online games in China, 1995–2015. *Games and Culture, 14*(3), 195–215.

Forward Industry Research (2019). 2019 China Esports Industry Report. Available: http://pdf.dfcfw.com/pdf/H3_AP202001231374539106_1.pdf

Gaming Publications Committee (GPC) & International Data Corporation (IDC) (2020, August). *2020 China Gaming Industry Report (January – June)*. Beijing: China Book Press.

Gaming Publications Committee (GPC) & International Data Corporation (IDC) (2019, December). *2019 China Gaming Industry Report*. Beijing: China Book Press.

GameTHK (2017). Twenty-three years of Nintendo's love affair with the Chinese market. Available: www.gamethk.com/news/detail/10265/6.html

Gamma Data (2020). 2019–2020 Chinese Game Enterprise Competitiveness Report. www.joynews.cn/toutiao/202005/0832430.html

Global Mobile Game Confederation (n. d.) About GMGC. Available: http://en.gmgc.info/

Golub, A., & Lingley, K. (2008). "Just like the qing empire": Internet addiction, MMOGs, and moral crisis in contemporary China. *Games and Culture*, *3*(1), 59–75.

Gong, Y. (2018). *China Animated Games Overseas Development Report*. Beijing: Social Sciences Academic Press.

Guancha, Zhe (2020, February 1). Nintendo said to be happy about its Switch sales in China. Available: www.guancha.cn/ChanJing/2020_02_01_534003.shtml

iResearch (2020). 2020 China's eSports Industry Report. Available: www.iresearchchina.com/content/details8_62007.html

Jiang, Q., & Fung, A.Y. (2019). Games with a continuum: Globalization, regionalization, and the nation-state in the development of China's online game industry. *Games and Culture*, *14*(7–8), 801–824.

Jin, D.Y. (2010). *Korea's Online Gaming Empire*. Cambridge, MA: The MIT Press.

Liao, S.X. (2016). Japanese console games popularization in China: Governance, copycats, and gamers. *Games and Culture*, *11*(3), 275–297.

Meyrowitz, J. (2005). The rise of glocality. New senses of place and identity in the global village. In K. Nyíri (ed.). *A Sense of Place: The Global and the Local in Mobile Communication in the 21th Century* (pp 21–30). Vienna: Passagen Verlag.

PRC Central Government (2000). Administrative orders on the management of digital game business venues. Available: www.gov.cn/gongbao/content/2000/content_60240.htm

Roudometof, V. (2016). *Glocalization: A Critical Introduction*. New York: Routledge.

Statistica (2020). Video Games Worldwide. Available: www.statista.com/outlook/203/100/video-games/worldwide#market-revenue.

Tai, Z. (2010). Setting the rules of play: Network video game policies and regulations in China. *Iowa Journal of Communication*, *42*(1), 45–71.

Tai, Z., & Hu, F. (2017). Mobile games in China: Ongoing industry transformations, emerging game genres, and evolving player dynamics. In D.Y. Jin (ed.) *Mobile Gaming in Asia: Politics, Culture and Emerging Technologies* (pp. 173–190). Dordrecht: Springer.

Yu, H. (2018). Game on: The rise of the esports Middle Kingdom. *Media Industries Journal*, *5*(1), 88–105.

Zhang, L. (2013). Productive vs. pathological: The contested space of video games in post-reform China (1980s–2012). *International Journal of Communication*, 7. Available: https://ijoc.org/index.php/ijoc/article/view/2066/1016

Zhao, Y., & Lin, Z. (2020). Umbrella platform of Tencent eSports industry in China. *Journal of Cultural Economy*, 1–17.

Zheng, Y., & Pan, R. (2012). From defensive to aggressive strategies: The evolution of economic nationalism in China. In A.P. D'Costa (ed.) *Globalization and Economic Nationalism in Asia* (pp. 680–714). Oxford: Oxford University Press.

22

TROLLING AND PRAISING THE ARAB SPRING ON TWITTER

Ahmed Al-Rawi

Introduction

This chapter deals with an empirical examination of public discourses in Arabic on the Arab Spring and it attempts to fill a gap in literature on this under-researched area. Previous research investigated the hashtag Arab Spring in English (Sieben, 2014) but no study has examined the use of the term exclusively in Arabic. Further, the data collected spans from the beginning of the Arab Spring protests in 2011 until late 2019. The study shows that the majority of Twitter users who reference the Arab Spring discuss it negatively, often trolling human rights activists in the region such as Jamal Khashoggi in order to discredit their cause. These trolls use common themes and conspiracy theories to appeal to a high number of users.

The study here is situated within the discussion of political trolling in the Arab world. Back in the early days of the Arab Spring, Ghannam (2012) advised Arab bloggers in 2011 not to use the hashtag of the country they were discussing to avoid facing unpleasant trolls. Though the public discussions were mostly directed at internet access and circumventing government control, a new cyberwar was starting in which Arab governments and political parties sought to control the narrative through social media manipulation, which included the use of trolls against any political opposition. Because of what they wrote online and did offline, activists in the region faced serious security risks (Ghannam, 2012).

The case of Bahrain in 2011 serves as a good example. Due to constant state surveillance of social media, many activists were tracked down, arrested, and even tortured (Al-Rawi, 2015). In this regard, Ghannam (2012) presented testimonials from Bahraini oppositional group members who faced clear harassment, including the case of prominent Bahraini blogger and activist, Hussain Yousif. "They told me that 'you are like an animal that we would kill and nobody would care for you. They have published my picture and my mobile number and said, 'Call this person and let him know what you think about him'" (p. 13). Yousif explained to the *New York Times* how trolls set schedules to tweet the same arguments using common abusive words and how they maintained doxxing practices whose goal is disclosing activists' personal details, including their phone numbers and places of residence (Ghannam, 2012).

In another study by Jones (2013), the author went even further and explored the way political institutions in Bahrain used methods like trolling to hassle activists. Jones found evidence of political trolling that ranged from hateful comments to death threats, after conducting a virtual ethnography between February 2011 and December 2011. Trolls' harassment included anonymous accounts tweeting an activist child's school name to scare her, while another male activist talked about five parody accounts devoted to mocking him. Others told Jones how such harassment stopped them from even expressing moderate political views. Respondents to the study confessed that in addition to not tweeting about the regime out of fear, some changed their Twitter privacy settings so that only their followers could see their tweets.

In addition to trolling, Jones addressed the use of doxxing in the way naming and shaming by pro-regime Twitter users was done, specifically in the case of a famous account named Hareghum. The word "Hareghum" (حارقهم) literally means "the one that burns them," and the user is considered a self-proclaimed defender of Bahrain and spends his days disclosing information about dissidents. This includes posting photos of people seen at anti-government rallies, circling their faces, and disclosing their addresses, places of work, and phone numbers (p. 79). It is important to note here that Twitter is not the only space for shaming activists in Bahrain, for similar groups were present on Facebook as well. Though Facebook managed to remove these groups more quickly, one page was reportedly responsible for the arrest of the poet Ayat al-Qurmez, after visitors of the page revealed information about her.

Turning to other Arab countries, Bradshaw and Howard (2017) found evidence showing the active use of cyber armies by Saudi Arabia, Syria, and Bahrain. After using systematic content analysis as well as reviewing credible research sources and consulting country experts, the authors found three main functional domains in which these cyber armies operate: "(1) strategies, tools and techniques of social media manipulation; (2) organizational form; and (3) organizational budget, behaviour and capacity" (p. 6). The study noted Saudi Arabia's involvement in spamming hashtags or hashtag poisoning. The authors also listed media reports claiming mobilization of bots by government actors in Saudi Arabia and Syria, where such accounts were used to "amplify marginal voices and ideas" and create "an artificial sense of popularity" (p. 11). Further, Al-Rawi also argued that the Syrian Electronic Army routinely targeted the Syrian opposition with hacking operations to support Bashar Assad's regime (Al-Rawi, 2014).

In the Arab world, political trolls and their activities have been described using a number of names, including "online seminars" (Darwish, Alexandrov, Nakov, & Mejova, 2017). Here, Darwish et. al note how it fits the Middle East by applying it to the case of Egypt. Online seminars are related to the coined Arabic term (lijan electroniyya), which can be translated into "electronic committees." A good example is found in public statements made by General El-Sisi of Egypt, who frequently claims that he can influence a social media agenda by deploying electronic brigades (p. 2). As per Darwish et al.'s empirical study, seminar users are actively involved in spreading political propaganda, often pretending to be normal users while advocating an agenda (p. 2). In other words, they act like sockpuppets because they pretend to be someone else to avoid detection and possibly enhance the effect of their messages.

Another notable example of trolling is related to the 2017 Qatari diplomatic crisis, as it introduced a new wave of polarized political activity between countries in the Gulf Cooperation Council (GCC). Due to some of Qatar's foreign policies, Saudi Arabia, the UAE, and Bahrain decided to cut diplomatic ties with Qatar in 2017. Al-Rawi's (2019) study on this cyberconflict shows how a diplomatic dispute between Qatar and other GGC states was reflected on the Twittersphere. Pro-Qatari Twitter users and trolls, for example, changed their profile pictures to use the image of Qatar's Emir and a unified solidarity statement, while on the other side anti-Qatari users started hashtags to attack Qatar and its Emir. In this regard, Saudi Arabia's former royal court advisor, Saud al Qahtani, created an army of trolls to fight Qatar's supporters and disseminated a viral Arabic hashtag called the blacklist to encourage Saudis to add names of alleged Qatari supporters and sympathizers. Similarly, Qatar deployed its own tactics. The Saudi information minister claimed that Qatar managed to hire 23,000 Twitter users to increase the divide in the region (Al-Rawi, 2019).

To sum up, online trolling in the Arab world has been ongoing for many years, especially after the beginning of the Arab Spring, and social media platforms have been weaponized by state-affiliated political actors to silence dissent. The media ecosystem remains divided along polarized politics, sectarian divisions, and ethnic groups, which is reminiscent of what Gitlin calls the divided public sphere or public sphericules (Gitlin, 1998).

Trolling and Praising the Arab Spring

In this study, I followed a mixed method to better understand the Arabic-language public discourses surrounding the Arab Spring on Twitter. First, I extracted 1,240,294 tweets collected from January 26, 2011 until July 24, 2019 (Figure 22.1) using a Python script. These tweets were posted by 283,530 unique users who sent 845,238 unique tweets. The highest volume of tweets was sent in 2013 (405,936), followed by 2012 (336,857), and 2011 (146,743). Due to API limitations of getting Twitter data, it is not clear how many tweets in total were sent by Twitter users to discuss the Arab Spring.

In addition, I used a Python script to extract the most frequent hashtags and terms used in the unique tweets to understand which terms are most referenced (Table 22.1). This offers an indication of the countries that received the most attention from the online public. Here, Egypt comes first in both English and Arabic (28,799 mentions) followed by Syria (25,785), Saudi Arabia (12,626), Tunisia (12,043), and Libya (7,295). The prominence of these countries shows the importance given to them by Twitter users. Interestingly, Saudi Arabia is the only one of these countries that did not witness large-scale protests. However, and as will be discussed below, Saudi Arabia is often mentioned in connection to trolling the Arab Spring's supporters. Table 22.1 also shows three phrases, two of which will be discussed below; the third one (no. 19) reads: "What have we gained from the Arab Spring", which is overwhelmingly negative in showing the shortcomings of the popular protests in the Arab world.

Due to the large dataset, I only focused on the unique tweets and most retweeted ones, because they offer a better understanding of the public engagement with the Arab Spring. In this regard, I qualitatively examined the top 100 most retweeted messages, which were sent 178,990 times, receiving 280,307 likes. These top tweets showed the existence of three distinctive online communities: (1)

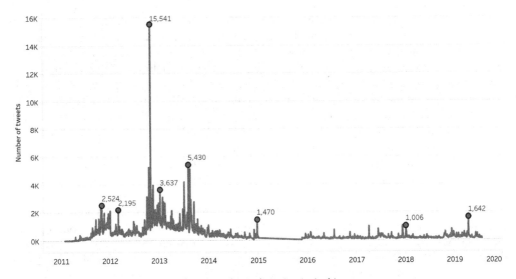

Figure 22.1 Distribution of tweets referencing the Arab Spring in Arabic

Table 22.1 The top 40 hashtags in the dataset

No	Hashtag	Frequency	No	Hashtag	Frequency
1.	#مصر	19,508	21.	#ksa	2,310
2.	#سوريا	14,590	22.	#syria	2,310
3.	#Syria	8,885	23.	#السودان	2,129
4.	#السعودية	8,564	24.	#الجزائر	2,040
5.	#تونس	8,407	25.	#الخليج	2,020
6.	#تعلمت_من_الربيع_العربي	7,538	26.	#فلسطين	1,955
7.	#Bahrain	7,380	27.	#Iran	1,855
8.	#Egypt	6,321	28.	#العرب	1,825
9.	#ليبيا	6,097	29.	#الإمارات	1,785
10.	#علمني_الربيع_العربي	5,831	30.	#مرسي	1,757
11.	#قطر	5,596	31.	#saudi	1,752
12.	#اليمن	5,354	32.	#تركيا	1,719
13.	#bahrain	4,727	33.	#GCC	1,709
14.	#البحرين	4,663	34.	#Yemen	1,697
15.	#العراق	4,057	35.	#غزة	1,689
16.	#الكويت	3,714	36.	#yemen	1,674
17.	#egypt	2,970	37.	#الامارات	1,608
18.	#ايران	2,895	38.	#No	1,606
19.	#بماذا_خرجنا_من_الربيع_العربي	2,840	39.	#لبنان	1,561
20.	#kuwait	2,578	40.	#الجزيرة	1,467

14% supportive of the Arab Spring, (2) 68% antagonistic against the Arab Spring, and (3) 18% neutral or unclear.

Here, 26,715 tweets mentioned the following message expressed in two different formats: "I learned from the Arab Spring" or "the Arab Spring taught me": (تعلمت_من_الربيع_العربي) and (علمني_الربيع_العربي). Figure 22.1 shows that on October, 28 2012 we have the highest number of tweets (15,541) because of these two trending hashtags, which were used as a kind of challenge. I then examined the most recurrent terms, and many of the most liked posts on what the Arab Spring taught people are very supportive of the protests. For example, the two most liked tweets (442) read as follows: "The Arab Spring taught me that oppression does not end with the fall of the head but it must be uprooted and its bases destroyed. Continue with your revolution, free people of Algeria." Another, which was retweeted 87 times, says: "I learned from the Arab Spring that the dictator does not want to admit that the reasons behind the revolution are the accumulation of injustice, oppression, persecution of people. Instead, he thinks it is a global external conspiracy." These tweets show that there is clear mistrust in the political establishment in the Arab world that is mostly characterized by its authoritarian rule. The other point is related to the discourse surrounding the protest, for we find that it is described as a revolution rather than a conspiracy. In other words, the top liked tweets are supportive of the Arab Spring movement and critical of different Arab regimes.

On the other hand, in the same dataset, we find that many other terms and most liked tweets show antagonistic views against the protests. For instance, some of the most recurrent terms include "the so-called Arab Spring" (2,247 times), "the consequences of the Arab Spring" (1,995), and "the alleged Arab Spring" (1,654) all of which are used in highly negative ways to discredit the popular protests. Also, the most liked tweets composed in different formats (257) mention: "I learned from the Arab Spring the validity of Ibn Taymiah's observation:[1] It is known that no group that revolted against a ruler has brought less moral corruption than what was originally there." As Ibn Taymiah is considered one of the founding fathers of the Salafi movement, which is based on a very strict interpretation of Islam including obeying the political ruler, this tweet implies a religious call and reminder to blindly respect political and religious authorities because doing so allegedly leads to more security, order, and safety. In fact, these are examples of appeals often used by Arab dictators to discredit any uprisings, and this notion is directly articulated in another popular tweet (62) that says: "I learned from the Arab Spring to be more supportive of our rulers after what we saw in other insecure countries which turned into jungles, allowing the strong to eat the weak."

Another salient theme that is very recurrent among this antagonistic community is the belief in a global conspiracy that allegedly created the Arab Spring revolts. Here, one user posted the following message, which was retweeted 159 times: "I learned from the Arab Spring that it is a deformed baby produced from a dubious marriage between America, the father, and the Muslim Brothers, the mother, with the blessing of Qaradawi and witnessed by Hamad. The marriage ceremony was in Doha." The tweet suggests that the USA orchestrated the Arab Spring with the help of the Muslim Brotherhood in Egypt. The latter group is regarded as a terrorist organization in Egypt and many GCC countries because of political differences. The reference to Yusuf al-Qaradawi, who is one of the leaders of the Muslim Brotherhood organization and is stationed in Qatar, is meant to connect him to Qatar's former Emir, Hamad Bin Khalifa Al-Thani, due to the financial and political support Qatar offers to the Muslim Brotherhood (Al-Rawi, 2017). Again, the implied conspiracy notion here is that the protesters' cause is invalid because they are blindly driven by foreign powers whose goal is to destroy the social fabric of Arab societies and spread political Islam.

It is important to note here that the majority of the 100 most retweeted posts were originally written by influencers and other famous people known for their antagonistic views against Qatar and the Arab Spring like Al Qahtani and Al Khalfan, who are mentioned below. Here, we find two polarized communities fighting for a space to discuss the merits and drawbacks of the Arab Spring, each of which tries to further its agenda and discourse surrounding the popular protests that engulfed the Arab world from 2011. In relation to the supportive community, most retweets were related to the anti-government protests in Sudan between December 2018 and July 2019, and I will provide below more details on the two polarized online communities.

As mentioned above, the dominant community is the one showing antagonism against the Arab Spring, constituting 68% of the top retweets. Here, the most retweeted post (7,956 times) reads as follows: "Saudi Arabia, Kuwait, and the UAE fulfilled all their obligations towards Jordan... Unlike the Hamadin regime [Qatar] that is known for its dirty scheme against Jordan during the Arab Spring." The negative association between Qatar and the Arab Spring is meant to highlight the idea that Qatar engineered the popular protests in many countries to spread political Islam and assist the Muslim Brothers with the help of its Al Jazeera channel. Incidentally, this particular tweet was sent by Saud Al Qahtani (@saudq1978), who is known as Mr. Hashtag or Prince of Darkness due to his active role in trolling Saudi Arabia's political dissidents and regime opponents (Al-Rawi, 2019, p. 1, 310). Al Qahtani was also implicated in the killing of the Saudi dissident journalist Jamal Khashoggi in Turkey (Al-Rawi, 2019). In the top retweets examined here, we found eight of Al Qahtani's other tweets referencing the Arab Spring included another negative statement against the Arab Spring and Qatar.

Incidentally, many tweets in our sample reference Jamal Khashoggi, such as the following one: "The destitute Muslim Brother, Khashoggi, defends the [anti-Saudi] intelligence cell, supports the Arab Spring, praises the [Muslim] brothers and Qatar despite their terrorism, and threaten to create opposition in the diaspora pic.twitter.com/e9xGwCpJiM." The message was posted by a Saudi user called @Alrad3sa, which means "Saudi counterattack", who tweeted seven times about the Arab Spring. This user, who is currently suspended for violating Twitter's rules, was part of Al Qahtani's troll army whose goal is to attack any online criticism against the Saudi Kingdom. Even after Khashoggi's assassination, attacks against him did not cease, for Dhahi Al Khalfan, deputy chief of Dubai police, who is known for his controversial tweets about Qatar, mentioned the following on October 22, 2018, just a few days after Khashoggi's death: "According to the Daily Post [sic], Khashoggi secretly created a large organization based in the US state of Delaware with branches in Turkey called DAWN that is funded by Qatar... to create a second Arab Spring wave." This message, which is the 10th most retweeted post (3,600), contains false information, for Al Khalfan[2] has fabricated the claim that DAWN is funded by Qatar. Other antagonistic retweets against the Arab Spring highlight a few issues including conspiracy theories that can be summed up in the following points:

- The protests are useless for they only bring chaos, destruction, and pain,
- Israel has exerted more power over the Middle East region because of the Arab Spring,
- The Arab Spring protesters are described as "cockroaches,' thugs, and brutes,
- The RAND organization planned to divide Saudi Arabia after 9/11 with the help of Qatar.
- The Arab Spring is a dark Winter whose goal is killing, violating people's honor, and looting their wealth.
- Iran reaped the fruits of the Arab Spring as it controls Arab affairs.
- Obama conspired with the Muslim Brothers to create the Arab Spring.
- Al Jazeera orchestrated the Arab Spring to spread political Islam all over the Arab world.

As mentioned above, some of the main targets of trolling include Qatar, which is often misspelled to sound like Qatarael (قطرائيل), which rhymes with the word Israel (اسرائيل) in Arabic to denote the two countries' close alliance in supporting the Arab Spring. Incidentally, many protesters also referenced Israel and its alliance with authoritarian Arab regimes, suggesting that both fear the Arab Spring revolutions due to their democratic outcomes. In addition, the Al Jazeera channel is routinely called "Al Khanzira" (الخنزيرة) or "female pig" to demean and discredit the news organization's coverage, which is often linked to serving Qatar's foreign policies and interests in the region.

Finally, the following tweet that was retweeted 1,416 times provides some insight into the gloating manner by which trolls negatively presented the outcomes of the popular protests, stating: "The Arab Spring is like a woman who endured her husband's infidelity for many years. When she exploded in his face and vented her anger, he mercilessly threw her into the street. The neighbors pitied her saying: 'At least she was living under a roof where she ate and drank for years, but she didn't thank her God for His blessing'." This tweet denotes a patriarchal outlook in which the people are expected to be passive followers of the powerful male leader who must rule the country without any objection. People, on the other hand, must remain grateful and appreciative of the kindness and protection of their leader even if he continuously acts aggressively. This tweet ties in well with the one that mentions Ibn Taymiah because religious directives are embedded in them. Another user tweeted an image showing dead Syrian children stating: "The Arab Spring passed from here, as they claimed" in order to create fear and ironically associate the uprising with death and social destruction.

On the other hand, the second community, which praises the Arab Spring and defends it, is much smaller, constituting 14% in the sample I examined from the most retweeted posts. In this respect, the most prominent user was Jamal Khashoggi himself, who posted 13 messages that were supportive of the Arab Spring. One of his messages was retweeted 1,437 times, expressing support for the popular protests in Iran and countering critical voices: "It is natural that I support the Iranian Spring like others who participated and supported the Arab Spring. Yet what can you say about others who opposed the Spring and viewed it as a conspiracy, while overlooking the voices of freedom in Damascus and Cairo and only hearing what happens in Mashhad and Tehran! Freedom has one banner." The tweet is meant to show Khashoggi critics' double standards, and it criticizes the Arab rulers who express direct and indirect support for the popular protests in Iran that aimed at creating political change, yet the same leaders vehemently opposed similar protests in their own countries.

This chapter provides an empirical analysis of the public discourses surrounding the Arab Spring in Arabic. I identified two main online communities that discuss this polarized political issue. The larger percentage of Twitter users are highly critical of the Arab Spring, often using conspiracy theories to discredit the protesters' cause. Political trolls have weaponized Twitter in different ways, such as creating a tightly knit online community to attack and silence oppositional groups and activists like

Jamal Khashoggi and subsequently dominate the public discourse. On the other hand, activists have a weaker voice and minor presence in the top retweeted messages, framing their uprising as a positive revolution whose progressive goal is spreading democracy and equality in the Middle East region. This political tension has resulted in an ongoing cyberwar waged along the divided public sphericules of social media. These discussions provide an excellent barometer on the kind of political polarization that occurs online because it is a contested issue especially for authoritarian regimes.

Future research needs to explore other social media platforms like Instagram, where the Arab Spring hashtag is also popular. Also, we need more studies that identify ongoing trolling activities combining different research approaches such as social network mapping and big data analysis.

Notes

1 Ibn Taymiah is also regarded as one of the forefathers of Wahhabism, which is the dominant Islamic doctrine in Saudi Arabia.
2 Al Khalfan is possibly referring here to the *Daily Beast* (Swan, 2018) not the *Daily Post*'s report.

References

Al-Rawi, A. (2014). Cyber warriors in the middle east: The case of the Syrian electronic army. *Public Relations Review, 40*(3), 420–428.

Al-Rawi, A. (2015). Sectarianism and the Arab Spring: Framing the popular protests in Bahrain. *Global Media and Communication, 11*(1), 25–42.

Al-Rawi, A. (2017). Assessing public sentiments and news preferences on Al Jazeera and Al Arabiya. *International Communication Gazette, 79*(1), 26–44.

Al-Rawi, A. (2019). Cyberconflict, Online Political Jamming, and Hacking in the Gulf Cooperation Council. *International Journal of Communication, 13*, 1301–1322.

Bradshaw, S., & Howard, P. (2017). Troops, Trolls and Troublemakers: A Global Inventory of Organized Social Media Manipulation. Oxford Internet Institute, pp. 1–37.

Darwish, K., Alexandrov, D., Nakov, P., & Mejova, Y. (2017, September). Seminar users in the Arabic Twitter sphere. International Conference on Social Informatics (pp. 91–108). Oxford Internet Institute. Oxford, UK: Springer.

Ghannam, J. (2012). *Digital media in the Arab world one year after the revolutions.* Center for International Media Assistance.

Gitlin, T. (1998). Public sphere or public sphericules? In T. Liebes & J. Curran (Eds.), *Media, ritual, identity* (pp. 168–174). London: Routledge.

Jones, M.O. (2013). Social media, surveillance and social control in the Bahrain uprising. Westminster Papers in Communication and Culture. DOI: http://doi.org/10.16997/wpcc.167

Sieben, J. (2014). *Twittering the #ArabSpring? An empirical content analysis of tweets.* Hamburg: Anchor Academic Publishing.

Swan, B. (2018, October 10). Jamal Khashoggi Wanted to Launch a Pro-Democracy Group. Then the Saudis Disappeared Him. The Daily Beast. Retrieved from www.thedailybeast.com/jamal-khashoggi-wanted-to-launch-a-pro-democracy-group-then-the-saudis-disappeared-him

23

RECEIVING UNFAMILIAR CULTURE IN POST-COLONIAL LATIN AMERICA IN THE DIGITAL AGE

Interpretations of Anime, Manga, and K-pop by Chilean Fans

Wonjung Min

Introduction

Geographically, Chile is an isolated region surrounded by deserts in the north, the Andes in the east, and the Pacific Ocean in the west. At the time of Spanish rule, Chile had nearly abandoned its land in subordination to the viceroyalty of Peru. After gaining independence, however, Chile's victory against its neighbors Peru and Bolivia in the Pacific War (1879–1884) allowed the country to achieve a solid foothold in the region. Much later, during the military regime (1973–1990), neoliberal policy was adopted, and Chile's economic development became a model approach in Latin America. Chile's political stability, which set it apart from other Latin American countries, also helped to secure its position in the region. A relatively smaller Indigenous population compared to neighboring countries, such as Peru and Bolivia, allowed Chile to establish its Europeanness as distinct from Peru and Bolivia, which had strong autochthonous cultures and were not primarily European (Prieto Larraín, 2020). At the same time, geographical isolation has given many Chileans little exposure to foreign cultures and thus may explain their lack of tact and empathy toward other cultures (Min, 2020).

This chapter will investigate the expansion of Asian popular culture in Latin America to analyze identity formation among Chilean fans of anime, manga, and K-pop as well as their interpretations of these elements of pop culture. It also considers why the massification of K-pop in Latin America is so strong in a region far from Korea and why the SM TOWN Live Concert was held in Chile rather than in Mexico or Brazil, which have larger populations. Centeno (1999) describes the Latin American identity as an imagined community, socially constructed through narrative, myths of origins, symbols, rituals, and collective memory, imagined by those who see themselves as part of that group (pp. 75–79). There is no identity without memory, and history is one way to preserve the memory of a society. However, memory is not the only way to represent (or imagine) the past and prepare for the future; monuments, rituals, literary works, and other cultural activities are also a means of remembering and forgetting (Rivero, Bellelli, & Bakhurst, 2000). How do monuments, rituals, literary works, and other cultural activities contribute to generating different memories for different classes, divided memories in the same society, and broken memories in Latin American—especially

Chilean—society after gaining independence? How do they affect the acceptance of unfamiliar cultures, such as Asian popular culture?

For Latin American countries such as Chile, independence from Spain in the late 19th century was not secured by aboriginal Indigenous peoples who had previously lived in the region but through the rebellion of Creoles (*Criollos* in Spanish), Spanish descendants born in the New World. Although different in each country, in most cases, settlers in Latin America formed *mestizo* cultures by eradicating, abolishing, absorbing, or blending various races and cultures. In his book *The Idea of Latin America*, Mignolo (2005) claims that the population of European or Latin descent effectively wiped out the Indian and Black populations following independence. Creoles, the protagonists of independence, sought to create a new European state on the new continent. For the Creoles, independence was marked by their desire for political autonomy and was not a synonym for revolution. However, the meaning of independence was different for each race and group, and in the process of state formation, there were attempts to create the types of countries that the elite groups wanted. The Creole elite of Chile, for example, aimed to create a white country. Hence, Chile's self-image has always been more European than indigenous (Stefoni, 2004). The country has denied a *mestizo* culture and has intentionally maintained a sovereign state, emphasizing a European cultural identity since its inception.

As part of its effort to construct a white country, the Chilean government began to receive immigrants from northern Europe, including Germany in the late 19th century. To actively attract German immigrants, the Chilean government established an immigration agency in Europe in 1882 that promised land for settler families (Gott, 2007). It actively recruited approximately 4,000 Germans to colonize the largely unoccupied provinces of southern Chile. Traditional *Criollos* and European immigrants formed an oligarchic elite group in Chile, a tradition that continues to this day. The German-speaking population of the south-central provinces of Chile is an ongoing source of both national pride due to its economic vigor and concern because of its persistence as a foreign enclave (Young, 1971).

Even today, Europe is considered a significant part of the heritage of Chile; elementary and secondary school textbooks start with the history of Europe and dedicate little space to the history of Indigenous peoples. Introducing the concept of *settler colonialism,* Gott (2007) observes that "Latin America shares these characteristics [Europeanism and a desire to 'whiten' the country] and clearly falls into the category of 'settler colonialism', even though the colonial powers are no longer present, having been forced out in the course of the nineteenth century" (p. 273). The Peruvian sociologist Quijano (2014) developed the concept of *colonialidad* or "coloniality," according to which societies retain or assume the pattern of global domination originating from European colonialism in the early 16th century even when they have become nominally independent. The adoption of racist ideas from Europe later in the 19th century in Latin America served to justify the increase in immigration and promotion of further wars of extermination (Gott, 2007). Cable News Network (CNN) Chile's program *Actualidad Central* serves as an example of ongoing coloniality in Chile. On September 20, 2015, *Actualidad Central* aired a special talk show to celebrate Chile's Independence Day, celebrated on September 18. The host's remarks about Chilean identity reveal its ambiguity:

> [There is a] feeling of not knowing what the cultural patterns are, without a clear national identity and denying who we are. We never define ourselves as mestizos. We try to erase our indigenous past and build myths about what we are; we are the English in South America, for example.

Similarly, the interview results for this chapter reveal that many Chilean fans of Asian popular culture identify themselves as Westerners, not as Latin Americans; for example, a 19-year-old female stated, "as I said before, as a Westerner," and a 27-year-old male said, "here in the West." How is Chile's Eurocentricity related to Chilean fans' imagining of Asia? This chapter hypothesizes that Latin

American, and specifically Chilean, fans of Asian popular culture form an imaginary Asia through media representations even while they live in an imagined Eurocentric society. Asians in Chile are often referred to as *chinos* (Chinese) (Min, 2020; Min et al., 2019). All people of Asian origin in Chile, including those born in the country, are considered to be Chinese. All fans of Asian popular culture in the country are considered outsiders because of the tendency for Chileans to believe that those who like *chinos* are akin to *chinos* (Min, 2020; Min et al., 2019). Chilean fans frequently also identify themselves as *chinos* but do not typically consume Chinese media; their interest is generally limited to Japanese anime and manga and Korean pop music, known as K-pop. In accordance with previous studies (Min, 2020; Min et al., 2019), most interviewees in the present study became aware of K-pop through Japanese anime and manga, and while these fans love and consume popular Asian culture, very few have visited Asia.

Following Chile's independence from Spain, various external cultures, such as North American hip-hop, Japanese anime and manga, and Korean popular cultures flowed into Chile and were met with both acceptance and rejection. In general, however, unfamiliar cultures have not been welcomed in Chilean society. Even Latin American trap and reggaeton have been scorned by older generations for their rebellious lyrics and inflammatory images. This chapter will describe how fans of Asian popular culture in Chile share an imaginary space and create bonds through an unfamiliar culture while they live in an imagined Eurocentric society. It also explores the development of imaginary cultural intimacy specific to digital media, primarily in the realm of social media.

Methodology

To understand Chilean interpretations of Asian popular culture, it is first necessary to consider how Eurocentrism and *chino*-ism in Latin America related to the formation of cultural identity in the region and this cultural identity determined by the legacy of Chile's socioeconomic status. In his article, "Global, Hybrid or Multiple? Cultural Identities in the Age of Satellite TV and the Internet," Straubhaar (2017) explores the impacts of today's global media on identity formation and how we should understand those impacts and the resultant identities. The shift from traditional local life after independence to modern interaction with mass media has produced identities that are multilayered; they encompass cultural-geographic elements that are local, regional, national, and transnational in relation to cultural-linguistic regions (Anderson, 1983). While Spanish colonization (1540–1810) coercively created a mixed race and led to cultural hybridization in Latin America, there were relatively fewer aboriginal Indians and mixed-race populations in Chile than in neighboring countries, such as Peru and Bolivia.

To reveal the influence of unsuccessful decolonization (Min, 2020), the existence of class in a democratic society, and imagery about Europe and Asia in Chilean media, in-depth interviews were conducted from July to December 2019. Prior to these interviews, analog data visualization was carried out in October 2018 during the 10th International Conference on Korean Studies, held at the Pontificia Universidad Católica de Chile. The conference participants were asked why they think Chilean people use the term *chino* and whether they also use the term. Participants wrote their answers on sticky notes on the wall during the conference. In total, 95 people (57 students, four professors, and 34 members of the public) replied to the analog data visualization. For the in-depth interviews, 36 self-identified interviewees aged 18–29 were chosen using the snowball method. The interviewees were divided into two groups—upper middle class and lower middle class—based on their socioeconomic status. A previous study (Min et al., 2019) had concluded that the socio-economic status of most K-pop fans in Chile was not high. Therefore, this study selected student participants from Pontificia Universidad Católica de Chile (PUC), Universidad Adolfo Ibáñez (UAI), and the University of Santiago, Chile (USACH), among others. PUC and UAI are politically conservative, elite universities, and the USACH is politically progressive.

The Past in the Present: Eurocentrism and *Chino*-ism

In *Imagined Communities*, Anderson (1983) states, "those born in the new continent were destined to be subordinates of those born in Europe for one reason only: they were irremediably criollos" (p. 57). The Creoles confronted the centralism of the old continent and modeled their own aristocracy in Chile, seeking to embody the enterprising spirit of those conquerors who sought a better future on the new continent. They created a mixed European and Chilean aristocracy with traditional values, liberal ideas, and a lack of aristocratic titles (Edwards, 1928). Hall (2016) describes the European presence in Caribbean cultural identity as the legacy of colonialism, racism, power, and exclusion. Just as Africa serves as an "imagined community" to which people feel a sense of belonging (Hall, 2016), for the founders of Latin American countries, Europe was the homeland of their identity and a utopian model to follow.

For the Chilean elite, the question of their legitimate status as Europeans was vital. German immigrants were crucial to the shaping of Chile after its independence because Spain's own European identity was ambiguous. Due to its geographic proximity to Morocco and Algeria and separation from France by the Pyrenees mountain range, Spain has long been dominated and influenced by Arabs, both racially and culturally. The founders of the Chilean government recognized Spain's precarious position in Europe and, after gaining independence, favored a policy of accepting northern European immigrants, including Germans, to create what they considered a truly white European country (Young, 1971). This legacy still has impacts today.

Fans of Asian popular culture do not consider an inability to distinguish different Asian peoples to be racist. Rather, they believe they are more open-minded than the average Chilean because they like Asian culture. The way that Chilean fans view Asia seems similar to the way they see their neighboring countries, in which the white population is not dominant. To the question of why Chileans use the term *chinos*, a 20-year-old female responds:

> Because they are all the same. That's why more than anything, I also called them [Asians] *chinos* until I realized that the eyes and physical features are different. But the majority of the people still call them *chinos* […] One goes to the Chinese restaurant and sees Chinese people, then some will bother them, calling them *chinos*. It is as if someone [were to ask] me if I were Peruvian.

This interviewee referenced eye form, a common feature for Asian stereotyping and revealed how Chileans think about Peru, which has a relatively larger indigenous population than Chile, implying that people who are not white are subordinate.

The first Asians in Latin America were Chinese *coolies* (a derogatory term for laborers), who arrived in Mexico in the 17th century; whether out of ignorance or confusion, the Spaniards called them *chinos* (Chou, 2004). Despite Spain's insecure position in Europe and its cultural assimilation of Arabs, the country's imagination regarding Asia was no different from the othering of non-Western cultures in other Western countries. Spain, which had neither colonized nor been colonized by Asia at that time, had an external orientation toward China (Prado-Fonts, 2018). The trafficking of Chinese *coolies* was expanded to Central and South America, and a Chinese community began to emerge in the northern part of Chile after the territories of Tarapacá and Antofagasta were taken from Peru and Bolivia in 1883 (Chou, 2004). Chileans followed the Mexicans and Spanish conquerors in regarding the *chinos* with an Orientalist view (Chou, 2004). Even today, for those who like Asian culture as well as those who do not know or care about it, all Asians are *chinos*: traditional *coolies* with slanted eyes (Min, 2020).

Another 20-year-old female fan described the derogatory meaning of the term *chinos*:

> Because they [Asians] are different, that is, because they are physically different. They are all with *ojos chinitos* [Chinese eyes] [...] They are also different in attitudes. They work hard, like the saying *trabajar como chinos* [to work like the Chinese]. I think all these show a closed mind.

The saying *trabajar como chinos* can be interpreted as stemming from the view of *chinos* as slaves, a cheap but hard-working labor force.

During the analog visualization of the data, one respondent stated that the use of the term *chino* in Chile "is like firmly establishing a distance between 'we' and 'others.'" According to Herzog (1998), during Spanish colonization,

> Spanish law did not define "insiders" and "outsiders" or distinguish them from each other. However, the existence of differences in membership status was expressed in some laws and administrative rulings that denied foreigners certain privileges implicitly granted only to members of the community. (p. 47)

This colonial tradition remains today. A 27-year female interviewee defined high class in Chile as "a mix between European ethnicity and one closer to it: blond and light eyes. There is also another type of aristocracy, which is from the Chilean colonial last name." Ongoing "othering" has been found in relationships between colonizers and colonized, and even in situations without colonization: the West has othered Spain, Spain has othered Latin American *criollos* (Creoles), and the Creole governors have othered aboriginal culture, any non-white people, and, sometimes, even themselves.

Chino-ism in the Digital Media Era

From the 1950s, when television was first introduced to Chile, American culture began to spread among Chilean audiences. It was the first foreign and non-European culture introduced to Chile. In his book *Meeting with the Yankee: North Americanization and Sociocultural Change in Chile 1898–1930*, Rinke (2004) claims that there were two phases of the cultural Americanization of Chile, the first occurring between 1900 and 1930 and the second between 1970 and 1990. From the beginning, North American cultures were associated with a combination of attractiveness and strangeness (or repudiation). While both acceptance and rejection remain, it seems that Chileans no longer consider American culture as foreign. A 28-year-old female said, "I think we are a bad copy of the United States." Only one respondent (a 28-year-old male) clearly said that Chile is Latin American. Although a 23-year-old male answered that Chile is part of the West, he contradicted himself by separating Chile and the West:

> The greeting that they [Asians] have is different from the Western one [...] a bit the same, but here in Chile and in the West, we tend to Westernize everything that comes from Asia such as approaching people, I think.

Japanese anime began to air on Chilean television in the 1990s, and since the spread of the internet, younger generations who watched Japanese anime on television have begun to turn to manga. When Japanese anime and manga were first introduced, there were many opinions about the impact of its violence on children and adolescents, and teachers prohibited children from watching anime (Cornejo Huerta & Jiménez Huerta, 2006). K-pop became popular from the early 2000s, with its youth fanbase growing steadily since 2010. K-pop has found acceptance in Chilean society, despite being more unfamiliar than anime and manga (Min, 2020; Min et al., 2019) due to Chile's shorter bilateral relationship with Korea than with Japan. While Chile has a relatively small population compared to other Latin American countries, such as Brazil, Mexico, Argentina, and Peru, its consumption of Latin American trap and Japanese anime and manga is the highest in the region (Bugueño, 2020). As a result, Chile has also become a mecca for K-pop and a place to record major K-pop programs, such as Music Bank and SM Live.

In Chile, Asian cultures are viewed differently from North American cultures because of geographic and cultural distance as well as racial prejudice. The Chileans interviewed in this study understood Asian popular culture as mainly comprising anime, manga, and K-pop; only one interviewee stated that he had started listening to Chinese pop. After all, whether Japanese anime, manga, or K-pop, all Asian popular culture is *chino* to Chilean fans. For this Chilean audience, the difference between Japanese anime and manga and K-pop is that Japanese culture was introduced in the analog era, during the 1990s, and has steadily grown in popularity ever since, while K-pop has expanded more rapidly and widely in the internet era.

The interview results demonstrate that consumers of Asian popular culture did not know the origin of what they were consuming. A priori, the globalized consumption of Asian popular culture began from ignorance. They began to obtain greater knowledge during the process of differentiation with respect to North American popular culture. A 26-year-old male fan put it this way:

> I listened to songs. I got on YouTube and found Super Junior. I knew that they were a K-pop band, but I had no idea who they were or who the members were. In 2014, the people I followed started to post on Tumblr and Twitter a lot about a group called EXO I started to inform myself and began to like K-pop.

The interviews revealed that the diffusion of various understandings of Asian culture was generated by globalization. Born after Chile's economic development and raised with television and the internet, the interviewees had more opportunities to connect with foreign cultures than older generations. The high internet penetration rate has made foreign pop culture, including that from Asia, easily accessible to everyone in the country. As a 23-year-old male stated:

> When I was a kid, my family had a computer at home, and we had a Super Nintendo emulator. I watched the video games and liked them. Video games caught my attention. [...] Later, I found strategic games like *Final Fantasy*, and I became a fan of that. I used to think about why those games are like that. After the video game, I found Japanese anime, which I could see when I bought a CD or DVD. I've been able to be closer to Asian popular culture since then.

Another interviewee (a 29-year-old male) discussed the prejudice against watching a large amount of anime:

> My parents watched anime, so when I was a kid, I watched what they watched. After I hadn't watched anime for a while, when I entered middle school, I thought maybe I could watch them again. I have never had any prejudice about the subject; therefore, I could watch them.

A significant part of the symbolic-dramatic matrix of popular culture has been appropriated by the cultural mass media industry, and it is possible to infer cultural expressions in reverse. That is, non-workers have been appropriating the symbolic-dramatic matrix of popular culture and the formats of technical reproduction of culture in the context of an industrial society, as well as diffusion, production, and circulation strategies, subverting the matrix's use and consumption as a mechanism of cultural domination. In Chile, there exists a tradition of recognizing Indian folk culture as pop culture. In the 20th century, new paradigms and concepts, such as popular culture versus traditional culture, guided scholarly research on these practices. Since the beginning of the 21st century, however, popular culture has been revalued as intangible cultural heritage, a category recognized by United Nations Educational, Scientific and Cultural Organization (UNESCO) in 2003 as a way to understand these types of knowledge and traditions in connection with local communities and their territories (Rivero, Bellelli, & Bakhurst, 2000). Donoso Fritz (2009) claims that the concept of folklore has been understood as the culture of the low-class, as *mestizo* popular culture, and as non-academic.

As the exotic is fascinating in itself, not knowing the language of the popular culture productions is not a significant problem for fans of Asian popular culture. The interviewees considered the language barrier to be difficult but also as having a positive effect, creating interest among fans in expanding their comprehension of other cultures. Moreover, with more widespread access to the internet, language barriers have become increasingly smaller and will continue to do so until they no longer represent a problem. A 25-year-old female fan stated that the cultural barrier eclipses the language barrier:

> When people do not know it, they see it as a problem, but the truth is that globalization and digital media have facilitated our lives in an incredible way. When a song of my favorite artist comes out, I can find the translations immediately on the internet. I can read the lyrics while listening to the music. I think the cultural barrier is bigger than the language barrier.

Interestingly, the socioeconomic status of K-pop fans was similar regardless of which university they attended, with most students belonging to the lower middle class. However, PUC and UAI interviewees stated that the most influential foreign cultures among young Chileans are American, Anglo-Saxon, Western, or Gringo cultures, though some interviewees stated that the influence of Asian culture, specifically Korean and Japanese culture, was growing. In contrast, the USACH respondents stated that the most influential foreign cultures among Chilean youth are Korean, Japanese, and, to a lesser extent, American.

Conclusion

In Chilean fans' imaginations, if Europe is the past, which has been left behind in the analog era of colonization, then Asia is the present, brought in by the age of digital globalization. In the 19th century, Chile's independence from Spain resulted in a class-based society run by elite Creole oligarchic groups. In the 20th century, the rise of neoliberalism during Augusto Pinochet's military regime strengthened social segregation. However, economic development has opened the possibility for many people to access the outside world through the internet, regardless of their socioeconomic status.

When the first Asian people known in Latin America arrived on the continent, Latin Americans indifferently followed the lead of the Spanish conquerors and called the Chinese workers *coolies*. In Chile, all Asians continue to be called *chinos*. People who like Asian popular culture are also called *chinos*, even though most fans of Asian popular culture consume Japanese anime and manga and/or K-pop, not Chinese popular culture. However, they distinguish between the derogative and affectionate meanings of the term.

Indian folklore has been understood to be popular culture, and any non-whites have not been welcomed into the imaginary European Latin America. Perhaps these factors are the reason why Asian popular culture is not acceptable in most of Chilean society. However, fans of Asian popular culture are broadening their horizons and building an imaginary society in the virtual world where they nurture imaginary cultural intimacy. The "*imaginary*" chino world of Chilean fans functions within their post-colonial context.

References

Anderson, B. (1983). *Imagined communities: Reflections on the origin and spread of nationalism.* Verso.

Bugueño, D. (2020, May 28). Hip-Hop in Chile: From Trap to Boom-Bap. bandcamp. https://daily.bandcamp.com/scene-report/chilean-hip-hop-list

Centeno, M.A. (1999). War and memories: Symbols of state nationalism in Latin America. *Revista Europea de Estudios Latinoamericanos y del Caribe, 66,* 75–105.

Chou, D.L. (2004). *Chile y China: Inmigración y relaiciones bilaterales (1845–1970)* [Chile and China: Immigration and bilateral relations]. Centro de Investigaciones Diego Barras Arana.

C.N.N. (2015, September 19). Actualidad Central: Los orígenes de la cultura chilena [Central News: The origins of Chilean culture] [Video]. YouTube. www.youtube.com/watch?v=TV9ILvgCPXw

Cornejo Huerta, S.A., & Jiménez Huerta, F.A. (2006). *Anime: Generando Identidad Cultural* [Anime: Generating cultural identity]. Bachelor's Thesis, Universidad Academia de Humanismo Cristiano, Chile.

Donoso Fritz, K. (2009). Por el arte-vida del pueblo: Debates en torno al folclore en Chile. 1973–1990 [For the Sake of Art and Life the People: Debates about Folklore in Chile, 1973–1990]. *Revista Musical Chilena,* Año LXIII, Julio-Diciembre, 2009, N° 212, 29–50.

Edwards, A. (1928). *La Fronda. Aristocrática en Chile.* Imprenta Nacional.

Gott, R. (2007). Latin America as a white settler society. *Bulletin of Latin American Research, 26*(2), 269–289.

Hall, S. (2016). *Cultural studies 1983: A theoretical history* (J. Slack & L. Grossberg, Eds.). Duke University Press.

Herzog, T. (1998). "A stranger in a strange land": The conversion of foreigners into members in colonial Latin America. In L. Roniger and M. Sznajder (Eds.), *Constructing collective identities and shaping public spheres: Latin American paths* (pp. 46–64). Sussex Academic Press.

Mignolo, W. (2005). *The idea of Latin America.* Welley.

Min, W. (2020). Mis chinos, tus chinos: The Orientalism of Chilean K-pop fans. *International Communication Gazette,* Article first published online: June 2, 2020.

Min, W., Jin, D.Y., & Han, B. (2019). Transcultural fandom of the Korean Wave in Latin America: Through the lens of cultural intimacy and affinity space. *Media, Culture & Society, 41*(5), 64–76.

Prieto Larraín (2020). *Branding the Chilean Nation Socio-Cultural Change, National Identity and International Image.* Doctoral thesis. Leiden University.

Prado-Fonts, C. (2018). Writing China from the rest of the West: Travels and transculturation in 1920s Spain. *Journal of Spanish Cultural Studies, 19*(2), 175–189.

Quijano, A. (2014). *Cuestiones y Horizontes: de la Dependencia Histórico-estructural a la Colonialidad/Descolonialidad del Poder* [Issues and horizons: From historical-structural dependence to coloniality/decoloniality of power]. CLACSO

Rinke, S. (2004). *Begegnungen mit dem Yankee: Nordamerikanisierung und sozio-kulturefler Wandel in Chile 1898–1990* [Meeting with the Yankee: North Americanization and sociocultural change in Chile 1898–1930]. Böhlau Verlag.

Rivero, A.R., Bellelli, G., & Bakhurst, D. (Eds.). (2000). *Memoria colectiva e identidad nacional* [Collective memory and national identity]. Biblioteca Nueva.

Stefoni, C. (2004). *Inmigrantes transnacionales: La formacion de comunidades y la transformacion en ciudadanos* [Transnational immigrants: The formation of community and the transformation into citizens]. FLACSO (Facultad Latinoamericana de Ciencias Sociales).

Straubhaar, J.D. (2017). Plenary 1. Global, hybrid or multiple? Cultural identities in the age of satellite TV and the Internet. *Nordicom Review, 29*(2), 11–29.

Young, G. (1971). Bernardo Philippi, initiator of German colonization in Chile. *The Hispanic American Historical Review, 51*(3), 478–496.

PART VI

Globalization, Migration, and Mobility

24

MULTILAYERED IDENTITIES AND COEXISTENCE OF PREFERENCES FOR NATIONAL AND US TELEVISION

Joseph Straubhaar, Vanessa de Macedo Higgins Joyce,
Melissa Santillana, and Luiz Guilherme Duarte

Global Flows of Television

Since the early 1970s, there has been considerable debate about the nature and meaning of international flows of television. Studies in the early 1970s showed that many countries imported most of their television, most of it from the US—beginning a strong debate about the one-way flow of television (Nordenstreng & Varis, 1974). Studies in the era showed the US as an imperial power in media, also dominating flows of film (Guback, 1984), news (Boyd-Barrett, 1980), music (Laing, 1986), and comics (Dorfman & Mattelart, 1972). Cultural imperialism was a strong argument, predicting an ever-increasing cultural domination of the developing and socialist worlds by the West, particularly the US (Schiller, 1969). That included increasing one-way media flows, penetration and ownership of cultural industries, and cultivating audiences into a consumer-oriented global paradigm by an increased reliance on advertising in television systems (Boyd-Barrett, 1977). Another related theoretical view of these phenomena, developed in Latin America, was that they reflected an economic and cultural dependence by developing countries there on the US (Beltran & Fox de Cardona, 1980; Fox, 1975).

However, subsequent research showed that a number of countries were beginning to produce much of their own programming, such as Brazil (Straubhaar, 1984), Egypt (Abu-Lughod, 1993), India (Agrawal, Joshi, & Sinha, 1986), and Mexico (Fernández & Paxman, 2000). Some studies began to show that national television was also more popular than US imports (Antola & Rogers, 1984). One of the theories developed to explain this preference for national programming was cultural proximity—that audiences would tend to prefer television programs that were most relevant and culturally similar to them, when countries could afford to produce them (Straubhaar, 1991). A similar, converse view, based in media economics, was that audiences would tend to reject cultural products that were too different or dissimilar, the theory of the cultural discount (Hoskins & Mirus, 1988).

Many of those emerging major producing countries also exported television to their neighboring regions. Brazil and Mexico began to dominate television trade within Latin America (Roncagliolo, 1996). Egypt dominated television flows within the Middle East (Amin, 1996). Hong Kong was then a major producer for much of the rest of Asia (To & Lau, 1995; Wilkins, 1998). These studies initiated a major round of research and theorization about the regionalization of television (Sinclair, Jacka, & Cunningham, 1996). Together these findings challenged one of the major tenets of cultural imperialism and dependency theories, that developing and non-Western countries would continue to depend on the US and Europe for most of their television programming.

However, many audiences continued to watch some US television, such as movies, cartoons, and action adventure series, programs that could not economically be produced in most developing countries, but which had loyal audiences cultivated during the long history of US cultural exports (Straubhaar, 2007). An even stronger argument for continued US presence was developed by Todd Gitlin, who argued that that same long history of US cultural penetration had made US culture the second culture of many people in the world (Gitlin, 1998). Research in Europe showed that while national programming was most preferred, US programming (not regional European programming) was the most frequent second choice (Buonanno, 2008). Furthermore, empirical audience research, conducted along with cultural proximity theory, showed that upper middle class and elite audiences often preferred foreign culture from the US or Europe, while middle, lower middle, and working classes tended to prefer national programs (Straubhaar, 1991). That fits one of the predictions of both cultural imperialism and dependency theories, that local and national elites would tend to be drawn into the cultures of former colonial powers in Europe or the US (Dos Santos, 1973).

These diverse tendencies are further reinforced by technological developments. Cheaper, more portable and easier to use waves of first transistor and now digitally based production technology have enabled more groups in more countries in the world to produce more of their own programming, reinforcing local and national bases of television (Straubhaar, 2007). However, first satellite/cable and now internet distribution technologies have also made global expansion easier for international television channels like CNN and HBO (Chalaby, 2005), or more recently streaming services, such as Netflix, Amazon Prime Video. and Disney+ (Lobato, 2018), bringing large amounts of imported programming to many places and those people who can afford satellite, cable, or internet-based television. This reinforces the class base of television flows, since many people either cannot afford these new forms of television, or as in the case of broadband internet, may simply not have access (Straubhaar, Castro, Duarte, & Spence, 2019).

So in terms of global and regional television flows, as well as generally rising national production in many parts of the world (Straubhaar 2007), an argument can be made for a complex multiplicity of flows that seem to correspond to complex arrangements of national identities that have been cultivated in most parts of the world by governments (Anderson, 1983), the ability of national producers to create a wide variety of genres, influence over time from global cultural powers, and the varied interests of social classes that may have been quite differently internationalized.

Multilayered Flows, Multilayered Audience Identities, and Television Consumption

The movement from traditional local life to modern interaction with mass media produced identities that were multilayered, with cultural geographic elements that are local, regional, and transnational based on enduring cultural linguistic regions (Sinclair, Jacka, & Cunningham, 1996), and national (Anderson, 1983). Both traditional and new media users around the world continue to strongly reflect these "modern" layers or aspects of identity while many also acquire new layers of identity that are transnational, US-influenced, or in some specific circumstances, global.

These increasingly multilayered identities are articulated with a variety of changing structures (Hall, 1997). Economies, political powers, social class, and geography strongly structure who can access which new channels. Media institutions themselves are becoming more complexly multilayered as they reach further geographically. Institutional models, such as commercial television networks, globalize, but are also localized and regionalized as they engage the specific histories and institutions of a variety of cultures, media traditions. and regulatory systems. Identities also layer up as people migrate, acculturate to new cultures, live abroad, travel, learn languages, join or leave religions, and, although the experiences are less directly personal and less intense, perhaps as they acquire access to new forms of media.

New layers form over the top of all others as structural circumstances permit or even dictate. Sometimes when we look at people, for instance, we are likely to see the newest layer as strongest. Many observers, when they look at a culture these days, see on top a new layer that they might call globalization. So seeing this as a new and highly visible layer, they might suppose that this is perhaps now the dominant layer, perhaps homogenizing all the others. Or perhaps even the dominant aspect of someone's identity or experience.

In this emerging model, people increasingly identify with multiple cultures at various layers or spaces. People identify with multiple cultural groups or symbols in different fields of activity (Bourdieu, 1984). People establish different identities at school and work, in sports or religion, with family and friends. In the process of learning from others, people form multiple layers of cultural capital, often specific not only to a field of activity, as Bourdieu (1984) predicted, but to different cultural layers.

All of these different layers of identity and culture will have varied connections to global, cultural linguistic, national, and local spaces and forces. A US soccer fan might begin to identify with European or Latin American teams and might seek out global soccer content on the internet or watch transnational soccer channels on satellite or cable TV. These different layers of identity and culture are based in varying combinations of cultural geography, institutional strategies and alliances, and cultural productions based on genre linked to institutions, nations and other cultural spaces.

Methodology

This study is based on secondary analysis of data from TGI Latina, a biannual marketing and media consumption survey conducted in eight Latin American countries by the Miami-based marketing intelligence firm Kantar Media, with fieldwork by IBOPE (Instituto Brasileiro de Opinião Pública e Estatística, in Portuguese) and its other subsidiaries in Mexico and South America.

The analysis presented in this chapter focuses on data from 2004 through 2014, which covered eight countries in Latin America: Argentina, Brazil, Chile, Colombia, Ecuador, Mexico, Peru, and Venezuela. For each country, a probability sample was projected to represent the total household and individual population in potential markets of interest. With the exception of Mexico, where the sample represents 20 cities across Mexico, most of the samples are limited to a few major metropolitan areas—eight in Brazil, far fewer in most other countries. This is important because people in major metro areas are richer, better educated, and more connected to a variety of communication technologies than are the national general population. For example, in 2012, 64% in the Kantar metro sample in Brazil had access to the internet, while the number in the general population was 44%. So, although the total number of respondents for all eight countries was 61,400, which represent a universe of more than 176 million people in the region covered, we have to remember that we can generalize to major metropolitan areas but not national general populations.

TGI Latina surveys are conducted door-to-door, with a combination of personal interviews and a paper survey left behind by the interviewer to be retrieved at a later date. Interviewers followed a skip pattern for sampling that was based on the physical location of respondents' homes. Since response rates were low among some important demographic groups—notably households at the bottom and at the top of the SES (socio-economic status) scales, and those in remote areas—TGI Latina weighted the responses to better represent the overall population.

235

Measurements

This study uses TGI Latina data to look at changes over time in respondents' self-reported interest in television programming from their own nation, the region, the US, and Europe. The theory of cultural proximity predicts that respondents would prefer first their own national programs and channels, then regional ones, then those of the US or Europe. This was represented in the surveys by *viewing interest for national, Latin American regional, US, and European television programs and films*. Four questions asked respondents to state their interest in television programs and films from (nation, region, etc.) on a scale from "very uninterested" to "very interested." We use the combined values "interested" and "very interested" to indicate interest in television programming from each of the four origins surveyed (national, regional, US, and European). We then examined the relationships between these scales of interest in programming to education, which we conceptually define as cultural capital; an index of socio-economic status, which we conceptually define as economic capital; and an index of forms of foreign language learning, which we conceptually define as linguistic capital.

Data Analysis

The TGI Latina 2004–2014 data was run through Choices 3, specially designed analysis software at Kantar Media. The team ran crosstabs of the designated indicators for viewing interest in US programming and the different capitals, and then used the Significance option in Choices 3 to calculate chi-square statistics and flag those significant at the .01 level. We used a more demanding level of significance, P=.01 versus P=.05, to limit the risk of Type I error.

Limitations

This study allows access to conceptually useful data but is limited in three important ways. First, it is a study of major metro areas, not national populations, as noted above. Second, in order to have access to the data, we had to analyze within the analytical programs of Kantar Media, which essentially limited us to cross-tabulations with significance analyzed by the chi-square statistics; more advanced statistical procedures and measures were not possible in Kantar's system. Third, because of the large sample size and our need to rely on cross-tabulation, we run some risk of Type I error here, finding false positives in significance due to our large sample (61,400).

The Context of Multichannel Viewing Growth

In overall terms, viewing options increased substantially from 2004 to 2014. The average proportion of households in all eight Latin American countries studied which had only broadcast television declined from 72 percent in 2004 to 45 percent in 2014. Households with cable television rose from 20 percent to 36 percent. Satellite television homes rose from 7 percent to 18 percent. Overall, there was a fairly steady growth in multichannel television in most of the eight countries, from a regional average under 30 percent to about 55 percent (Figure 24.1). There was a rapid uptake in Colombia, 2006–2009, while some others had ups and downs despite the general growth trend. The opportunity for viewing many more kinds of channels went up considerably in most metro areas in the analyzed countries from 2004 to 2014, diminishing the monopoly by national broadcast channels and providing more competition for national programming. So one could ask whether a decline in national cultural proximity or an increase in the attraction of US or European programming might be related to the increasing availability of those programs on cable or satellite multichannel television.

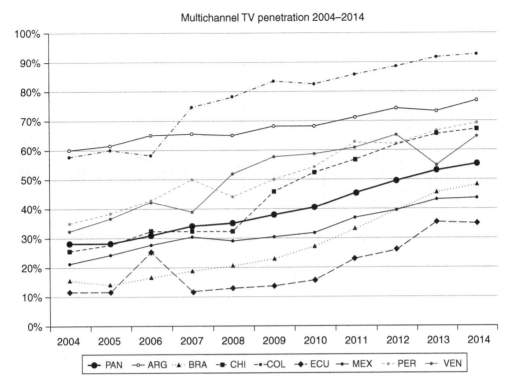

Figure 24.1　Multichannel Television Penetration, 2004–2014.

Preferences for National and Regional Television Programs

TGI Latina data from 2004 to 2014 show changes over time in respondents' overall interest in television from their own nation, compared to programming from the rest of the Latin American region, the US, and Europe. The theory of cultural proximity predicts that respondents would prefer first their own national programs and channels. It then predicted that after that, viewers would prefer regional programs, then those of the US or Europe.

In general, in all Latin American countries combined in 2014 (the set of columns at the left of Figure 24.2), 59 percent of respondents said they were interested or very interested in domestic television films or programs, while 52% said they were interested or very interested in US television programs and films, 31% said they were interested or very interested in other Latin American programing, and 30% said they were interested or very interested in European television programing. However, we do see some major differences between countries, visible in the other sets of columns by country. The countries are ranked left to right in terms of the level of their metro area audience's interest in national programming and some changes over time, which we examine below.

General Preferences for National Programming and Channels

In Latin America, audiences do indeed tend to prefer domestic content, at least in the case of seven out of eight Latin American countries surveyed (see Figure 24.2). Peru is an interesting exception in that preference for both national and US programming went up from 2004–2014, with preference for US programs slightly, but not significantly higher than for national ones. Overall, we see some

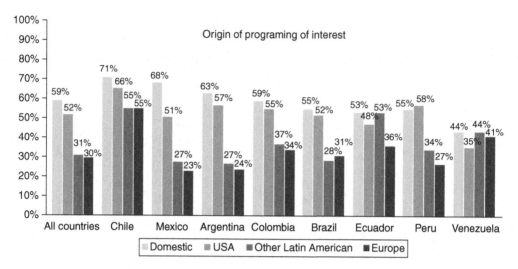

Figure 24.2   Latin American Television Viewing Interest by Origin in 2014.

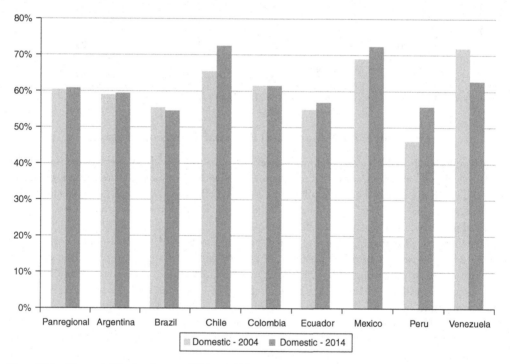

Figure 24.3   Domestic Viewing Interest, 2004 vs. 2014.

changes from 2004 to 2014, but also a large amount of stability in terms of preferences for national programs. Figure 24.3 shows the preferences for national programming, comparing 2004 to 2014.

Even though larger segments of most countries' audiences had increased viewing options in 2014 with the rapid growth in multichannel households 2010–2014, the audiences in most Latin American countries surveyed (with the exception of Venezuela) showed a strong continuing preference for domestic television programs, channels, and films. In Argentina, Brazil, and Peru, preference for national programming increased somewhat from 2004 to 2014. In Chile and Colombia, it continued almost unchanged, and in Ecuador and Mexico it declined slightly, while in Venezuela interest in national programming declined substantially, from 63 percent to 43.8 percent. In exactly those years, Venezuela went from being a strong producer of telenovelas to a net importer of them, with only one new national telenovela per year on average by 2014 (Acosta-Alzuru, 2015). The Venezuelan government shut down RCTV, a strong producer of telenovelas, in 2007, and later imposed conditions on content from another major producer, Venevision, that limited their willingness to invest in major productions (Acosta-Alzuru, 2015). These interventions could at least partially explain the Venezuelan audience's loss of interest in at least the entertainment aspects of national programming.

Genre Preferences and Domestic Bias

The idea of overall preference for national, regional, US or European programming might seem a bit abstract. To what degree do audience members surveyed in these Latin American countries actually think in those terms? Is asking people whether they tend to prefer national programs to US ones in general meaningful or valid? To verify the meaning of national origin preferences and to expand upon what they mean in terms of more concrete audience preferences, we compared the general preferences across the total sample in all eight countries for two kinds of specific national genres to the same preferences among those who had specified a greater preference for national programming (4 or 5 on a five-point scale). We looked at two genres in which survey respondents had a chance to prefer national vs. international versions of the same types of programming: news and telenovelas or soap operas.

News. Preferences for domestic news did not vary more than a couple of points between the general sample and those who specifically preferred national programming. Furthermore, these preferences stayed fairly constant from 2004 to 2014. Thus interest in national news did not vary much by preference for origin of programs or over time.

Telenovelas. For soap operas or telenovelas, there was a much larger, significant difference in preference between the general sample and those who opted for national programs. The general sample was less interested in soap opera by an average of five points, compared to those who preferred national programs in general, who were notably more interested in soap opera. This difference makes sense since the prime time telenovela is the flagship national program for most national networks in Latin America that have the audience size and economic wherewithal to produce them (J. Sinclair & Straubhaar, 2013). Interestingly, however, preference for national telenovelas also seems to have tapered off over time among both the general audience (from 45.9% in 2004 to 42.3% in 2014), and the audience more interested in national programming (from 50.9% in 2004 to 46.6% in 2014). One likely interpretation might be that telenovela interest in both groups declined somewhat as more options became available to them, as increasing numbers of people had access to multichannel television with its much greater variety of choices. However, this decline is relatively small: interest among the general audience is still over 42 percent in 2014, and interest among the audience with preference for national programming remained over 46 percent.

Regional Programming Preferences

In cultural proximity theory, regional television programming occupies a secondary position in audience preference. The theory presumes that national programming in most genres will be more popular if it is available, but that regional programming would be next in preference in genres where national production is not available. For much of the development of the Latin American regional television market, the most notable imported genres were telenovelas—that not every country could afford to produce (Rogers & Antola, 1985); highly produced variety shows like Televisa's *Siempre en Domingo* and *Sábado Gigante*; sports like soccer games; and comedy shows, as not every country

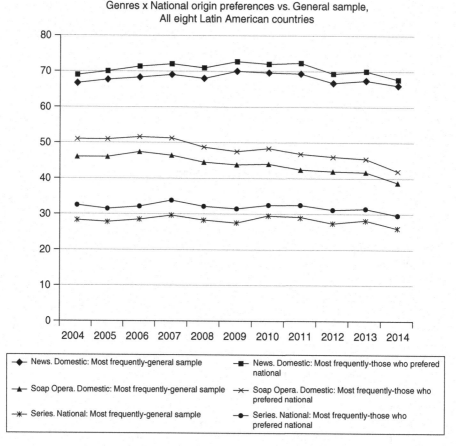

Figure 24.4 Genres x National Origin Preferences vs. General Sample in all Countries.

could afford scripted programs like the popular *El Chavo* from Mexico (Arriaga, 2006; Sinclair & Straubhaar, 2013).

In countries with large numbers of domestic television productions, like Mexico, Brazil, and Argentina, the distance between domestic and regional program preference is largest (Figure 24.5). This is because they have long been major producers of the main genre involved in Latin American television trade: telenovelas (Roncagliolo, 1995; Sinclair & Straubhaar, 2013). In Mexico, in 2014, over two-thirds of respondents stated they were interested or very interested in domestic programing, while over half stated they were interested or very interested in television programming from the US, and just over a quarter said they were interested or very interested in television programs from other Latin American countries, which was a notable increase from 2004. Like Brazil, Mexico had been a largely self-sufficient exporter of television to the rest of the region, but has begun to import more formats and do more co-production in the last decade. In Brazil, in 2014, over half stated they were interested or very interested in domestic programing, while a close half said they were interested or very interested in television programs from the US, almost a third said they were interested or very interested in television programs from Europe, and over a quarter said the same of programs from other Latin American countries.

The reverse is also true. Countries that produce the fewest telenovelas are the most interested in regional imports. That is notable in Chile, which produces some telenovelas but fewer than the major

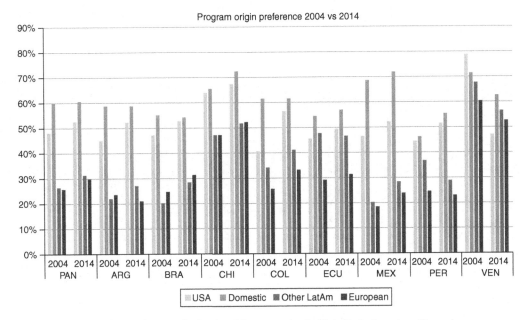

Figure 24.5 Changing Preferences for Regional Programming in Eight Latin American Countries.

producers, as well as in Ecuador, Peru, and Venezuela, which used to be a major producer but no longer is, as noted above.

National Program Preferences and SES

From its original development (Straubhaar 1991), one of the most widely acknowledged limits on cultural proximity among audience members has been social class (SES). National programs are fairly consistently popular across most audiences and audience segments. However, a number of in-depth interviews over the years 1989–2006 by Straubhaar in São Paulo and Salvador in Brazil led him to wonder if elite and upper middle class audiences were not somewhat less interested in national television and much more interested in finding alternatives to it through multichannel television (Straubhaar, 2003). As noted above, when SES is broken down into cultural capital, economic capital, and linguistic capital, each of those components has separate impacts, but it is useful to start with social class or SES as a whole.

Figure 24.6 indicates that, as a baseline for comparison, overall or average domestic or national preference across eight Latin American countries has not varied that much from 2004 (59.3 percent) to 2014 (59.2 percent), across most SES groups or social classes. This supports the idea of a relatively stable national preference based in cultural proximity over time. As Iwabuchi first observed, both primary cultural capital (national or local preference) and especially secondary cultural capital (regional or cultural linguistic group preference), are socially constructed and change over time (2002), as the examples of changing preferences in Peru and Venezuela over time above show.

However, in 2004, the top two SES groups in these eight Latin American countries had a significantly lower preference for national programming than the lowest 40 percent in SES terms, which had a significantly higher national preference. This pattern remained consistent across the years until 2014, although the differences were not always significant in statistical terms. A similar pattern was shown by better-educated audiences and by those who were well above average in their fluency in English.

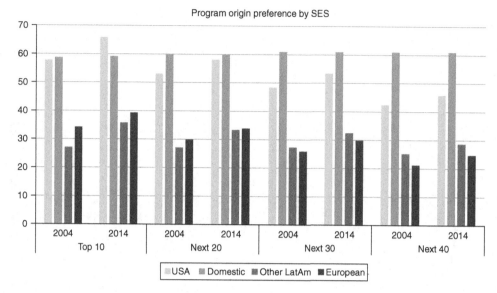

Figure 24.6 Domestic/National Viewing Interest x SES in eight Latin American countries, 2004–2014.

Analysis/Conclusion

In most countries, then, (with the exception of Peru, where US programming is preferred at higher rates than national programs—still unusual in Latin America), the concept of cultural proximity clearly applies when discussing national television preference in opposition to foreign television preference. It seems that at least in Latin American countries where national production has remained strong, national preference remains relatively high.

Examining the results, cultural proximity is still a good overall explanation for local/domestic programming preferences, as predicted by Straubhaar (1991) and others (Iwabuchi, 2001; Trepte, 2008); well over half of all respondents in all income groups stated they are interested or very interested in national television programming. Even the elites manifested an interest in national programming. While that was lower than their interest in US programming, elites' national interest remained much higher than their interest in European or regional/other Latin American programming. It is notable that the predictions by dependency theory and cultural imperialism theory that elites would be coopted into a more positive orientation to dominant cultures, like the US, seem to be true (Salinas & Paldan, 1979)

By contrast, the poorest 40 percent of this Latin American audience, across all eight countries, show a greater interest in national programming in relation to their interest in foreign television. This fits with earlier studies that found that national cultural proximity was strong overall, but varied by class (Straubhaar, 2003).

It is also worth noting that this sample of major metropolitan areas was biased toward audiences with greater income, greater education, more contact with foreign cultures, etc. than a national sample that would include more rural areas and smaller towns. This sample should be more challenging to cultural proximity, since it contains more people with the constituent elements of higher-class status that, as observed in this data, tends to reduce cultural proximity.

However, going into a bit more detail reveals that preference for one of the signature forms of Latin American television, the telenovela, has declined somewhat, particularly among those who say that they don't have an intrinsic preference for national production. Preference for national news, however, remains high. One possible explanation for this is that foreign entertainment can be substituted more easily for national entertainment than foreign news for national news in terms of proximity and relevance.

The take-up of multichannel pay TV has increased notably in Latin America, from 20 percent or less in most countries before 2000 (Reis, 1999), to approaching or exceeding 50 percent, in ten years. As internet penetration is growing even faster than pay TV in most Latin American countries, according to the same data from TGI Latina, national television producers face new competition from services such as Netflix in some of the areas where they had been strongest, like television drama, particularly telenovelas but also series in some countries.

One implication of these findings for cultural proximity theory is that it may have to be seen as less broad, covering all national production, and perhaps more as a continuing, but changing factor that may vary considerably by genre over time. Preliminary qualitative interviews among young people in the state of São Paulo by Straubhaar in 2015 show that US dramatic and comedy series are becoming increasingly popular among people under 40, and that national production of series, while increasing, has a hard time competing with the diversity and perceived quality of the series offered by the combination of pay TV and Netflix (Straubhaar, Higgins Joyce, Sinta, & Spence, 2015).

Indeed, given these factors, one might expect that, given the close geographical proximity, some common historical past, and somewhat close cultural ties, regional content would closely follow national preference, as predicted by earlier academic work on cultural proximity, noted above. However, it is US television programs, channels, and films that follow the national preference in most cases, with the exception of Peru, where preference for US programs surpasses national ones slightly, and Venezuela, where US programs are the least preferred, perhaps because of the campaign against US popular culture, along with other US global manifestations of power by the Chaves and Maduro governments (Petras, 2015).

A key theoretical issue raised here is the direct empirical challenge of these results to the secondary or regional aspect of cultural proximity. In Latin America in the past, when some genre such as drama or melodrama was underrepresented in national production, there was a tendency, particularly in the era of dominance by national broadcast networks, to import such programs from within the region (Rogers & Antola, 1985). That phenomenon, visible already in the 1970s–1980s, was part of what gave rise to cultural proximity theory (Straubhaar, 1991) and theorization about flows within geocultural regions (Sinclair, Jacka & Cunningham, 1996) in the first place. Furthermore, the combination of increasing national production and increasing regional flows in more expensive genres, like melodrama and scripted comedy, seemed to be part of what forestalled any rapid spread of pay TV in Latin America in the 1990s (Reis, 1999).

It seems that cultural proximity theory applied reasonably well to Latin American regional programming in the broadcast era, but it may well have changed since the late 2000s, in the pay TV, satellite/cable, and streaming television era that is now growing rapidly in Latin America with the growth of a large new lower middle class in many countries in the region (Ferreira et al., 2012). As noted above, upper and upper middle social classes have historically been more disposed to foreign television programming (Straubhaar, 2003). Parallel work from the same data analyzed here on preferences for US and European programming shows that higher levels of economic capital, cultural capital (education), and linguistic capital (intensive study of English) all connect to greater preference for foreign, non-regional television. Data reported here shows that socio-economic status, as a combined index of those factors, relates to lower preference for national programs and greater preference for foreign ones. Empirically, we know that considerable economic mobility has taken place after 2000, across the region but particularly in Brazil, Colombia, and Mexico (Joseph Straubhaar, Higgins Joyce, Sinta, McConnell, & Spence, 2015).

Many in the Latin American audiences increasingly have the money for pay TV and broadband internet. Many also are keeping their children in school much longer, so cultural capital, per se, which may be linked to greater comprehension of imported programming, is also increasing. These social factors among the audience create a dynamic in which technological options for other kinds of television viewing may have more impact now than before 2000.

Several authors who have worked with applying cultural proximity theory in other regions, such as East Asia (Iwabuchi, 2002), note that cultural proximity at the regional level is a very dynamic concept, changing as the relationships between countries in the region develop over time. Some countries, such as Chile, Peru, Colombia, and Mexico, are engaged in a greater economic and cultural approximation with the US, notably evidenced by the recent Pacific free trade negotiations, in which these countries participated. Brazil may also be moving somewhat more cautiously in this direction. Others, notably Argentina, Bolivia, Ecuador, and Venezuela, have supported more left-oriented governments, in which both commercial national stations and imported commercial channels have been under greater challenge and in which anti-US rhetoric is more visible. However, those governments have recently been under stress and challenge across Latin America, as the government change in Argentina in 2015 indicates, so this is also very dynamic over time. The region is moving in several different directions, as a wide variety of political commentators have noted, all with implications for television.

As noted above, audience preferences are also perhaps changing with new technologies that provide wider viewing choices, matched with increasing affluence and greater education, moving more people into the middle classes. Latin American upper middle classes have long diverged from broad popular sentiment to have a somewhat greater interest in imported US culture and television programs. It may be that Latin America is coming to resemble Europe, where national programming is most preferred, but regional programs lag behind preferences for US programs (Buonanno 2008).

References

Abu-Lughod, L. (1993). Finding a place for Islam: Egyptian television serials and the national interest. In C.A. Breckenridge (Ed.), *Public Culture* (pp. 494–512). Chicago, I.L.: Chicago Press.

Acosta-Alzuru, C. (2015). *De protagonista a extra: La telenovela venezolana.* Paper presented at the ALAIC, San Juan, Puerto Rico.

Agrawal, B.C., Joshi, S.R., & Sinha, A. (1986). *Communication Research for Development: The ISRO Experience.* Paper presented at the XV International Association of Mass Communication Research General Assembly and Conference, New Delhi, India.

Amin, H. (1996). Egypt and the Arab world in the satellite age. In J. Sinclair, E. Jacka, and S. Cunningham (Eds), *New Patterns in Global Television: Peripheral Vision, Oxford University Press, Oxford*, 101–125.

Anderson, B. (1983). *Imagined Communities: Reflections on the origin and spread of nationalism.* New York: Verso.

Antola, A., & Rogers, E.M. (1984). Television Flows in Latin America. *Comm Res,* 11(2), 183–202.

Arriaga, P. (2006). Pepito, El Chavo, and Bob Esponja. *Televizion,* 19 E, 30–31.

Beltran, L.R., & Fox de Cardona, E. (1980). *Comunicacion dominada: Estados Unidos en los medios de America Latina.* Mexico, D.F.: Instituto Latinoamericano de Estudios Transnacionales: Editorial Nueva Imagen.

Bourdieu, P. (1984). *Distinction: A social critique of the judgement of taste.* Harvard University Press.

Boyd-Barrett, O. (1977). Media Imperialism: Towards an International Framework for the Analysis of Media Systems. In J.E.A. Curran (Ed.), *Mass Communication and Society*: Arnold.

Boyd-Barrett, O. (1980). *The international news agencies.* Beverly Hills: Sage Publications.

Buonanno, M. (2008). *The age of television: Experiences and theories*: Intellect Books.

Chalaby, J. (2005). Towards an understanding of media transnationalism. In J. Chalaby (Ed.), *Transnational television worldwide: Towards a new media order* (pp. 1–13). London: I.B. Taurus.

Dorfman, A., & Mattelart, A. (1972). *Para leer al pato Donald*: Siglo XXI.

Dos Santos, T. (1973). The Crisis of Development Theory and Problems of Departure in Latin America. In H. Bernstein (Ed.), *Underdevelopment and Development: the Third World Today.* Baltimore: Penguin.

Fernández, C., & Paxman, A. (2000). *El tigre: Emilio Azcárraga y su imperio Televisa* : Grijalbo Mondadori.

Ferreira, F.H.G., Messina, J., Rigolini, J., López-Calva, L.-F., Lugo, M.A., & Vakis, R. (2012). *Economic Mobility and the Rise of the Latin American Middle Class.* Washington, DC: World Bank Group.

Fox, E. (1975). Multinational Television. *Journal of Communication,* 25(2), 122–127.

Gitlin, T. (1998). Under the Signs of Mickey Mouse and Bruce Willis. *New Perspectives Quarterly,* 15, 4–7.

Guback, T. (1984). International Circulation of U.S. Theatrical Films and Television Programming. In G. Gerbner & M. Siefert (Eds.), *World Communications* (pp. 153–163). New York: Longman Incorporated.

Hall, S. (1997). Old and New Identities, Old and New Ethnicities. In A.D. King (Ed.), *Culture, Globalization, and the World-System: Contemporary Conditions for the Representation of Identity* (pp. 41–68). Minneapolis: University of Minnesota Press.

Hoskins, C., & Mirus, R. (1988). Reasons for the US dominance of the International Trade in Television Programmes. In N.J. Smelser (Ed.), *Handbook of Sociology*: Sage.

Iwabuchi, K. (2001). Becoming "Culturally Proximate": The a/scent of Japanese Idol Dramas in Taiwan. In B. Moeran (Ed.), *Asian Media Productions*. Honolulu: University of Hawai'i Press.

Iwabuchi, K. (2002). *Recentering globalization: popular culture and Japanese transnationalism*. Durham: Duke University Press.

Laing, D. (1986). The Music Industry and the "Cultural Imperialism" Thesis. *Media, Culture, and Society, 8*, 331–341.

Lobato, R. (2018). Rethinking International TV Flows Research in the Age of Netflix. *Television & New Media, 19*(3), 241–256. doi:10.1177/1527476417708245

Nordenstreng, K., & Varis, T. (1974). *Television Traffic—A One-Way Street*. Paris: UNESCO.

Petras, J. (2015, 03.04). US and Venezuela: Decades of Defeats and Destabilization. Retrieved from http://petras.lahaine.org/?p=2023

Reis, R. (1999). What Prevents Cable TV from Taking off in Brazil? *Journal of Broadcasting & Electronic Media, 43*.

Rogers, E.M., & Antola, L. (1985). Telenovelas: A Latin American Success Story. *Journal of Communication, 35*(4), 24–35.

Roncagliolo, R. (1995). Trade integration and communication networks in Latin America. *Canadian Journal of Communications, 20*(3).

Roncagliolo, R. (1996). La integración audiovisual en América Latina: Estados, empresas y productores independientes. *Culturas en Globalización*, 41–54.

Salinas, R., & Paldan, L. (1979). Culture in the Process of Dependent Development: Theoretical Perspectives. In K. Nordenstreng & H.I. Schiller (Eds.), *National Sovereignty and International Communiations*. Norwood, NJ: Ablex Publishing Corp.

Schiller, H.I. (1969). *Mass Communication and American Empire*. Boston: Beacon.

Sinclair, J., & Straubhaar, J. (2013). *Television Industries in Latin America*. London: B.F.I./Palgrave.

Sinclair, J.S., Jacka, E., & Cunningham, S. (1996). *New Patterns in Global Television*. New York: Oxford University Press.

Straubhaar, J. (1984). The Decline of American Influence on Brazilian Television. *Communication Research, 11*(2), 221–240.

Straubhaar, J. (1991). Beyond Media Imperialism: Asymmetrical Interdependence and Cultural Proximity. *Critical Studies in Mass Communication, 8*, 39–59.

Straubhaar, J. (2003). Choosing national TV: cultural capital, language, and cultural proximity in Brazil. In M.G. Elasmar (Ed.), *The impact of international television: a paradigm shift* Mahwah, NJ: L. Erlbaum Associates.

Straubhaar, J. (2007). *World Television: From Global to Local*: Sage Publications.

Straubhaar, J., Higgins Joyce, V., Sinta, V., McConnell, C.L., & Spence, J.P. (2015). *Changing Class Formations and Changing Television Viewing: The New Middle Class, Television and Pay Television in Brazil and Mexico, 2003–2013*. Les enjeux de l'information et de la communication, (2), 207-223.

Straubhaar, J., Higgins Joyce, V., Sinta, V., & Spence, J.P. (2015). *Netflix as a new layer of global experience for Brazilian youth*. Paper presented at the Global Fusion conference, Texas A&M.

Straubhaar, J.D., Castro, D., Duarte, L.G., & Spence, J. (2019). Class, pay TV access and Netflix in Latin America: Transformation within a digital divide. *Critical Studies in Television, 14*(2), 233–254. doi:10.1177/1749602019837793

To, Y.m., & Lau, T.y. (1995). Global export of Hong Kong television: television broadcasts limited. *Asian Journal of Communication, 5*(2), 108–121.

Trepte, S. (2008). Cultural proximity in TV entertainment: An eight-country study on the relationship of nationality and the evaluation of U.S. prime-time fiction. *Communications, 33*(1), 1–25.

Wilkins, K. (1998). Hong Kong Television at the End of the British Empire. In B.T. McIntyre (Ed.), *Mass Media in the Asian Pacific* (pp. 14–28): Multilingual Matters Ltd.

25

GLOBALIZATION AND COPRODUCTION IN LATIN AMERICA[1]

Sophia A. McClennen

Coproduction simply designates films produced by two or more entities from different nations. And they are nothing new. In fact, the practice "first emerged with the Film Europe movement of the 1920s and early 1930s." (Jones and Higson, 2014). Generally coproductions are thought to solve two key dilemmas for filmmakers since they help raise financial resources, leverage incentives and tax breaks across a range of nations, and facilitate distribution in multiple markets. In essence, the idea is that the film benefits from a connection to the markets and resources of more than one nation.

At a very basic level film coproductions epitomize the global impact on local filmmaking, since these arrangements always involve interactions across states. Among the key issues at stake in studying them is the extent to which such arrangements diminish local creative control, develop a global aesthetic, and strengthen international market economies. Coproductions are generally thought to carry with them hegemonic implications for the simple reason that states with more funds to invest in culture send those resources to those with less, thereby reinforcing a core-periphery model of film investment and allowing states with more resources to control which films get made in "developing" economies.

This chapter explores the particular issues that arise when studying coproductions in the region of Latin America during the global era and argues that most scholars who have studied the increase in coproductions in the region have studied the phenomena according to prevailing paradigms that overemphasize the role of Spain as a source of neocolonial influence. It begins by offering a brief overview of the practice and a description of the critical paradigms that emerged in the 1960s to study it. It then analyzes the particular role of Spain and compares the role of Spain as a coproduction partner to two other funding models.

Coproduction in Latin America

The pattern for coproduction in Latin America began as a direct replica of the Spanish colonial project in the region. As Libia Villazana (2008) points out, "Latin American international film coproduction begins with a Spanish intervention, as does a large part of Latin American history. Thus, it started in 1931 with the establishment of the First Congress of Hispano American Cinematography (Primer Congreso Cinematográfico Hispanoamericano) held in Madrid, Spain." (p. 65). Beginning in those early years, the practice was fairly common but it would experience a tremendous upsurge in the 1990s when film industries across Latin America lost state support and were forced to find creative ways to participate in the global market. Coproduction, given those realities, was a logical response to a vulnerable and unsupportive home market.

Of course, it is not just the region of Latin America that has undergone these changes. Scholarship on coproduction has studied these trends globally. In a special issue of *Spectator* dedicated to the topic, Hyung-Sook Lee (2007) points out that "the current practices differ from those of the past in terms of the frequency of instances of coproduction, the diversified mediums and technologies involved, the wide geographical span that is interconnected through such cultural convergences, the widely multidirectional flow of capital, and the gradual decentrality of powers and influences among collaborators."(p. 7). Lee explains that the looming presence of Hollywood has created a wide variety of creative responses across the globe as filmmakers seek alternatives to the Hollywood model. Lee explains that coproductions tend to favor either outright corporate models or intra-regional alliances. Thus, the trends that take place across Latin America are by no means unique to the region.

In order to demonstrate that Latin American coproductions in the global era take a range of forms and defy traditional critical paradigms that consider coproductions as an "invasion" of foreign power into local creativity, this chapter maps out the key types of coproductions in the global era in order to study them in the Latin American context. The current coproduction model includes four basic practices: 1) coproductions with television stations from other nations, 2) multilateral coproduction bodies involving Latin American countries, Canada, and/or funds from European nations (such as the Dutch Hubert Bals fund), 3) corporate agreements and collaborations across film companies from Europe, the United States, Canada, and Latin America financed by multinational capital, and 4) coproductions "that receive direct public support" (Miller et al., 2005, p. 177) via transnational treaties. Miller et al. (2005) refer to the last two models as equity and treaty coproductions. As they point out, "international coproduction policies simultaneously inscribe and destabilize national descriptors of cultural value." (Miller et al., 2005, p. 177). One of the benefits to treaty coproductions is that the films can be considered "national" in more than one market. In contrast to "official" coproductions where there is a treaty in place, many films are internationally coproduced without a treaty or direct state investment. The fact that these various models coexist, at times within the same film, further complicates our ability to analyze the impact of the process.

Both Villazana (2008) and Miller et al. (2005) point out that the rise of coproductions in the 1990s was directly tied to efforts to resist Hollywood domination in the era of global markets, trade agreements, and state deregulation of culture industries. But Miller et al. (2005) also point out that "co-production results often surprise" since in some cases what appears to be a European film company is actually a shell for a large Hollywood studio. (p. 178). Primary concerns have been the ways that coproductions might interfere with creativity. There are numerous cases of producers insisting, for instance, on a set of actors or scenes that connect with the nation investing in the film. Such was the case in a number of Cuban films that received support from the Spanish Television station TVE, which demanded the inclusion of actors who would be familiar to their viewers. Funding from transnational film funds can be even more manipulative since these bodies often have explicit ideological motives behind their organizations.

This means, surprisingly, that purely corporate coproduction may be preferable and less manipulative since the goal is simply to make a profitable film. In another irony, global capital often funds films critical of global capital. Given the fact that political films from Latin America sell, this has meant that many corporate coproductions support films that criticize the very global economic system that produced them. This was the case with *Diarios de motocicleta* (*The Motorcycle Diaries*, 2004). As Steve Solot (2011) explains in a piece designed for Latin American audiovisual professionals, "Today the economic reality is that co-productions are used predominantly to compete in a global market and, therefore, focus on popular narratives that sell audiences to advertisers. In many cases, they do not reflect local cultural expressions or current political and economic changes." (paras. 9–10). In this way, coproductions create highly ambivalent funding models that support market realities but may not necessarily help develop creative opportunities for local film development.

As Michael Chanan (2016) explains, "a significant part of recent Latin American cinema has depended on international coproduction, a mechanism whose methods and effects are poorly understood." And Stephanie Dennison (2013b) suggests that the one element of coproduction different today is its sheer volume, since the recourse to transnational film funding is nothing new. (p. 23). To understand the critical context within which Latin American coproductions are assessed we have to consider the contributions of the New Latin American Cinema (NLAC) directors and their allies in third cinema, since these filmmakers became iconic representatives of Latin American film aesthetics and theory. For the third cinema filmmakers of the 1960s and 1970s, coproductions represented a real threat of cultural imperialism. A defining moment took place when the Committee on People's Cinema met in December 1973, in Algiers, under the chairmanship of Lamine Merbah to discuss the role of cinema in the third world and to offer a combined challenge to imperialism and neocolonialism. A number of Latin American directors were present, including Argentine Fernando Birri. One of the key issues they addressed was the problem of coproductions.

The conclusions of the committee were clear. In a statement issued as a result of their deliberations they declared that "coproductions must, first and foremost, be for the countries of the third world, a manifestation of anti-imperialist solidarity, although their characteristics may vary and cover different aspects." (Black Camera, 2010, pp. 5–14). Regarding the role of foreign investment from first world nations, the filmmakers were adamant: "We do not believe in coproductions in which an imperialist country participates, given the following risks: the imperialist country can shed influence through production methods which are foreign to the realities of our countries, and the examples of coproductions have given rise to cases of profit and the cultural and economic exploitation of our countries." (Black Camera, 2010, pp. 5–14). Following the legacies of cultural imperialism, the third cinema filmmakers were highly sensitive to the idea that their communities had been "invaded" by "foreign" films. And they had valid points since in almost every postcolonial context—especially within Latin America—Hollywood films were dominant for the filmgoing public in 1973.

The problem, though, was when these political filmmakers fought to remove global capitalist influence from their local culture industries, they failed to remember one of the tricky realities of feature filmmaking: it requires vast investment. Thus, their statement even ignored the realities within which these very same directors had to work. In fact, the story of the financing for the films of the NLAC reveals that the filmmakers were often put into situations where they had to receive funding from capitalist backers. In his study of the Brazilian film industry Randal Johnson (1984) explains that "production financing has traditionally been problematic in the under-capitalized Brazilian film industry, and Cinema Novo represented no exception to this rule. Its directors therefore devised collaborative forms of financing in which all actors and members of the crew participated in a share system." (p. 8). Even more interesting to note, he explains that many of the most political filmmakers adopted a pragmatic attitude toward film financing—and they showed little discretion for funding sources provided that they did not make ideological demands on them. This strategy meant that "a number of early Cinema Novo films, paradoxically, were financed by the National Bank of Minas Gerais, owned by the family of Magalhães Pinto, one of the civilian conspirators in the 1964 coup d'état. The cinema lent a certain amount of cultural prestige to the bank, which, in turn, made filmmaking possible."(Johnson, 1984, p. 8).

Consequently, there is a longstanding legacy of Latin American film projects that are overtly political in nature yet have had to engage the capitalist system to get funding. Yet, while the practice isn't new, the extent of it has ballooned, leading scholars to worry about the impact of coproductions on aesthetic independence. The current concern over the impact of foreign financing on film content has become more significant in the face of the ways that the neoliberal, global economic order increased coproductions and decreased state regulations protecting national film industries.

It is worth noting that the anxiety over coproduction is also present in the case of smaller film markets outside of Latin America that worry that they must defend themselves against "Americanization." For instance, UNESCO's (2005) "Convention on Cultural Diversity" was signed globally by 148 countries and was based on the principle that culture cannot be reduced to a commodity and should therefore be exempt from free trade deals such as the WTO Yet, "the treaty has also been criticized as a 'thinly disguised attempt […] to offer a shield against the spread of American culture [and] in particular Hollywood movies.'" (Morawetz et al., 2007, p. 427).

One of the interesting consequences of these concerns has been the way that Europe has defended itself against worries over Americanization in ways that place the European film industry more in alignment with Latin America against the invasion of Hollywood than in competition with it. One of Europe's key strategies has been to create cross-national funding alliances and agencies to support European film. Norbert Morawetz et al. (2007) point out that "in 2005 there were a staggering 182 of these support bodies in Europe (31 countries), providing a total amount of more than EUR 1.3 billion of public support (excluding tax incentives)." (p. 427). Thus the Europeans may be pouring more money into this problem than the Latin Americans, but there seems little doubt that both regions share the goal of an alternative market to that of Hollywood. Morawetz et al. (2007) and his team further point out that in common with the global south, the Europeans "also suffered a cycle of market failure and state intervention." (p. 427). Coproductions, then, were seen as a way to ensure that small markets were able to maintain some local production in the global film economy.

They also help the larger markets. UNESCO reports that the top coproducing nation is France and that almost half of all French films were coproductions in 2012 and 2013. (Albornoz, 2016, p. 24). Spain ranks around fifth with about 30% of its films in those years as coproductions. Mexico, in contrast, had only 20% of its films coproduced in 2012 and 7% in 2013. (UNESCO, n.d.). Argentina coproduced 17.7% in 2012 and 12.5% in 2013. (UNESCO, n.d.). Brazil, the third-largest film market in the region, coproduced 9.6% in 2012 and 15.5% in 2013. (UNESCO, n.d.). Thus, the idea that coproductions are a specific danger to the global south simply doesn't match up with the numbers. If we were to analyze these percentages as signs of influence, then the French would arguably have greater worries over cultural integrity than the nations of Latin America. UNESCO point out in their study that some nations, such as Cuba, only have any cinema at all due to coproductions. (Albornoz, 2016, p. 24).

The anxiety over coproductions, though, is not entirely in vain. In some cases, coproductions carry with them fairly specific content expectations. There has been further concern that coproductions soften cultural difference, creating cultural hybrids that have no geographical reference. As Sharon Strover (2016) explains, one example was the rise of the "euro-pudding"—the pan-European film funded by a variety of nations and aimed at a broadly defined European audience. In coproductions between Spain and Latin America this same practice has translated into concerns over what Dennison (2013b) refers to as "hispano-puddings." (p. 20). For example, coproduction alliances have often led to the casting of Spaniards in Latin American movies. Falicov (2007) notes that the economic imperatives of coproductions do carry with them content impact: "by delineating the various ways in which Spaniards enter into specific Latin American narratives, we find how it is that economic imperatives of funding can shape film narratives in specific ways." (p. 24). Teresa Hoefert de Turégano (2004) studies the case of Spanish coproduction policy in Latin America and concludes that there has been a clear incidence of Spanish influence in the region that has led to a "certain type of cinema". She explains that, after the United States, Spain is the second most important foreign power in the region, especially with regard to the telecommunications and culture industries. She points out that from 1986–1992 "Spanish television alone invested more than US $20 million in coproductions with Latin American countries. This is more than the Latin American governments combined invested in film production during those same years." (p. 23).

Coproductions Between Latin America and Spain

While Spain may have a smaller GDP than both Mexico and Brazil, it remains true that its influence on the film industry in the region outmatches its global economic prominence. It is important to note that the two primary vehicles for cinematic coproduction between Spain and Latin America are via either the media industry or the funding agency Ibermedia designed to help promote film from the region. The Conference of Iberian-American Cinematographic Authorities (CICA) approved in November 1997 a new funding scheme named Ibermedia. The first signing countries were Spain, Mexico, Argentina, Brazil, Venezuela, Cuba, Portugal, and Colombia. Its annual budget reaches $3.7 million. Between 1998 and 2004, Ibermedia invested in 160 coproductions. (Programa Ibermedia, n.d.).

Mar Binimelis Adell (2001) studies a decade of coproductions between Spain and Latin America (1997–2007) and notes, though, that the relationship is not simply a flow of Spanish influence south. She points out that the dominant role of the Spanish television station TVE has to be understood in context. The upsurge of their coproductions coincides with transitions in the media industry in the wake of the death of dictator Francisco Franco in 1975 and the advent of democracy in Spain in 1976 and a new constitution in 1978. While the Franco regime had held tight control over the media industry, the transition to democracy brought radical change. This was especially true in the case of TVE, which had formerly been under the direct control of the Ministry of Information and had effectively functioned as a propaganda arm for the government. In 1980 the Organic Law "established new 'democratic' mechanisms for regulating state-owned broadcasting media." (Gunther et al., 1999, p. 20). This was the context for the new directorship of Pilar Miró, who had herself been a film director, of TVE from 1986–1989. Miró launched a series of coproduction initiatives between the TV channel and film projects both within Spain and in Latin America. (Adell, 1997–2007, p. 159). Adell (1997–2007) further notes that these coproductions have to be read in conjunction with the European Union's efforts to strengthen their hold over their media industries. She explains that the implementation of European audio-visual regulations that required public television channels to invest in film revitalized an interest in Latin America. (Adell, 1997–2007, p. 163). She further notes that the coproduction relationship between Spain and Latin America has strengthened Spain's ability to export media content in the region. She sees the relationship as the development of a regional trade exchange, rather than a purely neocolonial enterprise. (Adell, 1997–2007, p. 166).

Dennison (2013b) suggests that the analysis of coproductions bifurcates between those examples where "it is possible to read the films as a self-referential critique of the constraints placed upon filmmakers by twenty-first-century film-making practices" and those where transnational, multi-lingual, or multi-accented films display "an off-putting social decontextualization."(p. 186). She concludes that stark binaries are not useful for understanding the impact of the coproduction process: "we should avoid the reductionist, binary trap of essentializing Latin America as Europe and the United States's other."(Dennison, 2013b, p. 193).

Alejandro Pardo (2007) attempts to offer a typology of the impact of Spanish-international collaborations and identifies four basic models.

- *(Inter)national Coproductions* are those films with a genuine national or local flavor (a strong taste of "Spanishness").
- *Foreign Financial Coproductions* would be exactly the opposite kind of movies to the previous ones. Here the investment is purely financial.
- *Multicultural Coproductions* represent the quintessential spirit of coproductions, because they are based on a real cultural exchange.
- *Internationally Oriented Coproductions* would be those films primarily designed for the international marketplace.

What's interesting to note is that after their significant overview of the various types of coproductions Pardo et al. conclude that overall these alliances are more about money than cultural influence. They note that, "almost 75% of Spanish international coproductions during the last five years have been designed on a strictly financial basis, without demanding necessarily a creative or cultural exchange." (Pardo 2007, p. 110). This leads them to conclude that worries over the connection between Spanish/Latin American coproductions and adjusted cinematic content are overblown given the fact that the "more frequent motivation to set up a coproduction project has been economic or financial rather than multicultural." (Pardo 2007, p. 110).

In general, though, scholars have noted that certain films are indeed influenced by these processes, even though the bulk of coproduced films are increasingly market-driven rather than content-limited. Perhaps the most market-oriented study is the one offered by Stuart McFadyen, Colin Hoskins, and Adam Finn (1988), who find that there is little evidence to support the claim that cultural distinctiveness is influenced by cross-national commercial investment. (p. 523–538). The problem, though, is that their pro-market approach misses some of the subtle ways that the global film industry is, in fact, creating broad aesthetic models. Hoefert de Turégano (2004) notes one persistent trend in Latin American/Spanish coproductions: the "emphatic tendency to both entrench national and cultural identities is infused with universalising references, to an increasingly formulaic degree." (p. 23). This pattern is a difficult trend for scholars unskilled in aesthetic analysis to identify, but it is a trend that is hard to dispute. She goes on to explain that "What is problematic is that within this particular context of independent production … many films seem to resemble each other, albeit seasoned with distinct cultural flavours, reflecting the dual homogenizing/differentiation process necessary to globalised cultural production through which capital expansion operates." (Turégano, 2004, p. 23). This means that the role of Spain may be less a sign of neoimperialism and more a sign of a globalizing trend where the foreign is marketed in globally recognizable ways.

But, before we jump to concluding that coproductions yield a new set of imagined communities, it is worth pausing to reflect on the bigger picture of film consumption. The Motion Picture Association of America (MPAA, 2015) notes that globally film consumption is on the rise. Data from 2015 show an 18% increase in box office revenue in the global market. (p. 4). But the bulk of this increase is related directly to the consumption of Hollywood product. The top ten films in Latin America in 2011 were almost all Hollywood blockbusters and these same ten films accounted for between 35 and 40% of all spectators in the world at large (González, 2013, Sect. Timeslide). A UNESCO study showed that the most-viewed feature films in theaters globally during 2012 and 2013 revealed the strong dominance of blockbusters from large Hollywood production and distribution companies. These films are almost entirely in English. (Albornoz, 2016, p. 28). The study further points out that five of the top films had budgets of $200 million or more and 60% had budgets over $100 million. A 2016 article in *The Hollywood Reporter* shows that the Mexican box office brought in $892 million and local films accounted for 6% of that market. In Argentina, local market share was about 13%. Discussing Brazil, the article points out that the nation "continues to grow in film production (more than 130 films in 2015), audiences (up 20 percent), theaters (250 new screens) and market share for local product (from 12 percent in 2014 to 13 percent in 2015)." (Mango and Hecht, 2016, Sect. Brazil). Despite that promising information, they quote a Brazilian producer who explains, "We only get to see lots of blockbusters in theaters. Then, when you make one art house film and try to enter these places, it seems as if the two don't combine." (Mango and Hecht, 2016, Sect. Brazil). Similarly "Argentina produces 100 features a year but most don't surpass 10,000 admissions or even get a commercial release, limiting market share at 10%, in line with indie imports." (Newbery, 2011, para. 7).

Given those market realities it is hard to grasp why the rise of the coproduction has tended to provoke such a critical reaction. In many ways coproductions exist to protect a small market share in a media economy that grossly favors the major media monopolies. I've also given some historical perspective on the situation and shown that the practice of coproductions and of capitalist funding for political films is nothing new. Yet, it remains the case that the directors of the NLAC are heralded as cinematic revolutionaries while the directors of the 1990s are often considered to be sell-outs to the global economy. Thus far, research on coproductions has failed to take seriously the complexities of the global film economy.

One of the reasons why scholarship on coproductions in Latin America is so complex is because there are so many financial models. To give a sense of the range of ways that foreign money flows into Latin American cinema this chapter analyzes three totally different models: 1) multilateral and altruistic film coproduction bodies that invest in and support Latin American filmmaking, such as Programa Ibermedia (an Ibero-American Aid Fund, conceived in 1989 and ratified in 1997); 2) production companies that seem locally based but are financed by transnational media capital such as Disney-funded Patagonik; and 3) treaty coproductions such as the one supported by MERCOSUR.

The Role of Ibermedia

Founded in 1997, Ibermedia (Programa Ibermedia) is sponsored by Spain, Portugal, and 18 member nations from Latin America. Each member nation contributes what it can, but at least $100,000, to the fund. Spain gives about $2 million and also supports the offices in Madrid. In 2008, Spain put in $3.3 million, or about 50% of the fund's resources. (Falicov, 2013, p. 68). Similar to Eurimages's desire to produce films aimed for the pan-European market, Ibermedia seeks to promote and develop projects for the Ibero-American market. They described their mission at the 1996 Summit of the Americas this way: "'The question is how one could contribute to the development of an Ibero-American film and television industry that is competitive in the world market, that is oriented towards the technological future, that is capable of projecting its own culture, and in addition, will contribute to creating employment and reducing the commercial deficit.'"(Falicov, 2013, p. 68). It's interesting to note that this description largely emphasizes the development of a market and industry over the development of a common culture.

In fact, Falicov (2013) notes that Ibermedia has two types of funding, one that is "technical-artistic" and carries with it a connection between a nation's investment and the percentage of actors and technicians that work on the film, and another that is purely financial. (p. 71). Alberto Elena et al. (2013) explain that Ibermedia functions on a "purely industrial model and gives priority to the economic prospects of the projects beyond any other consideration," a fact that imposes "severe aesthetic limitations in favour of conventional narrative cinema that follows the habitual industry formulas." (p. 153). Yet, rather than focus on the way that the films of Ibermedia conform to industry standards, it is more common for these films to be studied as examples of Spanish hegemony. Moreover, despite the fact that the financial coproductions mean that the profits go toward the nation with the economic leverage to invest, thereby reinforcing the core-periphery model of the global economy, it turns out that most scholars worry more over coproductions that are technical-artistic since these have more visible markers of potentially forced cultural affiliations.

Latin American coproductions are still largely dominated by Spain, even though other international and regional associations are on the rise. This means that it is the role of Spain—and specifically Spaniards—that most scholars key into in their research on Ibermedia. Villazana (2008) explains that the issue is related to the presence of Spanish artistic participants in coproduced films. (p. 71). The problem, she argues, stems from the reality that the bulk of these films are made in Latin America but must include Spanish talent: "this compulsory cooperation has brought to the fore the multiple inequalities that exist between Latin American countries and Spain." (Villazana, 2008, p. 73). Falicov (2013) focuses on four tropes of Spaniards that affect Ibermedia narratives: "the sympathetic Spaniard, the Spanish anarchist, the evil or racist Spaniard, and the Spanish tourist." (p. 73). Villazana (2008) further points out that in many of these cases the presence of the Spanish actor is awkward, or as in the case of Juan José Campanella's *Luna de Avellaneda* (*Avellaneda's Moon*, 2004) completely unexplained. (p. 76). Miriam Ross (2010) tries to understand the role of Spaniards in Ibermedia-funded Latin

Table 25.1 Latin American Films Released in Europe, 2000–2009

	Total Films	*Nationally Funded*	*Spain-coproduced*	*Ibermedia-funded*
Argentina	148	34	84	29
Brazil	58	22	0	5
Mexico	59	13	23	12
Cuba	24	0	15	10
Chile	31	7	7	1

Note: Table retrieved from Buquet (2012) Inserción internacional del cine latinoamericano.

American films according to contact zones that bring transnationality to the foreground. (p. 128). Elena et al. (2013), in contrast, study the role of Ibermedia in producing "hispanidad": "It is safe to say that the main theme of all of these coproductions has been and continues to be the recomposition of the great, albeit fractured, Hispanic family, a metaphorical, transoceanic and symbolically transhistoric recovery." (p. 154).

For Villazana (2008) the failure of Latin American nations to vigorously support their national film industries paved the way for Spanish domination; (p. 77) "Spain has become a faultless example of what the term neocolonialism embodies." (p.80). Yet, Elena et al. (2013) point out that such concerns overstate the significance and presence of Ibermedia coproductions. In fact, the realities of the limited reach of these films mean that the "impact on the region itself cannot be considered significant." And yet, they then qualify the statement by saying that Ibermedia "with all its defects and shortcomings has been the lifeline of film production in different countries of the region." (p. 153).

So which is it? Is Ibermedia keeping Latin American film alive, is it crushing it beneath the weight of Spanish neoimperialism, or is it unimportant? Before deciding, it is worth getting a sense of the scope of its funding. Ibermedia loans for production, which are ideally to be repaid, are not to exceed $200,000 nor exceed 50% of the total budget. In 2008, Ibermedia distributed a total of $6.5 million for 25 coproductions. In its first ten years of existence Ibermedia supported the production of about 250 films, an average of 25 per year. So, in practical terms we are not talking about excessive resources. Despite the fact that we often hear that the reason Spain is investing "heavily" in Latin American cinema is so that it can have content for European release, those numbers don't quite match up. Buquet (2012) explains that between 2000 and 2009 there were 311 Latin American films released in the European Union. (p. 185). Spain screened 237 of these films, an average of 24 per year. Of these 86 were nationally funded films and the rest were coproductions, most of them with Spain. (Buquet, 2012, p. 188). Of note is the fact that the films that were most successful were coproduced with the United States, not solely with Spain. Examples of these films were *Babel* (2006) and *El laberinto del fauno* (*Pan's Labyrinth*, 2006).

But here's the real catch: Buquet (2012) shows that Ibermedia-funded films are not really the bulk of Latin American films that reach Europe—a fact that upends the idea that Ibermedia is making films that dominate the way that Europeans, especially Spaniards, think about Latin America (p. 188) (see Table 25.1).

Ibermedia funded 167 of the films in the period studied by Buquet. Of these only 47 actually circulated beyond the country of origin—a fact that contradicts the notion that coproductions create images of the global south for western consumption.

The Role of Patagonik

In a vastly different example of coproduction from that of Ibermedia, we have the case of Disney-supported Patagonik, a production company co-owned with Argentina's Grupo Clarín. Between 1996 and 2000 Disney (through Buena Vista) proved that making films in Latin America could be profitable. Patagonik coproduced such internationally successful films as *Evita* (1996), *Cenizas del Paraíso* (*Ashes of Paradise*, 1997), *El hijo de la novia* (*Son of the Bride*, 2001), and *Nueve reinas* (*Nine Queens*, 2000). Villazana (2008) considers Patagonik to be an example of a hegemonic production house due to the combined investments of Disney and Telefónica and the fact that Patagonik films have also received Ibermedia support. While Villazana has a good point about Ibermedia's support of Patagonik films, the story of Patagonik is far more complex. While the production company benefits from foreign capital, it was also instrumental in reviving the Argentine film industry. It released a series of films that have been of extremely high quality and have had high aesthetic values as well.

A major reason for this is the connection between Patagonik and Pablo Trapero—a director who emerged as part of the New Argentine Cinema with his first feature, *Mundo grúa* (*Crane World*, 1999). Beginning with *Leonera* (*Lion's Den*, 2008), Trapero made three major films with Patagonik, all of which took up significant social issues within a more mainstream aesthetic. *Leonera* focused on the story of an incarcerated mother—a social justice issue that was not uniquely limited to Argentina but that raised important issues while not being overbearing and didactic in its treatment of the problem. The second film *Carancho* (*Vulture*, 2010) delves into the dark side of injuries from traffic accidents. There are 8,000 deaths and 120,000 people injured on Argentine roads annually. (French, 2012, para. 1). But rather than take this up in a morally heavy way, the film approaches the problem by focusing on two marginalized figures: an ambulance chaser and a nurse, who has to work extra shifts to make ends meet. The third film, *Elefante blanco* (*White Elephant*, 2012) follows two priests and a social worker who work in a marginalized slum in Buenos Aires. The film's title refers to a hospital project that never was completed, leaving a trail of corruption and the empty husk of a building. The empty building serves in the film as a symbol for corruption and its production of misery, but the symbolism avoids being overly heavy-handed, focusing equally on the challenges of the "outsiders" as well as those of the community. Trapero's films with Disney-funded Patagonik, then, were examples of a more commercial aesthetic that takes up serious issues in a way that is nuanced and complex.

Juan José Campanella also produced *El hijo de la novia* (*Son of the Bride*, 2001) with Patagonik, which was nominated for an Oscar. The irony was that the film was nominated as an Argentine film even though more than half of the funds that made the film came from outside of Argentina. Thus, it also shows another way that millennial globalization has complicated traditional geographies of power. The film does a good job of straddling a highly personal story of a son dealing with a midlife crisis and a mother with Alzheimer's against a story of the way that foreign capital is affecting Argentine local businesses. The common thread among these films is an aesthetically pleasing narrative that blends a personal relationship with a larger social concern. These films connect highly Argentine stories with tales that reveal the impact of the global economy. So, while it would be convenient to dismiss Patagonik as nothing more than a shill for multinational media investment, there is more to the story. These films are an excellent example of a way that foreign investment can be appropriated to support sophisticated and meaningful "local" culture.

The MERCOSUR Model

In a different model of Latin American coproduction in the global era we have the case of films supported through treaty coproduction facilitated by MERCOSUR. MERCOSUR (Mercado Común del Sur), or the Common Market of the South, was formed in 1991 out of a series of meetings that resulted in the "Tratado de Asunción" (Treaty of Asunción [Paraguay]) being signed by four South American nations: Argentina, Brazil, Paraguay, and Uruguay. Today it also includes Venezuela. Chile, Ecuador, Peru, and Colombia are associated states. (MERCOSUR, n.d.).

Table 25.2 MERCOSUR's Film Markets 2002–2005

Year	Spectators	MERCOSUR films that were not strictly national	National films with a MERCOSUR coproducer	MERCOSUR coproduction	Total films	Percent of market
2002	1,279,704	13	7	1	21	.96
2003	283,374	12	2	1	15	.19
2004	1,515,339	21	7	3	31	n/a
2005	573,912	19	14	1	34	n/a

Note: *Table retrieved from Aproximación al Mercado cinematográfico del MERCOSUR.*

The coordination of cultural policies for MERCOSUR was an explicit feature of the Cultural Integration Protocol by the end of 1996, but that measure did not directly address the audiovisual industry. In 2003 the MERCOSUR nations created RECAM (La Reunión Especializada de Autoridades Cinematográficas y Audiovisuales del MERCOSUR [Special Meeting of Cinematic and Audiovisual Authorities of MERCOSUR]), with the goal of "crear un instrumento institucional para avanzar en el proceso de integración de las industrias cinematográficas y audiovisuales de la región" [creating an institutional tool to advance the process of integrating the cinematic and audiovisual industries of the region]. (RECAM, n.d., para. 4). Yet, despite the idea of tying a trade agreement to cultural exchange, the results have been minimal. A study of the MERCOSUR film market focusing on Argentina, Brazil, and Chile, conducted by Octavio Getino and focusing on 2002–2005, showed that the total number of MERCOSUR films that circulated in the region was minimal (see Table 25.2):

We can note a trend toward more films and more viewers and we can see the effects of the 2003 agreements, but these numbers are still largely insignificant to the total market. To get a sense of the MERCOSUR market share consider this data (see Table 25.3):

This data shows that the ratio of MERCOSUR films to national films is still incredibly low. Most importantly it shows that those films that do reach screens attract very few spectators. As both Getino and Falicov note, it is not enough to make films that are connected to the region; distribution and exhibition policy also has to be coordinated to support the project.

Chanan et al. (2006) remind us that "cinema was transnational from the very start, and global in reach and operation by the 1930s." (p. 41). Dennison continues the argument by pointing out that "from early on in the history of Latin American film industries Italians, for example, were working in Brazil and North Americans were working in Mexico. Popular Latin American genre films such as melodrama and exploitation films were distributed throughout Latin America, with (Golden Age) Mexican cinema dominating the Latin American film market in the 1940s. Spain and Portugal were coproducing short films together as early as 1919, with the first feature film coproduction between the two countries being made in 1936." (Dennison, 2013a, p. 23). This all means that the transnational component of coproductions is nothing new and it shows no necessary signs of diluting the national.

This analysis of the complex, multi-faceted rise of coproductions in the global era unpacks the tendency to read globalization as either a threat to national culture or a new phase of globalized national culture. It shows the increasingly intricate web of geographic connections that define the global media industry and demonstrates that these connections don't always yield the outcomes we might expect. Transnational media alliances don't necessarily lead to films with transnational content. Coproductions across nations don't necessarily signify the end of national cinema. And, in some cases, these alliances preserve the national.

Table 25.3 National Film Versus MERCOSUR, 2002–2005

Country	Non-National MERCOSUR Films	MERCOSUR Coproductions	MERCOSUR Films Released	Spectators Reached	National Films Released
Argentina	15 non-national MERCOSUR films: - 11 Brazilian - 3 Chilean - 1 Uruguayan	15	30	20 of these films did not attract more than 10,000 spectators, and 8 did not reach 900.	205 national films released, reaching 17 million spectators.
Brazil	23 non-national MERCOSUR films: - 21 Argentine - 2 Chilean	14	37	22 of these films did not reach more than 25,000 spectators. 9 did not exceed 10,000.	151 national films released, reaching 55 million spectators.
Chile	30 non-national MERCOSUR films: - 24 Argentine - 5 Brazilian - 1 Uruguayan	9	39	26 of these films did not reach more than 5,000 spectators. 8 did not exceed 1,000.	51 national films released, reaching 3.7 million spectators.

Note: Table retrieved from Aproximación al Mercado cinematográfico del MERCOSUR.

Note

1 This chapter is drawn from my book, *Globalization and Latin American Cinema: Toward a New Critical Paradigm*; New York: Palgrave 2018.

References

Adell, M. (2001). La Geopolítica de las Coproducciones Hispanoamericanas. *Universitat Rovira I Virgili*. 1–469. www.tdx.cat/bitstream/handle/10803/51762/TESIS_DEF_COMPLETA.pdf.

Albornoz, L. (2016). Diversity and the Film Industry: An Analysis of the 2014 UIS Survey on Feature Film Statistics. *UNESCO Institute for Statistics*. Information Paper (29).

Black Camera (2010). Resolutions of the Third World Filmmakers Meeting, Algiers, December 5–14, 1973. Black Camera 2(1), 155–165. www.muse.jhu.edu/article/399812.

Buquet, G. (2012) Inserción internacional del cine latinoamericano en mercados de la Unión Europea. *Estudio de Producción y Mercados del cine Latinoamericano en la Primera Década del Siglo (XXI)185–197*. http://cinelatinoamericano.org/assets/docs/Cuaderno%207%20WEB.pdf.

Chanan, M. (2016) Review of Transnational Financial Structures in the Cinema of Latin America by Libia Villazana. www.libiavillazana.com/index-2.html.

Chanan, M., Dennison, S., Lim, S. (2006). *Latin American Cinema: From Underdevelopment to Postmodernism. Remapping World Cinema: Identity, Culture and Politics in Film*. Wallflower Press. 41.

Dennison, S. (2013a). *Contemporary Hispanic Cinema: Interrogating the Transnational in Spanish and Latin American Film*. Tamesis. 23.

Dennison, S. (2013b). Debunking Neo-imperialism or Reaffirming Neo-colonialism? The Representation of Latin America in Recent Co-productions. *Transnational Cinemas* (4)2, 186–193

Elena, A., Palacio, M., Türschmann, J. (2013). Family Affairs: Coproduction Policies between Spain and Latin America. *Transnational Cinema in Europe*. 153.

Falicov, T. (2007). Programa Ibermedia: Co-Production and the Cultural Politics of Constructing an Ibero-American Audiovisual Space. *Spectator* (27)2, 24.

Falicov, T. (2013). Ibero-Latin American Co-productions: Transnational Cinema, Spain's Public Relations Venture or Both? *Contemporary Hispanic Cinema: Interrogating the Transnational in Spanish and Latin American Film*. Woodbridge, Suffolk. 68–71.

French, P. (2012). Carancho—Review, *The Observer*. www.theguardian.com/film/2012/mar/04/carancho-pablo-trapero-review.

Getino, O. (n.d.). Aproximación al Mercado cinematográfico del MERCOSUR: Período 2002–2005. *RECAM*. 5–7. www.recam.org/_files/documents/aprox_al_mercado_cinemat_del_mercosur.pdf.

González, R. (2013). Mercados latinoamericanos de cine (2007–2012). *El Abordaje de Ideas Prensa*. http://elabordajedelasideasprensa.blogspot.mx/2015/02/mercados-latinoamericanos-de-cine-2007.html?view=timeslide.

Gunther, R., Montero, J., and Wert, J. (1999). The Media and Politics in Spain: From Dictatorship to Democracy. *Institut de Ciències Polítiques i Socials*. 20. http://citeseerx.ist.psu.edu/viewdoc/download?doi=10.1.1.540.2656&rep=rep1&type=pdf.

Johnson, R. (1984). *Cinema Novo x 5: Masters of Contemporary Brazilian Film*. University of Texas Press. 8.

Jones, H. and Higson, A. (2014, June). UK/European Film Co-Productions. 2. http://mecetes.co.uk/wp-content/uploads/2014/07/Jones-Higson-UK-European-Film-Co-productions.pdf

Lee, H. (2007). Hybrid Media, Ambivalent Feelings: Media Co-Productions and Cultural Negotiations. *Spectator*, (27) 2, 7. https://cinema.usc.edu/assets/054/10909.pdf.

Mango, A., Hecht, J. (2016). Latin America's Film Industry Paradox: 5 Countries with Loud Fest Titles (and Quiet Box Office Payoffs). *The Hollywood Reporter*. www.hollywoodreporter.com/lists/latin-americas-film-industry-paradox-864913/item/latin-america-brazil-864923.

McFadyen, S., Hoskins, C., and Finn, A. (1998). The Effect of Cultural Differences on the International Co-production of Television Programs and Feature Films. *Canadian Journal of Communication* (23)4, 523–538. www.uis.unesco.org/culture/Documents/ip29-diversity-film-data-2016-en.pdf.

MERCOSUR. (n.d.). Países del MERCOSUR. www.mercosur.int/innovaportal/v/7823/2/innova.front/paises-del-mercosur.

Miller, T., Govil, N., McMurria, J., Maxwell, R., Wang, T. (2005). *Global Hollywood 2* (London: British Film Institute), 177–178.

Morawetz, N., Hardy, J., Haslam, C., and Randle, K. (2007). Finance, Policy and Industrial Dynamics—the Rise of Co-Productions in the Film Industry. *Industry and Innovation* (14)4, 427.

MPAA. (2015). Theatrical Market Statistics 2015. *Motion Picture Association of America (M.P.A.A.)*. 4. www.mpaa.org/wp-content/uploads/2016/04/MPAA-Theatrical-Market-Statistics-2015_Final.pdf.

Newbery, C. (2011). Argentina Puts Up Barriers on Foreign Films. *Variety*. http://variety.com/2011/film/news/argentina-puts-up-barriers-on-foreign-films-1118042031/.

Pardo, A., Barriales-Bouche, S., and Salvodon, M. (2007). Spanish Co-Productions: Commercial Need or Common Culture? An Analysis of International Co-Productions in Spain from 2000 to 2004. *Zoom In, Zoom Out: Crossing Borders in Contemporary European Cinema*. Cambridge Scholars Publishing. 110.

Programa Ibermedia. (n.d.). www.programaibermedia.com/.

RECAM. (n.d.) ¿Qué es la RECAM?. www.recam.org/?do=recam.

Ross, M. (2010). South American Cinematic Culture: Policy, Production, Distribution and Exhibition. *Cambridge Scholars Publishing*. 120.

Solot, S. (2011). The New International Co-Production Scenario. *LATC—Latin American Training Center*. www.latamtrainingcenter.com/?p=2685&%3Blang=en.

Strover, S. (2016) Coproductions International. *The Museum of Broadcast Communications—Encyclopedia of Television*. www.museum.tv/eotv/coproductions.htm.

Turégano, H. (2004). The International Politics of Cinematic Coproduction: Spanish Policy in Latin America. *Film & History*. (34)2, 23.

UNESCO. (2005). The 2005 Convention on the Protection and Promotion of the Diversity of Cultural Expressions. http://en.unesco.org/creativity/sites/creativity/files/passeport-convention2005-web2.pdf.

UNESCO. (n.d). Data to Transform Lives. *UNESCO Institute for Statistics*. www.uis.unesco.org/DataCentre/Pages/country-profile.aspx?code=COL&%3Bregioncode=40520.

Villazana, L. (2008). Hegemony Conditions in the Coproduction Cinema of Latin America: The Role of Spain. *Framework: The Journal of Cinema and Media*, 49(2), 65–71. Retrieved October 28, 2020, from www.jstor.org/stable/41552527

26

TEMPORAL DIMENSIONS OF TRANSIENT MIGRATION STUDIES

The Case of Korean Visa Migrants' Media Practices in the US

Claire Shinhea Lee

Introduction

The rapid decline in transportation and telecommunications costs and the rapid development of new media technologies are encouraging drastic changes in the nature of migration. Rather than models of one-way mobility, settlement, and integration, migration studies have recognized the transnational mobility and the temporal fluidity of different types of migrant subjects, from high-skilled workers to low-skilled contract laborers and from refugees (asylum seekers) to marriage migrants (Robertson, 2014). Following this trend, the "mobility turn" have influenced the field by considering migration from a movement perspective and critiquing the static categories of analysis, for instance nation or ethnicity (Griffiths et al., 2013). This paradigm of focus on mobilities means reconsidering "spatial mobility, its patterns and manifestations" and within migration studies it generally indicates a transnational approach (Faist, 2013, p. 1,638). Moreover, scholars argue that we need to go beyond the prevailing economic approach (i.e. labor migrants as economic bodies) to include social behavior and mundane feelings of migration (Kõu et al., 2009).

It is in this context which I initiated my original project of *Mediatized Transient Migrants* (Lee, 2019), which explored the role of media in both the migratory processes and the transnational everyday lives of temporary skilled migrants[1]. Information communication technologies (ICTs) have played a crucial role in the lives of migrants by connecting migrants to their homeland, to the diasporic community, and to the host society. While migrants' transnational networking through media is not a new thing, in recent years the scale and forms of digital networking have altered a variety of migration dynamics (Leurs and Prabhakar, 2018). For instance, mobile (smart) phones have made available informal social networks that serve as significant sources of emotional, informational, and instrumental support for migrants (Chib and Aricat, 2017). Many scholars have conceptualized this new pattern of migrant communication infrastructure as "connected copresence" (Diminescu, 2008), "ordinary copresence" (Nedelcu and Wyss, 2016), or "ambient copresence" (Madianou, 2016).

In this project, I chose Korean middle-class visa-status migrants living in Austin, TX, as an empirical case study for several reasons. The first reason is the relatively large size of the Korean migrant population with little research on their media use, and the second is due to the characteristics of the

Korean community—common language, customs, values, and historic experiences as a group—which provide a good base for studying the nexus of homeland and hostland relations. Lastly, the remarkably high levels of internet use and rapidly developing media market of contemporary Korea make the sample case worth studying. Moreover, the study tried to complicate the traditional boundaries around categories of permanent and temporary migration and introduce the complex positionality of "middling" migration.

After completing my project, I realized how much this project was about "time" as much as about "space" and that temporality is crucial in understanding skilled visa-status migrants. As I developed the original study to a longitudinal one by conducting follow-up interviews, I found that during the last five years, among the 36 migrants I interviewed, ten of them returned to Korea, four married, three had babies, and 13 of them changed their immigration status. In this context, this chapter seeks to build introductory understandings of the temporal dimensions within the migration and media field through a specific case study of Korean middle-class temporary visa migrants.

Media and Migration: Digital Migration Studies and a Non-Media-Centric Approach

While migration scholars rarely had made the importance of media explicit in their work, media studies also had dealt with migration experience in a more restricted way such as remaining in the "effects" tradition: how coverage of immigration issues affects voting behavior or how host-country representations stimulate the desire to migrate (King & Wood, 2001). With current transnational mobility intertwined with the expanding scale, circulation, and impact of media consumption (Appadurai, 1996), studies have recognized the importance of the media's role in both the migratory processes and the transnational everyday lives of these migrants in three main ways: 1) media as an important source of information for potential migrants, 2) media representation of migrants in host-country media and the influence to migrants, and 3) migrants' use of homeland media and its role in the cultural identity and politics of diasporic communities (King & Wood, 2001, p. 1–2).

More recently, along with the social focus on migration issues and rapid development in ICTs, various disciplines such as sociology, anthropology, geography, and media and communication studies have become involved in the field of migration studies. In this context, some scholars are making an effort to systemize the field as "digital migration studies": an emerging research focus that seeks to understand relationships between migration and digital connectivity (Leurs and Prabhakar, 2018). There exist three paradigms of digital migration studies. The first paradigm mainly puts its interest on migrants who exist in cyberspace. Just like the early internet researchers who were interested in how people experiment and negotiate their online identities from their physical offline bodies in terms of gender, racial, and national identity, these scholars examined how migrant users imagine belonging to the cyber diasporic communities and the complications of doing virtual ethnography (Gajjala, 2004; Markham, 1998).

The second paradigm, often viewed as non-digital-media-centric, investigates migrants' physical places and everyday practices along with digital media consumption. Research in this categorization considers the broader social, spatial, and temporal context for media use and approaches contemporary migrant experiences in regard to power dynamics and the global-local complex (Georgiou, 2006, Madianou and Miller, 2012; Miller and Slater, 2000; Zijlstra and van Liempt, 2017). For example, Georgiou (2006) explored the role of media in the diasporic identity construction of Greek-Cypriot migrants in New York and London through interviews and participant observations and Madianou and Miller (2012) examined Filipino migrant mothers' distant mothering of their left-behind children in the Philippines through ICTs. More recently, Zijlstra and van Liempt (2017) studied the use of smartphones among Afghan, Iranian, and Syrian migrants during their border-crossings in Europe through trajectory ethnography. Lastly, in the third paradigm, migrants are increasingly datafied by new computational tools and techniques that extract data from users (Diminescu, 2008; Kok and Rogers, 2017).

While the three key paradigms have their own strengths, the first and the third paradigms tend to center digital technologies as the main object of the study and easily separate technology from other material, historical, and emotional factors. However, the second paradigm, which often utilizes an ethnographic approach to capture media practices in everyday settings, can in particular be highly valuable to describe the temporal formations of contemporary migration. In this matter, the present study aligns itself with the second paradigm digital migration studies.

Time, Temporality, and Temporariness

Migration has commonly been associated with space rather than with time, although all migration processes have complex temporal dimensions (Cwerner, 2001; Griffiths, Rogers, and Anderson, 2013; King et al., 2006). This is due to the classical ideas of migration as temporally linear (from home-land to the present hostland) and associated ideologies of assimilation and integration (Meeus, 2012). However, it is clear that contemporary migration complicates the boundaries between temporary and permanent and linear and circular. Due to the increasing but conflicting possibilities, uncer-tainties, and vulnerabilities of the global sphere, migration refers to dynamic processes and various temporalities.

For instance, the migration journey is more than the relative duration of travel time, but includes a variety of temporalities such as "waiting, accelerating, queuing, being still, stopping, and repeating" (Griffiths et al., 2013, p. 11). Migrant decision-making does not occur at a single moment in time and by complete individual agency but rather operates through "uncertain and surprising experiences of time" (Carling and Collins, 2018, p. 914). Moreover, especially in temporary migration (as both legal status and subjective status) the pathways become even more contingent, multi-directional, and varied in regard to different stages.

Despite some attention to time in the migration literature, including the detailed sociological framework of the "times of migration" (Cwerner, 2001), the comprehensive conceptual review of flows, ruptures, cycles, and synchronicity (Griffiths et al., 2013), previous works on the significance of life course and longitudinal studies (Collins and Shubin, 2015; King et al, 2006; Kobayasi and Preston, 2007; Kõu et al., 2009), the works focusing on liminal and suspended time (Conlon, 2011; Elliot, 2016) and border crossing as a temporal process (Axelsson, 2017), and research on times of immigra-tion policy and the temporalities of migrant agencies (Robertson, 2015b; 2019), in general, time and temporality are seldom used as central frameworks to understand migration. Especially in the field of media and migration, with most work focusing on mobility and identity (the spatial aspect) in the case of permanent migration, with the exception of studies focusing on generational differences (the temporal aspect) of diasporic audiences, the temporal dimensions in migration and the relation to media consumption remains limited.

In this chapter, expanding Shanti Robertson (2015b)'s conceptualization, I use "time" to refer to objective or quantitative time, which includes everyday work, leisure, and media time, or the length of time associated with a particular visa or work permit. In contrast, "temporality" refers to the experi-ence of time or time manifested in human experience (Hoy, 2009). Just as many scholars investigate spatiality, the human experience of space or place, in migration, temporality should be understood at the same level but in a different perspective. "Temporariness," in this study, can be understood in two ways: first referring to their factual immigration status of being temporary and thus the constraints placed on migrants by the state (Baubock, 2011), and second referring to migrants' subjective feelings and experiences in regard to their temporary situation. In the first case, temporariness indicates the opposite of permanency and in the second, temporariness may be substituted for terms like liminality or uncertainty.

Applying Temporal Concepts to Digital Migration Studies:
A Case Study Example

The original project of *Mediatized Transient Migrants* represented several aspects of time-oriented analysis throughout the study, mainly constituted of the media's ability to shape national and daily temporality (Moores, 2011; Scannell, 1996; Silverstone, 2003). In general, the 36 Korean visa-status migrants participated actively in Korean temporality through a wide spectrum of media practices: checking Korean news and Korean sports results every day, putting on live Korean broadcast television in their home, setting their mobile phone time zone with both US and Korean time, and using Korean-made calendars which indicated Korean holidays and events. These activities can be explained as the *synchronization* process (Lavi, 2012). However, even more than participating in this liveness of Korean temporality, the interviewees emphasized habitual media use that structured their own daily transnational time. This media routine often included pre-migration taken-for-granted media habits and thus related to home-country media consumption. For instance, many participants tried their best to fix their media timeline similar to their previous schedule back in the homeland by watching the Monday/Tuesday 10 p.m. drama and Saturday 5 p.m. show (in Korean timeline) exactly on Monday/Tuesday 10 p.m. and Saturday 5 p.m. in US time, utilizing the time-difference between the two countries and the quick update system through streaming or downloading. This practice could be an example of *periodicity* (Southerton, 2006) in which, although not simultaneous with Korean temporality, it connects to the rhythm of a distant place. Another example of media routine that structures transnational daily life was through *sequence* or in other words *media rounds* (Lavi, 2012). This meant that some kind of mundane media-consumption sequence was ritualized as a daily or weekly practice; for instance, several participants started their day by "holding their mobile phone --> visiting the Korean portal site --> skimming through all the news pages --> checking the trending keywords section" and others' (especially those who lived alone) meal times were closely associated with their media sequence (prepare their meal while downloading a Korean show --> connect the computer to the black screen -->eat meal while watching the show). In addition, I investigated how international students (F.1) conducted *media time squeezing* (Moshe, 2012) through self-media-planning in order to handle the shortage of time and keep up with the multichannel media affluence. Continuing and expanding this temporal approach to studying media and migration, here, I suggest two additional theoretical concepts that are especially useful in examining skilled temporary migration.

1) Life Course, Media Practices, and Migration Decision-Making
of Skilled Migrants

Life course perspectives can be used as a tool to explore the passage of time and the evolution of life trajectories of people (Kõu et el., 2009). For instance, geographers have used life course frame to explain an individual's life via the structures of events and transitions and migration scholars often adopt this approach to understand the influence of life paths, social networks, diasporas, and immigration policies on migration decision-making (Collins and Shubin, 2015). Scholars have argued that this migration "decision-making" is a "flow" and process rather than a singular event (Griffiths et al., 2013) and "drivers of migration" not only include the economic, political, demographic, social, and environmental features but also temporal factors. Acknowledging that the "decision to migrate" is a temporally informed process allows us to understand that these decisions are much more complex than a rational calculative one (Collins, 2018). Here in this study, I suggest that the conceptual framework of life course by Kõu et al. (2009)[2] is useful in investigating migration and media research, especially with "middling" migration populations such as the skilled migrants.

Korean temporary visa migrants discussed various "drivers of migration", including personal career path, strategic family planning, and employment issues. The combination of household paths and education–employment paths leading to migration decision were explicitly revealed for my dependent-visa participants. The fact that all ten dependent-visa-status migrants were women reveals how the macro, meso, and micro contexts together structure skilled-migration decision. For instance, most of them admitted that they followed their husbands' educational–employment path and many of them had to leave their job or study. Although this was not an easy decision, many of them pointed out the *timing* made much more sense for them to migrate to the US

> Hani (F2 --> H4): Since my husband and I discussed moving to the US for study abroad, it wasn't really hard to quit my job. And, anyways, I knew I had to have a baby.

> Dahyun (F2 --> permanent resident): We met in the same company as workers. I thought hard about moving to the US before marriage, but after marriage, I thought it was a natural process. We planned that I would have a baby during his study, and it happened.

Likewise, for dependent-visa women, the biological timescale of having a baby coincided with the institutional scale of their husbands' education–employment paths, and thus led to migration. Adding to these factors, media consumption functioned as a kind of driver for the migration for these women: most of the dependent women mentioned watching and loving American dramas before migration. However, interestingly, these migrants confessed that they do not watch American dramas any more after migration to the US

In this temporal migration journey, my study revealed that homeland media use was steeply increased when migrants dwelled in the US This was mainly due to the language and culture stress of Korean migrants who struggled to survive in the uneven global structure of transnational everyday lives. In fact, homeland media consumption provided my participants with some kind of onto-logical security that supported a sense of homeliness and daily reassurance (see Lee, 2019). Especially, I found that the F1-status international students who felt the most temporariness (usually no jobs and no houses yet) showed the most Korean media time compared to H1B or L1 skilled migrants. Moreover, homeland news consumption influenced in their decision of future trajectories. The more heavily they used homeland news, while they related and identified to their Korean (political) iden-tity strongly, migrants expressed that they did not want to go back to Korea since they consumed too much negative and dark news on Korean society. Then, conversely, when the ten migrants ended up returning to Korea, they all confessed that they consume less Korean media content compared to when they were in the US In this regard, the way media practices are influenced by and, at the same time, how media affect these life course paths is an important question for media scholars. When media practices are investigated in relation to the complex and multi-layered life course, we are able to understand the role of media better in temporary migration.

Although media practices may have influenced information gathering and emotional attachments regarding their migration path decisions, however, it is important to recognize that the actual migra-tion trajectories often did not result in the direction these migrants planned and imagined. This is true if we consider the fact that at the time of the original interviews (early 2014), except few, most of them expressed that they would like to stay in the US for quite a while, then go back to Korea far later. Previous studies on international students have tended to see their future trajectories as stay–return binary with push–pull factors (Bijwaard & Wang, 2016; Wu and Wilkes, 2017). While these studies introduced various factors, such as social ties, personal, economic, and professional, that influ-ence post-graduate migration decision, again in my study, I suggest that temporal factors, so to say *timing*, is critical in understanding post-migration routes. Below are quotes from follow-up interviews (five years later) with Minhyuck and Momo.

> Minhyuck (F1 --> OPT --> H1B --> Permanent resident --> migrated to Australia): I never knew that I would end up here when I was interviewed five years ago. Going through the hardships in the immigration process, I just had to quit my job in the US At that time, an offer came from Australia, and that is all. That was the only reason I came here.

Momo (F1 --> OPT --> H1B --> Returned to Korea): I remember my interview back then, and seriously, I have to confess that my media practices have changed so much! After I got a job and moved to a new place (more rural) where there were no Korean people around me, my Korean media consumption drastically decreased. Now back in Korea, still I don't consume that much.

Just like Minhyuck and Momo, most migration journeys did not follow their plan or intention, but at most times, people had to choose among the available options at an unpredictable moment. For instance, while middle-class visa migration is voluntary in nature, Chaeyoung (F2), Hyerin (F2), and Lisa (F2) all expressed strongly that they wanted to stay in the US yet ended up returning to Korea due to their husbands' career paths and family issues. More specifically, institutional time scales such as immigration policy changes due to the Trump administration and biological time scales such as parents' aging and sickness impacted their migration journey. In case of Jonghyun (L1) and Eunha (L2), within the five years they had to return to Korea and then move to Singapore and then to Saudi Arabia, all the migration processes dominantly controlled by the company's decision and timing.

2) "Staggered" Migration Processes, Experiences of Temporality, and Media Consumption

Robertson (2015a) refers to the experience of Asian migrants in Australia who go through a multi-stage migration of various temporary visas toward the hope of eventual permanent residency, as "staggered" forms of migration. This shifting migration pattern not only involves blurring of boundaries between temporariness and permanence but also unique experiences of temporality. Korean temporary visa-status migrants' contingent, multi-directional, and multi-stage pathways can be well explained through these *staggered* migration processes. Just like the Asian migrants in Australia, Korean visa migrants in the US were also governed by time. In this regard, I suggest that the concepts of *contingent temporality* and *indentured temporality* (Robertson, 2019) are effective in understanding visa-status migrants and their media practices.

Jungyeon (H1B --> Permanent resident): After we did the initial interview, finally and luckily, my family received the green card in fall of 2015. We migrated 22 years ago, so it was a long wait. My whole life has been affected by the immigration/visa status. I would have selected a different major if I wasn't concerned about the visa. I did accounting because many advised that it would have an advantage for getting a job and maintaining a sponsor for the visa. When I was searching for job, I don't know how many times I was refused due to my status. As soon as I got the green card, the first thing I did was quit my job and start the teacher certification. My friend told me that after receiving the green card, I look relaxed. Honestly, I think I've got much lazier since then. I realize that my unstable status kept me always busy and get-going. Sometimes, I even miss that speed and vigilance.

This follow-up-interview quote from Jungyeon reveals the long *waiting* process, and the everyday struggles she went through due to the migration governance. Jungyeon went through various visa stages throughout her life from F.1 (student) to H1B (temporary worker), first for two years and a second renewal for three years, and then finally to green card. Every step of immigration status change involved much stress, money, and even self-studied immigration law knowledge. For instance, at the last moment of receiving green card, due to her lawyer's sudden death, she had to figure out the Child Protection Act (CPA) by herself. If she had not done that, she would have opted out of the green card process, filed by her mom when she was a child, after waiting so long. Likewise, every step of her mundane life (choosing the major, traveling overseas, getting a job, dating, spending her leisure time) was disrupted and restructured by the unanticipated and unpredictable immigration status. Thus, what she experienced in every step of her migration journey until she received her green card was "contingent temporality," a "constant juggling of future on the biographic timescale across a dynamic institutional timescale" (Robertson, 2019, p.174). In addition, she recognizes that she experienced a different kind of speed of time, *tempo*, before and after being a permanent resident.

Going through this contingent temporality, my study found that these temporary migrants often found cyberspace as an alternative space to connect and belong without the feeling of temporariness or conditional acceptance. Jungyeon was a very active social media user who utilized Instagram, Telegram, Pinterest, and Facebook and confessed that these online communities have aided her to find true friends whom she could build relationships with regardless of her location or (immigration) status. Although she also had close friends offline, she expressed that at moments she felt a wall between those friends and her due to their permanent immigrant status in the US. They could never fully understand what she was going through due to this issue and she felt tired of explaining all the complications due to her status. However, with online communities who normally shared certain leisure interests and often lived in different countries or shared similar situations, she was free from the burden and difference.

The story of Yeri, who stayed in the US for nine years and returned to Korea, shows another experience of temporality: "indentured temporality" (Robertson, 2019), which indicates some forms of *stopping* or *delay* in migration trajectories or transnational daily lives.

> Yeri (F1 --> H1B --> Korea): I have to renew my visa every year. Almost every six months, I need to do all the paperwork. I was restricted to travel during the renewal process which takes about four–five months. I once couldn't even drive because my license had expired and my visa was still in the process. I had to literally ask for rides every time I had to buy things, go to the church, or meet someone. I spent more than $10,000 for the lawyer fee. Just going through all this process, I felt really exhausted.

Yeri, a post-doctoral student in higher education with a well-paid job, is easily regarded as an emancipated cosmopolitan elite migrant. However, her transnational daily life was often suspended or constrained by the institutional time scales of immigration policy. Time often functions as a border in temporary migrants' lives and sometime leaves migrants *stuck* in time, or even instantaneously illegal (Robertson, 2014). Especially, the visa migration reveals this border of time tangible in many ways: temporal limitations on duration of stay (five years for F1, 12 to 39 months for OPT (Optional Practical Training)), temporal eligibility criteria in the Child Protection Act, processing times for change of status (four months for OPT approval, more than a year for green card), temporal limitations on work rights (20-hour restriction for work in the school for F1, no work permit for dependent visa F2 and H4). Due to the conflict of these different time scales—biological, work-related, immigration law, family-related—migrants were *stopped* working or driving and *stuck* in isolated relationships or unhealthy marriages.

During this time of *stuckness* or *waiting*, many migrants confessed too much time or sometimes, at the opposite extreme, lack of time and thus increased anxiety and stress. In both ways, I argue that media consumption was a big part of how they dealt with time. For instance, participants consumed much Korean television as a tool for avoiding this stress or just to keep time going. This phenomenon was most explicit for migrants when they experienced transition (to a new place, new visa status, or new job) and as the temporariness of these temporary migrants represents, transitions frequently appeared in their everyday lives. More than two-thirds of my participants stated that they had increased their media use after migration to the US and the ten migrants who returned to Korea after the initial interview revealed that their media use was apparently reduced. Especially with the emergence of smart mobile phones, migrants in this study often confessed the fear of being addicted to Korean news or Korean television. This kind of media practice could be understood through their emotional emptiness and boredom during this indentured temporality. This hunger for media in migrants' daily lives has been similarly analyzed in a few studies (Christiansen, 2004; Gillespie, 1995; Smets, 2018) but I believe more concrete observation of the role of media in the experiences of temporality in temporary forms of migration is greatly needed and important.

Conclusion

When I conducted the initial interviews with my participants, I was in my F1 status trying to complete my degree. As time went by, my own personal immigration status went through changes: from F1 to OPT, and then to H4 (dependent of skilled migrant). The visa process journey at times allowed me to work (OPT), then *stopped* me from working (H4); other times I was *stuck* at home due to the expiration of my drivers' license and visa renewal process, and most of the time I was *waiting,* not knowing what the next step would be. I experienced the disadvantages of a temporary status in the job market and the fear of being illegal, just like my participants. I knew that although fully packed with knowledge completing my dissertation, I had no idea what my participants went through.

Temporality matters. It matters in media and migration studies, but also as we conduct our own research. I contend that a focus on temporality brings us an opportunity to maximize the three principles that Leurs and Prabhakar (2018) pointed out as the guidelines in doing digital migrant studies: relationality, adaptability, and ethics of care. As we examine the temporal aspects of media use and migration, we acknowledge the interlinked relationship of media and everyday lives, online and offline experiences, here (post-migration) and there (pre-migration), and place and time. Moreover, it becomes convenient to capture the constant and rapid changes in media technologies and practices. Last of all, admitting the temporal moments of the research and the temporariness of researcher, temporality as an analytical category allows us to embrace an ethics of care in conducting the study.

Notes

1 Based on qualitative interviews with 40 Korean middle-class temporary visa-status migrants living in the US, the project linked an emerging polymedia environment and transnational digital culture (i.e., cord-cutting practice and algorithmic culture) in order to interrogate mobility and migration in the globalization era. More specifically, the study looked into different visa categories—skilled workers (H1B., L1, OPT), academic graduate students (F1), and their accompanied dependents (F2, H4, L2)—and argued that the use of homeland media (social, news, and entertainment) allowed these migrants to make, connect to, and complicate home (Lee, 2019).

2 Life course is constituted by three inter-related paths: education—employment path, household path, and migration path. At the same time, life course is influenced and governed by three levels of contexts: micro (human capital or household members), meso (social networks or diasporas), and macro (migration policies or labor demand).

References

Appadurai, A. (1996). *Modernity Al Large: Cultural Dimensions of Globalization.* Minneapolis: University of Minnesota Press.

Axelsson, L. (2017). Living within temporally thick borders: IT professionals' experiences of Swedish immigration policy and practice. *Journal of Ethnic and Migration Studies,* 43(6), 974–990.

Baubock, R. (2011). Temporary Migrants, Partial Citizenship and Hypermigration. *Critical Review of International Social and Political Philosophy,* 14 (5): 665–693.

Bijwaard, G.E., & Wang, Q. (2016). Return migration of foreign students. *European Journal of Population,* 32(1), 31–54.

Carling, J., & Collins, F. (2018). Aspiration, desire and drivers of migration. Journal of Ethnic and Migration Studies, 44(6), 909–926.

Chib, A., & Aricat, R.G. (2017). Belonging and communicating in a bounded cosmopolitanism: The role of mobile phones in the integration of transnational migrants in Singapore. *Information, Communication & Society*, 20(3), 482–496.

Christiansen, C.C. (2004). News media consumption among immigrants in Europe: The relevance of diaspora. *Ethnicities*, 4(2), 185–207.

Collins, F.L. (2018). Desire as a theory for migration studies: temporality, assemblage and becoming in the narratives of migrants. *Journal of Ethnic and Migration Studies*, 44(6), 964–980.

Collins, F.L., & Shubin, S. (2015). Migrant times beyond the life course: The temporalities of foreign English teachers in South Korea. *Geoforum*, 62, 96–104.

Conlon, D. (2011). Waiting: Feminist perspectives on the spacings/timings of migrant (im)mobility. *Gender, Place & Culture*, 18(3), 353–360.

Cwerner, S.B. (2001). The times of migration. *Journal of Ethnic and Migration Studies*, 27(1), 7–36.

Diminescu, D. (2008). The connected migrant: an epistemological manifesto. *Social Science Information*, 47(4), 565–579.

Elliot, A. (2016). Paused subjects: Waiting for migration in North Africa. *Time & Society*, 25(1), 102–116.

Faist, T. (2013). The mobility turn: a new paradigm for the social sciences? *Ethnic and Racial Studies*, 36(11), 1637–1646.

Gajjala, R. (2004). *Cyber selves: Feminist ethnographies of South Asian women*. Walnut Creek: Rowman Altamira.

Georgiou, M. (2006). *Diaspora, identity and the media: diasporic transnationalism and mediated spacialities*. Cresskill, N.J.: Hampton Press.

Gillespie, M. (1995). Southall: Chota Punjab. *Television, Ethnicity and cultural change*, 29–47.

Griffiths, M., Rogers, A., & Anderson, B. (2013). Migration, time and temporalities: Review and prospect. *COMPAS Research Resources Paper*, 199–217.

Hoy, D.C. (2009). *The Time of Our Lives: A Critical History of Temporality*. Cambridge, MA: MIT Press.

King, R., & Wood, N. (2001). *Media and Migration: Constructions of Mobility and Difference*. London: Routledge.

King, R., Thomson, M., Fielding, T., & Warnes, T. (2006). Time, generations and gender in migration and settlement. *The dynamics of international migration and settlement in Europe*, 233(68), 29.

Kobayashi, A., & Preston, V. (2007). Transnationalism through the life course: Hong Kong immigrants in Canada. *Asia Pacific Viewpoint*, 48(2), 151–167.

Kok, S., & Rogers, R. (2017). Rethinking migration in the digital age: Transglocalization and the Somali diaspora. *Global Networks*, 17(1), 23–46.

Kõu, A., Bailey, A., & Van Wissen, L. (2009, September). Migrant biographies: A life course approach to high-skilled migration. In *XXVI IUSSP International Population Conference, Morocco* (Vol. 30).

Lavi, E. (2012). *Orientation to the nation: a phenomenology of media and diaspora* (Doctoral dissertation, Goldsmiths, University of London).

Lee, C.S. (2019). *Mediatized transient migrants: Korean visa-status migrants' transnational everyday lives and media use*. Lanham: Rowman & Littlefield.

Leurs, K., & Prabhakar, M. (2018). Doing digital migration studies: Methodological considerations for an emerging research focus. In *Qualitative research in European migration studies* (pp. 247–266). Springer, Cham.

Madianou, M. (2016). Ambient co-presence: transnational family practices in polymedia environments. *Global Networks*, 16(2), 183–201.

Madianou, M., & Miller, D. (2012). Polymedia: Towards a new theory of digital media in interpersonal communication. *International Journal of Cultural Studies*, 16(2), 169–187.

Markham, A.N. (1998). *Life online: Researching real experience in virtual space* (Vol. 6). Rowman Altamira.

Meeus, B. (2012). How to "catch" floating populations? Research and the fixing of migration in space and time. *Ethnic and Racial Studies*, 35(10), 1775–1793.

Miller, D., & Slater, D. (2000). *Internet*. Oxford: Berg Publishers.

Moores, S. (2011). That familiarity with the world born of habit: A phenomenological approach to the study of media uses in daily living. *Interactions: Studies in Communication & Culture*, 1(3), 301–312.

Moshe, M. (2012). Media time squeezing: the privatization of the media time sphere. *Television & New Media*, 13(1), 68–88.

Nedelcu, M., & Wyss, M. (2016). "Doing family" through ICT-mediated ordinary co-presence: transnational communication practices of Romanian migrants in Switzerland. *Global Networks*, 16(2), 202–218.

Robertson, S. (2014). Time and temporary migration: The case of temporary graduate workers and working holiday makers in Australia. *Journal of Ethnic and Migration Studies*, 40(12), 1915–1933.

Robertson, S. (2015a). Contractualization, depoliticization and the limits of solidarity: noncitizens in contemporary Australia. *Citizenship Studies*, 19(8), 936–950.

Robertson, S. (2015b). The temporalities of international migration: Implications for ethnographic research. In *Social transformation and migration* (pp. 45–60). Palgrave Macmillan, London.

Robertson, S. (2019). Migrant, interrupted: The temporalities of "staggered" migration from Asia to Australia. *Current Sociology*, *67*(2), 169–185.

Scannell, P. (1996). Radio, television, and modern life: A phenomenological approach.

Silverstone, R. (2003). *Television and everyday life*. London and new York: Routledge.

Smets, K. (2018). The way Syrian refugees in Turkey use media: Understanding "connected refugees" through a non-media-centric and local approach. *Communications*, *43*(1), 113–123.

Southerton, D. (2006). Analysing the temporal organization of daily life: Social constraints, practices and their allocation. *Sociology*, *40*(3), 435–454.

Wu, C., & Wilkes, R. (2017). International students' post-graduation migration plans and the search for home. *Geoforum*, *80*, 123–132.

Zijlstra, J., & van Liempt, I. (2017). Smart(phone) travelling: Understanding the use and impact of mobile technology on irregular migration journeys. International Journal of Migration and Border Studies, 3(2–3), 174–191.

27

ON THE POST-SOCIALIST MARKETIZATION OF THE PRESS IN CENTRAL AND EASTERN EUROPE

A View from Germany

Mandy Tröger

Introduction

"Since the press was and is subject to market principles, its role in the service of the public depends on the coincidences of the private sector. ... This is part of the paradoxes of our democratic society."

(European Parliament, April 1992, p. 13)

Underlining the intrinsic connection between a free press and a viable democracy, the European Parliament (EP), in 1992, emphasized that in spite of their "public task," newspapers were still "subject to the laws of the market" (Session documents 1992, p. 13). Its assumption was that a free market allowed competing voices to take their equal share in public debate. Acknowledging that market interests did not always go hand in hand with those of democratic societies, however, the EP pointed to self-regulation and other regulatory means that could be applied if needed.

It was no coincidence that the EP made its assessment of the free-press-paradox in 1992—in the midst of the post-socialist transition in Central and Eastern Europe (CEE). With political economic shifts following the end of Soviet rule, all CEE countries experienced structural reforms, not the least of their media and press. "The liberation of the media," wrote Peter Bajomi-Lázár in 2003, "was an axiom of the political transformation in the countries of East Central Europe" (p. 6). The freedom of media and the press were core demands of reform groups across the CEE At the time, also the International Press Institute (IPI) supported these developments. At its 39th annual conference in France in May 1990, 2,000 newspaper publishers and editors signed a resolution welcoming the blossoming of a "free and vibrant press in Hungary, Poland and Czechoslovakia" (cited in *Tagesspiegel*, 1990). A free press, it seemed, was finally to come to the informationally impoverished media landscapes of former Soviet countries. Though the conditions of change differed by region and country, Jakubowicz and Sükösd (2008) show that the press systems of all CEE countries soon faced a range of (economic, social, political, and technological) challenges in an "extremely compressed, short period of time" (p. 16). Many problems hit "immediately after communism fell" (ibid.).

This chapter looks at this immediate transition period in the light of foreign investments and changing ownership patterns in newly developing press markets. Already in the 1970s and 1980s, a growing body of work took a critical stance toward (Western) transnational capital flows in international media and communications (i.e. Schiller, 1969; Tunstall, 1977). This chapter adds to this critique by providing insights into what Armand Mattelart in 1994 called one of the "[t]wo major events" that further underscored the corporate-led transformation of the information world order, namely the "crumbling of the 'socialist bloc'" in the early 1990s (the other having been the Gulf War). In its aftermath, as Robert McChesney and Dan Schiller (2003) have shown, the "value of completed cross-border buyouts" in a global market for goods and services skyrocketed, rising "from less than $100 billion in 1987 to $1.14 trillion (current dollars) in 2000 " (p. 11). Linking this back to international communications, McChesney and Schiller argue that as part of this cross-border trade, also a transnational corporate-commercial communication system—closely tying control over the media to monopoly capitalism—spread globally (ibid.). This chapter shows how press markets took a central place in this process.

Already in April 1991, *The Economist* observed that "[n]o industry in Eastern Europe has attracted the interest of foreign investors or raised fears of foreign ownership like newspapers" (p. 70). As will be shown, however, the change of ownership was not the only thing that mattered. Early influences of Western market interests in media policies, reforming the press according to their needs, had long-term systemic consequences. This macro-level perspective, however, remains a missing piece to the puzzle when concerned with post-socialist press transitions.

According to Kasimierz Woycicki, chief editor of Polish newspaper *Życie Warszawa* (*Warsaw Life*) in 1990, the press transition in Poland at the time was shaped mainly by two issues: first, the search for new concepts of journalism and journalists, and, second, the question who was capable of implementing them (in Licht, 1990). Accordingly, much has been written about the democratization of the press and journalism (Balčytienė & Vinciūnienė, 2014, Dobek-Ostrowska & Głowacki, 2001, Klimkiewicz, 2009) as well as the relationship between mass media and democratic orientations in CEE countries (i.e. Voltmer, 2006). The underlying economic forces that shaped these processes and subsequent media structures remain side notes (i.e. Jakubowicz, 2001, Jakubowicz & Sükösd, 2008, Hrvatin & Petković, 2004).[1] This is because most accounts of post-socialist media transitions leave out (or rather take for granted) that a major driving force for structural reforms were Western corporate-commercial interests (Mappes-Niediek, 2003). It is still claimed to be "obvious that privatization and deregulation in these [CEE] countries are a necessary precondition" (Sturm, Muller & Dieringer 2000, p. 650) for general economic welfare. This includes the media.

During the immediate post-socialist period this meant that (Western) multinational media corporations, such as the News Corporation (Rupert Murdoch), the Mirror Group Newspapers (Robert Maxwell), or Hersant, early on moved into newly developing CEE markets. They bought out former party papers, founded new newspapers, and imported established formats from their "home" countries. In particular West German publishers, such as Axel Springer, Gruner + Jahr, Bauer, the WAZ-Group, and others took important roles in these acquisitions. Making use of their geographic proximity and their government-backed head-start in the German Democratic Republic (G.D.R.), they soon expanded to other CEE countries. The Axel Springer Publishing house, for instance, not only aimed at securing its "leading market position in Germany" by "means of a strong involvement in the GDR" (cited in *Die Welt*, 1990a), planning on a "massive investment program" for years to come (*Süddeutsche Zeitung*, 1990). "Axel Springer's internationalization", claims József Bayer, CEO of Axel Springer-Budapest in 1990, "began in Hungary" (Huth, 2019). The early setup of an office in Budapest was soon followed by the company's eastward expansion (Röper, 2006). Thereby, as Axel Springer CEO Peter Tamm put it, the publishing house was confident that it could "rely on market mechanisms" (cited in *Süddeutsche Zeitung*, 1990). His trust was not broken—with lasting consequences. "In total," concluded German media researcher Horst Röper in 2006, "German media companies are the leading media providers in almost every Eastern European transforming state" (p. 11). The question is how this dominance came about in the first place.

Based on extensive archival research, this chapter shows how early developments in the GDR set a strong precedent for press transitions in other CEE countries. As early as November 1989, West German economic groups shaped East German press reform by building market structures to their interest. They thereby hampered a profound structural change. East Germany then became the point of entry for various West German publishing houses, in particular Axel Springer, Bertelsmann, and the WAZ-Group, to other Eastern European markets. This chapter looks at the case of Hungary, which—like the GDR— became an early entrance point for major Western publishing houses. These corporations, also like in the GDR, soon took leading market positions and shaped the reform of the press to their advantage—generally in close relation with (former) political elites. Thus, while the initial goal of oppositional groups in both countries had been to break structural press monopolies, these corporations simply took them over or created new ones. This happened either because of insufficient regulatory means or because of intertwined political interests. These market strategies than impeded exactly those voices that had brought about democratic change.

The German Democratic Republic

In November 1989, hundreds of thousands of East Germans went to the streets protesting state repression, demanding free and democratic media. These protests brought down the Berlin Wall and set off a wave of progressive reforms, including in the media sector. Here, the reform goal was to break the information monopoly of the Socialist Unity Party (SED), which held about 70 percent of the newspaper production of the GDR (Tröger, 2019a).

On February 5, 1990, the Act on Freedom of Opinion, Information, and Media was passed. It prohibited censorship and declared the press to be free from political and economic monopolization. Every person and legal entity in the GDR had the right to publish, print, and distribute media (ibid.). This was followed by an explosion of newspaper startups: 16 new newspapers were founded at the beginning of February 1990 alone. Some were local initiatives of East German journalists and citizens, others were created in cooperation with publishers of the Federal Republic of Germany (FRG). By July 1990, about 100 new newspapers had been founded in a country with only 17 million people. Newspapers stood for democratic participation, diversity, and freedom of expression (Tröger, 2018, p. 65ff.).

In the meantime, established party newspapers (i.e. those of the SED) also claimed their political independence and went through internal reforms. The overall aim was to find new models of journalism and ownership. For that, by April 1990, three different institutions dealt exclusively with the reform of the GDR media: the non-partisan grassroots Media Control Council (MKR), the Ministry of Media Policy (MfM) created after the first free election on March 18, 1990, and the Committee for Press and Media of the People's Chamber. Media Minister Gottfried Müller emphasized that it was no solution to "simply adopt or imitate Western models and concepts" (cited in Wienert, 1990). Instead, new ways needed to be found and media freedom to be built domestically.

When on October 3, 1990, the GDR joined the Federal Republic, however, East Germany took over the media and press system of the FRG While much has been written about German unification, the interim period (November 1989 until October 1990), with its reform goals and struggles, has fallen out of history. This negligence is particularly surprising with regard to the media because the unification of press market far preceded Germany's political one.

A Market-Driven Press Reform

West German media corporations had begun to explore the East German market as early as November 1989. Already in December 1989, West German publishers started distributing their publications in the GDR, and by early March sporadic sales had turned into mass exports. As early as February 1990, the West German Ministry of the Interior (BMI) admitted, there was a need for regulation: taxes were not paid, prices not fixed. The BMI, however, "explicitly endorsed" these "activities of publishers in legal gray areas" (cited in Tröger, 2018, p. 254). It aimed at securing the flow of information for the first free GDR-election in March 1990, heavily financed by West German partisan interests. This laid the political foundation for a press transition shaped by West German corporate interests (Tröger, 2019b).

On March 5, 1990, the major publishing houses Axel Springer, Burda, Bauer, and Gruner + Jahr (G.+J., a subsidiary of the Bertelsmann media corporation) started systemic press imports. They single-handedly installed their own proprietary system. Dividing the GDR into four zones of distribution, the "Big Four" jointly distributed mainly their own publications, flooding the East German market. Illegal according to federal law, this scheme began only two weeks before the GDR population was to elect a new government, which left the interim government unable to act. Attempts at regulation were rejected or ignored (ibid., pp. 103–262).

The situation intensified shortly after the election when West German publishers aimed at gaining a competitive advantage by the use of predatory pricing to win future readers. This put additional pressures on East German newspapers, which struggled with outdated printing facilities, paper scarcity, and unreliable distribution infrastructures. When, on April 1, 1990 the GDR also ended press subsidies, most East German newspapers doubled or triple their prices and quickly turned to advertising for additional revenue, which made necessary West German expertise. This created early dependencies of the East German press (ibid., 86ff.).

By May 1990, almost all East German newspapers stood in joint venture negotiations with West German publishing houses. Their prime investment objects were the 14 former SED local newspapers, quasi-monopolies in their respective regions with extremely high circulation rates and unbroken structural privileges (i.e. paper, resources, etc.). "For weeks now, there has been a never ending stream of major publishing houses" aiming to secure their shares, wrote the union magazine *journalist* in May 1990 (cited in Tröger, 2018, p. 339). Officially, the negotiating parties closed agreements of intent. In reality, however, they put in place business relations that ranged from the acquisition of advertising, to the printing of newspapers in the FRG, to equity investments by the West German partners.

It was only in April 1991 when these joint ventures were turned into binding legal contracts by the trust agency (Treuhandanstalt, THA) administered by the German government. In doing so, the THA handed unaltered, former state press monopolies to major West German publishers, which soon further consolidated the East German market (Tröger, 2019a). The THA did this because it had little choice. The GDR market had been divided amongst corporate interests by May 1990. The regulatory means of the THA did not match economic realities and the BMI decided not to extend its political tasks to ensure press diversity by means of ownership policies.

The result was press concentration: of 120 new newspapers that had been founded in 1990 in the GDR, in November 1992, about 50 newspapers from about 35 publishers were left. To historian Konrad Dussel (2004), it was the consequence of the federal government's decision "against any experiment" (p. 245). Its price was the death of the newspapers. A sovereign East German press never developed.

Consequences for the Privatization of the Press in Central and Eastern Europe

Already in April 1990, the newly founded Association of Newspaper and Magazine Publishers of the GDR was pleading with publishers across Europe. They needed to take seriously concerns of market domination by the Big Four in the GDR "in their own interest, because in the next months to come, significant decisions are being made in the GDR for a future of a common Europe" (Verband der Zeitungs- und Zeitschriftenverleger der DDR, 1990). That same month, Springer announced it had taken over five out of 19 county newspapers in Hungary. Springer, however, was "not the only western media multi joining the Hungarian media circus," wrote the German newspaper *die tageszeitung* (1990a). Across Central and Eastern Europe, other Western media corporations, such as the WAZ-Group, the Mirror Group, or Hersant, followed.

Ágnes Gulyás (2000) has shown how, in a process frequently described as "self-privatization," most newspapers in Hungary were sold to multinational investors such as Bertelsmann, Hersant, and Springer. Already by the end of 1991, foreign press ownership reached 70 percent, and especially tabloid newspapers skyrocketed (p. 111ff, also Sükösd, 2000, Bajomi-Lázár, 2003). Also in Bulgaria, as Dobreva, Voltmer, and Pfetsch (2001) have shown, "[t]he media market underwent a rapid process of ownership concentration and many of the small outlets fell victim to economic pressure" (p. 179). In particular, the West German WAZ-Group managed to become so influential that "it forced local authorities to turn a blind eye at its obviously illegal monopoly on the market (owning a share of over 70%, whereas regulation puts a cap on 35%)" (ibid.). Also the Czechoslovakian media market was saturated by June 1990. More than 200 new newspapers and magazines had been registered with the Ministry of Culture in the Czech part alone. According to the news agency d.p.a. (1990), "especially local papers and political magazines had sprung up like mushrooms."[2] Ludmilla Stratecna, chief editor of the newspaper *Obzory* (*Horizons*), however, underlined that newspaper startups in Czechoslovakia were extremely difficult: paper scarcity and outdated printing technology made it almost impossible to compete with established party papers (in Licht, 1990) and those were bought up by multinational investors. Also in Lithuania and Estonia, "economic logics" soon became the driving force in press production and in matters of representation. A liberal market soon replaced concerns over censorship and political control with rapid financial gains and new criteria of news production (Balčytienė, 2006, 2011, Balčytienė & Lauk, 2005).

In Poland where, in February 1989, round table negotiations had started an unprecedented political transformation, privatization was administered by state institutions. Policies, however, lacked antitrust legislation and set no limitations on foreign ownership. Foreign acquisitions of newspapers and their mergers followed quickly (Bajomi-Lázár et. al., 2020). In particular Axel Springer found a strong foothold but also the French media giant Hersant entered the market. By May 1990, both corporations had had several exploratory talks, made declarations of intent, and closed deals. Hersant aimed not only to buy shares in exiting newspapers but, according to insiders in Warsaw, wanted "to enter big" (cited in *die tageszeitung*, 1990b)—with its own product range of newspapers and magazines. Accordingly, Bajomi-Lázár et. al. (2020) show that foreign owners generally "tended to 'clone' and bring to Poland products that had met commercial success in their respective countries" (p. 292). This was true also for other CEE markets, where according to media researcher Beate Schneider in 1992, "there is a tendency towards standardization" (Protocol, 1992, p. 4).

These processes went with such speed that it was impossible to keep track of them, not to speak of developments in neighboring countries. As one East German reporter put it in 1990, "in spite of international communication we know little of each other, we often have an unclear and distorted image of our neighbors' [media] problems" (cited in Licht, 1990). Jakubowicz and Sükösd (2008) argue that common to all post-socialist media systems, however, were processes of "demonopolization and (partial) remonopolization" as well as "commerzialization and marketization" (p. 16). These posses the authors argue, were necessary for other reforms to happen, such as democratization, pluralization, and professionalization (ibid.). This chapter argues differently. It shows how remonopolization and commerzialization came with a price, and this price was the loss of a democratic (grassroots) turn and a profound structural change in the media and press landscapes.

Reform of the Newspaper Industry in Hungary

In Hungary, press reform began as early as June 1989 when the last Communist government issued a decree abolishing licensing imposed upon print media. In consequence, thousands of new titles entered the market. In 1989 alone, 1,118 new publications were registered (Bajomi-Lázár, 2005).

By June 1990, there were about 2,000 newspapers, which made Hungary's press "extremely colourful" (*Mitteldeutsche Neuste Nachrichten*, 1990). Structurally, however, newspapers suffered from poor technological equipment and a shortage of money and other resources. Foreign capital became the early key for reform.

While the country had loosened its restrictions for foreign investments in the late 1980s, Antal Reger, a chief editor at the Hungarian Broadcasting Station, underlined that foreign investors were particularly fast in the press and media sector (in Licht, 1990). Already by March 1990, major media corporations such as the News Corporation owned by Rupert Murdoch, Axel Springer, and the Mirror Group Newspapers (Robert Maxwell) had acquired shares in different newspapers—the three were aiming to outpace one another: Maxwell had bought 40 percent of the country's fourth largest daily and former government organ *Magyar Hírlap* (*Hungarian Newspaper*) in February 1990 (*die tageszeitung*, 1990a). Murdoch had acquired 50 percent of the Reform Publishing House in January 1990, including a film magazine, a fashion magazine, a Hungarian press review, and the magazine *Reform*. The latter, founded in November 1988 with an initial circulation of 170,000 copies, was a tabloid paper that featured politically controversial stories in high-quality print. Its initial success, wrote *die tageszeitung* (1990a), had been "overwhelming. Each edition was completely sold out after a few hours; photocopies of 'Reform' were soon traded for horrendous prices." By March 1990, with the financial help of Murdoch, its circulation had climbed to 400,000 copies (ibid.). In addition, by March 1990, Murdoch had bought 50 percent of the afternoon daily *Mai Nap* (*Today*). The newspaper had launched in spring 1989 with a circulation of 100,000 copies. It had proved successful, in that the circulation rate of its direct competitor *Esti Hírlap* (*Evening Newspaper*) had dropped from 163,000 in January 1989 to 100,000 one year later (ibid.). Eventually, Maxwell bought 40 percent of *Esti Hírlap*, while *Mai Nap*—under Murdoch—held shares in Hungary's first commercial television station Nap TV and published a woman's magazine (ibid.; *Die Welt*, 1990b).

These examples only point to two broader developments: First, they sketch the competitive run of Western investors in the Hungarian press market. Second, they show that—like in the GDR— while politically the reorganization of Hungary's media was to be implemented by means of a media and information law, it practically took place as a market-driven reform intertwined with political interests. This was particularly true for Axel Springer.

Axel Springer

"Only because communism has been overthrown, we will not put up a sign saying 'Springer land' at the border" (cited in *die tageszeitung*, 1990c). This statement came from Dr. Péter Molnár, secretary of the Hungarian parliament committee for the privatization of the Hungarian press in April 1990. It was preceded by "one of the biggest media transactions in Eastern Europe" (*die tageszeitung*, 1990d) at the time, which major Hungarian news outlets simply named the "Springer scandal" (cited in *Berliner Zeitung*, 1990).

Already in February 1990, József Bayer had opened a Springer office in Hungary's capital Budapest, soon with a 70 percent holding of Axel Springer Germany (Huth, 2019). While Axel Springer-Budapest initially aimed for a joint venture with *Reform* (the magazine that was eventually bought by Murdoch), it soon changed direction toward the mass market. According to the oppositional Alliance of Free Democrats[3] in May 1990, Springer-Budapest aimed at taking over six county newspapers, five weeklies, ten city papers and more than 40 company newspapers, as well as several magazines and other publications (in *Berliner Zeitung*, 1990). By then, the publisher had already administered at least five of these take-overs. This, the Alliance argued, went against the material interests of the country. In an emergency motion, it demanded an "examination of Springer practices" (cited in ibid.) and asked for an investigation committee; its secretary became Dr. Péter Molnár.

According to Molnár, Springer's plans were legally and ethically questionable (in *die tageszeitung*, 1990c). The publisher's main targets were the former socialist county (megye) newspapers. Formerly independent, these newspapers had been taken over by the Communist Party (later Socialist Party) in the 1950s. Since the party had prohibited competing newspapers, these county newspapers had turned into profitable local monopolies (Bajomi-Lázár 2003, 2005). With the shifting political conditions and growing financial troubles of the Socialist Party in 1990, however, their financial stability was also in jeopardy. Springer wanted to claim them by means of a "legal trick" (*Mitteldeutsche Neuste Nachrichten*, 1990):

According to Hungarian antitrust law, anyone could establish (not buy) and distribute newspapers. In early 1990, Springer, thus, offered the six county newspapers with the highest circulation rates (between 50,000 and 90,000 copies) the opportunity to come out as "brand new newspapers" (cited in *die tageszeitung*, 1990c). They were to keep their editorial staff and printing houses. Subsequently, in April 1990, claiming their independence from the Socialist Party, these newspapers then simultaneously signed with Springer. Shortly after, they were renamed. These transfers, the Free Democrats claimed, had been "prepared and technically administered" by the Socialist Party (in *Berliner Zeitung*, 1990). József Bayer, CEO of Springer-Budapest, however, insisted in May 1990:

> We founded new newspapers, we did not buy old ones! In the end, the staff quit and joined us thereafter. And since no one was left to continue publishing the old newspapers, all subscriptions and advertising deals now fall to us.
>
> *(Cited in ibid.)*

This deal, Bayer emphasized, was a win-win situation. Springer was also to invest in printing technology and journalists did not fear for their jobs, because "[i]f you want to expand, you need staff!" (cited in ibid.). All Springer asked of its new employees was what it asked of all its journalists: a commitment to a democratic constitutional order, to the social market economy, and the rejection of any kind of totalitarianism.

Public responses ranged from admiring this "brilliant business trick" to warnings of a "clearance sale" in "Wild-East Hungary" to accusations of "fraud" (cited in *Mitteldeutsche Neuste Nachrichten*, 1990). The explosive nature of the deal was further increased by several oppositional groups insisting that the county newspapers were state *not* party property. Because the newspapers had been appropriated illegally in the 1950s, the party did not have the right of disposal. They asked the government for an "immediate moratorium for preserving communist property" (cited in *die tageszeitung*, 1990d). This did not stop Springer, however. In June 1990, it acquired its seventh county newspaper, *Somogyl Hírlap*, and became the publisher with the highest circulation rate in Hungary.

In response, the Association of Hungarian Newspaper Publishers protested against the "growing dependence on foreign capital" (cited in *Berliner Zeitung*, 1990) while the steering committee of the Journalist Association was concerned about "the partly unclear circumstance of the Springer takeover" (ibid.). What needed to be investigated were the links between the publisher and the Socialist Party. According to the party's treasurer András Fabriczki, a former classmate of Springer CEO, Bayer, this demand was an "impertinence" (cited in *die tageszeitung*, 1990c). To Molnár, however, it was "illicit to replace functions of a market economy with secrets pacts between former schoolmates" (ibid.). His committee, he underlined, was not against the privatization of the press but the Socialist Party had "made a pact with Springer" (ibid.) and that worked against market principles.

Bertelsmann & Co.

Other West German publishing groups also entered the Hungarian market. The business paper *Handelsblatt* made capital investments in the business paper *Világgazdaság* (*Global Economy*). Starting in June 1990, a license agreement gave *Világgazdaság* also secondary publication rights to help the developing market economy (*textintern*, 1990a). Likewise a subsidiary of Burda—World Wide

Advertising Burda—took over the advertising acquisition for the economic magazine *hvg* (Heti Vilaggazdasag) (*textintern*, 1990b).

By August 1, 1990, the German-based transnational Bertelsmann media corporation also entered the Hungarian market. It acquired 41 percent of the *Nepszabadzag* (*People's Freedom*), a "big fish" amongst Hungarian newspapers (*die tageszeitung*, 1990e). The former central organ of the Communist Party and leading daily in the country had a circulation of 360,000 copies. Initially, the newspaper had held talks with the German publishing group of the *Neue Westfälische* and had almost closed a deal in May 1990. This was when Bertelsmann "offered conditions favorable to the Hungarian side" (*Frankfurter Allgemeine Zeitung*, 1990) and bought shares for about US$ 2.5 million in the publishing house Hirlapkiado. Next to *Nepszabadzag*, Hirlapkiado published several dailies and magazines and had a total capital share of about US$ 6 million divided amongst Hungarian shareholders (e.g., banks, a book publisher, etc.). Bertelsmann brought in expertise in marketing and, above all, offered financial security in a media market that, according to the other shareholders, was defined by "aggressive foreign investors" (cited in ibid.; see also *die tageszeitung*, 1990e). To Bertelsmann, however, this was just the first step: it planned on establishing its book and music clubs, and on acquiring substantial shares in the broadcasting sector, and it was to succeed (Becker, 2017).

Conclusion

Though the specifics and outcomes differed by country with regard to the privatization of press markets or their levels of corruption, common to all press transitions in CEE countries was the implementation of the Western free-press model, the overall penetration of Western market interests and their products, and considerable foreign ownership and high market concentration. Here, the GDR and Hungary were prime examples for how transnational Western media corporations became the driving force behind early press reforms in 1989/1990. Though the spectrum of problems documented in this chapter sketched only a fraction of the larger transitional shifts, it has shown how the eastward expansion of Western corporate-commercial interests set early market-based limitations to what was politically possible. This was also because the introduced market logics to a centralized press left little room for competing ideas of a free press.

The GDR's unique geographic location, its sociopolitical proximity to the FRG, and the early interest of the federal government in German unification set the political frame for a market-driven take-over of the East German press by West German publishers. Therefore, it were not simple market forces that worked in favor of West German publishers, but it was the political will of the federal government that enabled them. This set the preconditions for the expansion of West German major publishing houses to other CEE markets. Hungary, with its early introduction of a multi-party system and liberalization of its economy, received help from the EC, which—in return—loosened restrictions on trade and taxes while offering financial help. Thus, Hungary opened its borders to foreign investors who soon invested heavily in the press market. Also this market-driven press reform happened within a set political frame. Here, the former state party prevented a bottom-up press reform by means of re-assigning its former press monopolies to Western economic interests (i.e., Axel Springer). Thus, the collaboration of West German media corporations with former party papers, and the take-over of former party monopolies for market means became a defining feature of the press reform in East Germany and Hungary.

This chapter has shown that nothing that happened in Central and Eastern Europe before, during, and after the post-socialist transition happened in isolation. Instead, CEE countries became battle grounds for various interests groups, East and West, but with strong influences of Western economic groups that shaped media reform according to their interests. These groups expanded and continued their long-established interests and disputes onto newly opened political arenas and economic markets. Thus, ideas and initiatives of how to rethink a free press based on socialist experiences were overrun, which made this period a lost window of opportunity. And this is where the free-press-paradox pointed at by the EP in 1992 worked against the interests of competing voices that make for a viable democracy. In the case of East Germany and Hungary, it did not break structural press monopolies but only changed their political justification.

Notes

1 Note: Current comparative studies document concentration processes and strong commercialization tendencies in different CEE media markets and their difference with regard to political cultures.
2 Until 1989, the whole country had had a total of 35 newspapers and magazines.
3 The second strongest parliamentary faction of the newly elected Hungarian parliament.

References

Balčytienė, A. (2006). *Mass Media in Lithuania: Changes, Development, and Journalism Culture*, Berlin: Vistas.
Balčytienė, A. (2011). Lithuania: Mixed Professional Values in a Small and Highly Blurred Media Environment. In J. Trappel, H. Nieminen, & L. Nord (eds.). *Media for Democracy Monitor: Leading News Media Compared*, pp. 175–203, Nordicom.
Balčytienė, A., & Lauk, E. (2005). Media Transformations: The Post-Transition Lesson in Lithuania and Estonia. In: *Informacijos Mokslai*, 33, pp. 96–110.
Balčytienė, A., & Vinciūnienė, A. (2014). Older and Newer Media in Transitional Democracies: Similarities and Differences in Media Functions and Patterns of Use, in I. Reifova, & T. Pavlickova, (eds.). *Working Title: CEECOM 2012 conference papers*, pp. 14–20. Cambridge Scholars Publishing.
Bajomi-Lázár, P. (2003). Freedom of the Media in Hungary, 1990–2002. PhD thesis. Central European University, Budapest.
Bajomi-Lázár, P. (2005). The Business of Ethics, the Ethics of Business. Hungary. Sajtószabadság Központ. Available online: http://sajtoszabadsag.mediakutato.hu/publikaciok/files/business_of_ethics.doc [May 10, 2020].
Bajomi-Lázár, P., Balčytienė, A., Dobreva, A., & Klimkiewicz, B. (2020). History of the Media in Central and Eastern Europe. In K. Arnold, P. Preston, & S. Kinnebrock (eds.). *The Handbook of European Communication History*, pp. 277–298, Hoboken, N.J.: Wiley.
Becker, J. (2017). Bertelsmann SE & Co. In B. Birkinbine, R. Gomez & J. Wasko (Eds.), Global Media Giants (pp. 144–162). New York: Routledge.
Berliner Zeitung (1990). Husarenritt durch Lücken im ungarischen Gesetzwerk. May 23, 1990.
Die Tageszeitung (1990a). Multis erobern Ungarns Medienmarkt. March 24, 1990.
Die Tageszeitung (1990b). Medienzaren in Polen. May 25, 1990.
Die Tageszeitung (1990c). Der Pakt mit Springer. July 11, 1990.
Die Tageszeitung (1990d). Ungarn—Springerland? June 4, 1990.
Die Tageszeitung (1990e). KP-Zeitung bei Bertelsmann. August 1, 1990.
Die Welt (1990a). Axel Springer Verlag mir Rekordinvestitionen. June 14, 1990.
Die Welt (1990b). [no title], May 22, 1990.
Dobek-Ostrowska, B., & Głowacki, M. (2001). *Making democracy in 20 years. Media and politics in Central and Eastern Europe*, Wydawnictwo Uniwersytetu Wrocławskiego.
Dobreva, A., Voltmer, K. & Pfetsch, B. (2001). Trust and Mistrust on Yellow Brick Road. Political Communication Culture in Post-Communist Bulgaria. In B. Dobek-Ostrowska & M. Głowacki (eds.). *Making democracy in 20 years. Media and politics in Central and Eastern Europe*, pp. 171–191. Wydawnictwo Uniwersytetu Wrocławskiego.
D.p.a. (1990). Medienmarkt in der CSFR explodiert. June 26, 1990, IISH/ID-Archive MKR, File 35f.
Dussel, K. (2004). *Deutsche Tagespresse im 19. und 20. Jahrhundert*. Münster.
European Parliament (1992). Session documents: Bericht des Ausschusses für Kultur, Jugend, Bildung und Medien über Medienkonzentration und Meinungsvielfalt, A3-0153/91, PE 152.265/endg., Europäisches Parlament, April 27, 1992, p. 13, Archiv des Liberalismus, FDP Medienkommission/24548.
Frankfurter Allgemeine Zeitung (1990). Bertelsmann beteiligt sich an Nepszabadzag. August 1, 1990.
Gulyás, Á. (2000). The development of the Tabloid Press in Hungary. In C. Sparks & J. Tulloch (eds.). *Tabloid Tales. Global Debates over Media Standards*, pp. 111–127. Lanham, MD: Rowman and Littlefield Publishers.
Hrvatin, S.B., & Petković, B. (eds.) (2004). *Media Ownership and Its Impact on Media Independence and Pluralism*. Peace Institute.
Huth, P. (2019). There was no business plan. *a_inside*, October 9, 2019. Available online www.axelspringer.com/en/tag/hungary [January 10, 2020].

Jakubowicz, K. (2001). Rude Awakening: Social and Media Change in Central and Eastern Europe. In: *the public*, 8/4, pp. 59–80.

Jakubowicz, K., & Sükösd, M. (2008). *Finding the Right Place on the Map. Central and Eastern European Media in a Global Perspective*. Intellect Books.

Klimkiewicz, B. (2009). Structural Media Pluralism and Ownership Revisited. The Case of Central and Eastern Europe. *Journal of Media Business Studies*, 6/3, pp. 43–62.

Licht, S. (1990, August 14). Ausgeprägte Verhaltensmuster müssen überwunden werden. *Neue Zeit*.

Mappes-Niediek, N. (2003). *Balkan-Mafia Staaten in der Hand des Verbrechens. Eine Gefahr für Europa*. Berlin: Ch. Links Verlag.

Mattelart, A. (1994). *Mapping World Communication*. Minneapolis: University of Minnesota Press, vii.

McChesney, R. & Schiller, D. (2003). The Political Economy of International Communications. Foundations for the Emerging Global Debate about Media Ownership and Regulation. Technology, Business and Society Programme, United Nations Research Institute for Social Development, Paper Number 11, October 2003. Available online: www.unrisd.org/80256B3C005BCCF9/(httpAuxPages)/c9dcba6c7db78c2ac1256bdf00 49a774/$file/mcchesne.pdf [October 10, 2020].

Mitteldeutsche Neuste Nachrichten (1990). Springer—Zeitungshai der Spitze. June 21, 1990.

Protocol (1992). Protokoll der 4. Sitzung des F.D.P. Medienbeirats am 20./21. November 1992 in Halle, Archiv des Liberalismus, FDP Medienkommission/24548.

Röper, H. (2006). Expansion in Osteuropa. *Menschen Machen Medien. Medienpolitische ver.di-Zeitschrift*, 7-8/6, 55, pp. 8–13.

Schiller, H. (1969). *Mass Communication and the American Empire*. New York: Augustus. M. Kelley Publishers.

Sturm, R., Muller, M.M., & Dieringer, J. (2000). Economic transformation in Central and Eastern Europe: towards a new regulatory regime?. In: *Journal of European Public Policy*, 7/4, pp. 650–662.

Süddeutsche Zeitung (1990). Im Medienmarkt werden die Karten neu gemischt. June 15, 1990.

Sükösd, M. (2000). Democratic Transition and the Mass Media in Hungary: From Stalinism to Democratic Consolidation. In G. Richard & A. Mugham (eds.). *Democracy and the Media. A Comparative Perspective*, pp. 122–164, Cambridge University Press.

Tagesspiegel (1990). Internationales Presseinstitut begrüßt freie Presse im Osten. May 10, 1990.

Textintern (1990a). Handelsblatt schliesst [sic] Lizenzvereinbarung mit Ungarn. No. 53, May 30, 1990.

Textintern (1990b). Ungarns Wirtschaftsblatt offen für westliche Inserenten. No 55/56, June 7, 1990, p. 4.

The Economist (1991). Eastern Europe's Newspapers: The Lure of Ink. April 20, 1991, p. 70.

Tröger, M. (2019a). Die Treuhandanstalt und die Privatisierung der DDR-Presse. In: *Aus Politik und Zeitgeschichte*. Bundesamt für politische Bildung, 35/37, pp. 34–39.

Tröger, M. (2019b). *Pressefrühling und Profit. Wie westdeutsche Verlage 1989/1990 den Osten eroberten*. Köln.

Tröger, M. (2018). *On unregulated Markets and the Freedom of Media. The Transition of the East German Press after 1989*. PhD thesis. University of Illinois at Urbana-Champaign.

Tunstall, J. (1977). *The media are American*. New York: Columbia University Press.

Verband der Zeitungs- und Zeitschriftenverleger der DDR (1990). Offener Brief. April 22, 1990, IISH/ID-Archive MKR, Box 1–4, File 1.

Voltmer, K. (ed.) (2005). *Mass Media and Political Communication in New Democracies*. London & New York: Routledge.

Wienert, K. (April 27, 1990). DDR-Minister will erst "hören und lernen". *Berliner Morgenpost*.

28

CULTURAL POLITICS OF GLOBAL ONLINE SUBSCRIPTION VIDEO-ON-DEMAND SERVICES IN CANADA

A Case Study of Netflix Canada

Taeyoung Kim

Introduction

The rise of online subscription video-on-demand (henceforth SVOD) businesses saw fundamental changes in the distribution practices of global media industries. SVOD involves "streaming," where media products are converted into digital codes and transmitted through high-speed internet and wireless communications, removing the need for physical platforms such as DVDs and video players (Evens & Donders, 2018). Indeed, US-based SVOD businesses such as Netflix and Amazon Prime interrupted the existing distribution systems of the film and television industries, where distributors delivered completed media goods from their production sites to aggregators who made such goods available to audiences (Jenner, 2016; Havens & Lotz, 2017). By bypassing barriers that interfered with content distribution, such as domestic regulations and technological standards, media products are now circulated worldwide to audiences through SVOD platforms.

The presence of US-led SVOD services in the Canadian mediascape is significant. After gaining success in the US market, Netflix began its SVOD service in Canada in 2010 as its first international market. The company's entry into the Canadian market became a sensation among Canadian audiences. As of 2016, Netflix benefited to the tune of $766 million, reflecting 70.8% of the nation's SVOD market revenue. Compared to 2012, when it earned $156 million in Canada, this was a five-fold increase (Taras, 2015; CRTC, 2017). The rise of Netflix's SVOD service caused upheaval in Canada's media industries. Given that much of the nation's broadcasting industry consists of several broadcasters cross-owned by telecommunication conglomerates including Bell, Rogers, and Quebecor Media, whose programming had been dependent on popular US television series, the entry of Netflix and other US-based SVOD services threatened the position of these conglomerates in the industry (Winseck, 2010; Taras, 2015). To maintain their presence in this burgeoning market, these companies introduced their SVOD platforms, although most of them were unsuccessful; more than half of the nation's Anglophone population subscribe to Netflix over local SVOD platforms (Taras, 2015; Lotz, 2018; Robertson, 2017, October 20; Statista, 2019). Such a high market share for this platform has reignited worries about the US' cultural invasion into Canada's cultural politics, which has been a longstanding issue throughout the country's history.

Despite concerns over Netflix's presence in the domestic market, different voices interpret Netflix as a partner for Canadian producers to globalize their content. For example, the Canadian Broadcasting Corporation (CBC), the nation's public broadcaster, began to distribute its titles such as *Intelligence, Kim's Convenience,* and *Anne with an E* to foreign markets—including the UK and the US—through Netflix as part of its globalization strategy. Moreover, as SVOD and its affordances of on-demand access, customized schedules, and engagement behaviors such as binge-watching transform the nature of television production and consumption, Canadian producers have no choice but to work with these online platforms to survive in the market (Lotz, 2018). Considering this, the Canadian government has provided benefits—including an exemption from charging goods and service tax (GST)—to Netflix in the expectation of its investment in Canadian content. Indeed, in return for the government's tax benefits, Netflix announced a $500-million investment plan to the Canada Media Fund (CMF) and other Canadian entrepreneurs over five years (2018–2022) to support Canadian film and television production. Granted, such exceptional measures in regulating this SVOD mogul at the federal level backfired, and several provinces including Québec responded by imposing their own provincial sales tax on Netflix starting in 2018 (Fletcher, 2017, October 3).

Controversies over Netflix's position in the Canadian mediascape raise several questions of how to interpret global SVOD services in the local context. In detail, how does this new platform interact with local characteristics? What are the characteristics of the relationship between this transnational online service and the domestic media landscape? As a case study of Netflix in Canada, this paper explores the characteristics of SVOD services by analyzing the catalogs of Netflix Canada. While the analysis focuses on the status of Canadian television programs on Netflix, it also explores the position of Canadian films in various international catalogs to cross-check the findings. Considering the roles and responses from local broadcasters and the Canadian government as major stakeholders in the nation's mediascape, the findings are expected to shed lights on the interactive dynamics of television landscapes in Canada in the era of SVOD that would reshape the nature of a key pillar in nation's cultural politics.

Methods

To understand the nexus of global platforms and local productions in online subscription video-on-demand services, this study analyzes catalogs of Netflix content as a primary source. In assessing distribution practices, many scholars have used schedules of television programs as indexes of broadcasting distribution that were available in newspapers or on the broadcaster's website (Williams, 2003). Concerning this, catalogs of SVOD platforms, which represent customized delivery of content, are one of the defining features of online subscription video-on-demand services (Lotz, 2017).

Since Netflix does not offer official catalogs for its content, this study uses several comparator websites including Netflixable[1], NewOnNetflix[2], Reelgood[3], Unogs[4], and What's New on Netflix[5] that introduce this SVOD service's collection unofficially and cross-checks each source to control reliability. In detail, this study focuses on which Canadian content—both films and television programs—is aggregated via Netflix, and employs unofficial Netflix catalogs of 24 countries.[6] This method—which uses unofficial archives and catalogs on the internet to investigate Netflix's collections—was already introduced by Lobato (2018) to analyze Netflix's content diversity. Based on the findings, it analyzes how various Canadian content is distributed through Netflix and the underlying dynamics that shape structured interactivity.

The Catalog of Netflix Canada: A Marginalized Position of Canadian Content

In recent years, the Canadian film and television industries have grown steadily, producing more than 700 television series and approximately 100 films per year. Even though the growth of these industries has been driven by outsourcing by Hollywood, including visual effects production and the utilization of Canadian cities and land as shooting locations as well as foreign investment, Canadian producers have strived to increase the amount of Canadian television series and films amongst the competition from the US industry.[7] Among Canadian content, the number of "online-first" productions— producers premiering their films and television series on certified online platforms including Netflix, not on broadcasters or in theaters—has been increased (Canadian MPA., 2018; 2019; 2020). Based on these facts, the following table 1 and table 2 explain how Canadian content is distributed through Netflix.

Overall, there are 29 Canadian television series and 73 films are available on Netflix's global catalogs. In terms of the company's Canadian catalog of 6,100 titles, there are only 29 Canadian films

Table 28.1 List of Canadian Television Content Aggregated via Netflix (as of September 2020, total 29 television series)[a]

Title	Genre	Available at
21 Thunder (2017, a CBC series)	Drama	Canada and 23 countries
Alias Grace (2017, a CBC series)	Drama	Canada and 23 countries
Anne with an E (2017–2019, a CBC series)	Drama	Canada and 23 countries
Backstage (2016–2017, Family Channel)	Drama	France, Germany, and 10 countries (except Canada)
Bitten (2016, Space)	Drama	France, Germany, and 23 countries (except Canada)
Bo on the Go! (2007–2011, a CBC series)	Cartoon	Israel, South Africa, and the US
Can You Hear me? (2018, a TéléQuébec series)★	Drama	Canada and 22 countries
Dragon's Den (2006–present, a CBC series)	Reality Show	Canada
Fangbone! (2016–2017, Family Chrgd)	Cartoon	France and 26 countries (except Canada)
Heartland (2017, a CBC series)	Drama	Canada and 16 countries
Heavy Rescue: 401 (2016–2017, Discovery Channel Canada and the Weather Channel Canada)	Reality Show	France and 28 countries (except Canada)
Highway thru Hell (2012, Discovery Channel Canada)	Reality Show	Australia and the UK
Inspector Gadget (2015, Teletoon)	Cartoon	France and 28 countries (except Canada)
Intelligence (2006–2007, a CBC series)	Drama	Canada and 5 countries
JPod (2008, a CBC series)	Sitcom	Australia and the UK
Justin Time (2016, Disney Channel Canada)	Cartoon	Canada and 22 countries
Kim's Convenience (2016–present, a CBC series)	Sitcom	Canada and 12 countries
Ma Gardienne est un Vampire (2011, Teletoon)★	Drama	France and 10 countries (except Canada)
Max and Ruby (2002, Treehouse)	Cartoon	Canada and 20 countries
Monster Math Squad (2012–2016, a CBC series)	Cartoon	Canada and 17 countries
My Perfect Landing (2020, Family Channel)	Drama	France and 18 countries (except Canada)
Oh No! It's an Alien Invasion (2014–2015, YTV)	Cartoon	France
Republic of Doyle (2010–2014, a CBC series)	Sitcom	Australia, India, UK, and US
Schitt's Creek (2015–present, a CBC series)	Sitcom	Canada and 5 countries
Strange Empire (2014–2015, a CBC series)	Drama	16 countries (except Canada)
The Next Step (2013, Family Channel)	Drama	Australia and 6 countries
Total Drama (2008, Teletoon)	Cartoon	Canada and 20 countries
Under Arrest (2016, KVOS-TV)	Reality Show	Canada and 16 countries
Workin' Moms (2018, a CBC series)	Sitcom	Canada

a ★ refers to French content.

Table 28.2 Canadian Films Distributed via Netflix (as of September 2020, total 73 films)[a]

Title	Genre	Accessible in
Across the Line (2015)	Drama	US
After the Ball (2015)	Comedy	India
American Hangman (2019)	Thriller	US
American Heist (2014)	Action	Canada and 7 countries
American Mary (2012)	Horror	Germany and Switzerland
Angels in the Snow (2015)	Drama	Hong Kong and 4 countries (except Canada)
Assault on Wall Street (2013)	Action	India
A Witches' Ball (2017)	Children	Canada and 31 countries
Bob's Broken Sleigh (2015)	Animation	Canada and 23 countries
Bon Cop, Bad Cop (2006)	Comedy	Canada and 31 countries
Bon Cop, Bad Cop 2 (2017)	Comedy	Canada and 31 countries
Braven (2018)	Thriller	Germany, Japan, and UK
Brick Mansions (2014)	Action	France and 5 countries (except Canada)
Bruno and Boots: Go Jump in the Pool (2016)	Drama	Canada and 26 countries
Bruno and Boots: The Wizzle War (2017)	Drama	Canada and 26 countries
Bruno and Boots: This Can't Be Happening at Macdonald Hall (2017)	Drama	Canada and 26 countries
Catwalk: Tales from the Cat Show Circuit (2018)	Documentary	France and 21 countries (except Canada)
Christmas Wedding Planner (2017) 18	Drama	Canada and 31 countries
Christmas with a View (2018)	Drama	Canada and 31 countries
Code 8 (2019)	Sci-fi	France, the Netherlands, and 19 countries
Cube (1997)	Indie	France and 8 countries (except Canada)
David Foster: Off the Record (2019)	Documentary	Australia, India, Japan, and UK
Goon (2011)	Comedy	Canada, UK
Goon: Last of the Enforcers (2016)	Comedy	Canada and 29 countries
Grave Encounters 2 (2012)	Thriller	Japan
Harvest Moon (2015)	Drama	Canada and 8 countries
Indian Horse (2017)	Drama	US
Into the Forest (2015)	Horror	US
Invisible Essence: The Little Prince (2018)	Documentary	Australia, France, UK, and US
I'll Be Home for Christmas (2016)	Drama	France and 20 countries (except Canada)
Jugaad (2017)	Documentary	Canada and 12 countries
Jusqu'au déclin (2019)★	Action	Canada and 31 countries
Kiss and Cry (2017)	Documentary	Canada and 31 countries
La légende de Sarlia (2013)★	Animation	Poland
Laurence Anyways (2012)	Drama	Korea
Les Affamés (2017)★	Horror	Canada and 26 countries
Long Time Running (2017)	Documentary	France and 30 countries (except Canada)
Love Jacked (2018)	Drama	France and 27 countries (except Canada)
Mean Dreams (2016)	Thriller	Czech Republic and the US
Michael Lost and Found (2017)	Documentary	Canada and 25 countries
Mission Kathmandu: The Adventures of Nelly and Simon (2017)	Animation	Argentina, Brazil, and Mexico
Mommy (2014)★	Drama	France
My Awkward Sexual Adventure (2012)	Comedy	Poland
My Life Without Me (2003)	Drama	Japan
October Gale (2014)	Indie	India
October Kiss (2015)	Drama	Canada and 9 countries

(continued)

Table 28.2 Cont.

Title	Genre	Accessible in
One Last Shot (1998)	Indie	Canada and 12 countries
Paper Year (2018)	Drama	US
Paranormal: White Noise (2017)	Thriller	UK
Perfect Sisters (2014)	Thriller	Germany and Switzerland
Playing Hard (2018)	Documentary	Canada and 31 countries
Punjab 1984 (2014)**	Drama	Canada and 26 countries
Romeo Ranjha (2014)**	Comedy	Canada and 9 countries
Room for Rent (2016) 36	Comedy	US
Rush: Beyond the Lighted Stage (2010)	Documentary	US and 8 countries
Serialized (2016)	Action	Germany, Switzerland
Spymate (2006)	Comedy	UK
Spookley the Square Pumpkin (2004)	Animation	Canada and 8 countries
Swearnet: The Movie (2014)	Comedy	Canada and 8 countries
The Accountant of Auschwitz (2018)	Documentary	France, Germany, and 29 countries (except Canada)
The Art of the Steal (2013)	Indie	Canada
The Body Remembers When the World Broke Open (2019)	Drama	Australia, UK, and US
The Captive (2014)	Thriller	Italy and Sweden
The Colony (2013)	Sci-fi	India
The Humanity Bureau (2018)	Sci-fi	UK
The New Romantic (2018)	Drama	US
There's Something in the Water (2019)	Documentary	Canada and 31 countries
Tom at the Farm (2013, French)	Indie	France
Transformer (2017)	Documentary	US
Trailer Park Boys: The Movie (2006)	Comedy	Canada and 15 countries
Turbo Kid (2015)	Action	France
What Keeps You Alive (2018)	Thriller	Australia and 7 countries (except Canada)
Why Knot (2016) 19	Documentary	Canada and 9 countries

a ★ refers to French-Canadian content and ★★ refers to Punjabi-Canadian content.

and 15 Canadian television series available, which is a highly marginalized outcome. In comparison to the amount of annual production of Canadian films and television programs, such a number indicates how this SVOD platform understands Canadian content in programming its catalog.

The lack of Canadian content promotion on Netflix is not, however, a new phenomenon; after Netflix launched its service in Canada, Miller and Rudniski (2012) found that the position of Canadian television series and films was highly marginalized in Netflix Canada's catalog, specifying that much of the programming was limited to content targeting family and children. In this regard, despite such a marginalized position in the catalog, there are several characteristics which reflect both Canadian media production and how Netflix employs Canadian films and television programs in its catalogs. In terms of television programs, the catalog continues to reinforce that CBC—including its French-language division Radio-Canada—continues to serve as a major distributor for Canadian producers in contrast to other private broadcasters whose programming depends on American content, even if many of CBC programs distributed through Netflix are produced by independent studios such as ITV Studios (*Schitt's Creek*) and Thunderbird Films (*Kim's Convenience*) (Taras, 2015). In addition to this, such a predominance of CBC content in Netflix's catalog reflects a close relationship between the broadcaster and this SVOD platform. Until recently, CBC co-produced several television series with Netflix, including *Anne with an E* (2017–2019) and *Alias Grace* (2017)—both television series based on Canadian original novels. Despite its criticism against the entry of US-led SVOD platforms that would fragment its advertising revenues and steal audiences from Canadian television, Netflix was understood as an important partner for CBC to reach global audiences and supply its production cost (CBC, 2017). For Netflix, CBC would be essential to diversify its distribution channel (Lobato, 2019).

Concerning Canadian television, another characteristic of Netflix Canada's catalog is a lack of French-language content. In previous years, Netflix offered several French-Canadian television series including *La théorie du K.O.* (2014–2015) and *Nouvelle Adresse* (2015) in its catalog. As of 2020, however, it discontinues distributing these and other French-Canadian content across the nation. On one hand, this may reflect the low number of Francophone subscribers in the nation compared to that of Anglophone subscribers across the nation.[8] On the other hand, this may indicate the strong presence of regional broadcasters like Radio-Canada and Videotron in the Francophone market that already provide streaming services with more French-language content (Ici.Tou.tv and illico.tv respectively).[9]

With this, cultural politics over official-language minorities is deeply related to the position of Netflix in Canada. Considering the history of disputes over cultural sovereignty of Québec and the Francophones, to promote and protect the production of French content held equal if not greater importance than their cultural identities for Francophone populations in Canada (Beauregard, 2018). In this regard, as long as that aggregation could be understood as the final stage of the distribution chain, the growing penetration of an Anglophone-dominated SVOD platform into the market could be an existential matter for Québécois as well as the Francophone population (Caldwell, 2008; Vonderau, 2015). This is well-exemplified by Québec's outrage at the Ministry of Canadian Heritage's decisions to forgive sales tax on Netflix since there was no guarantee of promoting French-language Canadian content in the platform (Hamilton, 2018, July 18). Thus, the marginalized position of Francophone Canadian content in Netflix Canada reflects the validity of some of the anxieties held by French language-speaking populations.

In terms of Netflix Canada's film collection, 18 out of 73 Canadian films distributed through Netflix are considered documentaries and independent movies. This reflects a tradition in Canadian media production that has focused on producing various genres of documentaries as part of developing authentic values of Canadian films and television, as the commercial market is already overwhelmed by imports from Hollywood (Hogarth, 2002). Considering the market power as well as capital strength and technological advantage of Hollywood films, Canadian films may not have competitive power in the market. As a consequence, in contrast to US commercial films, Canadian films began to represent various social movements including the New Left, the independence of Québec, feminists and queer activists, and immigrants (Druick, 2007). Indeed, public organizations like the National Film Board, which carries significant influence in film production, have supported Canadian filmmakers' efforts of diversification and their strategies to target niche markets. By emphasizing reality in its media products, Canadian films market themselves as more "memorable" films by focusing on short films and documentaries (Canada Media Fund, 2017, November 7).[10]

For Netflix, which has sought to diversify its catalog after major Hollywood studios suspended their license deals with the company, Canadian films were deemed as qualified resources to grow its catalog (Lobato, 2019). For years, the streaming platform has formed connections with Canadian producers through sponsoring the Toronto International Film Festival (TIFF), one of the largest events for Canadian filmmakers, leasing several film studio infrastructures in British Columbia and Ontario to shoot scenes of its film originals, and investing in funds designated for Canadian film production, etc. (Spangler, 2019; Friend, 2020). In addition to this, several Panjabi-language Canadian films like

Punjab 1984 and *Romeo Ranjha* could be beneficial for the company to attract audiences with a Panjabi background.

The Growing Presence of Netflix in Canadian Television and the State's Response

The findings from the catalog demonstrate how Canadian content is marginalized in a global SVOD platform's selection and how Netflix understands Canadian content in terms of providing local services. Contrary to expectations of the Canadian government and some industrial figures that Netflix would also benefit Canadian producers, the marginalized position of Canadian content in the catalog shows how this platform can reinforce preexisting imbalances in the nation's market, which is dominated by US cultural imports. Considering the position of television in Canadian cultural politics as the main medium for developing the nation's cultural identity through the production of Canadian content, the penetration of US SVOD services into Canadian households and the following decline of viewers of Canadian television is a matter of importance in the nation's entire mediascape (CBC, 2017). In response to this, CBC recently announced its intent to reconsider its partnership with Netflix, arguing that the relationship "hurt the long-term viability of our domestic industry (Benzine, 2019)". In this regard, understanding the state's response is crucial, as the Canadian government has recognized the position of Canadian television in the nation's cultural politics and is a major investor in producing Canadian films and television programs.

Throughout history, recognizing the film market would be overwhelmed by Hollywood commercial movies, Canadian bureaucrats expected television to be the main tool of developing a distinctive collective identity (Collins, 1990; Czach, 2010). In the belief that televisions would "bring Canadians together in sympathy and understanding" (The Royal Commission on National Development in the Arts, Letters, and Science, 1951, 49), they supported broadcasters to produce more Canadian content. In a similar vein, the state strived to protect the broadcasting market from its southern neighbor as it foresaw American television programs being a major threat to Canadian media and bureaucrats' efforts in constructing national identity. Thanks to support from the Canada Media Fund (CMF) and efforts from CBC and other Canadian broadcasters, the volume of Canadian television production has increased from 2,041 in 2009/2010 to 2,989 in 2016/2017. Overall, the amount of the nation's distributors' financing of Canadian films and television more than trebled from $155 million in 2009/2010 to $507 million in 2016/2017 (Canadian Media Producers Association (CMPA), 2020). In this context, the penetration of Netflix and other US SVOD services in the market would weaken not only Canadian broadcasters but also threaten the entire production chain of Canadian television.

While the power of SVOD services becomes more solid in the mediascape, the Canadian government's response to protect domestic players has been criticized as outdated and belated (CBC, 2017; Robertson, September 27, 2017; Benzine, 2019; CMPA., 2020). Much of this is based on the fact that foreign SVOD services are categorized as internet service providers, not as broadcasters, which makes them exempt from existing regulations. For instance, Netflix and US-based SVOD service providers are exempt from existing regulations over programming Canadian content. The recent arrangement of the United States-Mexico-Canada Trade Agreement (USMCA) and other multilateral trade pacts require the Canadian government to keep the internet, including SVOD businesses, open as part of "digital trade."[11] Although the government has strongly endorsed ideas of cultural exemption, where non-economic characteristics of cultural industries are intended to carry out the Canadian state's protectionist measures on imported cultural goods and services, such clauses on online goods and services that are built on the principles of free trade of online services and goods may challenge its arguments considering the digitalization of cultural industries (Goff, 2019).

In relation to this, the Canadian Radio-Television and Telecommunications Commission (CRTC)'s principles of net neutrality—"all traffic on the Internet should be given equal treatment by Internet providers with little to no manipulation, interference, prioritization, discrimination or preference given (CRTC, n.d.)"—also contribute to benefiting foreign SVOD platforms at the expense of undue effects on domestic internet service providers. Considering that Netflix's SVOD service is delivered through high-speed internet infrastructures managed by the aforementioned telecom vendors, such an outcome is paradoxical.

In sum, while domestic media companies are double bound to the principle of net neutrality and a series of television regulations, their American SVOD competitors enjoy the internet infrastructure with zero regulations (Gray & Lotz, 2012; CBC, 2017; Robertson, 2017, September 26). Meanwhile, the growing presence of Netflix in Canada in may worsen a structural asymmetry in cultural trade between Canada and the US by jeopardizing Canadian broadcasters and theaters which have functioned as outlets for Canadian media products.

Conclusion

In the digital media era, many countries have implemented various strategies to expand cultural exports to overturn their deficits in media markets dominated by US companies, but most of them were unsuccessful (Freedman, 2008). Despite their efforts, however, it becomes clear that more domestic markets become subject to the laissez-faire practices of US media conglomerates, a situation that has worsened since the development of several SVOD pioneers like Netflix. Thanks to the development of high-speed internet infrastructure and smart devices that bypass existing protectionist measures, providing a borderless environment for US media companies, Netflix and other US SVOD platforms have gained universal access to markets worldwide (Balbi & Magaudda, 2018; Elkins, 2018). The situation is not much different in Canada, as more than half of the population subscribe to Netflix and other foreign SVOD services and Canadian authorities continue to deregulate existing broadcasting regulations in the name of promoting convergence between broadcasters and telecommunications (Edge, 2011; Taras, 2015).

The findings of this analysis indicate that Netflix Canada's catalog represents distinctive characteristics of cultural politics in the nation. Most of all, it is evident the growing market power of SVOD businesses in Canada reinforces a structural asymmetry which has existed in the distribution of television and films in the domestic market. Along with their digital cutting-edge technologies, this reinforces the dominance of US capital in the market while outdated regulations fail to manage new SVOD service providers.

Of course, based on concerns, there are growing demands on regulating Netflix and other SVOD service providers from various stakeholders. Like Québec, several provinces are moving to impose an additional sales tax or value-added taxes—a so-called "Netflix Tax"—on Netflix's subscribers. In addition to this, major figures in the nation's media and telecommunication businesses, including Bell Media, CBC, and Corus Entertainment, have insisted the government solve reverse discrimination against domestic broadcasters and regulate foreign SVOD players (Benzine, 2019). Meanwhile, Canadian producers argue that these service providers should include more locally produced content in Netflix Canada's catalog (CMPA, 2020). In response to this, Netflix promises to customize its collections with local characteristics and invest in local content by financing original content from local productions, including its five-year $500 million investment in producing Canadian content. Moreover, the company announced its plan of investing $125 million in the production of French-language content. In spite of its commitments to Canadian cultural production, criticisms against this SVOD mogul over mistreating Canadian content continue to exist as the current catalog fails to represent Canadian content fairly with bypassing regulations on broadcasting Canadian content.

In this regard, although the market share of foreign SVOD players overwhelms that of local competitors and their collections neglect Canadian content, the tension between this global SVOD platform and local players over the nation's broadcasting market is still ongoing, which reflects cultural, economic, and political legacies in the nation's cultural politics. Considering the size of Canadian television businesses compared to their US competitors, the future of Canadian television may depend on how the government responds to Netflix and other foreign service providers as a regulator of the market and a longstanding patron of Canadian television production.

Notes

1 Netflixable provides catalogs of Netflix's 39 service regions. https://netflixable.com/
2 NewOnNetflix provides catalogs of Netflix Australia-New Zealand, Canada, UK, and the US https://newonnetflix.info/
3 Reelgood provides catalogs of US-based online streaming services as well as cable distributions. https://reelgood.com/source/netflix
4 Unog provides catalogs of Netflix's 24 service regions. https://unogs.com/
5 What's New on Netflix provides catalogs of Netflix's 30 countries such as Belgium, India, Norway, and Russia. https://whatsnewonnetflix.com/
6 This includes Canada and other countries such as Australia, Brazil, Czech Republic, France, Germany, Hong Kong, Hungary, India, Israel, Italy, Japan, Lithuania, Netherlands, Norway, Poland, Russia, Singapore, Slovakia, Spain, Sweden, Thailand, UK, and US
7 To categorize their products as "Canadian", producers are required to meet several criteria: the producer has to be Canadian; many of the key production functions requiring creativity, such as directing, music, photography, picture, and screenplay, should be performed by Canadians; at least three-fourths of the production cost should be paid for Canadian staffs, etc. (CRTC, 2016).
8 According to the CRTC (2017) survey, only 26% of Québec residents and 22% of the Francophone population subscribe to Netflix, much lower than in other provinces including Alberta (56%), British Columbia (50%), Saskatchewan (52%), Manitoba (53%), and Ontario (47%) as well as the nation's Anglophone population (50%).
9 In 2018, the Groupe V Média, National Film Board of Canada, and TV5 Québec agreed to add their Francophone content to the catalog of ICI.Tou.tv, a Francophone SVOD platform operated by Radio-Canada (Everlett-Green, 2018).
10 In terms of defining Canadian films, it does not include films that were outsourced from Hollywood, which has become a trend and accounts for 44.5% ($3.76 billion) of the total film and television production volume in 2017 (CMPA, 2018).
11 According to this trade pact, a digital product means "a computer program, text, video, image, sound recording, or other product that is digitally encoded, produced for commercial sale or distribution, and that can be transmitted electronically." Its Chapter 19 specifies parties should not impose discriminatory treatments or less-favorable measures on another party (USTR, 2018).

References

Balbi, G. & Magaudda, P. (2018). *A History of Digital Media: An Intermedia and Global Perspective*. New York, NY: Routledge.
Beauregard, D. (2018). *Cultural Policy and Industries of Identity: Québec, Scotland and Catalonia*. Cham: Palgrave Macmillan.
Benzine, A. (2019, October 8). "CBC will no longer work with Netflix to produce shows, says Catherine Tait". *Financial Post*. Retrieved from https://financialpost.com/telecom/media/cbc-will-no-longer-work-with-netflix-to-produce-shows-says-catherine-tait
Caldwell, J. (2008). *Production Culture: Industrial Reflexivity and Critical Practice in Film and Television*. Durham, N.C.: Duke University Press.
Canadian Broadcasting Corporation (2017). *A Creative Canada: Strengthening Canadian Culture in a Digital World*. Ottawa: Canadian Broadcasting Corporation.
Canada Media Fund (2017, November 7). "Back for more Canadian TV and films". Canada Media Fund. Retrieved from www.cmf-fmc.ca/en-ca/news-events/news/november-2017/back-for-more-canadian-tv-and-films
Canadian Media Producers Association (2018). Profile 2017: Economic Report on the Screen-Based Media Production Industry in Canada. Retrieved from https://cmpa.ca/wp-content/uploads/2018/02/Profile-2017.pdf

Canadian Media Producers Association (2019). Profile 2018: Economic Report on the Screen-Based Media Production Industry in Canada. Retrieved from https://cmpa.ca/wp-content/uploads/2019/03/Profile-2018.pdf

Canadian Media Producers Association (2020). Profile 2019: Economic Report on the Screen-Based Media Production Industry in Canada. Retrieved from https://cmpa.ca/wp-content/uploads/2020/04/CMPA_2019_E_FINAL.pdf

Canadian Radio-Telecommunication Commission (2016). So what makes it Canadian? Retrieved from https://crtc.gc.ca/eng/cancon/c_cdn.htm

Canadian Radio-Telecommunication Commission (2017). *Communications Monitoring Report 2017*. Ottawa: CRTC.

Canadian Radio-Telecommunications Commission (n.d.). Strengthening net neutrality in Canada. Retrieved from https://crtc.gc.ca/eng/internet/diff.htm

Collins, R. (1990). *Culture, Communication and National Identity: The Case for Canadian Television*. Toronto: University of Toronto Press.

Czach, L. (2010). The "turn" in Canadian television studies. *Journal of Canadian Studies*, 44(3), 174–180.

Druick, Z. (2007). *Projecting Canada: Government Policy and Documentary Film at the National Film Board*. Montreal & Kingston: McGill-Queen's University Press.

Edge, M. (2011). Convergence after the collapse: The "catastrophic" case of Canada. *Media, Culture & Society*, 33(8), 1266–1278.

Elkins, E (2018). Powered by Netflix: Speed test services and video-on-demand's global development projects. *Media, Culture & Society*, 1–18, https://doi.org/10.1177/0163443718754649

Evens, T. & Donders, K. (2018). *Platform Power and Policy in Transforming Television Markets*. Cham: Palgrave Macmillan.

Everlett-Green, R. (2018, May 18). Are Quebec media slightly ahead of our time? The Globe and Mail. Retrieved from www.theglobeandmail.com/canada/article-are-quebec-media-slightly-ahead-of-our-time/

Fletcher, R. (2017, October 3). "Quebec says it will impose sales tax on Netflix". *Global news*. Retrieved from https://globalnews.ca/news/3783322/quebec-says-it-will-impose-sales-tax-on-netflix/

Freedman, D. (2008). *The Politics of Media Policy*. Cambridge: Polity.

Friend, D. (2020, September 13). "With TIFF facing a tough year, Netflix makes a swift exit from festival season". CTV News. Retrieved from www.ctvnews.ca/entertainment/with-tiff-facing-a-tough-year-netflix-makes-a-swift-exit-from-festival-season-1.5102924

Goff, P. (2019). Canada's cultural exemption. *International Journal of Cultural Policy*, 25(5), 552 –567.

Gray, J., & Lotz, A. (2012). *Television Studies: Short Introductions*. Cambridge: Polity.

Hamilton, G. (2018, July 18). Once a rising star, Mélanie Joly demoted after missteps hurt Liberals in Quebec. *National Post*. Retrieved from https://nationalpost.com/news/politics/once-a-rising-star-melanie-joly-demoted-after-hurting-liberals-in-quebec

Havens, T., & Lotz, A. (2017). *Understanding Media Industries* (2nd ed.). New York, NY: Oxford University Press.

Hogarth, D. (2002). *Documentary Television in Canada: From National Public Service to Global Marketplace*. Montreal: McGill-Queen's University Press.

Jenner, M. (2016). Is this TVIV? On Netflix, TVIII and binge-watching. *New Media & Society*, 18(2), 257–273.

Lobato, R. (2018). Rethinking international TV flows research in the age of Netflix. *Television & New Media*, 19(3), 241–256.

Lobato, R. (2019). *Netflix Nations: The Geography of Digital Distribution*. New York, NY: New York University Press.

Lotz, A. (2017). *Portals: A Treatise on Internet-Distributed Television*. Ann Arbor, MI: University of Michigan Press.

Lotz, A. (2018). *We Now Disrupt This Broadcast: How Cable Transformed Television and the Internet Revolutionized It All*. Cambridge, MA: The Massachusetts Institute of Technology Press.

Miller, P., & Rudniski, R. (2012). Market impact and indicators of over the top television in Canada: 2012. Retrieved from https://crtc.gc.ca/eng/publications/reports/rp120330.htm#fig2-17

Robertson, S. (2017, September 26). A look at what's on the line for Canada's Cultural Industry. *The Globe and Mail*. Retrieved from https://beta.theglobeandmail.com/news/national/melanie-joly-set-to-unveil-her-vision-for-the-future-of-canadas-culturalindustry/article36406498/

Robertson, S. (2017, September 27). Canada should stop "subsidizing" US Internet giants, Péladeau says. *The Globe and Mail*. Retrieved from www.theglobeandmail.com/report-on-business/canada-should-stop-subsidizing-us-internet-giants-peladeau-says/article36405743/

Robertson, S. (2017, October 20). Netflix leads streaming in Canada. *The Globe and Mail*. Retrieved from www.theglobeandmail.com/report-on-business/industry-news/marketing/netflix-leads-streaming-services-in-canada/article36678928/

Royal Commission on National Developments in the Arts, Letters and Sciences 1949–1951. Report. Retrieved from www.collectionscanada.gc.ca/massey/h5-400-e.html

Statista (2019). Video streaming (SVoD). Retrieved from www.statista.com/outlook/206/108/video-streaming—svod-/canada

Spangler, T. (2019, February 19). "Netflix establishes production hub in Toronto, leasing nearly 250,000 square feet of studio space". *Variety*. Retrieved from https://variety.com/2019/digital/news/netflix-toronto-production-hub-canada-1203142537/

Taras, D. (2015). *Digital Mosaic: Media, Power, and Identity in Canada*. Toronto: University of Toronto Press.

United States Trade Representatives (2018). United States-Mexico-Canada Agreement. Retrieved from https://ustr.gov/trade-agreements/free-trade-agreements/united-states-mexico-canada-agreement

Vonderau, P. (2015). The politics of content aggregation. *Television & New Media*, 16(8), 717–733.

Williams, R. (2003). *Television: Technology and Cultural Form* (edited by Ederyn Williams). London: Routledge.

Winseck, D. (2010). Financialization and the "crisis of the media": The rise and fall of (some) media conglomerates in Canada. *Canadian Journal of Communication*, 35, 365–393.

INDEX

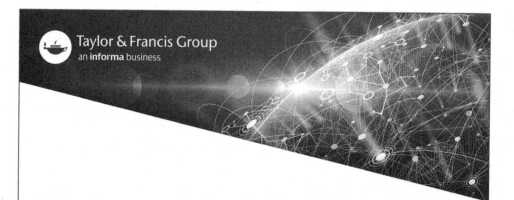

Printed in the United States
by Baker & Taylor Publisher Services